KU-635-401

**Edited and
designed by
Time Out Paris**
100 rue du Fbg-St-Antoine
75012 Paris
Tel: +33 (0)1.44.87.00.45
Fax:+33 (0)1.44.73.90.60
Email: editors@timeout.fr
www.timeout.com/paris

**For
Time Out Guides Ltd
Universal House
251 Tottenham Court Road
London W1T 7AB**
Tel: +44 (0)20 7813 3000
Fax:+44 (0)20 7813 6001
Email: guides@timeout.com
www.timeout.com

Editorial

Editor Paul Hines
Consultant Editor Natasha Edwards
Production Editor Alison Culliford
Editorial Assistants Amy Brooke, Kevin Money
Researchers Anna Brooke, Frances Dougherty, Jenny McVeigh, Natalie Whittle

Editorial Director Peter Fiennes
Series Editor Ruth Jarvis
Deputy Series Editor Jonathan Cox
Guides Co-ordinator Anna Norman

Design

Art Director Paris Richard Joy
Design Assistant Oliver Knight
Ad Design Philippe Thareaut, Edna Wargon

Group Art Director John Oakey
Art Director Mandy Martin
Art Editor Scott Moore
Picture Editor Kerri Littlefield

Advertising

Sales & Administration Manager Philippe Thareaut
Advertising Co-ordinator David Jordan
Advertising Executives Olivier Baenninger, Christa Halby

Group Commercial Director Lesley Gill
Sales Director Mark Phillips
International Sales Co-ordinator Ross Canadé

Administration

Managing Director Paris Karen Albrecht

Chairman Tony Elliott
Chief Operating Officer Kevin Ellis
Managing Director Mike Hardwick
Chief Financial Officer Richard Waterlow
Group Marketing Director Christine Cort
Marketing Manager Mandy Martinez
Group General Manager Nichola Coulthard
Guides Production Director Mark Lamond
Production Controller Samantha Furniss
Accountant Sarah Bostock

Contributors

History Michael Fitzpatrick, Paul Hines, Kevin Money, Colin Shaw (*A royal leg up*, Allis Moss; *Revving up*, Anna Brooke; *The Harkis*, Natalie Whittle). **The Surreal Thing** Paul Hines. **Architecture** Natasha Edwards. **Paris Today** Jon Henley (*2002's whoppers*, *...and floppers*, Kevin Money) **Security Fraud** Paul Hines. **State of the Art** Jenny McVeigh. **The Islands**, **Right Bank**, **Left Bank**, **Beyond the Périphérique** Amy Brooke, Anna Brooke, Alison Culliford, Natasha Edwards, Paul Hines, Kevin Money (*Heist cool*, Natalie Whittle; *Passages through time*, Kevin Money; *Paris, France's very own Southend*, Amy Brooke; *Bastille bother*, Natalie Whittle; *The art of the squat*, Sam Alexander; *The Seine*, Kevin Money; *La cage aux folles*, Elizabeth Bard; *ZAC's the way, uh-huh uh-huh*, Alison Culliford; *The under dogs*, Natalie Whittle). **Paris Power Strut** Sam Alexander. **Museums** Alison Culliford, Sophia Khan, Claire Tellier (*Time to remember*, Sophia Khan; *Primitive & Proper*, Kevin Money). **Accommodation** Kevin Money (*Smart about art*, Sam Alexander; *Hostel takeover bed*, Olivier Baenninger). **Restaurants** adapted from *Time Out Eating & Drinking in Paris Guide*. (*Big grec-fest*, Sam Alexander; *The British are coming*, Maryanne Blacker). **Bars, Cafés & Tearooms** Adapted from *Time Out Eating & Drinking in Paris Guide* (*Scratch 'n' snifters*, Kevin Money). **Shops & services** Amy Brooke (*Where to find the jeunes créateurs*, Amy Brooke; *Eau behave!*, Maryanne Blacker; *Paris' pulchritude parlours*, Alison Culliford, Christa Halby; *Vulgar? Me? Yep. Regal Rock Shop*, Maryanne Blacker; *Ice 'n' easy does it every time*, Lucia Scazzocchio; *Markets*, Kevin Money). **Festivals and Events** (*Pink, proud and politicised*, Anna Sansom). **Cabaret, Circus & Comedy** Sam Alexander (*Bar none*, Sam Alexander). **Children** Sophia Khan (*Babes in the wood*, *Children of the (digital) revolution*, Sophia Khan). **Clubs** Lucia Scazzocchio (*Girls on top*, *The promoters*, Lucia Scazzocchio). **Dance** Amy Brooke (*Dancing in the streets*, Amy Brooke). **Film** Elizabeth Bard, Simon Cropper (*Paris in the pictures*, Simon Cropper). **Galleries** Natasha Edwards (*Made in Paris?*, Natasha Edwards). **Gay & Lesbian** Toby Rose, Lucia Scazzocchio (*Pink prandial pleasures* Toby Rose; *Are you kidding?* Paul Hines). **Music: Classical & Opera** Stephen Mudge (*Summer notes*, Stephen Mudge). **Music: Popular music** David McKenna (*All you need is luvvies*, *French pop: crap, pap, or tip-top*, David McKenna). **Sport** Amy Brooke (*Martialing those inner resources*, *The sporting year 2003*, Amy Brooke). **Theatre** Sophia Khan (*When in Paris, act English*, Sam Alexander). **Trips out of Town** Louise Rogers (*Auvers and out* Kevin Money; *Up a lazy river*, Louise Rogers). **Directory** Amy Brooke, Alison Culliford, Frances Dougherty. **Index** Jenny McVeigh.

The Editor would like to thank: Hélène Hines,

Maps p398-407 by Mapworld, p410-412 courtesy RATP.

Photography by Karl Blackwell, Tom Craig, Adam Eastland, Oliver Knight, Jon Perugia, Alys Tomlinson. **Additional photography** Alison Culliford, Jean-Louis Faverole, Alison Harris, Colm Pierce, Natalie Whittle, Francesca Yorke. **Additional photos courtesy** Opéra National de Paris, Photothèque des Musées de la Ville de Paris, Mairie de Paris, Eurodisney, Hôtel de Crillon, Galerie Karsten Greve, Office du Tourisme de Chartres, Office du Tourisme de Dieppe.

© Copyright Time Out Group Ltd
All rights reserved

Contents

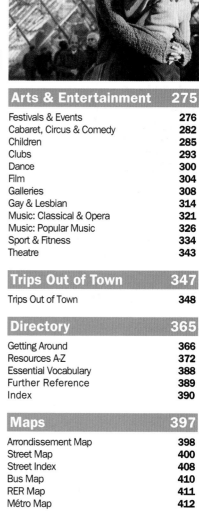

Introduction

Even a drugged and weary-from-the-violin Sherlock Holmes would have no problem applying deductive reasoning to solving the mystery of why, year after year, Paris is the world's number one tourist attraction. (And it is: in 2001, the latest year for which figures are available, 36 million people graced our city with their travellers' cheques). Sherlock would know – and here's an informative gem in a book that's brimming with them – that the barometer for the pull factor of any city is its OAPs: first across roads, first onto buses and first to get violent in queues, these survival machines prosper where the living is pleasing.

Paris has the world's most stylish oldies. Anywhere that can produce chain-smoking, won't-see-sixty-again dolly birds with Ramones bouffants, silver slingbacks and royal blue wrap-arounds, or aged gentlemen of the road who wear violent ginger wigs and T-shirts affirming that 'Masturbation Isn't Wrong' (both spotted near the Bastille on the morning of writing this Introduction) could be said to manifest a certain individuality of approach. That's the key to Paris' magnetism – its charisma.

This charisma manifests itself in all sorts of ways: in bricks-and-mortar beauty, in an almost arrogant range of cultural achievement that no other city can approach and in the attitude of the people who live here. Where else would have a Mayor with enough panache to build a beach in the middle of the city? (*See chapter* **Sightseeing**). Where else do school children take to the streets to march against far-right wingers? (*See chapter* **Paris Today**). Where else can you find a bar with its dedicated in-house chicken? (*See chapter* **Bars, Cafés & Tearooms**). Where else is crazy enough to risk having a museum dedicated to the postal service? (*See chapter* **Museums**). Nowhere else. So where else would you rather go? Nowhere else. It's elementary, isn't it?

ABOUT THE TIME OUT CITY GUIDES

The *Time Out Paris Guide* is one of an expanding series of *Time Out* City Guides produced by the people behind London's and New York's successful listings magazines. This 11th edition has been thoroughly revised and updated by writers resident in Paris who have striven to provide you with all the most up-to-date information you'll need to explore the city.

For events each week, see the *Time Out Paris* section (in English) inside French listings magazine *Pariscope*, available at all Paris-area newsstands. The quarterly *Time Out Paris Free Guide* is available in selected hotels, bars and visitor centres. For detailed reviews of 850 Paris restaurants, cafés and bars, buy the *Time Out Paris Eating & Drinking Guide*. Penguin's *Time Out Book of Paris Walks* features 23 themed itineraries by eminent writers and journalists.

THE LOWDOWN ON THE LISTINGS

We've tried to make this book as useful as possible. Addresses, telephone numbers, transport details, opening times, admission prices, credit card details and, where possible, websites, are all included. As far as possible, we've given details of facilities, services and events, all checked and correct at the time we went to press. However, arrangements can change at any time. Before you go out of your way, we'd advise you to telephone and check opening times, dates of exhibitions and other particulars. While every effort has been made to ensure the accuracy of the information contained in this guide, the publishers cannot accept responsiblity for any errors it may contain.

PRICES AND PAYMENT

The prices we've supplied should be treated as guidelines, not gospel. Inflation, fluctuations in exchange rates and sometimes even a mood-swing can cause prices to change. If you encounter prices that vary wildly from those we've quoted, ask whether there's a good reason. If not, go elsewhere. We have noted whether venues such as shops, hotels, restaurants, bars and clubs accept credit cards or not but have listed only the major cards – American Express (**AmEx**), Diners Club (**DC**), MasterCard (**MC**) and Visa (**V**). Note that shops, restaurants, cafés and museums often will not accept credit cards for sums of less than €15.

CROSS-REFERENCING

Where we mention important places or events also listed elsewhere in the guide, or in detail later in the chapter, they are highlighted in **bold**.

There is an online version of this guide, as well as monthly events listings for more than 30 international cities, at www.timeout.com.

THE LIE OF THE LAND

Paris is divided into 20 *arrondissements,* which form a spiral beginning at Notre-Dame and finishing at the Porte de Montreuil. Paris addresses include the *arrondissement* at the end of the postcode, following the prefix 750. We have referred to the *arrondissements* as 1st, 2nd, 3rd, 4th, etc. Chapters on **Accommodation**, **Sightseeing** and **Eating & Drinking** are divided into area categories that follow *arrondissement* guidelines. In the other listings categories, entries are in order of *arrondissement.* Addresses within the area covered on the **colour street maps** also have map references. An **arrondissement map** is on page 398.

TELEPHONE NUMBERS

All French phone numbers, including mobile (*portable*) numbers have ten digits. The area code for Paris is 01. From outside France, dial the country code (33) and leave off the zero at the beginning of the number.

ESSENTIAL INFORMATION

For all the practical information you might need – including getting yourself in the Paris mood, visa and customs information, disabled access, health and emergency telephone numbers, tips for doing business and dealing with French bureaucracy, a list of websites, a compendium of essential vocabulary, more information on the euro and the lowdown on the local transport network – see the **Directory** chapter at the back of this guide (*see p366*).

MAPS

We've included fully indexed colour maps to the city, including a map of Paris areas and *arrondissements,* plus public transport maps, at the back of the guide. We have printed a grid and page reference against all venues that appear on the maps.

LET US KNOW WHAT YOU THINK

We hope you enjoy the *Time Out Paris Guide* and we'd like to know what you think of it. We welcome tips for places that we should include in future editons and we value and take notice of your criticisms of our choices. There's a reader's reply card at the back of this book – or you can simply email us on editors@timeout.fr.

Advertisers

We would like to stress that no establishment has been included in this guide because it has advertised in any of our publications and no payment of any kind has influenced any review. The opinions in this book are those of *Time Out* writers and are entirely independent.

TRÈS CHEAP

'Low cost' car rental comes to Paris.

easyCar.com

easyCar.com

Paris Smart
@ Champs Elysées

easyCar.com

Book early
to pay less @

easyCar.com
low cost car rental online

PLACE VENDOME . GARE MONTPARNASSE . PORTE DE CHAMPERRET
PORTE DE VINCENNES . CHAMPS ELYSEES

In Context

History

Civil unrest, crooked leaders and inequality. As the man said, the more things change, the more they stay the same.

INTRODUCTION

The purpose of this chapter is to tell you about the main events, trends and personalities that have added up to create the Paris you'll find in 2003. It isn't meant to form the basis for your doctorate in French history, but if it clinches it for you, well, congratulations, doc; we won't tell anyone. Paris is a city whose history jumps out at you wherever you happen to look. Places mentioned in **bold** appear in other sections of the book (most often in the **Sightseeing** section). Please refer to the **Index** if you want to find out on which pages they can be found.

IT STARTED IN A BOG

Or rather a marshy plain punctuated by various dry hillocks, between the two meandering branches of the Seine (the now vanished northern arm ran just south of **Montmartre**). Into the Seine on the Left Bank ran the Bièvre, once a major river, now a canalised underground stream (although there is a campaign to have it uncovered).

The prehistoric Seine was also wider than today, but relatively easy to cross at this point, thanks to the islands from which Paris was to expand. The first visitors arrived in Paris a long time ago, long before guide books ('How did they manage?' you cry) and, clearly, long before the Customs. One of them lost a flint spear-tip on the hill we now call Montmartre, 120,000 years back, give or take a millennium. The still dangerous-looking weapon is to be seen today in the Stone Age Collection at the **Musée des Antiquités Nationales**.

Archaeologists are still arguing about who were the earliest settlers, and exactly which *arrondissements* were the most popular. What we do know is that there was a Stone Age weapons factory under present-day Châtelet, and the redevelopment of Bercy in the 1980s unearthed five Neolithic canoes, now high and dry in the **Musée Carnavalet**. The remains of mammoth, elk and deer which have been found on the Ile de la Cité suggest that it was a popular destination for Stone-Age picnickers. The unpredictable level of the river, however, probably forced people to place their dwellings on one of the area's many hills.

By 250BC, a canny bunch of Celts known as the Parisii had put the place on the map, and given the modern capital the makings of its name. Some Parisii kept going northwards and settled in what is now the English city of York. The ones who stayed behind became river traders and toll-bridge operators, wealthy enough to mint their own gold coins. The **Musée de la Monnaie** has a collection of their small change. Their most important *oppidum*, a primitive fortified town, was located on an island in the Seine, which is generally thought to have been the **Ile de la Cité**.

REVOLTING NEIGHBOURS

Superb strategic location and the capacity to generate hard cash got a town noticed. Julius Caesar arrived in southern Gaul as proconsul in 58BC and soon used the pretext of dealing with some pesky invading Germans to stick his Roman nose into the affairs of northern Gaul.

In 54BC the Eburones from the Meuse valley rebelled against the Romans, and soon other tribes joined in, including the Senones, neighbours of the Parisii. In the spring of 52BC Caesar called an Assembly of the Gauls at Paris, known to the Romans as Lutetia, but the city's early place in diplomatic mediation was not a resounding success: the following year, the Parisii rose up with the rest of Gaul.

Caesar had his hands full trying to deal with the great Gaul marauder Vercingetorix, so he sent his general Labienus with four legions and part of the cavalry to secure the passage of the Seine at Lutetia. Stopped in the marshes to the east by the combined forces of the Parisii and the Aulerques, the Romans retreated upstream as far as Melun. From there they were able to cross the river and advance directly toward Lutetia on the opposite bank.

The Parisii, however, had burned Lutetia and the wooden bridges. Menaced by the uprising of another tribe of Gauls, the Bellovaques, on his side of the river, Labienus had to improvise. Leaving one legion to make as much noise as possible, and under cover of a storm, Labienus managed to cross the Seine on hastily-constructed barges with three legions and take the Parisii by surprise. Now exposed on the plain, the Gauls were decimated, although a contingent of Parisii escaped the slaughter only to be defeated with Vercingetorix at the battle of Alesia.

SEIZED BY CAESAR

The surrender of Vercingetorix in 52BC left the Parisian region along with the rest of Gaul in Roman hands. During the first century AD, Lutetia was rebuilt on the Roman model with a rectilinear street pattern: the *cardo maximus* (main north-south street) is now the rue St-Jacques, the *decumanus maximus* (east-west) the rue Cujas. The port was located on the southern shore of the Ile de la Cité, while the Roman administration appears to have been based at the site of the **Palais de Justice**.

At its height, Roman Lutetia was a prosperous town of around 8,000 inhabitants. Apart from centrally-heated villas and a temple to Jupiter on the main island (remains of both are visible in the **Crypte Archéologique**), there were the sumptuous baths (now the **Musée de Cluny**), and the 15,000-seater **Arènes de Lutèce**, where gladiators, theatre troupes and circuses did their best to make up for the absence of television.

Christianity arrived in around 250 in the shape of Denis of Athens, who went on to become first bishop of Paris. Legend has it that he was decapitated by Valerian on Mons Martis, the mount of the martyrs, thus giving Montmartre its name. It was now that things really started to get nasty. Waves of barbarian invaders – Alamans, Francs and others – began crossing the Rhine from 275 onwards. They sacked more than 60 cities in Gaul, including Lutetia, where the population was decimated and the buildings on the Montagne Sainte-Geneviève were pillaged and burned. The bedraggled survivors used the rubble to build a rampart around the Ile de la Cité and to fortify the forum, although few citizens remained in the shadow of its walls.

It was at this unhappy time that the city was renamed Paris. Protected by the Seine and the new fortifications, its main role now was as a rear base for the Roman armies defending Gaul, and it was here in 360 that Julian was proclaimed emperor by his troops. In the same year, the first Catholic council of Paris was held, condemning the Arian branch of Christianity as heresy. The city's inhabitants, however, had more pressing concerns.

FRANK EXCHANGES

Around 450, with the arrival of the Huns in the region, the people of Paris prepared once again to flee. They were dissuaded by a feisty woman named Geneviève, who was famed in the Christian community for her fervent piety. Seeing the walls of the city defended against him, Attila turned back and was defeated soon afterwards. Geneviève modestly put it all down to the power of prayer.

In 464, Paris managed to resist another siege, this time by the Francs under Childeric. However by 486, after a further blockade lasting ten years, Geneviève had no option but to surrender the city to Childeric's successor, Clovis, who went on to conquer most of Gaul and founded the Merovingian dynasty. He chose Paris as capital of his new kingdom, and it stayed that way until the 7th century, in spite of various conflicts among his successors.

Under the influence of his wife, Clotilde, Clovis converted to Christianity. He founded and was buried in the basilica of the Saints Apôtres, later re-dedicated to Sainte Geneviève when the saviour and future patron saint of Paris was interred there in 512. All that remains of the basilica today is a single pillar in the grounds of the modern Lycée Henri IV; but there's a shrine dedicated to Sainte Geneviève and some relics in the fine Gothic church of **St-Etienne-du-Mont**, just next door.

Geneviève and Clovis had set a trend. The Ile de la Cité was still the heart of the city, but, under the Merovingians, the Left Bank was the up-and-coming area for fashion-conscious Christians, with 11 churches built here in the period (against only four on the Right Bank and one on the Ile de la Cité).

Not everyone was sold on the joys of city living, though. From 614 onwards, the Merovingian kings preferred their little p(a)lace in the *banlieue* at Clichy, or wandered the kingdom trying to keep rebellious nobles in check. When one of their number, Pippin 'the Short', decided to do away with the last Merovingian in 751, Paris was starting to look decidedly *passé*.

Pippin's son, Charlemagne, built his capital at Aix-la-Chapelle (now the German city of Aachen), while his successors, known as the Carolingian dynasty, moved from palace to palace, consuming the local production (much to the delight of the locals, one imagines).

Paris, meanwhile, was doing quite nicely for itself as a centre for Christian learning, and the city had grown to house a population of 20,000 by the beginning of the 9th century. This was the high point in the popularity and political power of the great abbeys like St-Germain-des-Prés, where transcription of the Latin classics was helping to preserve much of Europe's Roman cultural heritage. In the absence of the king, power in the Paris region was exercised by the Counts of Paris, at first minor royals or allies, later hereditary rulers. These counts were to have their hands full.

PILLAGE PEOPLE

In 845 the Vikings appeared before the walls, which had unfortunately not been repaired for the past few centuries. Unopposed, the Norsemen sacked the city, and king Charles II 'the Bald' (this was a compliment at the time), had to cough up 7,000 pounds of silver to get them to leave. Recognising a soft touch when they saw one, the Vikings returned to sack the city repeatedly between 856 and 869, burning churches with heathen abandon.

Deciding that matters were getting out of hand, Charles the Bald at last organised the defence of the city. Fortified bridges were constructed, the Grand Pont over the northern and the Petit Pont over the southern branch of the Seine, blocking the passage of the Viking ships further upstream.

In 885, Gozlin, bishop of Paris, had just finished repairing the Roman walls when the Vikings showed up once again; this time they found the city defended against them. After a siege lasting a year, the king Charles III 'the Fat' arrived at the head of an army but, deciding that discretion is indeed the better part of valour, handed over 700 pounds of silver and politely invited the Norsemen to pillage some other part of his kingdom. Impressed by his generosity, they returned in 889 and, failing to breach the walls of Paris, continued to ravage France until 911, when the region of Normandy was ceded to them.

The Count of Paris, Eudes, having performed valiantly in the siege of 885-886, was offered the royal crown when Fat Chas was deposed in 888. Although the Carolingians recovered the throne after his death in 898, Eudes' great-nephew, Hugues Capet, was finally elected king of France in 987, adding what remained of the Carolingian dominions to his territories around Paris.

THE MAGIC CAPET

Under the Capetian dynasty, although Paris was now at the heart of the royal domains, the city did not yet dominate the kingdom. Hugues was elected at Senlis and crowned at Noyon, while his successors divided their time between

Senlis, Paris, Étampes and Orléans, even as the importance of Paris grew.

Robert 'the Pious', king from 996 to 1031, stayed more often in the city than his father, restoring the royal palace on the Ile de la Cité, while Henri I (1031-1060) issued more of his charters in Paris than in Orléans. In 1112, the abbey of **Saint-Denis** replaced Saint-Benoît-sur-Loire as principal monastery, so confirming the pre-eminence of Paris over Orléans.

Paris itself still consisted of little more than the Ile de la Cité and small settlements under the protection of the abbeys on each bank. On the Left Bank, royal largesse helped to rebuild the abbeys of Saint-Germain-des-Prés, Saint-Marcel, and Sainte-Geneviève, although it took more than 150 years for the destruction wrought there by the Vikings to be fully repaired. The Right Bank, where mooring was easier, prospered from river commerce, and three boroughs grew up around the abbeys of Saint-Germain-l'Auxerrois, Saint-Martin-des-Champs and Saint-Gervais. Bishop Sully of Paris began building **Notre-Dame** in 1163.

The growing complexity of government during the 12th century, and the departure of kings on crusade, meant that the administration tended to stay in the palace of the Cité and the royal treasure in the fortress of the Temple

(built by the newly founded order of the Templars). The wisdom of this approach was confirmed by the disaster of Fréteval in 1194, where King Philippe Auguste was defeated by Richard the Lionheart, losing much of his treasure and his archives in the process.

This minor hiccup aside, the reign of Philippe Auguste (1180-1223) was to be a turning point in the history of Paris. Before, the city was a confused patchwork of royal, ecclesiastical and feudal authorities, exercising various powers, rights and privileges. Keen to raise revenues, Philip favoured the growth of the guilds, especially the butchers, drapers, furriers, haberdashers and merchants: so began the rise of the bourgeoisie with which Paris would become synonymous. When Philippe went on crusade in 1190, he nominated representatives of this new bourgeoisie to govern the city in preference to the feudal lords, even leaving them the keys to the royal treasure kept at the Temple. He also ordered the building of the first permanent market buildings at **Les Halles**.

At the same time he ordered the construction of a new city wall, first on the Right Bank to protect the commercial heart of Paris, and later on the Left Bank (chunks of his wall remain by the Lycée Charlemagne in the Marais and in rue Clovis in the Latin Quarter). At the western end

The Vikings attack, making the most of what amounted to a protection racket.

of the wall, Philip built a new castle, the **Louvre**, to defend the road from the ever-menacing Normandy, only 100 km away (and whose duke was also King of England). The Louvre was where he imprisoned his conquered enemies after the battle of Bouvines (1214) which set the seal on a remarkable reign.

THE GOLDEN AGE

Paris was now the principal residence of the king and the uncontested capital of France. No longer threatened by foreign invasion, the city found itself overrun by a new and altogether deadlier menace: lawyers. And barristers, bailiffs, prosecutors, sergeants, accountants, judges, clerks and all the bureaucratic paraphernalia of royal government.

To accommodate the growing royal administration, the Palace of the Cité, site and symbol of power for the previous thousand years, was remodelled and enlarged. The work was begun by Louis IX (later Saint Louis) in the 1240s, and continued under Philippe IV ('le Bel'). This vast architectural complex, of which the **Sainte Chapelle** and the **Conciergerie** can still be seen today, was inaugurated with great pomp at Pentecost 1313. Philippe invited Edward II of England and his Queen, Isabelle of France (kings were not above a bit of showing-off to the neighbours). The English were clearly impressed: they soon came back for a long stay.

The palace was quickly filled with functionaries, so the King spent as much of his time as he could outside Paris at the royal castles of **Fontainebleau** and, especially, **Vincennes**. The needs of the plethora of plenipotentiaries left behind to run the kingdom was met by a rapidly growing population in the city, piled into rather less chic buildings up to four storeys high.

Paris was also becoming a major religious centre: as well as the local clergy and dozens of religious orders, the city was home to the masters and students of the university of the **Sorbonne** (established in 1253), who were already gaining a reputation for rowdiness. An influx of scholars and pilgrims from all over Europe gave the capital an intellectual and cultural *cachet* it was never to lose.

By 1328, Paris had around 200,000 inhabitants, making it the most populous city in Europe. The fortifications of Philippe Auguste had already been overtaken by the growth of the city. However, that year was to be the last of the golden age: the line of Capetian kings spluttered to an inglorious halt as Charles IV died heirless, leaving the kingdom up for grabs.

Never ones to miss a trick, the English claimed the throne for the young Edward III, son of Philippe IV's daughter. Refusing to

Jeanne d'Arc: get yer Brits out for the boys.

recognise his descent through the female line (the country was no more a bastion of feminism in those days than it is now) the late king's cousin, Philippe de Valois, claimed the crown for himself as Philippe VI. So began the Hundred Years War, which, as every schoolchild knows, went on for a bit longer than that.

TROUBLE AND STRIFE

It went on for 116 years to be precise. To make matters worse, the Black Death, bubonic plague, ravaged Europe from the 1340s. Those not done for by this 'mad, tempestuous, monstrous, abominable, fearful, terrifying and treacherous disease', as the wordy royal surgeon Ambroise Paré put it (try getting that lot on your sick note), had to contend with food shortages, ever-increasing taxes, riots, repression, currency devaluations and marauding mercenaries.

Meanwhile, back in Paris, after growing together and supporting each other through the good times, the honeymoon period for the king and the bourgeoisie was coming to an end; and, like many an erstwhile happy couple, it was over money that they came to blows. Rich and populous, Paris was expected to bear the brunt of the war burden; and as defeat followed defeat (notably the disaster at Crécy in August 1346) the bourgeoisie and people of the city were increasingly exasperated by the futility of the sacrifices they were making.

When King Jean II le Bon called the Estates General (a sort of parliament) in November 1355 to beg for yet more money for the war effort, one Etienne Marcel, provost of the merchants of Paris, started making a name for himself as spokesman for the cities of the realm in favour of reform. By 1356 Jean II and the Estates General had failed to agree on a new tax system and the king devalued the currency again, something always guaranteed to rile a bourgeoisie accustomed to growing rich on fixed incomes from rents. As a result, the contingents of Paris, Rouen and Amiens were withdrawn from the royal army: which at least saved them from a whipping at the battle of Poitiers in October 1356, where Jean II was captured by the English and held for ransom, leaving the kingdom in a fix.

Taking advantage of the situation, Etienne Marcel seized control of Paris, hoping to force the Dauphin Charles to grant the city increased autonomy. By 1358, however, Marcel was well and truly hoisted on his own petard, dying at the hands of an angry mob. Charles went on to improve the defences of the Louvre and begin building the fort at **La Bastille**, not only to protect the city, but also to protect himself against its inflamed citizens. One day, the inflamed citizens would make their feelings abundantly clear on the site of this building.

By 1420, following the catastrophic French defeat at Agincourt, Paris was in English hands. In 1431, Henry VI of England was crowned King of France in Notre-Dame. He didn't last. Five years later, Henry and his army had been driven back to Calais by the Valois king, Charles VII. Charles owed his grasp on power to Jeanne d'Arc, a cross-dressing visionary peasant girl who led the victorious French in the battle of Orléans, only to be betrayed by her compatriots who decided she was getting too big for her boots. She was captured and sold to the English (see what we mean about the attitude towards feminism?) who had her burnt as a witch. Worse was to follow for the poor woman: Jeanne has since been adopted as the patron saint of France's extreme right-wing National Front party.

By 1436, Paris was once again the capital of France. But the nation was nearly ruined by war, still sharply divided politically, with powerful regional rulers continuing to threaten the monarchy. The ambitions of the Austrian Hapsburg dynasty represented a serious external worry. In a general atmosphere of instability, disputes over trade, religion and taxation were all simmering dangerously.

RENAISSANCE AND REFORMATION

In the closing decades of the 15th century, the restored Valois monarchs sought to reassert their position. A wave of building projects was the public sign of this effort, giving us such masterpieces as St-Etienne-du-Mont, St-Eustache and private homes like Hôtel de Cluny (which now houses the **Musée National du Moyen-Age**) and Hôtel de Sens.

Apart from his magnificent châteaux at **Fontainbleau**, Blois and Chambord, François 1er was responsible for transforming the Louvre from a fortress into a royal palace. He held open house for such luminaries as Leonardo da Vinci and Benvenuto Cellini. He also established the Collège de France to encourage humanist learning outside the control of the clergy-dominated universities.

Despite publicly burning heretics by the dozen, François was unable to stop the spread of Protestantism, launched in Germany by Martin Luther in 1517. Resolutely Catholic, Paris was the scene of some horrific violence against Huguenots, as supporters of the new faith were called. The picture was complicated by the political conflict opposing the Huguenot Prince de Condé and the Catholic Duc de Guise.

HACK UP A HUGUENOT

By the 1560s, the situation had degenerated into open warfare. Catherine de Médicis, the scheming Italian widow of Henri II, was the real force in court politics. It was she who connived to murder prominent Protestants gathered in Paris for the marriage of the king's sister on St Bartholomew's Day (23 August 1572). Catherine's main aim was to dispose of her powerful rival, Gaspard de Coligny, but the situation got out of hand, and as many as 3,000 people were butchered. Henri III attempted to reconcile the religious factions and eradicate the powerful families directing the conflict, but the people of Paris turned against him and he was forced to flee. His assassination in 1589 by the religious fanatic Jacques Clément brought the Valois line to an end.

MAKE MINE A BOURBON

Henri of Navarre promptly declared himself King Henri IV, getting the Bourbon dynasty off the mark. Paris was not impressed. The city closed its gates against the Huguenot king and the inhabitants endured a four-year siege by supporters of the new ruler. Henri broke the impasse by becoming a Catholic, being received into the church in 1593. It was he who gave the world 'Paris vaut bien une messe' (Paris is well worth a Mass).

The new king set about rebuilding his ravaged capital. He completed the **Pont-Neuf**,

A royal leg up (and over)

Being a powerful geezer's squeeze has never been a job for wimps: the lives of royal mistresses were ever risky. Take Agnès Sorel. Agnès, some-time close companion of Charles VII, was only 28 when she met her nemesis in the shape of Jacques Coeur, alchemist to the king. Mind you, she had her kicks along the way: the 15th century was a time for post-plague hedonism. Bodies not covered in pustules were much appreciated, and in the time allotted to her, Agnès blazed a taboo-breaking trail. The first woman to wear diamonds at court (steady, missus), she found it within herself to pose half-naked for a painting with one breast in, one out.

Having Catherine de Médicis as a rival could have been a huge disincentive for a lesser broad than another famous floozy, Diane de Poitiers, who was 20 years older than her bit on the side, Catherine's husband, Henry II. Forget de Médicis; cellulite and the southward sag were Di's enemies. The de Poitiers beauty regime involved bathing in dew and peeling a raw onion daily to cleanse her eyes. After Henry was killed in a jousting accident, Diane found herself having to survive in the Machiavellian jungle of the Médicis-controlled court. No fool, she took out the insurance policy of marrying off her daughter and grand-daughter to powerful men. Thus she managed to die of old age at her country home at Anet.

Then there was Madame de Maintenon, love interest of Louis XIV. Sun King? Get outta here: Stud King, more like. Louis had a bevy of children by various mistresses and had even dallied with his sister-in-law. His callous treatment of his victims had them rushing back for more. One cast-off, Madame de Montespan, had even resorted to black magic spells in a doomed attempt to get her man back, but no dice. Madame de Maintenon took a different approach: she relied on the sisterhood. She was a cheerful, matronly sort who was best of friends with the queen (Marie-Thérèse), who went so far as to die in her arms. La Maintenon finally married Louis on condition she never became queen. Title or no title, she had influence, albeit a sometimes baleful one. It was she who persuaded Louis to restrict the Huguenots' religious freedom, forcing their exile and seriously damaging the French economy.

As members of the current English monarchy know, having a bourgeois bit on the royal side never goes down well with hoi-poloi.

The pragmatic and comely **Madame de Pompadour.**

Louis XV's mistress, Madame de Pompadour, risked life, limb and dirty laundry when she travelled in public. Being pelted with mud and stones had not been part of the deal when a fortune-teller told the nine-year-old Jeanne-Antoinette Poisson (or Reinette – Little Queen – as she became known) that she would grow up to marry the king. Marriage didn't actually get a look-in, but a window of opportunity to become the royal mistress did open up in 1744 with the premature death of his current girlfriend. Reinette was in before you could say 'grab my fan'. Sadly, de Pompadour was never able to win the people over, and a large part of her problem was that she couldn't keep her nose out of things. She could have had a nice life organising banquets and buying furniture for Versailles, but no. Despite being a friend of Voltaire and a self-proclaimed patron of the arts, she sent any writer who annoyed her to jail and the genius of the painter Chardin went straight over her head. Nor did she do herself any favours by having a bash at diplomacy. When France disastrously formed the alliance with Austria that kick-started the Seven Years' War, La Pompadour, who'd transferred her energies from the bedroom to the stateroom, was blamed. She also carried the can for the loss of Canada.

Despite these high-profile blunders, there is a lesson for all women in the strategy she employed to hold down her position of favour with her man. La Pompadour took care of all the king's boring administrative duties and devoted a lot of her time arranging his debaucheries. Try it, girls.

the first bridge to span the whole of the Seine. He commissioned place Dauphine and the city's first enclosed residential square – the place Royale – now **place des Vosges**. The square was the scene of jousting competitions and countless duels.

Henri also tried to reconcile his Catholic and Protestant subjects, issuing the Edict of Nantes in 1598, effectively giving each religion equal status. The Catholics hated the deal, and the Huguenots were suspicious. Henri was the victim of at least 23 attempted assassinations by fanatics of both persuasions. Finally, in 1610, one François Ravaillac – a Catholic – fatally stabbed the king while he was stuck in traffic on rue de la Ferronnerie.

RICH PICKINGS FOR RICHELIEU

Since Henry's son, Louis XIII, was only eight at the time of his father's death, the widow, Marie de Médicis, took up the reins of power. We can thank her for the **Palais du Luxembourg** and the 24 paintings she commissioned from Rubens, now part of the Louvre collection.

Louis took up his royal duties in 1617, but Cardinal Richelieu, chief minister from 1624, was the man who ran France. Something of a schemer, he outwitted the king's mother, his wife, Anne of Austria, and a host of disgruntled princes and place-seekers. A wily administrator, Richelieu helped to strengthen the power of the monarch, and he did much to limit the independence of the aristocracy. The cunning cardinal was also a great architectural patron. He commissioned Jacques Lemercier to build what is now the **Palais-Royal**, and ordered the rebuilding of the **Sorbonne**.

The Counter-Reformation was at its height, and lavish churches such as the Baroque Val-de-Grâce were an important reassertion of Catholic supremacy. The 16th century was also *Le Grand Siècle*, a time of patronage of art and artists, even if censorship forced the brilliant mathematician and philosopher, René Descartes, into exile. The writer and adventurer, Cyrano de Bergerac (1619-55), was one of the celebrities of the period. Jean-Paul Rappeneau's wonderful film *Cyrano*, starring Gérard Depardieu, gives a largely fictitious view of the man, but a great sense of his turbulent times.

The first national newspaper, *La Gazette*, hit the streets in 1631, with Richelieu using it as a propaganda tool. The cardinal founded the **Académie Française**, a sort of literary think-tank which is still working, slowly, on the dictionary of the French language which Richelieu commissioned from them in 1634.

MAZARIN'S MACHINATIONS

Richelieu died in 1642; Louis XIII followed him a few months later. The new king, Louis XIV, was barely five years old. Anne of Austria became regent, with the Italian Cardinal Mazarin, a Richelieu protégé, as chief minister. Mazarin's nifty townhouse is now the home of the **Bibliothèque Nationale Richelieu**.

Endless wars against Austria and Spain had depleted the royal coffers, and left the nation drained by exorbitant taxation. In 1648, the royal family was chased out of Paris by a popular uprising, the *La Fronde*, named after the catapults used by some of the rioters. Parisians soon tired of the resulting anarchy. When Mazarin's army retook the city in 1653, the boy-king was warmly welcomed. Mazarin died in 1661 and Louis XIV, now 24 years old, decided he would rule France without the intervention of a chief minister.

THE SUN ALSO RISES

The Sun King was an absolute monarch. 'L'état, c'est moi,' (I am the State) was his egocentric vision of power. To emphasise his grandeur, the king embarked on wars against England, Holland and Austria. He also refurbished and extended the **Louvre**, commissioned **place Vendôme** and **place des Victoires**, constructed the Observatory and laid out the *grands boulevards* along the lines of the old city walls. The triumphal arches at **Porte St-Denis** and **Porte St-Martin** date from this time, too. But Louis' major project was the palace at **Versailles**, a massive complex which drew on the finest architectural, artistic and landscape-design talent of the age. Louis moved his court there in 1682.

Louis XIV owed much of his brilliant success to the work of Jean-Baptiste Colbert, nominally in charge of state finances, but eventually taking control of all the important levers of the state machine. Colbert was the force behind the Sun King's redevelopment of Paris..

The **Hôtel des Invalides** was built to accommodate the crippled survivors of Louis' wars, the **Salpêtrière** to shelter fallen women (*see p130* **La cage aux folles**). In 1702, Paris was divided into the 20 *arrondissements* or districts which survive to this day. Le **Procope**, the city's – perhaps the world's – first café, opened for business in 1686. Even if the original proprietor, Francesco Procopio dei Coltelli, wouldn't recognise it following a 1989 facelift, the place is still doing business in rue de l'Ancienne Comédie. Benjamin Franklin, Voltaire and Napoléon were customers.

Colbert died in 1683, and Louis' luck on the battlefield ran out. Hopelessly embroiled in the

War of the Spanish Succession, the country was devastated by famine in 1692.

The Sun King died in 1715, leaving no direct heir. His five-year-old great grandson, Louis XV, was named king, with Philippe d'Orléans as regent. The court moved back to Paris. Installed in the **Palais-Royal**, the regent set about enjoying his few years of power, hosting lavish dinners which regularly degenerated into orgies. The state, meanwhile, remained chronically in debt.

PARIS SEES THE LIGHT

While Philippe partied, some of the city's more sober residents were making Paris the intellectual capital of Europe. Enlightenment thinkers like Diderot, Montesquieu, Voltaire and Rousseau were all active during the reign of Louis XV. Literacy rates were increasing – 50% of French men could read, 25% of women – and the publishing industry was booming.

The king's mistress, Madame de Pompadour, encouraged him to finance the building of the **Ecole Militaire** and the laying out of place Louis XV, known to us as **place de la Concorde**. The massive church of **St-Sulpice** was completed in 1776. Many of the great houses in the area bounded by rue de Lille, rue de Varenne and rue de Grenelle (most now occupied by French government ministries)

date from the first half of the 18th century. The private homes of aristocrats and wealthy bourgeois, these were the venues for numerous *salons*, informal discussion sessions devoted to topics raised by Enlightenment questioning.

The Enlightenment spirit of rational humanism finally took the venom out of the Catholic-Protestant power struggle, and the increase in public debate helped to change views about the nature of the state and the place and authority of the monarchy. As Jacques Necker, Louis XVI's finance minister on the eve of the Revolution, put it, popular opinion was 'an invisible power that, without treasury, guard or army, gives its laws to the city, the court and even the palaces of kings.' Thanks to the Enlightenment, that power was about to change the history of Europe.

THE ROAD TO RUIN

The French Revolution was not the inevitable and historical moment which hindsight has bequeathed us (*see p15* **Revving up**).

One of its causes was French reaction to defeat in the Seven Years War (1756-63). Louis XV not only lost valuable colonies in India and Canada to England, he decided to establish Europe's largest army and navy to ensure that France would never again take a hammering. The cost of this military expansion was astronomical, and it was the ordinary people who paid. By the time Louis XVI came to the throne, the national purse was drained. Sick of being exploited, the Third Estate (the commoners) decided to form a National Assembly and began drafting a constitution.

BASTILLE DAY

On 14 July 1789, the storm broke. Early in the day, a crowd stormed **Les Invalides** and carried off tons of weapons. They then marched across town to the royal prison at the **Bastille**, for so long a hated symbol of repression. A pitched battle ensued, in which 202 people died. When the mob finally took control of the jail, they decapitated its governor, the Marquis de Launay, and freed its seven bemused prisoners – two lunatics, four forgers, and a gentleman who had been found in someone else's bed. It was a modest start, but the Revolution at least had its symbolic act of violence against the *ancien régime*. There was no going back.

The Bastille was eventually razed to the ground. It took 800 workers over three years to complete the destruction. Much of the stone went to construct the **Concorde** bridge.

A plaque on the westbound side of the tunnel of Line 1 of the Métro, 50 metres from Bastille station, marks the foundations of one of the prison's eight towers. Nothing else remains.

The big bang: storming the **Bastille.**

Revving up

When you look at the lives of most French people in spring 1789, you find yourself incredulous that it took them so long to get angry. From our vantage point, society was structured in a way that had self-destruction built in. The majority of the population (the so-called Third Estate, a huge, artificial grouping of the bourgeoisie, workers and peasants) was systematically used and abused by the First and Second Estates (respectively, the clergy and nobility): the Third Estaters generated most of France's increasingly important economic output, and they were footing the bill for the lavish expenditure of the other two sectors. The Third Estate was the only section of society that was barred from officer status in the army.

Unless you were a member of the lucky sperm club, social advancement was impossible. Guilds had a tight grip on the city economy, keeping the plum jobs in the family. Even the good news was bad – if you were a Third Estate city-dweller, medical advances meant that you were more likely than ever to live longer... but so were your neighbours, so more and more people were crowding your space. Nobles were oppressing you from above and your neighbours were treading on your toes. So, how to get out of the ghetto? Escape to the country? Country-dwelling Third Estaters spent 90% of their life on or under the poverty line. Write to your MP? 18th-century France was an absolute monarchy with no Parliament. There was a semi-representative institution, the Estates General, but it hadn't been convened since 1614: popular representation was a distant historical concept. It's surprising that society had held together for so long.

But there's no value in looking at the situation from our point of view and asking questions of people's reactions that implicitly expect them to share our reference points. We might recoil from the idea of absolute monarchy, but there's nothing wrong with the notion in principle, especially if your monarch conforms to your era's standards of fairness; and there's no reason to get agitated about having a crappy life if society teaches you that your lot is to have a crappy life.

So why, then, did France come over so savagely revolutionary in the summer of 1789, as opposed to, say, the winter of 1726 or, for that matter, the spring of 2002?

Let's start at the top. Louis XVI was the worst kind of absolute monarch, an absolute dick-head. By spring 1789, things were ripe for change. If the king had had the nous to introduce even the gentlest reforms, he might have won popular support. What he did was to call the Estates together for a bit of a pep talk and showed himself to be such a blithering geek that he wrote himself out of the game.

This was not a good time to reveal yourself as King No-brain. Economically, France was about to crash. Louis XVI's predecessors had engaged the nation in ruinously expensive wars, and their acts of monarchical contrition for such profligacy had been what, exactly? Building such extravagant courts as Versailles (*see chapter* **Trips Out of Town**). Financial difficulties were driving taxes up, and the Third Estate, which was having a harder-than-usual time due to a bad harvest, bore the burden. For what? Pretty palaces and meaningless overseas campaigns. A great deal of tax-payers' money had already been spent supporting the Americans in their war of independence against the British.

Crucially, French involvement in this war had more than economic repercussions on society. When soldiers drifted back to France in the mid- to late-1780s, their eyes had been opened by American revolutionary concepts. Suddenly, fancy ideas began to circulate in Paris: that there should be no taxation without representation; that all men should be equal; that it was right to take up arms against tyrants. These ideas went hand-in-glove with those of Rousseau and Voltaire, who – along with other exponents of the so-called Enlightenment – had fired up the bourgeoisie with the notion that reason was a more valid ideal than the dogma of divine right. Revolutionary pamphlets began to appear. The promulgation of these ideas was a key factor in the outbreak of revolution.

So was the aforementioned harvest. In July, starving farm labourers joined the angry crowds roaming Paris. The scene was set for confrontation when the city guilds formed their own militia to protect their members' homes. The weather turned oppressively hot. All that was needed was a spark. Someone had the idea of grabbing weapons from Les Invalides and turning over the Bastille. This idea uncorked an astonishing sequence of escalating violence that made history.

The guillotine, the sharp end of revolutionary zeal.

Life returned to 'normal' after the initial revolutionary success. The king visited the Hôtel de Ville on 16 July and delighted the crowd by accepting a tricolour badge. The attack on the Bastille and the spirit of revolt were, apparently, ignored. The city council voted to erect a statue to the king on the site of the hated prison. Louis made a mental note to leave town at the first opportunity.

As the summer wore on, there were isolated acts of violence and riot, and a lot of discussion. Sensing that the worst was to come, many noble families tried to move quietly out of France, thus adding thousands of domestic servants to the ranks of the angry unemployed.

Louis made his move on 21 June 1791, attempting to escape with his family to Germany. He was stopped at the town of Varennes and brought back to be imprisoned in the Tuileries. Financed by worried European monarchs, a Prussian army invaded France and advanced on Paris. The possibility of a negotiated settlement was no longer an option.

THE TERROR

The revolutionaries were anything but united. They fought among themselves for everything from immediate gain to increased political power. Those in the provinces deeply distrusted those in the capital. In September 1792, as the Prussians approached Paris, a wave of paranoia led to the massacre of at least 2,000 suspected traitors. Later in the same month, the monarchy

was formally abolished and the French Republic proclaimed. A citizens' army defeated the Prussians at Valmy.

The year 1793 saw the execution of Louis and his queen, Marie-Antoinette, as well as the brutal murder of those revolutionaries believed to be too moderate. In the *Grande terreur* of 1794, the guillotine stationed in place du Trône Renversé (now place de la Nation) dispatched 1,300 souls in six blood-sodden weeks.

The remaining years of the century saw more violence, famine and war, as the new republic fought off the armies of neighbouring monarchs, defeated royalist factions within France, and endured its own internal power struggles. When the dust settled, a young Corsican general emerged as the unlikely winner. The citizens' revolution had paved the way for dictatorship.

EMPIRE, ANYONE?

Napoléon gave France muscle and leadership. After a decade of murderous chaos, it was a winning combination. Boney had himself declared emperor in 1804, and knocked the stuffing out of Russia and Austria at Austerlitz the following year. 'If only it lasts,' his proud mother remarked. It didn't. On his way to the decisive disasters of Moscow and Waterloo, Napoleon gave France the *lycée* educational system, the Napoléonic Code of civil law, the Legion of Honour, the Banque de France, the **Pont des Arts**, the **Arc de Triomphe**, the

Madeleine church (he cunningly re-established Catholicism as the State religion), the **Bourse**, and the **rue de Rivoli**. He also instigated the centralised bureaucratic system which is still driving people mad. And so, with a remarkably lively CV, the Little Corsican died on the south Atlantic prison island of Sainte Helena in 1821.

ANOTHER ROUND OF BOURBONS
Having sampled revolution and military dictatorship, the French were now ready to give monarchy a second chance.

The Bourbons got back in business, briefly, in 1814, then again the following year, in the person of Louis XVIII, Louis XVI's elderly brother. The missing roman numeral goes to Louis' son, the XVII, who died in prison in 1795.

Several efforts were made to adapt the monarchy to the new political realities, but the forces unleashed during the Revolution, and the divisions which had opened in French society as a result, were not to be ignored.

When another brother of Louis XVI, Charles X, became king in 1824, he decided that enough royal energy had been wasted trying to reconcile the nation's myriad factions. It was time, Charles believed, for a spot of old-fashioned absolutism. The people responded with old-fashioned rebellion.

In July 1830, the king abolished press freedom and dissolved the Chamber of Deputies. Print workers took to the streets, and three newspapers defiantly published. Police attempts to seize copies led to full-scale rioting and the defection of Paris regiments. After three days of fighting in the streets (*Les Trois Glorieuses*), Charles X was forced to abdicate.

THE UMBRELLA KING
Another leftover from the *ancien régime* was now winched onto the throne – Louis-Philippe, Duc d'Orléans, who had some Bourbon blood in his veins. A father of eight who never went out without his umbrella, he was eminently acceptable to the newly powerful bourgeoisie. But the poor who had risked their lives in two attempts to change French society were unimpressed by the new king's promise to embrace a moderate and liberal version of the Revolutionary heritage. Trouble simmered.

BOURGEOIS BOOM TIME
The population of Paris doubled to one million over the first half of the 19th century. Most of the new arrivals were rural labourers come to work on the city's building sites. The middle classes were doing well, thanks to the late arrival of the industrial revolution in France, and the solid administrative structures inherited from Napoléon. The poor were as badly off as ever, only there were more of them.

ONCE MORE, WITH FEELING
When troops fired on a crowd of the unemployed on boulevard des Capucines on 23 February 1848, they triggered another

Napoléon – a constant battle to get his leg over.

revolution. The monarchy was no longer the target: this time the antagonists divided on class lines, rich against poor. The city was soon embroiled in barricade fighting. When the National Guard sided with the revolutionaries, Louis-Philippe stood down.

This workers' revolution ushered in the Second Republic. But in the elections of May 1848, provincial conservatives won the day against Paris progressives. When disappointed workers in the capital again took to the streets, they were massacred by government troops. As the pamphleteer Adolphe Karr said of the aftermath of the 1848 revolution, 'plus ça change, plus c'est la meme chose' (the more things change, the more they stay the same).

In December 1848, Louis Bonaparte – nephew of Napoléon – was elected president, winning 5.7 million of the seven million votes cast. By 1852, he had moved into the **Tuileries Palace** and declared himself Emperor Napoléon III.

HAUSSMANN'S HOUSES

The Second Empire was a bizarre fruit. Baudelaire and Flaubert were hauled into court for endangering public morals. No teacher could wear a beard – a sure sign of anarchist tendencies. The emperor appointed a lawyer as Préfet to oversee the reconstruction of Paris. Yet Little Napoléon, as Hugo called him, held on to power for 22 years, and the lawyer, Georges-Eugène Haussmann, went on to create the most magnificent city in Europe.

Haussmann's wide avenues were not only better ventilated and more hygienic than the squalid lanes they replaced; they were also more difficult to barricade. The tree-lined streets radiating from place de l'Etoile are the classic expression of Haussmann's vision, while the rich mix of styles in Charles Garnier's **Opéra** (designed 1861) is often seen as typical of Second Empire self-indulgence.

PULVERISED BY PRUSSIA

The emperor's attempt to remain neutral in the Austro-Prussian war ended in disaster. At Sedan, in September 1870, 100,000 French troops were forced to surrender to Bismarck's Prussians, and Napoléon III was imprisoned in Germany. He never came back. In the humiliating deal which put a temporary end to hostilities, France lost the industrial heartlands of Alsace and Lorraine to Germany.

Out of the ruins of the Second Empire rose the Third Republic, a hasty compromise given little chance of survival even by those who supported it. In fact, this makeshift constitution was to survive until 1940, thus becoming the most enduring in modern French history.

1871: A COMMUNE MISTAKE

Things started badly. Paris was surrounded by German forces, who had to be paid off to leave. The place was seething with revolt. The new president, Adolphe Thiers, had moved the seat of government to Versailles, further inflaming opinion in the city. On 26 March 1871, the Commune of Paris was proclaimed by an enthusiastic but ill-organised group of radicals. The city was immediately surrounded by government troops, and, to the amazement of the occupying Prussians, systematic slaughter became the order of the day. In a celebrated shoot-out in the cemetery of **Père Lachaise**, 147 communards were cornered and executed against the Mur des Fédérés, now a memorial to the insurrection.

In less than a week, an estimated 30,000 Parisians were summarily executed by Thiers' troops, with 40,000 more being taken prisoner. A third of the city was destroyed by fire. The Tuileries Palace (the fourth side of the great square of the Louvre) was so badly damaged it had to be demolished.

The capital, unlike the nation's 38,000 other municipalities, lost the right to elect a mayor, a situation which lasted until 1976. The tragic story of the Paris Commune is memorably documented in the collection of the **Musée d'Art et d'Histoire de St-Denis**.

LA BELLE EPOQUE

Thanks mainly to the huge economic boost provided by colonial expansion in Africa and Indo-China, the horrors of the Commune were soon forgotten in the self-indulgent materialism of the turn of the century.

The **Eiffel Tower** was built as the centrepiece of the 1889 Universal Exhibition. In 1891 the first line of the Métro opened, linking Porte Maillot and Vincennes in a miraculous 25 minutes. For the World Exhibition of 1900, the Grand and Petit Palais, the Pont Alexandre III and the Gare d'Orsay (now, **Musée d'Orsay**) were built to confirm France's position as a dominant world power. The first cinema had opened (1895), and nightclubs like the **Moulin Rouge** (1890) were buzzing. In 1906, the department store **Galeries Lafayette** was a glittering shrine to the new prosperity. Private cars made their noisy appearance.

AN AFFAIR TO REMEMBER

In 1894, a Jewish army officer, Captain Alfred Dreyfus, had been dismissed in disgrace from the army and deported to Devil's Island, convicted of selling state secrets to the Prussians. It was clear that the army had staged a cover-up, and that Dreyfus was innocent. Far from remaining a minor matter of military discipline, the affair rocked the French establishment to its self-satisfied roots.

Emile Zola famously championed the Jewish officer's cause, as did statesmen such as Georges Clemenceau and Jean Jaurès. The Catholic right wing sided with the army, and lost heavily when Dreyfus was proven innocent. The Affair laid bare a deep strain of anti-Semitism in Republican France. It led, indirectly, to the separation of Church and State, and to the long-term fragmentation of the political right. Moreover, it provoked a crisis of confidence in a national army still smarting from the disgrace at Sedan. Alfred Dreyfus was finally exonerated in 1906.

THE GREAT WAR

The Germans never made it to Paris in the course of the First World War. They were stopped 20 kilometres short by French victory in the Battle of the Marne, the city's taxi drivers famously ferrying reinforcements to the front. But the city, and French society generally, suffered terribly as a result of this war, despite the ultimate victory and the return of Alsace and Lorraine; 1.5 million French men and women died during the fighting; 200,000 more in the flu epidemic which swept Europe in 1918. The economy was ruined, the franc losing four-fifths of its value by 1920. And yet the Third Republic survived.

The interwar years were a whirl of activity in both artistic and political circles. Paris became the avant-garde capital of the world, spiritual home to Surrealism and Cubism. Hemingway, F. Scott Fitzgerald and Gertrude Stein made the city their home and source of inspiration. The Depression unleashed a wave of political violence, Fascists fighting Socialists and Communists for control. The election in 1936 of Léon Blum's Front Populaire saw the introduction of such social benefits as paid holidays for workers.

THE SECOND WORLD WAR

Paris was in German hands within weeks of the start of hostilities. The city fell without a fight (amazingly in hindsight, the Nazis had had a respect bordering on fear for the French army), and the Third Republic came to an end. A pro-German government in Vichy was headed by Maréchal Pétain, while a young army officer, Charles de Gaulle, went to London to organise the Free French opposition. For those happy to get along with the German army, the period of the Occupation presented few real hardships. Food was rationed and tobacco and coffee went out of circulation.

Each month during the winter of 1939-40, 800,000 Parisians still managed to go to the cinema. For those few who chose to resist, there were the Gestapo torture chambers at avenue

In Context

August 1944: is that a weapon in your pocket, or are you just feeling freshly liberated?

May 1968 – talking about a revolution.

Foch or rue Lauriston. The Vichy government was eager to please the Germans. From the spring of 1941, the French authorities deported Jews to the death camps, frequently via the internment camp at Drancy, in what prime minister Pierre Laval claimed was a necessary concession to his Third Reich masters.

In July 1942, 12,000 Jewish French citizens were rounded up in the Vélodrome d'Hiver, a sports complex on quai de Grenelle, and then dispatched to Auschwitz. In July 1994, a memorial to the victims was finally erected near the site of the long-demolished sports arena.

Paris survived the war practically unscathed, ultimately due to the bravery of one of its captors. On 23 August 1944, as the Allied armies of liberation approached the city, Hitler ordered his commander, Dietrich Von Choltitz, to detonate the explosives which had been set all over town in anticipation of a retreat. Paris would have been reduced to a cloud of dust. Von Choltitz had the courage to refuse, an inaction for which he would later be honoured by the French government.

On 25 August 1944, French troops, discreetly placed at the head of the US forces, entered the city. Late that afternoon General de Gaulle, sporting his London tan, vogued his way down the Champs-Elysées (*see p168* **Mémorial du Maréchal Leclerc**).

THE ALGERIAN WAR

The postwar years were marked by the rapid disintegration of France's overseas interests. Vietnam was lost in 1954.

When revolt broke out in Algeria two years later, almost 500,000 troops were sent in to protect national interests – including 700,000 French colonists. A protest by Algerian nationalists in Paris on 17 October 1961, led to the deaths of hundreds of people at the hands of the city's police. The extent of the violence was officially concealed for decades. A plaque commemorating the tragedy was unveiled at Pont St-Michel in 2001. Algeria became independent in 1962 (*see right* **The Harkis**).

MAY 1968

Charles de Gaulle's Fifth Republic was felt by many to be grimly authoritarian. There are certainly those who believe that he designed it to be an elected monarchy, which is interesting when you consider that it's the constitution that is still in use today. In the spring of 1968, students unhappy with overcrowded university conditions took to the streets of Paris at the same time as striking Renault workers. The protest turned violent, and six million people went on strike. The real significance of May '68 is still debated. Some see it as a youth phenomenon, pampered brats taking on the police before taking their rightful places as political leaders and captains of industry. Others would argue that it was a real crisis, one which fundamentally changed the nature of French political life. President de Gaulle certainly took it seriously at the time, fleeing to Germany on 29 May as the street violence reached its peak. It is astonishing how brazenly he laced up his running shoes at times of crisis. He came back, of course, and somehow won a huge victory in the June elections. But his career was effectively over. He died in retirement two years later.

THE MITTERRAND YEARS

Following the largely anonymous presidencies of Georges Pompidou and Valéry Giscard d'Estaing, the Socialist François Mitterrand took up the task in 1981. The verdict on Mitterrand is still not in, even among ardent socialists, but he left an indelible mark on Paris. We can thank him for his grands projets: I M Pei's **Louvre Pyramid**, the **Grande Arche de la Défense**, the **Opéra Bastille**, and the **Bibliothèque Nationale de France François Mitterrand**.

CHIRAC

Jacques Chirac (or, as he is known, Le Bulldozer) has led a charmed political life, as Mayor of Paris, prime minister, and President of the Republic. He has made every error open to a modern politician, demonstrated every hue of cynicism that has, outrageously, become allowable in the modern politician's public image, and has survived. While he was running for his second term in presidential office, for example, he was under investigation for no fewer than three sets of alleged criminal offences. He won.

Chirac currently presides over a right-wing government with a massive majority, even if voter participation in the 2002 elections was the lowest in French history, and many crucial decisions are now made by the European authorities in Brussels and Frankfurt.

Chirac has little to fear, beyond a couple of financial investigations which await the end of his presidential immunity in 2006.

France is 2003 is not without its challenges: on the domestic front, the fact that the far-right politician Jean-Marie Le Pen made such an impact on the 2002 presidential election is hardly indicative of a nation at ease with itself. France seems not to be aware of (or, at least, to want to be aware of) its diminished importance in the international hierarchy. The country now takes a distinct second place to Germany in terms of European Union policies, but does at least try to add a note of restraint to the application of the US's global policing activities.

The Harkis

The Harkis, Muslims who fought on the French side in the Algerian War of independence, were very much the losers of that savage conflict; it was after, not during, the war that they suffered most.

When French troops withdrew from Algeria in 1962, they left behind Harki soldiers in a country that saw them as traitors and collaborators. Capture, torture and death followed at the hands of the Algerian revolutionary army. Official figures estimate that 150,000 were slain; Harki associations put the figure higher.

The 40,000 Harkis who managed to flee Algeria came to France and found it to be something less than the promised land. They ended up living in the provinces in rudimentary internment camps set up by the government. Having left behind farms, land and possessions, the Harki communities faced both poverty and isolation. The Bias camp near Bordeaux was a typical case. It housed 13,000 Harkis between 1962 and 1975. When it was closed the Harkis were relocated to a separate housing estate where they were again excluded from French life. It was only in the late 1990s that Harkis gained full French citizenship. The legacy of the camps is 400,000 Harkis in France with over 30% unemployment, more than four times the national average. Owing to the lack of a French welcome, many of the younger generation Harkis lack the confidence to leave their communities.

The zeal of Harki groups battling to bring France to justice for the abandonment of their allies has recently been heightened. 25 September 2001 was the inaugural national Harki remembrance day (in 1999, the Harkis had been denied permission even to place a memorial wreath at the Arc de Triomphe). During the first remembrance ceremony, Jacques Chirac said, 'France has not given the Harkis their rightful due. It is time that the nation does its moral duty and acknowledges their sacrifice and their dignity'.

The country will soon have the chance to ease its conscience. In March 2002, French courts ruled that Harki associations' prosecution of the French for crimes against humanity was legally valid, and the case is due to be heard in 2003.

Defining moments

EARLY HISTORY

250 BC Lutétia founded on the Ile de la Cité by a Celtic tribe, the Parisii.
52 BC Paris conquered by the Romans.
260 AD St Denis executed on Mount Mercury.
360 Julian, Governor of Lutetia, is proclaimed Roman Emperor by his troops.
451 Attila the Hun nearly attacks Paris.
496 Frankish king Clovis baptised at Reims.
508 Clovis makes Paris his capital.
543 Monastery of St-Germain-des-Prés founded.
635 King Dagobert establishes Fair of St-Denis.
800 Charlemagne becomes first Holy Roman Emperor. Moves capital from Paris to Aix-la-Chapelle (Aachen).
845-880 Paris sacked by the Vikings.
987 Hugues Capet, Count of Paris becomes king of France.

THE CITY TAKES SHAPE

1136 Abbot Suger begins Basilica of St-Denis.
1163 Building of Notre-Dame begins.
1181 Philippe-Auguste establishes market at Les Halles.
1190-1202 Philippe-Auguste constructs new city wall.
1215 University of Paris recognised with Papal Charter.
1246-48 Louis IX (St-Louis) builds the Sainte-Chapelle.
1253 Sorbonne founded.
c1300 Philippe IV Le Bel rebuilds Conciergerie.
1340 Hundred Years War with England begins.
1357 Revolt by Etienne Marcel.
1364 Charles V moves royal court to the Louvre and builds Bastille and Vincennes fortresses.
1420-36 Paris under English rule; 1422 Henry V of England dies at Château de Vincennes.
1463 First printing press in Paris.

THE WARS OF RELIGION AND AFTER

1528 François 1er begins rebuilding the Louvre.
1572 23 Aug: St Bartholemew's Day massacre of Protestants.
1589 Henri III assassinated.

1593 Henri IV converts to Catholicism, ending Wars of Religion.
1605 Building of place des Vosges and Pont Neuf, the first bridge without houses atop it.
1610 Henri IV assassinated.
1635 Académie Française founded.
1643 Cardinal Mazarin becomes regent.
1648-53 Paris occupied by the *Fronde* rebellion.
1661 Louis XIV begins personal rule – and transformation of Versailles; fall of Fouquet.
1667 Paris given its first street lighting.
1671 Building of Les Invalides.
1672 Creation of the Grands Boulevards on line of Charles V's city wall. Portes St-Denis and St-Martin built.
1680 Comédie Française founded.
1682 Louis XIV transfers court to Versailles.
1685 Colbert commissions place des Victoires.

ROYALTY TO REPUBLICANISM

1700 Beginning of War of the Spanish Succession.
1715 Death of Louis XIV; Philippe d'Orléans becomes regent.
1751 First volume of Diderot's *Encyclopédie*.
1753 Place Louis XV (later Concorde) begun.
1785 Fermiers Généraux Tax Wall built.
1789 First meeting of Etats-Généraux since 1614.
1789 14 July: Paris mob takes the Bastille. Oct: Louis XVI forced to leave Versailles for Paris.
1791 21 June: Louis XVI attempts to escape Paris.
1792 September Massacres. 22 Sept: Republic declared. Royal statues removed.
1793 Execution of Louis XVI and Marie-Antoinette. Louvre museum opens to the public.
1794 The Terror – 1,300 heads fall in six weeks. July: Jacobins overthrown; Directoire takes over.
1799 Napoléon stages coup, becomes First Consul.
1804 Napoléon crowns himself emperor in Notre-Dame.
1806 Napoléon commissions the Arc de Triomphe.

1814 Napoléon defeated; Russian army occupies Paris; Louis XVIII grants Charter of Liberties.
1815 Napoléon regains power (the 'Hundred Days'), before defeat at Waterloo. Bourbon monarchy restored, with Louis XVII.
1830 July: Charles X overthrown; Louis-Philippe of Orléans becomes king.
1836 Completion of Arc de Triomphe.
1838 Daguerre creates first daguerreotype photos.
1848 Louis-Philippe overthrown, replaced by Second Republic. Most men get the vote. Louis-Napoléon Bonaparte elected President.

CULTURAL EVOLUTION

1852 Louis-Napoléon declares himself Emperor Napoléon III: Second Empire. Bon Marché, first department store, opens.
1853 Haussmann appointed Préfet de Paris.
1862 Construction of Palais Garnier begins. Hugo's *Les Misérables* published.
1863 Manet's *Déjeuner sur l'herbe* exhibited.
1866 *Le Figaro* daily newspaper founded.
1870 Prussian victory at Sedan; siege of Paris. Napoléon III abdicates.
1871 Commune takes over Paris; May: *semaine sanglante*.
1874 First Impressionist exhibition in Nadar's *atelier* on bd des Capucines.
1875 Bizet's *Carmen* at Opéra Comique.
1889 Paris Exhibition on centenary of Revolution: Eiffel Tower built. Moulin Rouge opens.
1894-1900 Dreyfus case polarises opinion.
1895 Dec: world's first public film screening by the Lumière brothers at the Jockey Club (Hôtel Scribe).
1900 Paris' *Exposition Universelle*: Grand Palais, Petit Palais, Pont Alexandre III built. First Métro line.
1904 Pablo Picasso moves to Paris.
1910 Floods in Paris.

THE WORLD WAR YEARS

1914 As World War I begins, Germans beaten back from Paris at the Marne.
1918 11 Nov: Armistice signed in the forest of Compiègne.
1919 Peace conference held at Versailles.
1927 La Coupole opens in Montparnasse.

1934 Fascist demonstrations.
1936-37 France elects Popular Front under Léon Blum; first paid holidays.
1940 Germans occupy Paris. 18 May: de Gaulle's call to arms from London.
1941-42 Mass deportations of Paris Jews.
1943 Nativity of Jean-Philippe Smet (aka Johnny Hallyday).
1944 25 Aug: Paris liberated.
1946 Fourth Republic established. Women given the vote.
1947 Christian Dior's New Look. The Marshall Plan gives post-war aid to France.
1949 Simone de Beauvoir's *The Second Sex* published.
1955-56 Revolt begins in Algeria; demonstrations on the streets in Paris.
1957 Opening of CNIT in new La Défense business district.
1958 De Gaulle President: Fifth Republic.

EUROPEAN UNION AND NEW WORLD ORDER

1959 France founder member of the EEC.
1962 Algerian War ends.
1968 May: student riots and workers' strikes in Paris and across France.
1969 De Gaulle resigns, Pompidou becomes President; Les Halles market closes.
1973 Boulevard Périphérique inaugurated.
1977 Centre Pompidou opens. Jacques Chirac wins first mayoral elections. Marie Myriam wins the Eurovision Song Contest with *L'oiseau et l'enfant*.
1981 François Mitterrand elected President; abolition of the death penalty.
1986 Musée d'Orsay opens.
1989 Bicentenary of the Revolution: Louvre Pyramid and Opéra Bastille completed.
1995 Jacques Chirac elected President.
1997 General election: Socialist government elected under Lionel Jospin.
1998 France wins football World Cup.
2001 Socialist Bertrand Delanoë elected Mayor. *Le Monde* declares 'We Are All Americans' following the destruction of the World Trade Center.
2002 The success of National Front leader Jean-Marie Le Pen in the first round of the presidential elections paves the way for Jacques Chirac's landslide re-election. Jean-Pierre Raffarin becomes Prime Minister as France chooses to be governed by the centre-right.

Paris Today

Jon Henley takes a snapshot of a Paris with its head stylishly in the sand after a tumultuous year in French politics.

Two pictures of Paris: in the first, a ragged army swarms over the monumental bronze statue at République. Clinging to its limbs, they brandish their banners and howl their anger and their shame before a crowd that stretches, for once quite literally, as far as the eye can see. In the second, small and smiling children make sandcastles opposite the Ile Saint-Louis while their parents doze on bright blue deckchairs. Palm trees whisper the length of a packed promenade and, where motorists usually hurtle along the Seine expressway, *pétanque* players get the beers in from a beach café.

Three months and a bare mile or so separate these constrasting photographs of city in peril (or so it thought at the time) and a city at play, proof if any were needed that you never know the French capital so well that it ceases completely to surprise you. And last year Paris, once again, did not disappoint.

By common accord, there had not been as many people on the city's streets since the student uprising of May '68. May Day 2002 fell midway between the two rounds of a traumatic

presidential election that provided one of the biggest upsets in postwar French history. '*Pas de problème*', the veteran newscaster Patrick Poivre d'Arvor rather strangely proclaimed as he broke the news, at 8pm precisely on Sunday 21 April: the exit polls showed beyond any doubt that Jean-Marie Le Pen, the perennial pariah of French politics, had knocked oh-so-earnest Socialist prime minister Lionel Jospin out of the race for the Elysée.

It was a problem, though. It wasn't that Jospin necessarily deserved to advance to the second round run-off: he is, when all's said and done, a lousy communicator who fought an ill-advised campaign wooing the centre ground. No, it was the fact that through a fatal mixture of apathy, disenchantment and Gallic bloody-mindedness (why else vote for Arlette Laguiller, a diminutive but dangerous Trotskyist fighting for the dictatorship of the proletariat and the overthrow of parliamentary democracy?), a nation fed up with the policies and personalities of its mainstream parties found itself faced with a choice for president between a sleaze-ridden incumbent who had achieved nothing of note in seven years in power and a bullying former paratrooper best known for his remark that the Nazi gas chambers were 'a detail of history'.

That's one way of looking at it, of course. Another is that this was the outcome of a fair democratic process and that if well over half the French electorate decided either to stay at home or to vote for a variety of no-hope candidates from the extreme left or the extreme right, that spoke volumes about the present state of French politics.

But to accept that would also be to accept that the five million-plus people who cast their vote for the leader of the racist National Front were in some way entitled to do so, that they may have had a legitimate grievance to make known, and that their voices might deserve to be heard. And that, in the country that likes to call itself the birthplace of human rights, would never do. So France, and Paris in particular, plunged into its well-practised protest routine. 'No Pasaran!' was the rather unoriginal rallying cry: the fascists shall not pass. A daily rolling wave of anti-Le Pen marches and rallies around the country culminated in the capital with a May Day spectacular that drew fully one million people – a few of whom chose to climb, very photogenically, onto that monumental statue in the Place de la République. And it was, no matter what you think of its rights and wrongs, magnificent. Everyone, from scandalised schoolkids through left-wing luminaries to ageing militants who remembered the communist demos of 1936, was there, and the sea of people was so vast that – despite being being forced by the weight of numbers to take two different routes – the head of the march had reached Bastille well before the middle had even left République.

But despite its undoubted grandeur, that picture is probably not the one I would choose as my defining image of Paris, anno 2002. For starters, the whole thing turned out to be a storm in a teacup: President Jacques Chirac was re-elected by a positively Stalinist majority a few days later as even staunch leftists voted for him to keep Le Pen out, and in June's general elections the National Front failed to win a single seat in the National Assembly. And second, the electoral rout of the Socialists left just one of their number holding his head high in a major public office: step forward Bertrand Delanoë, mayor of Paris. And third, Delanoë last summer did something so bold, so original, so pleasing and so very French that he made Paris forget all about its springtime traumas.

In 2001, the mayor took the unprecedented step of closing the *voie Georges-Pompidou*, the main urban expressway that since 1967 has run

In Context

2002's whoppers

A year's an aeon in popular culture. This lot had a fine old 2002.

Law and order was the big political issue of the year. Minister of the Interior, Nicolas Sarkozy, is seeking changes in the law to give more power to the police and sharpen the dentures of the nanny state. This dude means business.

Mayor Delanoë has had a good year, with praise for his Style-by-the-Sea, *Paris-Plage*. Public reaction to his being attacked during the *Nuit Blanche* proved his immense popularity. We look forward to more treats from our Bertie.

Cinema's latest cutie, Cécile de France, has been flashing her assets in *A+ Pollux*, *L'Auberge espagnole* and *Irène*, the Gallic take on *Bridget Jones*. Cécile's our tip for superstardom. Why? Looks, talent and, er, more looks.

After years snapping at the heels of French politics, Jean-Marie Le Pen found a stage barren enough for his far-right policies. He came, he saw, he shook the masses from their complacency; he didn't win.

...and floppers

And this lot had an *annus horribilis* – a veritable bummer of a year.

After the rather fey *Dieu est grand, et je suis toute petite* (God is big, and I am very small and simpering), Audrey Tautou, post-*Amélie*, has found serious acting rather more difficult to crack than her *crème brûlée*. We await her *Phèdre*.

Jean-Marie Messier, The Mister Big of French mass media, finally took a tumble after enraging the French cultural establishment by meddling in the affairs of Canal+, and slashing and burning the Vivendi Empire.

Honest, decent and dour, Lionel Jospin made a noble and dramatic exit after failing to unite the left for the big presidential push. The French opt for charisma every time. Lionel is now available for weddings and voice-overs.

Patrick Viera, France's midfield maestro, is Senegalese. He probably wished he played for the Lions of Teranga following France's first round departure from the World Cup. Oh dear. How sad. Never mind.

along the Right Bank of the Seine through the heart of historic Paris, to all traffic during the summer holidays. It was a hastily-planned and poorly-executed project that caused massive tailbacks and provoked the ire of a great many Parisian motorists. Last year, everyone was better prepared and Delanoë had refined the concept: several tons of sand, several more tons of pebbles, 130 parasols, 120 flags, 22 blue-and-white striped changing huts, 300 deckchairs and four summer cafés turned nearly 4km of road widely known as the shortest stretch of motorway in France into a beach, Paris-Plage.

The operation was a huge success. During six summer weeks, more than two million marvelling Parisians strolled along the quays, sunned themselves on the sand, tried their hand at boules, picnicked on the pebbles, and fought for the sun-loungers with determined German tourists (actually, that last bit isn't true. Paris-Plage took place in 'a formidable spirit of civic responsibility and mutual respect', according to the town hall press release.)

Everyone was impressed – even the right-wing town hall opposition which, having cruelly derided the €1.5m project, was utterly silenced by the event's overwhelming popularity and finished up by admitting it 'contained some interesting elements'. In few other cities would such an experiment be possible, let alone succeed. But Paris has always adored the grand gesture, and this one, besides marking a fine symbolic step in the mayor's ongoing battle with the automobile, was at the same time so unexpected, so obvious, so frivolous and such fun that grumblers were almost impossible to find. This summer, the operation will be expanded to include part of the Left Bank. By 2007, the end of his mandate, Delanoë hopes to have installed two large swimming pools immersed in the Seine, and by the end of the decade the banks of the river – listed as a Unesco World Heritage site – could be entirely car-free.

So if pressed, and for a variety of reasons, my vote for contemporary Paris pic of the year goes to the small and smiling children building sandcastles by the Seine.

Ultimately, you somehow expect massive and heartfelt (if possibly misguided) demonstrations in the city that toppled a monarchy and spawned a revolution. You don't expect to admire one of the world's finest urban panoramas from a makeshift beach in the middle of what is usually a motorway. But that, thankfully, is part of what makes Paris Paris.

Jon Henley is Paris correspondent for *The Guardian*.

Security Fraud

The new government is serious about fighting crime, but will its hard-line approach victimise *liberté*, *égalité* and *fraternité*?

In November 2002, Paris' prostitutes, decked out in Halloween masks, organised a demonstration. The reason that streetwalkers were walking the streets in anger for the first time in 25 years was the package of proposed legislative remedies to the major social problem that confronts France today: crime.

The matter has been a concern in Paris for some time. In 2001, crime in general was up by 7.2% on the previous year; murders and attempted murders up by 35%; violence against women up by 40%; pick-pocketing on the Métro up by 38%. On top of that, consider the fact that, in 1999, there were, proportionally, more crimes in France than there were in the US.

In 2002, violence in Paris went high-profile, with street clashes in April following right-winger Le Pen's showing in the presidential elections; on Bastille Day somebody tried to shoot President Chirac; in the early hours of 6 October, the Mayor, Bertrand Delanoë, was stabbed at a reception in the Hôtel de Ville, during the *Nuit Blanche*, an all-night party he had organised to allow Parisians to get out on the streets and let their hair down (not mow their Mayor down).

Almost more alarming than these statistics and events has been France's reaction to them. The people spoke clearly in the first round of the presidential elections in 2002, when Le Pen, hijacking the need for law and order as the fig leaf behind which he positioned his tumescent racism, progressed to the second-round vote.

The real beneficiary of the climate of concern was the eventual winner, Jacques Chirac. The most recent statistics available illustrate that he, centre-right prime minister, Jean-Pierre Raffarin, and – most particularly – Minister of the Interior Nicolas Sarkozy are certainly getting stuck in to the problem. Street crime in Paris has fallen steadily since Chirac's re-election: August 2002 alone saw it drop by 18%. Jean-Paul Proust, the Prefect of Police, puts this down to the 'Evaluation-Action' scheme, an initiative based on New York police procedures. To enforce the new approach, since May, the number of police on the streets has doubled.

All of this has to be good news for the law-abiding tourist. You should still take good care of your valuables (cameras, mobile phones, etc.), and, as in any city, you need to keep a close eye on your wallet or purse, especially on the Métro (particularly just as the carriage doors are closing, when villains can make a grab for your sparklers). Also, be wary of people 'accidentally' bumping into you and nabbing your cash; and, sad to say, be careful when you're helping people who appear to have had minor accidents – in some cases, this is a ruse to bring about close body contact (and thus ease of pick-pocketing). That said, a modest amount of street sense should keep you out of trouble.

The legal changes that mean good news for tourists do not necessarily mean the same thing for the republican ideal of *liberté, égalité* and *fraternité*. Sarkozy has proposed extensive changes in the penal code 'to protect public peace and security': squatters, beggars and prostitutes, for example, would be subject to new laws. Simply looking like a prostitute could get you six months in jail, courtesy of the proposed offence of 'passive soliciting'. That's what put the ladies on the march in November. The Paris headquarters of Act Up, the civil rights campaigning group, analyses the motivation behind throwing more police, more laws, more state power at social problems rather than attacking their economic causes thus: 'Today Sarkozy is dreaming of a totalitarian state... prostitutes will be forced underground and drug users will become criminals'. Of course, it's in the nature of such organisations as Act Up to view tough law enforcement with concern; but it's not just the weekend Guevaras who are worried. The Magistrates' Union has expressed its concern at Sarkozy's initiatives, labelling them as anti-republican. In October 2002, the Lawyers' Union joined the Magistrates and the League of Human Rights to impress upon the French government that if Sarkozy's proposals are adopted, they would promptly drag French society in the direction of a police state.

Why is it that the emphasis seems to be on

repression rather than prevention? There are two main reasons.

Firstly, prevention would rely on the healing of social wounds (such as poor assimilation of immigrants and a growing poverty gap). With the painful memory of Le Pen's law and order-based renascence still fresh in the national consciousness, it seems that politicians are simply too afraid not to appear tough on crime. Its social causes take a back seat. Yet those social causes exist, of course, and will continue to cause problems. French society is certainly hampered by a significant level of racism. In April 2002, *Le Monde* held a survey which showed that 87% of young French people acknowledged that Arabs of North African origin faced racism in France. At around the

Simply looking like a prostitute could get you six months in jail, courtesy of the proposed offence of 'passive soliciting'

same time, Jewish groups were cancelling trips to Paris because of a perception that France was anti-Semitic and unsafe to visit. Interestingly, the white, French-born contingent of November's prostitutes' march blamed the crackdown on their trade on African immigrant girls who, they claimed, are willing to do their job without resorting to condoms. Any country with an anti-Jewish and anti-Arab outlook would take some beating in a modern-day racism competition.

The second reason why repression is a more attractive option is that prevention would also necessitate an acknowledgement that at least a fair proportion of crimes is committed by the victims of racism and those who feel excluded by mainstream French society. On this score, the media and the intelligentsia join politicians in silence for fear of being labelled racist.

Ignoring the causes of crime will not make them go away. The American political writer Joe Klein has compared modern-day France to 1970s America, drawing parallels via such shared problems as an influx of immigrants who are resented by the host nation, a sluggish economy and alienated youth. These are social rifts that will take generations to heal; will the healing process really be assisted by incarcerating prostitutes?

So, as a visitor, you're less likely to be the victim of crime in Paris than you were one year ago. If you're worried about safety, a normal level of care should see you right. But if you're worried about civil liberties in France, it's time to read the small print on every new law.

State of the Art

Once it was all absinthe and abstractionism, but Paris no longer attracts the creative cream. Things went sour; here's how.

'Where does an artist like me have to go to be accepted? There must be somewhere. Where did the others go? Van Gogh, Renoir, Gogol, Rembrandt and all that mob? Where can I go to be appreciated? Of course! Paris!' Anthony Aloysius St John Hancock's triumphant realisation in the greatest cinematic satire of the Paris art world ever made, *The Rebel,* taps into a notion – that of Paris as the world's great nurturer of creative talent – that was outdated when the film was made in 1960 and yet still lingers in people's perception of the city.

For a period of about 50 years, starting from the last decades of the 19th century, the notion was true. The streets of Paris housed some of the greatest artists in the world. They revelled in the brothels of Montmartre, the cheap lodgings, the even cheaper French wine and, of course, the legendary Parisian cafés. *La vie de Bohème* proved irresistible to creative talent (and to bone-idle, talentless buffoons who wanted a piece of the action), and drew an ever-growing, increasingly international circle: Modigliani came from Italy, Picasso from Spain

and Rivera from Mexico. In the 1920s, big Ernie Hemingway set up camp and hobnobbed with emigré artists such as Gertrude Stein, James Joyce and F Scott Fitgerald. The joys of libertine Paris were not quite the only magnet for the talent influx, however: people such as Chagall and Zadkine, for example, fled from the fall-out of the Russian revolution because the city was reckoned to be politically *sympatico.*

It could have lasted. The reason it didn't is that the events of 1940 and the Occupation irreversibly changed Paris' image. The city was plunged into despair and shame – let's not forget that just a couple of miles to the north of the city was Drancy, a French-staffed internment camp for people on their way to Auschwitz (*see chapters* **History** *and* **Beyond the Périphérique**) – that weakened its hold over the cultural dynamics of the Western world. The artists previously so enamoured of the city woke up to find a morally compromised Paris. Of course, artists continued to live and work in the capital, but the lustre had gone. The author Serge Guilbaut describes the all-

In Context

Contemporary Voices: Bruno Dumont, artist in a squat

'Paris should be the centre of the cultural world, but there are many problems because artists cannot support themselves. Studio spaces are too expensive. That's why there's been an emergence of art squats. They bring life back to the arts in Paris and destroy the image of her as a pompous museum-city.'

pervading disillusionment: 'After the Second World War, few – including French painters – still believed in the formerly all-powerful Parisian Muse. She had been disrobed. She was still cute, but she had lost her mystery, her finery. She did not seduce any more.' The Muse had become a clapped-out hooker.

In this loss of innocence and its subsequent exodus lay the roots of the crises in contemporary French art. Most of the artists living in Paris had not been French, and even fewer were Parisian; the emigré withdrawal was catastrophic; and as the Parisian (and, thus, French) art world was falling into disrepair, America's was thriving. Enormously wealthy, the US was in a position to support and cultivate the arts. Moreover, *America* hadn't been found wanting morally – *America* hadn't surrendered and America hadn't collaborated. To make matters worse, even sex appeal had

migrated across the Atlantic, as the States offered up Marlon, Marilyn and Elvis.

Even under the dynamic husbandry of André Malraux, appointed the first Minister of Culture in 1959, Paris made little contribution to contemporary arts. The artist John Franklin Koenig, who was living and working in Paris from 1948, writes: 'The schools were poor and had insufficient programs; museums did not buy, and did not even seem interested in looking, especially when the art was contemporary. We fell into the old French pattern, in which no one bought the Impressionists, the Post-Impressionists and the different forms of non-figurative art until after the artists were well-respected or dead.' The American system of corporate, big bank and company sponsorship to help the arts and education had no precedent in France, and the state struggled to kick-start its artistic activity.

As ever, when an element of its cultural self-image is threatened, France hasn't gone down without a fight. Since the late 1960s, Paris has been trying to correct the deficit in its cultural output. Governments of the 1970s focused on a policy of cultural development which attempted to democratise and decentralise the arts; its showcase, the Pompidou Centre (*see chapter* **Museums**), opened in 1977. Georges Pompidou's dynamic approach called for 'a cultural centre in Paris which would be both a museum and a centre of creativity.' The 1980s, with Jack Lang as Minister of Culture, saw

The **Centre Pompidou**, an example of the wrapping being superior to the gift?

state-propelled cultural expansion – the budget was increased, and cultural policy opened up the realms of high art to circus, graffiti, photography, fashion and gastronomy. Lang argued that 'the basis of our thinking is that all the arts matter, even minor ones, and culture must be truly popular.' In 1982, Fiacre (Fonds d'incitation à la création), an organisation for the funding of artists, was created.

Artists working in Paris today can expect large subsidies from the government: financial aid for their first exhibition, and a grant of up to €7,600 for help in future artistic projects. In 2000, the budget for the Ministry of Culture and Communication was 2.4 billion euros. This is deployed offering support to young artists, improvement of their living conditions and help in accessing the international market.

Massive state and local subsidies, however, have failed to revive the contemporary French art market. In response to concerns about the country's place within an international market, the Ministry for Foreign Affairs recently commissioned a report by Alain Quémin. In his findings, Quémin highlighted the marginal

As ever, when an element of its cultural self-image is threatened, France hasn't gone down without a fight

presence of contemporary French artists in the permanent collections of the big cultural institutions. The importance of contemporary French art in international exhibitions is trailing behind Germany, who top the list, the United States who are second, and the Swiss, who are third. Where's France?

Just to twist the knife in a little deeper, the report identified the 100 best-known artists in the world in 2000: 33 came from America, 28 from Germany, eight from Britain and only four from France (Christian Boltanski, Daniel Buren, Sophie Calle and Pierre Huyghe – heard of them?). As one gallery owner in Paris explained to Quémin, the market for contemporary French art is simply unable to sustain itself: 'When I opened the gallery, I wanted to sell half French work and half foreign; it was a deliberate policy on my part to defend French artists. And yet in every way today, it is clear that one is forced to have at least half foreign work. I have more and more of it. I have to sell 70% foreign art and 30% French, not because I want to, but simply because of market forces.'

One of the reasons for this failure of the market in France is the lack of big collectors – of 'taste-makers' – to stimulate the market

Contemporary Voices: Diana Kami, artist
'The market here is very difficult because the French are afraid of spending money to invest in art. Compared to other countries, the French don't buy: they make good investments on well-known artists. But, on the other hand, you can always find somewhere to exhibit in Paris, in galleries or bars. And there are quite a few underground galleries who are willing to take a chance on young, unknown artists because they fall in love with their work.'

economically. The state provides an admirable amount of support, but the scene needs some private sector Monsieur or Madame Bigs (look at what Charles Saatchi did for the Young British Artists) to wade in with the cheque book and send art prices soaring. America, Germany, Italy and Switzerland all have their big collectors. But France remains in the doldrums, relying predominantly on state subsidies that do not raise media interest and therefore fail to attract a public audience.

In 1994 ADIAF (Association pour la Diffusion Internationale de l'Art Français) was set up, and is currently engaged in efforts to rectify the weak position of contemporary French art within the international market. It too supports artists living in France, but its main objective is to woo French collectors into the plastic arts, and its president, Gilles Fuchs, is one of the few active contemporary French collectors. In 2000, ADIAF was reponsible for setting up the Prix Marcel Duchamp, which gives France its first collectors' prize (like the Hugo Boss Prize in the United States and the Turner Prize in Britain).

For many French collectors, the market for contemporary art has no resilient value. There is a feeling in France that the flourishing home markets in America, Germany and Britain must have been created by some mysterious, faintly vulgar, Anglo-Saxon media machine that is off-limits to the French sensibility. But the real problem is that France, wallowing in its age-old rut of caution and cultural nostalgia, is refusing to cast more than a cursory glance over those of its artists who are actually alive and working. Meanwhile, the public conscience is eased by extensive state help – the life-support machine for a comatose market. The Paris scene has had a too-long attack of the Rip Van Winkles. The talent's out there, so's the inspiration, so's the cushy, state-subsidised life: Paris, it's time to wake up, put your teeth in and just smell that absinthe.

WHSmith

The English Bookshop

Books • Magazines • Guides
Videos & DVDs • Games • CD-Roms

1903-2003
This year we are celebrating a 100 years in Paris!

**WH Smith stock the entire range of
'Time Out' magazines and guides, including:**

- London's Time Out available on Wednesday of issue
- Eating & Drinking in London
- Eating & Drinking in Paris
- London Shopping & Services
- London Visitors' Guide
- Paris Visitors' Guide
- Film Guide
- Time Out New York every Thursday

**Plus Penguin Books' complete series
of Time Out City Guides.**

**248 rue de Rivoli, 1st. M° Concorde
Tel: 01.44.77.88.99 • Fax: 01.42.96.83.71
whsmith.france@wanadoo.fr • www.whsmith.fr
Open Mon-Sat 9am-7.30pm, Sun 1pm-7.30pm**

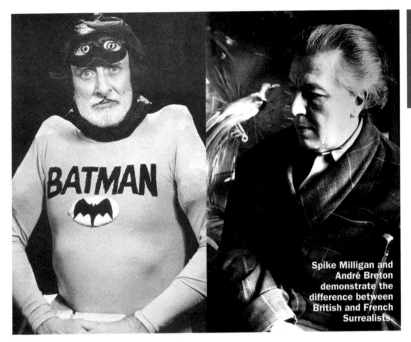

Spike Milligan and
André Breton
demonstrate the
difference between
British and French
Surrealists.

The Surreal Thing

You know what Surrealism is; but did you ever wonder how it
progressed from Parisian luvviedom to British laddism?

Spot the luvvie: **John Lennon**, **Spike
Milligan**, Ginger Geezer **Viv Stanshall**, **Vic
Reeves**. You can't, can you? There isn't one. So
the 64,000 euro question dangling hairily before
us is: how did Surrealism, an artistic movement
born in the 1920s to a coterie of Paris-based,
bourgeoisie blossoms manage to cross the
Channel and influence, not only the above-
mentioned geniuses (Lennon: 'To me,
surrealism is reality'), but many of Britain's
other most gifted and successful working-class
artists? How did it make that leap? How did it
avoid being numbed down or dumbed down?
Easy: it was unique among artistic movements
in that it was a sex and drugs and rock'n'roll
beast, and it arrived in the UK just when people
were sick – and about to get even sicker – of
everything that was supposed to make sense.

So let's talk about sex: surrealism had balls.
Blossoms its founders may have been, but the
talent they wielded in all sorts of artistic
spheres endowed the movement with a lot of
juice. Writers **Louis Aragon** and **Paul
Eluard**, film-makers **Luis Buñuel** and **Jean
Cocteau**, and painters **Joán Miró**, **Salvador
Dalí** and **René Magritte** comprised a
formidably gifted, impossible-to-ignore team.
Then there was the missionary vigour of the
movement's midwife **André Breton**, author of
the 1924 *Manifeste du surréalisme*. No mean
poet and critic himself, Breton was known as
the Pope of Surrealism, yet he seems to have cut
more of a Violet Elizabeth Bott dash, throwing
anyone who disagreed with him out of the gang,
launching purges and not being as fey as his
hairstyle would have you believe.

In Context

Breton, Aragon, Hilsum and Eluard wait for Dali to perfect the crackpot moustache.

A further clue to Surrealism's bawdy appeal to most Brits is rooted in its family tree: its lecherous old uncle was Sigmund Freud. From Freud came the lunatic juxtapositions that are all over Surrealism like a rash and the dominance of implication and association over literal meaning. But his most popular influence

Surrealism was like a winking, bosomy aunt who knows exactly what you get up to under the duvet

on the movement's appeal was his everything-puts-me-in-mind-of-sex thing. The Surrealists went for *that* in a big way; what a realistic, red-blooded and democratic stance to adopt. After all, don't we all have days like that, days when the sap is at high tide, and everything – even the family pet – conjures the red mist of lust? Certainly, from the evidence of their lives and their art, it seems that the Parisian Surrealists were, like the rest of us, a bunch of actual or would-be pervs. One could instance Marcel I-know-what-the-chicks-dig Duchamp, who famously sent his girlfriend a phial of semen as

a forget-me-not (well, they didn't have texting back then). Breton himself said that the movement was devoted to what he termed 'the omnipotence of desire', and there's something warm and inclusive about a movement that admits the naughty truth about us all. Surrealism was like a winking, bosomy aunt smelling of Baileys and chip fat who knows exactly what you get up to under the duvet and, what's more, encourages you to do it. Surrealism's mass appeal is its sex appeal.

Despite that, its early PR wasn't the sort of thing you can imagine arousing the interest of, say, a youthful Spike Milligan. Breton defined the movement in his *Manifeste* as, 'pure psychical automatism, which has the aim of expressing, whether verbally, in writing, or in some other manner, the actual functioning of thought freed from any control of the reason and any aesthetic or moral preoccupation'. The subsequent ideal was 'to transmute two seemingly contradictory states, dream and reality, into a sort of absolute reality, a surreality'. Eh? Look beyond the pretentiousness of the language and you'll see that Breton was describing a process exactly like that sought by many a Brit from a night out. Breton is talking about finding ways of doing nothing more mysterious than, in the current vernacular, getting off your tits and coming over all creative. Very appealing, even though many of us routinely have the more humble ambition of just getting off our tits as an end in itself. Then again, how many of us, returning home from a beano, have found ourselves moved to the act of creation? Be honest. Who has not, while in a state of 'pure psychical automatism', reeled off a poem, or a love letter, or a quick synopsis of a blockbuster? Voilà what the Surrealists called 'automatic writing', the loony outpourings of a trance state. Anyone can do that; you don't need A-levels or a posh education.

As for your rock'n'roll, well, early Surrealism couldn't strictly boast any, but it did go on the road. In 1936, almost 50,000 people visited the London run of the astonishingly successful International Surrealist Exhibition. Its highlight was surely when Salvador Dali's speech from within a diving suit was prematurely terminated due to his running low on oxygen and having to be cut out by a rescue team (shades of *Spinal Tap*'s Derek Smalls getting trapped in his pod there).

So these were not navel-gazing fancy lads: they were unpredictable nutters on the road, playing to big crowds. The Surrealists knew the value of a high profile, and Breton did as much for their public image as Epstein ever did for the Beatles'. There were also the many versions of the Manifesto and such magazines as *Littérature*, *La Révolution surréaliste* and, naturally, *Le Surréalisme au service de la révolution*.

Revolution? Aha, now that's a bit more Lennonesque, isn't it? That's a bit more working class hero and NHS glasses. Surrealism's powerful anti-bourgeois stance certainly had a lot of revolutionary things to say to British society in the 1930s, especially the layer that was routinely offered the shitty end of the stick. Imagine that you were from the class and generation whose members were coming to the bleak realisation that they were destined to be just what their dads had been 20 years earlier – canon fodder. Wouldn't a movement that had developed partly in disgust at the values and aspirations of a society that had produced the First World War have a distinct appeal to the class who'd fought it on behalf of the generals and politicians? Surrealism had a revolutionary enough-is-enough feel that extended to the individual as well as to the mass. Breton referred to it as being a campaign of systematic refusal against 'the whole series of intellectual, moral and social obligations that continually and from all sides weigh down upon man and crush him'. Ever felt like that? Ever grown tired of a life spent doing not much more than trying to keep

the boss off your back just so you can pay the bills for another year? Call that living?

Although the conditions were ideal in 1930s and 40s Britain for Surrealism to take root in working class consciousness, the beast had to change before it could go on to permeate much of modern-day UK popular culture. The key evolution of the working class British Surrealists is that they swapped the Parisians' reliance on seriousness (often psycho-sexual, but, really, what could be less deserving of a po face than the farce that is the old rumpy-pumpy?) for simply having a laugh. Breton gave us 'Surrealism uproots thought from an increasingly cruel state of thraldom'. Milligan gave us '*I'm Walking Backwards for Christmas*'. (The best Surrealist quote has to be, however, Dali's 'I don't do drugs – I *am* drugs'. Think about it, kids).

Watch a bit of Saturday morning children's TV, check out the YBAs, analyse the plot of your favourite soap or listen to the nonsensical claptrap at your next management briefing. In these increasingly crazy times, Surrealism's everywhere. Don't forget where it all started.

The best Surrealism

Paris locations
Studio 28 20 rue Tholozé, 18th, the cinema where a 1930 showing of Buñuel's *L'Age d'Or* sparked a right-wing riot. Oi, oi, oi!

Place Blanche 9th, centre of Breton's manor. He held court, he made plans and stratagems, he got tremendously pissed.

Rue La Fayette 9th, where, in 1926, Breton met the wandering wraith who inspired his *Nadja*. Bet she did.

Works
Manifeste du surréalisme, André Breton, 1924: laid it on the line.

Nadja, André Breton, 1928: Surrealism's first major novel, and it's set in Paris.

Un Chien Andalou, Luis Buñuel (with help from Dalí), 1928: eye-eye, not a film for the squeamish.

The Goon Show, Spike Milligan, Peter Sellers Harry Secombe, 1951-60: revolutionary radio show that influenced Peter Cook, John Lennon, Vic Reeves, Eddie Izzard, Liam Gallagher and, almost certainly, you.

In Context

Third-Empire fancy: Palais Garnier.

Architecture

It doesn't matter if you can't tell your apse from your alcove:
for architectural beauty, look up from the pavement.

THE ROMANESQUE

Medieval Paris was centred on the Ile de la Cité
and the Latin Quarter. The main thoroughfares
(rue St-Jacques and rue Mouffetard) followed
those of Roman Paris. Paris had several
powerful Romanesque abbeys outside the city
walls, but remains of this simple style are few.
The tower of **St-Germain des Prés**, topped
by a later spire, still has its rounded arches, and
some decorated capitals survive in the nave.

GOTHIC PARIS

Note: this section does not concern people who
like dressing in black, looking pallid and
listening to Bauhaus. Easy mistake to make,
though. 'Twas in the **Basilique St-Denis** that
the Gothic trademarks of pointed arches, ogival
vaulting and flying buttresses were first
combined. Vaulting allowed buildings to span
large spaces and let light in, hence an aesthetic
of brightness and verticality. A spate of
building followed with cathedrals at Chartres,
Sens and Laon, as well as **Notre-Dame**,
which incorporated all the features of the style:

twin-towered west front, soaring nave, intricate
rose windows and buttressed east end.

Shortly after work on Notre-Dame had begun,
Philippe-Auguste began the first **Louvre**, part
of whose keep can still be seen within the
museum complex. In the following century,
ribbed vaulting became more refined and
columns more slender, in the Rayonnant or
High Gothic style. Mason and architect Pierre
de Montreuil continued work on St-Denis, and
his masterpiece, the 1246-48 **Sainte-Chapelle**,
took Gothic to its height.

The later Flamboyant-Gothic style saw a
wealth of decoration. **Eglise St-Séverin**, with
its twisting spiral column, is particularly
original. The pinnacles and gargoyles of the
early-16th-century **Tour St-Jacques** and the
porch of **St-Germain-l'Auxerrois** are typical.
The **Tour Jean Sans Peur** is a rare fragment
of an early 15th-century mansion, while Paris'
two finest medieval mansions are the Hôtel de
Cluny (now **Musée National du Moyen-
Age**) and **Hôtel de Sens**.

THE RENAISSANCE

The influence of the Renaissance came late to Paris, and was largely due to François 1er. He installed Leonardo da Vinci at **Amboise** and brought over Primaticcio and Rosso to work on his palace at **Fontainebleau**. The pretty, hybrid church of **St-Etienne-du-Mont** shows that Renaissance style remained a largely superficial effect: the structure is Flamboyant Gothic, the balustrade of the nave and the elaborate roodscreen are Renaissance. A heavier hybrid is the massive **St-Eustache**. The **Hôtel Carnavalet**, altered by Mansart, and the **Hôtel Lamoignon**, both in the Marais, are Paris' best examples of Renaissance mansions.

THE ANCIEN REGIME

Henri IV built the **Pont Neuf** and **place Dauphine** on the Ile de la Cité and **place des Vosges** in the Marais. The latter were both symmetrical, with red brick vaulted galleries and very pitched roofs. The 17th century was a high point in French power; the monarchy desired buildings to reflect its grandeur: bonjour, Baroque, but even at **Versailles** the style never reached the excesses of Italy, as French architects followed Cartesian principles of harmony and balance.

The **Palais du Luxembourg** combines classic French château design with elements of the Pitti Palace in Marie de Médici's native Florence. Counter-Reformation churches such as the **Chapelle de la Sorbonne** followed the Gésu in Rome. The **Eglise du Val-de-Grâce**, designed by Mansart, and later Jacques Lemercier, is one of the grandest examples of Baroque architecture in Paris.

Nouveaux-riches flocked to build mansions in the Marais and the Ile-St-Louis. Those in the Marais follow a symmetrical U-shaped plan, with a secluded courtyard: look through the archways to the *cour d'honneur* of the **Hôtel de Sully**, Hôtel Libéral Bruand or Hôtel Salé (now **Musée Picasso**), where facades are richly decorated.

Under Colbert, Louis XIV's chief minister, the creation of stage sets to magnify the Sun King's power proceeded apace. The Louvre grew as Claude Perrault created the sweeping west facade, while Hardouin-Mansart's circular **place des Victoires** and **place Vendôme**, an elegant octagon, were both designed to show off equestrian statues of the king.

ROCOCO & NEO-CLASSICISM

In the early 18th century, the Faubourg-St-Germain overtook the Marais in fashion. Under Louis XV, the severe lines of the previous century were softened by rounded corners and decorative detailing, such as satyr masks over

doorways, at the Hôtel Chenizot (51 rue St-Louis-en-l'Ile) and **Hôtel d'Albret** (31 rue des Francs-Bourgeois). The main developments came in interior decoration, with the frivolous French rococo style. The finest example is the **Hôtel de Soubise**, with panelling, plasterwork and paintings by decorators of the day including Boucher, Restout and Van Loo.

From the 1750s, geometry was back as Ancient Rome inspired another monument to royal majesty, Jacques Ange Gabriel's neo-classical **place de la Concorde**; and Soufflot's domed **Panthéon** on a Greek cross plan was inspired by the one in Rome.

Utopian Claude-Nicolas Ledoux's **toll gates** played games with pure geometrical forms; circular at parc Monceau and La Rotonde de la Villette, and rectangular pairs at place Denfert-Rochereau and place de la Nation.

THE NINETEENTH CENTURY

The Revolution largely confined itself to pulling buildings down. Royal statues bit the dust, and churches became 'temples of reason' or grain stores. Napoléon, however, soon brought Paris back to a proper sense of its grand self. Land confiscated from aristocracy and church was built up. A stern classicism was preferred for the **Arc de Triomphe**, the Greek-temple-inspired **Madeleine** and Brongniart's **Bourse**.

By the 1840s, classical style was under challenge from a Gothic revival led by Eugène Viollet-le-Duc. Historical eclecticism ruled, though, with the neo-renaissance **Hôtel de Ville**, **Hôtel de la Païva** and **Eglise de la Trinité**. Hittorff chose Antique polychromy in the **Cirque d'Hiver**, while Byzantium and the Romanesque made a comeback from the 1870s.

The best Generics

Gothic groove
Hôtel de Cluny (5th). *See p117.*

Baroque'n'roll
Eglise de Val-de-Grace (5th). *See p117.*

Renaissance rood-ery
Eglise St-Etienne-du-Mont (5th). *See p116.*

Pseudo-Grecian naffness
Eglise de la Madeleine (8th). *See p85.*

Art Nouveau-la-la!
Chez Julien (10th). *See p90.*

Aerodynamism
Le CNIT (La Défense). *See p142.*

Breakthroughs in engineering made the use of iron frames increasingly popular. Henri Labrouste's reading room at the **Bibliothèque Ste-Geneviève** (1844-50), in the place du Panthéon, was one of the first to use iron for the entire structure. Stations like Hittorff's **Gare du Nord** (1861-65) and such massive stone structures as the Grande Galerie de l'Evolution (**Muséum d'Histoire Naturelle**) and **Musée d'Orsay** are but shells around an iron frame. The most daring iron structure of them all was of course the **Eiffel Tower**, built in 1889, then the tallest structure in the world.

BARON HAUSSMANN

Appointed Napoléon III's *Préfet de la Seine* in 1853, Haussmann was not an architect but an administrator. Aided by architects and engineers including Baltard, Hittorff, Alphand and Belgrand, he set about shooshing up Paris. Broad boulevards were cut through the old city. An estimated 27,000 houses were demolished and some 100,000 built. The boulevards answered communication and health problems in a city that had grown from 500,000 in 1789 to one million in 1850. They also ensured that the city could be more easily governed.

Haussmann constructed asylums, prisons, schools, churches (**Eglise St-Vincent de Paul**), hospitals, and the water and sewage systems. He landscaped the Bois de Boulogne and gave Paris its new market pavilions at Les Halles. Amid the upheaval, one building epitomised Second Empire style: Charles Garnier's sumptuous **Palais Garnier** opera of 1862-75. The city also acquired the Haussmannian apartment block, which lasted until well into the 20th century.

THE TWENTIETH CENTURY

The past century began with an outburst of extravagance for the 1900 Exposition Universelle. Laloux's Gare d'Orsay (now **Musée d'Orsay**) and the **Train Bleu** brasserie were ornate examples of the heavy beaux arts floral style and eclectic classical motifs of the period.

Art nouveau looked to nature and fluid forms. It is seen at its most flamboyant in Guimard's Métro stations, as well as in restaurants and brasseries, notably **Julien** and Maxim's. It was all a long way from the work of Henri Sauvage, innovative but too eclectic to be identified with any movement. After the geometrical Cité Commerciale Argentine flats (1904), his tiled apartment block at 6 rue Vavin (1911-12) was the first to use stepped-back terraces to get light into the different storeys. He went to a bigger social housing project in rue des Amiraux, tiled artists' studios-cum-flats in rue de la Fontaine, and the more overtly art

deco 1920s extension of **La Samaritaine**. Social housing began to be put up citywide, funded by philanthropists, such as the Rothschilds' estate in rue de Prague, 12th.

THE MODERN MOVEMENT

After World War I, two dudes rule – Auguste Perret and Le Corbusier. Perret stayed within a classical aesthetic, but his use of reinforced concrete gave scope for more varied facades, as in his flats and own office in rue Raynouard (16th) and the circular Conseil Economique et Social at place d'Iéna. Le Corbusier tried out his ideas in private houses, such as the Villa La Roche (**Fondation le Corbusier**). His Pavillon Suisse at the **Cité Universitaire** and **Armée du Salut** hostel in the 13th can be seen as an intermediary point between these villas and the mass housing schemes of his Villes Radieuses, which became so influential and so debased in projects across Europe after 1945.

Robert Mallet-Stevens is unrivalled for his elegance, most clearly on **rue Mallet-Stevens**. Paris is one of the best cities for Modern Movement houses and studios. Other examples include Adophe Loos' house for Dadaist poet Tristan Tzara in avenue Junot, 18th, supposedly the epitome of his maxim 'ornament is crime', Chareau's influential Maison de Verre (31 rue St-Guillaume, 7th, not visible from the

On a lighter note...

street), houses by Lurçat and Perret near parc Montsouris, Pierre Patout's steamboat-style apartments (3 bd Victor, 15th) and Studio Raspail at 215 bd Raspail by Elkouken.

The Modern Movement showed its influence in town halls, public housing and in numerous schools built in the socially-minded 1930s, while the love of chrome, steel and glass found its way into art deco brasseries including **La Coupole**, and the **Grand Rex** cinema.

POST-WAR PARIS

The aerodynamic aesthetic of the 1950s saw the 1958 **UNESCO** building, by Bernard Zehrfuss, Pier Luigi Nervi and Marcel Breuer. The shanty-towns that had emerged, many occupied by immigrant workers, cried out for a solution. In the 1960s and '70s, tower blocks sprouted in the suburbs (some solution) and new towns were created. Redevelopment inside the city was limited, but regulations allowed taller buildings, noticeably the Tour Montparnasse and in the 13th. Renzo Piano and Richard Rogers' high-tech **Centre Pompidou**, opened in 1977, was the first of the prestige projects that have become a trademark of modern Paris.

THE 1980S & BEYOND

Mitterrand's *grands projets* dominated the 1980s and early '90s as he sought to leave his stamp on the city with Nouvel's **Institut du Monde Arabe**, Sprecklesen's **Grande Arche de la Défense**, as well as Ott's more dubious **Opéra Bastille**, Perrault's **Bibliothèque Nationale** and Chemetov's Bercy finance ministry. Urban renewal has transformed previously industrial areas to return the balance of Paris eastwards. Stylistically, the word is 'transparency' – from I M Pei's **Louvre Pyramid**, and Nouvel's **Fondation Cartier**, to Armstrong Associates' Maison de la Culture du Japon – while also allowing styles as diverse as Portzamparc's **Cité de la Musique**, with geometrical blocks round an internal street. The city also invested in public housing: of note are the human-scale housing round parc de la Villette and parc André-Citroën, Piano's red-tile-and-glass ensemble in rue de Meaux (19th) and apartments for postal workers designed by rookie architects such as Frédéric Borel.

The most impressive buildings of the late 1990s have been either sacred or sporting. It's not easy to develop a new religious vernacular (there's a phrase to drop at your next dinner party); Architecture Studio at Notre-Dame de l'Espérance in the 15th and Botta at **Evry Cathedral** have responded well. Sports facilities have been boosted by Henri and Bruno Gaudin's streamlined Stade Charléty, Zublena and Macary's flying-saucer-like **Stade de**

Christian de Portzamparc's **Cité de la Musique.**

France and Architecture Studio's new copper-roofed Institut National du Judo. The Métro has also returned to style with Grumbach's and Khon's stations for the new Météor line.

Although the age of the *grands projets* is over, Chirac's Musée des Arts Premiers is under construction by the Seine. Paris has gained two footbridges: the **passerelle de Solférino** by French architect-engineer Marc Mimram and the future passerelle de Bercy by young Austrian architect Dietmar Feichtinger. Construction continues apace in the ZAC Rive Gauche around the new Bibliothèque Nationale and ZAC Alésia-Montsouris, but issues of conservation and conversion are at long last on the agenda: Valode et Pistre have rehabilitated the row of wine warehouses in the **Cour St-Emilion**, and the Compressed Air Building and Grands Moulins de Paris will be preserved within the ZAC Rive Gauche.

Moving indoors, the look of the new is back in favour (one could say that new is the new new), alongside the eternal neo-Louis and faux-Napoléons, as architect/designers such as Christian Biecher (**Sentou**, Joseph), Jakob and MacFarlane (**Georges**), Imad Rahouni (La Maison Blanche) or Paillard and Jumeau (**Nouveau Casino**) put their stamp on restaurant, shop and club interiors.

ABTA
No. W5344

ShortBreaks Ltd

NEED SOME TIME AWAY?

Short Break packages
quality hotels
central locations
unbeatable prices

020 8402 0007   www.short-breaks.com

Accommodation

Accommodation

The place you lay your *chapeau* makes a big difference to the quality of your stay. In Paris, you'll find memorable digs, whatever your budget.

Ah, hotel life. Filling the empty vodka bottles in the mini-bar with tap water; hastily covering those pasty nether regions when the maid ignores the do-not-disturb sign; trying to catch some zeds while the couple in the next room go in for some holiday oomphus-doomphus. You know you've had a break when you get back home and try on your complimentary shower cap collection. Paris has some of the most expensive – and best – hotels in the world, and at the moderate and cheap end of the scale, standards are good, with more bargain beds than most cities.

We haven't listed official star ratings – which usually reflect room size and the presence of a lift rather than decor, staff or atmosphere – because we don't think that that system would be of much practical use to you when you make your selection. Instead, we have divided the hotels into four categories, roughly representing the following price ranges for one night in a double room with shower/ bath facilities: **Deluxe** €300+; **Expensive** €200-€300; **Moderate** €100-€200; **Budget** up to €100. (All hotels are assumed to have amenities such as hairdryer and TV in the rooms and lifts and safes within the hotel).

In addition, all our **deluxe** hotels offer air conditioning, double glazed windows, bar(s) and restaurant(s) and can arrange baby-sitting; in-room services include a modem link and room service plus other pampering extras. **Expensive** hotels offer a similar standard of amenities and services. All the **moderate** hotels listed have a laundry, and in-room phone. At the **budget** hotels you can be assured of an in-room phone. Any additional services are listed below each review.

Please note that all hotels in France charge an additional room tax (*taxe de séjour*) of around €1 per person. Hotels are often booked solid during the major trade fairs and it's practically impossible to find a quality sleep during fashion weeks (January and early July for couture, March and October for *prêt-a-porter*). However, in quieter times, including July and August, hotels often offer attractively reasonable deals; phone ahead to find out. Same-day reservations can be made in person (for a small fee) at the Office de Tourisme de Paris (*see chapter* **Directory**).

The Islands

Expensive

Hôtel du Jeu de Paume
54 rue St-Louis-en-l'Ile, 4th (01.43.26.14.18/ fax 01.40.46.02.76/www.hoteldujeudepaume.com). M° Pont Marie. **Rates** single €152; double €210-€250; suite €450; breakfast €14. **Credit** AmEx, DC, MC, V. **Map** p406 K7.
Louis XIII ordered a tennis court to be built here in 1634, at a time when the Ile St-Louis was at the height of fashion. Subsequently a warehouse and then a craftsmen's workshop, in 1988 the timber-framed court was converted into a dramatic breakfast room, now filled with a wacky array (but it works) of modern and classical art, so you'll have lots to gaze at over your cornflakes. The rooms are sober in comparison, and fine for chilling out.
Hotel services *Baby-sitting. Bar. Conference services. Laundry. Sauna. Billiards. Gym. Internet.*

Hôtel du Jeu de Paume: art for breakfast.

Moderate

Hôtel des Deux-Iles
59 rue St-Louis-en-l'Ile, 4th (01.43.26.13.35/fax 01.43.29.60.25). M° Pont Marie. **Rates** single €128; double €146; breakfast €10. **Credit** AmEx, MC, V. **Map** p406 K7.
This refined, peaceful hotel in a 17th-century townhouse on Ile St-Louis has 17 rooms done up in faintly colonial style (which way to Happy Valley, eh?) with cane furniture, print curtains and a lovely fireplace in the lobby. The Hôtel de Lutèce up the road at No. 65 (01.43.26.23.52), under the same management, features a similar sense of period style.
Hotel services *Air con. Baby-sitting. Laundry.* **Room services** *Double glazing. Modem link. Radio.*

Budget

Hôtel Henri IV
25 pl Dauphine, 1st (01.43.54.44.53). M° Pont Neuf. **Rates** single €22-26 (no bathroom); double €30-€35 (no bathroom) €42-€57 (with bathroom); breakfast included. **Credit** MC, V. **Map** p406 J6.
The sign on the door claiming *'tout confort'* may hold a hint of irony, but for rock-bottom rates, this legendary hotel is a deluxe dive, situated on the attractive place Dauphine. After 250 years, the management have made a few concessions to modernity, installing its first en-suite rooms. It has a loyal following, so be sure to book a month in advance.

Hospitel Hôtel Dieu
1 pl du Parvis Notre Dame, 4th (01.44.32.01.00/ fax 01.44.32.01.16). M° Cité/Hôtel de ville **Rates** double €95.50; Breakfast €11. **Credit** MC, V. **Map** p406 J7.
Hospitel offers 14 rooms with a limited vista of the spires of Notre-Dame. The hotel is used by families of the hospital's in-patients and medical staff who have priority and usually take up about half the hotel's capacity. That distinctive hospital smell is not overpowering, the rooms are spotless and you couldn't ask for a better sightseeing base.
Hotel services *Air con.* **Room services** *Double glazing.*

The Louvre, Palais-Royal & Les Halles

Deluxe

Hôtel Costes
239 rue St-Honoré, 1st (01.42.44.50.00/ fax 01.42.44.50.01/www.hotelcostes.com). M° Tuileries. **Rates** double €460-€540; suite €620-€1150; breakfast. **Credit** AmEx, DC, MC, V. **Map** p401 G5.
We're talking posh, we're talking attitude and we're talking of the distinct possibility of bumping into A-listers, so don't forget your autograph book. This hotel boasts possibly the best pool in Paris, a sybaritic Eastern-inspired affair with an underwater CD system to enhance your *piscine* pleasure. We dare you to go down for a dip wearing your water-wings.
Hotel services *Bureau de change. Laundry. Fitness centre. Pool. Sauna. Nightclub.* **Room services** *CD-player. Fax. Radio. Wheelchair access.*

Hôtel de Crillon
10 pl de la Concorde, 8th (01.44.71.15.00/fax 01.44.71.15.03/www.crillon.com). M° Concorde. **Rates** single €480-€575; double €575-€855; suite €775-€5,100. **Credit** AmEx, DC, MC, V. **Map** p401 F4.
Fancy a bit of posh? This magnificent neo-classical palace, favoured by no less a goddess than Madonna, groans with marble, mirrors and gilt. The Ambassadeurs restaurant is sublime and the Winter Garden tearoom has a gorgeous terrace; the Institut Guerlain has its own beauty salon here.

Top ten — Hotels

Hôtel L'Anglois
Freaky furnishings, fantastic value. *See p47.*

Hôtel Axial Beaubourg
Where the velvet chairs purr 'Sit on me'. *See p48.*

Hôtel de Banville
Family warmth, charm and character. *See p56.*

Hôtel Henri IV
Kinda inexpensive, kinda nice. *See left.*

Hôtel Lenox
Just the place to start your novel. Again. *See p64.*

Hôtel des Saints-Pères
Chill-out in shopping heaven. *See p67.*

Hôtel Sofitel le Faubourg
As sweet and creamy as a bag of butterscotch. *See p45.*

Le Montalembert
Day and night curtains? Anti-glare lighting? *See p67.*

Timhotel Montmartre
Serious romance in Amélie-ville. *See p56.*

La Villa
Crocodile bedheads and kooky curtains. *See p60.*

Edouard VII
boutique hotel

Re-opening April 2003 after renovation works

Close to
the Louvre
and "fashion
Shops"

10% discount
on our rooms
for Time Out
readers

Edouard VII

★ ★ ★ ★

Special offers on our website www.edouard7hotel.com

39 avenue de l'Opéra, 2nd • Tel: 33 (0)1 42 61 86 02 • www.edouard7hotel.com

Hotel services *Fitness centre. Garden.* **Room services** *CD player. Fax.*

Hôtel Meurice
228 rue de Rivoli, 1st (01.44.58.10.10/ fax 01.44.58.10.15/www.meuricehotel.com). M° Tuileries. **Rates** single €600; double €720-€760; suite €950-€2,250; breakfast €32-€42. **Credit** AmEx, DC, MC, V. **Map** p401 G5.
Known as the hotel of kings – Queen Victoria and George VI were regulars and the Duke and Duchess of Windsor took refuge here after the abdication – this former bastion of English toffs is now back to its full glory. Revel in silk-laden Louis XVI rooms, acres of Italian marble and gold leaf paint galore, and don't forget that you're in a republic.
Hotel services *Fitness centre. Garden. Laundry.* **Room services** *CD-player. Fax. Room service (24-hr). Wheelchair access.*

Hôtel Sofitel le Faubourg
15 rue Boissy d'Anglas, 8th (01.44.94.14.00/ fax 01.44.94.14.28/www.accor-hotels.com). M° Concorde. **Rates** single €320-€354; double €380-€480; suites €502-€870; apartment €2,000; breakfast €27. **Credit** AmEx, DC, MC, V. **Map** p401 G4.
Serious *luxe* in this beautifully decorated hotel. Cream and white tones create a tranquil atmosphere, keeping the suits calm in readiness for their next power lunch. There is an attractive, intimate piano bar, and a skylit lobby, next to the impressive restaurant. Those fortunate souls with more money than sense pop over the road to neck a few cocktails in the Buddha Bar.
Hotel services *Health club. Laundry.* **Room services** *Triple glazing. Room service (24-hr). TV/VCR.*

Hôtel de Vendôme
1 pl Vendôme, 1st (01.55.04.55.00; fax 01.49.27.97.89; www.hoteldevendome.com). M° Concorde. **Rates** single €350-€490; double €410-€550; suites €840-€8,100; breakfast €25-€35. **Credit** AmEx, DC, MC, V. **Map** p401 G4.
In complete character with place Vendôme itself is this small but very *luxe* hotel located in the 1723 mansion of Pierre Perrin, secretary of the Sun King. During the 1998 refurbishment acres of marble were imported for the jewel-box foyer and bathrooms. There is also a piano bar where you can pretend to be Noel Coward or Gertrude Lawrence (or both).
Hotel services *Laundry.* **Room services** *Triple glazing. Fax. Radio. Room service (24-hr).*

Moderate

Hôtel Brighton
218 rue de Rivoli, 1st (01.47.03.61.61/fax 01.42.60.41.78/www.esprit-de-france.com). M° Tuileries. **Rates** double €109-€147; suite €183-€215 **Credit** AmEx, DC, MC, V. **Map** p401 G5.
Excellent value for its location, the marble and mosaic Hôtel Brighton dates back to the end of the 19th century when, for once in their history, France

and England shared a friendship. Book early and reserve one of the beautifully refurbished rooms overlooking the Tuileries gardens. The rest of the rooms are reasonably priced and spacious.
Hotel services *Bureau de change. Tea salon.* **Room services** *Double glazing. Hairdryer (some rooms). Room service (breakfast only).*

Hôtel des Tuileries
10 rue St-Hyacinthe, 1st (01.42.61.04.17/ fax 01.49.27.91.56/www.hotel-des-tuileries.com). M° Tuileries. **Rates** single €125-€190; double €140-€290; triple €205-€250; apartment €280-€360; breakfast €12. **Credit** AmEx, DC, MC, V. **Map** p401 G5
A delightful small hotel on a quiet street near the Tuileries gardens. Ethnic rugs, antique furniture and original pictures decorate the lobby and 26 rooms. The centrepiece is a listed spiral staircase. The cellar breakfast room gets natural light from an interior greenhouse. The fashion world has singled it out as a cool address, so book ahead. Here's hoping for a moment on the landing with a top model.
Hotel services *Air con. Baby-sitting. Bureau de change.* **Room services** *Double glazing. Radio. Room service (24hr). Safe. Wheelchair access.*

Budget

Hôtel du Cygne
3 rue du Cygne, 1st (01.42.60.14.16/ fax 01.42.21.37.02). M° Etienne Marcel or Châtelet. **Rates** single €76; double €91-€98; triple €105; breakfast €6. **Credit** AmEx, MC, V. **Map** p402 J5.
The Cygne occupies a renovated 17th-century building in pedestrianised Les Halles. Exposed beams abound, while antique furniture collected by the owners adds interest. Rooms are on the small side, but 'La Grande' under the eaves is delightful.
Hotel services *Bar.*

Hôtel de Lille
8 rue du Pélican, 1st (01.42.33.33.42). M° Palais Royal or Louvre-Rivoli. **Rates** single €35 (without bathroom); double €43 (without bathroom)-€50; triple €60 (without toilet)-€65; no breakfast. **No credit cards. Map** p401 H5.
You can't go wrong: slap-bang in Poshville, fake flowers and Toulouse-Lautrec prints hung hither and thither, every room spotless and all available at the most reasonable of reasonable prices.
Room services *Room service (24-hr).*

Hôtel Tiquetonne
6 rue Tiquetonne, 2nd (01.42.36.94.58/fax 01.42.36.02.94). M° Etienne Marcel. Closed August and over Christmas. **Rates** single €24 (without shower)-€36 (with shower);double €42; shower €5; breakfast €5. **Credit** MC, V. **Map** p403 J5.
On a cobbled street near Les Halles, this superb-value hotel has basic but clean rooms. Some are very large for the price, and high ceilings on the lower floors give even more of a sense of space. All doubles have bathrooms; some singles are without.

la villa
★★★★ Saint-Germain-des-Prés

A contemporary 4 star hotel in the
heart of Saint-Germain-des-Prés

29 rue Jacob, 6th
Tel: 01.43.26.60.00 - Fax: 01.46.34.63.63
e-mail: hotel@villa-saintgermain.com
web: www.villa-saintgermain.com

Hôtel de Banville
★★★

Charm and character of a French private house near the Champs Elysées.
Free unlimited high speed internet access from every room.
37 rooms and a suite - prices from €113 to €250

166 boulevard Berthier, 17th - Mº Porte de Champerret / RER Pereire
Tel: 33 (0)1.42.67.97.57 - Fax: 33 (0)1.44.40.42.77
e-mail: hotelbanville@wanadoo.fr - Web site: www.hotelbanville.fr

Opéra & the Grands Boulevards

Deluxe

Hôtel Victoires Opéra

56 rue Montorgueil, 2nd (01.42.36.41.08/
fax 01.45.08.08.79/www.victoiresopera.com).
Mº Sentier. **Rates** double €214-€364; suite €335-
€485; breakfast €12. **Credit** AmEx, DC,
MC, V. **Map** p402 J5.
Smart and spotless with spic, span and smiling staff,
the Victoires attracts a mixture of business and holiday makers. The tasteful brown/cream decor,
smoothly lit and dotted with unobtrusive artworks,
is immaculate, if unimaginative. However, if what's
on the outside counts you'll find all the pleasures of
Paris on colourful and authentic rue Montorgueil.
Room services *Radio. Wheelchair access.*

Moderate

Résidence Hôtel des Trois Poussins

15 rue Clauzel, 9th (01.53.32.81.81/
fax 01.53.32.81.82/www.les3poussins.com).
Mº St-Georges. **Rates** single €120; double €135-
€170; triple or quad €200; breakfast €10. **Credit**
AmEx, MC, V. **Map** p401 H2.
The Résidence wears its move upmarket well.
Between Opéra and Montmartre, it offers a rare
opportunity for self-catering. Of the 40 beamed, flo-
ral rooms, 24 are studios equipped with kitchens.
Hotel services. *Air con. Garden.*
Room services *Double glazing. Modem link. Room*
service. Wheelchair access (two rooms).

Budget

Hôtel L'Anglois (Hôtel des Croisés)

63 rue St-Lazare, 9th (01.48.74.78.24/fax
01.49.95.04.43). Mº Trinité. **Rates** double €86; suite
€94; breakfast €7.50. **Credit** AmEx, DC, MC, V.
Map p405 G3.
The 24 rooms of this great-value hotel have been
decorated individually with some rather eye-catching furniture; watch out for the delightful hidden
bathrooms in some of the larger rooms. There isn't
much natural light, but it makes a great base for a
shopping trip to the *grands magasins*. The hotel
changed its name after it was featured in the
Johnathan Demme film *Charade*.

Hôtel des Arts

7 cité Bergère, 9th (01.42.46.73.30/
fax 01.48.00.94.42). Mº Grands Boulevards.
Rates single €62-€65; double €65.50-€68.50; triple
€91; breakfast €5.50. **Credit** AmEx, DC, MC, V.
Map p402 J4.
In a tiny alley of hotels, this is the best, and most
unconventional, of the cheapies. Run by the friendly

Bernard family, the reception area is bohemian, with
a parrot, a bubbling fish tank, and a gaudy grandfather clock. The stairwells are covered with theatre
and museum posters. The 26 rooms vary in size and
species of flowery wallpaper.
Room services *Double glazing. Radio.*

Hôtel Chopin

46 passage Jouffroy or 10 bd Montmartre, 9th
(01.47.70.58.10/fax 01.42.47.00.70).
Mº Richelieu-Drouot or Grands Boulevards. **Rates**
single €62-€70; double €69-€80; triple €91; breakfast
€7. **Credit** AmEx, MC, V. **Map** p402 J4.
The Chopin was built with the passage Jouffroy in
1846 and forms part of its magical appeal. Behind
the entrance hall with its Chesterfield and piano is
a warren of salmon-coloured corridors and 36 rooms;
all (except one single) have en-suite bathrooms.

Hôtel Madeleine Opéra

12 rue Geffuhle, 8th (01.47.42.26.26/
fax 01.47.42.89.76). Mº Madeleine. **Rates** double
€75; breakfast €5. **Credit** DC, MC, V. **Map** p402 J4.
Wrought-iron furniture and English dailies in the
entrance bode well at this bargain find behind the
Madeleine church and the *grands magasins*. The 24
bedrooms are basic yet respectable.
Room services *Double glazing. Minibar.*

Hôtel Vivienne

40 rue Vivienne, 2nd (01.42.33.13.26/
fax 01.40.41.98.19). Mº Bourse or Grands
Boulevards. **Rates** single €48; double €75-€84; triple
€109; breakfast €6. **Credit** MC, V. **Map** p405 H7.
Soft yellows and oranges in the reception, wood
floors, chandeliers and wicker add to the charm of
this hotel. There's a lively bar below, and the hotel
is close to the Palais Garnier, the *grands magasins*
and pretty Galerie Vivienne.
Room services *Double glazing.*

The best Hotel views

Hôtel Eiffel Rive Gauche
Bargain digs with an Eiffel Tower view.
See p67.

Hôtel des Tuileries
Models stay here. Do we have to draw a
diagram? *See p45.*

Terrass Hôtel
Get an Eiffel from the bath. *See p56.*

Royal Fromentin
Under the bulbous gaze of Sacré-Coeur.
See p57.

Familia Hôtel
Birds-eye view of Quasimodo's love shack.
See p60.

Beaubourg & the Marais

Deluxe

Pavillon de la Reine

*28 pl des Vosges, 3rd (01.40.29.19.19/
fax 01.40.29.19.20/www.pavillon-de-la-reine.com).
M° Bastille or St-Paul.* **Rates** double €350-€570;
duplex €445-€570; suite €570-€700; breakfast €20-
€25. **Credit** AmEx, DC, MC, V. **Map** p406 L6.
Entered from the arcades of the place des Vosges,
Pavillon de la Reine is set back behind an enchanting formal garden. The 55 rooms and suites are all
tastefully decorated, but if you are booking in with
your current squeeze, ask for one of the duplexes,
decked out in purple velvet and taffeta, and hope
to emulate the *'petite nuit tellement intense'*
described by one customer in the guest book.
Hotel services *Bureau de change. Garden.
Laundry. Parking.* **Room services** *Room service
(24-hr). TV/VCR.*

Moderate

Hôtel Axial Beaubourg

*11 rue du Temple, 4th (01.42.72.72.22/fax
01.42.72.03.53/www.axialbeaubourg.com).
M° Hôtel de Ville.* **Rates** single €98-€112; double
€130-€160; breakfast €8. **Credit** AmEx, DC, MC, V.
Map p406 K6.
The new-look Axial Beaubourg has been stunning
passers-by with its red velvet armchairs and bell-
shaped lights seen through the windows.
Véronique Turmel has put a contemporary stamp
on this hotel while retaining features such as the
beams in the reception and first-floor bedrooms.
There are sparkling modern bathrooms, and the
personable charm of a family-run hotel is, happily,
much in evidence.
Hotel services *Air con.* **Room services** *Double
glazing. Modem point.*

Hôtel Caron de Beaumarchais

*12 rue Vieille-du-Temple, 4th (01.42.72.34.12/
fax 01.42.72.34.63/ www.carondebeaumarchais.com).
M° Hôtel de Ville.* **Rates** double €128-€142;
breakfast €9. **Credit** AmEx, MC, V. **Map** p406 K6.
Named after the 18th-century playwright who lived
just up the street, this charming hotel in the heart
of the Marais re-creates the refined tastes of
Beaumarchais' era, from gilded mirrors to Chinese-
style bathroom tiling. The 22 rooms are comfortable if not always so spacious as to bring on an
attack of agoraphobia.
Hotel services *Air con. Baby-sitting. Garden.*
Room services *Double glazing.*

Hôtel de la Bretonnerie

*22 rue Ste-Croix-de-la-Bretonnerie.com, 4th
(01.48.87.77.63/www.bretonnerie.com). M° Hôtel de
Ville.* **Rates** double €108-€148; suite €180;
breakfast €9.50. **Credit** MC, V. **Map** p406 K6.
With its beams, exposed stone and fine wrought

ironwork, this 17th-century *hôtel particulier* has
plenty of historic atmosphere and a sense of domestic calm, despite a central Marais location. Lavish
fabrics, rich colours and the odd four-poster bed
give a sense of individuality to the 29 suites and
bedrooms. Excellent value.

Hôtel de la Place des Vosges

*12 rue de Birague, 4th (01.42.72.60.46/
fax 01.42.72.02.64). M° Hôtel de Ville.* **Rates** single
€76-€84; double €101-€140; breakfast €6. **Credit**
AmEx, MC, V. **Map** p406 K6.
A few steps from the place des Vosges is this former muleteer's house, dating from the same period.
There is now an elegant reception, salon and breakfast area. The 16 bedrooms are plainer, but still
comfortable. There are views over the rooftops
from high-up rooms, but, to coin a phrase, the lift
doesn't quite go to the top floor.
Room services *Room service (24 hr).*

Hôtel St-Louis Marais

*1 rue Charles V, 4th (01.48.87.87.04/
fax 01.48.87.33.26/www.saintlouismarais.com).
M° Sully Morland or Bastille.* **Rates** single €90;
double €105-€120; breakfast €8. **Credit** MC, V.
Map p406 L7.
Built as part of a 17th-century Célestin convent, the
Hôtel St-Louis' thick walls offer a cosy welcome. 16
rooms are decorated in dark green or deep rose; terracotta floor tiles in half of them (the others have
plush carpets), tapestries on the walls and beams
add to its charm. Spacious single rooms are especially good value. There's a sister hotel on the Ile
St-Louis itself.
Hotel services *Baby-sitting. Meeting room.* **Room
services** *Double glazing. Fax. Modem link.
Wheelchair access.*

Hôtel St-Merry

*78 rue de la Verrerie, 4th (01.42.78.14.15/
fax 01.40.29.06.82). M° Hôtel de Ville.*
Rates double €146-€210; triple €250; suite €305;
breakfast €10. **Credit** MC, V. **Map** p406 K6.
Nestled against the Gothic church of the same
name, the 11-room, 17th-century St-Merry basks in
eccentricity. A confessional box serves as a phone
cubicle (what better place to phone the wife and get
a few things off your chest?) and the iron candelabras, stone walls and beams add to the charm.
The biggest surprise is the flying buttress straddling the bed in No. 9. Because it's a historic building there isn't a lift. Book in advance.
Hotel services *Baby-sitting.* **Room services**
Double glazing. TV in suite only.

Budget

Grand Hôtel Jeanne d'Arc

*3 rue de Jarente, 4th (01.48.87.62.11/
fax 01.48.87.37.31). M° St-Paul.* **Rates** single €64;
double €73; triple €107; quad €122; breakfast €5.80.
Credit MC, V. **Map** p406 L6.
The Jeanne D'Arc offers fabulous value, with more

Keeping a luxuriously low profile at **Pavillon de la Reine**. *See left*.

La Demeure
★★★

A peaceful neighborhood next to rue Mouffetard and the Latin Quarter, within walking distance of Saint Germain.

"Free breakfast offered to Time Out readers upon presentation of this ad"

Address: 51 blvd. St. Marcel, 13th - Tel: 33 (0)1.43.37.81.25 Fax: 33 (0)1.45.87.05.03
Email: la_demeure@netcourrier.com - Website: www.hotel-paris-lademeure.com

HOTEL
BRITANNIQUE
★★★

20 AVENUE VICTORIA, PARIS 1ST

www.hotel-britannique.fr
Tel: 33 (0)1.42.33.74.59 - Fax: 33 (0)1.42.33.82.65

genuine comfort than is standard in this price range. The style of the decoration is a little eccentric to some tastes, and the mirror in reception is truly bizzare, but the rooms are comfortable and good-sized. As a real bonus, the hotel's rather arthritic dog may well see you to your room.

Hôtel de la Herse d'Or
20 rue St-Antoine, 4th (01.48.87.84.09/ fax 01.48.87.94.01). M° Bastille. **Rates** single €32 (without bathroom); double €36 (without bathroom)- €54; breakfast €4. **Credit** MC, V. **Map** p406 L7.
Enter this 17th-century building down a stone-walled corridor, and you'll find a cheap hotel with good-sized rooms. The walls and floor are uneven to a pleasantly mind-altering extent. The two managers do a well-practised good-cop/bad-cop routine. **Room services** *Double glazing.*

Hôtel du Septième Art
20 rue St-Paul, 4th (01.44.54.85.00/ fax 01.42.77.69.10). M° St-Paul. **Rates** single €68; double €70-€120; breakfast €7. **Credit** AmEx, DC, MC, V. **Map** p406 L7.
'But what's the seventh art?' you cry. No it's not origami, it's cinema, and this hotel is a shrine to the golden age of Hollywood. This is a delightful place, and the black and white decor and almost wall-to-wall movie posters make for a very distinctive look. If the sedentary life of the cinephile is interfering with your circumference, fear not – there is now a room with fitness apparatus to work off the flab before you hit the next box of popcorn. **Hotel services** *Bar. Fitness room. Laundry.* **Room services** *Double glazing.*

The Bastille, eastern & north-eastern Paris

Moderate

Hôtel Beaumarchais
3 rue Oberkampf, 11th (01.53.36.86.86/ fax 01.43.38.32.86/www.hotelbeaumarchais.com). M° Filles du Calvaire or Oberkampf. **Rates** single €69-€85; double €99-€140; breakfast €7. **Credit** AmEx, MC, V. **Map** p402 L5.
This stylish hotel in the hip Oberkampf area was modernised by its architect owner, with brightly coloured walls, mosaics in the bathrooms, wavy headboards and Milan glass bedlamps. 33 rooms range from small singles to a good-sized suite; some overlook a pretty courtyard. **Hotel services** *Air con.* **Room services** *Double glazing. Room service (24hr).*

Libertel Terminus Est
5 rue du 8 mai 1945, 10th (01.55.26.05.05/fax 01.55.26.05.00/www.libertel-hotels.com). M° Gare de l'Est. **Rates** single €143-168; double €151-€213; suite €227-€382; breakfast €13. **Credit** AmEx, DC, MC, V. **Map** p402 K3.

One of the great railway hotels, the Terminus Est combines sleek, modern interior design with elements that evoke the age of steam: leather luggage handles on wardrobes, nostalgic photos, Edwardian-style bathroom fittings and a library in the lobby. **Hotel services** *Air con. Baby-sitting. Bar. Health club.* **Room services**. *Room service.*

Le Pavillon Bastille
65 rue de Lyon, 12th (01.43.43.65.65/fax 01.43.43.96.52/www.pavillon-bastille.com). M° Bastille. **Rates** double €130; suite €213; breakfast €12. **Credit** AmEx, DC, MC, V. **Map** p407 M7.
This hotel, set back behind an attractive courtyard opposite the Opéra Bastille, features bright, contemporary yellow and blue decor and exceptionally crisp-looking bedlinen. Try out the €24 Forfait VIP, for a bathrobe, bowl of fruit, slippers, and more flexible checking out times in addition to the half-bottle of white wine that greets all guests. Classy, eh? **Hotel services** *Air con. Bar. Patio.* **Room services** *Room service (24-hr). Wheelchair access. Non-smoking rooms.*

Budget

Résidence Alhambra
13 rue de Malte, 11th (01.47.00.35.52/ www.hotelalhambra.fr). M° Oberkampf. **Rates** single €54; double €59.50; breakfast €5.65. **Credit** AmEx, MC,V. **Map** p407 M7.
Flowery window boxes, a leafy garden and floral bedspreads create a cheerful mood at this hotel, which was renovated in 1999 but happily kept its prices low. The 58 bedrooms are simple but clean, and all have shower and WC.

Hotel Apollo
11 rue de Dunkerque, 11th (01.48.78.04.98/fax 01.42.85.08.78). M° Gare du Nord. **Rates** single €53; double €70; breakfast €6. **Credit** AmEx, DC MC,V. **Map** p407 M7.
Opposite the Gare du Nord, the Apollo is a great find. The 45 rooms have the rustic charm of a traditional railway hotel; rooms are decorated with large wardrobes and florid wall paper and are thankfully not invaded by the roar of the TGV. **Room services** *Double glazing.*

Hôtel Gilden Magenta
35 rue Yves Toudic, 10th (01.42.40.17.72/fax 01.42.02.59.66). M° République or Jacques Bonsergent. **Rates** double €63-€71; triple €75; quad €88; breakfast €6. **Credit** AmEx, DC, MC, V. **Map** p402 L4.
Apart from the Canal St-Martin, this isn't exactly the sightseer's idea of the perfect location, but for the price, you could certainly do a whole lot worse. The rooms are all perfectly clean, and there is an attractive garden terrace. The staff are friendly and helpful, but even they won't brave what is probably Paris' smallest lift. **Hotel services** *Parking.* **Room services** *Double glazing (some rooms). Room service.*

HÔTEL
★ ★ ★
Les Jardins d'Eiffel

A select 3 star hotel on the left bank ~ View of the Eiffel Tower
Close to Champs Elysées & St Germain

Air Conditioned Rooms ~ No Smoking Floors
32 Private Parking ~ Garden & Terrace

Special rates for Time Out Readers
Traditional: €90–€130
Executive: €98–€153
For your reservations call Marie:
33 (0)1.47.05.46.21

8 rue Amélie, 7th. M° Latour Maubourg
Tel: 33 (0)1.47.05.46.21
Fax: 33 (0)1.45.55.28.08
paris@hoteljardinseiffel.com
www.hoteljardinseiffel.com
Worldwide Reservation: Utell International U.I.

Rent your apartment in Paris

Champs-Elysées
Trocadéro
Opéra
Marais
Rive gauche

Bureau de Création - Paris - Photos . J.E. Fortunier

From 5 nights / Web instant visits
www.rentapart.com

France Appartements
97 avenue des Champs-Elysées - 75008 Paris
tel. 33 (0)1 56 89 31 00
fax. 33 (0)1 56 89 31 01
Comfort and privacy / Major credit cards accepted

FRANCE APPARTEMENTS

Hôtel de Nevers

53 rue de Malte, 11th (01.47.00.56.18/
fax 01.43.57.77.39/www.hoteldenevers.com).
M° République. **Rates** double €30-€46; triple €56;
€70; breakfast €4. **Credit** MC, V. **Map** p402 L4.
A good-value base ten minutes from the Marais and
within striking distance of Oberkampf, this hotel is
ideally placed for those wanting to make the most
of the capital's nightlife. Not only that, but if you're
in search of pussy, three languid cats welcome you
as one of the family. The vintage lift is a memorable
experience but all 34 rooms are clean and comfortable. The reception service isn't quite as efficient
now that the owners have hired outside help, but you
can't blame them for wanting a break.
Hotel services *Internet access.*

Hôtel des Sans Culottes

27 rue de Lappe, 11th (01.48.05.42.92/
fax 01.48.05.08.56). M° Bastille. **Rates** single
€53.50; double €61; breakfast included. **Credit**
AmEx, MC, V. **Map** p407 M7.
Slap bang in the middle of the touristy pub crawl
strip, rue de Lappe. Rooms are colourful, clean and
functional, if a little over-Airwicked. There is no lift,
so be careful belching back up the stairs in the middle of the night. The hotel is named after a group of
revolutionaries and its seedy status has everything
to do with its location and nothing to do with its
name. The hotel is attached to a popular restaurant
bearing the same name.
Hotel services *Parking.* **Room services** *Double
glazing.*

The Champs-Elysées & west

Deluxe

Four Seasons George V

31 av George V, 8th (01.49.52.70.00/
fax 01.49.52.70.10/www.fourseasons.com).
M° George V. **Rates** single €590-€810; double €650-
€880; triple €880; suite €1200-€9,000; breakfast €35-
€46. **Credit** AmEx, DC, MC, V. **Map** p400 D4.
While hardcore George V fans may lament the
Disneyfication of the hotel, there is no denying that
the new version churns out serious *luxe:* almost
over-attentive staff, glorious flower arrangements,
divine bathrooms and ludicrously comfy beds.
Hotel services *Fitness centre. Pool.* **Room
services** *CD-player. PlayStation.*

Hôtel Costes K

81 av Kléber, 16th (01.44.05.75.75/
fax 01.44.05.74.74.). M° Trocadéro. **Rates** single
€300; double €380; suite €460-€540; breakfast €19.
Credit AmEx, MC, V. **Map** p400 B5.
A Jagger-lips sofa greets you in the foyer of this
ultra-hip modern hotel. The rooms are beautifully
designed in a sleek, unconventional manner, with
individual artworks. The reception room and restaurant are spread out, rather bizzarely, around the
inner courtyard, adding to the sense of alienation on

The neo-classical **Hôtel de Crillon**. *See p43.*

entering the hotel, as your voice bounces unforgiv-
ingly off marble walls. Some of the staff act a bit
cooler-than-thou, but then they probably are.
Hotel services *Bureau de change. Health club.
Laundry. Pool.* **Room services** *CD player. Fax.
Radio. Room service (24hr). Wheelchair access.*

Hôtel Napoléon

*40 av de Friedland, 8th (01.56.68.43.21/fax
01.47.66.82.33/www.hotelnapoleonparis.com).*
M° Charles de Gaulle-Etoile. **Rates** single €245;
double €320-€550; suite €600-€1250; breakfast €22.
Credit AmEx, DC, MC, V. **Map** p400 D3.
It may be a mere step away from the Arc de
Triomphe but, with its orange awnings and gerani-
ums, the Napoléon has the old-fahioned grandeur of
a Riviera hotel from the 1920s. Inside, the same elegance pervades, along with a bustling reception.
Rooms are very individual and feature Empire furniture, Sèvres vases and framed documents carrying the signature of the Emperor himself.
Hotel services *Laundry.* **Room services** *Fax.*

Pershing Hall

49 rue Pierre-Charron, 8th (01.58.36.58.00/
fax 01.58.36.58.01/www.pershinghall.com).
M° George V. **Rates** double €380-€500; suite €720-
€1,000; breakfast €26. **Credit** AmEx, DC, MC, V.
Map p400 D4.
A recent addition to Paris' arsenal of luxury hotels,
Pershing Hall offers a clever mix of 19th-century
splendour and contemporary comfort, combined
with the intimacy of only 26 rooms. An eagle over

Hôtel de l'université PARIS

Step into history... This 17th century *hôtel particulier* has maintained its architectural integrity while providing 21st-century comfort and service. Explore the depths of the 12th century crypt, complete with tapestries and iron candelabras (also available for private parties).

Rooms from €80 to €240

Ideally situated in the heart of St-Germain, within 10 minutes walking distance from the Musée d'Orsay and the Musée du Louvre.

22 rue de l'université, 7th
Tel: 33 (0)1.42.61.09.39 - Fax: 33 (0)1.42.60.40.84
email: hoteluniversite@wanadoo.fr
web: www.hoteluniversite.com

A charming hotel, in the very heart of Paris, close to the Marais and Bastille Square

SINGLE €69-€85
DOUBLE €99
JUNIOR SUITE €140

3 rue Oberkampf, 11th.
M° Oberkampf, Filles du Calvaire
Tel: 01.53.36.86.86
Fax: 01.43.38.32.86

rerservation@hotelbeaumarchais.com
www.hotelbeaumarchais.com

the entrance is a reminder that this was once the American Legion's World War I HQ, but inside the emphasis is on warm colours and natural materials. You even get a blast of nature in the form of a dramatic vertical garden. Bedrooms, designed by Andrée Putman, offer stained grey oak floors, and bathrooms are particularily fine with geometric styling and copious towels.

Hotel services *DJ bar. Health spa.* **Room services** *CD-DVD player. Fax. Internet.*

Hôtel Royal Monceau

37 av Hoche, 8th (01.42.99.88.00/ fax 01.42.99.89.90/www.royalmonceau.com). Mº Charles de Gaulle-Etoile. **Rates** single €396-€534; double €442-€580; suite €610-€5,336; breakfast €27-€40. **Credit** AmEx, DC, MC, V. **Map** p401 H5.
Trompe l'oeil clouds on the ceilings, acres of marble and four florists arranging a gargantuan display in the lobby shout *'luxe'* at the Royal Monceau. The hotel recently amalgamated some rooms into 45 new suites. One belongs to Omar Sharif, who often enjoys an *apéro* in the English bar (but, please, no shouts of 'Oi, it's Doctor Zhivago!'). The Royal Monceau's other main boast is its fabulous health club Les Thermes, and there's a romantic garden restaurant.
Hotel services *Fitness club. Pool.* **Room services** *CD player. Fax. Internet. Radio. Wheelchair access.*

Expensive

Hôtel Radisson Champs-Elsyées

78 ave Marceau, 8th (01.53.23.43.43/fax 01.53.23.43.44/www.radissonsas.com). Mº Charles de Gaulle-Etoile. **Rates** double €225-€415; suite €690 **Credit** AmEx, DC, MC, V. **Map** p400 C4.
Many of the big hotel chains have invaded Paris, and Radisson now have this refined 24-room hotel near the Arc de Triomphe. The immaculate decoration is a kind of upmarket Ikea-style inside the rooms, and Wall-Street-office-block in the rest of the building. The rooms are perhaps a little small considering the price tag, but the staff are enthusiastic and the restaurant has an attractive terrace.
Hotel Services *Laundry.*

Hôtel Square

3 rue de Boulainvilliers, 16th (01.44.14.91.90/ fax 01.44.14.91.99/www.hotelsquare.com). Mº Passy/RER Kennedy-Radio France. **Rates** single or double €230-€370; suite €450; breakfast €18. **Credit** AmEx, DC, MC, V. **Map** p404 A7.
Though the polished granite curtain wall may look forbidding, the dramatic interior of this courageously modern hotel is welcoming, aided by the personalised service that comes with that extra gleam of sincerity that having to look after only 22 rooms brings. The exotic woods, quality fabrics and paint finishes are striking, with temporary exhibitions in the atrium by well-known artists, such as Ben and Viallat.

Smart about art

If the words 'hotel' and 'art' in the same sentence send a chill down your aesthetic spine, you are not alone. Full of tatty junk-shop 'finds' and framed Van Gogh original reproductions, hotel rooms are often the last resting place of many an overly-orange sunset and stuffed posing pooch. Thankfully, in Paris there are many hotels that have their artistic act together. Young artists are thick on the ground here, and savvy hoteliers are putting them to good use to attract the *'chouette'* set'.

Cleverly disguised as an expensive business hotel, the **Hôtel Scribe** boasts one of Paris' most forward-thinking programmes for the promotion of contemporary art. It sponsors several exhibitions a year, mostly in the realm of contemporary photography, and publishes a series of catalogues that would put most regional museums to shame. The Scribe has a distinguished history of catering to creative minds – Proust, Hemingway, Josephine Baker, and Lee Miller all dandied about here. More recently, Sam Taylor-Wood held a private bash here to celebrate her exhibition at the Centre National de la Photographie.

The zebra-print chairs and crushed-velvet sofas in the lobby of the **Artus Hôtel** are a sure sign that something hip is afoot. Young artists were commissioned to paint the doors of each room, lending individual character to smallish but charming quarters with terracotta walls, while the graffiti-style stairway, painted by American artist Jonone, is the epitome of slumming it in style. Back in the comfy lobby, the self-service bar allows you to invite friends and serve drinks as if you were in your own living room – and then sign it all to your tab like the big shot you are.

Hôtel Scribe

1 rue Scribe, 9th (01.44.71.24.24/Fax 01.42.65.39.97/www.accor-hotels.com). Mº Opera. **Rates** double €400-€440; single €340-€380; suite €500-€1,052; breakfast €25. **Credit** AmEx, MC, V.

Artus Hôtel

34 rue de Buci, 6th (01.43.29.07.20/ Fax01.43.29.67.44/www.artushotel.com). Mº Mabillon. **Rates** double €190-€235; duplex €300; suite €320; breakfast included. **Credit** AmEx, DC, MC, V.

Hotel services *Baby-sitting. Laundry.* **Room services** *CD player. Fax. Radio. TV/VCR. Wheelchair access.*

Moderate

Hôtel de Banville
166 bd Berthier, 17th (01.42.67.70.16/ fax 01.44.40.42.77/www.hotelbanville.fr). M° Porte de Champerret. **Rates** *single €127; double €150-€183; suite €244; extra bed €19; breakfast €11.* **Credit** AmEx, DC, MC, V. **Map** p400 C1.
Owner Marianne Moreau's mother and grandmother preceded her here, and the personal touches are proudly maintained. Each of the 38 rooms is individually designed and very feminine, with iron or brass beds and warm Italianate colours. La Chambre d'Amélie has a great rooftop view from the terrace. The 17th is one of the sleepiest *arrondissements* of Paris, however, so be prepared to get on the Métro if you want some va-va-voom.
Hotel services *Air con. Airport shuttle. Bar. Free unlimited Internet access.* **Room services** *Double glazing. Modem link. Radio. Room service (24hr).*

Hôtel Le Lavoisier
21 rue Lavoisier, 8th (01.53.30.06.06/ fax 01.53.30.23.00/www.hotellavoisier.com). M° St-Augustin. **Rates** *double €199; suite €245-€385; breakfast €12.* **Credit** AmEx, MC, V. **Map** p401 F3.
The 30-room Le Lavoisier is a classy affair. Decor is refined and warm, and the furniture mixes periods and styles to striking effect. A good location for watching leggy models strolling down the rue du Faubourg St Honoré or hob-nobbing with Jacques Chirac at the nearby Palais de L'Elysée.
Hotel services *Air con. Baby-sitting. Bar.* **Room services** *Double glazing. Internet connection. Modem link. Room service (24hr). Wheelchair access.*

Hôtel Regent's Garden
6 rue Pierre-Demours, 17th (01.45.74.07.30/ fax 01.40.55.01.42/www.bw-paris-hotels.com). M° Charles de Gaulle-Etoile or Ternes. **Rates** *single €150.30-€260.10; double €152.75-€260.10; breakfast €10.* **Credit** AmEx, DC, MC, V. **Map** p400 C3.
High ceilings and plush upholstery hark back to the Second Empire, when this house was built for Napoléon III's physician. There are 39 large bedrooms, some with gilt mirrors and fireplaces. With its walled garden, this is an oasis of calm just ten minutes from the hubbub of the Arc de Triomphe.
Hotel services *Air con. Baby-sitting. Bureau de change. Garden. Parking.* **Room services** *Double glazing. Modem link. Room service.*

Budget

Hôtel Keppler
12 rue Keppler, 16th (01.47.20.65.05/ fax 01.47.23.02.29/www.hotelkeppler.com).

M° Kléber or George V. **Rates** *double €80-€84; breakfast €5.40.* **Credit** AmEx, MC, V. **Map** p400 C4.
The high ceilings and spacious rooms are typical of this prestigious neighbourhood, but the prices aren't. There's a charming spiral staircase and a vintage lift. The reception and breakfast room are business-like, but subtle lighting adds atmosphere.
Hotel services *Bar.* **Room services** *Room service (24hr).*

Montmartre & Pigalle

Expensive

Terrass Hôtel
12-14 rue Joseph-de-Maistre, 18th (01.46.06.72.85/ fax 01.42.52.29.11/www.terrass-hotel.com). M° Place de Clichy. **Rates** *single €188-€214; double €225-€248; suite €302; breakfast included.* **Credit** AmEx, DC, MC, V. **Map** p401 H1.
Entering the rather dated lobby of the Terrass you may wonder what draws such stars as Pierce Brosnan and MC Solaar (the latter's a rap star, in France at least) to the hotel. Go up to the seventh floor and there's your answer – possibly the best view in the whole of Paris from the rooftop restaurant. Those in the know ask for room 704, from which you can lie in the bath and look out at the Eiffel Tower (of course, people on the Eiffel Tower can train their binoculars on you in the bath). Suite 802 is an apartment-sized winner.
Hotel services *Baby-sitting. Bureau de change. Laundry.* **Room services** *Some non-smoking rooms. Wheelchair access.*

Moderate

Timhotel Montmartre
11 rue Ravignan (Place Emile Goudeau), 18th (01.42.55.74.79/Fax 01.42.55.71.01/ www.timhotel.fr) M° Abbesses. **Rates** *double €110-€125; breakfast €8.50.* **Credit** AmEx, DC, MC, V. **Map** p402 H1.
Situated in the picturesque Place Emile Goudeau, this chain hotel has romantic weekend in Montmartre written all over it. And, if you do come over all ooh-la-la, you may not step out of the front door. The rooms are comfortable without being spectacularly plush; what you need to do is get yourself into one of the fourth- or fifth-floor numbers, and you'll get the benefit of stunning views of Paris.
Hotel services *Internet access.*

Villa Royale Pigalle
2 rue Duperre, 9th. (01.55.31.78.78/fax 01.55.31.78.70/royale@hotelsparis.fr). M° Pigalle. **Rates** *double €150; deluxe €210.* **Credit** AmEx, DC, MC, V. **Map** p402 H2.
The Villa Royale takes the notion of fitting in with its surroundings very seriously. Each room has been decorated individually, but none vary much from the basic principles of mock-baroque gaudiness. The

It's curtains for you at **Hôtel de Banville**. *See left.*

jewel in the crown is the starry Michou room, named after the cross-dressing revue club in nearby rue des Martyrs. Each room has a nifty device for refreshing one's clothes after a long spell schlepping around.
Room services *Plasma TV. Jacuzzi baths.*

Budget

Hôtel des Batignolles

26-28 rue des Batignolles, 17th (01.43.87.70.40/ fax 01.44.70.01.04/www.batignolles.com). M° Rome or Place de Clichy. **Rates** double €53-€63; triple €70; breakfast €4. **Credit** DC, MC, V. **Map** p401 F2.
This 1920s building still feels a bit like the girls' boardinghouse it once was, but provides a good base within easy reach of Montmartre. The Batignolles is simple, quiet and clean, with 33 spacious rooms and a tranquil courtyard.
Room services *Double glazing.*

Hôtel Eldorado

18 rue des Dames, 17th (01.45.22.35.21/fax 01.43.87.25.97/www.eldorado.cityvox.com). M° Place de Clichy. **Rates** single €39; double €54-€61; triple €77; breakfast €6. **Credit** AmEx, DC, MC, V. **Map** p401 F2.
Hidden behind place de Clichy in the fast-rising Batignolles area is a piece of real bohemia. Owner Anne Gratacos has decorated the 40 rooms individually – leopardskin here, a satin eiderdown there, velvet sofas and flea market finds. The 40 rooms are split between the main house and an annexe in the garden It is a hip address during the fashion shows.
Hotel services *Internet access. Restaurant.*

Hôtel Ermitage

24 rue Lamarck, 18th (01.42.64.79.22/ fax 01.42.64.10.33). M° Lamarck-Caulaincourt. **Rates** single €74; double €84; triple €107; quad €124; breakfast included. **No credit cards**. **Map** p401 H1.
This 12-room hotel is only five minutes from the Sacré-Coeur, but on a quiet street over the hill from the tourist madness of Place du Tertre. The rooms are large and endearingly over-decorated; some on upper floors have great views.
Room services *Double glazing.*

Royal Fromentin

11 rue Fromentin, 9th (01.48.74.85.93/fax 01.42.81.02.33/www.hotelroyalfromentin.com). M° Pigalle. **Rates** single €85; double €98; triple €119; breakfast included. **Credit** AmEx, DC, MC, V. **Map** p401 H2.
Bargain basement rock-star chic. Only aspiring superstars will fully appreciate the feel, views of Sacré-Cœur and illustrious guest book history within staggering distance of some of Paris' major music venues. Previous sleepers include the Spice Girls, Blondie and Nirvana.
Hotel services *Baby-sitting. Bar. Laundry.* **Room services** *Double glazing. Room service.*

Hôtel Regyn's Montmartre

18 pl des Abbesses, 18th (01.42.54.45.21/ fax 01.42.23.76.69/www.regynsmontmartre.com). M° Abbesses. **Rates** single €62-€78; double €73-€93; triple €98.50-€109; breakfast €6.85-€7.60. **Credit** AmEx, MC, V. **Map** p401 G1.
This is a great location opposite the Abbesses Métro

PARIS HOTELS
from 2 to 5 stars
at discounted rates

UP TO 65% OFF

Call free!

From Europe	00 800 1099 1099

Please quote special discount code : TI4

From USA	1 800 715 7666

www.hoteldiscount.com

Book online

More than 6300 hotels worldwide

HOTEL
TOLBIAC

A charming budget hotel listed in the following guides: Rough Guide, Lonely Planet, Interconnection.

SINGLE ROOMS FROM €21-€30
with or without shower

FOR 2 PERSONS: FROM ROOMS €29-€36
with or without shower

122 rue de Tolbiac, 13th.
M° Tolbiac
Tel: 01.44.24.25.54
Fax: 01.45.85.43.47
info@hotel-tolbiac.com
www.hotel-tolbiac.com

HÔTEL OPÉRA RICHEPANSE

★★★★

A Hôtel de Charme located in the heart of the most prestigious areas of Paris just minutes from Opéra, Concorde and shopping paradise Faubourg Saint-Honoré. Lavish Art Deco style prevails in this elegant 35 room, 3-suite establishment.

Rooms from €235 to €315 - Suites from €448 to €560

14 rue du Chevalier de St. George, 1st - M° Madeleine
Tel: 33 (0)1 42 60 36 00 - Fax: 33 (0)1 42 60 13 03
website: www.richepanse.com - email: richepanseotel@wanadoo.fr

Experience Rive Gauche and the Quartier Latin bustling with antique dealers and chic Parisian stores and restaurants. The Hôtel Lenox Saint Germain offers 34 en-suite bedrooms, an impressive breakfast buffet surrounded by vaults and frescoes, and the Lenox Club where the Jazzmen of the thirties live on.

Hôtel Lenox
SAINT GERMAIN
★★★

Rooms from €115 to €150 - Suites from €185 to €270

9 rue de l'Université, 7th - M° St Germain des Prés
Tel: 33 (0)1 42 96 10 95 - Fax: 33 (0)1 42 61 52 83
Website: www.lenoxsaintgermain.com - Email: hotel@lenoxsaintgermain.com

in the heart of Montmartre. There's a pretty breakfast room and six of the 22 rooms have superb views. **Hotel services** *Laundry. Lift.* **Room services** *Double glazing.*

The Latin Quarter & the 13th

Moderate

Les Degrés de Notre-Dame
10 rue des Grands-Degrés, 5th (01.55.42.88.88/ fax 01.40.46.95.34). Mº St-Michel Notre-Dame. **Rates** single €70; double €100-€140; studio €100; breakfast included. **Credit** MC,V. **Map** p406 J7.
Masses of dark wood and lovingly tended rooms make this hotel set back from the Seine a real find. If the ten hotel rooms are taken, ask about their two studios a few streets away from the hotel, where you can pretend to be a real Parisian. The studios come complete with washing machine, power shower and, in one flat, a conservatory filled with fresh flowers. **Hotel services** *Bar. Restaurant.* **Room services** *Double glazing. Modem link. Room service (24hr).*

Hôtel des Grandes Ecoles
75 rue du Cardinal-Lemoine, 5th (01.43.26.79.23/ fax 01.43.25.28.15/www.hotel-grandes-ecoles.com). Mº Cardinal Lemoine. **Rates** double €95-€120; breakfast €7. **Credit** MC, V. **Map** p406 K8.
A taste of the country in central Paris, this wonderful hotel, with 51 old-fashioned rooms, is built around a leafy garden where breakfast is served in the summer. The largest of the three buildings houses the reception area and an old-fashioned breakfast room with gilt mirror and piano. **Hotel services** *Garden. Lift. Parking.* **Room services** *Double glazing. Wheelchair access.*

Hôtel la Demeure
51 bd St-Marcel, 13th (01.43.37.81.25/ fax 01.45.87.05.03). Mº Les Gobelins. **Rates** double €105-€125; suite €179; breakfast €10. **Credit** AmEx, DC, MC, V. **Map** p406 K10.
This 43-room establishment was recently bought and totally revamped by a charming father-son team. Suites have sliding doors to separate sleeping and living space with direct Internet access from both. The wrap-around balustrades of the corner rooms offer lovely views of the city, and bathrooms feature either luxurious tubs, or elaborate shower heads with endless massaging possibilities. **Hotel services** *Air con. Baby-sitting. Parking.* **Room services** *ADSL Internet.*

La Manufacture
8 rue Philippe de Champagne, 13th (01.45.35.45.25/ fax 01.45.35.45.40/ www.hotel-la-manufacture.com). Mº Place d'Italie. **Rates** single €125; double €133-€199; triple €199; breakfast €7.50. **Credit** AmEx, DC, MC, V. **Map** p406 K10.
La Manufacture, revamped from scratch in 1999, is named after the nearby Gobelins tapestry works.

The designer got it just right: warm colours, modern but not too minimalist, squeaky-clean white-tiled bathrooms and perhaps the nicest breakfast room in Paris. Place d'Italie may not be in the heart of the action, but the location is quiet and not unattractive – plus it's only 15 minutes to Orly. **Hotel services** *Air con. Bar.* **Room services** *Double glazing.*

Hôtel du Panthéon
19 pl du Panthéon, 5th (01.43.54.32.95/ fax 01.43.26.64.65/www.hoteldupantheon.com). RER Luxembourg/Mº Cardinal Lemoine. **Rates** double €168-213; triple €198-229; breakfast €10. **Credit** AmEx, DC, MC, V. **Map** p406 J8.
An elegant, classy hotel with 34 individually decorated rooms which take their scheme from the *toile de Jouy* material print on the walls. Some rooms have impressive views of the Panthéon, others onto a charming courtyard, complete with chestnut tree. The Hôtel des Grands Hommes (01.46.34.19.60) next door is run by the same people. **Hotel services** *Air con. Baby-sitting. Bar. Bureau de change.* **Room services** *Double glazing. Modem link. Wheelchair access.*

Hôtel Résidence Henri IV
50 rue des Bernardins, 5th. (01.44.41.31.81/ 01.46.33.93.22/www.residencehenri4.com). Mº Maubert-Mutualité or Cardinal Lemoine. **Rates** double €123-€145; apartment 1 or 2 persons €153-€190; apartment 3 persons €183-€220; apartment 4 persons €213-€250; Breakfast €9. **Credit** AmEx, DC. **Map** p406 K7.
Hidden in a tiny cul-de-sac next to the leafy Square Paul Langevin, this 16-room hotel is decorated in the standard *belle époque* fashion, but with more genuine style than many similarly priced hotels. The apartment rooms are equipped with a handy mini-kitchen, although you may be reduced to eating on the beds in the smaller apartments.

Budget

Hôtel Esmeralda
4 rue St-Julien-le-Pauvre, 5th (01.43.54.19.20/ fax 01.40.51.00.68). Mº St-Michel or Maubert-Mutalite. **Rates** single €30; double €60-€80; triple €95; quad €105; breakfast €6. **No credit cards.** **Map** p406 J7.
This 1640 building (recently renovated) looks onto a tree-lined square and over the Seine to Notre-Dame. In the plant-filled entrance, the resident cat may be curled up in a velvet chair. Upstairs are 19 floral rooms with antique furnishings and uneven floors. Do book ahead. **Hotel services** *Room service.*

Familia Hôtel
11 rue des Ecoles, 5th (01.43.54.55.27/ fax 01.43.29.61.77/www.hotel-paris-familia.com). Mº Maubert-Mutualité or Jussieu. **Rates** single €69.50; double €86-€116; triple €139.50; quad €160;

breakfast included. **Credit** AmEx, DC, MC, V.
Map p406 J7.

An enthusiastic welcome awaits at this old-fashioned hotel whose balconies are hung with tumbling plants. Chatty owner Eric Gaucheron is immensely proud of the sepia murals and cherry wood furniture that feature in some of the 30 rooms. The Gaucheron family also owns the Minerve (01.43.26.26.04), just next door, offering the same fantastic package.
Room services *Double glazing. Minibar.*

St-Germain, Odéon & Montparnasse

Deluxe

Hôtel Bel-Ami

7-11 rue St-Benoît, 6th (01.42.61.53.53/ fax 01.49.27.09.33/www.hotel-bel-ami.com) M° St-Germain-des-Prés. **Rates** double €280-€400; suite €490; breakfast €18. **Credit** AmEx, MC, V
Map p405 H6.

With a super-stylish decor and pukka hotel pedigree (Grace-Leo Andrieu also put the *luxe* into The Lancaster and Le Montalembert), this is a favourite during fashion weeks. It's chic, muted minimalism for the most part, but the St-Germain-themed rooms have a warmer decor in memory of the jazz club once housed in the basement.
Hotel services *Laundry.* **Room services** *CD player. Fax. Radio. Room service (24hr). Wheelchair access.*

Hôtel Lutétia

45 bd Raspail, 6th (01.49.54.46.46/fax 01.49.54.46.00/www.lutetia-paris.com). M° Sèvres Babylone. **Rates** double €400-€530; suite €650-€2,300; breakfast €15-€19. **Credit** AmEx, DC, MC, V. **Map** p405 G7.

A masterpiece of art nouveau and early art deco architecture, the Lutétia opened in 1910 to accommodate shoppers coming to the Bon Marché. Today its plush bar and lively brasserie are still fine places for resting weary feet. Its 250 rooms, revamped in purple, gold and pearl grey, maintain a '30s feel.
Hotel services *Fitness centre. Laundry. Parking.*
Room services *Fax. Radio.*

Expensive

Hôtel de l'Abbaye

10 rue Cassette, 6th (01.45.44.38.11/ fax 01.45.48.07.86/www.hotel-abbaye.com). M° St-Sulpice. **Rates** double €185-€292; suite €355-€399; breakfast included. **Credit** AmEx, MC, V.
Map p405 G7.

This tranquil hotel was originally part of a convent. Wood panelling, well-stuffed sofas and an open fireplace make for a relaxed atmosphere but, best of all, there's a surprisingly large garden where breakfast is served in the warmer months. The 42 rooms

are tasteful and luxurious and the suites have rooftop terraces.
Hotel services *Bureau de change. Garden. Laundry.* **Room services** *Radio. Room service.*

L'Hôtel

13 rue des Beaux-Arts, 6th (01.44.41.99.00/ fax 01.43.25.64.81/www.l-hotel.com). M° St-Germain-des-Prés. **Rates** double €595-€687; suite €595-€687; breakfast €17. **Credit** AmEx, DC, MC, V.
Map p405 H6.

Longtime favourite with the fashion pack – poor old Oscar Wilde, pioneer of green velvet, died here – L'Hôtel has been taken well in hand by new owner Jean-Paul Besnard (a biologist, strangely). Jacques Garcia's revamp has restored the central stairwell to its former glory; Mistinguett's *chambre* retains its art deco mirror bed and Oscar's former resting place has, appropriately, green peacock murals. Don't miss the cellar swimming pool and *fumoir.*
Hotel services *Laundry. Pool. Steam room.* **Room services** *CD player. Fax.*

Relais Médicis

23 rue Racine, 6th (01.43.26.00.60/fax 01.40.46.83.39/ www.123france.com). M° Odéon/RER Luxembourg. **Rates** double €222-€258; single €188; breakfast included. **Credit** AmEx, DC, MC, V. **Map** p406 H7.

Near the Luxembourg Gardens, the very feminine Relais Médicis evokes an era of pennyfarthings and Gibson girls. The spacious bedrooms have windowside tables – just the job for a romantic breakfast. Piped classical music plays in a little drawing room – nice touch – and there is a courtyard topiary garden in which to write your postcards.
Room services *Radio.*

La Villa

29 rue Jacob, 6th (01.43.26.60.00/fax 01.46.34.63.63/ www.villa-stgermain.com). M° St-Germain-des-Prés. **Rates** double €240-€335; suite €440; extra bed €40; breakfast €14. **Credit** AmEx, DC, MC, V.
Map p405 H6.

What a find. There's something winkingly stylish about this hotel. It's like a long cool drink of something refreshing and naughty, and it's freshly renovated. Maybe it's the cool-to-the-nth faux crocodile skin on the bedheads or the crinkly taffeta on the taupe-coloured walls. This place is charismatic and likeable. Wonderfully, the room numbers are projected on to the floor in front of your door (in case it's a challenge to see straight when you make it back of an evening).
Hotel services *Laundry.* **Room services** *Modem link. Room service (24hr). Wheelchair access.*

Moderate

Hôtel d'Angleterre

44 rue Jacob, 6th (01.42.60.34.72/fax 01.42.60.16.93). M° St-Germain-des-Prés. **Rates** double €125-€210; suite €260; breakfast €9.15. **Credit** AmEx, DC, MC, V. **Map** p405 H6.

Low-key elegance prevails at this former British

Hostel takeover bed

Reasonable as the prices of staying in decent-quality Paris hotels are, there's a good case for allocating your budget to other areas of expenditure (booze, clothes you don't need but somehow couldn't live without, that piece of art you'll never get in your hold-all, etc, and that's before we've even considered shadier purchases). On a budget? Why not park your Wee Willy Winkie hat in a youth hostel? It doesn't have to be all grunge and off-white pillows in Paris.

The **MIJE** hostels are in 17th-century aristocratic Marais residences and former convents. Inside the plain-but-clean rooms, well-made beds have snow-white sheets and cosy blankets, while old stone walls echo with centuries of four-poster bed action. All rooms have a shower and a basin, but do make sure that you don't miss the 1am curfew. If you do, you'll be staying out all night. The rue de Fourcy branch even has a pleasant, in-house restaurant.

BVJ has clean rooms (with showers) and homely tartan quilts. Its Latin Quarter location and 24-hour access make it a good base from which to explore Paris. A flurry of cheap, potent wine, good conversation and *darbuka* beats (a Turkish drum, but you knew that) brightens up the bare communal quarters downstairs. Near the Sorbonne is the **Young & Happy Hostel**, a place which merits its name. You can buy a beer at the counter and strike the culture-vulture pose or catch up on your e-mail while reggae throbs from the speakers in the cramped lobby. Get into the community spirit, and the slightly tatty dorms and campsite antics in the washrooms won't seem to matter. Close to teeming Bastille, eastside enthusiasts can wash, lodge and breakfast in adequate surroundings at **L'Auberge Internationale des Jeunes**. If you should be unlucky enough to chance upon a yellow and abused-looking pillow, you can always rent sheets and pillow cases, but, of course, a certain amount of micro-bacteria is part of the fun. Street-side rooms have double glazing to take the edge off the noise.

If you want to really immerse yourself in Parisian student existence, the halls of residence at CROUS (Centre régional des oeuvres universitaires et scolaires) are open to under-26's during the summer months. See page 376 for details.

MIJE

Fourcy 6 rue de Fourcy, 4th (01.42.74.23.45/ fax 01.40.27.81.64/ www.mije.com). M° St-Paul. **Map** p406 L6. *Fauconnier 11 rue du Fauconnier, 4th (01.42.74.23.45). M° St-Paul.* **Map** p406 L7. *Maubisson 12 rue des Barres, 4th (01.42.74.23.45). M° Hôtel de Ville.* **Map** p406 K6. **Open** 7am-1am daily. **Rates** dorm €22 per person (18-30s sharing rooms); single €38; double €30; triple €25; membership €2.50; breakfast included. **No credit cards. Map** p402 K6.

BVJ/Quartier Latin

44 rue des Bernardins, 5th (01.43.29.34.80/ fax 01.53.00.90.91). M° Maubert-Mutualité. **Open** 24 hrs daily. **Rates** dormitory €25 per person; single €30; double €27; breakfast included. **No credit cards. Map** p406 K7.

Young & Happy Hostel

80 rue Mouffetard, 5th (01.45.35.09.53/ fax 01.47.07.22.24/ www.youngandhappy.fr). M° Place Monge. **Open** 8am-11am, 4pm-2am daily. **Rates** dormitory €19.50 per person; double €23 per person; breakfast included. **No credit cards. Map** p406 J9.

Auberge Internationale des Jeunes

10 rue Trousseau, 11th (01.47.00.62.00/ fax 01.47.00.33.16/ www.aijparis.com). M° Ledru-Rollin. **Open** 24hrs daily; rooms closed 10am-3pm. **Rates** Mar-Oct €14; Nov-Feb €13; breakfast included. **Credit** MC, V. **Map** p407 N7.

No nunsense dining at **MIJE**.

Accommodation

FIVE HOTELS IN THE HEART OF SAINT GERMAIN DES PRES

Welcome . Hôtel ★★

Excellent location in historic area.
All rooms have private bathroom/WC and TV.

Rooms from €70 - €120, breakfast €8

66 rue de Seine, 6th - M° St-Germain des Prés, Odéon, Mabillon
Tel: 01.46.34.24.80 - Fax: 01.40.46.81.59
www.welcomehotel-paris.com

Hotel de Seine ★★★

A peaceful haven just minutes from antique
dealers and art galleries.
Marble bathrooms, satellite TV.

Rooms from €120 - €180, breakfast €12

52 rue de Seine, 6th - M° St-Germain des Prés
Tel: 01.46.34.22.80 - Fax: 01.46.34.04.74
www.hotel-de-seine.com

Trianon Rive Gauche Hôtel ★★★

Parisian area made famous by artists and writers.
Bathrooms, satellite TV, direct telephone line,
bar, dry cleaning.

Rooms from €120 - €150, breakfast €9

1 bis rue de Vaugirard, 6th M° Odéon or Cluny
Tel: 01.43.29.88.10 - Fax: 01.43.29.15.98
www.trianon-rive-gauche.com

Hôtel des Deux Continents ★★★

Listed in Hôtel de Charme. Private bathrooms,
satellite TV, air-conditioning upon request.

Rooms from €135 - €190, breakfast €12

25 rue Jacob, 6th - M° St-Germain des Prés
Tel: 01.43.26.72.46 - Fax: 01.43.25.67.80
www.2continents-hotel.com

HÔTEL DES MARRONNIERS ★★★

Listed in Hôtel de Charme and Relais du Silence.
Private bathrooms, satellite TV, air-conditioning,
garden and veranda.

Rooms from €110 - €250, breakfast €12

21 rue Jacob, 6th - M° St-Germain des Prés
Tel: 01.43.25.30.60 - Fax: 01.40.46.83.56
www.hotel-marronniers.com

Hôtel de France ★★★

30 METRES FROM THE CHATEAU DE VERSAILLES
26 charming newly renovated rooms in harmony with
the ambiance of Versailles. Marble bathrooms,
satellite TV, air-conditionning upon request.

Rooms from €137 - €236, breakfast €11

5 rue Colbert, 78000 Versailles - Tel: 01.30.83.92.23
Fax: 01.30.83.92.24 - www.hotelfrance.versailles.com

Chic happens at **L'Hôtel**. *See p60.*

embassy where the US independence treaty was prepared in 1783. In need of excitement? Climb the listed staircase or bash out a few numbers at the grand piano in the salon. Some of the 27 rooms look over the hotel's ivy-strewn courtyard.
Hotel services *Baby-sitting. Bureau de change. Garden. Lift (not to all rooms).* **Room services** *Double glazing. Room service.*

Hôtel Aviatic

105 rue de Vaugirard, 6th (01.53.63.25.50./ fax 01.53.63.25.50/www.aviatic.fr). Mᵒ Montparnasse-Bienvenüe or St-Placide. **Rates** double €121-€191; breakfast €11. **Credit** AmEx, DC, MC, V. **Map** p405 H7.
This vintage hotel has been totally overhauled in the inimitable style of the Corbel sisters, creating a smart joint with bags of character. The polished floor in the lobby (ideal for precision skating) and hints of marble and brass give an impressive touch of glamour. The slightly more expensive 'supérieure' rooms are worth it for the extra space and solid, old-fashioned furniture. This hotel is very handy for access to the busy Montparnasse area.
Hotel services *Air Con. Baby-sitting.* **Room services** *Double glazing.*

Le Clos Médicis

56 rue Monsieur-le-Prince, 6th (01.43.29.10.80/ fax 01.43.54.26.90/www.closmedicis.com). Mᵒ Odéon/RER Luxembourg. **Rates** single €125; double €150-€180; triple €220; breakfast €10. **Credit** AmEx, DC, MC, V.**Map** p406 H7.
In a 1773 building built for the Medici family is this extremely stylish hotel designed by Jean-Philippe

Nuel. The brand-new decor is refreshingly modern and very chic, with taffeta curtains, chenille bedcoverings and antique floor tiles in the bathrooms.
Hotel services *Air con. Baby-sitting. Bar. Internet access.* **Room services** *Double glazing. Modem link.*

Hôtel du Danemark

21 rue Vavin, 6th (01.43.26.93.78/ fax 01.46.34.66.06). Mᵒ Notre-Dame-des-Champs or Vavin. **Rates** single €110; double €121-€150; breakfast €9. **Credit** AmEx, DC, MC, V. **Map** p405 G8.
Next to Henri Sauvage's 1912 Carreaux tiled appartment building is the newly decorated Danemark. With only 15 rooms, it has a sleek boutique-y look that blends in with nearby shops. The lobby features leather armchairs, and all the rooms have original oil paintings.
Room services *Double glazing. Room service (breakfast).*

Grand Hôtel de l'Univers

6 rue Grégoire-de-Tours, 6th (01.43.29.37.00/fax 01.40.51.06.45/www.hotel-paris-univers.com). Mᵒ Odéon. **Rates** single €170; double €180-€210; breakfast included. **Credit** AmEx, DC, MC, V. **Map** p406 H7.
15th-century beams, high ceilings and *toile*-covered walls are the trademarks of this hotel. *Côté Sud* fans will love the Manuel Canovas fabrics, but there are also mod-cons including a laptop for rent. The same helpful team also runs the Hôtel St-Germain-des-Près (36 rue Bonaparte, 6th/01.43.26.00.19/ www.hotel-st.ger.com), which boasts a medieval-themed room and the sweetest attic in Paris.

Hotel services *Air con.* Room services *Double glazing. Modem point.*

Hôtel Lenox

9 rue de l'Université, 7th (01.42.96.10.95/ fax 01.42.61.52.83/www.lenoxsaintgermain.com). M° St-Germain-des-Près. Rates double €112-€196; duplex €251-€266; breakfast €9-€12. Credit AmEx, DC, MC, V. Map p405 G6.

This venerable literary and artistic haunt (TS Eliot booked Joyce in on the recommendation of Ezra Pound) has been reborn with a wink to art deco and the jazz age. The Lenox Club Bar, open to the public, is a bravura creation with marquetry scenes of jazz musicians. Bedrooms, reached by a ride in an astonishing glass lift, have more traditional decor and ever-so-Parisian views.

Hotel services *Air con. Baby-sitting. Bar. Internet connection.* Room services *Double glazing. Radio.*

Hôtel des Marronniers

21 rue Jacob, 6th (01.43.25.30.60/ fax 01.40.46.83.56). M° St-Germain-des-Près. Rates single €110; double €150-€165; triple 205; breakfast €10-€12. Credit MC, V. Map p405 H6.

An oasis of calm in lively St-Germain, this hotel has a courtyard in front and a lovely conservatory and garden at the back, where you'll find the chestnut trees that give the hotel its name. The 37 rooms are mostly reasonably sized, with pretty canopies and fabrics.

Hotel services *Air con. Baby-sitting. Bar. Garden. Tea salon.* Room services *Double glazing.*

Budget

Hôtel Delambre

35 rue Delambre, 14th (01.43.20.66.31/fax 01.45.38.91.76/www.hoteldelambre.com) M° Edgar Quinet or Vavin. Rates single €65; double €80-€95; suite €140; breakfast €8. Credit AmEx, MC, V. Map p406 H7.

Elegant cast-iron touches in the 30 rooms give this friendly hotel an individual style, much updated from the 1920s when the 'Pope of Surrealism', André Breton (*see chapter* The Surreal Thing), lived here. The mini-suite in the attic is particularly pleasing.

Hotel services *Laundry.* Room services *Double glazing.*

Hôtel du Globe

15 rue des Quatre-Vents, 6th (01.43.26.35.50/ fax 01.46.33.62.69). M° Odéon. Closed August. Rates single or double €66-€100; breakfast €9. Credit MC, V. Map p406 H7.

The Globe is an appealing mix of styles. Gothic wrought-iron doors lead into florid corridors, and an unexplained suit of armour supervises guests from the tiny salon. Take heed: a small, winding staircase may lead to suitcase trouble.

Room services *Double glazing. Radio. Room service.*

Hôtel Istria-Montparnasse

29 rue Campagne-Première, 14th (01.43.20.91.82/fax 01.43.22.48.45). M° Raspail. Rates double €92-€106; breakfast €8. Credit AmEx, DC, MC, V. Map p405 G9.

If you're in Montparnasse in order to relive its artistic heyday, you can't do better than stay here – Man Ray, Kiki, Marcel Duchamp, Francis Picabia, Erik Satie and Louis Aragon all did. The Istria has been modernised since the days when the windswept-and-interesting mob graced its halls, but it still has great vats of charm with 26 simply furnished, compact rooms, a cosy cellar breakfast room and a comfortable living area. Film fans take note, the tiled artists' studios next door featured in Godard's *A Bout de Souffle.*

Hotel services *Garden. Laundry. Photocopier.* Room services *Double glazing. Room service (24hr).*

Hôtel de Nesle

7 rue de Nesle, 6th (01.43.54.62.41/fax 01.43.54.31.88/www.hoteldenesle.com). M° Odéon. Rates single €50-€70; double €70-€100; extra bed €12; no breakfast. Credit AC, MC, V. Map p406 H6.

The eccentric Nesle draws an international backpacker clientele. Madame regales visitors with tales of the Nesle's hippy past; Monsieur is responsible for the painted figures on the walls of the 20 rooms (from colonial to Oriental, Molière to the Knights Templar). There are no phones in rooms and no reservations are taken.

Hotel services *Garden. Terrace.* Room services *Double glazing.*

The 7th & the 15th

Deluxe

Hôtel Duc de St-Simon

14 rue de St-Simon, 7th (01.44.39.20.20/ fax 01.45.48.68.25). M° Rue du Bac. Rates double €220-€240; suite €320-€340; breakfast €14. Credit AmEx, DC, MC, V. Map p405 F6.

Step off the quiet side street into a pretty courtyard (where breakfast is served in the summer) – you'll be following in the footsteps of Lauren Bacall, Billy James and Toni Morisson. The 34 romantically decorated bedrooms include four with terraces above a leafy garden (sadly not accessible to visitors). A perfect pitch for the glamorous and amorous, though if you can do without a four-poster bed there are cheaper and more spacious rooms than the 'Honeymoon Suite'.

Hotel services *Laundry.* Room services *Room service. TV (on request).*

Le Montalembert

3 rue de Montalembert, 7th (01.45.49.68.68/ fax 01.45.49.69.49/www.montalembert.com). M° Rue du Bac. Rates double €320-€440; suite €490-€760; breakfast €20. Credit AmEx, DC, MC, V. Map p405 G6.

The **Hôtel des Saints-Pères** puts a ceiling on splendour. *See p67.*

depuis 1856
★ ★ ★
AVIATIC
H O T E L

Saint Germain des Prés

Special offers on our website www.aviatic.fr

105 rue de Vaugirard, 6th
Tel: 33 (0)1 53 63 25 50

10% discount
on our rooms
for Time Out
readers

RÉSIDENCE
ALMA-MARCEAU
★ ★ ★ ★
PARIS

The Résidence Alma Marceau★★★★ is a cluster of luxurious, well-equipped
1, 3 or 5-bedroom apartments, a few minutes walk from the Champs Elysées. The atmosphere is one of
homely comfort and refined elegance - ideal for putting up clients or friends. All apartments are individually decorated and offer spacious reception rooms, quiet bedrooms, marble bathrooms and fully equipped
kitchens. All apartments can be rented for a few days, or for longer periods.

For more information, get in touch with Mr Régis Maurin - Manager, or visit our website
www.residencealmamarceau.com

10% off for the Time Out readers

5 RUE JEAN GIRAUDOUX, 16TH - TEL: 33 (0)1.53.57.67.89 - FAX: 33 (0)1.40.70.06.70

A studiedly suave hotel. The atmosphere is part Zen, part minimalist cool; one could cite the lovingly-furnished bedrooms as an example. Each room is equipped with two sets of curtains (day and night) and special anti-glare lighting. The bar was the first of the newly trendy hotel bars to pull in the jet set, long before the likes of Costes.
Hotel services *Laundry.* **Room services** *Fax. Radio. TV/VCR.*

Expensive

Hôtel de l'Université

22 rue de l'Université, 7th (01.42.61.09.39/ fax 01.42.60.40.84/www.hoteluniversite.com). Mº Rue du Bac. **Rates** single €80-€125; double €150-€200; triple €200-€240; breakfast €9. **Credit** AmEx, MC, V. **Map** p405 G6.
Just a short walk from the Musée d'Orsay, this spacious 27-room hotel is full of antique wardrobes, warm colours, velvety carpets and soft furnishings. The elegant vaulted cellar rooms can be hired for functions.
Hotel services *Bureau de change. Laundry.* **Room services** *Double glazing.*

Moderate

Hôtel des Saints-Pères

65 rue des Saints-Pères, 6th. (01.45.44.50.00/fax 01.45.44.90.83). Mº St Germain des Prés. **Rates** double €105-€195; suite €280; Breakfast €11. **Credit** AmEx, MC, V. **Map** p405 G7.
Right in the middle of designer shopping heaven, this *hôtel particulier* built in 1658 by Gittard, one of Louis XIV's architects, is wonderfully calm. Discreet and low-key, the hotel has a charming garden, and a sophisticated, though small, bar. The most coveted room is No. 100, with its impressive 17th-century fresco by painters from the Versailles school. The room also features an open bathroom so you can also gaze at the myth of Leda and the Swan whilst splashing around.
Hotel services *Air con. Bar.* **Room services** *Double glazing.*

Budget

Hôtel Eiffel Rive Gauche

6 rue du Gros-Caillou, 7th (01.45.51.24.56/fax 01.45.51.11.77/www.123france.com). Mº Ecole Militaire. **Rates** double €85-€92; triple €110; quad €145; breakfast €7. **Credit** MC, V. **Map** p404 D6.
For the quintessential Paris view at a bargain price, ask for one of the upper floors of this well-situated hotel; you can see the Eiffel Tower from nine of the 30 rooms. They feature Empire-style bedheads and modern bathrooms. There is also a tiny, tiled courtyard with a bridge. The owner, Laurent Chicheportiche also has the Villa Garibaldi on the other side of the Ecole Militaire (48 bd Garibaldi, 15th; 01.56.58.56.58).
Room services *Double glazing. Radio.*

A suave snooze at the **Montalembert**. *See p54.*

AUBERGE INTERNATIONALE DES JEUNES

HOSTEL IN THE CITY CENTRE OF PARIS • BEST VALUE DOWNTOWN

€13
from
November
to February

€14
from March
to October

An ideal location for young people, a lively and safe area with many cafés and pubs. Laundromats, boulangeries and supermarkets nearby.

• Rooms from 2, 3 or 4 beds
• Breakfast included

YOU CAN BOOK BY FAX OR EMAIL. 10 rue Trousseau, 11th. M° Ledru Rollin, line 8.
Tel: +33 (0)1.47.00.62.00 • Fax: +33 (0)1.47.00.33.16
http://www.aijparis.com • email: aij@aijparis.com

www.rentoparis.com

LOOKING FOR A PLACE TO STAY IN PARIS?
(LONDON, MADRID, ROME)

WE HAVE EVERYTHING FROM HOTELS TO STUDIOS TO FOUR BEDROOM FURNISHED APARTMENTS AVAILABLE BY DAY, WEEK OR MONTH.

FOR MORE INFORMATION, GO TO WWW.RENTOPARIS.COM

Tel: +33(0)1.43.67.54.90 Fax: +33(0)1.43.67.73.04
E-Mail: contact@rentoparis.com

Grand Hôtel Lévêque
29 rue Cler, 7th (01.47.05.49.15/
fax 01.45.50.49.36/www.hotel-leveque.com).
Mº Ecole Militaire. **Rates** single €53; double €84-
€91; triple €114; breakfast €7. **Credit** AmEx, MC, V.
Map p404 D6.
Located on a largely pedestrianised market street
near the Eiffel Tower, the Lévêque is good value for
such a chic area. The tiled entrance is charming,
while the 50 rooms are well-equipped: there are
sparkling white bathrooms in all the doubles; singles just have a basin.
Room services *Double glazing. Modem link.*

Hôtel de Nevers
83 rue du Bac, 7th (01.45.44.61.30/
fax 01.42.22.29.47). Mº Rue du Bac. **Rates** double
€81-€91; breakfast €6. **No credit cards.**
Map p405 G6.
This characterful 11-room hotel was once part of a
convent. Everything is dinky and dainty, with mini-
wardrobes and neat bathrooms. Rooms are smart,
but the paintwork on the staircase has suffered regular torment as guests have to carry up their own
luggage (quite right, too: it builds character, what?).
If you can make it up to the fourth floor, there are
two rooms with tiny, charming terraces.
Room services *Double glazing.*

Bed & breakfast

Alcove & Agapes
Le Bed & Breakfast à Paris, 8bis rue Coysevox, 18th
(01.44.85.06.05/fax 01.44.85.06.14).
This B&B service offers more than 100 homes (€50-
€110 for a double) with hosts ranging from artists
to grandmothers.

Good Morning Paris
43 rue Lacépède, 5th (01.47.07.28.29/
fax 01.47.07.44.45). **Open** 9am-5.30pm Mon-Fri.
This company has forty rooms throughout the city.
Prices range from €38 for one person to €75 for
three.

Apart-hotels & short-stay rental

These can be a good way to free yourself from
the tyranny of over-attentive hotel staff,
particularly if you have small children or a
fabulously zinging sex life. A deposit is usually
payable on arrival. Small ads for private short-
term rentals can be found in the Anglophone
magazine *Fusac* or on its website www.fusac.fr.

Apparthotel Citadines
Central reservations 01.41.05.79.79/
fax 01.41.05.78.87/www.citadines.com **Rates**
studio from €87; apartment for four from €141.
Credit AmEx, DC, MC, V.
Seventeen modern complexes attract a mainly busi-

ness clientele. Rooms are on the cramped side, but a
kitchenette and table make them practical for those
with children. Discounts can be had for longer stays.
Room services *CD player. Dishwasher. Double*
glazing. Kitchen. Microwave.

Home Plazza Bastille
74 rue Amelot, 11th (01.40.21.20.00/
fax 01.47.00.82.40/ www.homeplazza.com).
Mº St-Sébastien-Froissart. **Rates** double €155-€198;
single €137; suite €295-€443; breakfast €18.
Credit AmEx, DC, MC, V. **Map** p402 L5.
Aimed at both business people and tourists, this
carefully constructed 'village' of 290 apartments
built around a street is reminiscent of a stage set.
Rooms are clean and modern with well-equipped
kitchenette and spacious bathrooms.
Hotel services *Air con. Bar. Business services.*
Garden. Parking. Restaurant.
Branch: Home Plazza St-Antoine, 289bis rue du
Fbg-St-Antoine, 11th (01.40.09.40.00/fax
01.40.09.11.55).

Paris Appartements Services
69 rue d'Argout, 2nd (01.40.28.01.28/
fax 01.40.28.92.01/www.paris.appartements-
services.fr). **Open** 9am-7pm Mon-Fri; 10am-noon Sat.
Rates studio from €61 per week; apartment from
€135 per week. **Credit** MC, V.
This organisation provides furnished studios and
one-bedroom flats in the 1st to 4th *arrondissements*,
with weekly maid service, and a 24-hour helpline.
The staff are bilingual.

The best For a treat

Hôtel Bel Ami
Follow the fashion pack for a dose of
minimalist luxury. *See p60.*

Hôtel Costes
An underwater sound system: need we say
more? *See p43.*

Hôtel Duc de St-Simon
Divinely dinky home to the rich and high-
profile *See p64.*

Hôtel Napoléon
Lose yourself in antique grandeur.
See p53.

Hôtel Royal Monceau
Wallow in pampered bliss in Les Thermes
health club. *See p55.*

Pavillon de la Reine
What could be more romantic than dossing
in place des Vosges? *See p48.*

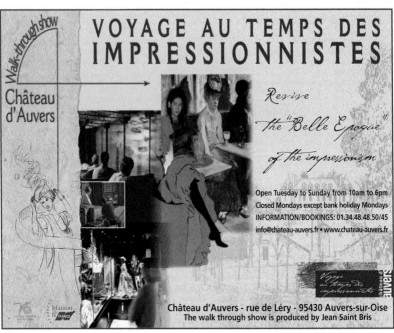

Walk-through show

VOYAGE AU TEMPS DES IMPRESSIONNISTES

Château d'Auvers

Revive

the "Belle Epoque"

of the impressionism

Open Tuesday to Sunday from 10am to 6pm
Closed Mondays except bank holiday Mondays
INFORMATION/BOOKINGS: 01.34.48.48.50/45
info@chateau-auvers.fr • www.chateau-auvers.fr

Château d'Auvers - rue de Léry - 95430 Auvers-sur-Oise
The walk through show is produced by Jean Saint Bris

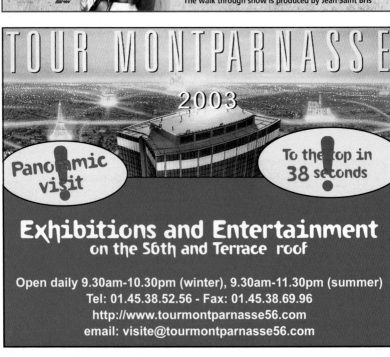

TOUR MONTPARNASSE

2003

Panoramic visit

To the top in 38 seconds

Exhibitions and Entertainment
on the 56th and Terrace roof

Open daily 9.30am-10.30pm (winter), 9.30am-11.30pm (summer)
Tel: 01.45.38.52.56 - Fax: 01.45.38.69.96
http://www.tourmontparnasse56.com
email: visite@tourmontparnasse56.com

Sightseeing

Introduction

Camera primed? Corn plasters firmly on? In the mood to be charmed?
Come on, then – let's investigate the most beautiful city in the world.

Paris is a compact capital city, its urban centre contained by the Périphérique and divided neatly by the Seine into the Left and Right banks, with Ile de la Cité and Ile St Louis in the middle. Parisians speak of their city in terms of *arrondissements*, a system that began with Napoléon and was continued when Baron Haussmann extended the outer limits of the city. Running from one to 20, the *arrondissements* begin at the Louvre and spiral out around the city in a snail-shell-like pattern which, once you can visualise it, does not take long to master. Parisians are more likely to refer to what *arrondissement* they live in than the name of the area itself. Some, such as the 16th (smart residential and embassy land) and the 6th (St-Germain), carry cachet; others are stereotyped (often by people who have never been there) as boring (the 15th) or unsafe (the 20th) – snobbery has a lot to answer for when dealing with *arrondissements*.

We have divided the Sightseeing chapter into five sections: The Seine, The Islands, Right Bank, Left Bank and Beyond the Périphérique. The Right and Left Bank sections are divided into areas which roughly follow *arrondissement*

guidelines, starting from the centre and working outwards in a clockwise direction. *Arrondissements* are given in all addresses. *See p398* **arrondissement map**.

The expressions *Rive Gauche* and *Rive Droite* are well known, but the old adage '*Sur la Rive Gauche on pense, sur la Rive Droite on dépense*' (on the Left Bank one thinks, on the Right Bank one spends money) has all but lost its relevance. While the Left Bank is still home to some of the country's greatest educational establishments, just as much, if not more, spending happens in St-Germain as in the Fbg-St-Honoré and the Marais, while plenty of intellectuals live in the left-wing 19th and 20th *arrondissements*.

A stronger distinction these days is between East and West, western Paris on both sides of the river still being home to the *haute bourgeoisie* and eastern Paris attracting new bohemians and genuine artists with its cheap rents, and pockets of uber-trendiness in the midst of working-class areas.

Getting around is both pleasurable and easy by Métro, bus or on foot (*see p365* **Directory**), or, for a lazy way to see the sights, what better than a riverboat cruise?

Top ten Sights you really must see

We know: you were dragged around them on the school trip to Paris, but the city's top ten tourist draws are enduringly alluring, so have a look at...

Notre-Dame de Paris Cathedral
This goth-rock classic remains a perennial favourite, and is currently number one in the tourist charts. *See p79.*

Basilique du Sacré-Coeur
Holding down the number two spot, this dome-tastic dazzler drags in Basilique-busting crowds by the bucket load. *See p107.*

Eiffel Tower
What can you say? Stand at the base and look up or stand and the top and look down – it's thrilling any way you take it. *See p131.*

Centre Georges Pompidou
Modern art and polemic exo-skeletal architecture still manage to pull in the punters. *See p153.*

Musée du Louvre
Does a tiny drop in visitors mean that Mona Lisa is finally losing her touch with the tourists? No way: the colossal number of gawpers cannot be smirked at. *See p148.*

Notre-Dame de Paris.

Cité des Sciences
This futuristic city never fails to ground its visitors with a magnetic attraction even Newton would be impressed by. *See p176.*

Musée d'Orsay
Paint-pot loads of art-lovers brush past this converted railway station every year. A little daub of heaven on earth. *See p155.*

Arc de Triomphe
A rather less than triumphant eighth position, but tourists still clamber up the Napoleonic staircase to see Paris at their feet. *See p102.*

Musée de l'armée
One emperor and his dog are rounding 'em up as tourists flock in to see where Napoléon and his four-legged friend lie just bones-apart. *See p168.*

Muséum d'Histoire Naturelle
The lot, from the first plip to the last plop. (From an original idea by mother nature). *See p177.*

Cité des Sciences.

Sightseeing

The Islands

Don't be fooled by the urbane gentility of it all; the Islands harbour tales of the emasculated, the incarcerated, the decapitated and the drug-crazed.

Ile de la Cité

In the 1st and 4th arrondissements.

The settlement that was to grow into Paris was founded on Ile de la Cité around 250 BC by the Parisii (*see chapter* **History**). It continued to be a centre of political and religious power into the Middle Ages.

When Victor Hugo wrote *Notre Dame de Paris* in 1831, the Ile de la Cité was still a bustling quarter of narrow medieval streets and tall houses: 'the head, heart and very marrow of Paris'. In that case, then, Baron Haussmann performed a marrow transplant; he supervised the expulsion of 25,000 people from the island, razing tenements and some 20 churches. The lines of the old streets are traced into the parvis in front of **Notre-Dame**. The people resettled to the east, leaving behind a few large, official buildings – the law courts, **Conciergerie**, **Hôtel-Dieu** hospital, the police headquarters and, of course, Notre-Dame.

The most charming spot is the western tip, where the **Pont-Neuf** spans the Seine. Despite its name – you know what's coming don't you – it is the oldest bridge in Paris, begun under the reign of Catherine de Médicis and Henri III in 1578 and taking 30 years in all to complete. Go down the steps to a leafy triangular garden known as the square du Vert-Galant. With a wonderful view of the river, it's a great spot for summer picnics, or you can take a boat trip from the *quai* with the Vedettes du Pont-Neuf (*see chapter* **Directory**). In the centre of the bridge is an equestrian statue of Henri IV, erected in 1635, destroyed in the Revolution and replaced in 1818 (make your mind up, eh?). On the island side of the bridge, the secluded place Dauphine, home to restaurants, wine bars and the **Hôtel Henri IV**, was built in 1607. It was commissioned by Henri IV, who named it in honour of his son, the dauphin Louis, the future King Louis XIII. The red brick and stone houses look out on both *quais* and square, whose third,

eastern side was demolished in the 1870s. André Malraux had a Freudian analysis of its appeal – 'the sight of its triangular formation with slightly curved lines, and of the slit which bisects its two wooded spaces. It is, without doubt, the vagina of Paris'.

The towers of the **Conciergerie** dominate the island's north bank. Along with the Palais de Justice, it was originally part of the Palais de la Cité, residential and administration complex of the Capetian kings. It stands on the site of an earlier Merovingian fortress and, before that, the Roman governor's house. Etienne Marcel's uprising prompted Charles V to move the royal retinue to the Louvre in 1358, and the Conciergerie was assigned a more sinister role as a prison where hapless souls awaited execution. The interior is worth visiting for its Gothic vaulted halls.

Sainte-Chapelle, Pierre de Montreuil's masterpiece of stained glass and slender Gothic columns, is nestled amid the nearby law courts. Surrounding the chapel, the Palais de Justice evolved alongside the Conciergerie. After going through security, you can visit the Salle des Pas Perdus, busy with plaintiffs and barristers, and sit in on cases in the civil and criminal courts. The Palais is still the centre of the French legal system, although it has long been rumoured that the law courts will be moved out to the 13th or 15th *arrondissement*.

Caged birds are on sale at the market (Sunday only) across the boulevard du Palais, behind the tribunal du Commerce at **place Louis Lépine**. For the rest of the week it's a flower market. The legal theme continues to the south with the Préfecture de Police, known by its address, quai des Orfèvres, and immortalised in Simenon's *Maigret* novels.

The **Hôtel-Dieu**, east of the market place, was founded as a hospital in the seventh century. During the Middle Ages your chances of survival here were, at best, slim, so it was clearly a model for today's NHS. The hospital was rebuilt in the 1860s on the site of a nearby foundling hospital.

Notre-Dame cathedral dominates the eastern half of the island. In front of the cathedral, the bronze marker known as **Kilomètre Zéro** is the point from which all distances are measured. The **Crypte Archéologique** under the parvis gives a sense of the island's multi-layered past, when it was a tangle of alleys, houses, churches and cabarets. Behind the cathedral is the **Mémorial de la Déportation**, a sobering reminder of the French citizens (and people who had fled from the Nazis in the hope of finding refuge in France) who perished in concentration camps. The capital's oldest love story unfolded at 9 quai aux Fleurs, where Héloïse lived with her uncle Canon 'Tony Soprano' Fulbert, who had her lover Abélard castrated. A medieval feel persists in the few streets untouched by Haussmann northeast of the cathedral, such as rue Chanoinesse and the rue des Chantres.

Cathédrale Notre-Dame de Paris

pl du Parvis-Notre-Dame, 4th (01.42.34.56.10). M° Cité/RER St-Michel. **Open** 8am-6.45pm Mon-Fri; 8am-7.45pm Sat-Sun; towers (01.53.10.07.02) 9.30am-5pm daily. **Admission** free; towers €5.50; €3.50 18-25s; free under-18s. **No credit cards.** **Map** p406 J7.

Keen to outdo the new abbey at St-Denis, Bishop Maurice de Sully decided to construct a grandiose new edifice in Paris. Begun in 1163, the Gothic masterpiece was not completed until 1345, straddling two architectural eras – the great galleried churches of the 12th century and the buttressed cathedrals that followed. Among its famous features are the three glorious rose windows and the doorways of the west front, recently cleaned and restored, with their rows of saints and sculpted tympanums depicting the *Last Judgement* (centre), *Life of the Virgin* (left), *Life of St-Anne* (right). In the 1630s Robert de Cotte destroyed the rood screen and choir stalls, making way for the new choir and grille completed only in 1708-25 for Louis XIV. During the Revolution, the cathedral was turned into a temple of reason and a wine warehouse, and the statues of the 28 Kings of Judah higher up the facade were destroyed, having been mistaken for statues of the kings of France – those seen today are replicas. Several of the originals were discovered in 1979 and are now on view at the **Musée National du Moyen Age** (*see chapter* **Museums**). The cathedral regained its ceremonial role for Napoléon's coronation as Emperor in 1804, but by the mid-19th century had fallen into such dilapidation that artists petitioned Louis-Philippe to restore the cathedral, which was masterfully done by Viollet-le-Duc. You can climb the north bell tower to a gallery adorned with gargoyles – well worth it for the view.

La Conciergerie

1 quai de l'Horloge, 1st (01.53.73.78.50). M° Cité/ RER Châtelet-Les Halles. **Open** *Apr-Sept* 9.30am-6.30pm daily; *Oct-Mar* 10am-5pm daily. **Admission** €5.49; €3.51 12-25s, students; free under-12s; €7.62 with Sainte-Chapelle. **No credit cards.** **Map** p406 J6.

Marie-Antoinette was held here during the Revolution and Danton and Robespierre also did a pre-guillotine pitstop. The Conciergerie looks every inch the forbidding medieval fortress, yet the pseudo-medieval facade was added in the 1850s. The 13th-century Bonbec tower survives from the Capetian palace, and the Tour de l'Horloge built in 1370, on the corner of boulevard du Palais, was the first public clock in Paris. The fortress became a prison under the watch of the Concierge. The wealthy had private cells with their own furniture; others were crowded together on beds of straw. A list of Revolutionary prisoners, including a hairdresser, shows that far from all victims were nobles. Marie-Antoinette's cell, the Chapelle des Girondins, contains her crucifix and a guillotine blade.

La Crypte Archéologique

pl du Parvis-Notre-Dame, 4th (01.43.29.83.51). Mº Cité/RER St-Michel. **Open** 10am-6pm; closed Mon. **Admission** €3.30; €2.20 over 60s; €1.60 under-26s; free under-14s. **No credit cards. Map** p406 J7.
The excavations under the parvis span 16 centuries, from the remains of Gallo-Roman ramparts to a 19th-century drain.

Mémorial de la Déportation

Square de l'Ile de France, 4th Mº Cité/RER St-Michel. **Open** 10am-6pm Tue-Sun; last ticket 5.30pm. **Admission** free. **Map** p406 J7.
This tribute to the 200,000 people deported to death camps during World War II can be found on the eastern tip of the island. A blind staircase descends to river level, where simple chambers are lined with tiny lights and the walls are inscribed with poetry. A barred window looks out onto the Seine.

Sainte-Chapelle

4 bd du Palais, 1st (01.53.73.78.50). Mº Cité/ RER Châtelet-Les Halles. **Open** *Apr-Sept* 9.30am-6.30pm daily; *Oct-Mar* 10am-5pm daily. **Admission** €5.49; €3.51 12-25s, students; free under-12s; €7.62 with Conciergerie. **Credit** (shop) MC, V. **Map** p406 J6.
Hoping to get canonised, kids? Follow the example of Louis IX. This devout monarch (1226-70) had a hobby of collecting holy relics. In the 1240s he bought what was advertised as the Crown of Thorns, and ordered Pierre de Montreuil to design a suitable shrine. The result was the exquisite High Gothic Sainte-Chapelle. The upper level, intended for the royal family and the canons, appears to consist almost entirely of stained glass. The windows depict Biblical scenes, and on sunny days coloured reflections dapple the stone. The lower chapel was for the use of palace servants. Guess what? They only went and made Louis a saint.

Ile St-Louis

In the 4th arrondissement.
Want to see how the other half live? The Ile St-Louis is one of the most exclusive residential addresses in the city. Delightfully unspoiled, it offers fine architecture, narrow streets and pretty views from the tree-lined *quais*.
For hundreds of years the island was a swampy pasture belonging to Notre-Dame and a retreat for fishermen, swimmers and courting couples, known as the Ile Notre-Dame. In the 14th century Charles V built a fortified canal through the middle, thus creating the Ile aux Vaches ('Island of Cows'). Its real-estate potential wasn't realised until 1614, when

speculator Christophe Marie persuaded Louis XIII to fill in the canal (now rue Poulletier) and plan streets, bridges and houses. The island was renamed in honour of the King's pious predecessor and the venture proved a huge success, thanks to society architect Louis Le Vau, who from the 1630s on built fashionable new residences on quai d'Anjou (including his own at No 3), quai de Bourbon and quai de Béthune, as well as the **Eglise St-Louis-en-l'Ile**. By the 1660s the island was filled and, unlike the Marais, where the smart reception rooms were at the rear of the courtyard, here they were often at the front to allow their residents riverside views.

The **rue St-Louis-en-l'Ile**, lined with quirky gift shops, quaint tearooms, lively stone-walled bars and restaurants and fine historic buildings, runs the length of the island. The grandiose Hôtel Lambert (2 rue St-Louis-en-l'Ile/1 quai d'Anjou) was built by Le Vau in 1641 for Louis XIII's secretary with interiors by Le Sueur, Perrier and Le Brun. At No 51, Hôtel Chenizot, look out for bearded faun adorning the rocaille doorway and the dragons supporting the balcony. The **Hôtel du Jeu de Paume**, at No 54 was once a real tennis court. Legendary ice cream shop **Berthillon** (No 31) often draws a queue down the street. There are great views of the flying buttresses of Notre-Dame at the western end, where a footbridge crosses to the Ile de la Cité. Here you will also find the **Brasserie de l'Isle-St-Louis**, which draws Parisians and tourists alike, so don't go if you're looking for some peace and quiet.

Baudelaire wrote part of *Les Fleurs du Mal* while living at the Hôtel de Lauzun. He and fellow poet Théophile Gautier also held meetings of their dope smokers' club here – the bloody hippies obviously thought it was clever. Earlier, Racine, Molière and La Fontaine spent time here as guests of La Grande Mademoiselle, cousin of Louis XIV. The *hôtel* stands out for its scaly sea-serpent drainpipes and *trompe l'oeil* interiors. There are further literary associations to be found at 6 quai d'Orléans, where the Adam Mickiewicz library-museum (01.43.54.35.61/open 2-6pm Thur) is dedicated to the Romantic poet, journalist and zealous campaigner for Polish freedom from Russia who lived in Paris 1832-40.

Eglise St-Louis-en-l'ile

19bis rue St-Louis-en-l'Ile, 4th (01.46.34.11.60). Mº Pont-Marie. **Open** 3-7pm Mon; 9am-noon, 3-7pm Tue-Sun. **Map** p406 L7.
Built 1664-1765, following plans by Louis Le Vau and completed by Gabriel Le Duc. The interior follows the classic Baroque model with Corinthian columns and a sunburst over the altar, and is a popular classical concert venue.

The Right Bank

Whether you want revolutionary resonance, modern-day militancy, *art de vivre* or architectural excellence, the *Rive Droite* is the bank that likes to say yes.

The Louvre to Concorde

In the 1st arrondissement.

It was in the 14th century that the Louvre and the secondary palaces of the Tuileries and Palais-Royal became the centre of royal power. Even today, the area has an atmosphere of genetically genteel stasis.

Now one of the world's great art museums, the **Palais du Louvre** (*see pp148-153*) has huge state rooms, fine courtyards and galleries stretching to the Jardin des Tuileries. Begun as a fortress and turned into a sumptuous Renaissance palace, the Louvre was designated a museum in 1793. Two hundred years later, Mitterrand's *Grand Louvre* scheme added I M Pei's pyramid in the Cour Napoléon, doubled the exhibition space, uncovered medieval remains and resulted in the subterranean Carrousel du Louvre shopping mall, auditorium and food halls. The pyramid's steel and glass structure creates mesmerising optical effects with the fountains, especially when it is floodlit at night.

On place du Louvre, opposite the palace, is **St-Germain-l'Auxerrois**, once the French kings' parish church and home to the only original Flamboyant Gothic porch in Paris, built in 1435. Mirroring it to the left is the 19th-century neo-Gothic 1st *arrondissement* town hall, alongside chic bar **Le Fumoir**.

Thanks to the *Grand Louvre* scheme, the **Musée des Arts Décoratifs**, the **Musée de la Mode et du Costume** and the **Musée de la Publicité** (*see chapter* **Museums**) have been rejuvenated, while the Arc du Carrousel, a mini-Arc de Triomphe built by Napoléon in 1806-09, has been restored. Through the arch

On reflection, louvrely: I M Pei's **Grand Louvre pyramid**.

▶ For detailed museum information and
opening times, turn to **Sightseeing:
Museums**, starting on page 147.
▶ For information on arts events turn to **Arts
& Entertainment**, starting on page 275.
▶ For shopping information turn to **Shops &
Services**, starting on page 235.

you can now appreciate the extraordinary
perspective through the **Jardin des Tuileries**
all along the Champs-Elysées up to the **Arc de
Triomphe** and beyond to the **Grande Arche
de la Défense**. Originally stretching to the
Tuileries palace, the Tuileries gardens were laid
out in the 17th century by André Le Nôtre and
remain a living space with cafés, ice-cream
stalls and summer fun fair. The gardens also
serve as a gallery for modern art sculptures.
Flanking the Tuileries overlooking **place de la
Concorde** stand the **Musée de l'Orangerie**,
and the **Jeu de Paume**, originally built for
playing real tennis, now used for contemporary
art exhibitions.

Along the north side of the Louvre, the rue
de Rivoli is remarkable for its arcaded facades.
It runs in a perfect line to **place de la
Concorde** in one direction, and to the Marais

in the other, where it becomes rue St-Antoine.
Despite the many souvenir shops, elegant, old-
fashioned hotels remain, along with gentlemen's
tailors, bookshops **WH Smith** and **Galignani**
and the famous tearoom **Angelina's**. The area
formed a little England in the 1830s-40s as
aristocracy, writers and artists flooded across
the Channel after the Napoleonic Wars. They
stayed at the **Hôtel Meurice** and dined in the
restaurants of the Palais-Royal.

Place des Pyramides, at the western end of
the Louvre where rue de Rivoli meets rue des
Pyramides, contains a shiny gilt equestrian
statue of Joan of Arc. One of four statues of her
in the city, this one is appropriated every year
on May Day as a symbol of French Nationalism
for the supporters of Jean-Marie Le Pen. Ancient
rue St-Honoré, running parallel to rue de Rivoli,
is one of those streets that changes style in
different districts – all smart shops towards
place Vendôme, local cafés and inexpensive
bistros towards Les Halles. At No 296, the
Baroque church of **St-Roch** is pitted with
bullet holes left by Napoléon's troops when they
crushed a royalist revolt in 1795. With its old
houses, rue St-Roch still feels like *vieux* Paris;
a couple of shops are even built into the side
of the church. Across the road, at 263*bis*, the

Sightseeing

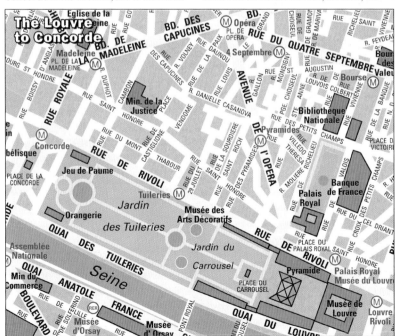

1670-76 Chapelle de l'Assomption has a dome so disproportionately large that contemporaries dubbed it 'dumb dome' (*sot dôme*), a pun on Sodom. Pause for laughter. Just west of here, much talked-about boutique **Colette** at No 213 has given some oomph to what was a staid shopping area, drawing a swarm of high-concept fashion boutiques such as Joseph, Mandarina Duck and **Marcel Marongiu**. For older Parisians it's the original Colette, novelist and naughty revue performer, who remains an icon of this area. Opposite is rue du Marché St-Honoré, where Le Rubis wine bar hosts the mob sampling the Beaujolais Nouveau every November. The street formerly led to the covered Marché St-Honoré, but that has been replaced by the shiny glass-and-steel offices of the BNP-Paribas bank.

Further west along rue St-Honoré lies wonderful, eight-sided **place Vendôme** (*see p85* **Heist cool**), one of Louis XIV's main contributions, with a perspective that now goes from rue de Rivoli up to Opéra. At the west end of the Tuileries, **place de la Concorde**, laid out to the glorification of Louis XV, is a masterclass in the use of open space. André Malraux may have been OTT when he called it 'the most beautiful architectural complex on this planet', but it's impossible not to be impressed by its grandeur. The winged Marly horses (these are actually copies of the originals, which are now in the Louvre) frame the entrance to the Champs-Elysées. The smart rue Royale, leading to the Madeleine, boasts superior tearoom **Ladurée** and the legendary Maxim's restaurant (featured in Lehár's opera *The Merry Widow*), which has a fabulous art nouveau interior. The rue Boissy d'Anglas offers smart shops and perennial fashion-haunt **Buddha Bar**; while the ultimate sporting luxuries can be found at Hermès on rue du Fbg-St-Honoré (westward extension of rue St-Honoré), as well as fashion names Yves Saint Laurent, Gucci, Guy Laroche, Karl Lagerfeld, Chloé, Lanvin and more. More tearooms and fine porcelain can be found in the Galerie Royale and Passage Royale.

Eglise St-Germain-l'Auxerrois
2 pl du Louvre, 1st (01.42.60.13.96). M° Pont Neuf or Louvre. **Open** 8am-8pm daily. **Map** p406 H6.
This pretty church was for centuries the royal church. Its architecture spans several eras: most striking though is the elaborate Flamboyant Gothic porch. Inside, note the 13th-century Lady Chapel and splendid canopied, carved bench designed by Le Brun in 1682 for the royal family. The church achieved notoriety on 24 August 1572, when the signal for the St-Bartholomew's Day massacre was rung from here.

Eglise St-Roch
296 rue St-Honoré, 1st (01.42.44.13.20). M° Pyramides or Tuileries. **Open** 8am-7.30pm daily. **Map** p401 G5.
This long church begun in the 1650s was designed mainly by Jacques Lemercier. The area was then the heart of Paris, and illustrious parishioners and patrons left funerary monuments: Le Nôtre, Mignard, Corneille and Diderot are all here. Look for busts by Coysevox and Coustou as well as Falconet's statue *Christ on the Mount of Olives*. There is a Baroque pulpit and a cherub-adorned retable behind the rear altar. In 1795, a shoot-out occurred in front of the church between royalists and conventionists – look out for the bullet holes which still pit the facade.

Place de la Concorde
1st/8th. M° Concorde. **Map** p401 F5.
Place de la Concorde is the largest square in Paris, with grand perspectives stretching east-west from the Louvre to the Arc de Triomphe, and north-south from the Madeleine to the Assemblée Nationale across the Seine. In 1792, the statue of Louis XV was removed from the centre and the revolutionaries' guillotine set up for the execution of Louis XVI, Marie-Antoinette and many more. Gabriel also designed the two colonnaded mansions on either side of rue Royale; the one on the west houses the exclusive Crillon hotel and the Automobile Club of France, the other is the Navy Ministry. The *place* was embellished in the 19th century with sturdy lamp posts, the Luxor obelisk, a present from the Viceroy of Egypt, and the tiered wedding-cake fountains that were recently splendidly restored. The best view is by night, from the terrace by the Jeu de Paume in the Tuileries gardens.

Place Vendôme
1st. M° Tuileries or Opéra. **Map** p401 G4.
Elegant place Vendôme got its name from the *hôtel particulier* built by the Duc de Vendôme previously on this site. Inaugurated in 1699, the eight-sided *place* was conceived by Hardouin-Mansart to show off an equestrian statue of the Sun King. This statue was torn down in 1792, and in 1806 the Colonne de la Grande Armée was erected. Modelled on Trajan's column in Rome and decorated with a spiral comic-strip illustrating Napoléon's military exploits, it was made out of 1,250 Russian and Austrian cannons captured at the battle of Austerlitz. During the 1871 Commune this symbol of 'brute force and false glory' was pulled down. The present column is a replica. Hardouin-Mansart only designed the facades; the buildings behind were put up by nobles and speculators. Today the square is home to Cartier, Boucheron, Van Cleef & Arpels, Trussardi and other prestigious jewellers and fashion names, as well as banks, the Justice Ministry and the Ritz hotel, from where Di and Dodi set off on their fateful last journey that summer night in 1997. Chopin died at No 12, in 1849.

Sightseeing

Comic relief at **Comédie-Française**.
See below.

Palais-Royal & Bourse

In the 1st and 2nd arrondissements.
Across the rue de Rivoli from the Louvre, past the **Louvre des Antiquaires** antiques superstore, stands the **Palais-Royal**, once Cardinal Richelieu's private mansion and now the Conseil d'Etat and Ministry of Culture. The **Comédie-Française** theatre stands on the southwest corner. The company, created by Louis XIV in 1680, moved here in 1799. The brass-fronted Café Nemours on place Colette is popular with thespians.

In the 1780s the Palais-Royal was a rumbustious centre of Parisian life, where aristocrats and the financially challenged inhabitants of the *faubourgs* rubbed shoulders. The coffee houses in its arcades attracted radical debate. Here Camille Desmoulins called the city to arms on the eve of Bastille Day. After the Napoleonic Wars, Wellington and Field Marshal von Blücher supposedly lost so much money at the gambling dens that Parisians claimed they had won back their entire dues for war reparations. Only haute cuisine restaurant Le Grand Véfour (which was founded as Café de Chartres in the 1780s) survives from this era, albeit with decoration from a little later. A more contemporary attraction at Palais-Royal is its

Métro entrance: artist Jean-Michel Othoniel has put a kitsch slant on Guimard's classic art nouveau design by decorating the aluminium struts with glass baubles.

Wander under the arcades to browse in an eccentric world of antique dealers, philatelists and specialists in tin soldiers and musical boxes. Look out for the Prince Jardinier, and vintage clothes specialist **Didier Ludot**. Go through the arcades to rue de Montpensier to the west, and the neo-Rococo Théâtre du Palais-Royal. Opposite, next to busy bar L'Entracte, is one of several narrow, stepped passages that run between this road and rue de Richelieu, which, with parallel rue Ste-Anne, is a focus of Paris' Japanese community.

Paris' traditional business district is squeezed between the elegant calm of the Palais-Royal and the frenzied Grands Boulevards. The Banque de France, France's central bank, has occupied the 17th-century Hôtel de Toulouse since 1811. Very little of the original remains, but its long gallery is still hung with old masters. Nearby, the pretty **place des Victoires** was designed, like place Vendôme, by Hardouin-Mansart, forming an intimate circle of buildings today dedicated to fashion. West of the *place*, explore the shop-lined, beautifully decorated galerie **Vivienne** and **galerie Colbert** (*see p88*, **Passages through time**) and temporary exhibitions at the **Bibliothèque Nationale Richelieu**. Luxury *épicerie* and wine merchant **Legrand** is on the corner of galerie Vivienne and rue de la Banque. Take a detour along the passage des Petits Pères to see Eglise Notre-Dame-des-Victoires, the remains of an Augustine convent with paintings by Van Loo.

Rue de la Banque now leads to the **Bourse** (stock exchange), behind a commanding neo-Classical colonnade. Otherwise the area has a relaxed feel, at weekends positively sleepy. For business lunches and after-work drinks, stockbrokers and journalists converge on the **Vaudeville** brasserie. Rue des Colonnes is a quiet street lined with graceful porticos and acanthus motifs dating from the 1790s. Across the busy rue du Quatre-Septembre is the 1970s concrete and glass HQ of Agence France-Presse, France's biggest news agency. This street and its continuation rue Réaumur were built up by the press barons with some striking art nouveau buildings. Most newspapers have since left, but *Le Figaro* remains in rue du Louvre.

The other side of the palace, off rue Jean-Jacques Rousseau, the **Galerie Véro-Dodat**, built by properous charcutiers of the same name in the Restoration, has a chequered floor and neo-classical shopfronts in excellent condition (*see p88*, **Passages through time**).

Bibliothèque Nationale Richelieu

58 rue de Richelieu, 2nd (01.53.79.53.79/www.bnf.fr).
Mº Bourse. **Open** Galeries Mansart/Mazarine during
exhibitions only 10am-7pm Tue-Sat; noon-7pm Sun.
Cabinet des Médailles 1-5.45pm Mon-Fri; 1-4.45pm
Sat; noon-6pm Sun. **Admission** Galerie
Mansart/Mazarine €5; €4 under-26s. Cabinet des
Médailles free. **Map** p401 H4.

The genesis of the French National Library dates
from the 1660s, when Louis XIV moved manuscripts
that could not be housed in the Louvre to this lavish Louis XIII townhouse. The library was first
opened to the public in 1692, and by 1724 the institution had received so many new acquisitions that
the neighbouring Hôtel de Nevers was added. Some
of the original painted decoration can still be seen in
Galeries Mansart and Mazarine, now used for exhibitions of manuscripts and prints. Antique coins
(originally known as '*médailles*') and curious royal
memorabilia collected by kings from Philippe-
Auguste onwards can be seen in the **Musée du
Cabinet des Médailles** (*see p172*). The complex
was transformed in the 1860s by the innovative
circular vaulted reading room designed by Henri
Labrouste, but the library is now curiously empty as
the books have been moved to the gigantic
Bibliothèque Nationale François Mitterrand
on the Left Bank (*see p136 and p380*), though
medieval manuscripts, maps, engravings, musical
scores and performing arts material remain here.

La Bourse

Palais Brongniart, pl de la Bourse, 2nd
(01.49.27.55.55/www.bourse-de-paris.fr). Mº Bourse.
Guided tours call a week in advance. **Admission**
€8; €5 students. **No credit cards**. **Map** p402 H4.

After a century at the Louvre, the Palais-Royal and
rue Vivienne, the stock exchange was transferred in
1826 to this building, a dignified testament to First
Empire classicism designed under Napoléon by
Alexandre Brongniart. It was enlarged in 1906 to
create a cruciform interior, where brokers buzzed
around a central enclosure, the *corbeille* (or crow's
nest). Computers have now made that design obso-
lete, but the daily dash for dosh means that the
atmosphere remains as frenetic as ever.

Louvre des Antiquaires

2 pl du Palais-Royal, 1st (01.42.97.27.00/
www.louvre-antiquaires.com). Mº Palais-Royal. **Open**
11am-7pm Tue-Sun. Closed Sun July-Aug.
Map p402 H5.

This upmarket antiques centre behind the facade of
an old *grand magasin* houses some 250 dealers (no,
clubbers: *antiques* dealers). Look for Louis XV furniture, tapestries, Sèvres and Chinese porcelain, silver and jewellery, model ships and tin soldiers.

Palais-Royal

main entrance pl du Palais-Royal, 1st (www.palais-
royal.org). Mº Palais Royal. **Open** gardens only
dawn-dusk daily. **Admission** free. **Map** p402 H5.

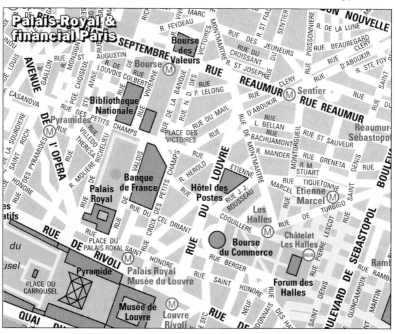

Built for Richelieu by Jacques Lemercier, the building was known as the Palais Cardinal. Richelieu left it to Louis XIII, whose widow, Anne d'Autriche, preferred it to the chilly Louvre and gave it its name when she came to live here with her son, the young Louis XIV. In the 1780s the Duc d'Orléans enclosed the gardens in a three-storey peristyle. Housing cafés, theatres, sideshows, shops and apartments, its arcades came into their own as a society trysting place. Today the gardens offer a tranquil spot in the heart of Paris, while many surrounding shops specialise in prints and antiques. The former palace houses the Conseil d'Etat and the Ministry of Culture. Daniel Buren's once-controversial installation of black and white striped columns of different heights graces the main courtyard; do take care if the old eyesight's a bit dodgy.

Place des Victoires

1st, 2nd. M° Bourse. **Map** p402 H5.
Louis XIV introduced the grand Baroque square in the form of circular place des Victoires, commemorating victories against Holland. It was designed in 1685 by Hardouin-Mansart to set off a statue of the king. The original disappeared in the Revolution and was replaced in 1822 with an equestrian statue by Bosio. Today, the sweeping facades shelter fashion names Kenzo and Thierry Mugler.

Opéra & the Grands Boulevards

Mainly in the 2nd, 8th and 9th arrondissements.
The wedding cake of Charles Garnier's **Palais Garnier** opera house (not to be confused with the *Laboratoire Garnier* of make-up fame), still looks freshly iced from its renovation. It evokes the mood of opera at its grandest, and it's not hard to see why the Phantom of the Opera legend started here. Garnier also designed the Café de la Paix, overlooking place de l'Opéra. Behind, in the Jockey Club (now **Hôtel Scribe**), the Lumière brothers held the world's first public cinema screening in 1895. The delightful wood-fronted emporium Old England is opposite on the boulevard des Capucines. Inside, the shop has antiquated wooden counters, Jacobean-style plaster ceilings and equally dated goods and service. The **Olympia** concert hall, at 28 boulevard des Capucines, the legendary venue of Piaf, Hallyday and other greats, was recently knocked down and rebuilt a few metres away (*see p326*). In 2001 it fell into the hands of the Vivendi group. Across the road at No 35, pioneering portrait photographer Nadar opened a studio in the 1860s, soon frequented by writers, actors and artists including Dumas *père*, Doré and Offenbach. In 1874 it was the setting for the first Impressionists' exhibition.

Pretty sidestreet rue Boudreau contains the 1880s **Théâtre de l'Athénée-Louis Jouvet** (*see p346*).

The **Madeleine**, a monument to Napoléon, stands like a classical temple at the end of the boulevard. Its huge Corinthian columns mirror the Assemblée Nationale over the Seine, while the interior is a riot of marble and altars. Many come to the *place* to ogle **Fauchon**, Paris' most extravagant delicatessen, **Hédiard**, **La Maison de la Truffe** and the other luxury foodstores, or for haute cuisine restaurant **Lucas Carton**, with art nouveau interior by Majorelle.

The *grands magasins* (department stores) **Printemps** and **Galeries Lafayette** opened behind the Palais Garnier in the late 19th century. Printemps still has an imposing domed entrance and Galeries Lafayette a stained-glass dome. Behind the latter, on rue Caumartin, stands the Lycée Caumartin, designed as a convent in the 1780s by Bourse architect Brongniart to become one of Paris' most prestigious lycées under Napoléon. West along Haussmann's boulevard is the small square containing the **Chapelle Expiatoire** dedicated to Louis XVI and Marie-Antoinette. Beyond the Second Empire church of **St-Augustin** is a clever exercise in cast iron by Baltard, architect of the Les Halles pavilions.

Choice of chair at **Palais-Royal**. *See p83.*

Chapelle Expiatoire

29 rue Pasquier, 8th (01.42.65.35.80).
M° St-Augustin. **Open** 1-5pm Thur-Sat. **Admission**
€2.50; free under 18. **Map** p401 F3.
The chapel was commissioned by Louis XVIII in
memory of his executed predecessors, his brother
Louis XVI and Marie-Antoinette. Their remains,
along with those of almost 3,000 revolutionary victims, including Philippe-Egalité, Charlotte Corday,
Mme du Barry, Camille Desmoulins, Danton,
Malesherbes and Lavoisier, were found in 1814 on
the exact spot where the altar stands. The year after
that, the bodies of Louis XVI and Marie-Antoinette
were transferred to the **Basilique St-Denis** (*see
p141*). The chapel draws ardent (if currently frus-
trated) royalists for a memorial service in January.

Eglise St-Augustin

46 bd Malesherbes, 8th (01.45.22.23.12).
M° St-Augustin. **Open** 10am-12.45pm, 3pm-6pm
Mon-Fri; 10am-noon, 4-7.30pm Sat; 10am-noon,
4-7.30pm Sun. **Map** p401 F3.
Designed by Victor Baltard in 1860-71, St-Augustin
is not what it seems. The domed, neo-Renaissance
stone exterior is merely a shell. Within, Baltard used
an iron vault structure; even the decorative angels
are cast in metal. Note the Bouguereau paintings in
the transept.

Eglise de la Madeleine

pl de la Madeleine, 8th (01.44.51.69.00).
M° Madeleine. **Open** 8am-6pm daily. **Map** p401 G4.
The building of a church on this site began in 1764.
In 1806, Napoléon sent instructions from Poland for
Barthélémy Vignon to design a 'Temple of Glory'
dedicated to his Grand Army. After the Emperor's
fall, construction slowed, but the church was finally consecrated in 1845. Inside are three-and-a-half
giant domes, a stunning organ (well, if you're going
to have an organ, have a stunner) and pseudo-
Grecian side altars amid a sea of multicoloured marble. The painting by Ziegler in the chancel depicts
the history of Christianity, Napoléon (ever the
shrinking violet) prominent in the foreground. This
is now a favourite place for society weddings.

Palais Garnier

pl de l'Opéra, 9th (box office 08.36.69.78.68/
www.opera-de-paris.fr). *M° Opéra.* **Open** 10am-5pm
daily. Guided tours in English (01.40.01.22.63) 1pm
and 2pm Tue-Sun €10; €5-€9 reductions.
Admission €6; €4 over 60s; free under 26s,
students. **No credit cards. Map** p401 G4.
The opera house is a monument to the Second
Empire *haute bourgeoisie*. Designed by Charles
Garnier in 1862, it has an auditorium for over 2,000
people. The exterior is opulent, with sculptures of
music and dance on the facade, Apollo topping the
copper dome and nymphs holding torches.
Carpeaux's sculpture *La Danse* shocked Parisians
with its frank sensuality, and in 1869 someone threw
a bottle of ink over its frankly none-too-horny marble thighs. The original is safe in the Musée d'Orsay.

Heist cool

Their exploits would impress the pinkest of
panthers. OK, we're not exactly talking
about dangling from a high tension line to
avoid laser beam booby traps, but Paris'
most recent crime wave has been
perpetrated by 'braqueurs' brimming with
brio. Having decided in recent years that
banks offer too much risk for too little
return, and having tired of the unglamorous
option of Bureaux de Change, ambitious
French criminals turned their attention in
spring 2002 to the unutterably elegant
Place Vendôme, where phallic monuments
and swish hotels jockey for attention with
France's most upmarket jewellers. In the
space of a few short weeks, something
like €11m worth of glittering, gem-
encrusted bracelets, watches, necklaces
and rings were lifted in six daring raids.

While some reactionaries settled for
common or garden ram-raiding, one
resourceful duo disguised themselves as
workmen before smashing a shopfront with
an ice axe and making off with two huge –
and hugely valuable – jewels. Fearful
jewellers have been forced to move their
most serious pieces to the back of their
shops, leaving in the front window the
equivalent of the Saturday night sparklers
of a Dagenham rapper. This has not foiled
the baddies – their ruses have simply
become more cunning. The pick of the
bunch have to be the two sophisticated
gents who attacked high-class jewellers
Fred with a canister of tear-gas hidden in a
bouquet of roses. These chancers made
off with a €6m haul.

The wonderfully named Brigade for the
Repression of Banditry (BRB) reckons many
pieces are stolen to order and probably
leave the country almost immediately,
while the remainder are probably taken to
workshops where the gems are removed
and the gold melted down, making the
gangsters' swag equally hard to trace. The
Association of Watchmakers and Jewellers
has even appealed to tough-guy Interior
Minister Nicolas Sarkozy to put the
frighteners on any putative Janet or John
Dillingers. So far, however, the efforts of
the old *Guillaume* to apprehend the person
or persons responsible for the dastardly
raids at the heart of Poshville have been
tragically Clouseau-esque.

Sightseeing

The Garnier hosts lyric productions as well as ballet. Visitors can see the library, museum, Grand Foyer, Grand Staircase and auditorium with its false ceiling, painted by Chagall in 1964. There's occasional talk of returning to the original, still underneath. (*See also p174, p300 and p325.*)

Quartier de l'Europe

This area north of Opéra around Gare St-Lazare was *the* Impressionist *quartier*, if hardly a tourist draw now. The exciting new steam age was depicted by Monet in the 1870s in *La Gare St-Lazare* and *Pont de l'Europe*; Caillebotte and Pissarro painted views of the new boulevards, and Manet had a studio on rue de St-Petersbourg. The area was known for its prostitutes; rue de Budapest remains a thriving red light district, while rue de Rome has long been home to Paris' stringed-instrument makers. Just east of Gare St-Lazare, check out the imposing **Eglise de la Trinité** and art nouveau brasserie Mollard.

Eglise de la Trinité

pl Estienne d'Orves, 9th (01.48.74.12.77).
M° Trinité. **Open** *Sept-June* 7.15am-8pm Mon-Fri; 9am-8pm Sat; 8.30am-1pm, 4.30-8pm Sun; *July-Aug* 11am-8pm Mon-Sat; 10.30am-1pm, 2pm-6pm Sun. **Map** p401 G3.
Dominated by the tiered wedding-cake belltower, this neo-Renaissance church was built 1861-67 by Théodore Ballu. Composer Olivier Messiaen (1908-92) was organist here for over 30 years. Guided tours on some Sundays. *Wheelchair access (call ahead).*

The Grands Boulevards

Contrary to popular belief, the string of Grands Boulevards between Madeleine and République (des Italiens, Montmartre, Poissonnière, Bonne-Nouvelle, St-Denis, St-Martin) were not built by Haussmann but by Louis XIV in 1670, replacing the fortifications of Charles II's city wall. The boulevards burgeoned after the Revolution, as new residences, theatres and covered passages were built on land repossessed from aristocrats or the church. The Grands Boulevards have long been a staple of Parisian literature, taking the traveller as they do through a cross-section of the city's sociology: a walk from Opéra to République, for example, will take you from luxury shops to the prostitutes of St Denis. Between boulevard des Italiens and rue de Richelieu is place Boieldieu and the **Opéra Comique** (*see chapter* **Music: Classical & Opera**), where *Carmen* was premiered in 1875. Alexandre Dumas *fils* was born across the square at No 1 in 1824.

The 18th-century *mairie* (town hall) of the 9th *arrondissement* (6 rue Drouot) was once home to the infamous *bals des victimes*, where every guest had to have had a relative lost to the guillotine. Having a dotted 'cut here' neck tattoo was not enough. The **Hôtel Drouot** auction house stands surrounded by specialist antique shops, coin and stamp dealers and wine bar Les Caves Drouot, where auction goers and valuers congregate. There are several grand *hôtels particuliers* on rue de la Grange-Batelière, which leads on one side down curious **passage Verdeau** and on the other back to the boulevards via picturesque **passage Jouffroy** and the colourful carved entrance of the **Grévin** waxworks (*see chapter* **Museums**). Across the boulevard look for **passage des Panoramas** (*see p88*, **Passages through time**). Wander down cobbled Cité Bergère, built in 1825 as desirable residences; though most are now budget hotels, the pretty iron and glass *portes-cochères* remain. The area is home to some wonderful kosher restaurants and the formerly infamous Folies-Bergère, where the high-kicking girls have recently returned to the stage. The palatial art deco cinema **Le Grand Rex** offers an interesting backstage tour. East of here are Louis XIV's twin triumphal arches, the **Porte St-Martin** and **Porte St-Denis**.

The best Snogging statues

Brancusi's *Kiss*
Catch this full body-slam snog on a gravestone in the Cimetière du Montparnasse. *See p133.*

Canova's *Eros + Psyche*
... which is preferable to Eros + Psycho. A spectacular marble of a kiss on the wing in the Louvre. *See p148.*

Le Cri
Approach this Cubist work in the Tuileries from Concorde; see a tortoise. Approach from the Louvre; see something très fruity. *See p81.*

Fontaine Médicis
A spot for amorous Parisians, encouraged by this dramatic sculpture in the Jardins du Luxembourg. *See p126.*

Eglise is the word at **la Madeleine**. *See p85.*

Le Grand Rex

1 bd Poissonnière, 2nd (cinema info
08.36.68.70.23/www.legrandrex.com). M° Bonne
Nouvelle. **Tour** Les Etoiles du Rex every 50 mins
10am-7pm Wed-Sun, public holidays, daily in school
holidays. **Admission** €7; €6 under-16s; €10.70 tour
and film; €9.20 under-16s. **Map** p402 J4.
Opened in 1932, the huge art deco cinema was
designed by Auguste Bluysen with fantasy Hispanic
interiors by US designer John Eberson. See behind
the scenes in the loony 50-minute tour. After a
presentation about the construction of the auditorium, visitors are shown the production room, taking in newsreel footage of Rex history and an insight
into film tricks with nerve-jolting Sensurround
effects. *Wheelchair access (call ahead).*

Hôtel Drouot

9 rue Drouot, 9th (01.48.00.20.20/ recorded
information 01.48.00.20.17). M° Richelieu-Drouot.
Open 10am-6pm Mon-Sat. **Map** p 401 H3.
A spiky aluminium and marble-clad concoction is
the unlikely setting for the hub of France's secondary art market, though now rivalled by
Sotheby's and Christie's. Inside, escalators whizz
you up to small salerooms, where medieval manuscripts, 18th-century furniture, Oriental arts, modern paintings and fine wines might be up for sale.
Details of forthcoming sales are published in the
weekly *Gazette de L'Hôtel Drouot*, sold at newsstands. Prestige sales take place at Drouot-
Montaigne. *Partial wheelchair access.*
Branches: Drouot-Montaigne, 15 av Montaigne, 8th
(01.48.00.20.80); Drouot Nord, 64 rue Doudeauville,
18th (01.48.00.20.90).

Porte St-Denis & Porte St-Martin

corner rue St-Denis/bd St-Denis, 2nd/10th; 33 bd
St-Martin, 3rd/10th. **Map** p402 K4.
These twin triumphal gates were erected in 1672 and
1674 at important entry points as part of Colbert's
strategy for the aggrandisement of Paris to the glory
of Louis XIV's victories on the Rhine. Modelled on
the triumphal arches of ancient Rome, the Porte
St-Denis is particularly harmonious, based on a
perfect square with a single arch, bearing Latin
inscriptions and decorated with military trophies
and battle scenes.

Les Halles & Sentier

In the 1st and 2nd arrondissements.
Few places epitomise the transformation of
central Paris more than Les Halles, wholesale
fruit and veg market for the city since 1181
when the covered markets were established by
king Philippe Auguste. In 1969 the trading
moved to a new wholesale market in the
southern suburb of Rungis, leaving a giant hole
– nicknamed *le trou des Halles* (a pun on bum-
hole). After a long political dispute it was filled
in the early 1980s by the miserably designed
Forum des Halles mall. One pavilion was
saved and reconstructed at Nogent-sur-Marne
(*see p141*). Warning to all luvvies: the Forum is
not the prettiest part of Paris. Hold onto your
handbag and prepare to spend at least half an
hour finding the way out once you're down
there. The rue Montorgueil market street is

Passages through time

Fact: debate has raged for decades over whether Southport, Lancashire's most elegant seaside resort, took its architectural inspiration from the boulevards of Paris, or whether, in fact, the opposite is the case. The question has never been resolved, but the similarities between the towns is nowhere more obvious than in Paris' glorious, glass-roofed galeries. Mostly built in the early 19th century, these havens for window shoppers allow astute pedestrians to make their way almost entirely under cover from the Grands Boulevards to the Palais-Royal, even though only 20 remain of the 100 that existed in 1840. Not all are examples of romantic splendour: the unprepossessing **Passage de Choiseul** (40 rue des Petits-Champs/23 rue St-Augustin, 2nd. M° Pyramides or Quatre-Septembre) was the childhood home of the writer Céline, who depicted it in *Mort à Crédit*, while **Passage Brady** (46 rue du Fbg-St-Denis/43 rue du Fbg-St-Martin, 10th. M° Château d'Eau or Strasbourg-St-Denis) is a small taste of India in one of the less salubrious quarters of Paris. It's best to visit in daytime: most are locked at night and on Sundays. Unlike Southport.

Galerie Véro-Dodat

2 rue du Bouloi/19 rue Jean-Jacques-Rousseau, 1st. M° Louvre or Palais Royal. **Map** p402 J5.
Véro and Dodat, prosperous *charcutiers*, built this beautiful arcade in the Restoration, equipping it with gaslights and charging astronomical rents. Attractions include the Café de l'Epoque, antique dolls and teddies at Capia, and By Terry cosmetics.

Galerie Vivienne & Galerie Colbert

6 rue Vivienne/4 rue des Petits-Champs & rue de la Banque, 2nd. M° Bourse. **Map** p402 H4.
Opened in 1826, Galerie Vivienne, with its stucco bas-reliefs and mosaic pavement still looks classy. There is a pretty tearoom, a silk orchid maker and several smart fashion shops. Running in a parallel L-shape is Galerie Colbert, with its glass dome.

Passage du Grand-Cerf

10 rue Dussoubs/145 rue St-Denis, 2nd. M° Etienne-Marcel. **Map** p402 J5.
This passage was built in 1835 and is notable for its height, wrought-iron works and hanging lanterns. It now houses unusual design shops including As'Art, PM & Co and La Corbeille, and hosts the biannual Puces du Design.

Passage Jouffroy & Passage Verdeau

10-12 bd Montmartre/9 rue de la Grange-Batelière, 9th. M° Richelieu-Drouot. **Map** p402 J4.
Built 1845-46, with a grand barrel-vaulted glass and iron roof. Within are the old-fashioned Hôtel Chopin, printsellers, antiquarian booksellers, Pain d'Epices dolls' houses, walking stick specialist Mr Segas and the curiosities of Thomas Boog. In the continuation, Verdeau, look for antique cameras and postcards.

Passage des Panoramas

10 rue St-Marc/11 bd Montmartre, 2nd. M° Richelieu-Drouot. **Map** p402 J4.
The earliest surviving passage is named after a novelty of the day: giant panoramic paintings that were viewed in a theatre, exhibited here when the passage opened in 1800. Take in the superb premises of Stern, engraver since 1830, L'Arbre à Cannelle tearoom, and Atelier Cesario Ceskam, a modern furniture craftsmen's studio.

altogether quainter. The market crowd and prostitutes of rue St-Denis continue to make this a colourful neighbourhood.

East of the Forum is place des Innocents, centred on the Renaissance Fontaine des Innocents. It was moved here from the city's main burial ground, nearby Cimetière des Innocents, which was demolished in 1786 after flesh-eating rats started gnawing into people's living rooms, and the bones transferred to the **Catacombes** (*see p134*). Pedestrianised rue des Lombards is a centre for nightlife, with bars, restaurants and the **Baiser Salé**, **Sunset** and **Duc des Lombards** jazz clubs (*see chapter* **Music: Rock, Roots & Jazz**). In ancient rue de la Ferronnerie, King Henri IV was assassinated in 1610 by Catholic fanatic François Ravaillac when the royal carriage was held up in the traffic. The street has now become an extension of the Marais gay circuit.

By the Pont-Neuf is **La Samaritaine** department store, currently converting to serious luxury after a takeover by LVMH. It has a fantastic art nouveau staircase and *verrière* (glazed roof). The Toupary restaurant and tearoom at the top also offers great views. From here the quai de la Mégisserie, lined with horticultural suppliers and pet shops, leads towards Châtelet. Looming over them is the

A step up at **Bourse du Commerce**. *See right.*

Eglise St-Eustache, with Renaissance motifs inside and chunky flying buttresses without. At the western end of the gardens is the circular, domed **Bourse du Commerce**. Hints of the market past linger in the 24-hour brasserie **Au Pied de Cochon**, and the all-night-bistro La Tour de Montlhéry.

The area west of Les Halles is packed with clothes shops: **Agnès b**'s empire – along most of rue du Jour – has been joined by more streetwise outlets such as **Kiliwatch** and **Le Shop**. East of here, pedestrianised rue Montorgueil, all food shops and cafés, is an irresistible place to while away a few hours. At 20 rue Etienne-Marcel, the **Tour Jean Sans Peur** is a strange relic of the fortified townhouse (1409-11) of Jean, Duc de Bourgogne, which has been restored and is now open to the public.

The ancient easternmost stretch of the rue St-Honoré runs into the southern edge of Les Halles. The Fontaine du Trahoir stands at the corner with rue de l'Arbre-Sec. Opposite, the fine Hôtel de Truden (52 rue de l'Arbre-Sec) was built in 1717 for a wealthy wine merchant. In the courtyard a shop sells historic issues of old papers and magazines. Running towards the Seine south of the gardens, ancient little streets such as rue des Lavandiers-Ste-Opportune and narrow rue Jean-Lantier show a human side of Les Halles that has yet to be destroyed in 'cleaning-up' programmes.

Bourse du Commerce

2 rue de Viarmes, 1st (01.55.65.78.41). M° Louvre. RER Les Halles. **Open** 9am-6pm Mon-Fri, limited access. **Tours** groups of up to 30, reserve in advance, 1½hr tour, €42 per group. **No credit cards**. **Map** p406 J5.
Now housing some of the offices of the Paris Chamber of Commerce (*see p374*), a world trade centre and a commodity market for coffee and sugar, the city's former main grain market was built in 1767 by Nicolas Le Camus de Mézières. It was later covered by a wooden dome and replaced by an avant-garde iron structure in 1809 – then covered in copper, now in glass. *Wheelchair access.*

Eglise St-Eustache

rue du Jour, 1st (01.40.26.47.99). M° Les Halles/RER Châtelet-Les Halles. **Open** *May-Oct* 9.30am-7.30pm daily; *Nov-Apr* 9.30am-7.30pm daily. **Tour** first Sun of every month 3pm, free (phone ahead). **Map** p406 J5.
This barn-like church (built 1532-1640) dominates Les Halles. Paintings in the side chapels include a *Descent from the Cross* by Luca Giordano; John Armleder's *Pour Paintings* added in 2000 give a contemporary touch. Works by Thomas Couture adorn the early 19th-century Lady Chapel. A favourite with music-lovers, the church boasts a magnificent 8,000-pipe organ (free recitals 5.30pm Sun).

Sightseeing

Forum des Halles

1st. M° Les Halles/RER Châtelet-Les Halles.
Map p402 J5.
As we said, this is not a place for those who simply cannot abide working-class living conditions, daahling. This labyrinthine concrete mall and site of a major Métro/RER interchange extends three levels underground and includes the Ciné Cité multiplex, the Forum des Images and a swimming pool, as well as mass-market clothing chains, branches of Fnac, Habitat and – a result of empty outlets – the Forum des Créateurs, a section given over to young designers. Saturdays become very crowded as gangs of teenagers descend on the place by RER.

Tour Jean Sans Peur

20 rue Etienne-Marcel, 2nd (01.40.26.20.28/tour. jeansanspeur.free.fr). M° Etienne-Marcel. **Open** termtime 1.30-6pm, Wed, Sat, Sun; school holidays 1.30-6pm Tue-Sun. **Tour** 2pm; €8. **No Credit Cards. Map** p402 J5.
This is the remnant of the townhouse of Jean Sans Peur, Duc de Bourgogne. Jean got his nickname (the fearless) from his exploits in Bulgaria. He was responsible for the assassination in 1407 of Louis d'Orléans, his rival and the cousin of Charles VI, which sparked the Hundred Years' War. Jean fled Paris but returned two years later to add this show-off tower to his mansion. The tower was also meant to protect him from any vengeance on the part of the widow of Louis d'Orléans (not so fearless, eh?), but it seems his card was fatally marked: in 1419 he was assassinated by a partisan of the future Charles VII. Today you can climb the multi-storey tower. Halfway up is a remarkable vault carved with naturalistic branches of oak, hawthorn and hops, symbols of Jean Sans Peur and Burgundian power.

Rue St-Denis & Sentier

For years the Sentier district was all crumbling houses, run-down shops and downmarket strip-joints. In recent years the prostitutes and peep-shows have been partly pushed back by energetic pedestrianisation and by the arrival of practitioners of another type of entrepreneurial activity that is prepared to do virtually anything for money – the start-ups.

The tackiness is gloriously unremitting along the traditional red-light district of rue St-Denis (and northern continuation rue du Faubourg-St-Denis), which snakes north from the Forum. Kerb-crawlers gawp at the neon adverts for *l'amour sur scène*, and size up defiantly dignified prostitutes in doorways.

Between rue des Petits-Carreaux and rue St-Denis is the site of the Cour des Miracles – a refuge where, after a day's begging, paupers would 'miraculously' regain use of their eyes or limbs. An abandoned aristocratic estate, it was a refuge for the underworld for decades until it was cleared out in 1667. The surrounding

Sentier district is the centre of the rag trade, and is correspondingly lively. Sweatshops churn out copies of catwalk creations and the streets fill with porters carrying linen bundles over their shoulders. Streets such as rue du Caire, d'Aboukir and du Nil, named after Napoléon's Egyptian campaign, are connected by a maze of passages lined with wholesalers. The area attracts hundreds of illegal and semi-legal foreign workers, trying to make their way in in a hostile environment.

Fbg-St-Denis to Gare du Nord

North of Porte St-Denis, which celebrates Louis XIV's victories on the Rhine, along the rue du Fbg-St-Denis, there's an almost souk-like feel, with its food shops, narrow passages and sinister courtyards. The brasserie **Julien** boasts one of the finest art nouveau interiors in Paris, while up dingy cobbled cour des Petites Ecuries, theatre-goers flock to **Brasserie Flo**. Garishly lit passage Brady is a surprising piece of India, full of restaurants, hairdressers and costume shops. Rue des Petites Ecuries was once known for saddlers but now has shops and cafés as well as top jazz venue **New Morning** (*see p333*).

The top of rue de Hauteville affords one of the most unexpected views in Paris. **Eglise St-Vincent de Paul**, with its twin towers and cascading terraced gardens, is about as close as Paris gets to Rome's Spanish Steps. Just behind, on rue de Belzunce, are the modern bistro Chez Michel and offshoot **Chez Casimir**.

Boulevard de Strasbourg was designed to give a grand perspective up to the Gare de l'Est and soon built up with popular theatres – the mosaic-filled neo-Renaissance Théâtre Antoine-Simone Berriau and the art deco Eldorado. At No 2, another neo-Renaissance creation houses Paris' last fan maker and the **Musée de l'Eventail** (*see p165*). Sandwiched between Gare de l'Est and Canal St-Martin stand the near-derelict remains of the Couvent des Récollets, currently being converted into an arts centre, and the park of Square Villemin.

Eglise St-Vincent de Paul

pl Franz-Liszt, 10th (01.48.78.47.47). M° Gare du Nord. **Open** 8am-noon, 5pm-7pm Mon-Sat; 9.30am-noon, 5pm-7.30pm Sun. **Map** p402 K2.
Imposingly set at the top of terraced gardens, the church was begun in 1824 by Lepère and completed 1831-44 by Hittorff, replacing an earlier chapel to cater to the newly populous district. The twin towers, pedimented Greek temple portico and evangelist figures on the parapet are in classical mode. The interior has a double storey arcade of columns, murals by Flandrin, and some rather natty church furniture by Rude.

Gare du Nord

rue de Dunkerque, 10th (01.53.90.20.20).
M° Gare du Nord. **Map** p402 K2.

The grandest of the great 19th-century train stations (and Eurostar terminal since 1994) was designed by Hittorff in 1861-64. A conventional stone facade, with Ionic capitals and statues representing towns served by the station, hides a vast, bravura iron and glass vault. Chaotic major building works have been going on for some time. Recently finished is the impressive refurbishment to the suburban lines section of the station that borders the rue du Faubourg-St-Denis, creating a light, airy space next to the grimy part that houses the Eurostar.

Beaubourg & the Marais

In the 3rd and 4th arrondissements.
Between boulevard Sébastopol and the Bastille lies Beaubourg – the area in which the Centre Pompidou landed in 1977 – and the Marais, built between the 16th and 18th centuries and now full of boutiques, museums and bars.

Beaubourg & Hôtel de Ville

Contemporary Parisian architecture began with the **Centre Pompidou**, opened in 1977. This international benchmark of inside-out high-tech is as much of an attraction as its contents, which include the impressive **Musée National de l'Art Moderne**. Out on the piazza is the **Atelier Brancusi**, the sculptor's reconstructed studio (*see p159*). On the other side of the piazza, peer down rue Quincampoix for its art galleries, bars and curious passage Molière. Beside the Centre Pompidou is place Igor Stravinsky, with the red brick **IRCAM** contemporary music institute (*see p324*) and the funky Fontaine Stravinsky, designed by the late Nikki de Saint Phalle and Jean Tinguely. On the south side of the square is the church of St-Merri, which has a Flamboyant Gothic facade complete with an androgynous demon leering over the doorway. Inside are a carved wooden organ loft, the joint contender for the oldest bell in Paris (1331) and 16th-century stained glass.

Beyond Châtelet looms the **Hôtel de Ville**, Paris' city hall and home to the mayor. The centre of municipal power since 1260, it overlooks a square of the same name, once known as place de Grève, beside the original Paris port. Protestant heretics were burnt in the *place* during the Wars of Religion, and rather grimly, the guillotine first stood here during the Terror, when Danton, Marat and Robespierre made the Hôtel their seat of government. Revolutionaries made it their base in the 1871 Commune, but the building was set on fire by the Communards themselves and wrecked during savage fighting. It was rebuilt on a grander scale in fanciful neo-Renaissance style with statues representing French cities along the facade, and could easily be thought to be a palace. Perish the very thought.

The cats and chicks all get their kicks at **place des Vosges.** *See p95.*

Sightseeing

Ducts deluxe at the **Centre Pompidou.** *See right.*

Centre Pompidou

rue Beaubourg, 4th (01.44.78.12.33).
Mº Hôtel de Ville or Rambuteau/RER Châtelet-Les
Halles. **Open** 11am-9pm Mon, Wed-Sun, holidays.
Closed Tue and 1 May. **Admission** €5.50-€8.50;
€3.50-€6.50 18-26; free under 18s. **Credit** (shop) V.
Map p406 K5/K6.

The primary colours and exposed pipes and air
ducts make this one of the most recognisable buildings in Paris. Commissioned in 1968, the centre is
the work of the Italo-British duo Renzo Piano and
Richard Rogers. Their 'inside-out', boilerhouse
approach put air-conditioning and lifts outside, leaving a freely adaptable space within. When the centre opened in 1977, its success exceeded all
expectations. After a revamp the centre reopened in
January 2000 with an enlarged museum, renewed
performance spaces, fashionable **Georges** restaurant and a mission to get back to the stimulating
inter-disciplinary mix of old (*see chapter* **Museums**).

Hôtel de Ville

Salon d'acceuil 2 rue de Rivoli, 4th (01.42.76.43.43).
Mº Hôtel de Ville. **Open** 10am-7pm Mon-Sat; 2-7pm
Sun. Free guided tour once a week. **Map** p406 K6.

The impressive Hôtel de Ville now forms a multiple
function as administrative centre, a place to entertain visiting dignitaries and, outside on the forecourt, a kind of people's palace where events such
as the World Cup are projected on a big screen, con-

cert, exhibitions and trade fairs held. Small exhibitions are held in the *Salon d'accueil,* the rest of the
building being out of bounds to the public except for
the guided tour. Mayor Delanoë himself has
eschewed palatial ostentation in favour of a dinky,
bijouette pad in the Marais.

Tour St-Jacques

pl du Châtelet, 4th. Mº Châtelet. **Map** p406 J6.

Much-loved by the Surrealists, this solitary
Flamboyant Gothic bell-tower is the remains of the
St-Jacques-La-Boucherie church, built for the powerful Butchers' Guild in 1523. Pascal carried out experiments on the weight of air here in the 17th century.
A weather station now crowns the 52-metre-high
tower, which can only be admired from outside.

The Marais

East of Roman rue St-Martin and rue du Renard
lies the Marais, a magical area whose narrow
streets are dotted with aristocratic *hôtels
particuliers,* art galleries, fashion boutiques and
stylish cafés. The city slows down here, giving
you time to notice the beautiful carved
doorways and the early street signs carved into
the stone. The Marais, or 'marsh', started life as
an uninhabited piece of swampy ground
inhabited only by a few monasteries and used

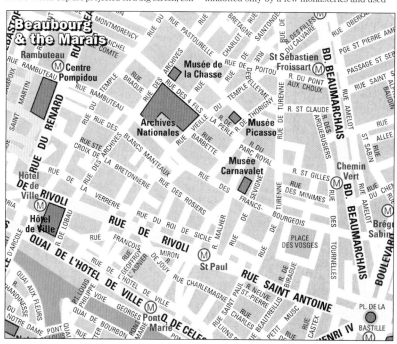

Coo d'état at **Hôtel de Ville**. *See p93.*

for market gardening. In the 16th century the elegant Hôtel Carnavalet and Hôtel Lamoignon sparked the area's phenomenal rise as an aristocratic residential district; Henri IV began constructing the **place des Vosges** in 1605. Soon nobles started building smart townhouses where famous literary ladies such as Mme de Sévigné and Mlle de Scudéry and influential courtesan Ninon de l'Enclos held court. The area fell from fashion a century later; happily, many of the narrow streets were essentially unchanged as mansions were transformed into industrial workshops, schools, tenements, even a fire station. It is now a lively, warm, international *quartier* that is a traditional home to minorities. It is here that you'll see Orthodox Jews shooting the breeze with out-and-about gay guys; this is no kind of ghetto; it's mixed, it's cool, and, to many, represents Paris at its best.

The rue des Francs-Bourgeois runs right through the Marais. The street soon forgets its Les Halles legacy in the food shops of rue Rambuteau; further on it is packed with elegant mansions and original boutiques. The tearoom **Les Enfants Gâtés** ('spoiled children') sums up the mood. For a little culture, seek out two of Paris' most elegant early 18th-century residences: Hôtel d'Albret (No 31) which is the venue for jazz concerts during the Paris quartier d'été festival (*see chapter* **Festivals & Events**) and Hôtel de Soubise (No 60), the national archives, where interiors by Boucher and Lemoine can be seen as part of the **Musée de l'Histoire de France** (*see p170*). On the

corner of the rue des Francs-Bourgeois and rue Pavée is the austere renaissance Hôtel Lamoignon. Built in 1585 for Diane de France, Henri II's illegitimate daughter, it now houses the **Bibliothèque Historique de la Ville de Paris** (*see p380*).

At the street's eastern end is the stunning place des Vosges. At one corner is the **Maison de Victor Hugo**, once occupied by the author (*see chapter* **Museums**). The luxurious **Ambroisie** restaurant is for special treats, while **Ma Bourgogne** offers simpler cuisine. An archway in the southwest corner leads to the elegant Hôtel de Sully which houses the **Patrimoine Photographique** (*see p176*).

Workaday rue du Temple, once the road leading to the Templars' church, is full of surprises. Near rue de Rivoli, the **Latina** specialises in Latin American films and holds tango *bals* in the room above. At No 41 an archway leads into the former Aigle d'Or coaching inn, now the Café de la Gare *café-théâtre*, Le Studio Tex-Mex and dance studios. Further north, the Hôtel de St-Aignan at No 71 contains the **Musée d'Art et d'Histoire du Judaïsme** (*see p167*).

The district's two most important museums are also in sumptuous *hôtels*. The **Musée Carnavalet** (*see p170*), dedicated to Paris history, runs across the Hôtel Carnavalet, once home to famous letter-writer Mme de Sévigné, and the later Hôtel le Peletier de St-Fargeau. Curiosities include faithful reconstructions of Proust's bedroom and the Fouquet jewellery shop. The Hôtel Salé on rue de Thorigny, built

Royale, the square's present name dates from the Napoleonic Wars, when the Vosges was the first region of France to pay its war taxes. Mme de Sévigné, salon hostess and letter-writer, was born here in 1626. At that time the garden was a place of duels and romantic trysts; now it attracts hot-shot *boules* players and sensitive types.

The Temple & Arts et Métiers

The northern, less gentrified half of the Marais towards place de la République is home to tiny local bars, costume-jewellery and rag-trade wholesalers, alongside contemporary art galleries (*see chapter* **Galleries**) and recently arrived fashion designers. The Quartier du Temple was once a fortified, semi-independent entity under the Knights Templar. The round church and keep have been replaced by Square du Temple and the Carreau du Temple clothes market. The keep became a prison in the Revolution, where the royal family were held in 1792. Rue de Bretagne is crammed with food shops; rue de Picardie boasts the **Web Bar** which runs exhibitions and concerts. The north-east corner of the Marais hinges on the **Musée des Arts et Metiers**, a science museum in a 12th-century chapel (*see p177*).

The St-Paul district

In 1559, Henri II was mortally wounded in a jousting tournament on what is now rue St-Antoine. He is commemorated in a grieving marble Virgin by Pilon in the Jesuit church of **St-Paul-St-Louis**. Towards the Bastille, the heavily domed church of the Visitation Ste-Marie was designed in the 1630s by Mansart. South of rue St-Antoine is a more sedate residential area known as St-Paul. There are still plenty of fine houses, but the overall mood is discreet. The Village St-Paul, a colony of antique sellers spread across small interlinked courtyards between rues St-Paul, Charlemagne and quai des Célestins, is a promising source of 1930s and 50s furniture, kitchenware and wine gadgets (open Mon, Thur-Sun). On rue des Jardins-St-Paul is the largest surviving section of the **wall of Philippe Auguste**. The infamous poisoner Marquise de Brinvilliers lived at Hôtel de Brinvilliers (12 rue Charles V) in the 1630s. She killed her father and brothers to inherit the family fortune and was only caught after her lover died – of natural causes.

Two of the Marais' finest mansions are on rue François-Miron: Hôtel de Beauvais, No 68, and Hôtel Hénault de Cantorbe, renovated to incorporate the **Maison Européenne de la Photographie** (*see p176*). At 17 rue Geoffroy l'Asnier, the Mémorial du Martyr Juif Inconnu

in 1656 and nicknamed after its salt tax collector owner, has been finely restored and extended to house the **Musée National Picasso** (*see p162*).

The Marais is also home to Paris' oldest Jewish community, centred on rue des Rosiers, rue des Ecouffes and rue Pavée (where there's a synagogue designed by Guimard). Originally made up mainly of Ashkenazi Jews who arrived after the pogroms (many were later deported during World War II), the community expanded in the 1950s and 60s with a wave of Sephardic Jewish immigration following French withdrawal from North Africa. As a result, there are now many falafel shops alongside the Jewish bakers and delis, such as Finkelstijn and Paris' most famous Jewish eatery, **Jo Goldenberg**; its exterior still bears the scars of a terrorist attack in the 1980s.

The lower ends of rue des Archives and rue Vieille-du-Temple are the centre of café life and happening bars, including cutesy **Petit Fer à Cheval** and cosmopolitan café **La Chaise au Plafond** in the neighbouring rue du Trésor. This area is the hub of Paris' gay scene (*see chapter* **Gay & Lesbian**).

Place des Vosges

4th. M° St-Paul. **Map** p406 L6.
The first planned square in Paris was built 1605-12 by Henri IV. The intimate square, with its beautifully harmonious red-brick-and-stone arcaded facades and steeply pitched roofs, is quite distinct from the pomp of later Bourbon Paris. Moreover, it is perfectly symmetrical. Originally the place

has been closed while a museum dedicated to the Holocaust is built. Down rue de Fourcy towards the river is the Hôtel de Sens, which now houses the **Bibliothèque Forney**, specialising in posters and postcards. Across from the tip of the Ile St-Louis the square Henri-Galli contains a rebuilt fragment of the Bastille prison and the Pavillon de l'Arsenal.

Eglise St-Paul-St-Louis

99 rue St-Antoine, 4th (01.42.72.30.32). M° Bastille or St-Paul. **Open** 9am-8pm Mon-Fri; 9-8.30pm Sat-Sun. **Map** p406 L6.

The domed Baroque Counter-Reformation church, completed in 1641, is modelled, like all Jesuit churches, on the Gesù in Rome, with its single nave, side chapels and three-storey hierarchical facade bearing (replacement) statues of saints Louis, Anne and Catherine. The hearts of Louis XIII and XIV were stolen from here in the Revolution. Most of the original paintings and furnishings were removed then too. In 1802 it became a church again and now houses Delacroix's *Christ in the Garden of Olives*.

Fortified wall of Philippe Auguste

rue des Jardins-St-Paul, 4th (www.philippe-auguste. com). M° Pont Marie or St-Paul. **Map** p406 L7.

King Philippe-Auguste (1165-1223) was the first great Parisian builder since the Romans, enclosing the entire city within a great wall. The largest surviving section, complete with towers, extends along rue des Jardins-St-Paul. Another chunk is at 3 rue Clovis (5th) and odd remnants of towers are dotted around the Marais and St-Germain-des-Prés.

Mainly in the 11th and 12th arrondissements.
Place de la Bastille, traditionally a boundary point between central Paris and the more proletarian east, has remained a potent symbol of popular revolt ever since the prison-storming that inaugurated the Revolution. Though still a favourite spot for demonstrations, the area has attracted new cafés, restaurants, galleries and bars since the 1980s and is now cusping as the in-place to get legless.

The site of the prison itself is now a Banque de France office and the gap left by the castle ramparts forms the present-day square, dominated by the massive **Opéra Bastille**. Opened in 1989 on the bicentennial of Bastille Day, it remains highly controversial, but productions sell out and, along with the creation of the Port de l'Arsenal marina to the south, it has contributed to the area's rejuvenation.

The cobbled rue de Lappe typifies the Bastille's transformation, as the last remaining furniture workshops, the 1930s Balajo dance hall, old Auvergnat bistro La Galoche d'Aurillac and grocer Chez Teil hold out against a dizzy array of gift shops and theme bars which teem with teens on weekends.

You can still catch a flavour of the old working-class district at the Sunday morning market on boulevard Richard Lenoir or up rue de la Roquette. Rue du Faubourg-St-Antoine still has furniture-makers' *ateliers* hidden up

No *pain*, no gain.

Sightseeing

Paris, France's very own Southend

That Bert Delanoë, the mayor fella, he doesn't half spoil us. In 2002, for one month, Paris metamorphosed into France's Southend-on-Sea. For a mere €1.5 million of taxpayers' money, Bertrand the Bold converted two miles of Seineside Right Bank into Paris-Plage, which aimed to reunite the capital with its famous, if somewhat pungent, waterway. The operation elicited criticism from taxi-drivers and residents stressing about jumbo jams and more areas for dogs to foul up with their mess. Despite this, operation Paris-Plage was such a success (over two million visitors in 2002) that it'll be back in 2003.

There were four beaches (two sand and two pebble), complete with 300 deckchairs, 150 parasols and 80 palm trees, 22 blue-and-white striped beach huts, beach volleyball, mobile ice-cream sellers and refreshment areas. Graffiti artists had their work on show along one section, and there were entertainers and DJs and live music to chill out to in the evening before the beach officially shut around 11pm.

The term 'beach' generally conjures up images of expanses of sand. This is what you tend to expect: sand, and lots of it. Last

year's inaugural Paris-Plage wasn't what you'd call sand rich, but that didn't stop Parisians and tourists from flocking here in their droves for that essential tan, caring little whether they parked their lithesome behinds on the last remaining square inch of concrete or a few grains of the much touted 'real beach' (actually an elongated sandpit). Apparently it's all about the concept. Give the Parisians a mere whiff of an idea and they're away with it. Call us hair-splitters, but it would have been nice to have had a paddle. Maybe this year Delanoë will make that possible,

too. If only Chirac would honour his election promise of drinking a glass of Seine water, we'd all feel confident enough to don our 'Kiss Me Kwick' hats and leg it down there.

Does this represent money well spent? It's a great idea and a fabulous consolation prize for all those for whom some time on a real beach is out of the question. And it's a stylish gesture, which is, of course, all very Parisian. But if all the Parisians need is a concept, then a huge sign with the word '*PLAGE*' emblazoned across it would have been a hell of a lot cheaper, wouldn't it?

Bastille bother

It is to France what the Forum was to Rome and what *Points of View* is to the BBC. All the Disgusteds-of-Paris (and there are a lot of those) come to place de la Bastille to have a bit of a moan. No need to say 'Meet me at that big green column with the jaunty gold angel on top, and we'll all throw our toys out of the pram': in troubled times, the venue for demos is taken as read.

'T was ever thus. The 1789 revolution started here, with a ruckus at Bastille jail. It ended with prison governer Marquis de Launay's head being paraded through the streets of Paris on a pike. The Bastille is heavy with revolutionary meaning: the *Colonne de Juillet* that now thrusts into the sky was installed in 1840, in memory of the grisly events of the 1830 uprising.

The Bastille remains a rallying point for the riled. Within minutes of the first round results of the 2002 Presidential elections having been announced, over a thousand people gathered to share their disbelief. For the next few days, there was an almost constant vigil at the Place. On 27 May, there was a rapidly organised anti-right wing march, and, a couple of days later, the May Day anti-Le Pen march (which overwhelmed the traditional annual workers' march from eastern Paris to Bastille) dwarfed all previous demos, with an estimated 900,000 people turning up. This time, the atmosphere was jovial, with dancing, bongo bands, massed loonies and costumed paraders having a laugh at the expense of the Le Penists.

You don't have to have a gripe to come to the place de la Bastille, but it sure helps. The *Motards en Colère,* the angry motorists brigade, marched here in 2002, as did Paris' hairdressers – save the mullet campaign perhaps?

passageways, while gaudy furniture stores line the street, but is being colonised by clothes shops and bars including **Barrio Latino** in a building worked on by Eiffel. Rue de Charonne has trendy bars, bistros and dealers in hip 60s furniture. Along with rue Keller, the patch is a focus for record shops, streetwear and, increasingly, young fashion designers (*see p243* **Where to find the jeunes créateurs**). There's still something of a village spirit as the in-crowd hangs out at the **Pause Café**.

However, the main thoroughfares tell only half the story. Behind narrow street frontages are cobbled alleys dating back to the 18th century and lined with craftsmen's workshops or quirky bars and bistros. Investigate the cours de l'Ours, du Cheval Blanc, du Bel Air (with hidden garden), de la Maison Brûlée, the passage du Chantier on Fbg-St-Antoine, or the rustic-looking passage de l'Etoile d'Or and the passage de l'Homme with old wooden shop fronts on rue de Charonne. This area originally lay outside the city walls on the lands of the Convent of St-Antoine (parts of which survive as the Hôpital St-Antoine), where in the Middle Ages skilled furniture makers were free from the city's restrictive guilds, beginning a tradition of free-thinking that made this area a powder keg during the Revolution.

Boulevard Beaumarchais separates rowdy Bastille from the elegant Marais. Look out for the polygonal **Cirque d'Hiver**, designed by Hittorff and still used today (*see p284*). Further east, on rue de la Roquette, a small park and playground surrounded by modern housing marks the site of the prison de la Roquette, where a plaque remembers the 4,000 resistance members imprisoned here in World War II.

Opéra Bastille

pl de la Bastille, 12th (box office 08.36.69.78.68/ guided visits 01.40.01.19.70/www.opera-de-paris.fr). M° *Bastille.* **Tour** phone for details. **Admission** €10; €8 over 60s; €5 under 26s.
No credit cards. Map p407 M7.

The Opéra Bastille, opened in 1989, has been controversial for several reasons: the cost, the scale, the architecture, the opera productions. Some thought it a stroke of genius to implant a high-culture edifice in a working-class area; others thought it typical Mitterrand skullduggery; still others found it patronising. Although intended as an 'opera for the people', that never really happened; opera and ballet are now shared with the Palais Garnier. (*See p300 and chapter* **Music: Classical and Opera**.)

Place de la Bastille

4th/11th/12th. M° *Bastille.* **Map** p407 M7.
Nothing remains of the infamous prison which, on 14 July 1789, was stormed by the forces of the plebeian revolt. Though only a handful of prisoners

Reflecting on a revolution: **Opéra Bastille**. *See left.*

remained, the event provided the rebels with gunpowder, and gave the insurrection momentum. It · remains the eternal symbol of the Revolution, celebrated here with a lively street *bal* every 13 July. The prison was quickly torn down, its stones used to build Pont de la Concorde. Vestiges of the foundations can be seen in the Métro; there's part of a reconstructed tower at square Henri-Galli, near Pont de Sully (4th). The Colonne de Juillet, topped by a gilded *génie* of Liberty, is a monument to Parisians killed in the revolutions of July 1830 and 1848.

South of the Bastille

A charming touch of inner-city quaintness is the **Viaduc des Arts**, a former railway viaduct now containing craft and design boutiques. Atop the viaduct, old ladies admire the roses and lovers spoon among the bamboo of the **Promenade Plantée**, which continues through the Jardin de Reuilly and east to the **Bois de Vincennes**. This is a wonderful walk if you need a break from the big-city hubbub, not least because its path lets you peek right into people's flats. Further along, avenue Daumesnil is fast becoming a Silicon Valley of computer outlets. At No 186, Eglise du St-Esprit is a curious 1920s concrete copy of the Hagia Sophia in Istanbul. At No 293 the **Musée des Arts d'Afrique et d'Océanie** (*see p163*) still stands, though its collection is in storage and will ultimately move to the new museum under construction on quai Branly (*see p171*).

As late as the 1980s, wine was still unloaded off barges at Bercy. This stretch of the Seine is firmly part of redeveloped Paris with the massive Ministère de l'Economie et du Budget and the **Palais Omnisports de Paris-Bercy** (*see chapter* **Sport**). At the eastern edge of the park, in striking contrast to the modern Ciné Cité multiplex, is Bercy Village. Forty-two *chais*, or brick wine warehouses, have been cleaned up and reopened as wine bars and cafés; the result is certainly lively, if somewhat antiseptic in a chinos and deck shoes kind of way. Particularly popular is Club Med World, where the themed bars and juggling barmen are intended to make you think of your next sunshine escape. A further group has been converted as the Pavillons de Bercy, containing the Musée des Arts Forains collection of fairground music and Venetian carnival salons (open to groups by appointment 01.43.40.16.22).

Bois de Vincennes

12th. M° Porte-Dorée or Château de Vincennes.
This is Paris' biggest park. Boats can be hired on the lake, there are cycle paths, a Buddhist temple, a racetrack, baseball pitch and flower gardens. It also contains Paris' main **Zoo** and the **Cartoucherie** theatre complex. The **Parc Floral** (01.43.43.92.95) has horticultural displays, free summer jazz and classical festivals, a picnic area, exhibition space, children's amusements and crazy golf. Next to the park is the imposing **Château de Vincennes** (*see p141*), where England's Henry V died in 1422.

Parc de Bercy (*see below*).

Sightseeing

The Champs-Elysées & west

In the 8th, 16th and 17th arrondissements.
The 'Elysian Fields' can be a disappointment on first, tourist-filled sight, but the avenue remains the symbolic gathering place of a nation – for any sporting victory, display of French medal-manufacturing prowess, 14 July celebration or attempt on the President's life.

Over the past few years the Champs-Elysées has gone through an astonishing renaissance. One of Jacques Chirac's worthier mayoral efforts was a major facelift here, with new underground car parks and smart granite paving. Upmarket shops and hotels have moved back in the past couple of years, including branches of Louis Vuitton, **Fnac**, the **Ladurée** tearoom and Marriott hotel, while a flock of stylish restaurants such as **Spoon, Food & Wine** and **Tagine** have drawn a fashionable, and affluent, crowd back to the surrounding streets. Most recently, Renault, a long-time resident, has upped the stakes with its **L'Atelier Renault**, incorporating a super-chic cocktail bar and restaurant within a showroom for concept cars and comtemporary design. At night there is an impressive vista stretching

Parc de Bercy

rue de Bercy, 12th. M° Bercy or Cour St-Emilion.
Map p407 N9/10.
Bercy park combines the French love of geometry with that of food. There's a large lawn and a grid with square rose, herb and vegetable plots, an orchard and gardens representing the four seasons.

La Promenade Plantée

av Daumesnil, 12th. M° Ledru Rollin or Gare de Lyon. **Map** p407 M8/N8.
The railway tracks atop the Viaduc des Arts have been replaced by a promenade planted with roses, shrubs and rosemary, offering a high-level view into Parisian lives. It continues at ground level through the Jardin de Reuilly and the Jardin Charles Péguy on to the Bois de Vincennes in the east. Rollerbladers are banned, but no one seems to have noticed.

Le Viaduc des Arts

15-121 av Daumesnil, 12th (www.viaduc-des-arts.com). M° Ledru-Rollin or Gare de Lyon. **Map** p407 M8/N8.
Under the arches of the Promenade Plantée, chic glass-fronted workshops now provide a showroom for designers and craftspeople. The variety is fascinating: from contemporary furniture and fashion designers to picture frame gilders, tapestry restorers, porcelain decorators, architectural salvage and a French hunting horn maker, as well as design gallery VIA and the late-opening **Viaduc Café**.

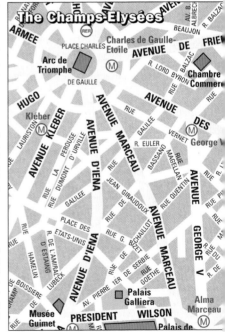

from floodlit place de la Concorde to the Arc de Triomphe, with the crowds lining up for the glitzy Lido cabaret, Queen nightclub and various cinemas.

The great spine of western Paris started life as an extension to the Tuileries gardens, laid out by Le Nôtre in the 17th century. By the Revolution, the avenue had been laid along its full stretch, but was more a place for a Sunday stroll than a thoroughfare. Shortly before the Revolution the local guard worried that its dark corners offered 'to libertines and people of bad intentions a refuge that they can abuse'. How's that for inadvertent PR?

It was during the Second Empire that the Champs-Elysées became a focus of fashionable society, military parades and royal processions. Bismarck was so impressed when he arrived with the conquering Prussian army in 1871 that he had a replica, the Kurfürstendamm, built in Berlin. Smart residences and hotels sprung up along its upper half, together with street lights, pavements, sideshows, concert halls, theatres and exhibition centres. The Prussian army in 1871 and Hitler's troops in 1940 both made a point of marching down it; but loud celebrations accompanied the allies' victory march along the avenue in 1944.

South of the avenue, the glass-domed **Grand Palais** and **Petit Palais**, both built for the 1900 *Exposition Universelle* and still used for major shows, create an impressive vista across elaborate Pont Alexandre III to Les Invalides. The rear wing of the Grand Palais opening on to avenue Franklin D Roosevelt contains the **Palais de la Découverte** (*see p178 and p290*), a fun science museum. Look out for the statues of Churchill and de Gaulle: Winnie's is butcher-than-thou, and Charlie's shows him capering along in fine mincing gait.

To the north are smart shops and officialdom. On circular place Beauvau a gateway leads to the Ministry of the Interior. The 18th-century Palais de l'Elysée, the official presidential residence, is situated at 55-57 rue du Fbg-St-Honoré. Nearby are the equally palatial British Embassy and adjoining ambassadorial residence, once the Hôtel Borghèse, home to Napoleon's favourite sister, Pauline.

The lower, landscaped reach of the avenue hides two theatres and haute cuisine restaurants, **Laurent** and Ledoyen, in fancy Napoléon III pavilions. At the Rond-Point des Champs-Elysées, Nos 7 and 9 give some idea of the splendid mansions that once lined the avenue. From here, the dress code leaps a few

Sightseeing

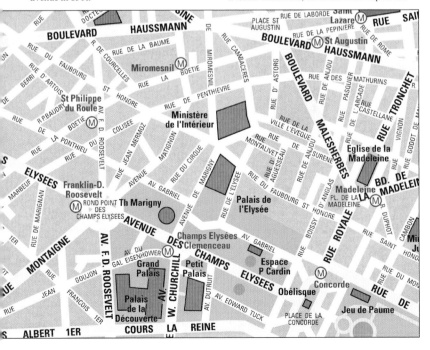

notches as avenue Montaigne reels off its array of fashion houses: Christian Dior, Chanel, Prada, Jil Sander, Loewe, Céline, Ungaro, Calvin Klein and more. Don't miss the lavish **Plaza Athénée** hotel and Auguste Perret's innovative 1911-13 **Théâtre des Champs-Elysées** concert hall topped by the fashionable **Maison Blanche** restaurant.

At the western end, the **Arc de Triomphe** towers above place Charles de Gaulle, better known as l'Etoile. Begun to glorify Napoléon, the giant triumphal arch was later modified to celebrate the armies of the Revolution. The *place* was commissioned later by Haussmann. It was from among the Bastille Day crowds here on 14 July 2002 that Maxime Brunerie whipped a .22 rifle from his guitar case and allegedly took a pot shot at Jacques Chirac. Mr Brunerie missed – hurling the guitar case itself might have been more effective – and was wrestled to the ground by tourists. The cops hadn't noticed a thing. From the top, look down on great swathes of prize Paris real estate: the swanky mansions along the grassy verges of avenue Foch or the prestige office buildings of avenues Hoche and Wagram.

Arc de Triomphe

pl Charles-de-Gaulle (access via underground passage), 8th (01.55.37.73.77). M° Charles de Gaulle-Etoile. **Open** *Apr-Oct* 10am-11pm daily; *Nov-Mar* 10am-10.30pm daily. Closed public holidays. **Admission** €7; €4.50 18-25s; free under-18s. **Credit** MC, V. **Map** p400 C3.

The Arc de Triomphe forms the centrepiece of Paris' grand east-west axis from the Louvre, through the Arc du Carrousel and place de la Concorde up to the Grande Arche de la Défense. The Arc is 50m tall, 45m wide and decorated with a giant frieze of battle scenes and sculptures including Rude's *La Marseillaise*. Commissioned by Napoléon in 1806 as a tribute to his own military victories, the arch was completed in 1836. In 1920 the Tomb of the Unknown Soldier was laid at the arch's base and an eternal flame burns to commemorate the dead of World Wars I and II. The manic drivers turn the place into a race track, but fortunately there is a subway. From the top, there's a wonderful view of the 12 avenues spreading out from l'Etoile.

Grand Palais

av Winston-Churchill, av du Général-Eisenhower, 8th (01.44.13.17.17/01.44.13.17.30). M° Champs-Elysées-Clemenceau. **Map** p401 E5.

Built for the 1900 *Exposition Universelle*, the Grand Palais was the work of three different architects, each of whom designed a facade. The famous golden horses are currently being restored, part of a major programme of work that will keep part of the building closed until 2005, although this remains Paris' main venue for bluckbuster exhibitions and home to the Palais de la Découverte.

Petit Palais

av Winston-Churchill, 8th (01.42.65.12.73). M° Champs-Elysées-Clemenceau. **Map** p401 E5.

This was also built for the 1900 *Exposition Universelle*, only here the style is rather more charmingly Rococo. The Petit Palais closed in February 2001 for extensive interior renovations, which are estimated to last three years; for the time being, some of the medieval exhibits are displayed in the Louvre.

Monceau & Batignolles

At the far end of avenue Hoche is intimate **Parc Monceau** (main entrance bd de Courcelles), with its neo-Antique follies and large lily pond. The park is usually full of neatly dressed children and nannies, and surrounded by some of the most costly apartments in Paris, part of the planned late 19th-century expansion of the city over the *plaine* Monceau. There are three museums which give an idea of the extravagance of the area when it was newly fashionable. These are **Musée Jacquemart-André** on boulevard Haussmann, **Musée Nissim de Camondo** (18th-century decorative arts) and **Musée Cernushi** (Chinese art). (*See chapter* **Museums**.) There are some nice exotic touches, such as the unlikely red lacquer Galerie Ching Tsai Too (48 rue de Courcelles, 8th), near the fancy wrought-iron gates of Parc Monceau, or the onion domes of the Russian Orthodox **Alexander Nevsky Cathedral** on rue Daru. Built in the mid-19th century when a sojourn in Paris was an essential part of the education of every Russian aristocrat, it is still at the heart of an emigré little Russia.

Famed for its stand during the Paris Commune, the Quartier des Batignolles to the northeast is much more working class, with the lively rue de Lévis street market, tenements overlooking the deep railway canyon and the attractive **square des Batignolles** park with its pretty church overlooking a small semi-circular *place*. The area is becoming increasingly fashionable. Rue des Dames contains the colourful **Eldorado** hotel, the **Lush** bar and antique bathroom shop **SBR**.

Alexander Nevsky Cathedral

12 rue Daru, 8th (01.42.27.37.34). M° Courcelles. **Open** 3-5pm Tue, Fri, Sun. **Map** p400 D3.

The edifice has enough onion domes, icons and incense to make you think you were in Moscow. This Russian Orthodox church was built 1859-61 in the neo-Byzantine Novgorod-style of the 1600s, on a Greek-cross plan by the Tsar's architect Kouzmine, architect of the St-Petersburg Beaux-Arts Academy. Services, on Sunday mornings and Orthodox saints' days, are in Russian.

Marvel arch: **Arc de Triomphe**. *See left.*

PLACE
CHARLES DE GAULLE

Cimetière des Batignolles

rue St-Just, 17th (01.53.06.38.68). M° Porte de Clichy. **Open** *Apr-Oct* 8am-6pm Mon-Fri; 8.30am-6pm Sat; 9am-6pm Sun; *Nov-Mar* closes at 5.30pm.
Squeezed between the Périphérique and the boulevard des Amiraux lie the graves of poet Paul Verlaine, Surrealist André Breton and Léon Bakst, costume designer of the Ballets Russes.

Trocadéro

South of the Arc de Triomphe, avenue Kléber leads to the monumental buildings and terraced gardens of the Trocadéro, with spectacular views over the river to the Eiffel Tower. The vast symmetrical 1930s **Palais de Chaillot** dominates the hill and houses four museums and the Théâtre National de Chaillot. Across place du Trocadéro is the small **Cimetière de Passy**. The Trocadéro gardens below are a little dilapidated, but the bronze and stone statues showered by powerful fountains form a spectacular ensemble with the Eiffel Tower and Champ de Mars across the river. To the west on Avenue du President Wilson is the Palais de Tokyo which houses, in one side, the **Musée de'Art Moderne de la Ville de Paris**, and in the other, the new **Site de Création Contemporaine** (*see p158*).

The none-too-lively area behind Trocadéro holds a few surprises. Hidden among the shops on avenue Victor-Hugo, behind a conventional-looking apartment block, is No 111, the Galerie Commerciale Argentine, a brick and cast-iron apartment block and shopping arcade, now mostly empty, designed by ever-experimental Henri Sauvage and Charles Sarazin in 1904.

Cimetière de Passy

2 rue du Commandant-Schloesig, 16th (01.47.27.51.42/www.findagrave.com). M° Trocadéro. **Open** 8am-5.45pm Mon-Fri; 8.30am-5.45pm Sat; 9am-5.45pm Sun. **Map** p400 B5.
Since 1874 this has been considered one of the most elegant places in Paris to be laid to rest. Maybe only Parisians could take an interest in matters of after-death chic. Tombs here include those of composers Debussy and Fauré, painters Manet and his sister-in-law Berthe Morisot, designer Ruhlmann and writer Giraudoux, as well as numerous generals and politicians.

Palais de Chaillot

pl du Trocadéro, 16th. M° Trocadéro. **Map** p400 C5.
Looming across the river from the Eiffel Tower, the immense pseudo-classical Palais de Chaillot was built by Azéma, Boileau and Carlu for the 1937 international exhibition and actually stands on the foundations of an earlier complex put up for the 1878 World Fair. It is home to the **Cinémathèque** rep cinema, **Musée de la Marine** (dedicated to marine

and naval history) and the **Musée de l'Homme** (ethnology, anthropology, human biology) in the western wing. The ex-**Musée des Monuments Historiques**, which used to be housed in the eastern wing, is due to reappear in 2004 as Cité de l'Architecture. The **Théâtre National de Chaillot** still lurks cosily in the eastern wing.

Passy & Auteuil

West of l'Etoile, most of the 16th *arrondissement* is pearls-and-poodle country, dotted with curios, avant-garde architecture and classy shops.

When Balzac lived at 47 rue Raynouard (now **La Maison de Balzac**, *see p173*), Passy was a country village where people came to take cures for anaemia at its mineral springs – a name reflected in the rue des Eaux. The **Musée du Vin** (*see p179*) is of interest for its location in the cellars of a wine-producing monastery that was destroyed in the Revolution.

West of the Jardins du Ranelagh (originally high-society pleasure gardens, modelled on the endearingly bawdy 18th-century London version) is the **Musée Marmottan**, which features a fabulous collection of Monet's late water lily canvases, other Impressionists and Empire furniture (*see p154*).

Next to the Pont de Grenelle is **Maison de Radio-France**, the giant Orwellian home to the state broadcasting bureaucracy, and a constant reminder of the huge role that the state still plays in people's lives, opened in 1963. You can attend concerts (*see p324*) or take guided tours round its endless corridors (*see p178*); employees nickname the place 'Alphaville', after the Godard film of that name.

From here, in upmarket Auteuil, go up rue Fontaine, the best place for specimens of art nouveau architecture by Hector Guimard. Despite extravagant iron balconies, **Castel Béranger** at No 14 was originally low-rent lodgings; Guimard designed outside and in, right down to the wallpaper and stoves. He also designed the less-ambitious Nos 19, 21 and tiny Café Antoine at No 17.

The area around Métro Jasmin is the place to pay homage to the area's other prominent architect, Le Corbusier. The **Fondation Le Corbusier** occupies two of his avant-garde houses in the square du Dr-Blanche. A little further up rue du Dr-Blanche, rue Mallet-Stevens is almost entirely made up of refined houses by Robert Mallet-Stevens.

West of the 16th, across the Périphérique, sprawls the **Bois de Boulogne**, a royal hunting reserve turned park which includes a boating lake and many kilometres of cycle lanes.

Material girls at **Marché St-Pierre**.
See p109.

Bois de Boulogne

16th (www.boisdeboulogne.com), Mº Porte-Dauphine or Les Sablons.

Covering 865 hectares, the Bois de Boulogne was the ancient Forêt de Rouvray hunting grounds. It was landscaped in the 1860s when grottoes and were created around the Lac Inférieur. The Jardins de Bagatelle (route de Sèvres à Neuilly, 16th/ 01.40.67.97.00/open 9am-5.30pm/8pm summer) are famous for their roses, daffodils and water lilies and contain an Orangerie where summer piano concerts are held. The **Jardin d'Acclimatation** is a children's amusement park (*see p286*). The Bois has two racecourses (Longchamp and Auteuil), sports clubs, the **Musée National des Arts et Traditions Populaires** and two restaurants. Packed at weekends with dog walkers and picnickers, at night it is transformed into a parade ground for transsexuals.

Castel Béranger

14 rue La Fontaine, 16th. Mº Jasmin. Closed to public.

Guimard's masterpiece of 1895-98 is the building that epitomises art nouveau in Paris. Guimard sought not just a new aesthetic but also explored new materials. Here you can see his love of brick and wrought-iron, asymmetry and renunciation of harsh angles not found in nature. Along with the whiplash motifs characteristic of art nouveau, there are still many signs of Guimard's earlier taste for fantasy and the medieval. Green seahorses climb up the facade and the faces on the balconies are supposedly a self portrait, inspired by Japanese figures to ward off evil spirits.

Fondation Le Corbusier

Villa La Roche, 10 square du Dr-Blanche, 16th (01.42.88.41.53/www.fondationlecorbusier.asso.fr). Mº Jasmin. **Open** 1.30pm-6pm Mon; 10am-12.30pm, 1.30pm-6.30pm Tue-Fri. Closed Aug. **Admission** €2.40; €1.60 13-18s; free under 12s.

This house, designed by Le Corbusier in 1923 for a Swiss art collector, shows the visionary architect's ideas in practice with its strip windows, roof terraces, built-in furniture, split volumes and an unsuspected use of colour. Adjoining Villa Jeanneret – also by Le Corbusier – houses the Foundation's library.

Les Serres d'Auteuil

3 av de la Porte d'Auteuil, 16th (01.40.71.75.23). Mº Porte d'Auteuil. **Open** 10am-6pm (summer); 10am-6pm (winter). **Admission** €0.80. **No credit cards.**

These romantic glasshouses were opened in 1895 to cultivate plants for Parisian parks and public spaces. Today there are seasonal displays of orchids and begonias. Best of all is the steamy tropical central pavilion with palm trees, birds and a pool of Japanese ornamental carp.

Montmartre & Pigalle

Mainly in the 9th and 18th arrondissements.

Montmartre, away to the north on the tallest hill in the city, is the most unabashedly romantic district of Paris. Despite the onslaught of tourists who throng Sacré-Coeur and place du Tertre, it's surprisingly easy to get away from the hubbub. Climb and descend quiet stairways, peer into little alleys and deserted squares or

Sacre-Coeur:
a magnificent
penitence.
See right.

explore streets like rue des Abbesses, rue des Trois Frères and rue des Martyrs with its boho shops and young, arty community.

For centuries, Montmartre was a quiet, windmill-packed village. As Haussmann sliced through the city centre, working-class families began to move out in search of accommodation and peasant migrants poured into industrialising Paris from across France. The hill was absorbed into Paris in 1860, but remained fiercely independent. Its part in the Paris Commune is commemorated by a plaque on rue du Chevalier-de-la-Barre.

From the 1880s artists moved in to the area. Toulouse-Lautrec patronised Montmartre's bars and immortalised its cabarets in his posters; later it was frequented by artists of the Ecole de Paris, Utrillo and Modigliani.

The best starting point is the Abbesses Métro, one of only two in the city (along with Porte Dauphine) to retain its original art nouveau glass awning designed by Hector Guimard. Across place des Abbesses as you emerge from the station is the art nouveau church of St-Jean de Montmartre, with its turquoise mosaics around the door. Along rue des Abbesses and adjoining rue Lepic, which winds its way up the *butte* (hill), are many excellent food shops, wine merchants, busy cafés, including the heaving **Sancerre**, and offbeat boutiques. Along impasse Marie-Blanche there's a strange neo-Gothic house. The famous **Studio 28** cinema, opened in 1928, is on rue Tholozé. Buñuel's *L'Age d'Or* had a riotous première here in 1930.

In the other direction from Abbesses, at 11 rue Yvonne-Le-Tac, is the Chapelle du Martyr where, according to legend, St Denis picked up his head after his execution by the Romans in the third century. Around the corner, the cafés of rue des Trois Frères are popular for an evening drink. The street leads into place Emile-Goudeau, whose staircases, wrought-iron street lights and old houses are particularly evocative, as is the unspoiled bar **Chez Camille**. At No 13 stood the Bateau Lavoir. Once a piano factory, it was divided in the 1890s into a warren of studios where artists lived in penury, among them Braque, Picasso and Juan Gris. Among the ground-breaking works of art created here was Picasso's *Demoiselles d'Avignon*. The building burned down in 1970 but has been reconstructed. Further up the hill on rue Lepic are the village's two remaining windmills. The Moulin du Radet was moved here in the 17th century from its hillock in rue des Moulins near the Palais-Royal.

On top of the hill, dozens of so-called artists compete to sketch your portrait or try to flog lurid sunset views of Paris; **Espace Dalí** (*see* *p159*) on rue Poulbot offers a slightly more illustrious alternative. Just off the square is the oldest church in the district, St-Pierre-de-Montmartre, whose columns have grown bent with age. Founded by Louis VI in 1133, it is a fine example of early Gothic, and a contrast to its extravagant neighbour and Montmartrian landmark, **Sacré-Coeur**.

On the north side of place du Tertre in rue Cortot is the quiet manor housing the **Musée de Montmartre** (*see p172*), devoted to the area and its former inhabitants, with original Toulouse-Lautrec posters. Dufy, Renoir and Utrillo all had studios here. Nearby in rue des Saules is the Montmartre vineyard. The grape-picking each autumn is an annual ritual (*see chapter* **Festivals & Events**).

Further down the hill amid rustic, shuttered houses is the **Lapin Agile** cabaret at 22 rue des Saules, another legendary meeting point for Montmartre artists which is still going strong today. A series of pretty squares leads to rue Caulaincourt, towards the **Cimetière de Montmartre**, a curiously romantic place. Winding down the back of the hill, the wide avenue Junot is lined with exclusive houses, among them the one built by Adolf Loos for Dadaist poet Tristan Tzara at No 15.

Montmartre is the starting-point of our 15km round-Paris walk (*see p142* **Paris Power Strut**).

Cimetière de Montmartre

20 av Rachel, access by stairs from rue Caulaincourt, 18th (01.43.87.64.24/www.findagrave.com).
M° Blanche. **Open** *16 Mar-5 Nov* 8am-6pm Mon-Fri; 8.30am-6pm Sat; 9am-6pm Sun and holidays; *6 Nov-15 Mar* 8am-5.30 pm Mon-Fri, 8.30am-5.30pm Sat; 9am-5.30pm Sun and holidays. **Map** p401 G1.

Here you will find the graves of Sacha Guitry, Truffaut, Nijinsky, Berlioz, Degas, Greuze, Offenbach, Feydeau, Dumas *fils* and German poet Heine, reflecting the area's artistic past. There's also La Goulue, first great star of the cancan and model for Toulouse-Lautrec, celebrated beauty Mme Récamier, and the consumptive heroine (umbrellas at the ready when she had a coughing fit) Alphonsine Plessis, inspiration for Dumas' *La Dame aux Camélias* and Verdi's *La Traviata*. Mementos are still left daily for Egyptian pop diva Dalida.

Sacré-Coeur

35 rue du Chevalier-de-la-Barre, 18th (01.53.41.89.00). M° Abbesses or Anvers. **Open** Crypt/dome 6am-11pm daily. **Admission** Crypt and dome €4.60; €2.45 6-16s, students; free under-6s. **No credit cards. Map** p402 J1.

The sugar-white dome is one of the most visible landmarks in Paris. Begun as an act of penance after the nation's defeat by the Prussians in 1870 (let it go, guys), Sacré-Coeur wasn't finished until 1919. A jumble of architects worked on the mock Romano-Byzantine edifice. The view from the dome is breathtaking. Inside is an interior of sparkly mosaics.

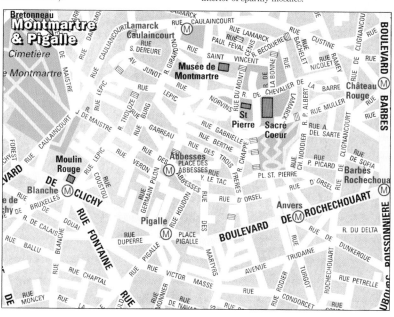

The art of the squat

The opportunity to attach the adjective 'cultural' to any activity always hurls Parisian sophisticates into tremors of joy. So it's not surprising, then, that when a mob of painters, dancers, musicians and all-round creative types chance upon a 'space' in which to delve deep and then pour forth, opinion formers should label those spaces 'centres of popular artistic exchange to enrich and invigorate the urban territory'. In the last 18 months, the artistic squat, which has been a Parisian phenomenon for years (illustrious forebears of today's scene include **Squart**, **Hôpital Ephémère** and **Les Frigos**), has blossomed as a growth area.

'It's logical', explains Jeremy from Anglophone squat **In Fact** (51 rue de Châteaudun, 9th/ Mº Trinité. See www.kilometerzero.org for details of events). 'Ten per cent of all properties in Paris are uninhabited. We artists need a place to live and work. So we break in.' And the owners? 'They pay the bills.'

Not just any old dauber can throw their leg through an open window and get stippling: squatting is a craft in itself, and you have to know what you're doing. First, you have to find a property that is definitely abandoned; shifting your knitting machine into the living room of a family who are enjoying a TV dinner in front of *Loft Story* could result in a breach of the peace. Once you've broken in (mind your nails), put the Hoover round and get the air fresheners pumping. Next, change the locks. Then, visit the neighbours ('Hello, I'm Jeremy from In Fact...'), the local town hall and the police and inform them that you intend to put your new living space to constructive, non-lucrative use. Then do your stuff. If your activities are judged to be beneficial to the community, local courts will grant you a period of grace.

Your building's owner might even enter into a 'contract of trust', whereby the squat can continue until a mutually agreed date. On the other hand, he might just send the boys round; and, don't forget, you should always be ready for that artists' rite of passage, the police raid.

Chez Robert-Electron Libre (59 rue de Rivoli, 1st/Mº Châtelet) is slap bang in the 1st *arrondissement* and a mere potter's wheel's throw from the Hôtel de Ville. The achievement of the Libre crew is considerable: a space that was teeming with rats and dead pigeons in 1999 is now teeming with modern art lovers – 40,000 of them passed through its portals in 2002. On sales days auctioneers peer owlishly over horn-rimmed specs and smart-looking buyers tug their ear lobes to the tune of several hundred euros per lot.

Despite this lurch towards respectability (Mayor Delanoë is even considering buying the space for the artists), there's still something wonderfully chaotic about the place. Perhaps it's the girl diligently wall-papering a toilet with copies of a Trotskyite newspaper; or could it be the family of chickens clucking it up in the indoor farm?

Paris' artistic squats are crammed with colour, creativity and surprises; the successful ones are run by committed people with big ideas, people who want to provide an alternative look at an increasingly uniform arts scene. So let us not be cynical. The Parisians are just being, well, a bit Parisian when they call the phenomenon 'the democratisation of culture through direct urban-collective action'. The quality of some of the works and the warmth that visitors encounter suggest that, between you and us, they might well be on to something.

Pigalle

Pigalle has long been the sleaze centre of Paris. Cue the stampede. By the end of the 19th century, of the 58 houses on rue des Martyrs, 25 were cabarets (a few such as Michou and Madame Arthur remain today); others were dubious hotels used for illicit liaisons. The **Moulin Rouge**, once the image of naughty *fin-de-siècle* Paris, has become a cheesy tourist draw. Its befeathered dancers still cancan across the stage but are no substitute for La Goulue and Joseph Pujol – the *pétomane* who could pass wind melodically.

This brash area has recently become a trendy night spot. The Moulin Rouge's old restaurant has become the **MCM Café**, while the **Folies Pigalle** cabaret is a club famed for its afters. What was once the Divan Japonais, depicted by Toulouse-Lautrec, has been transformed into **Le Divan du Monde**, a nightclub and music venue, while the old **Elysée Montmartre** music hall puts on an eclectic array of rock and pop concerts and club nights.

La Nouvelle Athènes

Just south of Montmartre and bordered by the area around Gare St-Lazare lies this mysterious, often overlooked *quartier* once beloved of artistes of the Romantic era. Long-forgotten actresses and *demi-mondaines* had mansions built here. Some of the prettiest can be found in tiny rue de la Tour-des-Dames, which refers to one of the many windmills owned by the once-prosperous Couvent des Abbesses. Wander through the adjoining streets and passageways to catch further angles of these miniature palaces and late 18th-century *hôtels particuliers*, especially on rue de La Rochefoucauld.

The area round the Neo-Classical Eglise Notre-Dame-de-Lorette was built up in Louis-Philippe's reign and famous for its courtesans. From 1844 to 1857, Delacroix had his studio at 58 rue Notre-Dame-de-Lorette (next to the house, at No 56, where Gauguin was born in 1848). The painter later moved to place de Furstenberg in the 6th *arrondissement* (now Musée Delacroix).

Just off rue Taitbout stands square d'Orléans, a remarkable housing estate built in 1829 by English architect Edward Cresy. This ensemble of flats and artists' studios attracted the glitterati of the day, including George Sand and her lover, Chopin. The **Musée de la Vie Romantique** (*see p174*) in nearby rue Chaptal displays the writer's mementoes in a perfect setting. Take in place Gustave-Toudouze, with pleasant tearoom Thé Folies, and glorious circular place St-Georges, home to the true Empress of Napoléon III's Paris, the notorious madame Païva, who lived in the neo-Renaissance No 28, thought outrageous at the time of its construction.

The **Musée Gustave Moreau**, meanwhile, is grounds alone for a visit. Fragments of *la bohème* can still be gleaned in the area, though the Café La Roche, where Moreau met Degas for drinks and rows, has been downsized to the forgettable La Jaconde on the corner of rues de La Rochefoucault and La Bruyère. Degas painted most of his memorable ballet scenes round the corner in rue Frochot and Renoir hired his first decent studio at 35 rue St-Georges. A few streets away in Cité Pigalle, a collection of studios, stands Van Gogh's last Paris house (No 5), from where he moved to Auvers-sur-Oise (*see p356* **Auvers and Out**). There is a plaque here, but nothing on the building in rue Pigalle where titchy Toulouse-Lautrec drank himself to death in 1903.

La Goutte d'Or

For a very different experience, head for Barbès-Rochechouart Métro station and the area north of it. Zola used the area as a backdrop for *L'Assommoir*, his novel set among the district's laundries and absinthe cafés – think Dickensian and you're there.

Now it is primarily an African and Arab neighbourhood, and it can seem like a colourful slice of Africa or a state under constant police siege, with frequent sweeps on drug dealers. Down rue Doudeauville, you'll find African music shops, rue Polonceau has African grocers and Senegalese restaurant Chez Aïda, while square Léon is the focus for **la Goutte d'Or en Fête** every June, which tries to harness some of the local talent (*see p278*). Some bands, such as Africando and the Orchestre National de Barbès, have become well known across Paris. There is a lively street market under the Métro tracks (Mon, Wed, Sat morning), with stalls of exotic vegetables and rolls of African fabrics. This area also houses the legendary bargain store **Tati**, where you can buy clothes for unbelievably low prices, while Mayor Delanoë has tried to inject a bit of class by designating **rue des Gardes** 'rue de la mode' to encourage young designers. From here rue d'Orsel leads back to Montmartre via **Marché St-Pierre**. The covered market hall is now used for exhibitions of naïve art, but in the street, outlets such as Dreyfus and Moline vie for custom with discount fabrics.

On the northern edge of the city at Porte de Clignancourt is Paris' largest flea market, the **Marché aux Puces de St-Ouen** (*see chapter* **Shops & Services**).

Cute canal work: **Canal St-Martin.**

North-east Paris

In the 10th, 11th, 19th and 20th arrondissements.
The old working-class area north and east of
République is in transformation, mixing
pockets of charm with grotty or even dangerous
areas. The main tourist attraction is **Père
Lachaise** cemetery, but if you look further
afield you'll find fascinating pockets of a Paris
that you might have through had disappeared
decades ago. Ménilmontant and Belleville, once
villages where Parisians escaped at weekends,
were absorbed into the city in 1860.

Canal St-Martin to La Villette

Canal St-Martin, built 1805-25, begins at the
Seine at Pont Morland, disappears underground
at Bastille, then re-emerges at rue du Faubourg-
du-Temple east of place de la République. This
stretch has the most charm, lined with shady
trees and crossed by iron footbridges and locks.
Over the past year or so, property prices have
begun to rise as bobos and Eurostar commuters
have begun to follow yer actual artistes.

You can take a boat up the canal between the
Port de l'Arsenal and the Bassin de la Villette
(*see p372*). Between the fifth and sixth locks at
101 quai de Jemmapes is the **Hôtel du Nord**,
which inspired Marcel Carné's 1938 film. East
of here is the Hôpital St-Louis (main entrance
rue Bichat), founded in 1607 to house plague
victims and built as a series of isolated
pavilions to stop disease spreading. Behind the
hospital, the rue de la Grange-aux-Belles housed
the infamous Montfaucon gibbet, built in 1233,
where victims were hanged and left to the
elements. Today the street contains music cafés
Chez Adel (No 10) and Apostrophe (No 23).
Only the inconspicuous Le Pont Tournant, on

The best | Verdant venues

Buttes Chaumont
Grottoes galore. *See p112.*

Jardin Naturel
...it's as wild the French get. *See p114.*

Parc de Belleville
For those with a head for heights. *See p112.*

Parc Monceau
Corinthian columns for classicists. *See p102.*

Promenade plantée
Roses among the rooftops. *See p100.*

Square des Batignolles
Pretty, and great for train-spotting. *See p105.*

the corner with quai de Jemmapes overlooking the swing bridge, still seems to hark back to canal days of old.

To the east is the Parti Communiste Français, on the place du Colonel-Fabien, a surrealistic, curved glass curtain raised off the ground on a concrete wing, built in 1968-71 by Brazilian architect Oscar Niemeyer with Paul Chemetov and Jean Deroche. To the north, place de Stalingrad was landscaped in 1989 to expose the Rotonde de la Villette, one of Ledoux's grandiose toll houses which now houses exhibitions and archaeological finds. Here the canal widens into Bassin de la Villette, built for Napoléon in 1808, bordered by new housing developments, as well as some of the worst of 1960s and '70s housing. At the eastern end of the basin is an unusual 1885 hydraulic lifting bridge, the Pont de Crimée. Thursday and Sunday mornings inject some vitality with a canalside market, place de Joinville. East of here, the Canal de l'Ourcq (created in 1813 to provide drinking water, as well as for freight haulage) divides: Canal St-Denis runs north through St-Denis towards the Seine, Canal de l'Ourcq runs through La Villette and suburbs east. The area has been revitalised since the late 1980s by the brilliant **Cité des Sciences et de l'Industrie** science museum, the activity-filled postmodern **Parc de la Villette** and by the superbly designed **Cité de la Musique** concert hall and music museum.

Parc de la Villette

au Corentin-Cariou, 19th. M° Porte de la Villette, or av Jean-Jaurès, 19th. M° Porte de Pantin. **Map** p403 inset.

La Villette's programmes range from avant-garde music to avant-garde circus. The site of Paris' main cattle market and abattoir, it was to be replaced by a high-tech slaughterhouse but was then, to the disappointment of many, turned into the **Cité des Sciences et de l'Industrie**, a futuristic, interactive science museum. Outside are the shiny spherical **Géode** cinema and Argonaute submarine. Dotted with red pavilions or *folies*, the park itself is a postmodern feast (guided tours 08.03.30.63.06, 3pm Sun in summer). The *folies* serve as glorious climbing frames in addition to such uses as first-aid post, burger bar and children's art centre. Kiddies shoot down a Chinese dragon slide and a meandering suspended path follows the Canal de l'Ourcq. As well as the big lawns, which are used for an open-air film festival in July and August, there are ten themed gardens with evocative names such as the Garden of Mirrors, of Mists, of Acrobatics and of Childhood Fears. South of the canal are the **Zénith**, used for pop concerts, and the Grande Halle de la Villette, part of the old meat market now used for trade fairs, exhibitions and the **Villette Jazz Festival**. It is winged by the Conservatoire de la Musique music school on one side and on the other the **Cité de la Musique**, designed by Christian de Portzamparc, with its concert halls, rehearsal rooms and **Musée de la Musique**. (*See chapters* **festivals & Events**, **Museums**, **Cabaret & Circus**, **Children**, **Music: Classical & Opera**, **Music: Popular Music**, **Theatre**).

Ménilmontant & Charonne

Once just a few houses on a hill where vines and fruit trees were cultivated, Mesnil-Montant expanded with bistros, workers' housing and knocking shops. It became part of Paris in 1860 with Belleville, and has a similar history. Today it's a thriving centre of alternative Paris, as artists and young Parisians have moved in. Flanking boulevard de Ménilmontant, **Cimetière du Père Lachaise** is generally thought to be the most illustrious burial site in Paris. South of here, rue de la Réunion ends in the deliberately unkempt **Jardin Naturel**.

The area mixes 1960s and 70s monster housing projects with older dwellings, some gentrified, some derelict. Below rue des Pyrénées, the Cité Leroy or Villa l'Ermitage are cobbled cul-de-sacs often housing artists' studios. At its junction with rue de Ménilmontant there is a bird's-eye view into the centre of town. Follow rue Julien-Lacroix to place Maurice-Chevalier and 19th-century Notre-Dame-de-la-Croix church.

While side streets still display male-only North African cafés, the rue Oberkampf is home to some of the city's most humming bars. The cutting edge may already be moving elsewhere, but young international trendies have followed the artists and **Le Mécano**, **Mercerie** and **Scherkhan** bars have succeeded the success of **Café Charbon** and **Le Cithéa** club. Offbeat art shows are put on at **Glassbox**, while a more cultural concentration has evolved on rue Boyer with the **Maroquinerie** literary café.

East of Père-Lachaise is Charonne, which joined Paris in 1859. The medieval Eglise St-Germain de Charonne, place St-Blaise, is the city's only church, apart from St-Pierre de Montmartre, still to have its own graveyard. The rest of Charonne, centred on rue St-Blaise, is a prettified backwater of quiet bars and bistros. Cross the Périphérique at Porte de Montreuil for the **Puces de Montreuil** (*see chapter* **Shops & Services**), the junkiest of the Paris fleamarkets.

Cimetière du Père Lachaise

main entrance bd de Ménilmontant, 20th (01.55.25.82.10). M° Père-Lachaise. **Open** *16 Mar-5 Nov* 8am-6pm Mon-Fri; 8.30am-6pm Sat; 9am-6pm Sun and holidays; *6 Nov-15 Mar* 8am-5.30pm Mon-Fri; 8.30am-5.30pm Sat; 9am-5.30pm Sun and holidays. **Map** p403 P5.

With thousands of tightly packed tombs arranged along cobbled lanes and tree-lined avenues, this is said to be the world's most visited cemetery. Named after the Jesuit Père de la Chaise, Louis XIV's confessor, it was laid out by the architect Brongniart in 1804. It was never meant to be 'just' a cemetery, and was designed as somewhere for talking a walk or

having a quiet ponder. The presumed remains of medieval lovers Abélard and Héloïse were moved here in 1817, along with those of Molière and La Fontaine, in a bid to gain popularity for the site. Famous inhabitants soon multiplied: Sarah Bernhardt, Delacroix, Ingres, Bizet, Balzac, Proust, Chopin, Colette and the singing sheep, Piaf. Jim Morrison, buried here in 1971, still attracts a flow of spaced-out pilgrims. Oscar Wilde's headstone, carved by Epstein, is a winged, naked, male angel which was considered so offensive that it was neutered by the head keeper, who used the offending member as a paperweight. The Mur des Fédérés got its name after 147 members of the Paris Commune of 1871 were lined up and shot against it. Further up the hill is a series of moving Holocaust memorials.

Belleville

This lively area was incorporated into the city in 1860 and became a work and leisure place for the poorer classes. Despite attempts to dissipate workers' agitation by splitting the former village between the 11th, 19th and 20th *arrondissements*, it was the centre of opposition to the Second Empire. Cabarets, artisans, and workers' housing typified *fin-de-siècle* Belleville.

On boulevard de Belleville, Chinese and Vietnamese shops rub shoulders with Muslim and Kosher groceries, couscous and felafel eateries. On the small streets off the rue de Belleville, old buildings hide courtyards and gardens. Rue Ramponneau mixes new housing and relics of old Belleville. At No 23 an old iron smithy has become **La Forge**, a squat for artists, many of whom are members of La Bellevilloise association, which is trying to save the area from redevelopment and preserve its original charm. Rue Sainte-Marthe is a delightful cobbled road lined with multi-ethnic restaurants and *chanson* venue **Le Panier**. There is also the modern but charming **parc de Belleville** with its Maison des Vents devoted to birds, kites and (almost) all things airborne.

Up the avenue Simon Bolivar is the eccentric **Parc des Buttes-Chaumont**, one of the most attractive feats of Haussmann's designers. East of the park are a number of tiny, hilly streets lined with small houses and gardens.

Parc des Buttes-Chaumont

rue Botzaris, rue Manin, rue de Crimée, 19th. M° Buttes-Chaumont. **Map** p403 N2.
This wonderland is possibly the perfect meeting of nature and the artificial, with its meandering paths and vertical cliffs. It was designed by Haussmann in the 1860s on the distinctly unpromising site of a granite quarry, rubbish tip and public gibbet. With all that froth and mania safely in the past, waterfalls now cascade out of a man-made cave, which even has its own fake stalactites. (*See also p287.*)

The Left Bank

The *Rive Gauche* has stopped living off its Sorbonne, Sartre and '68 reputation: it's back with a ZAC, futuristic parks and vibrant restaurants.

The Latin Quarter

In the 5th arrondissement.

This section of the Left Bank east of boulevard St-Michel is probably so named because students here spoke Latin until the Revolution. Another theory is that it alludes to the vestiges of Roman Lutétia, of which this area was the heart. The first two Roman streets were on the site of present-day rue St-Jacques (later the pilgrims' route to Compostella) and rue Cujas. The area still boasts many medieval streets, scholarly institutions and the city's most important Roman remains: the Cluny baths, now part of the **Musée National du Moyen Age**, and the **Arènes de Lutèce** amphitheatre.

Quartier de la Huchette

The boulevard St-Michel, at one time symbolic of student rebellion, has been taken over by fast-food giants and downmarket shoe and clothes chains. Bonjour, capitalism. You'll find more Greek restaurants and cafés than evidence of medieval learning down rue de la Huchette and rue de la Harpe. Look out for 18th-century wrought-iron balconies and carved masks on the latter street. Find, too, rue du Chat-Qui-Pêche, supposedly Paris' narrowest street, and rue de la Parcheminerie, named after the parchment sellers and copyists who once lived here. Sticking up amid the tourist paraphernalia is Paris' most charming medieval church, the **Eglise St-Séverin**, which has an exuberant Flamboyant Gothic vaulted interior.

Across the ancient rue St-Jacques is **Eglise St-Julien-le-Pauvre**, built as a resting place for pilgrims in the 12th century.

By the river, back from the *bouquinistes*, or booksellers, lining the *quais*, expats with leather patches sewn onto the elbows of their tweed jackets congregate at English bookshop **Shakespeare & Co** (37 rue de la Bûcherie).

A medieval garden is the latest attraction at the **Musée National du Moyen Age – Thermes de Cluny**, across boulevard St-Germain. A Gothic mansion built over ruined

Rue Mouffetard: the snazziest market in Paris. *See p117.*

Roman baths, the museum now houses a quite magnificent collection of medieval art.

East of here, place Maubert, now a morning marketplace (Tue, Thur, Sat), was used in the 16th century to hang Protestant heretics. The little streets between here and the *quais* are among the city's oldest. Rue de Bièvre charts the course of the river Bièvre, which flowed into the Seine in the Middle Ages. Religious foundations once abounded; remnants of the Collège des Bernardins can be seen in rue de Poissy. On quai de la Tournelle there's food for all budgets, from the illustrious **Tour d'Argent** (No 17) to the Tintin shrine *café-tabac* Le Rallye (No 11). Below, numerous houseboats are moored at a former dock for hay and wood.

Eglise St-Julien-le-Pauvre

rue St-Julien-le-Pauvre, 5th (01.43.54.52.16). Mº Cluny-La Sorbonne. **Open** 9.30am-noon, 3-6.30pm Mon-Sat; 9.30am-6.30pm Sun. **Map** p406 J7.
Formerly a sanctuary for pilgrims en route for Compostella, the present church dates from the late 12th century. Originally part of a priory, it became the university church when colleges left Notre-Dame for the Left Bank. Since 1889 it has been used by the Greek church. Ignore the poorly maintained exterior; the interior is well worth a visit. One of the trees in the garden is said to be the oldest in Paris.

► For detailed museum information and opening times, turn to **Sightseeing: Museums,** starting on page 147.
► For shopping information turn to **Shops & Services,** starting on page 235.
► For information on arts events turn to **Arts & Entertainment,** starting on page 275.

Eglise St-Séverin

1 rue des Prêtres-St-Séverin, 5th (01.42.34.93.50). Mº Cluny-La Sorbonne or St. Michel. **Open** 11am-7.45pm Mon-Fri; 8am-9.30pm Sat; 9am-9.30pm Sun. **Map** p406 J7.
Primitive and Flamboyant Gothic styles merge here. The double ambulatory is famed for its 'palm tree' vaulting and unique double spiral column. Next door are the remains of the charnel house. The bell tower has the oldest bell in Paris (1412). Do have a look at the modern stained glass windows.

Musée National du Moyen Age – Thermes de Cluny

6 pl Paul-Painlevé, 5th (01.53.73.78.00/ www.musee-moyenage.fr). Mº Cluny-La Sorbonne. **Open** 9.15am-5.45pm Mon, Wed-Sun. **Admission** €5.50; €4 18-25s, all Sun; free under-18s, CM. **Credit** (shop) V. **Map** p406 J7.

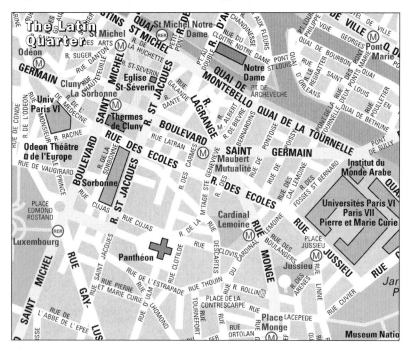

The museum is famed for its Roman remains and medieval art, most notably the Lady and the Unicorn tapestry cycle. The museum itself, commonly known as Cluny, is also a rare example of 15th-century secular Gothic architecture. It was built – atop a Gallo-Roman baths complex dating from the second and third centuries – by Jacques d'Amboise in 1485-98 for lodging priests at the request of the Abbé de Cluny. With its main building behind a courtyard, it set new standards for domestic comfort and was a precursor of the Marais *hôtels particuliers*. The baths are the finest Roman remains in Paris: the vaulted *frigidarium* (cold bath), *tepidarium* (warm bath) and *caldarium* (hot bath) are visible. A printer, a laundry and cooper set up here in 1807, before it became a museum in 1844. The new medieval garden is inspired (as are many of us) by courtly and saintly love; it is planted with species found in medieval treatises, tapestries and paintings. (*See chapter* **Museums**.)

The Sorbonne & the Montagne Ste-Geneviève

The days of horn-rims, pipes and student goatees are long gone. In the 1980s, an influx of well-heeled residents put accommodation in this warren of narrow streets beyond some students' reach. At least the intellectual tradition persists: the Montagne Ste-Geneviève is a concentration of academic institutions, from the **Sorbonne** to research centres to Grandes Ecoles such as the Ecole Normale Supérieure; students throng in countless specialist book stores and the art cinemas of rue Champollion and rue des Ecoles.

The district began its long association with learning in about 1100, when a number of scholars, including high-pitched Pierre Abélard, began to live and teach on the Montagne, independent of the established Canon school of Notre-Dame. This loose association of scholars began to be referred to as a university. The Paris schools attracted scholars from all over Europe, and the 'colleges' – really just student residences – multiplied, until the University of Paris was given official recognition with a charter from Pope Innocent III in 1215.

By the 16th century, the university – now known as the **Sorbonne**, after the most famous of its colleges – had been co-opted by the Catholic establishment. A century later, Cardinal Richelieu rebuilt it, but it slid into decay again. After the Revolution, when the university was forced to close, Napoléon revived the Sorbonne as the cornerstone of his new, centralised education system. The university participated enthusiastically in the uprisings of the 19th century, and was also a seedbed of the May 1968 revolt. Nowadays the Sorbonne is decidedly less turbulent. The present buildings

are mostly 19th century; only the Baroque Chapelle de la Sorbonne, where Richelieu is buried, survives from his rebuilding.

Look out for the independent **Collège de France**, also on rue des Ecoles, which was founded in 1530 by a group of humanists led by Guillaume Budé with the patronage of François 1er. For intellectual fodder, neighbouring Brasserie Balzar attracts a fascinatingly varied clientele.

Climb up rue St-Jacques, winding rue de la Montagne-Ste-Geneviève or take rue des Carmes, with the Baroque chapel of the Syrian church, and rue Valette past the brick and stone entrance of the Collège Ste-Barbe, where Ignatius Loyola and later Montgolfier and Eiffel studied, to place du Panthéon. The huge domed **Panthéon**, originally commissioned by Louis XV as a church to honour the city's patron, Ste-Geneviève, was converted in the Revolution into a secular temple for France's *grands hommes*. *Grandes femmes* (kicking off with Marie Curie) were only admitted from 1995, suggesting, perhaps, that women's lib(erté) was not high on the list of revolutionary priorities. In October 2002, a new tenant, Alexandre Dumas, moved in, with the kind of ceremonial hullabaloo befitting such a notorious womaniser (and author). In the surrounding square, also conceived by the Panthéon's architect, Soufflot, is the elegant *mairie* (town hall) of the 5th *arrondissement*, mirrored by the law faculty. On the north side, the Bibliothèque Ste-Geneviève university library, built 1844-50 by Labrouste, has medieval manuscripts and an iron-framed reading room. On the other side of the square is the **Hôtel des Grands-Hommes**, where Surrealist André Breton invented 'automatic writing' in the 1920s (*see chapter* **The Surreal Thing**).

Sightseeing

The best Dead'uns

Samuel Beckett
Long pause. (**Montparnasse** *see p133*).

Count Hyacinthe Hugues Timoléon de Cossé-Brissac
Not that famous, but what a name. (**Panthéon** *see p118*).

Napoléon's pooch
Ruff luck, Boney. (**Les Invalides** *see p129*).

Jean-Paul Sartre
Ex-existent existentialist. (**Montparnasse** *see p133*).

Puvis flair at the **Panthéon**.

Pascal and Racine, and the remains of Paris' patron saint, Ste Geneviève, are buried at **St-Etienne-du Mont**, on the northeast corner of the square. Jutting up behind is the Gothic-Romanesque Tour de Clovis. Further along rue Clovis is a chunk of Philippe-Auguste's 12th-century city wall. Hemingway lived on both rue du Cardinal-Lemoine and rue Descartes (plaque at No 74 rue du Cardinal-Lemoine). James II resided at No 65 in the severe buildings of the former Collège des Ecossais, founded in 1372 to house Scottish students and where James' II brain also resided until it was desecrated and subsequently lost by mobs during the French Revolution. Some people have no respect for other people's property. At No 75 hides the charming **Hôtel des Grandes-Ecoles**. Also in the area, in the Rue des Irlandais, is the new Centre Culturel Irlandais. Inhabiting the old Irish College building (which has undergone a £7 million refurbishment), the centre aims to strengthen Franco-Irish relations and presents a programme of films, concerts, plays and spoken word events that display the variety and depth of Irish culture. This is one serious cultural centre: it even has its own writer (Claire Keegan) and painter (Fionna Murray) in residence.

Collège de France
11 pl Marcelin-Berthelot, 5th (01.44.27.12.11). Mᵒ Cluny-La Sorbonne. **Map** p406 J7.
Founded in 1530 thanks to the patronage of François 1ᵉʳ, the college's purpose is to teach knowledge in the making rather than fact. Lectures – which are free and open to the public – can include such eminent names as Claude Lévi-Strauss, Emmanuel Le Roy Ladurie, Jean-Claude Pecker and Jacques Tits.

Eglise St-Etienne-du-Mont
pl Ste-Geneviève, 5th (01.43.54.11.79). Mᵒ Cardinal-Lemoine/RER Luxembourg. **Open** 9am-noon, 2-7pm Mon-Sat; 9am-noon, 2.30-7pm Sun. **Map** p406 J8.
Ste-Geneviève saved the city from Attila the Hun in 451; her shrine here has been a popular pilgrimage place since the Dark Ages. The present church was built in an amalgam of Gothic and Renaissance styles between 1492 and 1626, and originally adjoined the abbey church of Ste-Geneviève. The facade mixes Gothic rose windows with classical columns. The stunning Renaissance roodscreen, with its double spiral staircase and ornate stone strapwork, is the only one left in Paris. Ste-Geneviève's elaborate brass-covered shrine is to the right of the choir, surrounded by plaques giving thanks for her miracles.

Le Panthéon
pl du Panthéon, 5th (01.44.32.18.00). RER Luxembourg. **Open** *summer* 10am-6.30pm daily; *winter* 10am-6.45pm daily. **Admission** €7; €4.50 18-25s; free under-18s. **Credit** MC, V. **Map** p406 J8.

Soufflot's neo-classical megastructure was the architectural *Grand Projet* of its day, commissioned by a grateful Louis XV to thank Ste Geneviève for his recovery from illness. But events caught up with its completion in 1790, and post-Revolution it was re-dedicated as a 'temple of reason' and the resting-place of the nation's great men. The austere crypt of greats includes Voltaire, Rousseau, Victor Hugo and Zola. New heroes are added rarely: Pierre and Marie Curie's remains were transferred here in 1995, she being the first woman to be interred in her own right. André Malraux, writer, Resistance hero and De Gaulle's culture minister, arrived to keep her company in 1996. Alexandre Dumas wormed his way in in 2002. Inside you can admire the Greek columns and domes, as well as 19th-century murals depicting the saint's life by symbolist painter Puvis de Chavannes and which were a formative influence on Picasso's blue period. Do brave the steep spiral stairs up to the colonnade, and you'll be rewarded with some truly wonderful views across the city. The reconstruction of Foucault's pendulum also hangs here. The pendulum, hung from the 'eye of God', proves that the earth does indeed spin on its axis. Therefore, while you watch the pendulum swing, the building, and you, are moving around the pendulum and not vice-versa. Are you keeping up here? The central area has been cordoned since a woman was struck by a piece of falling Panthéon, so you may want to bring your own hard hat.

La Sorbonne

17 rue de la Sorbonne, 5th (01.40.46.22.11/ www.sorbonne.fr). M° Cluny-La Sorbonne.
Map p406 J7.
Founded in 1253 by Robert de Sorbon, the University of the Sorbonne was at the centre of the Latin Quarter's intellectual activity from the Middle Ages until the dramatic events of May 1968, when it was occupied by students and stormed by the CRS (riot police). The authorities subsequently splintered the University of Paris into several less-threatening outposts, but the Sorbonne remains home to the Faculté des Lettres. Rebuilt by Richelieu and reorganised by Napoléon, the present buildings mostly date from 1885 to 1900 and include a labyrinth of classrooms and quaint lecture theatres, as well as an observatory tower. The elegant dome of the 17th-century chapel dominates place de la Sorbonne; Cardinal Richelieu is buried inside. This is only open to the public during exhibitions or concerts.

The rue Mouffetard area

Place de la Contrescarpe has been a famous rendezvous since the 1530s, when writers Rabelais, Ronsard and Du Bellay frequented the Cabaret de la Pomme de Pin at No 1. It is still known for its lively cafés, and is a great spot for people-watching over a glass of wine or three. **Rue Mouffetard**, originally the road to Rome and one of the oldest streets in the city, winds

off to the south. Cheap bistros, knick-knack shops and crowds of tourists have moved in and changed the vibe in what Hemingway rather poncily described as 'that wonderful narrow crowded market street, beloved of bohemians'. There is a busy street market (Tue-Sat and Sun morning) on the lower half. It's particularly seething at weekends when the market spills on to the square and around the cafés in front of the **Eglise St-Médard**. There's another busy market at place Monge (Wed, Fri, Sun morning). From 1928-29 George Orwell stayed at 6 rue du Pot-de-Fer. Then an area of astounding poverty, it is now lined with cheap bars and restaurants. Public schoolboy Orwell deigned to work as a *plongeur* (washer-upper), and his experiences are vividly depicted in *Down and Out in Paris and London*. The restored houses along **rue Tournefort** bear no relation to the cheap garrets described in Balzac's *Le Père Goriot*.

Beyond rue Soufflot is one of the most picturesque stretches of the rue St-Jacques. Here you'll find several ancient buildings. Note the elegant *hôtel* at No 151. There are also some very good food shops, the vintage bistro Perraudin and Aussie bar Café Oz. Rue d'Ulm houses the elitist Ecole Normale Supérieure, which was occupied by the unemployed in January 1998; in an echo of 1968, several students joined in. And what then, you cry, in terms of social change? Nothing. Oh, well. *Plus ça change*, as the man said.

Turn off up hilly rue des Fossés-St-Jacques to discover place de l'Estrapade, tucked behind the Panthéon. The square has a dark past: the estrapade was a wooden tower from which deserters were dropped in the 17th century. To the west, broad rue Gay-Lussac (a hotspot of May '68 and now about as revolutionary as a subscription to *Home & Garden*) leads to the **Jardins du Luxembourg**. Further down rue St-Jacques is another eminent landmark, the **Val-de-Grâce**, the least-altered and most ornate of all Paris' Baroque churches. Leading up to this, at No 6 rue du Val-de-Grâce, is the former home of Alfons Maria Mucha, the Czech art nouveau painter who is most famous for his Sarah Bernhardt posters.

Eglise St-Médard

141 rue Mouffetard, 5th (01.44.08.87.00). M° Censier-Daubenton. **Open** 8am-12.30pm, 2.30-7pm Tue-Sat; 4-7pm Sun. **Map** p406 J9.
The original chapel here was a dependency of the Abbaye de Ste-Geneviève; rebuilding at the end of the 15th century created a much larger, late Gothic structure. Some of the capitals were fluted to suit 1780s neo-classical fashion.

Eglise du Val-de-Grâce

*pl Alphonse-Laveran, 5th (01.40.51.47.28). RER
Port-Royal.* **Open** Call to arrange guided visits noon-
6pm, Tue, Wed, Sat, Sun. **Admission** €4.60, €2.30
6-12s, free under-6s. **No credit cards. Map** p406 H9.
Anne of Austria vowed to erect 'a magnificent
temple' if God blessed her with a son. He presented
her with two. The resulting church and its Benedic-
tine monastery – now a military hospital and the
Musée du Service de Santé des Armées devoted to military medicine (*see chapter* **Museums**) –
were built by François Mansart and Jacques
Lemercier. Expensive and built over decades, this is
the most luxuriously Baroque of the city's 17th-
century domed churches. The swirling colours of the
dome frescoes painted by portrait artist Pierre
Mignard in 1669 (and for which Molière wrote a eulo-
gy) are meant to prefigure heaven.

The Jardin des Plantes district

The quieter eastern end of rue des Ecoles is a
focus for Paris' Muslim community, major
academic institutions and home to several
Roman relics. Old-fashioned bistros on rue des
Fossés-St-Bernard contrast with the brutal
1960s-70s slab architecture of Paris university's
campuses VI and VII (known as Jussieu), now
the subject of a major regeneration project.
Between the Seine and Jussieu is the strikingly
modern glass **Institut du Monde Arabe**,
which has a busy programme of concerts and
exhibitions and a restauarant with a great view
over the city. The **Jardin Tino Rossi**, along
the river, contains the slightly dilapidated
Musée de la Sculpture en Plein Air.
  The Paris mosque is not far away up rue
Linné. You may want to stop off at the **Arènes
de Lutèce**, the Roman amphitheatre. The
central arena and many tiers of stone seating
were discovered in 1869 during the building of
rue Monge. Their excavation started in 1883,
due to the archaeological zeal of Victor Hugo.
The wonderfully pretty, green-roofed **Mosquée
de Paris** was built in 1922, partly inspired by
Granada's Alhambra, though its popular and
beautiful Moorish tearoom has, sadly but
inevitably, become a favourite with the
bourgeois brigade, more intent on studying
their Ceylon than their Koran.
  The mosque looks out on to the **Jardin
des Plantes**, Paris' superb botanical garden.
Established in 1626 as a garden for medicinal
plants, it features an 18th-century maze, a
winter garden brimming with rare species and
the brilliantly renovated Grande Galerie de
l'Evolution of the **Muséum National
d'Histoire Naturelle**. There's also the
Ménagerie, an unlikely by-product of the
Revolution, when royal and noble collections of
wild animals were impounded.

Arènes de Lutèce

*entrances rue Monge, rue de Navarre, rue des
Arènes, 5th. Mº Cardinal-Lemoine or Jussieu.*
Open 8am-5.30pm winter; 8am-10pm summer.
Map p406 K8.
The Roman arena, where roaring wild beasts and
tough-guy gladiators met their deaths, could seat
10,000. The site was discovered in 1869 and now
incorporates a romantically planted garden. These
days, it attracts skateboarders, footballers and
boules players, so the blood-and-thunder factor has
probably gone down a notch or two, but the macho
preening is alive and kicking.

Institut du Monde Arabe

*1 rue des Fossés-St-Bernard, 5th (01.40.51.38.38)
(www.imarabe.org). Mº Jussieu.* **Open** Museum
10am-6pm Tue-Sun. *Library* 1-8pm Tue-Sat. *Café*
noon-6pm Tue-Sun. **Admission** roof terrace, library
free. Museum €3; free under-12s. Exhibitions €6.86;
€5.34 students, over-60s. **Map** p406 K7.
A clever blend of high-tech steel, glass architecture
and Arab influences, this wedge-shaped *Grand
Projet* was designed by French architect Jean Nouvel
in 1980-87 with seemingly endless shuttered windows inspired by the screens of Moorish palaces.
They look like (and are designed to act as) camera
apertures according to the amount of available light.
Inside is a comprehensive collection of Middle Eastern art, archaeological finds, exhibition spaces, a
library and café. The Institute runs a programme of
dance and classical Arab music. It's well worth nipping up to the roof for some great views of the city.

Jardin des Plantes

*pl Valhubert, rue Buffon or rue Cuvier, 5th
(01.40.79.30.00). Mº Gare d'Austerlitz or Jussieu.*
Open Main garden daily-sunset; Mon, Wed-Sun,
summer 10am-6pm; winter 10am-5pm (Alpine garden
Apr-Sept 8am-11am, 1.30-5pm; greenhouses Apr-Sept
1-5pm Mon, Wed-Fri; 10am-5pm Sat and Sun;
ménagerie Apr-Sept, 9am-5/6pm, Mon-Sat; 9am-
6.30pm Sun; Gallery of Evolution 10am-6pm, late
night Thur until 10pm, closed on Tues; other galeries
Apr-Sept, Mon, Wed-Fri, 10am-5pm, Sat/Sun 10am-
6pm). **Admission** free; greenhouses €2.29;
Ménagerie €4.57-€3.05. **Map** p406 L8.
Although small and slightly run-down, the Paris
botanical garden is a great place to visit, containing
more than 10,000 species, and including tropical
greenhouses and rose, winter and Alpine gardens.
Begun by Louis XIII's doctor as the royal medicinal
plant garden in 1626, it opened to the public in 1640.
It also contains the **Ménagerie**, a small zoo, and the
Muséum National d'Histoire Naturelle, including the magnificently renovated 1880s Grande
Galerie de l'Evolution. Several ancient trees on view
in the gardens include a false acacia planted in 1636
and a cedar planted in 1734. A plaque on the former
laboratory announces that this is where Henri Bec-
querel discovered radioactivity in 1896. Let's hope
he was wearing his lead undies. *See also chapters*
Museums *and* **Children**.

Arabian sights at **Institut du Monde Arabe.**

La Mosquée de Paris

1 pl du Puits-de-l'Ermite, 5th (01.45.35.97.33/ tearoom 01.43.31.38.20/Turkish baths 01.43.31.18.14/www.mosquee-de-paris.com).
M° Censier-Daubenton. **Open** tours 9am-noon, 2-6pm Mon-Thur, Sat, Sun (closed Muslim holidays); tearoom 10am-midnight daily; restaurant noon-3pm, 7-10.30pm daily; baths (women) 10am-9pm Mon, Wed, Sat; 2-9pm Fri; (men) 2-9pm Tue; 10am-9pm Sun. **Admission** €2.30; €1.50 7-25s, over-60s; free under-7s; tearoom free; baths €15-€35-.
Credit MC, V. **Map** p406 K9.

The mosque's stunning green-and-white square minaret oversees the centre of the Algerian-dominated Muslim community in France. Built 1922-26 in Hispano-Moorish style, with elements inspired by the Alhambra and Fez's Mosque Bou-Inania, the mosque is a series of buildings and courtyards in three sections: religious (grand patio, prayer room and minaret, all of which are for serious worshippers as opposed to inquisitive tourists); scholarly (Islamic school and library); and, entered from rue Geoffroy-St-Hilaire, commercial (domed *hammam* or Turkish baths, relaxing Moorish tearoom and souvenir and bird-cage shop).

St-Germain & Odéon

St-Germain-des-Prés is where the great legend of Paris café society and intellectual life grew up. Verlaine and Rimbaud drank here; a few generations later, Sartre, Camus and de Beauvoir scribbled their first masterpieces and musicians congregated around writer, critic and trumpeter Boris Vian in Paris' postwar jazz boom. Self-proclaimed Lizard King and erotic politician Jim 'I'll-see-if-a-bath-perks-me-up' Morrison spent most of his final days on the planet here in the summer of 1971.

Earnest types still vogue their way down the road ostentatiously bearing weighty tomes and the literati still gather on terraces – to give TV interviews – but the area is so expensive that any writers here are either well-established or rich. Luxury fashion groups have moved in: Armani took over the old Drugstore, Dior a bookshop, Cartier a classical record shop and Louis Vuitton unpacked its bags at place St-Germain; since the All Jazz Club and La Villa

The Seine

Inland cities are rarely much cop without a decent river. Paris without the Seine would be – well, for a start, what would we do with all the bridges? And what would the Parisians do without the Right Bank and the Left Bank?

The Right-Left delineation has long been vital to the way in which Parisians see themselves and their city. In the 1950s and 1960s, Left Bank meant intellectual, revolutionary, creative; in the 1980s and 1990s it meant old fart; now it's waking up again (*see p134* **ZAC's the way, uh-huh, uh-huh**). People under 30, who won't remember when the Left Bank was all jazz goatees and existentialism, nonetheless mourn the passing of the black polo neck days. Right Bank used to mean business and money-making; now, its eastern *quartiers* are where the would-be and actual groovers hang out. The city's evolution follows a standard pattern: working class and/or immigrant populations energise an area; middle-class professionals move in, attracted by the vibe, and their collective drabness kills that vibe; things move on elsewhere.

In the geographical sense, Paris was created by the Seine, which, in a prehistoric frenzy, hollowed out a basin that was tailor-made for traders to set up stall in. That was dandy for the ancient loadsamoney brigade, but the river also, of course, created a way in for marauding

hordes. Marauding always facilitates fast-track urban development.

The Seine still represents the main thoroughfare for today's pillaging mobs – tourists – as the majority of Paris' most famous landmarks lie conveniently on its banks. A river trip between, say, the Pont des Invalides and the Pont d'Austerlitz offers arguably the best sightseeing blast on the planet (the Grand Palais, Assemblée Nationale, Jardin des Tuileries, Musée d'Orsay, the Louvre, Notre-Dame, to mention but the heavy mob). If you do take the *bateau* option (*see chapter* **Directory**), you might

Jazz Club closed, musicians have crossed the river. It didn't happen without a fight from the boho traditionalists, though it has to be said that the fight was a 'powder puffs at dawn' affair: in 1997 a band of intellectuals with time on their hands founded 'SOS St-Germain' in an attempt to halt the tides of change. They turned out to be nothing more than a well-meaning bunch of Cnuts, though even some of the fashionistas seemed to jump camp – Sonia Rykiel joined the campaigners and Karl Lagerfeld opened his own photography gallery on rue de Seine. Nevertheless, St-Germain now almost rivals the avenue Montaigne for its designer boutiques. You can't fight evolution.

From the boulevard to the Seine

Hit by shortages of coal during World War II, Sartre descended from the ivory tower of his apartment on rue Bonaparte to save a bundle on heating bills. 'The principal interest of the **Café de Flore**,' he noted, 'was that it had a stove, a nearby Métro and no Germans.' Although

you can now spend more on a few coffees there than on a week's heating, the Flore (172 bd St-Germain) remains an arty favourite and hosts *café philo* evenings in English. Its rival, **Les Deux Magots** (6 pl St-Germain-des-Prés), now provides for an interesting cross-section of tourists. At No 151 is politicians' favourite **Brasserie Lipp**; at No 170 is the late-night bookshop and intelligentsia pick-up venue **La Hune**. Art nouveau fans should look out for the brasserie Vagenende (No 140).

Traces of the cloister and part of the Abbot's palace remain behind the church on rue de l'Abbaye. Built in 1586 in red brick with stone facing, it prefigures the place des Vosges. The charming place Furstenberg (once the stableyard of the Abbot's palace), now shades upmarket furnishing fabric stores and the house and studio where the painter Delacroix lived (*see chapter* **Museums**). Rue de l'Echaudé shows a typical St-Germain mix: bistro cooking at L'Echaudé-St-Germain (No 21). Ingres, Wagner and Colette lived on rue Jacob; its elegant 17th-century *hôtels* now contain

spare a thought for those who rest in its waters. Rather, you might spare a thought for how certain of them got there. On 17 October 1961, a demo was held near Bonne Nouvelle Métro station by Algerian immigrants, in protest at France's refusal to grant independence to its North-African colony. The CRS, the hard men of France's police force, were quick to the scene and quick to use live ammunition to protect their nation's *liberté*, *egalité* and, of course, *fraternité*. While contemporary newspapers reported three deaths, it is now widely believed that as many as 300 protestors were murdered that night.

Their bodies were dumped in the Seine. Still waters, eh? Ironically, today there is a dedicated river police force whose job it is to retrieve anyone who topples in while pricking sausages at a Seineside barbie, or wrap in tin foil those among the bodies beautiful who've had too much of the sun on the tanning *quais*. The river may meander along a seductive route, but beware, o potential skinny-dipper: Jacques Chirac promised that it would be clean by 1995. Eight years later, you're still advised against slipping into your flippers, unless, of course, you believe in the healing properties of sewerage.

Sightseeing

Stone poses at **Eglise St-Sulpice**. *See p126.*

specialist book, design and antiques shops, pleasant hotels and bohemian throwbacks including *chansonnier* bistro Les Assassins.

Further east, the rue de Buci hosts a street market, running into rue de Seine with a lively scene centred around the **Bar du Marché** and **Les Etages** cafés. Hotel La Louisane, on the same road, played host to jazz gods Chet Baker and Miles Davis and Existentialism deities Sartre and De Beauvoir. Rue Bonaparte (where Manet was born at No 5 in 1832), rue de Seine and rue des Beaux-Arts are still packed with small art galleries specialising in 20th-century abstraction, tribal art and art déco furniture (*see chapter* **Galleries**). Oscar Wilde complained about the wallpaper and then turned up his tootsies at what was then the Hôtel d'Alsace, now the renovated and still fashionably over-the-top **L'Hôtel** in rue des Beaux-Arts. La Palette and Bistro Mazarin are good stopping-off points with enviable terraces on rue Jacques-Callot. Rue Mazarine, with shops of lighting, vintage toys and jewellery, is now home to Conran's brasserie **L'Alcazar** (No 62) in a former cabaret. The **Ecole Nationale Supérieure des Beaux-Arts**, Paris' main fine-arts school and a former monastery, is at the northern end of rue Bonaparte. On the quai de Conti stands the **Institut de France**, recently cleaned to reveal its crisp classical decoration. Next door stands the neo-classical Hôtel des Monnaies, formerly the mint (1777-1973) and now the **Musée de la Monnaie**, a coin museum. Opposite, the iron Pont des Arts footbridge leads across to the Louvre.

Coffee was first brought to Paris in 1686 (Paris without coffee? Seems like Eden with no fruit tree or a Big Mac without a slice of gherkin) at Café Procope on rue de l'Ancienne-Comédie. Once frequented by Voltaire, Rousseau, Benjamin Franklin, revolutionary Danton and later Verlaine, it is now an attractive restaurant aimed at tourists; it contains some remarkable memorabilia, including Voltaire's desk and a postcard from Marie-Antoinette. The back opens on to the twee cobbled passage du Commerce St-André, home to toy shops, jewellers and chintzy tearooms. In the 18th century, Dr Joseph-Ignace Guillotin first tested out his notorious execution device – designed to make public executions more humane and destined to come in more than a little handy in revolutionary Paris – in the cellars of what is now the Pub St-Germain (currently undergoing refurbishment). The first victim was reputedly a sheep. Jacobin regicide Billaud-Varenne was one of those who felt the blade of Dr Guillotin's invention. His former home (45 rue St-André-des-Arts) was an incongruous location for the first girls' *lycée* in

Paris, the Lycée Fénelon, founded in 1883 ('Me? A girls' school? With *my* reputation?'). Formerly a 'des res', today rue St-André-des-Arts is lined with gift shops, crêperies and an arts cinema. Escape the main thoroughfare and make for the quiet side streets, such as rue des Grands-Augustins, rue de Savoie and rue Séguier, home to printers, bookshops and dignified 17th-century buildings. On the corner of rue and quai des Grands-Augustins, the restaurant Lapérouse still boasts a series of private dining rooms, where gentlemen like to entertain their *demi-monde* mistresses; while Les Bookinistes offers contemporary flavours. The turreted Hôtel de Fécamp, at 5 rue de Hautefeuille, was the medieval townhouse of the abbots of Fécamp, begun in 1292. Rue Gît-le-Coeur ('here lies the heart') is so-called, legend has it, because one of Henri IV's mistresses lived here. At No 9 is the now rather luxurious Hôtel du Vieux Paris, or the 'Beat Hotel', where William Burroughs revised *The Naked Lunch*. You thought it was a first draft, too, huh?

Ecole Nationale Supérieure des Beaux-Arts (Ensb-a)

13 quai Malaquais, 6th (01.47.03.52.15). M° Odéon or St-Michel. **Open** courtyard 9am-5pm Mon-Fri; exhibitions Tue-Sun 1-7pm. **Admission** exhibitions €4; €2.50 students, children, free under-12s. **Credit** V. **Map** p405 H6.

Paris' most prestigious fine-art school is installed in what remains of a 17th-century convent, the 18th-century Hôtel de Chimay and some later additions. After the Revolution, the buildings were trans-formed into a museum of French monuments, then in 1816 into the *Ecole*. Today it often puts on exhibitions (*see chapter* **Museums**).

The best Métros

Abbesses
One of two remaining Guimard art nouveau entrances. Amélie Poulain finds love here. (*Line 12, 18th arrondissement*).

Arts et Métiers
Very Jules Verne. (*Lines 3 and 11, 3rd arrondissement*).

Assemblée Nationale
Wall-to-wall French history. (*Line 12, 7th arrondissement*).

Louvre-Rivoli
A seriously statuesque station. (*Line 1, 1st arrondissement*).

Institut de France

23 quai de Conti, 6th (01.44.41.44.41/www.institut-de-france.fr). Mᵒ St-Germain-des-Prés. **Guided tours** Sat, Sun (call ahead for times). **Admission** €3.05. **No credit cards. Map** p406 H6.

The building was constructed by Mazarin as a school. In 1805 the five academies of the Institut (Académie Française, Académie des Inscriptions et Belles-Lettres, Académie des Sciences, Académie des Beaux-Arts, Académie des Sciences Morales et Politiques), were transferred here. Inside is Mazarin's ornate tomb by Hardouin-Mansart, and the Bibliothèque Mazarine. Access to the library is open to anyone over 18 who turns up with ID, two photos and €15.24 for a one-year library card. The Académie Française, the zealous (nay: jealous, nay: pointless) guardian of the French language was founded by Cardinal Richelieu in 1635 with the perhaps somewhat xenophobic aim of preserving the sacrosanct purity of French from all those corrupting outside influences. English, for example. The Immortals, as the members of the Academy are still pompously known, pluckily refuse to surrender and have never stopped trying to impose archaic rules on a language and a population which is embracing multi-cultural influences.

Eglise St-Germain-des-Prés

3 pl St-Germain-des-Prés, 6th (01.43.25.41.71). Mᵒ St-Germain-des-Prés. **Open** 8am-7.45pm Mon-Sat; 9am-8pm Sun. **Map** p405 H7.

This, ladies and gentlemen, is the oldest church in Paris. On the advice of Germain (later bishop of Paris), Childebert, son of Clovis (would you call your child Bert?), had a basilica and monastery built here around 543; it was originally called the Church of St Vincent and then came to be known as St-Germain-le-Doré because of its copper roof. During the Revolution the abbey was burnt and a saltpetre refinery installed; the spire was only added as part of a clumsy 19th-century restoration. Despite all this, most of the present structure is 12th-century, and some ornate carved capitals and the tower remain from the 11th. Tombs to keep an eye out for include that of Jean-Casimir, deposed king of Poland, who became abbot of St-Germain in 1669, and Scottish nobleman William Douglas. Under the window in the second chapel is philosopher and mathematician René Descartes' funeral stone; his ashes (bar those from his skull) have been lodging here since 1819.

St-Sulpice & the Luxembourg

South of boulevard St-Germain between Odéon and Luxembourg is a quarter that epitomises civilised Paris, full of historic buildings and interesting shops. Just off the boulevard lies the covered market of St-Germain, once the site of the medieval St-Germain Fair. Following redevelopment it now houses an underground swimming pool, auditorium, food hall and a shopping arcade. There are bars and bistros along rue Guisarde, nicknamed *rue de la soif* (street of thirst) thanks to its regular swarm of merry carousers. Rue Princesse and rue des Canettes are a beguiling mix of lively bistros, including Mâchon d'Henri and Brasserie

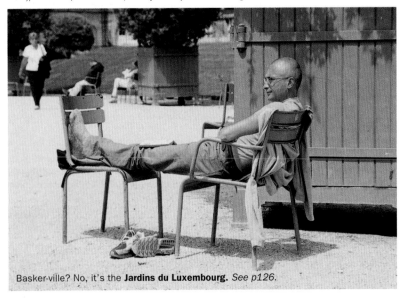

Basker-ville? No, it's the **Jardins du Luxembourg.** *See p126.*

Sightseeing

Fernand, budget eateries, Italian pizzerias and late-night haunts known to a determined – if unsteady – few: the Birdland bar, Bedford Arms and notoriously elitist nightspot **Club Castel**.

Pass the fashion boutiques, antiquarian book and print shops and high-class patisseries (note the huge queue outside Pierre Hermé, the supposed international emperor of patisserie) and you come to **Eglise St-Sulpice**, a surprising 18th-century exercise in classical form with two uneven turrets and a colonnaded facade. Delacroix painted the frescoes in the first chapel on the right. The square contains Visconti's imposing, lion-flanked Fontaine des Quatre Point Cardinaux (thus named because of the statues of Bossuet, Fénélon, Massilon and Flechier, none of whom, curiously enough, was actually a cardinal) and is used for an antiques fair and a poetry fair every summer. The **Café de la Mairie** remains a favourite with intellectuals and students, while amid shops of religious artefacts, the chic boutiques along place and rue St-Sulpice include Yves Saint Laurent, Christian Lacroix, **Agnès b**, **Vanessa Bruno**, **Muji**, perfumer Annick Goutal, the

furnishings of Catherine Memmi and milliner **Marie Mercié**. Prime shopping territory continues to the west: clothes shops on rue Bonaparte and rue du Four and leather, accessory and fashion shops on rue du Dragon, rue de Grenelle and rue du Cherche-Midi. If you spot a queue in the latter street, it's most likely for **Poilâne**'s designer bread. **Au Sauvignon**, at the busy carrefour de la Croix-Rouge, is a perfect place for people watching. 115 priests were killed in 1792 in the chapel of St-Joseph des Carmes (70 rue de Vaugirard), once a Carmelite convent, now hidden within the Institut Catholique. To the east lies wide rue de Tournon, lined by some grand 18th-century residences, such as the elegant Hôtel de Brancas (now the **Institut Français de l'Architecture**) with figures of Justice and Prudence over the door. This street opens up to the **Palais du Luxembourg**, which now serves as the Senate, and its adjoining park.

Returning towards boulevard St-Germain, you pass the neo-classical **Odéon, Théâtre de l'Europe**, built in 1779 and currently closed for renovation. Beaumarchais' *Marriage of Figaro* was first performed here in 1784. The semi-circular place in front was home to revolutionary hero Camille Desmoulins, at No 2, now *La Méditerranée* restaurant, designed by Jean Cocteau. Another hangout among the antiquarian bookshops on rue de l'Odéon is Le Bar Dix. Joyce's *Ulysses* was first published next door (No 12) by Sylvia Beach at the legendary **Shakespeare & Co** in 1922.

Up the street, at 12 rue de l'Ecole-de-Médecine, is the colonnaded neo-classical Université René Descartes (Paris V) medical school, also home to the **Musée d'Histoire de la Médicine** (*see chapter* **Museums**). The Club des Cordeliers cooked up revolutionary plots across the street at the Couvent des Cordeliers (No 15). Marat, one of the club's leading lights, met an undignified end in the tub at his home in the same street, when he was stabbed by Charlotte Corday. Look out for the sculpted doorway of the neighbouring *hôtel* and the domed building at No 5, once the barbers' and surgeons' guild. Climb up rue André-Dubois to rue Monsieur-le-Prince for the popular budget restaurant Polidor at 41, which has been feeding students and tourists since 1845 and, near the boulevard St-Michel, the **3 Luxembourgs** arts cinema.

Eglise St-Sulpice

pl St-Sulpice, 6th (01.46.33.21.78). Mᵒ St-Sulpice.
Open 8am-7pm daily. Good **Map** p405 H7.
If you look, you will notice that one of the church's two towers is shorter (actually a good five metres) than the other: designed by an architect with one leg longer than the other? No. It is, in fact, unfinished. The grandiose Italianate facade – and the towers – were designed by Jean-Baptiste Servandoni, although he died, in 1766, before the other tower was completed. Altogether, it took 120 years (starting from 1646) and six architects to finish the church; the *place* in front of the building and the fountain were designed in the 19th century by Visconti. Look out for three wonderful paintings by Delacroix in the first chapel: *Jacob's Fight with the Angel, Heliodorus Chased out of the Temple* and *St-Michael Killing the Dragon*. These lend a wonderfully sombre atmosphere to the interior.

Jardins and Palais du Luxembourg

pl Auguste-Comte, pl Edmond-Rostand or rue de Vaugirard, 6th. Mᵒ Odéon/RER Luxembourg.
Open dawn-dusk daily. **Map** p405 H8.
The *palais* was built in the 1620s for Marie de Médicis, widow of Henri IV, by Salomon de Brosse, on the site of the former mansion of the Duke of Luxembourg. Its Italianate, rusticated style was intended to remind her of the Pitti Palace in her native Florence. In 1621, she commissioned Rubens to pro

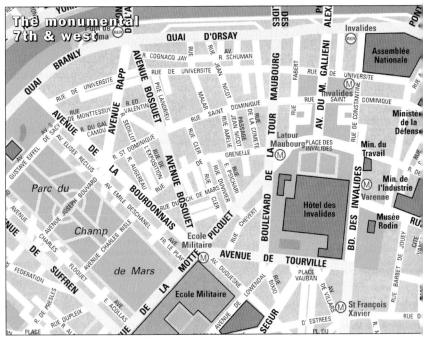

duce for the palace the 24 huge paintings celebrating her life (in various stages of undress) that are now in the Louvre. Reworked by Chalgrin in the 18th century, the *palais* now houses the French parliamentary assembly, the Senate. The gardens are the real draw today: part formal, with terraces and gravel paths, part 'English garden' of lawns, they are the quintessential Paris park. The garden is peopled with diverse sculpted *dramatis personae,* from the looming Cyclops on the 1624 Fontaine de Médicis, to queens of France, a mini Statue of Liberty and a monument to Delacroix. There are orchards, containing over 300 varieties of apples and pears, and an apiary where you can take courses in beekeeping (always impresses the ladies, that one, especially when they see the hat). The **Musée du Luxembourg** in the former Orangerie is used for art exhibitions. Most interesting, though, are the people: chess players, joggers in suspiciously tight shorts and martial arts practitioners; children on ponies, in sandpits, on roundabouts and playing with the old-fashioned sailboats on the lake. Then, there are the crazy old weirdos. There are positively the chicest tennis courts on the Left Bank *boules* pitches, a café and a bandstand, while the park chairs are the domain of book lovers, those looking for romance and those who seem quite recently to have chanced upon it and want the world to share their joy. (*See also chapter* **Children**).

Sunny and chairs: **Eglise St Germain-des-Prés.**

Sightseeing

The monumental 7th & west

Mainly 7th arrondissement, parts of 6th and 15th.
Townhouses spread out westwards from St-Germain into the 7th *arrondissement*, as the vibrant street and café life subsides in favour of tranquil residential blocks and government offices. The 7th easily divides into two halves: the more intimate Faubourg St-Germain to the east, with its historic mansions and fine shops and, to the west of Les Invalides, an area of windswept wide avenues and, of course, the **Eiffel Tower**.

The Faubourg St-Germain

Often written off by notorious old bore Proust as a symbol of staid, *haute bourgeoise* and aristocratic society, this area remains home to some of Paris' oldest and grandest families (*vive la Révolution!*), though most of its 18th-century *hôtels particuliers* have now been taken over by embassies and government ministries. You can admire their stone gateways and elegant courtyards, especially on rues de Grenelle, St-Dominique, de l'Université and de Varenne. Among the most beautiful is the Hôtel Matignon (57 rue de Varenne), residence of the Prime Minister; the facade is sometimes visible through the heavily guarded entrance portal.

Used by the French statesman Talleyrand for lavish receptions, it boasts the biggest private garden in Paris. The Cité Varenne at No 51 is a lane of exclusive houses with private gardens. You'll have to wait for the open-house *Journées du Patrimoine* (*see chapter* **Festivals and Events**) to see the decorative interiors and private gardens of others such as the Hôtel de Villeroy (Ministry of Agriculture, 78 rue de Varenne), Hôtel Boisgelin (Italian Embassy, 47 rue de Varenne), Hôtel d'Estrées (residence of the Russian ambassador, 79 rue de Grenelle), Hôtel d'Avaray (residence of the Dutch ambassador, 85 rue de Grenelle) or Hôtel de Monaco (Polish Embassy, 57 rue St-Dominique). Then there's rue du Bac where Bon Marche, Paris' oldest department store can still be found. Continuing westward along the Seine, facing the Pont de la Concorde and the place de la Concorde across the river, is the **Assemblée Nationale**, the lower house of the French parliament. Beside the Assemblée is the Foreign Ministry, often referred to by its address, the quai d'Orsay. Beyond it stretches the long, grassy esplanade leading up to the golden-domed **Invalides**, the vast military hospital complex which now houses the **Musée de l'Armée** and **Napoléon's tomb**. The two churches inside – St-Louis-des-Invalides and the Eglise du Dôme – glorify French monarchs. Stand with your back to the dome and you'll see that the esplanade gives a striking perspective across cherubim-laden **Pont Alexandre III** to

the Grand and Petit Palais, all three constructed for the 1900 *Exposition Universelle*.

Just beside Les Invalides, a far cosier place to visit (in fact, it's one of the city's major chill-out spots if you feel like taking things easy for a while) is the **Musée Rodin**, housed in the charming 18th-century Hôtel Biron and its romantic gardens. Rodin was invited to move here in 1908 on the understanding that he would bequeath his work to the state. As a result, you can now see many of his great sculptures, including *The Thinker* and *The Burghers of Calais*. You can also see the works of Rodin's talented pupil, Camille Claudel.

Assemblée Nationale

33 quai d'Orsay, 7th (01.40.63.60.00/ www.assemblee-nat.fr). M° Assemblée Nationale. **Open** 8.40-11.40am and 2-5pm Mon, Fri and Sat **Guided tours** all day approximately every 20 minutes; ID required. **Map** p405 F5.
The Palais Bourbon has held parliament's lower house since 1827. The palace was extended by the Prince de Condé, who added the Hôtel de Lassay, now official residence of the Assembly's president. Inside, the library is decorated with Delacroix's *History of Civilisation*. Visitors can attend debates.

Chapelle de la Médaille Miraculeuse

Couvent des Soeurs de St-Vincent-de-Paul, 140 rue du Bac, 7th (01.49.54.78.88). M° Sèvres-Babylone. **Open** 7.45am-1pm, 2.30-7pm Mon-Sat; 7.30am-2pm, 2.30-7pm Sun. **Map** p405 F7.
In 1830 saintly Catherine Labouré was visited by the Virgin, who gave her a medal which performed

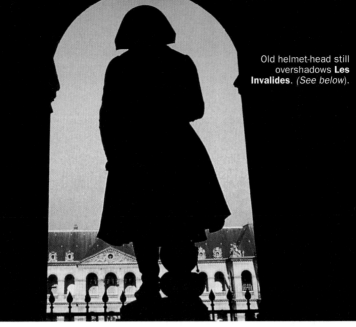

Old helmet-head still overshadows **Les Invalides**. *(See below).*

many miracles. Attracting over two million faithful every year, the kitsch chapel – a concoction of statues, mosaics and murals, and the embalmed bodies of Catherine and her mother superior – continues to be one of France's most visited pilgrimage sites. Reliefs recount the story of the nun's life.

Les Invalides

esplanade des Invalides, 7th (01.44.42.54.52/Musée de l'Armée 01.44.42.37.67/www.invalides.org). *M° Invalides.* **Open** Apr-Sept 10am-6pm daily; Oct-Mar 10am-5pm daily. **Admission** courtyard free. Musée de l'Armée & Eglise du Dôme €6; €4.50 students under 26; free under-18s, CM. **Credit** MC, V. **Map** p405 E6.

Despite its imposing gilded dome, the Hôtel des Invalides was (and in part still is) a hospital. Commissioned by Louis XIV to care for the war-wounded, at one time it housed up to 6,000 invalids – hence the name. The foundations were laid in 1671 and the design is Bruand's baby. Now the *hôtel* contains the **Musée de l'Armée** (*see chapter* **Museums**), with its staggering display of wartime paraphernalia, and Musée de l'Ordre de la Libération. Since 1840 the Baroque Eglise du Dôme has been dedicated to the worship of Napoléon, whose body is alleged to have been brought here from St Helena (there is now some doubt as to whose body is actually in the tomb; we could be looking at an exhumation). The church of St-Louis, known as the Church of the Soldiers, is decorated with captured flags and its crypt filled with the remains of military men. Cannon barrels are everywhere but it's worth a wander through the gardens and the principal courtyard, with its grandiose arcades and sundials, to get an idea of the power of royal patronage.

Musée d'Orsay

1 rue de la Légion d'Honneur, 7th (01.40.49.48.14/ recorded information 01.45.49.11.11/www.musee-orsay.fr). *M° Solférino/ RER Musée d'Orsay.* **Open** 10am-6pm Tue, Wed, Fri, Sat; 10am-9.30pm Thurs, 9am-6pm Sun. **Admission** €7; €5 students, over-60s, Sun; free under-18s; free first Sun of month. **Credit** (shop) AmEx, MC, V. **Map** p405 G6.

Originally a train station, beautifully designed by Victor Laloux to coincide with the 1900 *Exposition Universelle*, the Orsay is now home to masterpieces by Monet, Degas, Renoir, Gauguin and Van Gogh among others. Look out for the statues representing Toulouse, Bordeaux and Nantes, the towns the station originally served. By the 1950s, the platforms were too short for modern trains and the station was threatened with demolition. At this point, it became home to a theatre (the Renault-Barrault), and Orson Welles' film version of *The Trial* was shot here. It was saved in the late 1970s when President Giscard d'Estaing decided to turn it into a museum spanning the fertile art period 1830-1914. The interior was redesigned by Italian architect Gae Aulenti, and the main attraction is the skylit Impressionist gallery on the upper floor. *See also p155.*

West of Les Invalides

To the west of the Invalides is the massive **Ecole Militaire,** the military academy built by Louis XV to educate the children of penniless officers. It would later train Napoléon. Still used by the army, it is closed to the public. Opposite its south entrance are the Y-shaped

La cage aux folles

Since its founding in 1656, a tremendous throng of beggars, loons and ladies of the night – not to mention the People's Princess – have passed through the gates of La Salpêtrière. Now one of the showpieces of the French hospital system, it was in its time last call for the underbelly of French society.

In the 17th century, 'hospitals' had almost nothing to do with medicine in the modern sense. La Salpêtrière was founded as a kind of shelter or almshouse for women, where all kinds of 'undesirables' – the old, crippled, insane, or just plain poor – could receive care from the state, and more importantly, be segregated from the society they might pollute. Good intentions quickly became expedient solutions, and by 1679 the hospital also included a prison for prostitutes. Women were rounded up in the slums of Faubourg Saint-Antoine and Faubourg Saint-Marcel for charges as diverse as blasphemy, perversion and alchemy. Overcrowding soon lead to drastic solutions; beginning in 1680, prostitutes were chosen – often paired with men from Le Bicêtre – and shipped to the wilds of the colonies. No wonder Baton Rouge is such a party town.

The Revolution was bound to find its way to La Salpêtrière, gathering place of society's most humble elements. On 3 September 1792 a drunken mob descended on the gates, intending to liberate the prostitutes, but the scene rapidly deteriorated into full-scale debauchery. Some 600 women were raped in a two-day orgy, ending on the evening of 4 September with the murder of 35 women on the hospital grounds.

Until the 19th century, mental illness was viewed either as demonic possession or a failure of the will. The insane were grouped together with prostitutes, beggars, and petty criminals as the dregs of society. Little attempt at cure or classification was made, and 'patients' were regularly chained and left to rot. In 1795, Philippe Pinel arrived at La Salpêtrière, and in a gesture that many consider the beginning of modern psychology, freed the insane from their chains.

Work on the causes and classification of mental illness continued here with Esquirol, and culminated in Charcot's studies of hysteria. A pioneer in the field of neurology, Charcot was among the first to explore how psychology and physiology worked together to produce the symptoms of mental disease. Famous for his dramatic teaching style, he gave lectures on hysteria featuring nubile women who could faint on command. Among the students was the young Sigmund Freud.

La Salpêtrière's most famous visitor was more elevated than the traditional clientele. On 31 August 1997 Princess Diana was pronounced dead here after her car crash. Management have avoided naming the exact spot to which she was delivered, so as not to encourage its becoming a shrine.

Today, not much is left of the revolutions, medical and otherwise, that occurred here, but the old loony bin has broadened its activities. Charcot's library can be visited by appointment, and the chapel hosts classical music concerts at the weekends. The *Festival d'automne* uses the chapel to host big-name contemporary art exhibitions by the likes of Bill Viola, Anish Kapoor, and Jenny Holzer.

Chapelle St-Louis-de-la-Salpêtrière

47 bd de l'Hôpital, 13th (01.42.16.04.24). M° Gare d'Austerlitz. **Open** 8.30am-6.30pm daily. **Map** p406 L9.

UNESCO building, constructed in 1958, and the Modernist Ministry of Labour. But it's not all officialdom and bureaucracy: there's the old-fashioned bistro Thoumieux at 79 rue St-Dominique; at No 129, an arcaded square featuring the attractive Fontaine de Mars; smart food shops in rue Cler and one of Paris' prettiest street markets on the avenue de Saxe.

This area was once far more industrial. The corner of rue Surcouf and rue de l'Université is the site of the Manufacture du Gros Caillou, where France's first cigarettes were made in 1845. From the north-western side of the Ecole Militaire begins the vast **Champ de Mars**, a market garden converted into a military drilling ground in the 18th century. It's a popular place for Bastille Day celebrations, and it houses the beautiful **Mur pour la Paix**, erected in 2000 against the backdrop of the **Tour Eiffel** to celebrate the hopes brought by the new millenium. How long ago that seems. People are invited to leave their own messages for peace.

Les Egouts de Paris

entrance opposite 93 quai d'Orsay, by Pont de l'Alma, 7th (01.53.68.27.81). M° Alma-Marceau/ RER Pont de l'Alma. **Open** 11am-4pm Sat-Wed. Closed three weeks in Jan. **Admission** €3.80; €3.05 students, over 60s; €2.30 5-12s; free under 5s, CM. **Map** p404 D5.
For centuries the main source of drinking water in Paris was the Seine, which was also the main sewer. Thankfully, construction of an underground sewerage system began in 1825. Today, the Egouts de Paris is perhaps the smelliest museum in the world; each sewer in the 2,100km system is marked with a replica of the street sign above. Please note that the *Egouts* can be closed after periods of heavy rain. Believe us, it's for the best.

Eiffel Tower

Champ de Mars, 7th (01.44.11.23.45/recorded information 01.44.11.23.23/www.tour-eiffel.fr). M° Bir-Hakeim/RER Champ-de-Mars. **Open** Sept-9 June 9.30am-11pm daily; 10 June-Aug 9am-midnight. **Admission** By lift 1st level €3.70; €2.10 3-12s; 2nd level €6.90; €3.80 3-12s; 3rd level €9.90; €5.30 3-12s; free under-3s. By stairs (9.30am-6.30pm) 1st & 2nd levels €3. **Wheelchair access (1st & 2nd levels only).Credit** AmEx, MC, V. **Map** p404 C6.
It's hard to miss the Eiffel Tower. At 300m tall, when built in 1889 for the *Exposition Universelle,* it was the tallest building in the world. Now, with its aerial, it reaches 321m. The view of it from Trocadéro across the river is monumental, but the distorted aspect from its base most dramatically shows off the graceful ironwork of Gustave Eiffel and brings home its simply massive scale. Be prepared for a long wait for the lifts (which travel 100,000km a year). Even in the middle of winter, there's no shortage of people prepared to queue. In fact the number of visitors has led to a plan to add five levels of exhibition space by excavating beneath the tower. Those hardy souls

who go on to the top can view Eiffel's cosy salon and enjoy amazing panoramas: over 65km on a good day. At night the city lights against the Seine live up to their romantic image – and the queue is shorter. You can eat at the **Altitude 95** bistro on the first level or the super-smart **Jules Verne** on the second.

UNESCO

pl de Fontenoy, 7th (01.45.68.10.00/www.unesco.org). M° Ecole-Militaire. **Open** 9.30am-2.30pm Mon-Fri (For groups of six people). **Map** p404 D7.
The Y-shaped UNESCO headquarters was built in 1958 by a multinational team. A giant construction in concrete and glass, it is the combined work of a group of architects of three nationalities: American, Marcel Breuer, Italian, Pier Luigi Nervi and French, Bernard Zehrfuss, who in turn were selected by an

Cimetière du Montparnasse. *See p133.*

High-flying herbs in **Jardin de L'Atlantique.**

du Japon stands near the Pont Bir-Hakeim on quai Branly. The riverfront, with its tower block developments, was the scene of some of the worst architectural crimes of the 1970s. Further west there is hope: the sophisticated headquarters of the Canal+ TV channel (2 rue des Cévennes) are surrounded by fine modern housing, and the **Parc André Citroën**.

Parc André Citroën
rue Balard, rue St-Charles, quai Citroën, 15th.
M° Javel or Balard. **Open** dawn-6pm Mon-Fri; 9am-6pm Sat, Sun, holidays. **Map** p404 A9.
This park is a fun, 21st-century take on a French formal garden. It comprises glasshouses, computerised fountains, waterfalls, a wilderness and gardens with different-coloured plants and even sounds. Stepping stones and water jets prove that this is a garden for pleasure as well as philosophy. There's also a panoramic Paris in miniature.

Maison de la Culture du Japon
101 bis quai Branly, 15th (01.55.33.51.90).
M° Bir-Hakeim. RER Champ de Mars Tour Eiffel.
Open noon-7pm Tue, Wed, Fri, Sat; noon-8pm Thur.
Admission free. **Map** p404 C6.
Built in 1996 by the Anglo-Japanese architectural partnership of Yamanaka and Armstrong, this opalescent glass cultural centre reflects Paris' large Japanese community. There is a full programme of exhibitions, theatre and film, plus a library, authentic Japanese tea ceremony and a shop.

Montparnasse & beyond

Mainly 6th and 14th arrondissements, parts of 13th and 15th.
The legends of Montparnasse began in the early 1900s, when artists such as Picasso, Léger and Soutine fled to 'Mount Parnassus' from the rising rents in Montmartre. They were joined by Chagall, Zadkine and other escapees from the Russian Revolution and also by Americans, including Man Ray, Henry Miller, Ezra Pound and Gertrude Stein. Between the wars the neighbourhood symbolised modernity.
Today, Montparnasse is a less festive place. The high-rise **Tour Montparnasse**, is the most visible of several atrocious projects of the 1970s; at least there are good views from the top. The old Montparnasse railway station witnessed two events of historical significance: in 1898 a runaway train went out of control and burst through its facade; the Germans surrendered Paris here on 25 August 1944. In the summer of 2002, the station became the focus of a short-lived and cruel spectator sport: the middle lane of the station travelator was briefly speeded up in order to cope with increased traffic. It was almost immediately closed and blocked off, following the felling of various old dears who were unable to handle

international committee of five which included Swiss and Le Corbusier. It's worth visiting for the sculptures and paintings by Picasso, Arp, Giacometti, Moore, Calder and Miró. Inside it buzzes with palpable postwar idealism that can now add an air of poignancy. Behind there's a Japanese garden, with a concrete contemplation cylinder by Japanese minimalist architect Tadao Ando – just the sort of environment in which to experience a devastating attack of depersonalisation.

Village Suisse
38-78 av de Suffren/54 av de la Motte-Picquet, 15th (01.43.06.44.18). M° La Motte-Picquet-Grenelle.
Open 10.30am-1pm; 2-7pm Mon, Thur-Sun.
Map p404 D7.
The mountains and waterfalls created for the Swiss Village at the 1900 *Exposition Universelle* have long since gone, but the village lives on. Rebuilt as blocks of flats, the street level has been colonised by some 150 boutiques offering high-quality antiques and collectables. The village and its gardens are particularly popular on Sundays, but no matter when you go, if your doctor has advised you to avoid all forms of excitement, this is the place for you, sports fans.

Fronts de Seine

Downstream from the Eiffel Tower, the 15th *arrondissement* is rarely high on the tourist agenda. The high-tech **Maison de la Culture**

Sightseeing

the new velocity (to the glee of the assembled jackals who, within days of the fast lane's introduction, were taking bets on how long the frail would manage to stay upright). One of the fallen lost control of her shopping trolley and caused a domino-effect cascade.

Nearby, the ever-saucy rue de la Gaîté is known for its strip joints, but if you don't fancy the T&A routine, boulevard Edgar-Quinet has pleasant cafés and an organic street market (Wed, Sat mornings). The boulevard du Montparnasse still buzzes at night, thanks to its many cinemas and brasseries: the Dôme at No 108, now a fish restaurant and bar; giant art deco brasserie **La Coupole** at No 102, which opened in 1927; and opposite, classic late-night café **Le Select**. The boulevard also houses the main entrance to the Cimetière du Montparnasse. Further east, literary café **La Closerie des Lilas** was a favourite with everyone from Lenin and Trotsky to Picasso and Hemingway.

A more recent addition is the glass and steel **Fondation Cartier** by Jean Nouvel on boulevard Raspail, an exhibition centre for contemporary art. There are shoe, food and children's shops on rues Vavin and Bréa, which lead to the **Jardins du Luxembourg**. Stop for a coffee at Café Vavin and look at Henri Sauvage's white tiled apartment building at **6 rue Vavin**, built in 1911-12.

Cimetière du Montparnasse
3 bd Edgar-Quinet, 14th (01.44.10.86.50). M° Edgar-Quinet or Raspail. **Open** 16 Mar-5 Nov 8am-6pm Mon-Fri; 8.30am-6pm Sat; 9am-6pm Sun; 6 Nov-15 Mar 8am-5.30pm Mon-Fri; 8.30am-5.30pm Sat; 9.30am-5.30pm Sun. **Map** p401 G9.
The roll-call reads like a who-was-who of Left Bank cultural life. Pay homage to writers Jean-Paul Sartre and Simone de Beauvoir, Baudelaire, Maupassant, Tzara, Beckett, Ionesco and Duras; composers César Franck and Saint-Saëns; sculptors Dalou, Rude, Bartholdi, Laurens (with his own sculpture *Douleur* on the tomb) and Zadkine; Captain Alfred Dreyfus, and Mr and Mme Pigeon forever reposing in their

bed. From cinema and showbiz are Jean Seberg, star of *A bout de souffle,* and Serge Gainsbourg. Brancusi's sculpture *Le Baiser* (The Kiss), adorns a tomb in the north-east corner.

Jardin de l'Atlantique
entry from Gare Montparnasse or pl des Cinq-Martyrs-du-Lycée-Buffon, 15th. M° Montparnasse-Bienvenüe. **Open** dawn-dusk daily. **Map** p405 F9.
Perhaps the hardest of all Paris' gardens to find, the Jardin de l'Atlantique, opened in 1995, takes the Parisian quest for space airbound with an engineering feat suspended 18 metres over the tracks of Montparnasse station. It is a small oasis of granite paths, trees and bamboo in an urban desert of modern apartment and office blocks. Small openings allow you to peer down on the trains below.

Tour Maine-Montparnasse
33 av du Maine, 15th (01.45.38.52.56). M° Montparnasse-Bienvenüe. **Open** 9.30am-10.30pm daily. **Admission** exhibition/terrace €7.55; €6.40 students, over-60s; €5.18 5-14s; free under-5s. **No credit cards. Map** p405 F9.
Built in 1974 on the site of the former Gare Montparnasse, this steel-and-glass monster, at 209m high, is lower than the Eiffel Tower, but more central. A lift whisks you up to the 56th floor, where you'll find a display of aerial views of Paris. Classical concerts are held on the terrace.

Denfert-Rochereau & Montsouris
A spooky kind of burial ground can be found at place Denfert-Rochereau, entrance to the **Catacombs**. The bones of six million people were transferred here just before the Revolution from overcrowded Paris cemeteries to a network of tunnels that spreads under much of the 13th and 14th *arrondissements.* The entrance is next to one of the toll gates of the Mur des Fermiers-Généraux built by Ledoux in the 1780s. A bronze lion, sculpted by Bartholdi of Statue of Liberty fame, dominates the traffic junction. The nearby rue Daguerre is the focus of local life with its cafés and street market.

One of the big draws here is the **Parc**

The best ▶ Places for pondering

Cimetière du Montparnasse
High-achievers or apparent low-lifers, everybody checks into the Wooden Waldorf one day. *See p133.*

La Mosquée de Paris
A magnificently atmospheric place in which to gather your thoughts, whatever your faith. *See p120.*

Musée Rodin
You think therefore you are (in a museum surrounded by stunning sculpture, including *Le Penseur*). *See p128.*

Parc André Citroën
Stretch out and chill on the grass or pose pensively among the water features. *See p132.*

Montsouris. On its opening day in 1878 the man-made lake inexplicably emptied and the engineer responsible committed suicide. Around the western edge of the park are small streets such as rue du Parc Montsouris and rue Georges-Braque that were built up in the early 1900s with charming villas and artists' studios. On the southern edge of Montsouris is the **Cité Universitaire**, home to 6,000 foreign students.

Les Catacombes

1 pl Denfert Rochereau, 14th (01.43.22.47.63) M° *Denfert-Rochereau* **Open** 11am-4pm Tue; 9am-4pm Wed-Sun. Closed public holidays. **Admission** €5; €3.30 over 60s; €2.60 students, 14-26s; free under-14s. **No credit cards. Map** p405 H10.

These miles of dark, subterranean passages have existed since Roman times. Towards the end of the 18th century many of the old over-crowded Paris cemeteries suffered from overflow and corpses started to shoot into people's cellars. Decency and hygiene meant that something had to be done; the bodies were transferred here with delicacy and taste. Neatly arranged stacks of bones are interspersed by tidy rows of skulls, while mottoes and quotations inscribed on stone tablets add reflections on death that must have brought tears to the eyes of many a Goth. There are supposedly bits of some six million people down here, including many victims of the Revolutionary Terror. Don't be deterred by the warning at the entrance to the ossuary: 'Stop! This is the empire of death!'. It's all very Vincent Price and not at all terrifying.

ZAC's the way, uh-huh, uh-huh

Take it from us: the 13th *arrondissement* is about to become the coolest area in Paris. 'But how? Through which means of urban regeneration?' you ask. Through four: the construction of the Bibliothèque Nationale de France breathed life into what had become the sort of place blues men wail about, a desolate area formerly taken up by lonesome railway yards; the continual pull of the floating club, the **Batofar**; the artsy scene growing up around **rue Louise Weiss;** and, most influentially, the **ZAC-Rive Gauche** project.

This project, which is now beginning to blossom after a decade's hard slog (it was launched back in the days when Jacques Chirac was Mayor), will culminate in the creation of a new university, the none-too-

catchily named Université de Paris VII Denis Diderot. The ambition and scope of the project is impressive; this is the biggest building programme in Paris since the construction of La Défense. The area will house the Diderot University, the National Institute of Oriental Languages and Civilisations and a study and research centre for sports science. The aim is to create nothing less than a 21st-century Latin Quarter. Students and faculties will co-exist with the 'real world', in the form of atelier-dwellers and businesses, who've been encouraged to move into the area in order to prevent it becoming too rarified. Could this demolition of the ivory tower existence be the death-knell for the student pseud? Bring it on! Whatever the genre of student it fosters, the university will cater for over 25,000 students and 4,000 teaching staff when it opens in 2004. Architecturally, the project's not all slash and burn; existing industrial buildings in the area, such as Les Frigos former refrigerated warehouses (now containing artists' studios), and the majestic Grands Moulins de Paris, partly burnt down in 1996, will be incorporated. A new main street, the avenue de France, is being constructed over the railway tracks. Currently much of the area resembles a building site as new office buildings and appartment complexes appear overnight, shops open and roads change names. Temporary building site it may be, but it's no dump, as grafitti artists have moved in in force and coloured the place in. It's going to be fascinating to see if the theory behind the whole project will live up to its aim; if it does, the ZAC Rive Gauche will give the entire Left Bank a completely new image.

Cité Universitaire

bd Jourdan, 14th. (www.ciup.fr). RER Cité Universitaire.
The Cité Universitaire is an odd mix. The 40 pavilions spread across lanscaped gardens were designed in supposedly national style, some by architects of the country like the De Stijl Collège Néerlandais by Willem Dudok; others in exotic pastiche like the Asie du Sud-Est pavilion with its Khmer sculptures and bird-beak roof. The Swiss (1935) and Brazilian (1959) pavilions are by Le Corbusier.

Parc Montsouris

bd Jourdan, 14th. RER Cité-Universitaire.
The most colourful of the capital's parks. Laid out by Alphand, its gently sloping lawns descend towards an artificial lake, with turtles and ducks and a variety of trees and flowerbeds.

A growing flotilla of music bars moored on the Seine – the Batofar, Péniche Blues Café and Péniche Makara – is also providing signs of new life in the air, bringing in the clubbers, who just might help those student types relax a bit. Across the railway, an art nucleus called ScèneEst is burgeoning among the offices and housing developments. Further vivacity comes via the artsy mob: many gallery spaces are clustered around rue Louise Weiss, which held a five-year anniversary party in 2002, showcasing the modern installations and conceptual works of an international spectrum of young artists (*see chapter* **Galleries**). Overlooking the boulevards des Amiraux, Le Corbusier's Armée du Salut hostel (12 rue Cantagrel, 13th/01.53.61.82.00) points to earlier urban planning.

The 15th arrondissement

Tranquil and residential and with a Mona Lisa-style inscrutable allure, the 15th, centred on the shopping streets of rue du Commerce and rue Lecourbe, is Paris' largest *arrondissement* and probably the one that has the least for the tourist. Having said that, it's worth making a detour to visit **La Ruche** ('beehive'), designed by Eiffel as a wine pavilion for the 1900 exhibition and resituated here as artists' studios. Nearby on rue des Morillons the **Parc Georges Brassens** was opened in 1983. **Porte de Versailles** is home to Paris' international exhibition centre which was created in 1923 to house the Foire de Paris, previously held at the Champ de Mars. It attracts millions of visitors and is now the fourth-largest exhibition space in Europe, hosting everything from agricultural expositions to fashion shows.

Parc Georges Brassens

rue des Morillons, 15th. M° Porte de Vanves.
Map p404 D10.
Built on the site of the former Abattoirs de Vaugirard, parc Georges Brassens prefigured the industrial regeneration of parc André Citroën and La Villette. The gateways crowned by bronze bulls have been kept, as have a series of iron meat market pavilions, which house a busy antiquarian and second-hand book market at weekends. The interesting Jardin des Senteurs is planted with aromatic species while, in one corner, a small vineyard produces 200 bottles of Clos des Morillons every year.

La Ruche

passage de Dantzig, 15th. M° Convention.
Map p404 D10.
Peek through the grille or sneak in behind an unsuspecting resident to see the former wine pavilion, rebuilt here by philanthropic sculptor Alfred Boucher to be let out as studios for struggling artists. Chagall, Soutine, Brancusi and Modigliani all spent periods here, and the 140 studios are still much sought after by artists.

The 13th arrondissement

The 13th *arrondissement*, not hitherto recognised as Paris' most happening area, is set to become the city's focal point of fun (*see left*, **ZAC's the way, uh-huh, uh-huh**).

Gobelins & La Salpêtrière

Its image may be of tower blocks, but the 13th also contains some historic parts, especially where it borders on the 5th. The **Manufacture Nationale des Gobelins** is home to the French state weaving companies. The gear

Sightseeing

produced here continues a tradition dating back to the 15th century. The river here became notorious for its pollution, while the slums were depicted in Hugo's *Les Misérables*. The area was finally tidied up in the 1930s. On rue des Gobelins, the so-called **Château de la Reine Blanche** is a curious medieval relic.

The busy road intersection of place d'Italie has seen more developments with, opposite the town hall, the Centre Commercial Italie 2, a bizarre high-tech confection designed by Japanese architect Kenzo Tange, which contains the **Gaumont Grand Ecran Italie** cinema.

Château de la Reine Blanche
17 rue des Gobelins, 13th. M° Gobelins. **Map** p406 K10. Through a gateway you can spot the turret and first floor of an ancient house. The curious relic is named after Queen Blanche of Provence who had a *château* here, but was probably rebuilt in the 1520s for the Gobelins. Blanche was also associated with the Couvent des Cordeliers (a centre of theological teaching), of which a fragment survives on the corner of rue Pascal and rue de Julienne.

Manufacture Nationale des Gobelins
42 av des Gobelins, 13th (01.44.08.52.00). M° Gobelins. **Open** visits by guided tour only, 2.15 and 2.30pm Tue-Thur (90 mins); reserve in advance on 01.44.54.19.33 **Admission** €7.62; €6.10 7-24s. **No credit cards. Map** p406 K10.
Named after Jean Gobelin, a dyer who previously owned the site, the factory was at its wealthiest during the *ancien régime* when tapestries were produced for royal residences under artists such as Le Brun and Oudry. Today tapestries are still woven and visitors can watch weavers work. The guided tour (in French) through the 1912 factory helps you to understand the weaving process and takes in the 18th-century chapel and the Beauvais tapestry workshops. Arrive 30 minutes before the tour.

Chinatown

South of the rue de Tolbiac is Paris' main Chinatown, centred between the '60s tower blocks along avenues d'Ivry and de Choisy, and home to an Asian community. The bleak modern architecture could make it depressing if you're affected by that sort of thing (and what about the people who have to live here?), yet it's a fascinating piece of South-East Asia sur Seine, lined with restaurants, Vietnamese *pho* noodle bars and Chinese patisseries, as well as the large Tang Frères supermarket on avenue d'Ivry. Less easy to find is the Buddhist temple hidden in an underground car park beneath the tallest tower block (Autel du la culte de Bouddha, av d'Ivry, opposite rue Frères d'Astier-de-la-Vigerie, open 9am-6pm daily). Come here for the traditional lion and dragon dances at Chinese New Year (*see chapter* **Festivals and Events**).

La Butte aux Cailles and the developing east

In contrast to Chinatown, the villagey Butte aux Cailles is a neighbourhood of old houses, winding cobblestone streets and funky bars and restaurants. This workers' neighbourhood, home in the 1800s to many small factories, was one of the first to fight during the 1848 Revolution and the Paris Commune. The Butte has preserved its insurgent character and has resisted the aggressive forces of city planning and construction companies. The cobbled rue de la Butte-aux-Cailles and the rue des Cinq-Diamants are the HQ of the arty, *soixante-huitard* bohemian forces. The cottages built in 1912 in a mock-Alsatian style at 10 rue Daviel were one of the earliest public housing schemes in Paris. Further south, explore passage Vandrezanne, the square des Peupliers, the rue Dieulafoy and the streets of the Cité Florale.

The Butte offers a selection of relaxed, inexpensive bistros: Le Temps des Cérises, run as a cooperative, busy **Chez Gladines** and more upmarket Chez Paul. Several feisty bars, including **La Folie en Tête** and Le Merle Moqueur, provide music and cheap beer on tap to a youthful crowd spilling on to the pavement.

Bibliothèque Nationale de France François Mitterrand
quai François-Mauriac, 13th (01.53.79.53.79/www.bnf.fr). M° Bibliothèque or Quai de la Gare. **Open** 10am-8pm Tue-Sat; noon-7pm Sun. Closed two weeks in Sept/Oct and two weeks in Aug. **Admission** day €3; annual €30; student €15. **Credit** MC, V. **Wheelchair access. Map** p406 M10.
Opened in December 1996, the new national library (dubbed 'TGB' or *Très Grande Bibliothèque*) was the last of Mitterrand's *Grands Projets* and also the most expensive. It certainly seems imperial in its ambition. The architect, Dominique Perrault, was criticised for his curiously dated-looking design, which hides readers underground and stores the books in four L-shaped glass towers. He was also criticised for forgetting to include blinds to protect the books from sunlight; they had to be added after construction. In the central void is a garden (filled with 140 trees, uprooted from Fontainebleau at a cost of 40 million francs). Those who are interested in such minor details as the destination of tax-payers' money will be relieved to hear that nowhere near enough dosh was channelled into the prosaic activity of making things work. The research section opened in autumn 1998, whereupon the computer system failed and staff promptly went on strike. The library houses over ten million volumes, and has room for 3,000 readers. Books, newspapers and periodicals are on public access to anyone over 18. There are regular concerts and exhibitions. (*for other libraries see p380.*)

Beyond the Périphérique

Just outside Paris lies an intriguing suburban mix. You'll find sites of national triumph, sites of national shame, des-res heaven and housing estate hell.

Boulogne & the west

Paris' most conventionally desirable suburbs lie to the west, where the middle classes built expensive properties between the wars. Decentralisation also means that La Défense, Neuilly, Boulogne, Levallois and Issy-les-Moulineaux have become work locations for Paris residents, notably in the advertising, media and service industries, so week days see an influx of sharp suits and business bouffants.

Neuilly-sur-Seine is the most sought-after residential suburb. Smart apartment blocks have gradually replaced the extravagant mansions built around the **Bois de Boulogne**.

Boulogne-Billancourt is the main town in the region outside Paris. In 1320 the Gothic Eglise Notre Dame was begun in tribute to a statue of the Virgin washed up at Boulogne-sur-Mer. By the 18th century, Boulogne was known for its wines and laundries and, early in the 20th century, for its artist residents (Landowski, Lipchitz, Chagall, Gris), while Billancourt was

known for cars, aviation and cinema. The former Renault factory has been sitting in the Seine like a school disco wallflower since it closed in 1992, but it has a big future as the Fondation Pinault contemporary art museum, which it will finally become in 2006. Near the Bois de Boulogne are elegant villas, and some fine examples of 1920s and 30s architecture. The **Musée des Années 30** (*see p168*) focuses on artists and architects who lived in the town at the time. Across the Seine, the **Parc de St-Cloud** is surrounded by villas. South of St-Cloud is Sèvres, site of the **Musée National de Céramique** (*see p165*).

The **Château de Malmaison** at Rueil-Malmaison was loved by Napoléon and Joséphine. The eccentric Château de Monte Cristo (01.30.61.61.35) at Port Marly was built for Alexandre Dumas with a tiled Moorish room. In the grounds, the Château d'If folly is inscribed with the titles of his many works.

St-Germain-en-Laye is a smart suburb with a château, where Henri II lived in style with his wife Catherine de Médicis and his

Les Jardins Albert Kahn

14 rue du Port, 92100 Boulogne (01.46.04.52.80).
M° Boulogne-Pont St Cloud. **Open** *May-Sept* 11am-
7pm Tue-Sun; *Oct-Apr* 11am-6pm Tue-Sun.
Admission €3.30; €2.20 13-25s, over-60s; free
under-13s, disabled. **Credit** V.
With red bridges, Japanese shrines, Alsatian forests
and cascading streams, the gardens created by
financier Albert Kahn (1860-1940) should be twee,
yet somehow never are. There's an enormous ·
variety crammed in a small space. *Wheelchair access.*

Parc de St-Cloud

92210 St-Cloud (01.41.12.02.90). M° Pont de St
Cloud. **Open** *Mar-Apr* 7.30am-8.50pm daily; *May-*
Aug 7.30am-9.50pm daily; *Sept-Oct* 7am-8.50pm
daily; *Nov-Feb* 7.30am-7.50pm daily. **Admission**
free; €3.50 cars. **No credit cards.**
This is another classic French park laid out by Le
Nôtre, and all that remains of a royal château that
belonged to 'Monsieur', brother of Louis XIV. There
are complex avenues that meet in stairs, long perspectives, a great view over Paris from the Rond-
Point du Balustrade and a series of pools and ·
fountains: most spectacular is the Grande Cascade,
a multi-tiered feast of dolphins and sea beasts
(switched on 2pm, 3pm, 4pm Sun in June).

Villa Savoye

82 rue de Villiers, 78300 Poissy (01.39.65.01.06/
www.fondationlecorbusier.asso.fr). RER Poissy + 15
min walk. **Open** *1 Mar-31 Oct* 10am-5.30pm Tue-
Sun; *2 Nov-28 Feb* 10am-5pm Tue-Sun. **Admission**
€4; €2.50 18-25s; free under-18s. **Credit** MC, V.
Built in 1929 for a family of rich industrialists, this
luxury house with its sculptural spiral staircase and
roof terraces is perhaps Le Corbusier's most successful work. Inside are some seminal pieces of
Modernist furniture. *Wheelchair access.*

La Défense

La Défense's skyscrapers and walkways create
the feeling of another world. The area is lively,
though: business in the week, and filled with
visitors at the weekend.

La Défense is named after a stand against the
Prussians in 1870: in 2001, its martial
associations were underlined when the tensions
caused by dreadful social conditions and the
failure of French society to assimilate its
immigrant population erupted into a two-hour
gang battle. Ironically, La Défense has been a
showcase for French business since the mid-
50s, when the triangular CNIT exhibition hall
(01.46.92.11.11/open 9am-6pm Mon-Sat) was
built for trade shows, but it was the **Grande**
Arche that gave the district a true monument.
More than 100,000 people work here, and
another 35,000 live in the futuristic blocks of
flats on the southern edge. None of the
skyscrapers display any great architectural

La Défense: other worldly. *See right.*

mistress Diane de Poitiers. Here Louis XIV was
born, Mary Queen of Scots grew up, and the
deposed James II lived for 12 years. Napoléon
III turned the château into the **Musée des**
Antiquités Nationales (*see p164*). Outside,
its park forms a famous weekend promenade.
The **Musée Départemental Maurice**
Denis (*see p154*) has a collection of Nabi
and Post-Impressionist art.

Further west, the town of Poissy merits a
visit for its Gothic Collégiale Notre Dame (8 rue
de l'Eglise), much restored by Viollet-le-Duc,
and Le Corbusier's avant-garde **Villa Savoye**.

Château de Malmaison

av du Château, 92500 Rueil-Malmaison
(01.47.49.48.15). M° Grande Arche de la Défense/
RER La Défense. **Open** *Oct-Mar* 10am-5pm daily;
Apr-Sept 10am-5.45pm daily. **Admission** Short visit
€4; €2.50 18-25s; free under 18s; Long visit €4.50;
€3.50 18-25; free under 18s. **No credit cards.**
This was Napoléon and Joséphine's love nest.
Bought by Joséphine in 1799, it was the Emperor's
favourite retreat during the Consulate (1800-03).
After the couple's divorce, Napoléon gave the
château to his ex, who died here in 1814. Following
his defeat at Waterloo, Boney paused for one last
visit to the château before sloping off to exile. All
that historical-romantic relevance has not gone to
waste: today the château is open, not only for sightseeing purposes, but as a wedding venue, too.

The under dogs

Et in arcadia doggo. What must befall Titus, Brutus, Ramses and Virgil also robs us of dear Poupy, Poupette, Teddy and Chouchou. Fate spares no dog. When souls have flown, bones must be buried. The aforementioned pooches are among the 55,000 who have been spared the indignity of the back garden and rest in the Père Lachaise of animal graveyards, the Cimetière des Chiens.

Founded in 1899 by French feminist Marguerite Durand, the cemetery lies on the northern edge of Paris, on a small river island. Tall trees flutter as visitors traverse a stone gateway, topped at each end by bushy-tailed statues. The Seine, like time, marches solemnly alongside. Rather spookily, the cemetery is also crawling with cats – alive, and staring at visitors from headstone perches – it's all very Edgar Allen Poe. The felines belong to one of the keepers, who nod in recognition to regular mourners as they drift in, making sometimes daily vigils to their beloveds' gravesides.

It's hard to know what to do in a graveyard full of unknowns, particularly when flowers are being offered and memorial photos polished not far away. The graves themselves, each intensely personal, are fascinating: Some have chosen portraits of the furry faithful, others gnomes, trinkets and statues – everything speaks of uninhibited devotion. One lucky canine named 'Arry' has a bowl of tennis balls ready for play on top of his grave – the torture must be immense. Sultan Galant vom Hatzfeld (1981-96) reposes in a resplendent shrine of Corinthian columns and shiny marble. One can only imagine what kind of dog he was (although it has to be something fairly high maintenance).

Other graves say it with words (which almost always exceed a dog's core understood vocab of 'bifteck', 'promenade' and 'NON!'). 'Your boundless affection was the light of my life; I am so unhappy without you and your wonderful gaze,' chokes the owner of Youpi. And, more simply: 'For you, my loyal Pussy, I will always have eternal tenderness.' Words fail one.

All the '*fidèle compagnons*' are buried via some kind of funeral – it's not just a dead dog, a grieving owner and a shovel. Music is not unusual at the ceremonies. The cemetery proves that dog-love can be poignant. One grave pays tribute to 'our only friend.'

Underneath (aptly named) Faust's grave is the assertion that he was 'too intelligent to live'. So why did he dash out into the road, then? 'Disappointed by humans, never by my dog,' spits the epitaph of Liang. Not much mushy feeling there. It's a far cry from the indulgent philanthropy of Durand, who was so kind she also set up a summer rest-house for the benefit of over-worked female journalists. Imagine.

But, bone-picking aside, this is a caring and sharing kind of place. Who could fail to be touched by the tear-jerking statue of Barry the St-Bernard, who, in true selflessness, saved the lives of 40 people, and was killed by the 41st? Or by the tomb of a stray who died at the cemetery gates, or by the grave of 'Petit Boby', who only lasted ten months? It's a dog's life, clearly.

Cimetière des Chiens

4 pont de Clichy, 92600 Asnières (01.40.86.21.11). M° Mairie de Clichy. **Open** 16 Mar-14 Oct 10am-6pm Mon, Wed-Sun; 15 Oct-15 Mar 10am-4.30pm, Mon, Wed-Sun. Admission €3; €1 6-12s. **No credit cards**.

Sightseeing

distinction, although together they make an impressive sight. A recent wave of development has seen westward growth and includes a new 40-storey tower by Pei Cobb Freed and a church by Franck Hammoutène. The Info-Défense kiosk (01.47.74.84.24/ open Apr-Oct 10am-6pm, Nov-Mar 9.30am-5.30pm Mon-Fri) in front of CNIT has maps and guides of the area.

La Grande Arche de la Défense

92400 Paris la Défense (01.49.07.27.57/ www.grandearche.com). M° La Défense. **Open** *Apr-Sept* 10am-8pm; *Oct-Mar* 10am-7pm. **Admission** €7; €5.50 under 18s, students. **Credit** AmEx, MC, V. Completed for the bicentenary of the Revolution in 1989, the Grande Arche, designed by obscure Danish architect Johan Otto von Spreckelsen, is now a major tourist attraction. A stomach-churning ride in high-speed glass lifts soars up through the 'clouds' to the roof where there is a fantastic view into Paris. Outside on the giant forecourt are fountains and sculptures by artists including Miró, Serra, Calder and César's *Thumb. Wheelchair access.*

St-Denis & the north

Amid the suburban sprawl stands one of the treasures of Gothic architecture: the Basilique St-Denis, where most of France's monarchs were buried. St Denis also boasts the innovative **Musée de l'Art et d'Histoire de St-Denis** (*see p170*) in a scrupulously preserved Carmelite convent, a busy covered market, and some fine modern buildings, such as Niemeyer's 1989 HQ for Communist newspaper *L'Humanité* and Gaudin's extension to the town hall. Across the canal is the elegant **Stade de France**, designed for the 1998 Football World Cup. The département of Seine St-Denis also has a lively cultural life, with a buzzing theatre scene and prestigious jazz and classical music festivals. Le Bourget, home to Paris' first airport contains the **Musée de l'Air et de l'Espace** (*see p177*). North of Sarcelles, Ecouen, noted for its Renaissance château, now the **Musée National de la Renaissance** (*see p166*), gives glimpses of a rural past. Enghien-les-Bains, set around a large lake where you can hire rowing boats and pedalos, provided a pleasure haven in the 19th century with the development of its spa, a casino (the only one in the Paris region) and a racecourse. In the centre of the St-Denis suburb is the memorial to the people who died in the World War II internment camp at **Drancy**.

Basilique St-Denis

6 rue de Strasbourg, 93200 St-Denis (01.48.09.83.54). M° St-Denis-Basilique. **Open** *Apr-Sept* 10am-6.15pm Mon-Sat; noon-6.15pm Sun. *Oct-Mar* 10am-5.15pm Mon-Sat; noon-5.15pm Sun. **Admission** nave free. Royal tombs €5.50 per person (€4.50 per person in a group); €3.50 18-25s, students, over 60s; free under-18s. Guided tours 11.15am, 3pm Mon-Sat, 12.15pm Sun. **No credit cards.**

Legend has it that when St-Denis was beheaded, he picked up his head and walked to Vicus Catulliacus (now St-Denis) to be buried. The first church, parts of which can be seen in the crypt, was built over his tomb in around 475. The present edifice is the first example of true Gothic architecture. The basilica was begun by Abbot Suger in the 12th century. In the 13th, master mason Pierre de Montreuil erected the spire and rebuilt the choir, nave and transept. This was the burial place for all but three French monarchs between 996 and the end of the *ancien régime*, so the ambulatory is a museum of French funerary sculpture. During the Revolution in 1792, the tombs were desecrated and the royal remains thrown into a pit nearby.

Eglise Notre Dame du Raincy

av de la Résistance, 93340 Le Raincy
(01.43.81.14.98). SNCF/RER E Raincy-Villemomble.
Open 10am-noon, 2-6pm Mon-Sat; 10am-noon Sun.
Auguste Perret's little-known modernist master-piece was built 1922-23 as a modest war memorial. In place of conventional stained glass, the windows are coloured glass blocks that create fantastic reflections on the interior.

Le Mémorial de la Déportation du Camp de Drancy

15 rue Arthur Fontaine, 93700 Asnières
(01.48.95.35.05). M° Mairie de Clichy.
In 2001, the French government made the remains of Drancy, the camp in which people were interned in World War II, into an historic monument. It was not before time. This site was originally built as a housing estate in the 1930s. In August 1941, 4,232 Jews – many of whom had fled to France hoping for refuge from oppressive regimes elsewhere in Europe – were interned at the unfinished concrete camp. From here, most of the inmates were customarily shipped to Auschwitz (a total of some 70,000 people in all). The internment camp was staffed by French Gendarmes. A small memorial exhibition was opened in 1989, and there is a memorial sculpted by Shelomo Selinger.

Stade de France

rue Francis de Pressensé, 93200 St-Denis
(01.55.93.00.00/www.stadefrance.fr). M° St-Denis Porte de Paris/RER B La Plaine-Stade de France/RER D-Stade de France St-Denis. **Open** 10am-6pm daily. **Admission** €6 adults; €4.50 children; free under 6s. *Coulisses du Stade* (10am, 2pm, 4pm) €14; €10 6-17s, students; free under-6s (visit in English 2pm). **Credit** MC, V.
The Stade de France, designed by Zublèna, Macary, Regembal and Constantini, was built in an astonishing 31 months – just in time for the French team's 1998 football World Cup triumph. Happily, it was not demolished following their 2002 World Cup disaster. Its bleak saucer-like steel and aluminium roof has become a landmark. (Paris St-Germain play, of course, at Parc des Princes, sports fans). *Wheelchair access.*

Vincennes & the east

The more upmarket residential districts in the east surround the Bois de Vincennes, such as Vincennes, home to Paris' main zoo. Joinville-le-Pont and Champigny-sur-Marne draw weekend crowds along the banks of the Marne.

Château de Vincennes

av de Paris, 94300 Vincennes (01.48.08.31.20).
M° Château de Vincennes. **Open** Oct-Mar 10am-noon, 1.15pm-5pm daily; *Apr-Sept* 10am-noon, 1.15 - 6pm daily. **Admission** Short visit €4; €2.50 18-25s; free under 18s; Long visit €5.50; €3.50 18-25; free under 18s. **No credit cards.**
An imposing curtain wall encloses this medieval fortress. The square keep was begun by Philippe VI and completed by Charles V, who also began rebuilding the newly-renovated Flamboyant-Gothic Sainte-Chapelle. Louis XIII had the Pavillon du Roi and Pavillon de la Reine built by Louis Le Vau.

Pavillon Baltard

12 av Victor Hugo, 94130 Nogent-sur-Marne
(01.43.24.76.76/www.pbpa.net). RER Nogent-sur-Marne. **Open** during salons/exhibitions only.
When Les Halles was demolished someone had the foresight to save one of Baltard's iron and glass market pavilions and resurrect it in the suburbs.

Sceaux & the south

Bordering Paris, the 'red' suburb of Malakoff houses many artists. Sceaux was formerly the setting for a château built for Louis XIV's finance minister Colbert. The present building housing the Musée de l'Ile de France (01.46.61.06.71) dates from 1856. At Châtenay-Malabry, the 1930s Cité de la Butte-Rouge garden-city estate was a model of its time for social housing. The south-eastern suburbs boomed during 19th-century. Ivry is famed for social policies, such as the L'Atelier housing projects. The bleak new town of Evry is of note for housing estates like Les Pyramides and the modern **Cathédrale de la Résurrection**.

Arcueil Aqueduct

Spanning the Bièvre valley through Arcueil and Clamart, this impressive double-decker structure brings water from Wissous to Paris. A Roman structure existed a few metres from this one. In 1609 Henri IV decided to reconstruct the aqueduct, and by 1628 it provided water for 16 Paris fountains.

Cathédrale de la Résurrection

1 clos de la Cathédrale, 91000 Evry (01.64.97.93.53). SNCF Evry-Courcones. **Open** 10am-noon, 2-6pm Mon-Sat; 2.30-7pm Sun.
Completed in 1995, this was the first new cathedral in France since the war. Mario Botta's rather heavy, truncated, red-brick cylindrical form seeks to establish a new aesthetic for religious architecture.

Sightseeing

Paris Power Strut

Tired of those fey and feeble city strolls? Then get your trotting boots around this one: it knackers the parts other walks simply cannot reach.

When you do a walk, you want to feel you're doing a walk, not some lightweight lollop, right? So how's about a 15-mile, seven-hour circular trot around the whole of Paris? This little belter is an event in itself, and, of course, if you don't fancy the whole stroll in one shot, we've broken it down into the eminently do-able chunks you'll find below. Get up early. Wear trainers. Take water. Think positive. To make things easier for you, we've put the roads you should look out for in **bold**.

Montmartre – Boulevard de Clichy

Sit on the steps of **Sacré-Coeur** for a view of the terrain to be covered. Take a deep breath, shake hands – your own if necessary – and turn to face the domes. Walk to the left of them up **rue du Chevalier-de-La-Barre**. Keep bearing left until you get to the charming **place du Tertre**. Make for the opposite corner of the square, to the right of the blue *salon de thé*, and down the steps of **rue du Calvaire**. Left, then **rue Drevet** and more steps. Cross **rue des Trois-Frères** and bear right at London Groove. This is real romantic Paris territory; think Amélie and accordion music.

Further on you'll emerge in **place des Abbesses** with its red brick church (St-Jean de Montmartre) and art nouveau Métro awning. A good mix of tourists and locals frequent this square. Head right of the church along **rue des Abbesses** and at no. 31 go left down **rue Germain-Pilon**. Imposing ladies in fur coats do the strutting here, but again you're a bit early for all that, especially now that Mr Sarkozy has made it dodgy even to smile at a lady of the night in the morning (*see chapter* **Paris Today**). You'll soon come out on **bd de Clichy**: dirty photos, plastic willies (great for that souvenir for grandma) and murky theme pubs. Glance to your right and you'll see the masts of the Moulin Rouge. Resist temptation: go left and then take the first right at Folies Pigalle down **rue Pigalle**.

Pigalle – Opéra

Phew! What a relief to leave all that filth behind! Walk 250 yards then fork left down **rue de La Rochefoucauld** and continue past rows of typical Parisian shutters into the relatively tourist-free 9th *arrondissement*. This quarter was home to Van Gogh, Renoir and

Toulouse-Lautrec. At 12 rue de La Rochefoucauld, turn right down **rue de la Tour des Dames**. You'll come out at the grimy Eglise de la Trinité. The front is nicer, as is the little park you'll find there; it's well worth a pause for a calf-stretch/play in the sandpit.

Next target is **rue de Mogador**, opposite the church and to the right of the café of the same name. Admittedly it's not picture-postcard. Nor is **bd Haussmann** where it comes out, but press on, for poshness is to come. The ornate building in front of you is the back entrance to the Opéra Garnier – skirt round the edge for the altogether sparklier full-effect. From the traffic island opposite look out for oft-ignored 'naked-man-with-lute' on the top of the opera. Next, hunt around for the building with the Rolex sign and head immediately to the left of it down **rue de la Paix**.

Place Vendôme – Eiffel Tower

Aim for the column ahead of you, past jewellery shops and flash hotels. The comic-strip round the edge recounts Napoléon's victory over the Prussian foe. To Napo's right you'll see the Ritz and the Ministry of Justice. Beyond the square cross **rue de Rivoli** and enter the metal gates of the **Jardin des Tuileries**. Having passed violent statues 'lions slaying hippo' and 'lions slaying small pig', head right to **place de la Concorde**, venue for big-box-office Revolution guillotinings. Beyond the obelisk is a view bang up the Champs-Elysées to the Arc de Triomphe. How about that for a bit of city planning? Bear left towards the river.

The next half-hour couldn't be easier: stick to the Concorde side of the Seine and go towards the Eiffel Tower. Go via the riverbank or greenery at road level. Either way, the route's a doddle, so try a bit of speed-walking to make up time. You might just pause at the bronze flame just past **Pont d'Alma** that has become an unofficial shrine to Princess Diana. From this spot you've a view all the way back to Sacré-Coeur, which should give you a morale boost.

Battle on along **av de New-York**. If giant raftloads of lazy tourists glide by, ignore them. You're a winner! Cross the Seine on the pedestrian bridge and find your way to the base of the Eiffel Tower. Climbing it would be a bad move today.

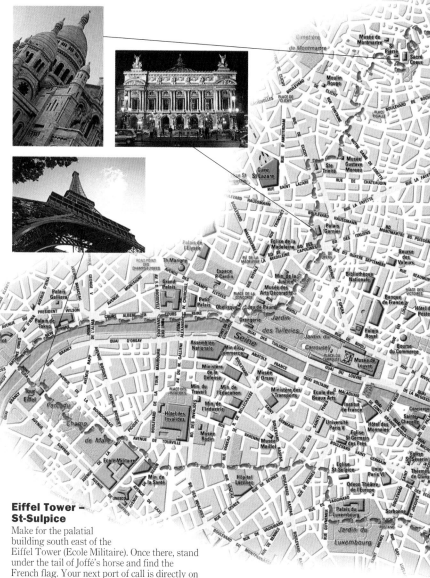

Eiffel Tower –
St-Sulpice

Make for the palatial
building south east of the
Eiffel Tower (Ecole Militaire). Once there, stand
under the tail of Joffé's horse and find the
French flag. Your next port of call is directly on
the other side, but unless you're a general in the
French army, you'll have to take the long way
round. Go right, hug the wall until you can line
up the flag with the Eiffel Tower and stand
with the stubby obelisk at 12 o'clock. Take the
road at 10.30 (**rue d'Estrées**). Once past the
gleaming dome of Invalides it crosses two
streets and turns into **rue de Babylone**.

   Stick to this for half-a-mile: past the exotic-
looking Pagode cinema, the back entrance of

Matignon and a poo-free walled-garden (both at
number 34ish), then slide past le Bon Marché
and a play-park. Rue de Babylone turns into rue
de Sèvres where it crosses bd Raspail, but just
keep going. This is boutique land: if you're
doing this walk with someone who likes clothes
shopping, be firm. Beyond a half-horse/half-
man sculpture with amazing genitals turn right
down **rue du Vieux-Colombier** and head for
the circular towers of St-Sulpice.

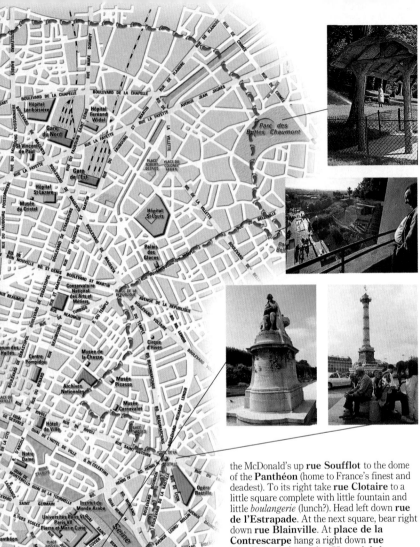

the McDonald's up **rue Soufflot** to the dome of the **Panthéon** (home to France's finest and deadest). To its right take **rue Clotaire** to a little square complete with little fountain and little *boulangerie* (lunch?). Head left down **rue de l'Estrapade**. At the next square, bear right down **rue Blainville**. At **place de la Contrescarpe** hang a right down **rue Mouffetard**. At number 55 turn left down **rue Ortolan**. Stick to the left-hand side of **place Monge**, turn left, then immediately right down **rue Lacépède** and all being well you'll see the greenery of the **Jardin des Plantes**.

Enter the gardens through the metal gates. Attention: the rest of this paragraph will tax your sense of direction. Head sharp right up a path, then take the steepest route up, which should bring you to a mini-bandstand thing. From the bandstand face the skyscraper; your next targets, the Seine and pont d'Austerlitz, are at 3 o'clock from this at the other end of the gardens. Be brave.

Jardins du Luxembourg – Jardin des Plantes

In front of the fountain turn right down **rue Bonaparte** and keep going when it turns into **rue Guynemer**. Enter the **Jardins du Luxembourg** on the left and cut directly across them. Once out of the gardens, aim left – why not enliven things with a skip here? – at

Pont d'Austerlitz – République

Leave the gardens through more metal gates and cross **pont d'Austerlitz** opposite. On the other side, look left for Notre-Dame and a glimpse of the Eiffel Tower; if you were standing under that two hours ago you're on track. Go left a few yards until you see a column with a shiny top: Bastille. Go down **bd de la Bastille** towards it but, opposite no. 16, take the road left down to the port and stroll past big boats. At **place de la Bastille** have a gander at the rad skaters and BMXers.

Follow the direction of Liberté's flaming torch (look up!) to **rue St-Antoine**. At number 36, head right to **place des Vosges**. At Louis VIII's horse make for the left-hand corner of the square and **rue des Francs-Bourgeois**. Welcome to the Marais: Jewish eateries, cool gay bars and trendy shops all rolled into one cuddly area. For kosher aromas, take the third left down **rue Pavée**, then right down **rue des Rosiers**. You'll soon come out on **rue Vielle-du-Temple**. Turn right and stick to it. Opposite number 132 (a derelict chocolate shop) take **rue de Turenne**. Notice the Marais' money and fashion slip away. When rue de Turenne runs out, head past a particularly yellow letterbox to **rue Béranger**. **Passage de Vendôme** (number 18) will bring you out on the vast roundabout that is **République**. Aim middle right for **rue du Faubourg-du-Temple**. You'll be relieved to know the squiggling is over. Now it's straight – straight uphill for a mile. Ha!

Rue du Faubourg du Temple – Buttes Chaumont

Don't be alarmed if your brain devises canny questions for which you find no response: 'Why am I spending my holiday doing this?' Or 'Why don't I just get the nearest Métro home?' Block out those losers' thoughts! Instead, contemplate the incredible mix of colours and cultures to be found up rue du Faubourg-du-Temple.

When it crosses bd de Belleville and becomes **rue de Belleville** keep climbing (don't get your boulevards and your rues confused). Opposite 57 rue de Belleville hangs a comment about advertising by the artist Ben Vautier (translation: 'don't trust words'). Trust ours. Look back down rue de Belleville for a glimpse of the Eiffel Tower. For an even better view, at number 64, nip 500 yards up **rue Piat** and back again. If such diversions are unthinkable just take it from us that it's a good view and go left along **rue Rébeval**. Bear immediately right (**rue de l'Equerre**) then canter up steps to **av Simon Bolivar**. Head left to greenery and go through gates of the **parc des Buttes Chaumont**.

Same problem: how to give directions through a park designed for strollers to lose themselves in? Like this: stick left when you enter, past a restaurant and a bridge, then take the first path on your left and keep going down until you reach the lake. This entirely man-made park was designed by Haussmann on the site of an old rubbish tip, so the boy did well. At the lake, go under an arch to the caves, complete with waterfalls and fake stalactites. From beyond the caves – or anywhere else if you give up on the caves – take the steps sharp right up to the small pavilion at the highest point in the middle of the lake. From inside you'll have a view over industrial suburbs and the familiar domes of Sacré-Coeur. The end is in sight. So is the Mairie of the 19th *arrondissement* (stately building with mini bell tower, other side of lake). This is your next target. Take steps down through rock, cross suspension bridge, bear right.

Mairie du 19th – Sacré-Coeur

We know: It hurts. Just hang on in there. Think Kate Bush: don't give up. Take **av Laumière**, left of the Mairie. At the bottom of the hill, past M° Laumière, turn left, then right down **rue Euryale-Dehaynin**. Cross the canal on the pedestrian bridge on your left and once on the other side head right towards the black-and-white theatre-boat Abracadabra. Is a boat a stupid landmark? What if it's sailed off? Walk along **quai de la Seine** anyway and at number 67 take **rue Riquet** and stay on it. You can be sure you're among the first tourists wilfully to take a stroll in this neck of the woods.

Once you've crossed a thick band of railway tracks rue Riquet starts to get more attractive. This is a bit of straightforward Paris, without the tourists of Montmartre, the cash of Rive Gauche or the hip-exotic of Belleville. Carry on when Riquet turns into **rue Ordener**. More railway tracks, one of which leads to London Waterloo. At a long colourful wall feels left down **rue Marcadet**. At number 38 turn left onto **rue Labat**. If you walk on the left-hand pavement you can glimpse those domes. Labat crosses Barbès, Clignancourt, Custine, Lambert but just keep going until you can't go any further because of a wall and a sign saying '**rue Bachelet**'. Go briefly down hill to the right. Steps. Climb them. More steps. Must. Keep. Walking. Round Sacré-Coeur. Et voilà!

Last instructions: find a bar close by, have a drink or three and groan. Well done. You've probably got blisters, you almost certainly won't be able to walk normally for days, but when someone asks you 'how was Paris?', you can reply: 'Paris was mine!'

paris museum pass
carte musées-monuments

Valid for 1, 3 or 5 days, the Paris museum pass gives wait-free admission to see the permanent collections of 60 museums and sights in and around Paris.

On sale in museums, monuments, metro stations and at the Paris Tourist Office.

inter Musées

Tuck into Time Out's pick of 850 top Paris bars, cafés and restaurants!

From the editors of this guide, 164 pages packed with honest, authoritative reviews of 850 of the city's finest bistros, brasseries, bars, boutiques and cafés. Fully indexed, with original colour photos throughout.

Just €7.95/£5.99 at good bookshops and newsagents.

Or send your address with VISA number + expiry date to:
Time Out, 100 rue du Fbg-St-Antoine, 75012 Paris.
Fax: +33 (0)1.44.73.90.60 / E-mail: distribution@timeout.fr

Museums

From dreamy Impressionist doodlings to conceptual challenges with bits of wood and string, everything for a full-on art attack hangs out in Paris.

Passing the time at the **Musée d'Orsay**. *See p155.*

To visit Paris and not go to any museums is scandalous. Well, it'd be bit of a shame; Paris is where many of the great names became great. Surrealism, Cubism, art nouveau and art deco all developed here. Then there's the talent: Monet, Matisse, Rodin, Degas, Lautrec – all French. Then there's the artists who made Paris their home away from home: Picasso, Dali, Kandinsky, Chagall, Giacometti, Brancusi, Modigliani; there must have been something inspirational in the drinking water, or maybe the booze was cheap and the chicks were friendly. Whatever, Paris has the cred and it's almost drunk with museums.

So what's new, seeing that Modern and even Post-Modern aren't so, well, modern anymore. A visit to one of the many contemporary art spaces, like the **Palais de Tokyo** (*see p164*) or the **Plateau** (*see p165*), will set you straight

with their frequently changing shows of video and installation art. But there's no need to overdo the arty side of things. Temper your cultural agenda with a visit to the Planetarium at the **Cité des Sciences et de l'Industrie** (*see p177*) or slurp some wine at the **Musée du Vin** (*see p179*). Paris is a heavy-duty pitstop for ground-breaking exhibitions, and 2003 is no exception. This year's major exhibitions include a Chagall show at the **Galeries Nationales du Grand Palais** (*see p158*) plus an Italian-themed year at the **Louvre** (*see p146*), including exhibitions on Michaelangelo, da Vinci and 16th-century Italian art. 2003 is also Year of Algerian culture, which will be celebrated throughout France; Paris events include exhibitions of Algerian art and history at the **Institut du Monde Arabe** (*see p176*) **Musée de l'Histoire de France** (*see p171*).

PARIS CARTE MUSEES ET MONUMENTS

According to scientific theory, the most time a lay person can spend in a museum is one-and-a-half hours before longing for a coffee and a sit-down. However, if you do opt for death by cultural overdose, the best-value way to do it is with the **Carte Musées et Monuments** (CM). Coming in handy one-day (€15), three-day (€30) or five-day (€45) formats, it allows entry into 70 museums and monuments all over Paris (although you have to pay extra for special exhibitions) and allows you to jump queues. It's available from museums, tourist offices, branches of Fnac and main Métro and RER stations. For further information, visit www.intermusees.com. In our listings CM indicates whether the card is accepted. Museum musing is one of the cheaper ways to while away a few hours in Paris. You're unlikely to pay more than €6 admission, and there's often a reduced rate for students, children and over-60s – although you'll probably need an ID card or passport to prove your status. In any case, all the permanent collections at municipal-run museums are free and a reduced rate is usually applicable on Sundays. All national museums are completely free on the first Sunday of the month and most museums throw open their doors for the annual *Printemps des Musées* (Springtime of the Museums), which usually falls on a Sunday in April (more information on 01.40.15.36.00/www.culture.gouv.fr). Thousands also turn out for the annual

Journées des Patrimoines (national heritage days), 20-21 September in 2003, for the chance to see behind the normally closed doors of some of the capital's oldest and most beautiful buildings. More information on 01.40.15.37.37/www.jp.culture.fr.

Jostling with busloads of tourists and their hand-held cameras takes the joy out of the museum experience, so try to visit on weekdays, or take advantage of the '*nocturnes*' (late night opening) that most of the big museums offer. Pre-booking is essential before 1pm at the Grand Palais, and it's also possible to pre-book the Louvre and other major exhibitions. Most museums close on either Monday or Tuesday, and most ticket counters – and, more unfairly, some loos – shut 30-45 minutes before closing (you may find yourself being shooed out, gently but firmly, a good 15 minutes before the official closing time).

The Louvre

entrance through Pyramid, Cour Napoléon, 1st (01.40.20.50.50/recorded information 01.40.20.51.51/www.louvre.fr). Mº Palais Royal. **Open** 9am-6pm Thur-Sun; 9am-9.45pm Mon, Wed. Closed Tue. **Admission** €7.50 (until 3pm); €5 after 3pm, Sun; free under-18s first Sun of month; CM. Temporary exhibitions vary between €3.80-€5.50. Package deal, €8-€10. **Credit** MC, V. **Map** p406 H5. The labyrinthine Louvre is the museum to end all museums: just when you think you've

Louvre among the ruins.

mastered it, you turn a corner and discover another awesome staircase or a series of rooms. Its breadth is mind-boggling but that also means that there's something for everyone (if only you can find it), including Renaissance painting, grandiose battle scenes, Antique sculpture, Egyptian mummies, medieval jewels, courtly tapestries – and that's aside from the building itself. Neck pains are the price you pay for admiring the marvellous ceiling: ornate gilt-work snakes around most of the one-time royal palace, and the ceiling paintings rival anything on the walls. A circular room in Sully portrays Icarus, with the wax on his wings melting, plunging directly, seemingly, onto those of us below. The Louvre is a marvellous architectural hybrid: its intricately carved brickwork gives the impression that it has been constructed entirely of custard cream biscuits, whilst the futuristic Pyramid, surrounded by gently lapping water, is the glassy-eyed sentinel.

The original Louvre was built by Philippe Auguste in the 1190s as part of his Paris defences; by the mid-14th century it had been turned into a royal residence. Remains of walls and turrets, including the Charles V library tower, lay buried beneath the new palace for centuries. Much of it has now been unearthed and can be seen in the underground complex, including the ancient heart of Philippe Auguste's fortress, the vaulted Salle St-Louis with its central supporting column and carved grotesque head. Subsequent rulers all had their ha'penny worth to add. In the 1540s, François 1er asked Pierre Lescot to begin a Renaissance palace (now the western wing of the enclosed Cour Carrée). Continued by his successors, the different facades are carved with royal monograms – H interlaced with C and D for Henri II, his queen Catherine de Médicis and favourite Diane de Poitiers. Suave devils, or were they trying to stir it for poor old Henri? Henri IV and Louis XIII completed the Cour Carrée and built the wing along the Seine. The pedimented facade along rue du Louvre was added by Perrault under Louis XIV. Louis brought in Le Vau and Le Brun to refurbish the interior, with a sumptuous suite for his mother Anne of Austria (which she'd be delighted to know now houses Roman antiquities). After Louis XIV's court left for Versailles, the royals abandoned the palace and the apartments were often occupied by artists and state servants. Still, people just couldn't resist touching the place up. After the Revolution, Percier and Fontaine, Napoléon's architects, added a grand stairway of which only the ceilings of the one-time landing remain (now Salles Percier and Fontaine). At the Emperor's command, they also built the galleries along rue de Rivoli,

complete with imperial figures, although it was Napoléon's nephew, Napoléon III, who added the Cour Napoléon.

The art collection was first opened to the public in 1793, but the Ministry of Finance remained in the palace until the 1980s, when the ministers were dragged kicking and screaming out of their lavish apartments and over to the much less glamourous 12th *arrondissement*. The space they left enabled the Louvre's latest transformation, which began with the opening of the Richelieu Wing in 1993. I M Pei's weird but undeniably stunning glass pyramid opened in 1989 to a chorus of disapproval from traditionalists, who now seem to have been partially won over – but who cares what traditionalists think? It serves as a dramatic main entrance to one of the world's most celebrated museums.

USERS' TIPS

• The museum is divided into three wings: Denon (down the Seine side), Richelieu (down the Rivoli side), and Sully, which joins them up and runs around the Cour Carrée at the end. Pick up a plan at the information desk – you'll need it.
• Jump the worst of the queues and enter via the Carrousel from rue de Rivoli or from Palais-Royal Métro (advance tickets can also be bought at the Virgin Megastore inside the Carrousel).
• Get organised: tickets can be bought in advance at Fnac, Carrefour, Auchan and Virgin ticket offices or on the web. If buying on the spot, credit card ticket machines can be quicker than the tills.
• Tickets are valid all day: you can leave the museum and re-enter if you wish.
• Staff shortages mean that some rooms are closed on a weekly basis – check on 01.40.20.51.51 or www.louvre.fr.
• Grab a bite at the elegant Café Richelieu, the Café Denon or the Café Mollien, which has an outdoor terrace in summer. Under the pyramid there's a sandwich bar, café and the Grand Louvre restaurant serving classic French cuisine. Alternatively, take a breather outside at the **Café Marly** (*see p214*), which overlooks the pyramid and serves trendy brasserie-style food. The Restorama in the Carrousel du Louvre has multiple self-service outlets, ranging from Lebanese and pizza to cheese and wine.
• Shopaholics, have your credit cards ready; the Louvre has excellent art book, postcard, poster and gift shops (with reproductions of many Louvre items), a special children's art bookshop, as well as several stalls around the museum where you can buy museum guides. And there's always the Carrousel shopping centre.
• Finally…don't try to see everything on one visit. Let yourself be beguiled – you're bound to get lost within the first 20 minutes, so use it as an excuse to discover the unexpected.

The Collections

Ancient Egypt

Sully: ground and 1st floors; Richelieu: ground floor.

Announced by the Giant Sphinx in pink granite, the Egyptian department immediately divides into two routes. The Thematic Circuit presents Nile culture (fishing, agriculture, hunting, daily and cultural life, religion and death); one of the biggest draws is the famous Mastaba of Akhethetep, a richly decorated burial chamber from Sakkara dating back to around 2,400BC. Six small sphinxes, a row of apes from Luxor and the lion-headed goddess Sekhmet recreate elements of temple complexes, while massive stone sarcophagi, mummies, amulets, jewellery and jars of entrails (yum!), are all part of a vivid display on funeral rites and the journey to resurrection in the next world.

Meanwhile, the Pharoah Circuit takes a chronological approach, from the Seated Scribe and other stone figures of the Ancient Empire, via the elongated painted wood figures of the Middle Empire to the New Empire with its animal-headed statues of gods and goddesses, papyrus scrolls and hieroglyphic tablets. Look out for the double statue of the God Aman protecting Tutankhamun, and the black diorite 'cube statues' of priests and attendants. The collection has its origins in Napoléon's Egyptian campaign of 1798-99 and the work of Champollion, the French linguist and Egyptologist, who deciphered hieroglyphics in 1824.

Oriental Antiquities & Islamic art

Sully: 1st floor; Richelieu: lower-ground floor; 1st floor.

Amid Cypriot animalistic vases and carved reliefs from Byblos, there are two breathtaking palace reconstructions: the great court, *c.*713BC, from the palace of Sargon II at Khorsabad (in present-day Iraq) with its giant bearded and winged bulls and friezes of warriors and servants, and the palace of Darius I at Susa (now Iran), *c.*510 BC, with its fantastic glazed-brick reliefs depicting rows of archers, lions and griffins, along with all sorts of bowls, statues and other artefacts. Islamic decorative arts include early glass, fine 10th-to-12th-century dishes decorated with birds and calligraphy, traditional Iranian blue and white wares, Iznik ceramics, intricate inlaid metalwork from Syria, carpets, screens, weapons and funerary stele.

Greek, Roman & Etruscan antiquities

Denon: lower ground floor, ground floor; Sully: ground floor, 1st floor.

The *Winged Victory of Samothrace*, a headless Greek statue dating back to the 2nd-century BC, stands sentinel at the top of the Daru staircase, and the rest of the Greek, Roman & Etruscan collection is no less awe-inspiring. This section is also home to the 2.3m-high *Athena Peacemaker* and the *Venus de Milo*, and is overflowing with gods and goddesses, swords and monsters. The huge collection is made up of pieces amassed by François 1er and Richelieu, plus the Borghese collection (acquired in 1808), and the Campana collection of thousands of painted Greek vases and small terracottas.

Etruscan civilisation of central Italy spans roughly the 7th century BC until submission to the Romans in the 1st century AD. The highlight is the *Sarcophagus of the Cenestien Couple, c.*530-510BC, in painted terracotta, which depicts a smiling couple reclining at a banquet. Roman antiquities include a vivid relief of sacrificial animals from a temple in Rome, intricately carved sarcophagi, mosaic floors and the Boscoreale Treasure, fabulous silverwork excavated at a villa near Pompeii.

French painting

Richelieu: 2nd floor; Sully: 2nd floor; Denon: 1st floor.

There are around 6,000 of the most famous paintings in the world on show here, and it really is exciting to see the real thing with your own eyes (over the shoulder of tourists who want to see the real thing with their own camcorder). The most impressive paintings, physically as well as aesthetically, are the massive 18th/19th-century canvases hanging in the Grand Galerie in the Denon wing. Here art meets politics with Gros' suitably dashing *Napoléon visitant le champ de bataille d'Eylau (Napoleon at the Battle of Eylau)*, David's absolutely enormous *Sacre de Napoléon (Coronation of Napoleon I)* and Delacroix's flag-flying frenzy, *La Liberté Guidant le Peuple (Liberty Leading the People)*. Photojournalism has nothing on Géricault's technically beautiful but emotionally disturbing *Le Radeau de la Méduse (The Raft of the Médusa)*: turning his artistic vision to the shocking true story of the abandoned men who resorted to cannibalism and murder after an 1816 shipwreck, he manages to contrast hope (there is a tiny hint of a boat on the horizon) with despair (the one old man who looks out of the canvas, surrounded by the dead and the dying). A little further on, but just as horrifying, is Girodet's *Le Déluge (The Deluge)*, where a wild-eyed man tries to cling onto a woman who is being pulled down by her own children. Famous Biblical and historical scenes rub shoulders with portraits of aristocracy and grand depictions of those great moments from classical mythology, even if the Sphinx in Ingres' *Oedipus Explaining the Enigma* looks like more of a pussy cat than a man-eater.

History of art fanatics will have a field day: here you can find the earliest known non-religious French portrait (*c.*1350: an anonymous portrait of Jean Le Bon), the *Pièta de Villeneuve-les-Avignon* attributed to Enguerrand Quarton, Jean Clouet's *Portrait of François 1er* (marking the influence of the Italian Renaissance on portraiture), and works from the Ecole de Fontainebleau, including the anonymous *Diana the Huntress*, an elegant nude who bears a more than passing resemblance to Diane de Poitiers, Henri II's mistress. Poussin's religious and mythological subjects epitomise 17th-century French classicism, in works full of erudite references for an

audience of cognoscenti. Don't miss Charles Le Brun's wonderfully pompous *Chancellier Seguier* and his four grandiose battle scenes, in which Alexander the Great stands in for Louis XIV. The 18th century begins with Watteau's *Gilles and the Embarkation for Cythera*. Works by Chardin include sober still lifes, but also delicate figure paintings. If you're used to the sugary images of Fragonard, don't miss the *Fantaisies,* which forego sentimentality for wonderfully fluent, broadly-painted fantasy portraits, intended to capture moods rather than particular likenesses. Also in the Sully wing are sublime Neo-Classical portraits by David, Ingres' *La Baigneuse* (*The Bather*) and *Le Bain Turc* (*Turkish Bath*), portraits and Orientalist scenes by Chassériau and landscapes by Corot.

French sculpture

Richelieu: ground floor.

French sculpture is displayed in and around the two glazed sculpture courts created as part of the Grand Louvre. A tour round the different medieval regional schools takes in the *Virgins* from Alsace, 14th-century figures of Charles V and Jeanne de Bourbon that originally adorned the exterior of the Louvre and the late 15th-century *Tomb of Philippe Pot*, an effigy of Burgundian knight carried by eight black-clad mourners. Fine Renaissance memorials, fountains and portals include Jean Goujon's friezes from the Fontaine des Innocents. In the Cour Marly, pride of place goes to Coustou's *Chevaux de Marly*, two rearing horses being restrained by their grooms, plus two slightly earlier equestrian pieces by Coysevox, all originally sculpted for the favourite royal château at

Marly-le-Roi. In Cour Puget are the four bronze captives by Martin Desjardins, Clodion's Rococo frieze and Pierre Puget's twisting, Baroque *Milo of Croton*. Amid 18th-century heroes and allegorical subjects, look for Pigalle's *Mercury and Voltaire*.

Italian painting

Denon: 1st floor.

The Venetian paintings section is undergoing an overhaul at present, but Veronese's monumental, lavishly coloured *Noces de Cana* (*Wedding Feast at Cana*) still heralds your arrival. Two rooms of fragile Renaissance frescoes by Botticelli, Fra Angelico and Luini open the Italian department. Cimabue's *Madonna of the Angels, c.*1270, combines the composition of Byzantine icons with the Renaissance's modelling of form. Look out also for Fra Angelico's *Coronation of the Virgin* and Mantegna's *Calvary, St-Sebastian* and bacchanal scenes. Highlights of the Sienese school include Simone Martini's *Christ Carrying the Cross* and Piera della Francesca's *Portrait of Sigismondo Malatesta*. Florentine High Renaissance treasures include Raphael's *Belle Jardinière* Virgin and Child, and two lovely small paintings depicting dragon slayers St George and St Michael. Leonardo's *Virgin of the Rocks* and *Virgin, Child and St-Anne* are also present, but needless to say it's the *Mona Lisa* (known in France as *La Joconde*), who hogs the limelight. She's almost impossible to look at for many reasons: because of her familiarity, because after all the hype she's still pretty small, because of the bullet-proof glass protecting her, because of the camera-clicking crowds ever before her… but she certainly has that *je ne sais*

quoi, even though she's not what you'd call a Page Three stunna. As of 2003, at the grand old age of 500 or so, she will finally be old enough to have her own room, which should be able to accommodate even more goggle-eyed tourists than usual. Other highlights in this section include Caravaggio's Baroque masterpiece *The Fortune Teller*, the celebrated *Fête Champêtre* attributed to Titian, and the magnificent fruit and leaf heads of Arcimboldo's *Four Seasons*, plus paintings by Tintoretto, Lotto and Bronzino.

Italian sculpture
Denon: ground floor, lower ground floor.
Michelangelo's *Dying Slave* and *Captive Slave* (sculptures originally planned for the tomb of Pope Julius II in Rome) are the real show-stealers here, but other Renaissance treasures include a painted marble relief by Donatello, Adrien de Vriesse's gleaming, elongated bronze *Mercury and Psyche* and Giambologna's *Mercury*. Benevenuto Cellini's heavy-looking *Nymphe of Fontainebleau* relief can be found on the Mollien staircase.

Northern schools
Richelieu: 2nd floor; Denon: lower ground floor.
The northern Renaissance includes Flemish altarpieces by Memling and Van der Weyden, Bosch's fantastical, proto-Surrealist *Ship of Fools*, Metsys' *The Moneylender and his Wife*, which combines a complex moral message, lively everyday detail and visual games, as well as the northern Mannerism of Cornelius van Haarlem. The Galerie Médicis is devoted to Rubens' Médicis cycle. The 24 canvases commissioned in the 1620s for the Palais de Luxembourg by Marie de Médicis, widow of Henri IV, mix historic events and classical mythology for the glorification of the queen. But look also at Rubens' more personal, glowing portrait of his second wife *Hélène Fourment and her Children*, along with Van Dyck's *Charles I and his Groom* and peasant-filled townscapes by Teniers.

Dutch paintings in this wing include early and late self-portraits by Rembrandt, his *Flayed Ox* and the warmly glowing nude *Bathsheba at her Bath*. There are Vermeer's *Astronomer* and *Lacemaker* amid interiors by De Hooch and Metsu, and the meticulously finished portraits and *trompe l'oeil* framing devices of Dou, plus works from the Haarlem school.

German paintings in small side galleries include portraits by Cranach, Dürer's *Self-Portrait* and Holbein's *Anne of Cleves*.

The rooms of Northern and Scandinavian paintings include Caspar David Friedrich's *Trees with Crows*, the sober, classical portraits of Christian Købke and pared-back views of Peder Balke. A small but high-quality British collection includes landscapes by Wright of Derby, Constable and Turner and portraits by Gainsborough, Reynolds and Lawrence. Northern sculpture (Denon, lower-ground floor), ranges from Erhart's Gothic *Mary Magdalene* to the Neo-Classical work of Thorvaldsen.

Decorative Arts
Richelieu: 1st floor; Sully: 1st floor
The decorative arts collection runs from the Middle Ages to the mid-19th century, often with royal connections. Many of the finest medieval items came

Georges Town: **Centre Pompidou.** *See above right.*

from the treasury of St-Denis amassed by the powerful Abbot Suger, counsellor to Louis VI and VII, among them *Suger's Eagle* (an amazing antique porphyry vase with gold mounts), a serpentine plate surrounded by precious stones and the sacred sword of the kings of France, dubbed 'Charlemagne's sword' by the Capetian monarchs as they sought to legitimise their line.

The Renaissance galleries take in ornate carved chests, German silver tankards, and the *Hunts of Maximilien*, twelve 16th-century Brussels tapestries depicting months, the zodiac and hunting scenes. 17th and 18th-century French decorative arts are displayed in superb panelled rooms, and include characteristic brass and tortoiseshell pieces by Boulle. Later displays move on to the elaborate Rococo 'monkey commode' – fair sets the mind a-wandering, doesn't it – of Crescent and parquetry by Leleu, as well as French faïence and porcelain, silverware, watches and scientific instruments. Napoléon III's opulent apartments, used until the 1980s by the Ministry of Finance (who said France doesn't have a monarchy?), have been preserved with chandeliers and upholstery intact.

Tribal Art
Denon: ground floor.
A small display in the Pavillon de Flore augurs what is to come in the future Musée du Quai Branly (*see p171* **Primitive & proper**). Items range from Benin bronze heads from Nigeria and Polynesian carved wood statues to pot-bellied terracotta figures from Mexico. This is definitely the place to enthuse museum-weary children.

Other museums

Fine art

Centre Pompidou (Musée National d'Art Moderne)
rue St-Martin, 4th (01.44.78.12.33/ www.centrepompidou.fr). M° Hôtel-de-Ville or Rambuteau/RER Châtelet-Les Halles. **Open** 11am-9pm Mon, Wed-Sun (until 11pm for some temporary exhibitions). Closed Tue, 1 May. **Admission** €5.50; €3.50 18-26s; free under-18s; CM. Temporary exhibitions (includes museum) €6.50-€8.50; €4.50-€6.50 18-26s; one day package €10, €8 18-26s. **Credit** MC, V. **Map** p406 K6.

The newly-enlarged and renovated galleries of the Pompidou Centre now incorporate architecture and design as well as its unparalleled collection of fine art. The sheer scale of the Centre's holdings means that only a small proportion can be seen at any one time, so there is a partial rehang every year. Level four kicks off with post-1960s art by the likes of Yves Klein, Dubuffet, the late Nikki de Saint-Phalle (she of the fabulous fountain sculptures in the square outside), Jasper Johns and the perennial wrapper, Christo, plus sections dedicated to contemporary architecture and design by Rem Koolhaas and Jean Prouvé, amongst others. Performance art spaces, video lounges and installation areas, such as the one currently dedicated to Sarkis' *I Love My Lulu*, add to the mix. Level five takes a step back and roughly covers the period from 1905 to 1960: a memorable

Sightseeing

journey through the making of art history, encompassing Primitivism, Fauvism, Cubism and Bauhaus right up to American Colour-Field painting and Abstract Expressionists. Here you'll find works by Matisse, Picasso, Mondrian, Kandinsky, Klee, Rothko and Bacon. The photography collection also has an impressive roll call, including Brassaï, Kertesz, Man Ray, Cartier-Bresson and Doisneau. 2003 promises major shows on Philippe Starck (Feb-May) and French semiologist Roland Barthes (until Mar). *See also chapters* **Architecture, Sightseeing: Right Bank** and **Film**. *Auditorium. Café. Children's workshops. Cinema. Guided Visits. Restaurant. Shops. Wheelchair access.*

Musée d'Art Moderne de la Ville de Paris

11 av du Président-Wilson, 16th (01.53.67.40.00). M° Iéna or Alma-Marceau. **Open** 10am-5.30pm Tue-Fri; 10am-7pm Sat, Sun (collection); 10am-6.30pm Tue-Sun (temporary exhibitions). Closed Mon, 1 Jan, 1 May, 25 Dec. **Admission** permanent collection free. Temporary exhibitions vary between €3-€7; free under-13s. **Credit** MC, V. **Map** p404 D5.
This monumental museum was built for the 1937 Exposition Universelle and forms the other half of the **Palais de Tokyo**, now a cutting edge contemporary art space (*see p162*). It's home to the municipal collection of modern art and is particularly strong on the Cubists, Fauves, the Delaunays, Rouault, Schwitters and Ecole de Paris artists Soutine, Modigliani and Van Dongen. The postwar section goes from Support-Surface, the torn-poster works of Villegle and compressions by César and Arman, 70s conceptual art (Boltanski, Messager, Gette, Gilbert & George) and Arte Povera to videos by young artists (Huyghe, Bournigault) and Tania Mourad's humming, white-domed meditation room. For most of 2003, the permanent collection will be closed for renovation work, although the museum's dynamic temporary exhibitions will be keeping up the good work. In 2003 look out for exhibitions of Turner Prize-winning British artist Steve McQueen and seminal Russian artist Kasmir Malevitch. *Bookshop. Café. Concerts. Wheelchair access*

Musée Cognacq-Jay

Hôtel Donon, 8 rue Elzévir, 3rd (01.40.27.07.21). M° St-Paul. **Open** 10am-6.15pm Tue-Sun. Closed Mon, some public holidays. **Admission** permanent collection free. Temporary exhibitions vary between €2.50-€5; free under-13s. **No credit cards.** **Map** p406 L6.
This intimate museum in a carefully restored *hôtel particulier* houses the collection put together in the early 1900s by Ernest Cognacq, founder of La Samaritaine, and his wife Louise Jay. Their tastes stuck mainly to the French 18th-century, focusing on outstanding French Rococo artists such as Watteau, Fragonard, Boucher, Greuze and pastellist Quentin de la Tour, although some English (Reynolds, Lawrence, Romney), Dutch and Flemish (an early Rembrandt, Ruysdael, Rubens), and a

sprinkling of Canalettos and Guardis have slipped in too. Pictures are displayed in panelled rooms alongside furniture, porcelain, tapestries and sculpture of the same period.
Bookshop. Children's workshops.

Musée Départemental Maurice Denis, 'Le Prieuré'

2bis rue Maurice Denis, 78100 St-Germain-en-Laye (01.39.73.77.87). RER A St-Germain-en-Laye. **Open** 10am-5.30pm Tue-Fri; 10am-6.30pm Sat, Sun. Closed Mon, 1 Jan, 1 May, 25 Dec. **Admission** €3.80; €2.20 12-25s, students, over-60s; free under-12s; CM. With temporary exhibition: €5.30; €3.80 12-25s, students, over-60s; free under-12s. **No credit cards.**
Out in the elegant commuterland of St-Germain-en-Laye, this former royal convent and hospital became home and studio to Nabi painter Maurice Denis, who also decorated the chapel in the garden, in 1915. This remarkable collection comprises paintings, prints and decorative objects by the Nabis – the name means 'Prophets' – who counted Sérusier, Bonnard, Vuillard, Roussel and Valloton among their number. Seeking a renewed spirituality in painting, they took inspiration from Gauguin and Toulouse-Lautrec, who also have some paintings on show here.

Musée Jacquemart-André

158 bd Haussmann, 8th (01.42.89.04.91/ www.musee-jacquemart-andre.com). M° Miromesnil or St-Philippe-du-Roule. **Open** 10am-6pm daily. **Admission** €8; €6 7-17s, students; free under-7s; CM. **Credit** MC, V. **Map** p405 E3.
The magnificent collection gathered by Edouard André and his wife Nélie Jacquemart is as worth visiting for its illustration of the life of the 19th-century *haute bourgeoisie* as for the treasures they unearthed. The ground floor reception rooms take in the circular Grand Salon, rooms of tapestries and French furniture, Boucher mythological fantasies, the library (with Dutch paintings including Rembrandts), the smoking room hung with English portraits, and the magnificent polychrome marble winter garden with double spiral staircase. On the stairway three recently restored Tiepolo frescoes from the Villa Contarini depict the arrival of Henri III in Venice. Upstairs, what was to have been Nélie's studio became their 'Italian museum', an exceptional Early Renaissance collection that includes Uccello's *St George and the Dragon*, Mantegna's *Ecce Homo*, a superb Schiavone portrait, a Carpaccio panel and Della Robbia terracottas. Even the tea room has a Tiepolo ceiling! The free audio guide is both useful and atmospheric. A Picasso exhibition in 2003 will add a splash of Modernism to the mix.
Audio guide in six languages. Bookshop. Café (11.30am-6pm). Partial wheelchair access.

Musée Marmottan – Claude Monet

2 rue Louis-Boilly, 16th (01.42.24.07.02/ www.marmottan.com). M° La Muette. **Open** 10am-6pm Tue-Sun. Closed Mon, 1 Jan, 1 May, 25 Dec. **Admission** €6.50; €4 8-25s, over-60s; free under-8s. **Credit** MC, V. **Map** p404 A6.

Sightseeing

Michel Monet bequeathed 165 of his father's works, plus sketchbooks, his palette and family photos, to the Musée Marmottan, including a breathtaking series of late water lily canvases, now on display in a special circular room. The collection also contains the definitive Monet, *Impression Soleil Levant*, which gave the Impressionist movement its name. There are also canvases by Sisley, Renoir, Pissarro, Manet, Caillebotte, Berthe Morisot, the 19th-century Realists and the Wildenstein collection of medieval illuminated manuscripts. The recently restored ground- and first-floor salons house smaller Monets, early 19th-century gouaches, a Sèvres porcelain geographical clock and First Empire furniture.
Shop. Wheelchair access.

Musée de l'Orangerie
Jardin des Tuileries, 1st (01.42.97.48.16).
M° Concorde. **Open** in 2004. **Map** p403 F5.
Monet's eight, extraordinarily fresh, huge, late *Nymphéas* (water lilies), conceived especially for two oval rooms in the Orangerie, were left by the artist to the nation as a 'spiritual testimony'. The museum is closed until 2004 for a major overhaul. On reopening the Jean Walter and Paul Guillaume collection of Impressionism and the Ecole de Paris will also go on show again, plus furniture and decorative objects.

Musée National d'Orsay
1 rue de la Légion d'Honneur, 7th (01.40.49.48.14/ recorded information 01.45.49.11.11). M° Solférino/ RER Musée d'Orsay. **Open** 10am-6pm Tue, Wed, Fri, Sat (from 9am June-Sep); 10am-9.45pm Thur; 9am-6pm Sun. Closed Mon, 1 Jan, 1 May.

Admission €7; €5 18-25s, all on Sun; free under-18s; CM. Exhibitions (museum included) €8.50; €6.50 18-25s, all on Sun; free under-18s. **Credit** (shop) AmEx, MC, V. **Map** p405 G6.
A Beaux-Arts train station, built for the 1900 Exposition Universelle, was saved from demolition to become the Musée d'Orsay, the Paris museum devoted to the pivotal years from 1848 to 1914. Architect Gae Aulenti remodelled the interior, keeping the iron-framed coffered roof and creating galleries off either side of a light-filled central canyon. There are some organisational drawbacks: the Impressionists and Post-Impressionists are knee-deep in tourists upstairs, while too much space is given downstairs to Couture's languid nudes or Meissonier's history paintings – but it somehow manages to maintain its open-plan feel. The museum follows a chronological route, starting on the ground floor, running up to the upper level and finishing on the mezzanine, highlighting continuities between the Impressionists and their forerunners and their revolutionary use of light and colour.

Running down the centre of the tracks a central sculpture aisle takes in monuments and maidens by artists including Rude, Barrye and Carrier-Belleuse, but the outstanding pieces are by Carpeaux, including his controversial *La Danse* for the facade of the Palais Garnier. The Lille side, on the right of the central aisle, is dedicated to the Romantics and history painters: Ingres and Amaury-Duval contrast with the Romantic passion of Delacroix's North African period and the cupids of Cabanel's *Birth of Venus*. Further on are examples of early Degas, and works by Gustave Moreau and Puvis de Chavannes.

Sightseeing

Musée d'Art Moderne de la Ville de Paris: it is what it says on the can. *See left.*

The first rooms to the Seine side of the central aisle are given over to the Barbizon landscape painters Corot, Daubigny and Millet. One room is dedicated to Courbet, with *The Artist and his Studio*, his monumental Burial at Ornans and his show-stopping *L'Origine du Monde* (*The Origin of the World*). This floor also covers pre-1870 works by the Impressionists and their precursor Boudin.

Upstairs holds the main attraction, the Impressionists, with masterpieces by Pissarro, Renoir and Caillebotte, Manet's once controversial *Déjeuner sur l'Herbe*, several of Monet's paintings of Rouen cathedral, and works by Degas. The riches continue with the Post-Impressionists. Among the boiling colours and frantic brushstrokes of Van Gogh are his *Church at Auvers* and his last painting, *Crows*. This is where you will find the primitivist jungle of the Douanier Rousseau, the gaudy, vivacious Montmartre lowlife depicted by Toulouse-Lautrec, the colourful exoticism of Gauguin's Breton and Tahitian periods, as well as works by Cézanne, Seurat, Signac and Redon.

On the mezzanine are the Nabis painters – Vallotton, Denis, Roussel, Bonnard and Vuillard. Several rooms are given over to art nouveau decorative arts, including furniture by Majorelle, silverware, and Gallé and Lalique ceramics. Paintings by Klimt and Burne-Jones reside here, and there are also sections on architectural drawings and early photography. The sculpture terraces include busts and studies by Rodin, heads by Rosso and bronzes by Bourdelle and Maillol. *See also p129.*

Audioguide. Bookshop. Café-restaurant. Cinema. Guided tours. Library. Wheelchair access.

Exhibition centres

Visiting one of Paris' non-museum exhibition centres has lots of advantages: the shows are often less crowded, offer a smaller but specialised look at interesting subjects, and are often significantly cheaper (or even free). Most venues are only open to the public during exhibitions, so check listings in *Pariscope* before dropping by. Cultural centres often put on exhibitions that can make a welcome change to a regular museum-goer's agenda: Centre Culturel Calouste Gulbenkian (Portugal – 51 av d'Iéna, 16th/01.53.23.93.93). Centre Culturel Suisse (32-38 rue des Francs-Bourgeois, 3rd/01.42.71.38.38). Centre Wallonie-Bruxelles, 127 rue St-Martin, 4th/01.53.01.96.96). Goethe Institut (Germany – 17 av d'Iéna/16th/ 01.44.43.92.30 and Galerie Condé, 31 rue de Condé, 6th/01.40.46.69.60). Institut Finlandais (60 rue des Ecoles, 5th/01.40.51.89.09). Centre Culturel Irlandais (6 rue des Irlandais, 5th/01.58.52.10.30). Institut Néerlandais (121 rue de Lille, 7th/01.53.59.12.40). Maison de l'Amérique Latine (217 bd St-Germain, 7th/01.49.54.75.00).

Bibliothèque Forney

Hôtel de Sens, 1 rue du Figuier, 4th (01.42.78.14.60). M° Pont-Marie. **Open** 1.30-8.30pm Tue-Fri; 10am-8pm Sat. Closed Mon, Sun, public holidays. **Admission** free. Exhibitions €3; €1.50

Horseplay: discover what goes into an equestrian statue at **Musée Bourdelle**. *See p160.*

Sightseeing

students under 28, over-60s; free under-12s.
No credit cards. Map p406 L7.
Set in the turrets of the oldest mansion in the Marais, the library specialises in the applied and graphic arts and has a wing given over to temporary displays.

Bibliothèque Nationale de France – Richelieu

*58 rue de Richelieu, 2nd (01.53.79.81.26/
www.bnf.fr). M° Bourse.* **Open** 9am-6pm Mon-Sat.
Closed Sun, two weeks in Sept, public holidays.
Admission €5; €4 students, 13-25s; free under-13s.
Crypte free. **Credit** AmEx, MC, V. **Map** p405 H4.
Within the old Bibliothèque Nationale, the Galeries Mansart and Mazarine take in all works on paper from medieval manuscripts and historic water-colours to photography and contemporary prints. A new gallery, La Crypte, is used for contemporary and graphic art. *Wheelchair access.*

Bibliothèque Nationale de France – François Mitterrand

*quai François-Mauriac, 13th (01.53.79.59.59/
www.bnf.fr). M° Bibliothèque or Quai de la Gare.*
Open 10am-7pm Tue-Sat; noon-7pm Sun. Closed
Mon, two weeks in Sept, public holidays.
Admission €5; €4 students, 13-25s; free under-13s.
Credit MC, V. **Map** p407 M10.
The gigantic new library could not be more of a contrast to its historic parent but it shares a similarly erudite programme, including photography, artists' books and an ongoing exhibition cycle on writing. *Café. Wheelchair access.*

Chapelle St-Louis de la Salpêtrière

*47 bd de l'Hôpital, 13th (01.42.16.04.24). M° Gare
d'Austerlitz.* **Open** 8.30am-6.30pm daily.
Admission free. **Map** p406 L9.
Libéral Bruand's austere 17th-century chapel provides a fantastic setting for contemporary art, notably to date installations by Viola, Kawamata, Kapoor and Holzer for various Festivals d'Automne. *Wheelchair access.*

Espace Paul Ricard

*9 rue Royale, 8th (01.53.30.88.00/
www.espacepaulricard.com). M° Concorde.* **Open**
10am-7pm Mon-Fri. Closed weekends, some public
holidays. **No credit cards. Map** p405 F4.
The purveyor of *pastis* here promotes contemporary art, notably with the Prix Paul Ricard – young French artists shortlisted by an indepedent curator for an annual prize – held to coincide with FIAC each autumn. Other shows have included new German painters and contemporary design.

Fondation Cartier pour l'art contemporain

*261 bd Raspail, 14th (01.42.18.56.72/recorded info
01.42.18.56.51/www.fondation.cartier.fr).*
M° Raspail. **Open** noon-8pm Tue, Wed-Sun. Closed
Mon. **Admission** €5; €3.50 under-25s, students,
over-60s; free under-10s. **Credit** AmEx, MC, V.
Map p405 G9.
Jean Nouvel's jaw-dropping 1990s glass and steel

building, which combines an exhibition centre with Cartier's offices up above, is as much a work of art as the quirky installations inside. Monographic shows by contemporary artists and photographers (Pierrick Sorin, Eggleston, Takashi Murakami) alternate with wide-ranging multicultural, century-crossing themes, such as 'Birds' or 'the Desert'. The fact that the themes are identified saves you the effort of trying to work out what the hell's going on. Architect-turned-philospher-and-critic Paul Virilio has wanted to put together a multi-disciplinary project based on the concept of 'Accidents' for ten years: at last you can catch it in 2003 (until March).
Bookshop. Wheelchair access.

Fondation Coffim

*46 rue de Sévigné, 3rd (01.44.78.60.00/
www.fondation-coprim.com). M° St-Paul.* **Open**
10am-6pm Mon-Fri; 2-6pm Sat. Closed Sun, Aug,
public holidays. **Admission** free. **Map** p406 L6.
The gallery belonging to property developer Coprim moved recently to a former print workshop in the Marais; the new environment is super-smart and shiny. The bent is mostly towards contemporary figurative painting – Gérard Garouste, Combas, et al – and the foundation also runs a prestigious annual competition for young artists. *Bookshop.*

Fondation EDF - Espace Electra

6 rue Récamier, 7th (01.53.63.23.45/www.edf.fr).
M° Sèvres-Babylone. **Open** noon-7pm Tues-Sun.
Closed Mon, public holidays, between exhibitions.
Admission free **No credit cards. Map** p405 G7.
This former electricity substation, owned by the French electricity board, is used for varied, well-presented exhibitions, from garden designer Gilles Clément to pioneer film-maker Georges Méliès.

Fondation Icar

*159 quai de Valmy, 10th (01.53.26.36.61/
www.icarfoundation.org). M° Colonel Fabien or
Château Landon.* **Open** 1-7pm Wed-Sun. Closed
some public holidays, Aug, Sept. **Admission** free.
Map p402 L3.
American-funded Icar puts on occasional, but always intriguing, exhibitions of American conceptual art, plus related music and lectures, in strikingly converted, light-filled former industrial premises alongside the Canal St-Martin.

Fondation Mona Bismarck

34 av de New-York, 16th (01.47.23.38.88).
M° Alma-Marceau. **Open** 10.30am-6.30pm Tue-Sat.
Closed Mon, Sun, Aug, public holidays. **Admission**
free. **Map** p404 C5.
Good old Mona (née Strader, but she married well, and often): the Fondation provides a chic setting for eclectic exhibitions of everything from Etruscan antiquities to North American Indian art, often lent by prestigious foreign collections. One of the three main exhibitions of 2003 will be of ancient Italian ceramics from the Art History Museum of Geneva.

Sightseeing

Galeries Nationales du Grand Palais

3 av du Général-Eisenhower, 8th (01.44.13.17.17/ www.rmn.fr). M° Champs-Elysées-Clemenceau. **Open** 10am-8pm Mon, Thur-Sun; 10am-10pm Wed. Pre-booking compulsory before 1pm. Closed Tue, 1 May, 25 Dec. **Admission** €8-€10; €5.50-€8 18-26s, all on Mon; free under-13s. **Credit** MC, V. **Map** p405 E5.

Paris' premier venue for blockbuster exhibitions is a striking leftover from the 1900 *Exposition Universelle* but it still has plenty of life left in it. The glass-domed central hall is closed for restoration, but two other exhibition spaces remain. Highlights of 2003 include major shows featuring the work of Chagall, Vuillard and Gauguin.

Audioguides. Shop. Café. Cinema. Wheelchair access.

Halle St-Pierre – Musée d'Art Naïf Max Fourny

2 rue Ronsard, 18th (01.42.58.72.89/ www.hallesaintpierre.org). M° Anvers. **Open** 10am-6pm daily. Closed 1 Jan, 1 May, 25 Dec, Aug. **Admission** €6.50; €5 students 12-26; free under-4s. **Credit** (shop) AmEx, DC, MC, V. **Map** p406 J2.

The former covered market in the glorious shadow of Sacré-Coeur specialises in *art brut* (a term coined by Dubuffet to describe self-taught *singuliers*, including the mentally ill, who used poor or idiosyncratic materials) and *art-naïf* (self-taught artists who use more traditional techniques) from its own and other collections. Two shows run until the end of July 2003: *Oeil pour oeil* (*An Eye for an Eye*), which explores the often visionary 'savage eye' of *art brut* creators, and a restrospective of the weird and magical world of Jephan de Villiers.

Bookshop. Café/restaurant. Children's workshops.

Jeu de Paume

1 pl de la Concorde, 8th (01.47.03.12.50). M° Concorde. **Open** noon-9.30pm Tue; noon-7pm Wed-Fri; 10am-7pm Sat, Sun. Closed Mon, some public holidays. **Admission** €6; €4.50 students, 13-18s, over-60s; free under-13s. **Credit** MC, V. **Map** p405 F5.

When the Impressionist museum moved from here to the Musée d'Orsay, the former royal real tennis court was intelligently redesigned for modern and contemporary art shows. Retrospective-style shows held here have included César, Arman and Morellet with occasional excursions into architecture. This year the sure-fire crowdpuller will be a major show on Magritte (Feb-June).

Bookshop. Café. Cinema. Wheelchair access.

Musée-atelier Adzak

3 rue Jonquoy, 14th (01.45.43.06.98). M° Plaisance. **Open** hours vary, call in advance. **Admission** free. The eccentric house and studio built by the late Roy Adzak harbours traces of the conceptual artist's plaster body columns and dehydrations. Now a registered British-run charity, it gives (mainly foreign) artists a first chance to exhibit in Paris.

Partial wheelchair access.

Musée National du Luxembourg

19 rue de Vaugirard, 6th (01.42.34.25.95). M° St-Sulpice/RER Luxembourg. **Open** 10am-11pm Mon, Fri; 10am-7pm Tue-Thur; 10am-8pm Sat, Sun. **Admission** €9; €6 students; €4 8-12s; free under 8s. **Credit** MC, V. **Map** p405 F7.

This small but imposing museum was the first public gallery in France when it opened in 1750 and was later a forerunner of the Musée National d'Art Moderne. After several years in the wilderness, a more coherent and imaginative policy is now in evidence, under the stewardship of the national museums and the French Senate: 2002's once-in-a-lifetime Raphael exhibition had queues stretching around the block, and the 2003 exhibitions, focusing on Modigliani (until March) and Gaughin (Apr-June), look set to be just as amazing.

Café. Shop. Wheelchair access.

Palais de Tokyo: Site de Création Contemporaine

13 av de New-York, 16th (01.47.23.54.01/ www.palaisdetokyo.com). M° Iéna or Alma-Marceau. **Open** noon-midnight Tue-Sun. Closed Mon, some public holidays. **Admission** €5, €3. **Map** p404 B5.

Otherwise known as 'the other bit' opposite the Musée d'Art Moderne de la Ville de Paris, this adventurous venue, started by Jérôme Sans and Nicolas Bourreaud, aims to change the face of the contemporary art scene. Its late opening hours show an effort to be more in tune with the lifestyles of city-dwellers, and the reasonably-priced canteen-style café-restaurant is open to the museum space. Proclaimed 'a laboratory for contemporary art', the building has been stripped back to its concrete shell, revealing a skylit central hall, and permitting the coexistence of exhibitions and installations, fashion shows and performances.

Bar. Restaurant. Shop. Wheelchair access.

Passage de Retz

9 rue Charlot, 3rd (01.48.04.37.99). M° Filles du Calvaire. **Open** 10am-7pm Tue-Sun. **Admission** €6; €4 students under 26, over-60s; free under-12s. **Credit** (over €10) MC, V. **Map** p406 L5.

This gorgeous Marais mansion was resurrected as a gallery eight years ago. Its 750m² bright, open-plan exhibition space, designed by Sylvain Dubuisson, has hosted exhibitions and installations by contemporary artists, architects, designers and photographers. Wooden floors, a glass roof and walled garden give it a relaxing vibe. Pop into the designer café, if only to see the extraordinary silver sponge bar, which looks for all the world like an enormous bosom, or alternatively a Zeppelin.

Bookshop. Café. Partial wheelchair access.

Pavillon des Arts

101 rue Rambuteau, 1st (01.42.33.82.50). M° Châtelet-Les Halles. **Open** 11.30am-6.30pm Tue-Sun. Closed Mon, public holidays. **Admission** €5.50; €4 students, over-60s; €2.50 8-26s; free under-8s. **No credit cards**. **Map** p406 K5.

...nogtastic **Musée National Rodin**. *See p162.*

This gallery in the Forum des Halles hosts varied exhibitions from contemporary photography to Turner to Paris history.
Wheelchair access.

Le Plateau

corner of rue des Alouettes and rue Carducci, 19th (01.53.19.84.10). Mº Buttes Chaumont/Jourdain. **Open** 2-7pm Wed-Fri, 11am-7pm Sat- Sun. Closed between exhibitions. **Admission** free.

This new contemporary art space, opened in spring 2002, has become the low-budget challenger to the Palais de Tokyo. Born out of a campaign by local associations for a community-based arts centre in northeast Paris and the search for an exhibition space for the FRAC d'Ile de France (Fonds Régional d'Art Contemporain), the small exhibition space has still managed to pull the crowds looking for 'real' art. Exhibitions from the FRAC collection alternate with artist-curated shows and projects with local artists' groups, complemented by experimental cinema, contemporary music and dance.

One-man shows

Atelier Brancusi

piazza Beaubourg, 4th (01.44.78.12.33 www.centrepompidou.fr). Mº Hôtel de Ville or Rambuteau/RER Châtelet-Les Halles. **Open** 2-6pm Mon, Wed-Sun. **Admission** (included with Centre Pompidou – Musée National d'Art Moderne) €5.50; €3.50 18-26s; free under-18s, first Sun in month. **Credit** AmEx, MC, V. **Map** p406 K6.

When Constantin Brancusi died in 1956 he left his studio in the 15th *arrondissement* and all its contents to the state. Rebuilt outside the Centre Pompidou, the studio has been faithfully reconstructed. His fragile works in wood and plaster, including his endless columns and streamlined bird forms, show how Brancusi revolutionised sculpture.

Atelier-Musée Henri Bouchard

25 rue de l'Yvette, 16th (01.46.47.63.46/ www.musee-bouchard.com). Mº Jasmin. **Open** 2-7pm Wed, Sat. Closed last two weeks of Mar, June, Sept and Dec. **Admission** €4; €2.50 students under-26; free under-6s. **No credit cards**.

Prolific sculptor Henri Bouchard moved here in 1924. Lovingly tended by his son and daughter-in-law, his dusty studio, crammed with sculptures, casts and moulds, sketchbooks and tools, gives an idea of the official art of the time. Bouchard began with Realist-style peasants and maidens, but around 1907-09 he moved to a more stylised, pared down, linear modern style, as seen in his reliefs for the Eglise St-Jean-de-Chaillot and the monumental *Apollo* for the Palais de Chaillot. One of the highlights of 2003 will be an exhibition devoted to women in Bouchard's sculptures.
Partial wheelchair access.

Espace Dalí Montmartre

11 rue Poulbot, 18th (01.42.64.40.10). Mº Anvers or Abbesses. **Open** 10am-6.30pm daily; *July-Aug* 10am-9pm daily. **Admission** €7; €6 over-60s; €5 8-25s, students; free under-8s. **Credit** (shop) AmEx, DC, MC, V. **Map** p405 H1.

The black-walled interior, artistically programmed lighting and specially composed soundtrack make

Pablo's palace: **Musée Picasso**. *See p162.*

it clear that this is a high-marketing presentation of the artist's work. Don't expect to see Dalí's Surrealist paintings; the museum concentrates on his sculptures and sketches (many from the tacky end of his career) and his literary tributes to La Fontaine, Freud, de Sade, Dante and *Don Quixote*.
Shop.

Fondation Dubuffet

137 rue de Sèvres, 6th (01.47.34.12.63/ www.dubuffet-fondation.com). M° Duroc.
Open 2-6pm Mon-Fri. Closed weekends, Aug, public holidays. **Admission** €4; free under 10s. **No credit cards. Map** p405 E8.
You literally have to travel up a garden path (very charming, so it's not too traumatic) to reach this museum tucked away in an old three-storey mansion. Set up by the controversial artist and one-time wine merchant just a decade before his death, the foundation ensures that there is a significant body of his works permanently accessible to the public. There is a changing display of Dubuffet's playful and exuberant drawings, paintings and sculptures, plus models of the architectural sculptures from the Hourloupe cycle.
Archives (by appointment). Bookshop.

Musée Bourdelle

16-18 rue Antoine-Bourdelle, 15th (01.49.54.73.73). M° Montparnasse-Bienvenüe or Falguière. **Open** 10am-5.40pm Tue-Sun. Closed Mon, public holidays. **Admission** Permanent collection free. Temporary

exhibitions €4; €3 students, over-60s; free under-13s. **No credit cards. Map** p405 F8.
Rodin's pupil, sculptor Antoine Bourdelle, produced monumental works including the Modernist relief friezes at the Théâtre des Champs-Elysées, inspired by Isadora Duncan and Nijinsky. Housed around a small garden, the museum includes the artist's studio and apartments, a 1950s extension revealing the evolution of Bourdelle's equestrian monument to General Alvear in Buenos Aires, and a new wing by Christian de Portzamparc housing bronzes such as his studies of Beethoven in various guises that embody different aspects of creative genius.
Bookshop. Children's workshops. Reference library (by appointment). Wheelchair access.

Musée National Delacroix

6 pl Furstenberg, 6th (01.44.41.86.50/www.musee- delacroix.fr). M° St-Germain-des-Prés. **Open** 9.30am- 12.30pm, 2-5pm Mon, Wed-Sun. Closed Tue, 1 Jan, 1 May, 25 Dec. **Admission** €4; €2.60 18-25s, all on Sun; free under-18s, first Sun of month; CM. **Credit** MC, V. **Map** p405 H6.
The pretty place Furstenberg, where Delacroix moved in 1857 to be nearer to the Eglise St-Sulpice where he was painting murals, has just had a dust-off in time for 2003. The Louvre and the Musée d'Orsay house his major paintings, but the collection displayed in his apartment and studio includes small oil paintings, some free pastel studies of skies and sketches, and still maintains some of the atmosphere of the studio as it must have been in his day. Other displays relate to his friendships with Baudelaire and George Sand.
Bookshop.

Musée National Hébert

85 rue du Cherche-Midi, 6th (01.42.22.23.82). M° St-Placide or Vaneau. **Open** 12.30-6pm Mon, Wed-Fri; 2-6pm Sat, Sun and public holidays. Closed Tue, 1 Jan, 1 May, 25 Dec. **Admission** €3; €2.44 18- 25s; free under-18s, first Sun of month; CM. **No credit cards. Map** p405 F7.
Ernest Hébert (1817-1908) was a painter of Italian landscapes and figurative subjects, who started off with hilariously uptight pious portraits and lachrymose depictions of sentimental shepherdesses, before turning towards brightly coloured, Symbolist-influenced muses and Impressionist-tinged ladies. Although Hébert was fairly successful in life, for most people the watercolours and oils are unremarkable and soon begin to drag a bit. However, if nothing else, they remain an interesting testament to 19th-century taste, and the run-down house, built in 1743, has a certain (run-down) appeal.

Musée-Jardin Paul Landowski

14 rue Max Blondat, 92100 Boulogne-Billancourt (01.46.05.82.69/www.mairie-boulogne-billancourt.fr). M° Boulogne-Jean Jaurès. **Open** 10am-noon, 2-5pm Wed, Sat, Sun. Closed some public holidays. **Admission** €2. **No credit cards.**
Sculptor Landowski (1875-1961) had the great good fortune to win the Prix de Rome in 1900, and there-

Time to remember

On 16 and 17 July 1942, 12,884 Jews, 4,051 of them children, were arrested in Paris by the French police under the orders of the Vichy government and rounded up in the Vélodrome d'Hiver in the 15th (now marked by a plaque on quai de Grenelle). The Vél d'Hiver has come to symbolise the zeal of Vichy France in following – and exceeding – Nazi orders. A quarter of France's wartime Jewish population was murdered in the Holocaust but the tragedy has been shamefully played down by governments seeking to distance the French state from the Vichy regime. Some amends were made under Chirac, with an admission in 1995 that the French state was responsible and the sentencing to prison in 1998 of an ex-Vichy official. For a city so horrendously affected by the tragedy, however, it is surprising that Paris has not up to now had its own Holocaust museum. The **Musée d'Art et d'Histoire du Judaïsme** (*see p176*) has some fine examples of art and artefacts but doesn't tackle history beyond the beginning of the 20th century. The city has two holocaust memorials – the moving but notably discreet **Mémorial de la Déportation** (*see p80*) and the **Mémorial du Martyr Juif Inconnu** in the Marais, and it is the latter that has been chosen as the site for the Musée de la

Shoah, scheduled to open in 2004. The **Centre de Documentation Juive Contemporaine**, housed in the memorial, will be closed till 2004 but a small display can be seen at a temporary address (*see below*). The project also encompasses the building of a wall In Jerusalem stone containing a full list of names of the 76,000 Jews deported from France between 1942 and 1945, for which extensive research had to be done comparing the original Gestapo reports with other sources.

October 2002 saw another boost for Jewish culture in Paris with the opening of the **Maison de la Culture Yiddish**. It has an impressive media centre with 8,000 books, 4,000 recorded songs and a nearly 1,000 videos and, true to its *raison d'etre*, runs Yiddish language courses as well as klezmer music, singing and even Yiddish cookery.

Mémorial du Martyr Juif Inconnu (future Shoah Museum)

17 rue Geoffroy-l'Asnier, 4th (www.memorial-cdjc.org). Mº St Paul. **Temporary display:** *37 rue de Turenne, 3rd (01.42.77.44.72).*

Maison de la Culture Yiddish

18 passage St-Pierre Amelot, 11th (01.48.03.20.17/www.yiddishweb.com). Mº Oberkampf. **Open** 9.30am-7pm Mon-Fri; 2-5pm Sat, Sun.

after was kept busy with state commissions. Landowski was not a man who thought small or sat around twiddling his chisel: most of his work treats both classical and modern themes on a monumental scale. One of his most intriguing creations is *Temple*: four sculpted walls depicting 'the history of humanity'. About a hundred sculptures are on show in this pleasant garden and studio.

Musée Maillol

59-61 rue de Grenelle, 7th (01.42.22.59.58/ www.museemaillol.com). M° Rue du Bac. **Open** 11am-6pm Mon, Wed-Sun. Closed Tue. **Admission** €7; €5.50 students; free under-16s. **Credit** (shop) AmEx, MC, V. **Map** p405 G7.

Dina Vierny was only 15 when she met Maillol (1861-1944) and became his principal model for the next decade (nudge-nudge, wink-wink), idealised in such sculptures as *Spring, Air* and *Harmony*. In 1995 she opened this delightful museum over the renovated 18th-century Hôtel Bouchardon, displaying Maillol's drawings, pastels, engravings, tapestry panels, ceramics and his early Nabis-related paintings, as well as sculptures and terracottas. A 20th-century treasure trove, the museum also displays works by Picasso, Rodin, Gauguin, Degas and Cézanne, a whole room of Matisse drawings, some rare Surrealist documents and multiples by Marcel Duchamp and Jacques Duchamp-Villon. Vierny has also championed Russian artists from Kandinsky and Poliakoff to Ilya Kabakov, whose installation *The Communal Kitchen* recreates the atmosphere and sounds of a shared Soviet kitchen. German artist Christian Schad is the focus of the first exhibition of 2003 (until February), with Raoul Dufy hot on his heels (Mar-Jun).
Bookshop. Café. Wheelchair access.

Musée Gustave Moreau

14 rue de La Rochefoucauld, 9th (01.48.74.38.50). M° Trinité. **Open** 10am-12.45pm, 2-5.15pm Mon, Wed-Sun. Closed Tue, some public holidays. **Admission** €3.40; €2.30 18-25s, Sun; free under-18s; CM. **Credit** AmEx, MC, V. **Map** p405 G3.

Easily the looniest of all the one-man museums, this is not only where Symbolist painter Gustave Moreau (1825-98) lived, worked and taught, but was also designated by the artist to become a museum after his death – as was inevitable given that the enormous double-storey studio is stuffed to the gills with his paintings, finished or otherwise. Thousands more of his drawings and watercolours can be pulled out from shutters on the walls. His mind in retreat, Moreau developed a personal mythology, filling his detailed canvases with images of St John the Baptist, St George, the divinely lascivious Salomé, mystical beasts, strange plants and fantastical architecture. It's also a chance to see the dinky private apartment where he lived with his parents, which he arranged symbolically in their memory.
Bookshop.

Musée National Picasso

Hôtel Salé, 5 rue de Thorigny, 3rd (01.42.71.25.21). M° Chemin-Vert or St-Paul. **Open** *Apr-Oct* 9.30am-6pm Mon, Wed-Sun; *Nov-Mar* 9.30am-5.30pm Mon, Wed-Sun. Closed Tue, 25 Dec, 1 Jan. **Admission** €5.50; €4 18-25s; free under-18s, first Sun of month; CM. **Credit** (shop) AmEx, MC, V. **Map** p404 L6.

This unparalleled collection of Picasso's paintings and sculpture was acquired by the state in lieu of inheritance tax and is housed in one of the grandest Marais mansions. The collection represents all phases of the master's long and varied career, showing Picasso's continual inventiveness and life-affirming sense of humour. Masterpieces include a gaunt, blue-period self-portrait, studies for the *Demoiselles d'Avignon*, *Paolo as Harlequin*, his Cubist and classical phases, the surreal *Nude in an Armchair*, lively beach pictures of the 1920-30s, portraits of his favourite models Marie-Thérèse and Dora Maar, and the unabashedly ribald pictures he produced in later years. The unusual wallpaper collage, *Women at their Toilette*, gets its own small room, and there are also prints and ceramics, minotaur etchings, and Picasso's collection of tribal art – juxtaposed with 'primitive' wood figures that he actually carved himself. Take the time to concentrate on his bizarrely wonderful sculptures, from the vast plaster head on the staircase and the spiky *Project for Monument to Apollinaire* to the *Girl on a Swing*. Look closely at the sculpture of an ape – its face is actually made out of a toy car. This museum is an astonishing testament to one man's bewilderingly inventive genius, but with this amount of material even Picasso can get repetitive. A few paintings by Matisse and Douanier Rousseau take the pressure off.
Audiovisual room. Bookshop. Outdoor café May-Oct. Wheelchair access.

Musée National Rodin

Hôtel Biron, 77 rue de Varenne, 7th (01.44.18.61.10/www.musee-rodin.fr). M° Varenne. **Open** *Apr-Sept* 9.30am-5.45pm Tue-Sun (gardens 6.45pm); *Oct-Mar* 9.30am-4.45pm (gardens 5pm) Tue-Sun. Closed Mon, 25 Dec, 1 Jan, 1 May. **Admission** €5; €3 18-25s, all on Sun; free under-18s, first Sun of month; CM. Gardens only €1. **Credit** MC, V. **Map** p405 F6.

The Rodin museum occupies the *hôtel particulier* where Rodin lived at the end of his life. *The Kiss*, *Cathedral*, the *Walking Man*, portraits and early terracottas are indoors, accompanied by several works by Rodin's mistress and pupil, Camille Claudel. To top it off, the walls are hung with paintings by Van Gogh, Monet, Renoir, Carrière and Rodin himself. But it's the gardens that most people seem to love, perhaps because they do away with museum claustrophobia, or perhaps because they're spotted with shady trees, and full of unexpected treasures. Look out for the *Burghers of Calais*, the elaborate *Gates of Hell*, the *Thinker*, *Orpheus* under a shady stretch of trees, and several unfinished nymphs emerging from their marble prison. Fans can also visit Villa des Brillants at Meudon (01.41.14.35.00; *May-Oct,*

Sightseeing

1-6pm Fri-Sun, museum and gardens €2, gardens only €1), where Rodin worked from 1895.
Bookshop. Garden café. Partial wheelchair access. Visits for visually handicapped (by appointment).

Musée Zadkine

100bis rue d'Assas, 6th (01.43.26.91.90). M° Notre-Dame-des-Champs or Vavin/RER Port Royal. **Open** 10am-6pm Tue-Sun. Closed Mon, public holidays. **Admission** Permanent collection free. Temporary exhibitions €4; €3 students, over-60s; €2 under-26s; free under-13s; CM. **No credit cards. Map** p405 G8.
Works by the Cubist sculptor Ossip Zadkine are displayed around this tiny house and garden near the Jardins du Luxembourg. Zadkine's compositions include musical, mythological and religious subjects and his style varies with the materials: bronzes tend to be geometrical, wood more sensuous, flowing with the grain. Sculptures are displayed at eye level, along with drawings and poems by Zadkine and some paintings by his wife, Valentine Prax. There are also temporary exhibitions of contemporary art. *Partial wheelchair access.*

Architecture & urbanism

Institut Français d'Architecture

6 rue de Tournon, 6th (01.46.33.90.36/ www.archi.fr/IFA-CHAILLOT). M° Odéon. **Open** (during exhibitions) 12.30-7pm Tue-Sun. **Admission** free. **No credit cards. Map** p406 H7.
Exhibitions examine 20th-century architects or aspects of the built environment, with an emphasis on Modernist pioneers and current projects. In 2004

the IFA and the Musée des Monuments (currently closed) merge as the new Cité de l'Architecture et du Patrimoine in the Palais de Chaillot (for more information visit www.archi.fr/IFA/chaillot).
Lectures. Library. Partial wheelchair access (call ahead).

Musée des Années 30

Espace Landowski, 28 av André-Morizet, 92100 Boulogne-Billancourt (01.55.18.46.45). M° Marcel Sembat. **Open** 11am-6pm Tue-Sun. Closed Mon, 15-31 Aug, public holidays. **Admission** €4.10; €3.10 students, over-60s; free under-16s. **No credit cards.**
The Musée des Années 30 is a reminder of what an awful lot of second-rate art was produced in the 1930s. There are decent Modernist sculptures by the Martel brothers, graphic designs and Juan Gris still lifes and drawings, but the highlights are the designs by avant-garde architects including Perret, Le Corbusier, Lurçat and Fischer.
Guided visits 2.30pm Sun. Shop. Wheelchair access.

Musée des Arts d'Afrique et d'Océanie

293 av Daumesnil, 12th (01.44.74.84.80/recorded information 01.43.46.51.61). M° Porte Dorée.
Opening times & admission Not known at time of going to press. **No credit cards.**
Its collection of Aboriginal and Pacific island art, African masks and statues has gone into storage in preparation for the new Musée des Arts Premiers (*see p171* **Primitive & Proper**), but the shell of this extraordinary museum is still open to architecture fans. Designed for the 1931 Exposition Coloniale, it has an art deco bas-relief glorying in France's colonial past and two art deco rooms by

Jean Nouvel's glass-fronted **Fondation Cartier**. *See p157.*

Sightseeing

Ruhlmann with fantastic murals by Ducos de la Haille. Happily for the crocodiles, the basement still houses its rather noisy aquarium.

Pavillon de l'Arsenal

21 bd Morland, 4th (01.42.76.33.97/www.pavillon-arsenal.com). M° Sully-Morland. **Open** 10.30am-6.30pm Tue-Sat; 11am-7pm Sun. Closed Mon, 1 Jan. **Admission** free. **Credit** (shop) MC, V. **Map** p406 L7.
This centre presents imaginative exhibitions on urban design and architecture, often looking at Paris from unusual perspectives, be it that of theatres, hidden courtyards or the banks of the Seine. There's a 50m² model of Paris, and a permanent exhibition '*Paris, la ville et ses projets*' on the historic growth of the city.

Decorative arts

Musée des Antiquités Nationales

Château, pl du Charles de Gaulle, 78100 St-Germain-en-Laye (01.39.10.13.00/www.musee-antiquitiesnationales.fr). RER A St-Germain-en-Laye. **Open** 9am-5.15pm Mon, Wed-Sun. Closed 25 Dec, 1 Jan. **Admission** €4; €2.60 students 18-25; free under-18s, first Sun of month; CM. **Credit** (shop) MC, V.
Thousands of years spin by from one cabinet to the next in this awe-inspiring museum tracing France's rich archaeological heritage: some of the early Paleolithic animal sculptures existed long before the Ancient Egyptians. Artefacts from the Romans in Gaul are more familiar but of fine quality. The redesigned Neolithic galleries feature statue-menhirs, female statues and an ornate tombstone from Cys-la-Commune. Exhibits are well presented and full of curiosities, like the massive antlers from a prehistoric Irish deer or the set of 18th-century cork models of ancient sites. The museum also hosts a couple of interesting temporary exhibitions each year, which are included in the entry price.
Guided visits. Shop. Wheelchair access.

Musée des Arts Décoratifs

Palais du Louvre, 107 rue de Rivoli, 1st (01.44.55.57.50/www.ucad.fr). M° Palais Royal. **Open** 11am-6pm Tue-Fri (until 9pm Wed); 10am-6pm Sat, Sun. Closed Mon, some public holidays. **Admission** €5.40; €3.90 18-25s; free under-18s; CM. **Credit** MC, V. **Map** p406 H5.
This rich collection of decorative arts is currently undergoing a major facelift as part of the Grand Louvre project. So far only the Renaissance and Middle Ages galleries are open; the remaining departments are scheduled for completion in 2004. In addition to 16th-century Venetian glass and Flemish tapestries, there are two reconstructions of period rooms: a panelled Gothic Charles VIII bedchamber and a Renaissance room. The religious art collection includes a wonderful altarpiece of the life of John the Baptist by Luis Borassa. Temporary exhibitions often feature aspects of 20th-century design or contemporary artist-designers.
Library. Shop. Wheelchair access (105 rue de Rivoli).

The Lady and the Unicorn tapestry cycle, one of the treasures of **Cluny**. *See right.*

Musée National de la Céramique

pl de la Manufacture, 92310 Sèvres (01.41.14.04.20). M° Pont de Sèvres. **Open** 10am-5pm Mon, Wed-Sun. Closed Tue, public holidays. **Admission** €4; €2.60 18-25s; free under-18s, all on Sun; CM. **Credit** (showroom) MC, V.

Founded in 1738 as a private concern, the porcelain factory moved to Sèvres from Vincennes in 1756 and was soon taken over by the state. Finely painted, delicately modelled pieces that epitomise French Rococo style, together with later Sèvres, adorned with copies of Raphaels and Titians, demonstrate extraordinary technical virtuosity. The collection also includes Delftware, Meissen, Della Robbia reliefs, Hispano-Moorish pieces and wonderful Ottoman plates and tiles from Iznik.
Shop and showroom. Wheelchair access.

Musée du Cristal Baccarat

30bis rue de Paradis, 10th (01.47.70.64.30/ www.baccarat.fr). M° Poissonnière. **Open** 10am-6pm Mon-Sat. Closed Sun, public holidays. **Admission** €3; free under-12s. **Credit** (shop) AmEx, DC, MC, V. **Map** p406 H5.

This is the showroom of celebrated glassmaker Baccarat, with a museum attached. The main attraction is in seeing which fallen head of state or deposed monarch used to drink out of Baccarat glasses – many a champion of the people seems to have got sloshed via Baccarat. There are also some kitsch but technically magnificent pieces produced for the great exhibitions of the 1800s and the superb Art Deco services designed by Georges Chevalier. Baccarat transferred its workshops here in 1832; the street remains full of glass and china outlets.

Musée de l'Eventail

2 bd de Strasbourg, 10th (01.42.08.90.20). M° Strasbourg-St-Denis. **Open** 2-6pm Mon-Wed. **Workshop** 9am-12.30pm, 2-6pm Mon-Fri. Closed Aug, public holidays. **Admission** €5; €2.50 under 12s. **No credit cards. Map** p406 K4.

The fan-making Hoguet family's collection is housed in the workshop and neo-Renaissance showroom, and you may well see fans being made (now generally for fashion shows) as you walk around. Exhibits go from 18th-century fans with mother-of-pearl and ivory sticks to early 20th-century advertising fans and contemporary designs by Karl Lagerfeld. There's also a display on the techniques and materials used to make these luxury items – which, until the French Revolution, only the nobility were permitted to use.

Musée Galliéra: Musée de la Mode de la Ville de Paris

Palais Galliéra, 10 av Pierre 1er de Serbie, 16th (01.56.52.86.00). M° Iéna or Alma-Marceau. **Open** during exhibitions 10am-6pm Tue-Sun. Closed Mon, public holidays. **Admission** (includes audioguide) €7; €5.50 over-60s; €3.50 13-26s; free under-13s. **Credit** MC, V. **Map** p404 C5.

Opposite the Musée d'Art Moderne de la Ville de Paris is this fanciful 1890s mansion housing the administrative offices of the state's vast costume collection. The two ground-floor rooms hold changing exhibitions, ranging from the history of *toile de Jouy* to the annual Modes à Suivres (early Sept), where the creations of young designers are showcased at the same time as they hit the shops.

Musée National du Moyen Age – Thermes de Cluny

6 pl Paul-Painlevé, 5th (01.53.73.78.00/www.musee-moyenage.fr). M° Cluny-La Sorbonne/RER St-Michel. **Open** 9.15am-5.45pm Mon, Wed-Sun. Closed Tue, 1 Jan, 1 May, 25 Dec. **Admission** €5.55; €4 18-25s, all on Sun; free under-18s, first Sun of month; CM. **No credit cards. Map** p406 J7.

Occupying the Paris mansion of the medieval abbots of Cluny and the remains of a Roman bathing establishment, the museum of medieval art and artefacts retains a domestic scale suitable for the intimacy of many of its treasures. Most famous is the mesmerising *Lady and the Unicorn* tapestry cycle: six, late 15th-century Flemish *mille-fleurs* tapestries depicting convoluted allegories of the five senses, beautifully displayed in a special circular room. Other textiles include fragile Coptic embroidery and Edward III's emblazoned saddle cloth. Elsewhere there are enamel bowls and caskets from Limoges, ornate gold reliquaries, stained glass, carved ivory, medieval books of hours, wooden chests and locks, Nottingham alabasters, and Flemish and German wood carving. One room is devoted to chivalry and everyday life at the end of the Middle Ages. The heads of the kings of Judah from Notre-Dame cathedral, mutilated in the Revolution under the mistaken belief that they represented the kings of France and rediscovered (minus their noses) in 1979, are the highlight of the sculpture collection. *See also p114.*
Bookshop. Concerts. Guided tours in English 2pm Wed; 11.45am Sat.

Musées des Parfumeries-Fragonard

9 rue Scribe, 9th (01.47.42.93.40) and 39 bd des Capucines, 2nd (01.42.60.37.14). M° Opéra. **Open** 9am-5.30pm Mon-Sat. Closed Sun, 25 Dec. (Apr-Oct rue Scribe open daily). **Admission** free. **Credit** AmEx, MC, V. **Map** p405 G4.

Get on the scent at the two museums showcasing the collection of perfume house Fragonard. The five rooms at rue Scribe range from Ancient Egyptian ointment flasks to Meissen porcelain scent bottles, while the second museum contains, among others, bottles by Lalique and Schiaparelli. Both have displays on scent manufacture and an early 20th-century 'perfume organ' (which sounds saucier than it actually is) with rows of ingredients used by 'noses' to creating those stimulating concoctions.
Shop.

Musée de la Publicité

Palais du Louvre, 107 rue de Rivoli, 1st (01.44.55.57.50/www.ucad.fr). M° Palais Royal. **Open** 11am-6pm Tue, Thur-Fri; 11am-9pm Wed; 10am-6pm Sat, Sun. Closed Mon, some public

Sightseeing

It's a glass act at the **Musée du Cristal Baccarat**. *See p165.*

holidays. **Admission** €5.40; €3.90 18-25s; free under-18s; CM. **Credit** MC, V. **Map** p405 H5.
The advertising museum holds an enormous collection of posters, promotional objects and packaging, only a small fraction of which can be seen at one time. Temporary exhibitions go from individual graphic designers to 20th-century Chinese posters, while the multimedia space allows you to access historic posters by the likes of Toulouse-Lautrec. The distressed interior by Jean Nouvel was inspired by the city: the result is contemporary yet respectful.
Archives. Café. Shop. Wheelchair access.

Musée Nissim de Camondo
63 rue de Monceau, 8th (01.53.89.06.40/ www.ucad.fr). M° Villiers or Monceau. **Open** 10am-5pm Wed-Sun. **Admission** €4.57; €3.05 18-25s; free under-18s; CM. Closed Mon, Tue, some public holidays. **Credit** MC, V. **Map** p405 E3.
The collection, put together by Count Moïse de Camondo, is named after his son Nissim, killed in World War I. Moïse replaced the family's two houses near Parc Monceau with this palatial residence in 1911-14, and lived here in a style more in keeping with his love of the 18th century. Grand first-floor reception rooms are stuffed with furniture by leading craftsmen of the Louis XV and XVI eras, huge silver services and sets of Sèvres and Meissen porcelain, Savonnerie carpets and Aubusson tapestries. Nissim de Camondo's bedroom, the kitchens and servants' quarters are also open to the public.
Bookshop.

Musée de la Mode et du Textile
Palais du Louvre, 107 rue de Rivoli, 1st (01.44.55.57.50/www.ucad.fr). M° Palais Royal. **Open** 11am-6pm Tue, Thur-Fri; 11am-9pm Wed; 10am-6pm Sat, Sun. Closed Mon, some public holidays. **Admission** €5.40; €3.90 18-25s; free under-18s; CM. **Credit** MC, V. **Map** p406 H5.
Housed in the Palais du Louvre (but entered separately), the Musée de la Mode boasts the richest collection of 20th-century fashion worldwide, including the entire archives of Vionnet and 5,000 original drawings by Schiaparelli – obviously, only a fraction can be seen at one time. The museum may be more for those who live for fashion, but it's also about fashion for life, including designs that pave the way for future wardrobe must-haves by the likes of Comme des Garçons or Junya Watanabe. The crowd-puller in 2003 is sure to be the Jackie Kennedy exhibition, with more than 70 of the outfits she wore from 1959-1963 plus documents, films and photos. There's a parallel exhibition on how the 60s turned fashion on its head in Paris (until March).

Musée National de la Renaissance
Château d'Ecouen, 95440 Ecouen (01.34.38.38.50/www.musee-renaissance.fr). SNCF from Gare du Nord to Ecouen-Ezanville, then bus 269. **Open** 9.45am-12.30pm, 2-5.15pm Mon, Wed-Sun. Closed Tue, 1 Jan, 1 May, 25 Dec. **Admission** €4; €2.60 18-25s, Sun; free under-18s, first Sun of the month, CM. **No credit cards.**
The Renaissance château built 1538-55 for Royal

Constable Anne de Montmorency and his wife Margaret de Savoie is the authentic setting for a wonderful collection of 16th-century decorative arts. There are some real treasures arranged over three floors of the château (some parts only open in the morning or afternoon, so phone ahead if you have things you particularly want to see). Best of all are the original painted chimneypieces, decorated with caryatids, grotesques, Biblical and mythological scenes. Complementing them are Limoges enamels, armour, embroideries, rare painted leather wall hangings, and a magnificent tapestry cycle depicting the story of David and Bathsheba. This year's exhibition in the salle des tissues will be of fabulously embroidered priestly garb. Later in 2003, in an exhibition partnered by the Louvre, the Croatian Renaissance will be explored.

Bookshop. Wheelchair access (call ahead).

Musée de la Serrurerie – Musée Bricard

Hôtel Libéral Bruand, 1 rue de la Perle, 3rd (01.42.77.79.62). Mº St-Paul. **Open** 2-5pm Mon; 10am-noon, 2-5pm Tue-Fri. Closed Sat, Sun, Aug, Sept, public holidays. **Admission** €5; €2.50 students, over-60s; free under-18s. **No credit cards**. **Map** p406 L6.

Knockers, anyone? This museum, belonging to Bricard locksmiths, is housed in the cellars of the elegant mansion that architect Libéral Bruand built for himself in 1685. The collection focuses on locks and keys (Freud would have had a field day) from

Roman times to the end of the 20th century, finely wrought or engraved in the style of the time. It also takes in window fastenings, hinges, tools and elaborate, gilded door handles from Versailles, complete with Louis XIV's trademark sunburst.

Ethnology, folk & tribal art

See also p171 **Primitive & proper.**

Musée d'Art et d'Histoire du Judaïsme

Hôtel de St-Aignan, 71 rue du Temple, 3rd (01.53.01.86.53/www.mahj.org). Mº Rambuteau. **Open** 11am-6pm Mon-Fri; 10am-6pm Sun. Closed Sat, some Jewish holidays. **Admission** €6.10; €3.81 18-26s, students; free under-18s. **Credit** (shop) AmEx, MC, V. **Map** p406 K6.

Opened in 1998 in a Marais mansion, this museum originated from the collection of a private association formed in 1948 to safeguard Jewish heritage, so much of which had been dessecrated in the Holocaust. Displays bring out the importance of ceremonies, rites and learning, and show how styles were adapted across the globe through some fine examples of Jewish decorative arts: a silver Hannukah lamp made in Frankfurt, finely carved Italian synagogue furniture, a painted wooden sukkah cabin from Austria, embroidered Bar Mitzvah robes, Torah scrolls and North African dresses to name but a few. There are also documents and paintings relat-

ing to the emancipation of French Jewry after the Revolution, and the Dreyfus case, from Zola's *J'Accuse* to anti-Semitic cartoons. An impressive array of paintings by the early 20th-century avant-garde and the Ecole de Paris includes El Lissitsky, Mané-Katz, Modigliani, Soutine and Chagall. This museum does not deal with the Shoah (Holocaust), with the exception of a work by Christian Boltanski that commemorates the Jews who were living in the Hôtel St-Aignan in 1939, 13 of whom died in concentration camps. (*See also p161* **Time to Remember**.)
Auditorium. Café. Library. Shop. Wheelchair access.

Musée National des Arts et Traditions Populaires

6 av du Mahatma-Gandhi, 16th (01.44.17.60.00). M° Les Sablons. **Open** 9.30am-5pm Mon, Wed-Sun. Closed Tue, some public holidays. **Admission** €4; €2 10-25s, students, over-60s; free under-10s, first Sun of month; CM. **No credit cards.**
In contrast with its 1960s buiding, this centre of French folk art in the Bois de Boulogne spotlights the traditions and popular culture of pre-industrial France. Rural life is depicted through agricultural tools, household objects and costumes. The liveliest sections are those devoted to customs and beliefs – a crystal ball, tarot cards, thunder stones and early medicines – and popular entertainment. Visit now – it's due to move to Marseille in 2008.
Auditorium. Library/sound archive (by appointment). Shop. Wheelchair access.

Musée Dapper

35bis rue de Paul Valéry, 16th (01.45.00.01.50). M° Victor-Hugo. **Open** 11am-7pm Wed-Sun. Closed Mon and Tue, some public holidays. **Admission** €5; €2.50 students, 16s-25s; free under-16s. **Credit** MC, V. **Map** p404 B4.
This small specialist museum makes a refreshing change from the conventional Paris pit stops. The Fondation Dapper began in 1983 as an organisation dedicated to preserving sub-Saharan art. Reopened in 2000 after a renovation, the new Alain Moatti-designed museum includes a performance space, bookshop and café. A glass bridge leads you into the reception area, underneath is the café, a mixture of red lacquer and brown hues. The exhibition space houses two themed exhibitions every year covering Africa and the African diaspora.
Wheelchair access.

Musée de l'Homme

Palais de Chaillot, pl du Trocadéro, 16th (01.44.05.72.72). M° Trocadéro. **Open** 9.45am-5.15pm Mon, Wed-Sun. Closed Tue, public holidays. **Admission** €5; €3 4-16s, students under 27, over-60s. **Credit** (shop) MC, V. **Map** p404 B5.
Hiving off the human biology, anthropology and ethnology sections of the Muséum National d'Histoire Naturelle, the Musée de l'Homme begins with world population growth, going on to consider birth control, death, disease, genetics and racial distinction before turning to tribal costumes, tools, idols and ornaments from all over the world, arranged by con-

tinent. The displays could do with some labelling in English, but the variety of the collections, including a shrunken head, a stuffed polar bear and a reconstruction of a Mayan temple, makes for ideal escapism on a rainy day. The museum will close in 2004, when the collection moves to the new Musée du Quai Branly (*see p171* **Primitive & proper**). *Café. Cinema. Lectures. Library. Photo Library. Wheelchair access (call ahead).*

History

Mémorial du Maréchal Leclerc de Hauteclocque et de la Libération de Paris & Musée Jean Moulin

23 allée de la 2e DB, Jardin Atlantique (above Grandes Lignes of Gare Montparnasse), 15th (01.40.64.39.44). M° Montparnasse-Bienvenüe. **Open** 10am-6pm Tue-Sun. Closed Mon, public holidays. **Admission** Permanent collection free. Exhibitions normally €4; €3 students, over 60s; €2 under 25s; free under 13s; CM. **No credit cards.** **Map** p405 F9.
2003 marks not only the centenary of the birth of Free French Forces commander General Leclerc, but also 60 years since the death of left-wing Résistance hero, Jean Moulin, following his capture and torture by the Gestapo. This rooftop double museum all about World War II and the Résistance will be hosting special commemorative exhibitions for the occasion. There is also extensive documentary material here, backed up by film archives (in the first part captions are translated into English, though the translations disappear in the Résistance room). An impressive 270° slide show relates the liberation of Paris and memorable documents include a poster exhorting Frenchmen in occupied France to accept compulsory work service in Germany – to act as 'ambassadors of French quality'.
Bookshop. Lectures. Research centre. Wheelchair access (call ahead).

Musée de l'Armée

Hôtel des Invalides, esplanade des Invalides, 7th (01.44.42.37.72/www.invalides.org). M° Varenne or Latour-Maubourg. **Open** *Apr-Sept* 10am-6pm daily; *Oct-Mar* 10am-5pm daily. Closed first Mon of month, 1 Jan, 1 May, 1 Nov, 25 Dec. **Admission** €7; €5.50 students under 26; free under-18s, CM. **Credit** MC, V. **Map** p405 E6.
After checking out Napoléon's tomb under the vast golden dome of Les Invalides, many tourists don't bother to follow up with the army museum (included in the ticket). If you are interested in military history, the museum is a must, but even if sumptuous uniforms and armour are not your thing, the building is in itself a splendour. Besides military memorabilia, the rooms are filled with fine portraiture (don't miss Ingres' masterpiece, *Emperor Napoléon on his Throne*), some well-recreated interiors, as well as the newly reopened museum of maquettes of fortifications. The World War I rooms are particularly immediate and moving, the conflict brought vivid-

Brothers in arms at the **Musée des Arts d'Afrique et d'Oceanie**. *See p163*.

ly to life by documents and photos. The General de Gaulle wing, opened in 2000, at last gives World War II the coverage it deserves, taking in not only the Free French forces and the Résistance but also the Battle of Britain and war in the Pacific, and alternating weaponry, uniforms and curious artefacts with some blood-chilling film footage. *See also p129. Café. Concerts. Films. Lectures. Shop.*

Musée d'Art et d'Histoire de St-Denis

22bis rue Gabriel-Péri, 93200 St-Denis (01.42.43.05.10). M° St-Denis Porte de Paris. **Open** 10am-5.30pm Mon, Wed-Fri (until 8pm Thur); 2pm-6.30pm Sat, Sun. Closed Tue, some public holidays. **Admission** €4; €2, over-60s; free under-16s. **No credit cards**.
This prizewinning museum in the suburb of St-Denis is housed in a former Carmelite convent which, in the 18th century, numbered Louis XV's daughter Louise de France among its incumbents. Although there are displays of local archaeology, prints about the Paris Commune, Modern and Post-Impressionist drawings and documents relating to the poet Paul Eluard who was born in the town, the most vivid part is the first floor where the nuns' austere cells have been preserved.
Partial wheelchair access.

Musée du Cabinet des Médailles

58 rue de Richelieu, 2nd (01.53.79.81.26/ www.bnf.fr). M° Bourse. **Open** 1-6pm daily. Closed Sun, two weeks in Sept, public holidays. **Admission** free. **Credit** MC, V. **Map** p406 H4.
On the first floor of the old Bibliothèque Nationale is the anachronistic Cabinet des Médailles. This collection of coins and medals is actually for specialists, but efficient sliding magnifying glasses help bring exhibits to life. Probably the most interesting aspects for the general public are the museum's parallel Greek, Roman and medieval collections, where oddities include the Merovingian King Dagobert's throne and Charlemagne's chess set (what a fun guy he must have been), nestling among Greek vases and miniature sculptures from all periods.
Shop. Partial wheelchair access.

Musée Carnavalet

23 rue de Sévigné, 3rd (01.44.59.58.58/www.paris-france.org/musees). M° St-Paul. **Open** 10am-6pm Tue-Sun. Closed Mon, some public holidays. **Admission** Free. Temporary exhibitions €5.50; €4 over-60s; €2.50 14-26; free under-14s; **Credit** (shop) AmEx, MC, V. **Map** p406 L6.
An unexpected treasure in the heart of the Marais, this magnificent building houses some 140 rooms dedicated to the history of Paris, from pre-Roman Gaul to the 20th century. Built in 1548, and transformed by the celebrated architect Mansart in 1660, it became a museum in 1866 when Baron Haussmann had a twinge of conscience about all the buildings being destroyed to make way for his new boulevards. He persuaded the city to buy the Hôtel

Carnavalet to preserve some of the more beautiful interiors, and the rest is history!
Displays are chronological. The original 16th-century rooms house the Renaissance collections with portraits by Clouet, and furniture and pictures relating to the Wars of Religion. The first floor covers the period up to 1789 with furniture, applied arts and paintings displayed in restored, period interiors. The bold colours, particularly in the oval boudoir from the Hôtel de Breteuil (1782), may come as a shock to those with pre-conceived ideas about subdued 18th-century taste. Interesting interiors include the Rococo cabinet painted for engraver Demarteau by his friends Fragonard, Boucher and Huet in 1765 and the Louis XIII-style Cabinet Colbert.
The collections from 1789 onwards move into the Hôtel Le Peletier de Saint-Fargeau next door, acquired in 1989. The Revolutionary items are the best way of getting an understanding of the convoluted politics and bloodshed of the period. There are portraits of all the major players, prints, objects and memorabilia including a bone model of the guillotine, Hubert Robert's gouaches and a small chunk of the Bastille prison. Highlights of the later collections include items belonging to Napoléon, views of Paris depicting the effects of Haussmann's programme, the ornate cradle given by the city to Napoléon III on the birth of his son, the art nouveau boutique designed by Mucha in 1901 for jeweller Fouquet and the art deco ballroom of the Hôtel Wendel painted by Catalan artist José-Maria Sert. Rooms devoted to literature finish the tour with portraits and room settings, including Proust's cork-lined bedroom.
Not much remains of the original interior of the Hôtel Le Peletier except the elegant grand staircase and one antique panelled cabinet; its newly restored *orangerie*, the only surviving 17th-century one in Paris, now houses Neolithic dug-out canoes excavated at Bercy amongst other Gallo-Roman archaeological finds. The museum is well-known for its temporary exhibitions, too. 2003 starts off with a fabulous tribute to the silk creations of the Maison Prelle, from the mid 18th century to today, and a retrospective of the life and work of lacqueur artisan Pierre Bobot, in the year of the centenary of his birth.
Bookshop. Guided tours. Lectures. Reference section (by appointment). Wheelchair access.

Musée de l'Histoire de France

Hôtel de Soubise, 60 rue des Francs-Bourgeois, 3rd (01.40.27.62.18/www.archivesnationales.culture.gouv. fr/chan). M° Hôtel-de-Ville or Rambuteau. **Open** 10am-5.45pm Mon, Wed-Fri; 1.45-5.45pm Sat, Sun. Closed Tue, some public holidays. **Admission** €3.50; €2.50 18-25s; free under-18s. **No credit cards**. **Map** p406 K6.
Housed in one of the grandest Marais mansions, this museum is to be renovated with a view to new presentation that favours the plurality of historical interpretations. In the meantime, a changing selection of historical documents and artefacts cover not just major political events – the Wars of Religion, the French Revolution – but also social issues and

quirky aspects of daily life, from the founding of the Sorbonne to an ordonnance about umbrellas or World War I postcards. The Hôtel de Soubise also boasts the finest Rococo interiors in Paris. The apartments of the Prince and Princesse de Soubise were decorated in the 1730s with superb plasterwork, panelling and paintings by artists including Boucher, Natoire, Restout and Van Loo. An exhibition exploring the history of Algeria, from the end of the Ottoman period through to present Franco-Algerian relations, runs from June-November, 2003.
Shop.

Musée de la Marine

Palais de Chaillot, pl du Trocadéro, 16th (01.53.65.69.69/www.musee-marine.fr). Mº Trocadéro. **Open** 10am-6pm Mon, Wed-Sun. Closed Tue, some public holidays. **Admission** €6; €4 under-25s, over-60s; €3 6-18s; free under-6s; CM. Admission with exhibition: €7; €5.40 under-25s, over 60s; €3,85 6-18s; free under 6s. **Credit** (shop) AmEx, MC, V. **Map** p404 B5.

French naval history is explored, from detailed carved models of battleships and Vernet's imposing series of paintings of the ports of France (1754-65) to a model of a nuclear submarine. There's also the Imperial barge, built when Napoleon's delusions of grandeur were reaching their zenith in 1810, carved prows, old maps, antique and modern navigational instruments, ships in bottles, underwater equipment and romantic maritime paintings. A new area is devoted to the modern navy. The current two-year-long exhibition, 'Queen Mary 2: the Birth of a Legend,' is a 'real-time' exhibition detailing how to go about creating the biggest (and most expensive) transatlantic cruise-liner ever – due to be sailing the seven seas in 2004. This exhibition might be as close as you're going to get to the liner with its thousand or more cabins, five pools, a gym, a library, a hospital and even – get this – a planetarium. 2003 is also the year of the biennial salon of the sea-inspired art (May-Sept). While all this is happening, renovation work will also be taking place (due for completion in 2005), although all rooms remain open.
Shop.

Musée de la Monnaie de Paris

11 quai de Conti, 6th (01.40.46.55.35/ www.monnaiedeparis.fr). Mº Odéon or Pont-Neuf. **Open** 11am-5.30pm Tue-Fri; noon-5.30pm Sat, Sun. **Admission** €3 (€6 with audioguide); €2.20 students; free under-16s, over-60s, all on first Sun of month; CM. **Credit** (shop) MC, V. **Map** p406 H6.

Housed in the handsome Neo-Classical mint built in the 1770s by Jacques-Denis Antoine, this high-tech museum tells the story of France's coinage from pre-Roman origins to the present day through a series of sophisticated displays and audiovisual presentations. The history of the French state is, of course, directly linked to its coinage, and the museum is informative about both.
Shop. Visit to atelier (2.15pm Wed, Fri reserve ahead).

Primitive & proper

If you display a war mask from the Ivory Coast behind a sheet of glass, are you protecting the vital heritage of African culture, or are you saying 'Look at those wacky savages – aren't they just the greatest!'? Was the tribal chief asked nicely for that ceremonial headgear, or was he in fact one of the many victims of imperialism? You can just picture the beads of perspiration forming on the brow of the President of the Republic, Jacques Chirac, as he wrestled with these cultural dilemmas. The shrunken heads at the Musée de l'Homme were getting distinctly tatty, and the collections at the Musée des Arts d'Afrique et d'Océanie were starting to overflow their galleries. Jacques the lad proclaimed his desire 'to give to the arts of Africa, the Americas, Oceania and Asia their proper place in the museums of France'. The proper place he and his ministers chose was Quai Branly, right next to the Eiffel Tower, in the 7th. Construction has already begun here for a state-of-the-art museum by architect of the moment, Jean Nouvel, which will re-house the old museums' collections and a pedagogical centre for post–colonial studies. One has to wonder at the location of the new museum. The 7th is the ministers' 'hood, home to everyone from Alain Juppé to the Assemblée Nationale itself. Yet its population is whiter than a polar bear's arse; it has the vibrant ethnic buzz of a Freemasons' convention in Surrey. The museum claims it will be a resource centre 'particularly accessible to the countries from which the collections originally came'. Would it not have made more cultural sense to build the museum in Barbès or Belleville, where Parisian immigrants actually live, and where a celebration of the cultures from which they originate would perhaps give a much-needed boost to race relations? The 40,000m^2 new museum must be welcomed for giving space to the collections, many of which have remained in dusty storerooms for decades, but many will lament the passing of fabulously musty **Musée de l'Homme** (*see p168*) and the wacky and original **Musée des Arts d'Afrique et d'Océanie** (*see p162*) which is currently Paris' most splendid white elephant.

Green peace at **Musée Carnavalet**. *See p170.*

Musée de Montmartre

12 rue Cortot, 18th (01.46.06.61.11). M° Lamarck-Caulaincourt. **Open** 11am-5pm Tue-Sun. Closed Mon, 1 Jan, 1 May, 25 Dec. **Admission** €3.81; €3.05 students, over-60s; free under-8s. **Credit** (shop) MC, V. **Map** p405 H1.

At the back of a peaceful garden, this 17th-century manor is a haven of calm after touristy Montmartre. Aiming to preserve documents and artefacts relating to the historic hilltop, the collection consists of a room devoted to Modigliani (who lived in rue Caulaincourt), the reconstructed study of composer Gustave Charpentier, some original Toulouse-Lautrec posters, porcelain from the short-lived factory at Clignancourt and a tribute to the local cabaret, the Lapin Agile. The studios above the entrance pavilion were occupied at various times by Renoir, Émile Bernard, Raoul Dufy and Suzanne Valadon with her son Maurice Utrillo.

Musée du Montparnasse

21 av du Maine, 15th (01.42.22.91.96). M° Montparnasse-Bienvenüe or Falguière. **Open** *during exhibitions* Wed-Sun. **Admission** €3.81; €3.05 students under-26, over-60s; free under-15s. **No credit cards. Map** p405 F8.

The Musée du Montparnasse opened in 1998 in one of the last remaining alleys of artists' studios in the area. In the 1930s and 40s it was home to Marie Vassilieff, who opened her own academy and canteen where penniless artists – including regulars Picasso, Modigliani, Cocteau, Matisse and Zadkine – came for cheap food. Trotsky and Lenin were also among her guests.

Musée de la Poste

34 bd de Vaugirard, 15th (01.42.79.23.45/ www.laposte.fr). M° Montparnasse-Bienvenüe. **Open** 10am-6pm Mon-Sat. Closed Sun. **Admission** €4.50; €3; free under 12s. **Credit** V. **Map** p405 E9.

This is a tad more interesting than it sounds. Although belonging to the state postal service, it is more than just a company museum. Amid uniforms, pistols, carriages, bicycles, letter boxes, portraits, official decrees, cartoons and fumigation tongs emerge some fascinating snippets of history: during the 1871 Siege of Paris, hot-air balloons and carrier pigeons were used to get post out of the city and *boules de Moulins*, balls containing hundreds of microfiche letters, were floated down the Seine in return, mostly never to arrive. The second section gives a survey of French and international philately. Philately will get you nowhere.

Musée de la Préfecture de Police

4 rue de la Montagne Sainte-Geneviève, 5th (01.44.41.52.50/www.prefecturepolice-paris.interieur.gouv.fr). M° Maubert-Mutualité. **Open** 9am-5pm Mon-Fri; 10am-5pm Sat. Closed public holidays. **Admission** free. **No credit cards. Map** p406 J7.

Rather spookily located upstairs in a hideous police station, the history of Paris is viewed via crime since the establishment of the Paris police force in the 16th century. You need to read French to best appreciate the assorted warrants and edicts, but there are plenty of evocative murder weapons. Among eclectic treasures are prisoners' expenses from the Bastille including those of dastardly jewel thief the Comtesse de la Motte, the exploding flowerpot planted by

Louis-Armand Matha in 1894 in a restaurant on the rue de Tournon, and the gory Epée de Justice, a 17th-century sword blunted by the quantity of noble heads chopped.

Musée de la Résistance Nationale

Parc Vercors, 88 av Marx Dormoy, 94500 Champigny-sur-Marne (01.48.81.00.80/ www.musee-resistance.com). RER A Champigny-St-Maur then bus 208. **Open** 9am-12.30pm, 2-5.30pm Tue-Fri; 2-6pm Sat, Sun. Closed Mon, weekends in Aug, Sept. **Admission** €3.81, €1.91 free under-16s. **No credit cards**.

Occupying five floors of a 19th-century villa, the Résistance museum starts at the top with the pre-war political background and works down, via defeat in 1940, through German occupation and the rise of the *maquis*, to victory. Given the way the Résistance movement has captured the imaginations of people around the globe, it's slightly odd that no effort is made for foreign visitors: hundreds of photographs aside, the bulk of the material consists of newspaper archives, both from official and clandestine presses, with no translations. Three short archive films and a few solid artefacts are more accessible, with a sobering wall of machine guns and pistols, a railway saboteur's kit (cutters to chop through brake pipes, sand to pour into gearboxes and logs to lay across tracks) and a homemade device for scattering tracts. Displays steer clear of wallowing in collaborationist disgrace and of Résistance hero tub-thumping.

Literary

Maison de Balzac

47 rue Raynouard, 16th (01.55.74.41.80). M° Passy. **Open** 10am-6pm Tue-Sun. Closed Mon, public holidays. **Admission** Collection free. Temporary exhibitions €3.30; €2.20 over-60s, €1.60 14-26s; free under-13s. **No credit cards. Map** p404 B6.

Honoré de Balzac (1799-1850) rented a flat at this address in 1840 to avoid his creditors and established a password to sift friends from bailiffs. The museum is spread over several floors, and although the displays are rather dry, the garden is pretty and gives an idea of the sort of country villa that lined this street when Passy was a fashionable spa. A wide range of memorabilia includes first editions, letters, corrected proofs, prints, portraits of friends and Polish mistress Mme Hanska, plus a 'family tree' of Balzac's characters that covers several walls. The study houses his desk, chair and the mono-grammed coffee pot that fuelled all-night work on much of *La Comédie humaine.* *Library (by appointment).*

Maison de Chateaubriand

La Vallée aux Loups, 87 rue de Chateaubriand, 92290 Chatenay-Malabry (01.47.02.08.62). RER B Robinson + 20 min walk. **Open** (guided tours only except Sun) *Apr-Sept* 10am-noon, 2-6pm Tue-Sun; *Oct-Mar* 2-5pm Tue-Sun. Closed Mon, Jan, 25 Dec.

Admission €4.50; €3 students, over-60s; free under-12s. **No credit cards**.

In 1807, attracted by the quiet Vallée aux Loups, René, Vicomte de Chateaubriand (1768-1848), author of *Mémoires d'outre tombe* (*Memoirs from Beyond the Grave*), set about transforming a simple 18th-century country house into his own Romantic idyll and planted the park with rare trees as a reminder of his travels. Most interesting is the over-the-top double wooden staircase, based on a maritime design, a reminder of the writer's noble St-Malo birth, and the portico with two white marble Grecian statues supporting a colonnaded porch. Anyone familiar with David's *Portrait of Mme Récamier* in the Louvre will find the original chaise longue awaiting the sitter, who was one of Chateaubriand's numerous lovers – no doubt to the discomfort of his

The best Nudes

The **Musée de l'Erotisme** (*see p179*), in the vicinity of the Moulin Rouge of course, houses seven floors of art, objects and artefacts dedicated to the most abiding of all human interests: nookie. If you're scared of being seen nipping in for a gander, here are some corporeal delights, located in more seemingly innocent places:

The Thinker

A man with a nice body and possibly a brain. Rodin's pensive body-builder in the garden at the **Musée Rodin**. *See p162.*

Olympia

Manet's groundbreaking portrait of a prostitute which caused a scandal back in 1865, in the **Musée d'Orsay**. *See p155.*

Venus de Milo

The luscious goddess of love still attracts as many admirers as ever at the **Louvre**. *See p148.*

L'Origine du Monde

Gustave Courbet's sexually explicit, faceless woman was painted over a century ago, but is still leaves viewers speechless at the **Musée d'Orsay**. *See p155.*

Nude study of Balzac

Yes, one of the great literary figures shows off his cruet set. And a sturdy, determined looking chap he is too (**Musée Rodin**). *See p162.*

Femme au Fauteil Rouge

Ladies, let's hope it never gets this bad... (**Musée Picasso**). *See p162.*

stern wife, Céleste. After a politically inflammatory work Chateaubriand was ruined and in 1818 had to sell his beloved valley.

Concerts/readings (spring, autumn). Shop. Tearoom.

Musée de la Vie Romantique

16 rue Chaptal, 9th (01.48.74.95.38). M° Blanche or Saint-Georges. **Open** 10am-5.40pm (6pm in summer) Tue-Sun. Closed Mon, public holidays. **Admission** permanent collection free. Temporary exhibitions €4.50, €3 over-60s, students under 26; €2.20 under-18s; CM. **No credit cards. Map** p405 G2.

When Dutch artist Ary Scheffer lived in this villa, this area south of Pigalle was known as the New Athens because of the concentration of writers, composers and artists living here. Baronne Aurore Dupin – better known as George Sand (1804-76) – was a frequent guest at Scheffer's soirées, and many other great names crossed the threshold, including Sand's lover, Chopin, Delacroix and composers Charpentier, Liszt and Rossini. The museum is charming, with a lovely rose garden and tearoom, but literary detectives on the trail of the great George Sand, novelist and proto-feminist, might be disappointed: the watercolours, lockets and jewels she left behind reveal little of her ideas or her affairs. In the courtyard, Scheffer's studio is used for exhibitions; in 2003 look out for one that has managed to reunite for the first time some of the most beautiful and sophisticated creations by 19th-century master goldsmiths and jewellers François-Désiré and son.

Archives. Bookshop. Children's workshops. Concerts. Tearoom.

Musée Mémorial Ivan Tourguéniev

16 rue Ivan Tourguéniev, 78380 Bougival (01.45.77.87.12). M° La Défense, plus bus 258. **Open** 10am-6pm Sun; by appointment for groups during the week. **Admission** €4.60; €3.80 12-26s; free under-12s. **No credit cards.**

The datcha where novelist Ivan Turgenev lived for several years until his death in 1883 was a gathering spot for composers Saint-Saëns and Fauré, divas Pauline Viardot (with whom Turgenev was in love throughout his life) and Maria Malibran, and writers Henry James, Flaubert, Zola and Maupassant. Letters and editions (mainly in Russian) are on the ground floor, and above there's the music room where Viardot held court, as well as the writer's deathbed. The guided tour (in French) is worthwhile.

Bookshop. Concerts. Guided tours 5pm Sun, all year round.

Maison de Victor Hugo

Hôtel de Rohan-Guéménée, 6 pl des Vosges, 4th (01.42.72.10.16). M° Bastille. **Open** 10am-6pm Tue-Sun. **Admission** €5.50; €4 students; €2.50 13-26s; free under-13s. **No credit cards.**

The intense, prolific Victor Hugo lived here from 1832 to 1848, and the house has now been turned into a museum for France's favourite son. You can see first editions of his books, nearly 500 drawings, and, more bizarrely, Vic's home-made furniture, some of which he carved with his own teeth. Terrible

thing, gum splinters. The museum also holds varying exhibitions on themes related to Hugo.

Giftshop.

Musée Edith Piaf

5 rue Crespin-du-Gast, 11th (01.43.55.52.72). M° Ménilmontant. **Open** by appointment 1-6pm Mon-Wed; 9am-noon Thurs (call two days ahead). Closed June, Sept. **Admission** donation. **No credit cards. Map** p407 N5.

Les Amis d'Edith Piaf run this tiny two-room museum in a part of Paris that the archetypal French singer knew well. The memorabilia on show exudes love for the 'little sparrow', her diminutive stature graphically shown by a lifesize cardboard cut-out. Her little black dress and tiny shoes are particularly moving, and letters, posters and photos provide a personal touch. There's also a sculpture of the singer by Suzanne Blistène, wife of Marcel, who produced most of Piaf's films.

Library. Shop.

Musée de la Musique

Cité de la Musique, 221 av Jean-Jaurès, 19th (01.44.84.44.84/www.cite-musique.fr). M° Porte de Pantin. **Open** noon-6pm Tue-Thur, Sat; noon-7.30pm Fri; 10am-6pm Sun. Closed Mon, some public holidays. **Admission** €6.10; €4.57 18s-25s; €2.29 6-18s; free under-6s, over-60s; CM. **Credit** MC, V. **Map** p407 insert.

Alongside the concert hall in the striking modern Cité de la Musique, the innovative music museum houses a gleamingly restored collection of instruments from the old Conservatoire, interactive computers and scale models of opera houses and concert halls. On arrival you are supplied with an audio guide in a choice of languages. Don't be a precious old luvvie and spurn this offer, for the musical commentary is an informative joy, playing the appropriate music or instrument as you approach the exhibit. Alongside the trumpeting brass, curly woodwind instruments and precious strings are more unusual items, such as the Indonesian gamelan orchestra, whose gurgling, percussive sounds influenced the work of both Debussy and Ravel. Some of the concerts in the museum's amphitheatre use historic instruments from the collection. *See also p111 and p323.*

Audioguide. Library. Shop. Wheelchair access.

Musée de l'Opéra

Palais Garnier, 1 pl de l'Opéra, 9th (01.40.01.24.93). M° Opéra. **Open** 10am-6pm daily. **Admission** €6; €4 10-25s, students, over-60s; free under-10s. **No credit cards. Map** p405 G4.

The magnificently restored Palais Garnier houses small temporary exhibitions relating to current opera or ballet productions, and a permanent collection of paintings, scores and bijou opera sets housed in period cases. The entrance fee includes a visit to the auditorium (if rehearsals permit).

Guided tours in English.

Oriental arts

Musée National des Arts Asiatiques – Guimet

6 pl d'Iéna, 16th (01.56.52.53.00/ www.museeguimet.fr). M° Iéna. **Open** 10am-6pm Mon, Wed-Sun. Closed Tue. **Admission** (includes temporary exhibition and free audioguide) €7; €5 students, 18-25s, Sun; free under-18s, first Sun of month; CM. **Credit** (shop) MC, V. **Map** p405 E5.

The reopened museum of Asian art was the success story of 2001, as it emerged enlarged and rejuvenated from five years of renovation. Founded by Lyonais industrialist Emile Guimet in 1889 to house his collection of Chinese and Japanese religious art, and later incorporating the Oriental collections from the Louvre, Musée Guimet boasts some 45,000 objects from Neolithic times on in a voyage to Asia that conveys the flow of religions and civilisations. Lower galleries focus on India and Southeast Asia, centred on the stunning collection of Hindu and Buddhist Khmer sculpture from Cambodia. Amid legions of calmly smiling Buddhas and the striking seventh-century Harihara, a half-Shiva, half-Vishnu figure, you can't miss the massive *Giant's Way*, part of the entrance to a temple complex at Angkor Wat, where two female demi-goddesses hold a seven-headed cobra. Upstairs, Chinese antiquities include mysterious jade discs, an elephant-shaped Shang dynasty bronze pot, lively terracotta figures, horses and camels found in tombs, fragile paintings from Dunhuang and later Chinese celadon wares and porcelain. Other rooms contain Afghan and Pakistani glassware and sculpture, Tibetan mandalas and statues, Japanese Buddhist sculpture, paintings and lacquer and ceramics, as well as Moghul jewellery, caskets, fabrics and miniatures. *Auditorium. Guided visits. Library. Restaurant. Shop. Wheelchair access.*

Musée Cernuschi

7 av Velasquez, 8th (01.45.63.50.75). M° Villiers or Monceau. **Map** p405 E2.

Closed until 2004 for renovation, this collection of Chinese art was amassed by erudite banker Henri Cernuschi on a long voyage to the Far East in 1871. It ranges from Neolithic terracottas and legions of Han and Wei dynasty funeral statues to refined Tang celadon wares, Sung porcelain, fragile paintings on silk, bronze vessels and jade amulets.

Musée de l'Institut du Monde Arabe

1 rue des Fossés-St-Bernard, 5th (01.40.51.38.38/ www.imarabe.org). M° Jussieu. **Open** 10am-6pm Tue-Sun. Closed Mon, 1 May. **Admission** €4; €3 12-25s, students, over-60s; free under-12s; CM. Temporary exhibition prices vary. **Credit** MC, V. **Map** p402 K7.

Opened in 1987 as one of Mitterrand's *Grand Projets*, the institute of the Arab world brings together a library, cultural centre, exhibitions and the 'Museum of Arab Museums', displaying items on long-term loan from museums in alternating Arab countries alongside its own permanent collection. The objects cover a huge geographical and historical span.

Medallion men at the **Musée de la vie Romantique**. *See left*.

Particularly strong are the collections of early scientific instruments, 19th-century Tunisian costume and jewellery and contemporary fine art.
Bookshop. Cinema. Lectures. Library. Tearoom. Wheelchair access.

Photography

Centre National de la Photographie
Hôtel Salomon de Rothschild, 11 rue Berryer, 8th (01.53.76.12.32/www.cnp-photographie.com). M° Charles de Gaulle-Etoile or Georges V. **Open** noon-7pm Mon, Wed-Sun. Closed Tue, 1 May, 25 Dec. **Admission** €4.60; €2.30 10-25s, over-60s; free under-10s. **Credit** MC, V. **Map** p404 D3.

The distinguished-looking National Photography Centre, in the middle of the somewhat snobby 8th, actually takes a strong contemporary line: recent retrospectives have included Sam Taylor-Wood, Stephen Wilks and Han-Peter Feldman. Many of the exhibitions have more in common with the risk-taking shows put on at the Palais de Tokyo; in fact, one of the 2003 highlights is sure to be a joint collaboration with the Palais, showing work by Lyonnaise photographer, installation artist and video-maker Franck Scurti. Also to look forward to in 2003, up-and-coming Paris-based talent Martine Aballéa, and disquieting Czech photographer Václav Stratil. Short video programmes are screened in the café every day from 4pm and the pleasant garden is open to all.
Café. Wheelchair access (call ahead).

Edithpus complex: confront yours at the **Musée Edith Piaf**. *See p174.*

Maison Européenne de la Photographie
5-7 rue de Fourcy, 4th (01.44.78.75.00/ www.mep-fr.org). M° St-Paul or Pont-Marie. **Open** 11am-8pm Wed-Sun. Closed Mon, Tue, some public holidays. **Admission** €5; €2.50 students, over-60s; free under-8s, all 5-8pm Wed. **Credit** (over €9.15) MC, V. **Map** p406 L6.

The MEP's setting, in a restored Marais mansion and minimalist modern extension, is ideal in scale for photography exhibitions. The permanent collection includes Martin Parr's wicked snapshots of middle-class British life, landscapes and cityscapes by Italian Gabriele Basilico, a host of American black-and-white classics and show-stoppers like Helmut Newton's says-it-all *Big Nude*. An energetic venue, it organises the citywide biennial Mois de la Photo (next in 2004) and the Art Outsiders (new media art on the web) festival in September, plus big retrospectives like last year's William Klein.
Auditorium. Café. Library. Wheelchair access.

Patrimoine Photographique
Hôtel de Sully, 62 rue St-Antoine, 4th (01.42.74.47.75/www.patrimoine-photo.org). M° Bastille. **Open** 10am-6.30pm Tue-Sun. Closed Mon, some public holidays. **Admission** €4; €2.50 students, under 25s, over-60s; free under-10s, under-25s, over-60s; free under-10s. **No credit cards.** **Map** p406 L7.

A small gallery devoted to photographic heritage, located in a stunning Marais *hôtel*. Shows usually take an historical angle (Cecil Beaton, Jacques-Henri Lartigue, Lucien Hervé), or a theme (the Egyptian pyramids, crime photography).

Science, medicine & technology

La Cité des Sciences et de l'Industrie
La Villette, 30 av Corentin-Cariou, 19th (01.40.05.80.00/01.40.05.12.12/www.cite-sciences.fr). M° Porte de la Villette. **Open** 10am-6pm Tue-Sat; 10am-7pm Sun. Closed Mon, public holidays. **Admission** €7.50; €5.50 7-16s, students under 25, over-60s; free under-7s; all on Sat; CM. **Credit** MC, V. **Map** p407 insert.

The ultra-modern science museum at La Villette has been riding high since its opening in 1986 and pulls in over five million visitors a year. Explora, the permanent show, occupies the upper two floors, whisking visitors through 30,000m² of 'space, life, matter and communication', where scale models of satellites including the Ariane space shuttle, planes and robots make for an exciting journey. There's an impressive array of interactive exhibits on language and communication, enabling you to learn about sound waves and try out different smells. Pretend to be a weatherman in the Espace Images, try out the delayed camera and other optical illusions in the Jeux de Lumière, or draw 3D images on computer.

Sightseeing

The hothouse 'garden of the future' investigates futuristic developments in agriculture and bio-technology. There is naturally a section devoted to man's conquest of space, too, which lets you experience the sensation of weightlessness. Other sections feature climate, ecology and the environment, health, energy, the ocean and volcanoes. The Automobile gallery looks at the car both as myth and technological object, with driving simulator and displays on safety, pollution and future designs. The lower floors house temporary exhibitions, a documentation centre and children's sections. The Louis Lumière cinema shows films in 3-D, and there's a restored submarine moored next to the Géode.
Bookshop. Café. Cinema. Conference centre. Library (multimedia). Wheelchair access & hire.

Musée de l'Air et de l'Espace

Aéroport de Paris-Le Bourget, 93352 Le Bourget Cedex (01.49.92.71.99/recorded information 01.49.92.71.71/www.mae.org). M° Gare du Nord then bus 350/M° La Courneuve then bus 152/RER Le Bourget then bus 152. **Open** *May-Oct* 10am-6pm; *Nov-Apr* 10am-5pm Tue-Sun. Closed Mon, 25 Dec, 1 Jan. **Admission** €6; €4.05 8-16s, students; free under-8s. **Credit** MC, V.

The air and space museum is a potent reminder that France is a technical and military as well as cultural power. Housed in the former passenger terminal at Le Bourget airport, the collection begins with the pioneers, including fragile-looking biplanes, the contraption in which Romanian Vivia succeeded in flying 12 metres in 1906, and the strangely nautical command cabin of a Zeppelin airship. Outside on the runway are Mirage fighter planes, a Boeing 707, an American Thunderchief with painted shark-tooth grimace and Ariane launchers 1 and 5. Within a vast hangar, walk through the prototype Concorde 001 and view wartime survivors, a Spitfire and German Heinkel bomber. Further hangars are packed with military planes, helicopters, commercial jets, bizarre prototypes, stunt planes, missiles and satellites. A section is devoted to hot air balloons, invented in 1783 by the Montgolfier brothers and swiftly adopted for military reconnaissance. Recent additions to the museum include a new and improved planetarium and the 'Espace' section, dedicated to space travel. Most captions are summarised in English.
Shop. Wheelchair access (except new 'Espace' building).

Musée des Arts et Métiers

60 rue Réaumur, 3rd (01.40.27.22.20). M° Arts et Métiers. **Open** 10am-6pm Mon, Wed-Sun; open until 9.30pm Thurs. Closed Tue, some public holidays. **Admission** €5.50; €3.80 under-18s, students under-26; over-60s; free under-5s. **Credit** MC, V. **Map** p406 K5.

The successful combination of 12th-century structure and 21st-century technology and design reflects the museum's aim – to demonstrate the history and future of the technical arts. A new permanent exhibition looking at seven aspects of science and technology has been created from the museum's vast collection of more than 80,000 machines and models. Throughout, videos and interactive computers explain the science behind the exhibits and at the end of each section there is a workshop for budding young scientists and technophobes alike to get to grips with what is on display. Most impressive is the chapel, where an elaborate glass and steel staircase enables you to climb right up into the nave. There, amid the stained glass, you can gaze down upon the wonders of man's invention, which include Blériot's plane and the first steam engine.

Musée de l'Assistance Publique

Hôtel de Miramion, 47 quai de la Tournelle, 5th (01.46.33.01.43). M° Maubert-Mutualité. **Open** 10am-6pm Tue-Sun. Closed Mon, Aug, public holidays. **Admission** €4; €2 students, over-60s; free under-13s, CM. **No credit cards. Map** p406 K7

The history of Paris hospitals, from the days when they were receptacles for abandoned babies to the beginnings of modern medicine with anaesthesia, is explained in a lively fashion through paintings, prints, various grisly medical devices and a reconstructed ward and pharmacy; texts in French only.

Musée d'Histoire de la Médecine

Université René Descartes, 12 rue de l'Ecole-de-Médecine, 6th (01.40.46.16.93). M° Odéon. **Open** *15 July-Sept* 2-5.30pm Mon-Fri; *Oct-13 July* 2-5.30pm Mon-Wed, Fri, Sat. Closed Sun, public holidays. **Admission** €3.05; free under-12s. **No credit cards. Map** p406 H7.

The medical faculty collection covers the history of medicine from ancient Egyptian embalming tools through to a 1960s electrocardiograph. There's a gruesome array of serrated-edged saws and curved knives used for amputations, stethoscopes and syringes, the surgical instruments of Dr Antommarchi, who performed the autopsy on Napoléon and the scalpel of Dr Félix, who operated on Louis XIV.

Muséum National d'Histoire Naturelle

36 rue Geoffroy-St-Hilaire/2 rue Bouffon, pl Valhubert/57 rue Cuvier, 5th (01.40.79.30.00/ www.mnhn.fr). M° Gare d'Austerlitz or Jussieu. **Open** Grande Galerie: 10am-6pm Mon, Wed, Fri-Sun; 10am-10pm Thur. Other galleries: 10am-5pm Mon, Wed-Fri; 10am-5pm Sat, Sun Apr-Sep. Closed Tue, 1 May. **Admission** Grande Galerie €7; €5 5-16s, students, over-60s; free under-5s (with temporary exhibition €9 and €5. Other galeries each €5; €3 5-16s, students, over-60s; free under-5s. **No credit cards. Map** p406 K9.

The brilliantly renovated Grande Galerie de l'Evolution has taken Paris' Natural History Museum out of the dinosaur age. Architect Paul Chemetov successfully integrated modern lifts, stairways and the latest lighting and audiovisual techniques into the 19th-century iron-framed structure. As you enter, you will be confronted with the 13.66m-long skeleton of a whale: the rest of the ground floor is dedicated to other sea creatures. On the first floor are the mammals, including Louis XVI's rhinoceros, stuffed on a wooden chair frame. Videos and interactive computers give information on life in the wild. Glass-sided lifts take you up through suspended birds to the second floor, which deals with man's impact on nature and considers demographic problems and pollution. The third floor traces the evolution of species, with a galery of endangered and extinct species. The separate Galerie d'Anatomie comparée et de Paléontologie contains skeletons of virtually every creature you can imagine and there are also galeries of mineralogy and geology. The butterfly gallery is temporarily closed. *See also p288. Auditorium. Bookshop. Café. Library. Wheelchair access (Grande Galerie).*

Musée Pasteur

Institut Pasteur, 25 rue du Dr-Roux, 15th (01.45.68.82.83/www.pasteur.fr). Mº Pasteur. **Open** 2-5.30pm Mon-Fri. Closed weekends, public holidays, Aug. **Admission** €3; €1.50 students. **Credit** V. **Map** p405 E9.

The apartment where the famous chemist and his wife lived for the last seven years of his life (1888-95) has hardly been touched since his death; you can still see their furniture and possessions, family photos and a room of scientific instruments. The highlight is the extravagant, Byzantine-style mausoleum on the ground floor housing Pasteur's tomb, decorated with mosaics of his scientific achievements.

Musée de Radio-France

Maison de Radio-France, 116 av du Président-Kennedy, 16th (01.56.40.15.16/01.56.40.21.80/www.radio-france.fr). Mº Ranelagh/RER Kennedy-Radio France. **Open** guided tours 10.30am, 11.30am, 2.30pm, 3.30pm, 4.30pm Mon. **Admission** €3.80; €3 8s-25s, students, over-60s. **No credit cards. Map** p404 A7.

Audio-visual history is presented with an emphasis on French pioneers such as Branly and Charles Cros, including documentary evidence of the first radio message between the Eiffel Tower and the Panthéon. Particularly interesting is the London broadcast of the Free French with its delightfully obscure coded messages. From the museum you can see people recording radio programmes below.

Musée du Service de Santé des Armées

pl Alphonse-Laveran, 5th (01.40.51.40.00). RER Port-Royal. **Open** noon-6pm Tue, Wed for groups; 1.30-6pm Sat, Sun for individuals. **Admission** €4.60; €2.30 6-12s; free under-6s. **No credit cards. Map** p406 J9.

The museum traces the history of military medicine, via recreations of field hospitals and ambulance trains, and beautifully presented antique medical instruments. The section on World War I brings a chilling insight into the true horror of the conflict, when many buildings were transformed into hospitals and, ironically, medical science progressed in leaps and bounds.

Palais de la Découverte

av Franklin D Roosevelt, 8th (01.56.43.20.21/www.palais-decouverte.fr). Mº Franklin D Roosevelt. **Open** 9.30am-6pm Tue-Sat; 10am-7pm Sun. Closed Mon, 1 Jan, 1 May, 14 July, 15 Aug, 25 Dec. **Admission** €5.60; €3.65 5-18s, students under 26; free under-5s. Planetarium €2.50. **Credit** AmEx, MC, V. **Map** p405 E5.

Join hordes of schoolkids at Paris' original science museum, housing designs from Leonardo da Vinci onwards. Replicas, models, audiovisual material and real apparatus are used to bring displays to life, whilst permanent exhibits cover biology, astronomy, chemistry, physics and earth sciences. There are even regular 'live' experiments. The Planète Terre space shows developments in meteorology, while one room is dedicated to the sun. If that gets you in an astro-mood, then be sure to take in one of the various shows at the planetarium too. *See also p290. Café. Experiments. Shop. Wheelchair access.*

Eccentricities

Musée de la Chasse et de la Nature

Hôtel Guénégaud, 60 rue des Archives, 3rd (01.53.01.92.40). Mº Rambuteau. **Open** 11am-6pm Tue-Sun. Closed Mon, public holidays. **Admission** €4.60; €2.30 16-25s, students under 26, over-60s; €0.75 5-16s; free under 5s. **No credit cards. Map** p406 K5.

It may seem a strange thing to find in the middle of town, but housed on three floors of a beautiful 17th-century Mansart mansion is a collection of objects under the common theme of hunting (nature, not counting the alarming array of stuffed animals, doesn't get much of a look-in). The highlight is the wonderfully ornate weapons: crossbows inlaid with ivory and mother-of-pearl, rifles decorated with hunting scenes; all reminders that hunting's accoutrements were important status symbols. There's a huge display of bird and animal studies by France's first great animalier painter Alexandre-François Desportes, as well as his portrait of Louis XIV's favourite hunting dogs. *Bookshop. Wheelchair access.*

Musée de la Contrefaçon

16 rue de la Faisanderie, 16th (01.56.26.14.00). Mº Porte-Dauphine. **Open** 2-5pm Mon-Thur; 9.30am-noon Fri; 2pm-6pm Sun. Closed Sat, public holidays. **Admission** €2.30; free under-12s. **No credit cards. Map** p404 A4.

This small museum set up by the French anti-counterfeiting association puts strong emphasis on the penalties for forgery. Although the oldest known forgery is displayed (vase covers from *c.*200 BC), the focus is on contemporary copies of well-known brands – Reebok, Lacoste, Vuitton, Ray Ban – with the real thing displayed next to the fake. Even Babie doll, Barbie's illicit clone, gets a look-in. The French government's concept of *liberté* may well find a home here in 2003.

It's all about discovery at the **Palais de la Découverte**. *See left.*

Musée de la Curiosité
11 rue St-Paul, 4th (01.42.72.13.26/
www.museedelamagie.com). M° St-Paul or Sully
Morland. **Open** 2-7pm Wed, Sat, Sun (longer during
school holidays). Closed Mon, Tue, Thur, Fri.
Admission €7, €5 3-12s; free under-3s.
No credit cards. Map p405 L7.
The magic tricks start in the queue and get more
complicated as you work your way through this cabinet of curiosities dedicated to the history of magic.
Going as far back as Ancient Egypt, there is a broad
selection of the tools of the trade, ranging from
wands to boxes for cutting sequinned ladies in half.
The welcome is enthusiastic and friendly, and the
guides are passionate about their art.

Musée de l'Erotisme
72 bd de Clichy, 18th (01.42.58.28.73). M° Blanche.
Open 10am-2am daily. **Admission** €7; €5 students
under 25; under-18s not admitted. **Credit** MC, V.
Map p401 H2.
Opened in 1997 by a collector of erotic art, this museum in the centre of red light Pigalle houses diverse
erotic oeuvres, sacred and profane, include painting,
sculpture, graphic art and *objets d'art* from Latin
America, Asia and Europe. The labelling, however,
is minimal, leaving their origin, age and purpose (if
any) to your imagination.
Shop. Wheelchair access.

Musée de la Franc-Maçonnerie
16 rue Cadet, 9th (01.45.23.20.92). M° Cadet.
Open 2-6pm Tue-Sat. Closed Mon, Sun, some public
holidays, July, Aug. **Admission** €2; free under-12s.
No credit cards. Map p405 H3.
At the back of the Grand Orient de France (French
Masonic Great Lodge), a school-hall type room
traces the history of freemasonry from medieval
stone masons' guilds to the present via prints of
famous masons (General Lafayette and 1848 revolutionary leaders Blanc and Barbès). If you're not
already in on the funny handshakes, don't expect
anything to be given away.
Bookshop. Wheelchair access (call ahead).

Musée du Vin
Rue des Eaux, 16th (01.45.25.63.26/
www.museeduvinparis.com). M° Passy. **Admission**
€6.50; €5.90 over-60s; €5.70 students; under 14s free.
Credit (shop/restaurant) AmEx, DC, MC, V.
Map p404 B6.
This museum is aptly housed in the vaulted cellars
of a wine-producing monastery destroyed in the
Revolution. The ancient bottles, vats, corkscrews
and cutouts of medieval peasants making wine are
quickly seen, but at the end your patience is rewarded with a tasting. This *dégustation* is not designed
to result in inebriation.
Restaurant (noon-3pm). Shop. Partial wheelchair access.

dALEA

High-end dinners and snacks

13 boulevard Edgar Quinet, 14th
M° Edgar-Quinet, Vavin or
Montparnasse
Tel: 01.40.47.02.43
Fax: 01.40.47.02.33

odessa
c a f e

Modern bistrot / Cocktail-bar
(15 different beers on tap, 60 different whiskies)

28 rue d'Odessa, 14th
Tel: 01.43.20.64.84
M° Edgar-Quinet, Vavin or Montparnasse

Traditional Bistrot,
blackboard menu, lunch specials

23 rue d'Odessa, 14th
M° Edgar-Quinet, Vavin or Montparnasse
Tel: 01.42.18.01.55
Fax: 01.43.35.19.75

cafe **Lutetia**

Charming Brasserie
with a "railway" theme

49 rue Linois, 15th - M° Charles Michel
Tel: 01.45.77.65.65

Eat, Drink, Shop

Restaurants

They do a mean cuisine here. Gastronomical standards are astronomical. When food fetishists' faces hit the soup, they don't go to heaven; they come to Paris.

Eat, Drink, Shop

Parisian cuisine has too much strength in depth ever to become an endangered species, but, a couple of years ago, it did seem to be too much up its own parson's nose to be anything but traditionally classy. It was static. Not so now: the food scene is exhibiting those intriguing quirks that signify a spurt of evolution. To mention just a few examples of how things are broadening out, you can now find French cuisine that doesn't lay the foundations for a trip to the cardiac care unit at such low-fat joints as **Hiramatsu** (*see right*); Pascal Barbot at **l'Astrance** (*see p197*) is waging a stand against elitism by introducing Australian influences to his French dishes; bistros continue to surprise with young chefs such as Thierry Breton and Nicholas Vagnon (*see p201*) turning out brilliant food from small kitchens. There's a new vivacity in Paris, and you'll benefit from that wherever you choose to square your elbows.

Except for the very simplest restaurants, it is wise to book ahead. This can usually be done the same day as your intended visit. More time should be allowed for haute cuisine restaurants, which need to be booked weeks in advance and checked the day before. On the clothing front, anything bar your gym gear should be fine, but Parisians look smart when they go out, so denim could make you stick out. All bills include the service charge, so only tip if you're bowled over. In this chapter, we use the terms *menu* and *prix-fixe* to denote set meals, where you get a starter, main and dessert for one price.

For further listings see the *Time Out Paris Eating and Drinking Guide*.

The Islands

Brasseries

Brasserie de l'Isle St-Louis
55 quai de Bourbon, 4th (01.43.54.02.59).
M° Pont-Marie. **Open** noon-1am Mon, Tue, Fri-Sun;
5pm-1am Thur. Closed Aug. **Average** €30.
Credit MC, V. **Map** p406 K7.
Once beyond this brasserie's idyllic terrace, a rustic world of dark wood and mounted animal heads transports you far from the city. Seating is elbow-to-elbow, as punters cram in to taste Alsatian classics like *coq au Riesling*, hen roasted with potatoes and apples and *choucroute garnie*.

International

Japanese/French: Hiramatsu
7 quai de Bourbon, 4th (01.56.81.08.80). M° Pont Marie. **Open** noon-2pm, 8-10pm Tue-Sat. **Average** €120. **Prix fixe** €92. **Lunch menu** €46. **Credit** AmEx, DC, MC, V. **Map** p406 K7.
Hiroyuki Hiramatsu's spectacular new restaurant seats only 18. The food is a tribute to French haute cuisine, with the difference that it is almost all low-fat and rich produce is used healthily. Try sublime Nippo-French dishes like a salad of raw pigeon breast, Savoy cabbage and *foie gras*, poached at the table in hot stock, and a stunning coffee-cream-brown-sugar take on cappuccino for dessert.

The Louvre, Palais-Royal & Les Halles

Bistros & brasseries

L'Ardoise
28 rue du Mont-Thabor, 1st (01.42.96.28.18).
M° Concorde or Tuileries. **Open** noon-2.15pm,
6.30-midnight Wed-Sun. Closed 25 Dec-3 Jan, one week in May, three weeks in Aug. **Average** €30.
Prix fixe €30. **Credit** MC, V. **Map** p401 G5.
Never mind the non-existent decor; it's Tour d'Argent-trained chef Pierre Jay who merits attention. The blackboard menu balances fish and meat, classic and creative, with mains such as calf's liver cooked in sherry vinegar and swordfish in an orange-flavoured butter sauce. Jay's Burgundy roots are reflected in the mostly under-€30 wine list.

Le Gavroche
19 rue St-Marc, 2nd (01.42.96.89.70). M° Bourse or Richelieu-Drouot. **Open** 7am-2am Mon-Sat. **Average** €30. **Lunch menu** €13. **Credit** V. **Map** p402 H3.
If you dream of the Paris you know from the silver screen – a smouldering, carefree sensualists' paradise where no one worries about cholesterol – come to this charming, old-fashioned *bistro à vins*, famed for its gargantuan *côte de boeuf* for two accompanied by a huge pile of freshly cooked *frites*.

Le Petit Flore
6 rue Croix-des-Petits-Champs, 1st (01.42.60.25.53).
M° Palais Royal or Louvre Rivoli. **Open** 6am-8pm Mon-Sat. Food served Mon-Sat noon-2.30pm Mon-Sat. Closed Aug. **Prix fixe** €12. **Credit** DC, MC, V.
Map p402 H5.

Here you will find classy touches not normally associated with a budget menu. The terrace is bordered by a sea of flowers. Inside, cosy tables are dressed with smart white tablecloths. The €12 lunch *menu* includes hearty traditional fare such as *magret*, *confit* and *entrecôte*, served with steaming *frites*.

Au Pied de Cochon

6 rue Coquillière, 1st (01.40.13.77.00/ www.pieddecochon.com). M° Les Halles. **Open** 24-hrs daily. **Average** €40. **Credit** AmEx, DC, MC, V. **Map** p402 H5.

Once your crispy trotter arrives, it may not be immediately obvious what to do next; don't hesitate to ask for a bit of advice. Le Pied de Cochon has oysters and all the other usual brasserie food for those who refuse to partake in the foot-fest. *Wheelchair access.*

Le Souletin

6 rue La Vrillière, 1st (01.42.61.43.78). M° Palais Royal. **Open** noon-2.30pm, 8-10.30pm Mon-Fri; noon-2.30pm Sat. **Average** €30. **Credit** V. **Map** p402 H5.

This friendly little bistro offers one of the most authentic Basque menus in Paris. Start with a plate of Basque charcuterie or *pipérade*, followed by squid, *axoa* (veal cooked with onions, tomatoes and peppers), or *poulet basquaise*. Finish up with *brebis d'Ossau*, the delicious Pyrenean ewe's milk cheese, or the iced parfait of Izarra, a Basque liqueur.

Le Tir Bouchon

22 rue Tiquetonne, 2nd (01.42.21.95.51). M° Etienne-Marcel. **Open** noon-2.30pm, 8-11pm Mon-Fri; noon-2.30pm, 8-11.30pm Sat; 8-11pm Sun. Closed 25 Dec and 1 Jan. **Average** €40. **Lunch menu** €12.50, €20. **Credit** AmEx, MC, V. **Map** p402 J5.

The food at this unpretentious bistro on a small, cobbled road is as warm and welcoming as its ochre colours and candle-lit tables. The wide variety of main courses might include a baked pike-perch in a creamy crayfish sauce and a tender venison steak topped with a melted slice of *foie gras*.

Contemporary/trendy

Restaurant Etienne Marcel

34 rue Etienne-Marcel, 2nd (01.45.08.01.03). M° Etienne-Marcel. **Open** 11.30am-1am daily. **Average** €40. **Credit** AmEx, MC, V. **Map** p402 J5.

The terrace facing streetwise rue Etienne-Marcel gives the latest Costes brothers venture an edgier-than-usual vibe. The designer building-works decor by artists Huyghe and Parreno features 70s hard, boxy plastic chairs and bald light fixtures. A hi-tech juke box allows punters to choose music for their soirée and the food pushes fusion as far as the French are currently prepared to go.

Macéo

15 rue des Petits-Champs, 1st (01.42.97.53.85). M° Bourse or Palais Royal. **Open** noon-2.30pm, 7-11pm Mon-Fri; 7-11pm Sat; 12-30-11pm Sun. **Average** €50. **Prix fixe** €35, €38 (dinner only). **Lunch menu** €25, €34. **Credit** MC, V. **Map** p402 H5.

Macéo has one of the best wine lists in Paris. A cosmopolitan crowd out for a good time throngs the gorgeous room with its wedding-cake mouldings, and the modern market menu is often excellent – for vegetarians too. If only they would realise that the sometimes abysmal service can mar what is usually an otherwise lovely meal.

Step back in time at the **Brasserie de l'Isle St-Louis**. *See left.*

Menu Lexicon

Agneau lamb. **Aiguillettes** (*de canard*) thin slices of duck breast. **Aïoli** garlic mayonnaise. **Aligot** mashed potatoes with melted cheese and garlic. **Aloyau** beef loin. **Anchoïade** spicy anchovy and olive paste. **Andouillette** sausage made from pig's offal. **Ananas** pineapple. **Anguille** eel. **Asperge** asparagus. **Aubergine** aubergine/eggplant.

Ballotine stuffed, rolled up piece of meat or fish. **Bar** sea bass. **Bavarois** moulded cream dessert. **Bavette** beef flank steak. **Béarnaise** sauce of butter and egg yolk. **Beignet** fritter or doughnut. **Belon** smooth, flat oyster. **Biche** venison. **Bifteak** steak. **Bisque** shellfish soup. **Blanc** breast. **Blanquette** 'white' stew made with eggs and cream. **Boudin noir/blanc** black (blood)/white pudding. **Boeuf** beef; – **bourguignon** beef cooked Burgundy style, with red wine, onions and mushrooms; – **gros sel** boiled beef with vegetables. **Bouillabaisse** Mediterranean fish soup. **Bourride** a *bouillabaisse*-like soup, without shellfish. **Brochet** pike. **Bulot** whelk.

Cabillaud fresh cod. **Caille** quail. **Canard** duck. **Cannelle** cinnamon. **Carbonnade** beef stew with onions and stout or beer. **Carré d'agneau** rack of lamb. **Carrelet** plaice. **Cassis** blackcurrants; blackcurrant liqueur. **Cassoulet** stew of white haricot beans, sausage and preserved duck. **Céleri** celery. **Céleri rave** celeriac. **Cèpe** cep mushroom. **Cervelle** brains. **Champignon** mushroom; – **de Paris** button mushroom. **Chateaubriand** thick fillet steak. **Chaud-froid** a sauce used to glaze cold dishes. **Chèvre** goat; goat's cheese. **Chevreuil** young roe deer. **Choucroute** sauerkraut, served *garni* with cured ham and sausages. **Ciboulette** chive. **Citron** lemon. **Citron vert** lime. **Citronelle** lemongrass. **Civet** game stew. **Clafoutis** batter filled with fruit, usually cherries. **Cochon de lait** suckling pig. **Coco** large white bean. **Colin** hake. **Confit de canard** preserved duck. **Contre-filet** sirloin steak. **Coquelet** baby rooster. **Coquille** shell. **Coquilles St-Jacques** scallops. **Côte** chop; – **de boeuf** beef rib. **Crème brûlée** creamy custard dessert with caramel glaze. **Crème Chantilly** sweetened whipped cream. **Crème**

fraîche thick, slightly soured cream. **Cresson** watercress. **Crevettes** prawns (GB), shrimp (US). **Croque-madame** sandwich of toasted cheese and ham topped with an egg; **croque-monsieur** sandwich of toasted cheese and ham. **En croûte** in a pastry case. **Cru** raw. **Crudités** assorted raw vegetables. **Crustacé** shellfish.

Daube meat braised in red wine. **Daurade** sea bream. **Désossé** boned. **Dinde** turkey. **Duxelles** chopped, sautéed mushrooms.

Echalote shallot. **Eglefin** haddock. **Endive** chicory (GB), Belgian endive (US). **Entrecôte** beef rib steak. **Epices** spices. **Epinards** spinach. **Escabèche** sautéed and marinated fish, served cold. **Escargot** snail. **Espadon** swordfish. **Estouffade** meat that's been marinated, fried and braised.

Faisan pheasant. **Farci** stuffed. **Faux-filet** sirloin steak. **Feuilleté** 'leaves' of (puff) pastry. **Filet mignon** tenderloin. **Fines de claire** crinkle-shelled oysters. **Flambé** flamed in alcohol. **Flétan** halibut. **Foie** liver; – **gras** fattened goose or duck liver. **Forestière** with mushrooms. **Au four** baked. **Fraise** strawberry. **Framboise** raspberry. **Fricassé** fried and simmered in stock, usually with creamy sauce. **Frisée** curly endive. **Frites** chips (GB); fries (US). **Fromage** cheese; – **blanc** smooth cream cheese. **Fruits de mer** shellfish. **Fumé** smoked.

Galette round flat cake of flaky pastry, potato pancake or buckwheat savoury *crêpe*. **Garni** garnished. **Gelée** aspic. **Gésiers** gizzards. **Gibier** game. **Gigot d'agneau** leg of lamb. **Gingembre** ginger. **Girolle/chanterelle** small, trumpet-like mushroom. **Glace** ice cream. **Glacé** frozen or iced. **Goujon** breaded, fried strip of fish; also a small catfish. **Gras** fat. **Gratin dauphinois** sliced potatoes baked with milk, cheese and garlic. **Gratiné** browned with breadcrumbs or cheese. **A la grècque** vegetables served cold in the cooking liquid with oil and lemon juice. **Cuisses de grenouille** frogs' legs. **Grillé** grilled. **Groseille** redcurrant. **Groseille à maquereau** gooseberry.

H aché minced. **Hachis Parmentier** shepherd's pie. **Hareng** herring. **Haricot** bean; **– vert** green bean. **Homard** lobster. **Huître** oyster.

I le flottante whipped egg white floating in vanilla custard.

J ambon ham; **– cru** cured raw ham. **Jarret** ham shin or knuckle. **Julienne** vegetables cut into matchsticks.

L angoustine Dublin Bay prawns, scampi. **Lapin** rabbit. **Lamelle** very thin slice. **Langue** tongue. **Lard** bacon. **Lardon** small cube of bacon. **Légume** vegetable. **Lièvre** hare. **Limande** lemon sole. **Lotte** monkfish.

M âche lamb's lettuce. **Magret** duck breast. **Maison** of the house. **Maquereau** mackerel. **Marcassin** wild boar. **Mariné** marinated. **Marmite** small cooking pot. **Marquise** mousse-like cake. **Merguez** spicy lamb/beef sausage. **Merlan** whiting. **Merlu** hake. **Meunière** fish floured and sautéed in butter. **Miel** honey. **Mignon** small meat fillet. **Mirabelle** tiny yellow plum. **Moelle** bone marrow; **os à la –** marrow bone. **Morille** morel mushroom. **Moules** mussels; **– à la marinière** cooked with white wine and shallots. **Morue** dried, salted cod; **brandade de –** cod puréed with potato. **Mousseline** hollandaise sauce with whipped cream. **Myrtille** bilberry/blueberry.

N avarin lamb and vegetable stew. **Navet** turnip. **Noisette** hazelnut; small round portion of meat. **Noix** walnut. **Noix de coco** coconut. **Nouilles** noodles.

O euf egg; **– en cocotte** baked egg; **– en meurette** egg poached in red wine; **– à la neige** see *Ile flottante*. **Oie** goose. **Oignon** onion. **Onglet** cut of beef, similar to *bavette*. **Oseille** sorrel. **Oursin** sea urchin.

P alourde type of clam. **Pamplemousse** grapefruit. **Pané** breaded. **En papillote** cooked in a packet. **Parfait** sweet or savoury mousse-like mixture. **Parmentier** with potato. **Paupiette** slice of meat or fish, stuffed and rolled. **Pavé** thick steak. **Perdrix** partridge. **Persil** parsley. **Petit salé** salt pork. **Pied** foot (trotter). **Pignon** pine kernel. **Pintade/**

pintadeau guinea fowl. **Pipérade** Basque dish of green peppers, onions, Bayonne ham and tomatoes, often served with scrambled egg. **Poivre** pepper. **Poivron** red or green (bell) pepper. **Pomme** apple. **Pomme de terre** potato. **Pommes lyonnaises** potatoes fried with onions. **Potage** soup. **Pot-au-feu** boiled beef with vegetables. **Potiron** pumpkin. **Poulet** chicken. **Poulpe** octopus. **Pressé** squeezed. **Prune** plum. **Pruneau** prune.

Q uenelle light, poached fish (or poultry) dumpling. **Quetsche** damson. **Queue de boeuf** oxtail.

R agoût meat stew. **Raie** skate. **Râpé** grated. **Rascasse** scorpion fish. **Réglisse** liquorice. **Rillettes** potted pork, goose, salmon or tuna. **Ris de veau** veal sweetbreads. **Riz** rice. **Rognons** kidneys. **Rôti** roast. **Rouget** red mullet.

S t Pierre John Dory. **Salé** salted. **Sandre** pike-perch. **Sanglier** wild boar. **Saucisse** sausage. **Saucisson sec** small dried sausage. **Saumon** salmon. **Seiche** squid. **Selle** (*d'agneau*) saddle (of lamb). **Suprême** fillets (of chicken) in a cream sauce. **Supion** small squid.

T agine slow-cooked North African stew. **Tapenade** Provençal olive and caper paste. **Tartare** raw minced steak (also tuna or salmon). **Tarte aux pommes** apple tart. **Tarte Tatin** warm, caramelised apple tart cooked upside-down. **Timbale** dome-shaped mould, or food cooked in one. **Tisane** herbal tea. **Tournedos** small slices of beef fillet, sautéed or grilled. **Tourte** covered pie or tart, usually savoury. **Travers de porc** pork spare ribs. **Tripes** tripe. **Tripoux** dish of sheep's offal and sheep feet. **Truffes** truffles. **Truite** trout.

V acherin cake of layered meringue, cream, fruit and ice cream; a soft, cow's milk cheese. **Veau** veal. **Velouté** stock-based white sauce; creamy soup. **Vichyssoise** cold leek and potato soup. **Volaille** poultry.

Cooking time (La cuisson)

Cru raw. **Bleu** practically raw. **Saignant** rare. **Rosé** pink (said of lamb, duck, liver, kidneys). **A point** medium rare. **Bien cuit** well done.

Au Bon Saint-Pourçain

*"Expect better-than-average
home cooking"*
Time Out with Pariscope 2002

*Open daily noon-2pm, 7.30-10.30pm
Closed Sundays
10 bis rue Servandoni, 6th - Tel: 01.43.54.93.63
Mº Odeon or Saint-Sulpice.*

**Asian-fusion recommended
by several major
gastronomic guides.
Open Mon-Fri noon-2pm,
daily 7pm-11pm**

**12 rue de Richelieu, 1st.
Mº Palais Royal
Tel: 01.42.61.49.48 - 01.42.60.96.18**

l'Écurie

Miny welcomes you to
her charming Parisian
restaurant in the
heart of the
Quartier Latin.

58 rue de la Montagne
Sainte-Geneviève, 5th.
(on the corner of rue Laplace)
Tel: 01.46.33.68.49
Mº Maubert-Mutualité
Open Mon, Wed-Sat noon-3pm,
7pm-midnight.
Tue, Sun 7pm-midnight

Au
Grain
de
folie

Montmartre's
Vegetarian Restaurant

*24 rue de La Vieuville, 18th
Mº Abbesses Tel: 01.42.58.15.57
Open daily noon-2.30pm,
evenings 7.30-11.30pm
(Winter 7-10.30pm)*
Complimentary tea/coffee with this ad

Fish

Iode
48 rue d'Argout, 2nd (01.42.36.46.45). M° Sentier.
Open 12.30-3pm, 8.30-11.30pm Mon-Fri; 8.30-11.30pm
Sat. **Average** €30. **Credit** MC, V. **Map** p402 J4.
Something fishy has been going on – ha ha – in this
new-wave Breton bistro. Big hits are the creamy,
carefully seasoned tartare of grenadier and a pile of
crisp deep-fried baby squid. If the fare's on the point
of filling you up, finish with a berry and citrus salad
in a light mint syrup; heartier appetites could try
crêpes Suzette washed down with a glass of cloudy
draught cider.

Haute cuisine

Les Ambassadeurs
*Hôtel de Crillon, 10 pl de la Concorde, 8th
(01.44.71.16.16/www.crillon.com). M° Concorde.*
Open noon-2.30pm, 7-10.30pm daily. **Average**
€145. **Prix fixe** €135. **Lunch menu** €62 (Mon-Fri).
Credit AmEx, DC, MC, V. **Map** p401 F5.
With its view over place de la Concorde, chandeliers
and acres of marble, the Crillon's main restaurant is
one of the most opulent dining establishments in
Paris. Chef Dominique Bouchet ensures that the food
is as exalted as the setting, aestheticising customers
into submission with superb dishes like truffle salad,
cannelloni stuffed with lamb in tomato and black
olive sauce, and sea bass with grilled olives. Desserts
are sublime, including the *truffe glâcée* with fresh
thyme ice cream. *Wheelchair access.*

International

Cambodian: La Mousson
*9 rue Thérèse, 1st (01.42.60.59.46). M° Pyramides
ou Palais Royal.* **Open** noon-2.30pm, 7.15-10.15pm
Mon-Sat. **Average** €23. **Prix fixe** €15.10, €19.10.
Lunch menu €11.60, €16. **Credit** MC, V.
Map p401 H5.
The tiny cook, known to her faithful customers as
Lucile, moved to Paris in 1975 and has been recre-
ating Khmer flavours ever since. Try authentic
Cambodian dishes like *amok*, a soothing steamed
fish dish made with coconut milk, galangal, lemongrass and kaffir lime leaf, and, for the adventurous,
ta peir (fermented black rice) as dessert.

Italian: La Bocca
*59 rue Montmartre, 2nd (01.42.36.71.88).
M° Sentier or Etienne Marcel.* **Open** noon-2am daily.
Average €25. **Credit** MC, V. **Map** p402 K4.
Perch on the tiny terrace, or, if the weather's iffy,
drop down at a tiled table inside at this casually hip
Italian. Food is fresh and seasonal: an antipasti plate
of grilled vegetables is generous enough for two, and
linguine Siracusa with garlic, chilli, basil and dried
tomatoes is utterly delicious. The espresso is top-
notch, aided no doubt by the turn-of-the-century
Victoria Arduino coffee machine.

Opulent dining at **Les Ambassadeurs**.

Japanese: Laï Laï Ken
7 rue Ste-Anne, 1st (01.40.15.96.90). M° Pyramides.
Open noon-10pm Mon-Sat; 6-10pm Sun. **Average**
€14. **Prix fixe** €13. **Credit** AmEx, MC, V.
Map p401 H5.
The large number of Japanese diners inside testify
to this being one of best Japanese eateries on the rue
Ste-Anne. *Ramen* – noodle soup with bamboo shoots
and pork slices – is the way to go; otherwise, take
your pick from an extensive menu. Above all, don't
miss the sublime *age gyoza*, deep-fried pork and garlic dumplings in a crispy rice pastry wrapper, preferably accompanied by large cans of Asahi beer.

Opéra & the Grands Boulevards

Bistros & brasseries

L'Alsaco
*10 rue Condorcet, 9th (01.45.26.44.31/
www.alsaco.net). M° Poissonnière.* **Open** 7-11pm
Mon, Sat; noon-2.30pm, 7-11pm Tue-Fri. Closed last
two weeks in July, Aug. **Average** €30. **Prix fixe**
€19, €29 (dinner only). **Lunch menu** €19.
Credit MC, V. **Map** p402 J2.
This cosy *winstub* run by a jolly, almost cartoon
host, is one of the best places in Paris to try Alsatian
food. There is little point in ordering *à la carte* – the

Eat, Drink, Shop

Have a vine time at **Macéo**. See p183.

menus incorporate most dishes and are better value. If things are getting wintry outside, try *bäckaofa*, a warming, hearty beef and potato stew not entirely dissimilar to the Irish version. They have some excellent Alsatian wines, too. *Wheelchair access.*

Le Bistrot d'Anglas

29 rue Boissy d'Anglas, 8th (01.42.65.63.73). M° Madeleine. **Open** 9am-10pm Mon-Fri, noon-3pm Sat. Closed Aug. **Average** €23. **Lunch menu** €15.70. **Credit** MC, V. **Map** p401 F4.
The service at this unprepossessing bistro is too frequently brusque bordering on the downright rude. So why would you go there? Because if you're sore-footed, faint and hungry in this area of designer boutiques and fashionable eateries you will be mighty glad of its good-value *plat du jour* – dishes like *tagliatelles aux écrevisses* with plenty of juicy crayfish or the *assiette du pêcheur* with a timbale of saffron-laden risotto rice.

Brasserie Flo

7 cour des Petites-Ecuries, 10th (01.47.70.13.59). M° Château d'Eau. **Open** noon-3pm, 7pm-1.30am daily. **Average** €38. **Prix fixe** €30 (dinner only). **Lunch menu** €21. **Credit** AmEx, DC, MC, V. **Map** p402 K3.
This restaurant is the foundation of Jean-Paul Bucher's Flo empire, which has breathed new life into Paris' old brasseries. Main courses include tender Scottish salmon with chunks of bacon, baked whole garlic cloves and bright-green spinach, and juicy roast veal with morels, served with a crisp and creamy rice galette. Hedonists can finish their meal with the decadent *coupe* Flo, cherry ice cream drowned in cherry liqueur. *Wheelchair access.*

Chez Jean

8 rue St-Lazare, 9th (01.48.78.62.73). M° Notre-Dame-de-Lorette. **Open** noon-2pm, 7.30-10.30pm Mon-Fri; 7-10.30pm Sat. Closed two weeks in Aug. **Average** €33. **Prix fixe** €32. **Credit** MC, V. **Map** p401 H3.
In the mood for some sedate, discerning dining? Want to pretend to be Bryan Ferry for a while? The engaging Jean has created a pleasant oasis whose menu changes at least monthly so you can come back again and again and again. Once you've planted yourself on the deep red banquettes, you'll find the staff need no prompting to deliver the next carafe or another basket of homemade bread; and you'll need no prompting to get stuck in. The dishes – such as tender fresh skate fillet on a warm bed of ratte potatoes or young guinea fowl roasted with peach slices and oversized shallots – is of the same high standard as the service.

Le Vaudeville

29 rue Vivienne, 2nd (01.40.20.04.62). M° Bourse. **Open** noon-3pm, 7pm-1am daily. **Average** €32. **Prix fixe** €30.50 (dinner only). **Lunch menu** €21.50. **Credit** AmEx, DC, MC, V. **Map** p402 H4.
Just opposite the Bourse, and thus very handy for the Opéra, the Grands Boulevards and the *grands magasins*, this delightful standby with its art deco interior is always kicking up a buzz. The brasserie fare is sophisticated, cashed-up yuppie comfort food that still tickles the palate. The dozen *spéciales N° 3* oysters are meaty enough to make a dinner in themselves (as they should do at €27), while the grilled fresh cod is salty and satisfying with its sturdy mashed potatoes dribbled with truffle sauce.

Contemporary/trendy

Trendy: L'Envue
39 rue Boissy-d'Anglas, 8th (01.42.65.10.49).
M° Madeleine. **Open** 8am-11pm Mon-Sat. **Average**
€30. **Credit** AmEx, DC, MC, V. **Map** p401 F4.
Video clips from the catwalk shows play over the
bar at this new restaurant in a part of Paris that desperately needs troughing options beyond plastic
corner café and haute cuisine. The menu is ideal for
picking at, with a seafood platter of sea bass sashi-
mi, salmon tartare and *rillettes, brandade de morue*
and a similar vegetable plate. The dessert menu
delivers treats like baba sponge with roasted
pineapple, which you personally douse with rum –
you may raise eyebrows if you pour more than a
bottle's worth and request a drinking straw.

Bon 2
2 rue du Quatre Septembre, 2nd (01.44.55.51.55).
M° Bourse. **Open** 8am-2am Mon-Sat. **Average** €35.
Prix fixe €30.50 (dinner only). **Lunch menu** €22.
Credit AmEx, DC, MC, V. **Map** p402 H4.
The Bourse location of Philippe Starck's second Bon
gives it a more business-like atmosphere than the
original in the 16th and you can keep an eye on your
bonds with the electronic indexes running above the
oyster bar. The menu features breakdowns of the
health-giving properties of the various dishes, from
vitamins to laxative properties (with a tongue-in-
cheek '*bon pour morale*' for the puddings, which are
courtesy of Ladurée). 32-year-old Richard Pommies'
cooking is international but with a certain Provençal
slant – as in the bowl of sweet roast vegetables
served with the excellent fennel-stuffed fillet of *bar*.

Haute Cuisine

Lucas Carton
9 pl de la Madeleine, 8th (01.42.65.22.90/
www.lucascarton.com). M° Madeleine. **Open** 8-10.30pm
Mon, Sat; noon-2.30pm, 8-10.30pm Tue-Fri. Closed
Aug. **Average** €200. **Lunch menu** €64.
Credit AmEx, DC, MC, V. **Map** p401 G4.
In one of the most sumptuous dining rooms in Paris
(plum-coloured banquettes and art nouveau partitions with glass-encased butterflies) Lucas Carton
delivers a hard-to-equal luxury eating experience.
The €64 *menu d'affaires* is not as business-like as
it sounds with adventurous starters such as a
carpaccio of tuna flavoured with shallot, pink ginger, aromatic oil and a crunchy spiced *tuile*. If you're
feeling flush go *à la carte* and sample Alain
Senderens' signature duck *à l'Apicius*.

International

Italian: Paparazzi Opéra
6 square de l'Opéra Louis Jouvet, 9th (01.40.07.92.56).
M° Opéra. **Open** noon-2.30pm, 7.45-11.30pm Mon-
Sat. **Average** €25. **Credit** AmEx, DC, MC, V.
Map p401 G4.
This annexe of the famous pizzas-so-big-they're-
served-on-two-plates pizzeria nearby makes a move
upmarket with a cool Milanese decor and more varied menu. Start off with antipasti (but then you
would, wouldn't you?), and then go with one of the
famous crusty pizzas. They also offer a nice choice
of pastas, and an original jacket potato with truffles
and pancetta (Italian bacon).

Beaubourg & the Marais

Bistros

Baracane
38 rue des Tournelles, 4th (01.42.71.43.33).
M° Bastille or Chemin Vert. **Open** noon-2.30pm,
7pm-midnight Mon-Fri; 7pm-midnight Sat. **Average**
€23. **Prix fixe** €22, €36. **Lunch menu** €8, €13.
Credit MC,V. **Map** p406 L6.
This venue affords a respite from the Bastille and
Place des Vosges crowds. Starters include a smoky
Jerusalem artichoke soup with bacon. Mains keep
the positive momentum going: a fresh trout pan-
fried with hazelnuts, parsley and butter, and a
hearty pastry-wrapped *croustade* of roasted feta,
mushrooms and green vegetables. Generous
desserts arrive as part of the €22 *menu*. Fine service
and fabulous value.

Au Bourguignon du Marais
52 rue François-Miron, 4th (01.48.87.15.40).
M° St-Paul. **Open** noon-3pm, 7.30-11pm Mon-Fri;
noon-5pm (brunch) Sat. **Average** €38. **Prix fixe**
€22.10 (brunch only). **Credit** AmEx, DC, MC, V.
Map p406 K6.
This stylish dining room with friendly and efficient
staff serves delightfully pleasing food. Try a starter
of tender sautéed *girolles* with cured ham and
parmesan shavings on a bed of rocket. An unmissable main is the seared tuna steak, glistening wan-
tonly in a herb vinaigrette with steamed spinach on
the side. Resistance is futile. Fans of Burgundy will
relish the wine list.

Chez Janou
*2 rue Roger-Verlomme, 3rd (01.42.72.28.41). M°
Chemin Vert.* **Open** noon-2am daily. **Average** €23.
No credit cards. Map p406 L6.
There is something southern about Chez Janou, from
the help-yourself nibbles to the friendly but frenetic staff who happily clean up around diners while
the latter finish that second or third bottle of wine.
The tuna tartare served with an onion marmalade,
and the duck, are always excellent, and sweet tooths
should not miss the chocolate mousse: where else in
Paris – or anywhere – do you get to help yourself to
as much as you want?

Le Pamphlet
*38 rue Debelleyme, 3rd (01.42.72.39.24). M° St-
Sébastien-Froissart.* **Open** noon-2.30pm, 8-11pm
Mon-Fri; 8-11pm Sat. **Prix-fixe** €27. **Credit** MC, V.
Map p406 L5.
Beyond the excellent contemporary bistro cooking
with a Basque-Béarnais slant, what everyone likes
about this bistro is the calm atmosphere. The menu
changes often and tastefully, with traditional
starters such as cream of lentil soup poured over a
scallop of foie gras, and less traditional ones like
tempura prawns with salad. Main courses run to
beautifully prepared dishes like sole meunière with
a gratin of Jerusalem artichokes.

Les Petits Marseillais
72 rue Vieille-du-Temple, 3rd (01.42.78.91.59).
M° Rambuteau. **Open** noon-2.30pm, 8-11pm daily.
Average €34. **Credit** AmEx, MC, V. **Map** p406 K6.
Ever since this cosy place run by two childhood
friends from Marseille – they're the muscular guys
behind the bar – opened, it's been packed with a hip,
friendly, mixed crowd that chats easily between
tables. They serve the type of food you'd get if you
were lucky enough to snag an invitation to a
cabanon (privately owned sea shack – try saying
that when you're breaking in new dentures): sautéed
squid, roast lamb, and tagliatelle with pistou sauce
and hunks of parmesan.

Contemporary/trendy

Georges
Centre Pompidou, 6th floor, rue Rambuteau, 4th.
(01.44.78.47.99). M° Rambuteau. **Open** noon-2am
Mon, Wed-Sun. **Average** €46. **Credit** AmEx, DC,
MC, V. **Map** p406 K5.
Here is another of the Costes brothers' successful
scene centrals, peopled by staff that must have been
genetically engineered to look so perfect. Daytime
sees exhibition escapees and casual diners while
night-time is more a Gucci groove. The food is fine,
but prices are on the high side. The cup-full of gaz-
pacho is chilled and spicy, and the artichoke hearts
with salmon slices are perfect for a hot summer's
day. *Wheelchair access.*

International

Australian: Bennelong
*31 bd Henri IV, 4th, (01.42.71.07.71). M° Bastille or
Sully-Morland.* **Open** noon-3pm, 7.30-10.30pm Tue-
Fri; 7.30-10.30pm Sat; 7.30-10pm Sun. **Average** €40.
Prix fixe (dinner only) €28.95-€38.10. **Lunch
menu** €20. **Credit** AmEx, MC, V. **Map** p406 L7.
Wizard of Oz Jean-Paul Bruneteau was born in
France but spent 30 years in Australia where he pioneered the use of 'bush' foods in his restaurants.
Foodies are the beneficiaries of his innovation. Opt
for the smoked emu salad followed by fillets of tender, just-cooked kangaroo or, if that's a tad too
authentic, a punchy, finely balanced Thai chicken
curry or a beautifully cooked *daurade*. An extensive
vegetarian menu is offered on Sunday nights.

Jewish: Chez Marianne
*2 rue des Hospitalières-St-Gervais, 4th
(01.42.72.18.86). M° St-Paul.* **Open** 11am-midnight
daily. **Average** €15. **Credit** MC, V. **Map** p406 L6.
Chez Marianne has long set the standard by which
all other Jewish restaurants in Paris are judged.
Assiettes composées, plates of four to six Middle
Eastern and Central European Jewish specialities,
are served with baskets of delicate pumpernickel
and rye bread. Don't leave without trying the houmous and tahini, and have a good guzzle of the full-
bodied Israeli non-kosher lager, Maccabee.

Eat, Drink, Shop

Couscous kisses at **404**. *See p193.*

Le Polidor

In the heart of the Quartier Latin, just a few steps away from the Panthéon, the Sorbonne and Boulevard St. Michel

Enjoy fine French cuisine in a superb historic surrounding dating back to 1845

Prix fixe: €18, à la carte: avg. €20 Lunch menu: €9

41 rue Monsieur-le-Prince, 6th, M° Odéon. Tel: 01.43.26.95.34
Open Mon-Sat noon-2.30pm, 7pm-1am, Sun noon-2.30pm, 7pm-11pm

"The service is really splendid...a comfortable and pleasant spot" – Time Out Paris with Pariscope

Traditional Bistro with a cuisine to savour at a price to remember. Set in a wonderful, leaf swept Avenue just off the Seine

Ardoise lunch time set-menu €18.80 (starter + main course or -main course + dessert) Carte €40

Restaurant Nabuchodonosor

6 avenue Bosquet, 7th M°Alma Marceau • Tel: 01.45.56.97.26 Fax: 01.45.56.98.44 • www.nabuchodonosor.net
Closed Saturday lunch and all day Sunday

North African: 404

69 rue des Gravilliers, 3rd (01.42.74.57.81). M° Arts et Métiers. **Open** noon-2.30pm, 8pm-midnight Mon-Fri; noon-2.30pm (brunch), 8pm-midnight Sat, Sun. Closed at lunch in Aug. **Average** €27. **Lunch menu** €17 (Mon-Fri); brunch €21 (Sat, Sun). **Credit** AmEx, DC, MC, V. **Map** p406 K5.

Londoners will already be familiar with owner Momo's formula: riad-chic decor, remixed Moroccan sounds from his own CDs and succulent North African specialities. On a recent visit, the food was a bit hit-and-miss, although the chicken tagines – one with pear, the other with preserved lemon and olives – were good. The politeness and infectious energy of the grooving staff, however, make it hard to fault the mood. Reservations required.

Vegetarian

Le Potager du Marais

22 rue Rambuteau, 3rd (01.44.54.00.31). M° Rambuteau. **Open** noon-3pm, 7-11pm Mon-Sat. **Average** €15. **Prix fixe** €14.48. **Lunch menu** €9.91. **Credit** AmEx, MC, V. **Map** p406 K5.

Fresh pastas, soups and daily fish specials are made with organic ingredients and flavourful yet light seasonings. For main dishes, try the stuffed tomato, the curried tofu penne, or a cep ravioli with olive oil and herbs. Portions are a little on the small side, or was it just the lack of calories? Either way, don't miss out on desserts of poached pear, smothered in chocolate, or the flower-scented crème brûlée.

La Verte Tige

13 rue Ste-Anastase, 3rd (01.42.77.22.15). M° St-Sébastien-Froissart. **Open** noon-2.30pm, 7.30-10.30pm Tue-Sat, 12.30-4pm Sun. Closed Aug. **Average** €15. **Prix fixe** €16 (evenings, Sat and Sun lunch). **Credit** MC, V. **Map** p406 L5.

This vegetarian restaurant is in a class of its own. The chef has taken traditional Iranian dishes and subtracted the meat elements: thus the *espinada* – a spinach purée with fried onions, garlic and yoghurt that has just the right tang. Mains include a varied vegetarian platter and couscous with tofu sausage – there is also a €8 *plat du jour* each weekday.

The Bastille & eastern Paris

Bistros & brasseries

Chardenoux

1 rue Jules-Vallès, 11th (01.43.71.49.52). M° Charonne. **Open** noon-2.30pm, 8-10.30pm Mon-Fri; 8-10.30pm Sat. Closed Aug. **Average** €30. **Credit** AmEx, MC, V. **Map** p407 N7.

Chardenoux's etched glass and belle époque painted ladies keep it up there among Paris' most romantic restaurants, but it's the food that makes it a favourite of many Parisians. Chef Bernard Passavant is good at potent, flavour-packed sauces. If you're lucky you might get as dish of the day ten-

der *biche* (doe) in a wonderful red wine and blackcurrant concoction, accompanied by potato purée dyed purple with blackcurrants, and sautéed *trompette de la mort* mushrooms. *Wheelchair access.*

L'Encrier

55 rue Traversière, 12th (01.44.68.08.16). M° Ledru-Rollin or Gare de Lyon. **Open** noon-2.15pm, 7.15-11pm Mon-Fri; 7.15-11pm Sat. Closed Aug. **Average** €20. Prix fixe €13 (dinner only), €14, €17.80. **Lunch menu** €10. **Credit** MC, V. **Map** p407 M8.

This small restaurant with bare stone walls and open kitchen is buzzing most mealtimes. Suits predominate at lunch, with a cosier crowd in the evening. The bargain €10 *menu* features starters such as fromage blanc with grated radish or *potage de légumes* while mains include steaks and a chunky Montbéliard sausage with cabbage. Turn up early as they don't take reservations. *Wheelchair access.*

Les Jumeaux

73 rue Amelot, 11th (01.43.14.27.00). M° Chemin Vert. **Open** noon-2.30pm, 7.30-10.30pm Tue-Sat. Closed Aug. **Prix fixe** €30 (dinner only). **Lunch menu** €24. **Credit** MC, V. **Map** p406 L6.

As its name suggests, this restaurant is run by identical twins, one ducking and diving in the kitchen while his brother meets and greets a sophisticated local crowd. The three-course *menu* for €30 features precise and imaginative cooking: a *fricassée d'escargots* and an unusual but successful camembert brick, pink veal kidney served on a bed of stewed beetroot or moist and tasty rabbit. And the finely aged cheeses are selected with just the same care.

Paris Main d'Or

133 rue du Fbg-St-Antoine, 11th (01.44.68.04.68). M° Ledru-Rollin. **Open** noon-3pm, 8pm-midnight Mon-Sat. Closed Mon in Aug. **Average** €22. **Lunch menu** €11. **Credit** MC, V. **Map** p407 M7.

A regular bistro by day, this turns into a lively Corsican by night. The menu, titled '*dossier Corse, confidentiel*', refers to the islanders' reputation for skullduggery and the air of playful mystery is compounded by the fact that many of the dishes use uniquely Corsican ingredients. Try veal in Vico honey (Vico is a region), the delicious *pignata marina* (a kind of bouillabaisse) or the roast kid.

Le Square Trousseau

1 rue Antoine-Vollon, 12th (01.43.43.06.00). M° Ledru-Rollin. **Open** Tue-Sat noon-2.30pm, 8-11.30pm. **Average** €38. **Lunch menu** €20, €25. **Credit** MC, V. **Map** p407 N7.

This restaurant would be worth visiting for its superb 1900s interior alone, but what makes the place a must is its *joie de vivre*. It's a favourite with a media and film crowd, perhaps because it is itself a readymade set. The food, though, is for real, with satisfying mains including plump farm chicken served with a mini, creamy risotto, or tender strips of duck in a delicious cherry sauce. The relatively steep wine prices may come as a surprise, but the selection shows expertise.

Eat, Drink, Shop

Le Train Bleu

Gare de Lyon, Louis-Armand, 12th (01.43.43.09.06).
M° Gare de Lyon. **Open** 11.30am-3pm, 7-11pm daily.
Average €49. **Prix fixe** €39.64. **Credit** AmEx,
DC, MC, V. **Map** p407 M8.
Few places better evoke the blowsy elegance of the
Belle Epoque than this spectacular station restau-
rant. Decorated with tile murals to celebrate the
World Fair of 1900, it serves surprisingly decent
food. Try dishes like lobster with mixed salad, a veal
chop au gratin, the first-rate cheese tray and gigan-
tic *baba au rhum. Wheelchair access.*

International

Sardinian: Sardegna a Tavola

1 rue de Cotte, 12th (01.44.75.03.28).
M° Ledru-Rollin. **Open** 7.30-11.30pm Mon; noon-
2.30pm, 7.30-11.30pm Tue-Sat. **Average** €30.
Lunch menu €14.94. **Credit** AmEx, MC, V. **Map**
p407 N7.
This Sardinian restaurant gets better and better.
The good-value lunch *menu* includes thinly sliced
charcuterie and chunky vegetables. Then comes
ravioli stuffed with ricotta and mushrooms in thick,
tomato-mushroom sauce, and farfalle pasta with
mint, crushed almonds, fresh chilli pepper and plenty of olive oil. For dramatic effect try the black pasta
with squid in its ink – tastes delicious too.

Thai: Bali Bar

9 rue St-Sabin, 11th (01.47.00.25.47). M° Bastille.
Open noon-3pm, 7.30pm-11.30am Tue-Fri; noon-
3pm,7.30pm-2am Sat, Sun. **Average** €30. **Prix fixe**
€33.54. **Lunch menu** €14.48. **Credit** DC, MC, V.
Map p407 M6.

You'll love the Bali Bar. Lubricate yourself with a
cocktail and then hit starters such as a basket of
steamed pork and prawn dumplings. Among classic Thai fare is the *yam neua*, a spicy salad of rare
beef, shallots, mint and coriander. Service is occasionally haphazard, but staff are good-humoured
and good enough fun to make it seem kind of charming. *Wheelchair access.*

North African: Au P'tit Cahoua

24 rue des Taillandiers, 11th (01.47.00.20.42).
M° Bastille. **Open** noon-2pm, 7.30-11.30pm Mon-Sat;
7.30-11.30pm Sun. **Average** €30. **Prix fixe** €9.
Credit AmEx, MC, V. **Map** p407 M6.
The rather baroque décor and beautifully made
Moroccan food create an appealing atmosphere that
pulls an interesting crowd of young trendies and
locals. Try the lamb with prunes, chicken with preserved lemons or very good couscous, and finish up
with a honey-drenched pastry for dessert. The original address (39 bd St-Marcel, 13th, 01.47.07.24.42)
has décor that recreates a Berber tent if you fancy a
nibble under canvas.

The Champs-Elysées and west

Bistros & brasseries

L'Angle du Faubourg

195 rue du Fbg-St-Honoré, 8th (01.40.74.20.20).
M° Ternes or George V. **Open** noon-2.30pm, 7-11pm
Mon-Fri. Closed 27 July-21 Aug. **Average** €61. **Prix
fixe** €42.69 (dinner only). **Lunch menu** €35.06.
Credit AmEx, DC, MC, V. **Map** p400 D3.

Next stop **La Gare**. *See right.*

The offshoot of renowned Taillevent produces excellent contemporary bistro food in a relaxed minimalist decor of Tuscan-red walls and black wood tables. Chef Stéphane Cosnier does great modern dishes such as vegetable salad served on finely sliced tomme cheese and roasted cod with a 'condiment' of *brandade de morue*.

Passiflore

33 rue de Longchamp, 16th (01.47.04.96.81).
M° Trocadéro. **Open** noon-2pm , 8-10.30pm Mon-Fri;
8-10.30pm Sat. **Average** €35. **Credit** AmEx, MC, V.
Map p400 B5.
Chef Roland Durand has a hit on his hands with his new bistro. Durand has real talent for using Asian and other exotic cuisines as an inspiration for delicious modern French dishes such as pumpkin-stuffed ravioli in mulligatawny soup, cream of spinach with *boudin antillais* (blood sausage), a chicken *tourte* and a pastilla of pears in lemon grass.

Le Bistro des Vignes

1 rue Jean-Bologne, 16th (01.45.27.76.64). M° Passy
or La Muette. **Open** noon-2.30pm, 7-10.30pm Mon-Thur, Sun; 7-11pm Fri, Sat. **Average** €26.
Credit AmEx, MC, V. **Map** p400 B6.
On a quiet street across from Notre-Dame de Passy, Le Bistrot des Vignes is making a subdued noise of its own. The artichoke-heart salad garnished with smoked salmon and poached egg is not to be missed. Duck confit is flavourful without being greasy, though the real prize goes to the heavenly garlic potatoes that come with it. *Wheelchair access.*

Bistro d'à Coté Flaubert

10 rue Gustave-Flaubert, 17th (01.42.67.05.81/
www.michelrostang.com). **Open** 12.15-2.30pm daily,
7.30-11pm. Closed one week in mid-Aug. **Average**
€46. **Lunch menu** €27. **Credit** AmEx, MC, V.
Map p400 D2.
Michel Rostang pioneered the star chef's bistro in this old *épicerie*, where he serves sophisticated bistro food that reflects haute cuisine roots. A *pressé* of asparagus, sundried tomatoes and *coppa* ham accompanied by a raw artichoke and parmesan salad, for instance, creates fantastic textures. Main courses are simpler but well prepared, with the emphasis on fine-quality meat. For puds the pots of chocolate that have become a Rostang classic.

La Gare

19 chaussée de la Muette, 16th (01.42.15.15.31).
M° La Muette. **Open** 12.30-3pm, 7.30-11.30pm daily.
Average €33. **Prix fixe** €19, €24. **Credit** AmEx,
DC, MC, V. **Map** p400 A6.
This was once a train station of the *Petite Centure*, the railway circling Paris built by Napoléon III. The menu, while still dominated by the rotisserie specialities, has been refined. A *pince de tourteau* (crab claw) with an avocado mousseline, and black truffle risotto are among the starters, while no-nonsense main courses such as leg of lamb slide down a treat. *Wheelchair access.*

Big *grec*-fest

Forget *le croque monsieur* and *le jambon-beurre*. Don't even consider *le Big Mac*: the authentic Parisian fast-food has to be *le grec*. Greek, you cry? Feta cheese parcels? A charcoaled something drizzled with olive oil, perhaps? Nope, exotic as it sounds to an untrained ear, your *sandwich grec* is your basic kebab and chips, served the length and breadth of Paris by Turks, Egyptians, Moroccans, Tunisians and, occasionally, even Greeks.

The classic kebab and chips *à la française* bears only a passing resemblance to the processed gunk that you might be familiar with. It has four core elements: bread – fluffy, baked on premises, preferably one hour before eating; meat – lamb or veal seasoned with herbs and spices, grilled on a 'rotating grill spike' and served fresh; salad – lettuce, tomato, onion (more tea, vicar?); sauce – *blanche* (*fromage frais* and yoghurt), but ketchup and mayonnaise are acceptable. Wash that lot down with a mint tea and a sticky honey cake and you're well and truly *grec'ed* up and ready for anything… anything leisurely.

Grecs can be eaten on the hoof or *sur place* and you can grab one for four euros or less. There's a high concentration of *grec*-purveyors around St-Michel (5th) and rue Marx-Dormoy (18th). Ahmed at **Simdbad** (14 av de St-Ouen, 17th/M° La Fourche/01 42 93 91 68/open 11am-10pm Mon-Sat) is particularly fine and you can watch Egyptian TV with his regulars while you munch.

If you haven't eaten for a week try *le complet* at **Sahara de Magreb** (75 rue de Mazagran, 10th/M° Bonne Nouvelle/open 9am-8pm daily), all the usual lashings plus an egg and melted cheese.

A lighter, more sophisticated sandwich is on offer for the same price at **Au Cœur du Liban** (56 rue de Lancry, 10th/ M° Jacques Bonsergent/01 42 02 59 09/open noon-midnight daily, restaurant upstairs). Pita bread, no chips, tender chicken with a garlic sauce or beef and lamb (with the fat removed, but you could always bring some lard and smear it on) and a lemon sauce. 'This isn't a *grec*,' the owner insists, 'this is a *libanais!*'. Fair enough. The *libanais* are delicious, nutritious and they even leave room for a little *grec*-sized snackette.

Brasserie du Louvre

Anytime of day, experience the tasty flavour
of Paris at the Brasserie du Louvre, ideally
located between the "Comedie Française"
and the Louvre Museum.

Menu €26 (including wine), €31,
€12 (children)

Terrasse and Air Conditioning - Open daily 7am to midnight

Continuous service from midday to midnight

1 Place André Malraux, 1st - Reservation: 01.42.96.27.98
M° Palais Royal Musée du Louvre

Les Ormes

8 rue Chapu, 16th (01.46.47.83.98). M° Exelmans.
Open 12.15-2pm, 7.30-10pm Tue-Sat. **Average** €34.
Prix fixe €28.97. **Lunch menu** €21.34, €25.91.
Credit AmEx, MC, V. **Map** p404 A10.
The lusty cooking of talented young chef Stéphane
Molé is worth a nibble. The brief, good-value *prix-
fixe* changes almost daily, but typical dishes include
quenelles de brochet (pike-perch) with *sauce améri-
caine*, snails and wild mushrooms with a sorrel *timbale* and pumpkin soup garnished with morsels of
sautéed lamb sweetbreads. Desserts are excellent,
and the wine list offers many bargains.

Contemporary/trendy

L'Astrance

4 rue Beethoven, 16th (01.40.50.84.40). M° Passy.
Open noon-2pm, 8-10.30pm Wed-Sun; 8-10.30pm
Mon, Tue. Closed one week in Feb. **Average** €52.
Prix fixe €65, €80. **Lunch menu** €29. **Credit**
AmEx, DC, MC, V. **Map** p404 B6.
Tucked away in a surprisingly hip space, young
chef Pascal Barbot is a major new talent.
Antipodean experience at Ampersand in Sydney
shows up in chic, minimalist and delicious dishes
like scallops in peanut cream sauce and red mullet
cooked in a banana leaf and served with tamarind
sauce and a gratin of bananas.

La Maison Blanche

*15 av Montaigne, 8th (01.47.23.55.99). M° Alma-
Marceau.* **Open** noon-2.30pm, 8pm-midnight daily.
Closed Aug. **Average** €76. **Credit** AmEx, MC, V.
Map p401 E4.
The Pourcel twins of Montpellier have revived this
roof-top restaurant. The slick white decor is brac-
ingly modern, and there are friendly young waiters
dressed in black and a superb menu. Starters star,
with dishes such as sea urchins stuffed with dressed
crab and garnished with caviar or tarte Tatin of
shallots with grilled red mullet; desserts are brilliant.

Market

*15 av Matignon, 8th (01.56.43.40.90). M° Champs-
Elysées Clemenceau.* **Open** noon-3pm, 6.30-10.30pm
Mon-Thur, Sun; noon-3pm, 6.30-11.30pm Fri, Sat.
Average €80. **Lunch menu** €39. **Credit** AmEx,
MC, V. **Map** p401 E4.
Bankrolled by Luc Besson and sporting a slick
Manhattan-style decor, Market serves fusion food
that is as close to the sophisticated modern cooking
in New York or San Francisco as anything you'll
find in Paris. Try first-rate dishes such as fontina
and black truffle pizza and mains such as lobster
with Thai herbs and duck breast with sesame juice.

Shozan

*11 rue de La Trémoille, 8th (01.47.23.37.32).
M° Franklin D. Roosevelt or Alma-Marceau.* **Open**
noon-2.30pm, 7-10.30pm Mon-Fri. **Average** €61.
Prix fixe €60, €75 (dinner only). **Lunch menu**
€22, €29. **Credit** AmEx, DC, MC, V. **Map** p400 D4.

Some of the most delicious and original cooking in
Paris is to be found at this elegant restaurant . Try
the *sushi de foie gras* – small pieces of grilled foie
gras on seaweed-wrapped rounds of rice with
rhubarb and apple chutney – or tuna steak with a
crust of buckwheat, and sesame-caramel wafers layered with grapefruit and a verbena infusion.

Spoon, Food & Wine

*14 rue de Marignan, 8th (01.40.76.34.44).
M° Franklin D. Roosevelt.* **Open** noon-2pm, 7-11pm
Mon-Fri. Closed last week in July and first three
weeks in Aug. **Average** €50. **Credit** AmEx, DC,
MC, V. **Map** p401 E4.
When Alain Ducasse's world-food bistro with its
'mix and match' concept opened it had the effect of
a fire alarm going off in a wax museum. Since then,
Paris has changed – and, impressively, so has
Spoon. The eclectic menu includes such offerings as
a sublime *mousse d'étrilles* (velvet swimming crab),
spare ribs with *sauce diable* and potato chips or
grilled loin of rabbit with its liver and kidneys.

Haute cuisine

Guy Savoy

*18 rue Troyon, 17th (01.43.80.40.61/
www.guysavoy.com). M° Charles de Gaulle-Etoile.*
Open noon-2pm Mon-Fri, 7.30-10.30pm; 7.30-
10.30pm Sat. Closed Aug. **Average** €230. **Prix fixe**
€188, €235. **Credit** AmEx, DC, MC, V. **Map** p400 C3.
The relative informality makes this like no other
haute cuisine restaurant in Paris. The €188 *menu
prestige* involves an eight-course selection of seasonal dishes designed to show off the range of the
kitchen, such as a delicate yet earthy slice of
suprême de volaille de Bresse, stuffed with foie gras
and artichoke heart and studded with truffle, or John
Dory, roast on the bone and served with salsify and
shallot confit. The food is not faultless, but you will
be surprised and at times dazzled by it.

Laurent

*41 av Gabriel, 8th (01.42.25.00.39/
www.le-laurent.com). M° Champs-Elysées-
Clemenceau.* **Open** 12.30-2pm, 7.30-10.30pm Mon-Fri;
7.30-10.30pm Sat. **Average** €120. Prix fixe €65,
€130 **Credit** AmEx, DC, MC, V. **Map** p401 E4.
This pastel-pink 19th-century pavilion serves as
a luxurious lunch canteen for France's political
and business elite. The pace is more relaxed in
the summer, when meals are served on the pretty
terrace, or in the evening, when gastronomes take
time to savour consultant chef Joël Robuchon's
menu, prepared by Philippe Braun. Dishes may
appear simple, but in terms of quality of
ingredients, precise timing and depth of flavour,
the food is some of the best in the world. The
good value €65 *menu du pavillon* (available at
lunch and dinner) offers a selection from the carte
in smaller portions, and the excellent sommelier
will enable you to find satisfaction at around €50.
Wheelchair access.

Le Cinq

Four Seasons Hôtel George V, 31 av George V, 8th
(01.49.52.70.00). M° George V. **Open** noon-2pm
daily, 7.30-10.30pm. **Average** €130. **Credit** AmEx,
DC, MC, V. **Map** p400 D4.

Ex-Taillevent chef Philippe Legendre is now one of
the finest in France and has toned down his use of
luxury produce for discerning palates. What could
be more 'rustic chic' than an hors d'oeuvre of baby
mackerel with mustard oil and cress? Sure, Legendre
knows his way around the noblest products of the
French larder – turbot, sea bass, lobster, scallops,
the finest meats, truffles, and so on – but the fun here
really begins when he starts mixing different gen-
res. What's more, Le Cinq has found a brilliant compromise between intrusive American-style service
and the traditionally Parisian lofty distance.

Pierre Gagnaire

6 rue Balzac, 8th (01.58.36.12.50/
www.pierre-gagnaire.com). M° George V. **Open**
noon-2pm, 7.30-10pm Mon-Fri; 7.30-10pm Sun (Oct-
Apr only). Closed mid July-mid Aug. **Average** €160.
Prix fixe €195. **Lunch menu** €95. **Credit** AmEx,
DC, MC, V. **Map** p400 D4.

You need a good few hours to fully savour the fruits
of Pierre Gagnaire's exuberant creativity. The
amuse-bouches could be mistaken for Zen art, and
starters are bold: cold, raw gambas in deeply
flavoured olive sauce; bok choy with foie gras and
a rooster's *sot-l'y-laisse* (a tantalising morsel also
known as the 'oyster'), anybody? Main courses are
intriguing: pink suckling lamb rubbed with ewe's
milk curd and *nicchia* capers, served with toasted

rice, Shanghai cabbage with *petit gris* snails and fen-
nel shoots. Sounds obscene, tastes great. Then there
is *le grand dessert*, Gagnaire's seven-plate extravaganza. Gagnaire is often accused of over-experimen-
tation, and his food does demand concentration, but
France definitely needs at least one chef like him.

International

Indian: Kirane's

85 av des Ternes, 17th (01.45.74.40.21). M° Porte
Maillot. **Open** noon-2.30pm, 7-11.30pm daily.
Average €27. **Prix fixe** €27, €30.50 (dinner only).
Lunch menu €13, €15.50. **Credit** AmEx, DC, MC,
V. **Map** p400 B3.

One of the few places in Paris where'll you find
authentic Indian fare. A good way to start is the
mixed tandoori featuring juicy chunks of chicken,
fat prawns, moist salmon and succulent pieces of
lamb. The lamb rogan josh is a masterpiece of finely balanced spices while royal salmon *hara* is an
attractive coral wedge of grilled, marinated fish in
an aromatic green sauce.

North African: Tanjia

23 rue de Ponthieu, 8th (01.42.25.95.00).
M° Franklin D. Roosevelt. **Open** noon-3pm, 8pm-2am
Mon-Fri; 8pm-2am Sat, Sun. Closed Aug. **Average**
€46. **Prix fixe** €50, €58. **Lunch menu** €20. **Credit**
AmEx, DC, MC, V. **Map** p401 E4.

The food is better than you'd expect at this very
trendy Moroccan, and the staff are pleasantly
attitude-free. The assorted starters for two – pricey
at €16 a head but sufficient to feed a small army –

Creative genius **Pierre Gagnaire** adds that final sprig. *See above.*

Five-star service at **Le Cinq**. *See left.*

include *briouats* (turnovers) of gambas, chicken and chèvre, aubergine caviar, and salads. Then it's on to pigeon *pastilla* (crispy pastry with ground pigeon and almonds) and generous servings of mild lamb *tagine* (cooked ten hours with 25 spices) or couscous with organic veggies. Try the fig ice cream.

Spanish: Rosimar
26 rue Poussin, 16th (01.45.27.74.91). M° Michel-Ange-Auteuil. **Open** noon-2pm, 7-10pm Mon-Fri. **Average** €30. **Prix fixe** €28.20. **Credit** AmEx, MC, V.
In business in this serene street for 14 years, this family-run Spanish restaurant looks as if it owes more to disco than flamenco with its decor of pink tablecloths, black chairs and chrome ceiling. The food is delicious, though – try snails in garlic and parsley, roasted red peppers or the excellent paella.

Montmartre & Pigalle

Bistros

Le Bouclard
1 rue Cavalotti, 18th (01.45.22.60.01). M° Place de Clichy. **Open** noon-2.30pm, 7-11.30pm Mon-Fri; 7-11.30pm Sat. **Average** €45. **Lunch menu** €15, €22. **Credit** AmEx, DC, MC, V. **Map** p401 G2.
This traditional-style bistro a short walk from the Moulin Rouge highlights French rural cooking, with dishes such as cassoulet and prized regional meats. Owner Michel Bonnemort also makes tourists feel at home by offering European culinary landmarks

such as Spanish serrano ham and swordfish carpaccio. Vegetarian dishes are on the menu, and the ever-so-British apple crumble. It's eclectic but generally successful, especially if you stick to French dishes.

Chez Toinette
20 rue Germain-Pilon, 18th (01.42.54.44.36). **M°** *Abbesses.* **Open** 8-11pm Tue-Sat. **Average** €24. **Credit** V. **Map** p402 H2.
With its limited seating and even more limited opening hours, fabulous cuisine, discreet candle-lit atmosphere and ridiculously low prices, you may think you've died and gone to heaven at Chez Toinette. Timeless Provençal mains are heightened by the slightest designer touches. An autumn speciality is the sublimely aromatic *côtelette de marcassin*, baby wild boar cutlet smothered in wild mushrooms, bay leaves and coriander, and the baked chocolate and pear tart merits a full-page review to itself. Reserve even on weekdays.

La Fourchette des Anges
17 rue Biot, 17th (01.44.69.07.69). M° Place de Clichy. **Open** 7-11pm Mon-Sat. **Prix fixe** €18.50, €23. **Credit** MC, V. **Map** p401 G2.
This little restaurant on one of Paris' newly hip streets serves Provencal-influenced food in a rather romantic setting. Try dishes such as *cassolette de ravioles* (a rich, layered gratin of pasta, cheese and béchamel sauce), or spinach and scallops wrapped in crisp brik pastry and served in a pool of anise-infused cream, chunky boeuf with *foie gras* or leg of lamb fragrantly seasoned with just the right amount of thyme. An apple and Calvados charlotte provides a light, almost ethereal ending to the meal.

SUSAN´S PLACE

**Europe's Finest Chili! • 'Spécialité d'or' for Texas Nachos
• Vegetarian Mexican Dishes**

Susan will welcome you with Fajitas & a big Mexican starter for two with a
homemade Margarita. Try the delicious vegetarian dishes. Don't miss
Susan's excellent homemade desserts and the Mexican coffee...explosive!

**51 rue des Ecoles, 5th (near bd St Michel). Tel: 01.43.54.23.22
Open Tue-Sat noon-2.15pm, 7-11.30pm. Sun dinner only. Closed Mondays**

Auberge
"d'chez eux"

DON'T MISS ONE OF THE BEST CLASSIC
FRENCH BISTROS IN PARIS!

Complete Lunch Menu... €28 / €33.50

*Cuisine Bourgeoise • Foie Gras • Cassoulet
Confits • Frogs' Legs • Great choice of desserts*

"(...) heady" –Time Out Paris Guide 2002

(Just off Place des Invalides) www.chezeux.com

2 avenue de Lowendal, 7th • Mᵒ Ecole Militaire • Tel: 01.47.05.52.55

La Mascotte
52 rue des Abbesses, 18th (01.46.06.28.15).
M° Abbesses. **Open** noon-3pm, 7-11pm daily.
Average €28. **Prix fixe** €14, €24. **Credit** AmEx,
MC, V. **Map** p402 H2.
Ever since the highly caloric (and some would say
saccharine) *Amélie Poulain* made everyone curious
about Montmartre again, this good neighbourhood
brasserie has been crowded. Here you find quality
escargots and really first-rate oysters, delicious *fruits
de mer*, and main courses such as *sole meunière* with
chive-and-tarragon brightened mash, *petit salé* and
steaks. The simple wine list is full of good buys, too,
but be patient with the service – your reward is a
good meal with a gentle bill. *Wheelchair access.*

Aux Négociants
*27 rue Lambert, 18th (01.46.06.15.11). M° Château-
Rouge.* **Open** noon-2.30pm Mon; noon-2.30pm, 7.30-
10.30pm Tue-Fri. Closed Aug. **Average** €24. **Credit**
AmEx, MC, V. **Map** p402 J1.
Don't be put off by the cramped tables or the prime
view of the public toilets outside; this place belongs
to a dying breed of rustic bistros. The attitude to
food is generous, the rabbit pâté starter left on the
table in its Pyrex dish with a large pot of cornichons
to help yourself. The approach to wine is equally
down-to-earth – you order a bottle and return what
you haven't drunk, paying according to how many
markers have been revealed.

La Table de Lucullus
*129 rue Legendre, 17th (01.40.25.02.68).
M° La Fourche.* **Open** 12.30-2pm, 7.30-11pm Mon-
Sat. Closed Aug. **Average** €40. **Lunch menu** €16.
Credit MC, V. **Map** p401 F1.
Self-taught Nicholas Vagnon has a keen palate,
demonstrated by a market menu that is inventive
without ever missing a beat. Starters might include
langoustine carpaccio or brilliantly garnished foie
gras and main courses run to haddock with artichoke hearts and a hearty but delicate casserole of
shredded lamb, cracked wheat, fresh mint and dried
fruit. In season, figs garnished with raspberries are
the perfect finishing touch. Reservation is essential.
Wheelchair access.

Fish

Ty-Coz
*35 rue St-Georges, 9th (01.48.78.42.95).
M° St-Georges.* **Open** noon-2pm, 7-10pm Tue-Sat.
Average €46. **Prix fixe** €26 (dinner only). **Credit**
AmEx, MC, V. **Map** p402 H3.
Breton Ty-Coz is the place for superlative seafood:
the problem is what to choose; a whole fresh crab
glistening on a bed of iodine-packed seaweed is as
much of a must as the fillet of golden smoked haddock with a side dish of beautifully cooked mushrooms and courgettes with colourful strips of carrot,
beans and a sprinkling of parsley. And, for a faultless dessert, try a *crêpe* that oozes melted chocolate.

International

Indian: Kastoori
*4 pl Gustave Toudouze, 9th (01.44.53.06.10). M° St-
Georges.* **Open** 6.30-11.30pm Mon; 11.30am-2.30pm,
6.30-11.30pm Tue-Sun. **Average** €16. **Prix fixe**
€13 (dinner only). **Lunch menu** €8. **Credit** MC, V.
A tabla soundtrack and colourful throws and cush-
ions give this restaurant a cosy feel, and in summer
you can spill onto the leafy terrace. The food is sat-
isfactory rather than brilliant but very reasonably
priced, especially the €13 four-course *menu*. The
strong, velvety and exotic Goa milkshake (pineapple, mango and papaya) is a sumptious end to a
meal. Alcohol is not served but you can bring your
own with no corkage charge.

Polish: Mazurka
*3 rue André-del-Sarte, 18th (01.42.23.36.45).
M° Anvers or Château Rouge.* **Open** 7pm-midnight
Mon, Tue, Thur-Sun. **Average** €23. **Prix fixe**
€17.53. **Credit** AmEx, MC, V. **Map** p402 J1.
This endearing, red velvet restaurant, nestled in the
foothills of Montmartre, oozes Krakovian hospitali-
ty and charm. The menu revolves around standard
Polish fare, homemade and elegantly prepared.
Serenaded by a duo crooning Polish (and sometimes
Russian) folk songs, enjoy blinis, borscht, silky
pierogi, pickled herring, stuffed cabbage and
sausage flambé and the poppy-seed gâteau sernik.

Vietnamese: Le Sourire de Saigon
*54 rue du Mont-Cenis, 18th (01.42.23.31.16).
M° Jules Joffrin.* **Open** 7.30-11pm daily. **Average**
€30. **Credit** AmEx, MC, V. **Map** p402 H1.
Popular with showbiz types like Claude Lelouch and
Richard Berry, this tiny Vietnamese place garland-
ed with fairy lights serves up some excellent food.
Chef Sau Dong once cooked for the emperor Bao Dai,
and she does wonderful nems, fried wontons and
soups to start, followed by elegantly subtle main
courses like Saigon-style carmelised monkfish or
skewered beef with angel-hair noodles.

North-east Paris

Bistros & brasseries

Chez Casimir
*6 rue de Belzunce, 10th (01.48.78.28.80). M° Gare
du Nord.* **Open** noon-2pm, 7-11.30pm Mon-Fri.
Average €28. **Prix-fixe** €30 including wine.
Credit MC, V. **Map** p402 K2.
Thierry Breton deserves a medal for this place,
where pre-Eurostar passengers can savour a last
taste of France. Typical dishes run to a fricassée of
white asparagus dressed with herbs, meat juice and
vinegar, Aubrac steak with diced potatoes, poached
cherries with homemade vanilla ice cream, and an
easy-going wine list. Protegé Philippe Tredgeu is in
the kitchen; Breton's own delicious cooking can be
tasted at Chez Michel, down the road at No.10.

AZABU

麻布

"Chefs cook under eager gazes around the teppan-yaki table, making some superb food, mains of grilled fish or prawns are both top-notch"
-Time Out Paris with Pariscope (2002)

3 rue André Mazet, 6th. M° Odéon
Open noon-2pm, 7-10pm
except Monday (all day) and Tuesday lunch
Tel: 01.46.33.72.05

Restaurant
Arabo - Andalou

Open daily
for dinner: 6.30pm-1am
and wed, thu & sat
for lunch: noon-2.30pm

130 rue Saint-Maur, 11th
M° Parmentier
Tel: 01.48.05.97.71

Bistro des Capucins

27 av Gambetta, 20th (01.46.36.74.75). M° Père Lachaise. **Open** 12.15-1.45pm, 7.30-9.45pm Tue-Sat. **Average** €25. **Prix fixe** €20. **Map** p403 P5.

Just across the street from Père Lachaise cemetery (so within staggering distance if you've been overcome with grief at the Lizard King's grave), this has rapidly become one of the best tables in eastern Paris, thanks to the first-rate cooking of chef Gérard Fouché who trained at Le Grand Véfour. The intriguingly diverse crowd gives off a pleasant convivial buzz. There's a certain southwestern heartiness to Fouché's menu (he's from Bordeaux), but his precision and creativity elevate this place well beyond *bistro du coin* rank.

La Boca

12 rue de la Fidélité, 10th (01.53.24.69.70). M° Gare de l'Est. **Open** noon-2.30pm, 7.30pm-midnight Mon-Sat; 7.30pm-midnight Sun. **Average** €25. **Prix fixe** €13, €19.50. **Lunch menu** €11.60. **Credit** V. **Map** p402 K3.

In the increasingly in-demand Canal St-Martin area, this relaxed, friendly restaurant and its clever decor (incorporating art nouveau, *belle époque* and 1950s) is currently a big hit with local trendy young things. Start out with one of Gégé's cocktails (he's the grinning bartender with the jazz-man look) and then opt for classics like carrot flan with chive sauce, tomato-stuffed ravioli in pistou sauce or rabbit terrine with onion jam.

The décor is as divine as the food at **Julien**.

La Boulangerie

15 rue des Panoyaux, 20th (01.43.58.45.45). M° Ménilmontant. **Open** noon-2pm, 7.30-11pm Mon-Fri; 7.30pm-midnight Sat; noon-3pm Sun. **Average** €20. **Prix fixe** €18 (evening only). **Lunch menu** €15. **Credit** MC, V. **Map** p403 P4.

La Boulangerie offers just about everything you could ask of a restaurant: a warm setting in a former bakery, helpful waiters, and imaginative cooking at a very reasonable price. The *croustillant de grenadier* shows the chef's creativity – a *brandade*-like potato and white fish purée wrapped in crisp brik pastry and served with a creamy Noilly butter sauce. Rearrange your taste buds with a freshly made apple sorbet with apple liqueur.

Les Fernandises

19 rue de la Fontaine-au-Roi, 11th (01.48.06.16.96). M° République. **Open** noon-2pm, 7.30-11pm Tue-Sat. Closed Aug. **Average** €30. **Prix fixe** €21. **Lunch menu** €17. **Credit** MC, V. **Map** p403 M4.

One for the *fromage*-ophiles. Here, there are eight varieties of excellent camemberts (handy to know, just in case you thought it was your dining partner's feet). Pre-cheese treats include poultry-laden starters – a salad laced with strips of tender duck and chicken livers on warm lentils – a nicely crisped duck breast paired with *gratin dauphinois*, and a tasty roast pigeon. If you've still got room for dessert, there's a *tarte aux pommes flambée* that's well worth ordering. The wine list is reasonably priced and there is a good selection of Calvados. Book ahead.

Julien

16 rue du Fbg-St-Denis, 10th (01.47.70.12.06). M° Strasbourg St-Denis **Open** noon-3pm, 7pm-1.30am daily. **Average** €40. **Prix fixe** €30. **Lunch menu** €21. **Credit** AmEx, DC, MC, V. **Map** p402 K2.

The gorgeous Cuban mahogany interior of this popular brasserie dates from 1890, and the mood is permanently festive over platters of foie gras and other southwestern delights, which also include a very good *cassoulet d'oie* (preserved goose in white beans) The regulars always finish up with the profiteroles in hot chocolate sauce.

International

Indian: New Pondicherry

189 rue du Fbg-St-Denis, 10th (01.40.34.30.70). M° Gare du Nord. **Open** noon-10.30pm daily. **Average** €10. **Prix fixe** €7.50, €9.50. **Credit** AmEx, V. **Map** p402 K2.

According to those who've travelled to southern India, the food served at this friendly place, named after the former French colony, is spot-on authentic. Idli, a fat spongy cake of rice and lentil flour, is served as in India with spicy red paste and coconut chutney. Similarly good is the *vadai*, warm spiced lentil fritters, while mains are the dosai (filled pancake) and biryani (rice casseroles). No booze, so bring your own or drink *lassi*, the sweet or salted yoghurt drinks.

Eat, Drink, Shop

Platter chatter at **Le Buisson Ardent**.

Eat, Drink, Shop

Italian: Chez Vincent

5 rue du Tunnel, 19th (01.42.02.22.45). M° Botzaris.
Open noon-2.30pm, 8-11pm Mon-Fri; 8-11.30pm Sat.
Average €35. **Credit** AmEx, DC, MC, V. **Map** p403 N2.
Up in the heights near the Parc des Buttes-
Chaumont lurks the griddle whence floweth some of
the most authentic Italian cooking in Paris. Don't be
dismayed by the phoney decor – the authenticity
comes from the theatrically open, neon-lit kitchen
and the antipasto bar. Don't believe us? Try the beef
carpaccio, deep-fried squid and gambas in a superb
celery and caper sauce.

North American: Blue Bayou

111-113 rue St-Maur, 11th (01.43.55.87.21).
M° Parmentier or St-Maur. **Open** 11am-2pm,
7.30pm-12.30am Tue-Sat; 11am-2pm Sun. **Average**
€20. **Lunch menu** €8.50. **Credit** AmEx, MC, V.
Map p403 M3.
Reflecting the resurrection of Cajun pride brewing
deep in the swamps of Louisiana, this Oberkampf
restaurant makes a rather strident point of insisting
that it is Cajun and not American. That being said,
beyond their fine *jambalaya* (stewed sausage, peppers and chicken served on rice), and decent *gumbo*,
this is also a great place for a hefty, succulent burger,
which comes with a nice potato gratin.

The Latin Quarter & the 13th

Bistros & brasseries

L'Avant-Goût

26 rue Bobillot, 13th (01.53.80.24.00). M° Place
d'Italie. **Open** noon-2pm, 7.30-11pm Tue-Fri.
Average €26. **Lunch menu** €14, €26. **Credit** MC, V.
Map p406 K10.
Chef Christophe Beaufront presides over one of the
best contemporary bistros in Paris. Typical of his
magical touch are dishes such as an onglet of veal
with roasted unpeeled garlic cloves, salad and potato gratin, *galinette* with fried ginger chips and confit vegetables and tomato stuffed with oxtail on a
bed of *ravioles de Royan*. Desserts include a
meringue with fine powder of walnuts and a
moelleux au chocolat with vanilla ice cream.

L'Equitable

1 rue des Fossés St-Marcel, 13th (01.43.31.69.20).
M° Censier Daubenton. **Open** noon-2.30pm, 7.30-
11pm Tue-Sat. Closed three weeks in Aug. **Average**
€30. **Prix fixe** €28. **Lunch menu** €20.50. **Credit**
AmEx, V. **Map** p406 K9.
The talent of chef Yves Mutin makes this restaurant
with its provincial bare walls and bright paintings
worth a visit. Starters of asparagus with poached
egg in mousseline sauce and a superb rabbit and
pine nut terrine are followed by mains of veal steak
and baby vegetables in a herb pesto sauce and cod
in *sauce vierge* with anchovy-spiked aubergine
purée. Finish up with the roasted peach.

Au Petit Marguery

9 bd du Port-Royal, 13th (01.43.31.58.59).
M° Gobelins. **Open** noon-2.30pm, 7.30-10.15pm Tue-
Sat. **Average** €30. **Prix fixe** €33.60. **Lunch menu**
€25.20. **Credit** AmEx, MC, V. **Map** p406 J9.
This old-fashioned bistro is one of the few surviving outposts of a chain of the same name that thrived
in Paris during the 1920s. The *prix fixe* menu, featuring lots of game in season, is superb, with dishes like purée of partridge and juniper berries and a
superb *lièvre à la royale* (a dome of rich, shredded
hare's meat in a magnificent sauce of its blood and
offal mixed with wine). Otherwise feast on excellent
quality meat and alcoholic desserts.

Le Buisson Ardent

25 rue Jussieu, 5th (01.43.54.93.02). M° Jussieu.
Open noon-2pm, 7.30-10.30pm Mon-Fri. Closed Aug.
Prix fixe €28. **Lunch menu** €15. **Credit** AmEx,
DC, MC, V. **Map** p406 K8.
'The burning bush', is a fine example of a sophisticated 21st-century bistro. On a busy midweek
lunchtime the tall room hums with a mixed crowd
of tourists, business people and academics. The
cooking is traditional but with modern twists and
presentation: tomato *millefeuille* with feta, *rognon de*
veau entier, *crème brûlée* with chestnut cream.

L'Ecurie

2 rue Laplace, 5th (01.46.33.68.49). M° Maubert-Mutualité. **Open** noon-2pm, 7pm-midnight daily. **Average** €20. **Prix fixe** €15. **Lunch menu** €11.50. **No credit cards. Map** p406 J8.

Humble L'Ecurie is hidden on a village-like, tranquil square, and in summer its pavement terrace is a superb place to sip the complimentary sangria and Calvados that begin and end a meal. This restaurant is a reminder of why simple, fresh-off-the-grill food makes us happy, whether it's tomato and red peppers à la provençale, saddle of lamb with rosemary or rump-steak with pepper. Check out the cellars.

Table de Michel

13 quai de la Tournelle, 5th (01.44.07.17.57). M° Maubert-Mutualité. **Open** 7-11pm Mon; noon-2.30pm, 7-11pm Tue-Sat. Closed Aug. **Average** €35. **Prix fixe** €27. **Lunch menu** €19. **Credit** AmEx, MC, V. **Map** p406 K7.

Michel, who used to run a traditional French restaurant on the Butte-aux-Cailles, is now doing his personal take on Franco-Italian fusion cuisine. This includes a luscious *feuilleté d'escargots*, a perfectly cooked, pungent *risotto aux cèpes* and a winning tagliatelle au foie gras, which all goes down very well with a bottle of his exceptional Chianti. Mind you, what wouldn't?

Chez René

14 bd St-Germain, 5th (01.43.54.30.23). M° Maubert-Mutualité. **Open** 12.15-2.15pm, 7.45-10.45pm Tue-Fri; 7.45-10.45pm Sat. Closed Aug. **Average** €40. **Prix fixe** €39.50 (dinner only). **Lunch menu** €28. **Credit** MC, V. **Map** p406 J7.

These days it's not René but his son Jean-Paul who chats with the diners, but there's still the same heavy silver cutlery, thick starched linen, black-jacketed waiters and honest hard work that started in 1957. The *coq au vin* is the reason for coming here, with its dark, succulent sauce made just with flour, butter, jus and wine. Similar skills go into the *boeuf bourguignon*, but you might want to give puddings a miss in favour of the cheese.

Le Réminet

3 rue des Grands-Degrés, 5th (01.44.07.04.24). M° Maubert-Mutualité or St-Michel. **Open** noon-2pm, 7.30-11pm Mon, Thur-Sun. Closed two weeks in Aug. **Average** €30. **Prix fixe** €17 (dinner only, Mon, Thur). **Lunch menu** €13 (Mon, Thur, Fri). **Credit** MC, V. **Map** p406 J7.

Hugues Gournay does some excellent cooking in his minuscule kitchen, situated behind a cosy dining room with its two crystal chandeliers, red velvet curtains and bouquet of flowers on the bar. Specials change regularly, and recently included a superb starter of house-smoked salmon in dill cream on a crispy potato galette and main courses of sautéed scallops with young leeks and pan-fried steak with Cuban-style black beans.

Haute cuisine

La Tour d'Argent

15-17 quai de la Tournelle, 5th (01.43.54.23.31/ www.tourdargent.com). M° Pont Marie or Cardinal Lemoine. **Open** 7.30-9.30pm Tue; noon-1.30pm, 7.30-9.30pm Wed-Sat. **Average** €145. **Lunch menu** €60. **Credit** AmEx, DC, MC, V. **Map** p406 K7.

Don't let the classy (and glassy) surroundings and the views-to-die-for make you think you can't afford this. You can, and you deserve it – but only at lunchtime. The lunch *prix fixe* offers some Tour d'Argent classics, plus contemporary dishes and a selection of wine. Starters of a 'mosaic' of *foie gras* and rabbit flavoured with Sauternes wine, and langoustine tails in a tangy curry sauce with salad will get you going, and follow your instincts for the main. For afters, a *millefeuille* of fresh raspberries and strawberries, perhaps? *Wheelchair access.*

The best Restaurants

For a porker's pinky
Trot along to Au Pied de Cochon. *See p183.*

For posh nosh if you have the dosh
Les Ambassadeurs. *See p187.*

For eating in Starck surroundings
Phil-boy's done Bon 2 up a treat. *See p189.*

For filling your platter
Portions as they should be at Chez Janou. *See p190.*

For a nice slice of kangaroo
Hop down to Bennelong. *See p190.*

For star gazing
The big cheeses hang at Laurent. *See p197.*

For a decent Ruby Murray
That rare beast the authentic Anglo-Indian-style curry at Kirane's. *See p198.*

For soul food
One word: Bojangles. *See p201.*

For some large fromage
Les Fernandises is the beez-kneez for cheese. *See p203.*

For gorgeous Gallic grub
One word: Allard. *See p207.*

For just desserts
Two words: Violon d'Ingres. *See p211.*

Eat, Drink, Shop

"Probably the best vegetarian feast in Paris"
- Time Out Paris Eating & Drinking Guide 2002

La Victoire Suprême du cœur

VEGETARIAN RESTAURANT

CENTRAL PARIS

41 Rue des Bourdonnais, 1st
M° Châtelet
Tel: 01.40.41.93.95

Monday to Saturday: Noon - 2.30pm & 7pm - 10pm

The two most authentic Indian restaurants in Paris

Nirvana · Inde   **KIRANE'S**

6 rue de Moscou, 8th   85 avenue des Ternes, 17th
M° Liege or Europe   M° Porte Maillot
Tel: 01.45.22.27.12   Tel: 01.45.74.40.21

Open daily   Open daily
noon-2.30pm, 7pm-11pm   noon-2.30pm
closed Sunday   7pm-11.15pm

International

Chinese: Tricotin

15 av de Choisy, 13th (01.45.84.74.44). Mº Porte de Choisy. **Open** 9am-11.30pm daily. **Average** €15. **Credit** MC, V.

At the far end of Chinatown's main strip is a rare gem, as appealing to the palate as it is easy on the pocket. Canteen-style tables teem with families, students and couples feasting on a colourful and steaming array of Chinese, Thai, Cambodian and Vietnamese delicacies. A peek into the kitchen reveals chefs in white uniforms preparing food in rhythmic unison. You will marvel that such delicious, inexpensive and speedily-made dishes can also be so beautifully presented, but book to avoid a wait, especially for larger groups.

Brazilian: Botequim

1 rue Berthollet, 5th (01.43.37.98.46). Mº Censier Daubenton. **Open** noon-2pm, 8-11.30pm Mon-Sat; 8-11:30pm Sun. **Average** €30. **Credit** MC, V. **Map** p406 J9.

A *botequim* is a small, scruffy neighbourhood bar that serves food. Import such a concept to Paris and it's bound to get dressed up a bit. Mains are huge but if you want a starter, try the panaché, a sampling of well-prepared Brazilian snacks. As a main, there really is no avoiding the superb *feijoada*, Brazil's national dish made from several cuts of fresh and salted meats stewed with black beans and served with rice, garlicky sautéed greens, orange slices and grainy manioc flour. A selection of Brazilian confections will seduce your sweet tooth.

Greek: Les Délices d'Aphrodite

4 rue de Candolle, 5th (01.43.31.40.39). Mº Censier-Daubenton. **Average** €30. **Prix fixe** €30.50 (dinner only), €10-€30 (selection of mezedes). **Lunch menu** €16.50. **Credit** AmEx, MC, V.

If you know what real Greek food is like you'll recognise it here; if not, prepare for a discovery. The meze are fresh and aromatic. Mains include dishes such as *pastitsio* (pasta, ground pork, tomatoes and béchamel sauce) and keftedes, airy deep-fried balls of ground lamb served with diced courgettes and carrots in tomato sauce. If you don't like retsina go for the gorgeous red that is the Nemea.

St-Germain & Odéon

Bistros & brasseries

Allard

41 rue St-André-des-Arts, 6th (01.43.26.48.23). Mº Odéon or RER St-Michel. **Open** noon-2.30pm, 7-11pm Mon-Sat. Closed three weeks in Aug. **Average** €50. **Prix fixe** €30.50. **Lunch menu** €22.80. **Credit** AmEx, DC, MC, V. **Map** p406 H7.

With vanilla-coloured walls and big zinc bar, this traditional bistro has a delicious pre-war feel, confirmed when the kitchen sends out the glorious Gallic grub you dream of finding in Paris. Start with sliced Lyonnais sausage, or maybe a sautée of wild mushrooms; then chose between three classics: roast shoulder of lamb, roast Bresse chicken with sautéed ceps or roast duck with olives. Finish up with the *tarte fine aux pommes.* Wheelchair access.

Eat, Drink, Shop

Lipp-smacking fare at the politicos' favourite brasserie. *See p208.*

Au Bon Saint-Pourçain

10bis rue Servandoni, 6th (01.43.54.93.63).
Mº St-Sulpice or Mabillon. **Open** noon-2.30pm, 7.30-
10.30pm Mon-Sat. **Average** €30. **No credit cards.**
Map p405 H7.
The host is notoriously impatient to the point of virtually telling you what you want to order, so it's a
ditherers' delight; the wine list is even quicker: not
much beyond the eponymous €13 house red from
the Allier/Loire Valley, but people still keep coming
back for the generously portioned, solid bistro fare.
Young rabbit in aspic with a tomato coulis, roast
chicken in a dark mushroom and tarragon gravy
and *brandade de morue* are an example of what
you'll get here. The crème brûlée is excellent.

Brasserie Fernand

13 rue Guisarde, 6th (01.43.54.61.47). Mº Mabillon.
Open noon-2.30pm, 7pm-midnight Mon-Sat. Closed
Aug. **Average** €30.50. **Credit** MC, V.
Map p405 H7.
More of a bistro than a brasserie, Fernand is more
relaxed than many of its neighbours, with a jolly
patron who occasionally sings. The blackboard
reads like a round-up of bistro standards, but they
are prepared with imagination: a Provençal-inspired
'tarte' of warm goat's cheese and pistou over gently
melted courgettes, onions and tomatoes; oxtail parmentier and entrecôte with a pile of bone marrow
and excellent purée. *Wheelchair access.*

Brasserie Lipp

151 bd St-Germain, 6th (01.45.48.53.91/
www.brasserie-lipp.fr). Mº St-Germain-des-Prés.
Open 11.30am-1am daily. Closed 24, 25 Dec.
Average €40. **Credit** AmEx, DC, MC, V.
Map p405 G6.
The bill of fare is pretty banal, but Lipp thrives on
the fact that people of fame and influence have
always come here – once it was Mitterrand and Giscard d'Estaing, now it is more likely to be well-
known actors and film producers. Best bets from the
main courses are the three cuts of beef or *plats du
jour*, and at least you get to eat off exquisite ceramics using chunky art deco crockery. The downside
is that if you're Mr and Mrs Nobody, you'll likely as
not be seated upstairs, well removed from the action.

Contemporary/trendy

Ze Kitchen Galerie

4 rue des Grands-Augustins, 6th (01.44.32.00.32).
Mº St-Michel. **Open** noon-2.30pm, 8-11pm Mon-Fri;
8-10.30pm Sat. **Average** €50. **Lunch menu** €27,
€35. **Credit** AmEx, DC, MC, V. **Map** p406 H7.
Aside from ze dreadful name, this is an attractive,
comfortable modern bistro with a pleasant menu
organised around four themes – soup, cru (as in raw
fish), pasta and a la plancha (grilled). Try the red
tuna tartare with lemon grass, pasta shells stuffed
with diced mushrooms and Mimolette cheese, duck-
ling cooked a la plancha in red onion juice and
coriander, and caramel macaroon.

Le Salon d'Hélène

4 rue d'Assas, 6th (01.42.22.00.11). Mº Sèvres-
Babylone. **Open** 12.30-2pm, 7.30-10pm Tue-Sat
(evenings only in Aug). **Average** €60. **Prix fixe**
€60, €135. **Credit** AmEx, MC, V. **Map** p405 G7.
At the casual downstairs salon beneath her restaurant, Hélène Darroze has abandoned the *entrée-plat-
dessert* format for an array of inventive tapas-sized
dishes. You can order the *plat du jour* from upstairs
but it's more interesting to choose the tapas, where
Darroze updates south-western classics with Japanese and Mediterranean influences. There are also
mini desserts. *Wheelchair access.*

Fish

La Méditerranée

2 pl de l'Odéon, 6th (01.43.26.02.30/www.la-
mediterranee.com). Mº Odéon. **Open** noon-2.30pm,
7.30-11pm daily. **Average** €46. **Prix fixe** €24.50,
€29. **Credit** AmEx, MC, V. **Map** p406 H7.
Burgundy velvet seats, wall paintings by Manuel
Vertès and Christian Bérard and Jean Cocteau plates
conjure up the era when the Côte d'Azur was
colonised by artists and literati. The €29 *menu* is
well-thought-out: a lightly blanched courgette
stuffed with a nicely fishy *brandade*, perhaps, then
a roast perch just crisp on the outside on a bed of hot
aubergine caviar, and crème renversée topped with
egg white, accompanied by apple compote.

International

Italian: La Brasseria Italiana

81 rue de Seine, 6th (01.43.25.00.28). Mº Odeon.
Open 8-11pm Mon; noon-2.30pm, 8-11pm Tue-Sat.
Average €35. **Lunch menu** €16, €23. **Credit**
AmEx, MC, V. **Map** p406 H6.
Though this restaurant puts another nail in the cof-
fin of what used to be a thriving market street, it's
welcome for its serious kitchen and friendly service
and attractive setting. Try starters of grilled vegetables (aubergine, courgette, pepper, baby onion)
with Scamorza cheese and delicate courgette flowers stuffed with herbed ricotta (rather overwhelmed
by heavy breading), and main courses such as risotto with nettles, a wonderful old-fashioned summer
dish, or linguine with girolles and bacon.

Japanese: Yen

22 rue St-Benoît, 6th (01.45.44.11.18). Mº St-
Germain-des-Prés. **Open** 7.30-11pm Mon, Sun; noon-
2pm, 7.30-10.30pm Tue-Sat. **Average** €45. **Lunch**
menu €18.50, €30.50. **Credit** AmEx, DC, MC, V.
Map p406 H6.
The menu here is divided into appetisers, starters
and the speciality of cold or hot soba (buckwheat
noodles). Eating the noodles is a slightly complex
procedure but the food is so good you'll soon find
yourself slurping straight from the bowl. The ginger and green tea ice creams finish off the meal
superbly. *Wheelchair access.*

The British are coming

Wait a blooming minute: the supposed inventors of gastronomy taking cooking classes from the masterminds of mushy peas, boiled spuds and grey beef? How can it be? Oh, in this brave new global world, it be.

Come on down, the rice is right! Yes, come on down, channel-hopping queen and king of Brit TV cuisine... Delia Smith and Jamie Oliver. In an act of extreme cultural generosity, both those Brits are giving a guiding hand – publishing giant Hachette has translated their cookbooks for the French market.

Admittedly, the French, ever sensitive to any form of foreign invasion, might be a tad resistant to the charms of these saucy *anglais*. Smith's nationality has been downplayed, she's referred to only as 'Delia', in the same lofty vein as Colette, Dalida, Barbara and Marie-Antoinette (all well known for their cooking prowess).

Delia's cookbook *La Cuisine facile d'aujourd'hui* or 'Simple Cooking Today', champions the back-to-basics style of cooking, from how to boil an egg to *rösti* 'bubble and squeak'. This is food that all self-respecting Gauls should be able to whip up in a jiffy. But, in 2003, how many really can?

Such is the apparent poverty of French cooking that there's a shrieking demand for the kind of straightforward approach to cooking that dependable Delia embodies. Even in France, where eating is a cultural act, the domestic traditions that used to be handed down from mother to daughter have all but disappeared. But do daughters these days really want to cook like their mothers?

France, unlike Britain, the US or Australia, has no television chefs popularising cooking by tossing about 'well wicked' bunches of herbs and legs of lamb proclaiming that 'Ith not me thath naked, me old darlingth, ith the food, innit'. French chefs tend to be dignified despite their very silly, very tall chef's hats. They're not about adding cornflour to their hollandaise to make sure it doesn't curdle or creating posh nosh for the masses.

French cookery books fall into two categories: too basic or too much (the *Larousse Gastronomique* weighs in at almost 3,000 pages and super chef Alain Ducasse's cooking bible is 1,024 pages). The French just want something in between – yes, even when it comes to food.

Publisher Hachette thinks that French how-to-cook books are too basic and too traditional. Delia, by comparison, is simple and modern, mixing cooking influences from all over the world. An old-fashioned French *pot-au-feu* positively pales next to Delia's Thai chicken with coconut cream or pork with Jamaican sauce. Jamie, too, represents the new contemporary British cuisine. That Essex boy with the mockney accent is *so* fusion.

However, Delia's no-nonsense approach is not without its detractors. Food critic Egon Ronay once described her approach as 'the missionary position of cooking' – surely a horrifying concept for the saucy French.

Alain Passard, chef at top-rated L'Arpège (*see p212*), professes never to have heard of Delia and is somewhat surprised by her audacity. The French, he says, know how to choose good products and that's much more important than a new cookbook. He suggested that 'this woman of yours take a step or two back'. Steady: that's how wars start. Most French chefs insist that British cuisine makes no impact in France but Delia and Jamie just might change all that, and if they don't, pale-but-interesting Nigella Lawson is coming in 2003. Anyone for some pukka cookin' lessons, innit?

Jamie Oliver, purveyor of pukka tucker.

Eat, Drink, Shop

Restaurant Chez Vong

10 rue de la Grande Truanderie, 1st
M° Etienne Marcel
Parking Sébastopol: 35-37 bd Sébastopol
Tel: 01.40.39.99.89 - Fax: 01.42.33.38.15
e-mail: chez.vong@wanadoo.fr
website: www.chez-vong.com
Open Mon-Sat, noon-2.30pm & 7pm-12.30am
Closed on Sunday

6 rue d'Antin, 2nd. M° Opéra
Tel: 01.42.61.25.52 - Fax: 01.42.60.33.92
e-mail: passy.mandarin@wanadoo.fr
website: www.passy-mandarin.com
Open daily, noon-2.45pm & 7pm-11.15pm

Le Pachyderme • Restaurant • Cocktail-Bar
Open daily 9am-2am

2 bis boulevard Saint-Martin, 10th • M° Republique
Tel: 01.42.06.32.56

Latin American: Fajitas

15 rue Dauphine, 6th (01.46.34.44.69). M° Odéon.
Open noon-11pm Tue-Sun (7-11pm Mon, June-Aug only). **Average** €25. **Prix fixe** €18.50. **Credit** AmEx, MC, V. **Map** p406 H7.
A Mexican/American husband-and-wife team run this colourful restaurant in St-Germain. Miguel cooks deliciously fresh northern Mexican dishes with some southern specials among the starters. The guacamole is spectacular and the signature *fajitas* with beef and chicken are a magnificent main. Miguel is a champion of the *fajita*'s untapped potential (who is this philosopher king?): they even feature as puddings – the banana and caramel version is, and you'll think we're exaggerating, ambrosial.

The 7th & the 15th

Bistros & brasseries

L'Affriolé

17 rue Malar, 7th (01.44.18.31.33). M° La Tour Maubourg. **Open** noon-2.30pm, 7.30-10.30pm Tue-Sat. Closed three weeks in Aug. **Prix fixe** €30. **Lunch menu** €19. **Credit** AmEx, MC, V. **Map** p404 D6.
This bustling contemporary bistro attracts devoted neighbourhood regulars who come to feast on a good-quality market menu. It changes weekly, and though not every dish is perfect, the cooking is generally appealing, with dishes like sautéed girolles and stuffed baby cabbage. There's an admirable assortment of reasonably priced wines, the best of which is the Coteaux du Tricastin.

Le Bamboche

15 rue de Babylone, 7th, (01.45.49.14.40). M° Sèvres Babylone. **Open** noon-2pm, 7-11pm Mon-Fri.
Average €45. **Credit** MC, V. **Map** p405 F7.
This little gem owned by chef Claude Colliot, a remarkable cook, continues to refine a stunningly inventive repertoire. Madame Colliot runs the softly lit dining rooms with precision and humour and dishes such as veal chop in hazelnuts and succulent pigeon breast with Szechuan pepper and beetroot caramel offer subtle but spectacular pleasures. For dessert, you can wrap your fangs around possibly the best *millefeuille* in town.

Le Sept/Quinze

29 av de Lowendahl, 15th (01.43.06.23.06). M° La Motte Picquet Grenelle. **Open** noon-2.30pm, 8-11pm Mon-Fri; 8-11pm Sat. **Average** €35. **Prix fixe** €24. **Lunch menu** €22, €16. **Credit** MC.V. **Map** p404 D8.
A young team runs this attractive dining room where ochre walls create a Mediterranean allure. Inventive dishes are often Provençal, occasionally Italian and Spanish. Daily specials may include a delicious homemade vegetable soup with a dab of saffron aïoli or linguine with goat's cheese and roasted pinenuts.

Nabuchodonozor

6 av Bosquet, 7th (01.45.56.97.26). M° Alma Marceau. **Open** noon-2.45pm, 7.30-11pm Mon-Fri; 7.30-11pm Sat. Closed three weeks in Aug. **Average** €30. **Lunch menu** €18.80. **Credit** AmEx, MC, V. **Map** p404 D5.
The cigar-wielding Eric Rousseau makes his customers feel instantly at home in this elegant restaurant whose wine board attests to his passion. Chef Thierry Garnier's *carte* is an inventive take on traditional French cuisine, with meticulously prepared dishes such as a rich, creamy chestnut soup with earthy-tasting snails, and *daube provençale* among the main courses. *Wheelchair access.*

Classic

Violon d'Ingres

135 rue St-Dominique, 7th (01.45.55.15.05). M° Ecole-Militaire or RER Pont de l'Alma. **Open** 7-10.30pm Mon, Sat; noon-2.30pm, 7.10.30pm Tue-Fri. Closed three weeks in Aug. **Average** €80. **Lunch menu** €39. **Credit** AmEx, MC, V. **Map** p405 D7.
Details such as the bread, canapés and amazing *petits fours* all indicate that Christian Constant's banjo is perfectly tuned. Starters include a tomato and seafood *millefeuille*, prepared with such culinary dexterity that it seems a shame to cut into it. Desserts can be spectacular – how about souffléed potatoes lightly caramelised and filled with a coffee crème pâtissière, served beside a fluffy liquorice mousse and topped with hot chocolate sauce?

Contemporary/trendy

Caffè

74 bd La-Tour-Maubourg, 7th (01.47.53.80.86). M° La-Tour-Maubourg. **Open** noon-2.15pm, 8-10.15pm Mon-Sat. **Average** €40. **Credit. Map** p405 E5.
This artfully brick-alcoved space offers superb Franco-Italian fusion cooking. A great example of what the kitchen's up to is risotto Milanese topped with pan-fried foie gras, saffron providing a perfect foil for the rich foie gras. Portions are generous and you shouldn't miss the homemade caramel ice cream. The Montepulciano stands out on a short but interesting wine list.

L'Esplanade

52 rue Fabert, 7th (01.47.05.38.80). M° La Tour-Maubourg. **Open** noon-1am daily. Café 8am-2am. **Average** €60. **Credit** AmEx, MC, V. **Map** p405 E6.
The view is stunning (Les Invalides, beautifully floodlit at night), the interior sumptuous (Jacques Garcia, naturally), the food modish (raw tuna with soy and wasabi, steamed vegetables), and the waitresses uniformly stylish and skinny. L'Esplanade is vintage Costes. The only thing that varies is the clientele, with the profusion of gold buttons giving off a glare almost as distracting as Napoléon's dome.

La Cagouille: scaling the heights of fish food. *See right.*

Fish

La Marine de Thiou
*3 rue Surcouf, 7th (01.40.62.96.70). M° La Tour-
Maubourg.* **Open** noon-3pm, 8pm-11pm Mon-Fri,
8pm-11pm Sat. **Average** €50. **Credit** AmEx, MC, V.
Map p405 E6.
Since the original Thiou moved to 49 quai Orsay, the
talented Thai chef has transformed this address into
a Eurasian seafood restaurant with appealing if
expensive results. Try langoustine-stuffed ravioli in
lemon sauce, John Dory cooked in banana leaf,
prawns sautéed with garlic and chilli peppers.

Haute Cuisine

L'Arpège
*84 rue de Varenne, 7th (01.45.51.47.33/
www.alain-passard.com). M° Varenne.* **Open** 12.30-
2.30pm, 8pm-1am Mon-Fri. **Average** €240. **Prix
fixe** €300. **Credit** AmEx, MC, V. **Map** p405 F6.
With much fanfare, chef Alain Passard recently
decided to return meat to his haute cuisine menu,
having previously gone all fish and veggie. But it's
still the most vegetarian haute cuisine table in town,
with dishes like saffron and nasturtium-petal soup.
If you eat crustaceans the lobster sautéed in mustard with a garnish of tiny red onions is a must.

Le Jules Verne
*Second Level, Eiffel Tower, Champ de Mars, 7th
(01.45.55.61.44). M° Bir-Hakeim or RER Champ de
Mars.* **Open** 12.15-1.45pm, 7.15-9.45pm daily.
Average €100. **Lunch menu** €49 (Mon-Fri).
Credit AmEx, DC, MC, V. **Map** p404 C6.
Along with soaring views over the city from the

Eiffel Tower itself, you'll enjoy an exciting array of
contrasting tastes and textures, courtesy of chef
Alain Reix. Luxury ingredients are plentiful and are
sure to feature on the extravagant *menu dégustation*
(€110). The fine wines are likely to give your wallet
a hammering, but you'll be too giddy to care.

International

Chinese: Chen
*15 rue du Théâtre, 15th (01.45.79.34.34).
M° Charles Michels.* **Open** noon-2.30pm, 7.30-
10.30pm Mon-Sat. **Average** €70. **Prix fixe** €75.
Lunch menu €40. **Credit** AmEx, MC, V.
Map p404 B7.
Here the finest French produce, much of it *appella-
tion d'origine contrôlée,* is blended with Chinese technique. Star dishes include courgette flowers stuffed
with crab mousse in a sauce of fresh crab meat, and
frogs' legs sautéed in salt and Szechuan pepper, plus
main courses like rock lobster in ginger.

Lebanese: Restaurant Al Wady
*153-155 rue de Lourmel, 15th (01.45.58.57.18).
M° Lourmel.* **Open** noon-3pm, 7-midnight daily.
Average €25. **Lunch menu** €10, €13. **Credit**
AmEx, MC, V. **Map** p404 B9.
If you don't have the courage for lamb's brain or the
lsnat (tongue served either hot or in a salad) don't
worry – there are 47 other appetisers to choose from.
How about *spécial moutabal,* a delicately smoked
aubergine caviar crowned with walnuts and pome-
granate seeds, or *fattouche* salad laced with lip-puck-
ering chilli and lemon? Main courses are very meaty
and the *meze* make a fine meal in themselves.

Mauritian: Chamarel

13 bd de La-Tour-Maubourg, 7th (01.47.05.50.18).
M° Invalides. **Open** noon-2pm, 8-10pm Mon-Fri;
8-10pm Sat. **Average** €60. **Credit** AmEx, MC, V.
Map p405 E5.

Working with friendly Mauritian *maître d'hôtel*
Antoine Heerah, Jérôme Bodereau shows off his
impressive skills at this amusing if rather formal
new restaurant. Though he's wielding seasoning
constellations that are not part of his indigenous
palette, Bodereau does a good job of creating the curried nuances that dominate the cuisine of this Indian
Ocean island. The chicken roasted with curry leaves
under its skin is a treat.

Montparnasse & beyond

Bistros & brasseries

Contre-Allée

83 av Denfert-Rochereau, 14th (01.43.54.99.86).
M° Denfert-Rochereau. **Open** noon-2pm, 7.30-
10.30pm Mon-Fri, Sun; 8-10.30pm Sat. Closed
Christmas. **Average** €35. **Prix fixe** €25-€35.
Credit AmEx, MC, V. **Map** p405 H10.

This modern bistro, whose name means the parallel
streets that run alongside the wide avenues of this
district, can be the stuff of dreams as the garden has
been lit up to give a rush of green from the back windows and you can dine under the stars. The menu
is full of imaginative Mediterranean fare and caters
as much for those who want to eat healthily, lightly, even meatlessly as for the hearties. *Wheelchair
access.*

La Coupole

102 bd du Montparnasse, 14th (01.43.20.14.20).
M° Vavin. **Open** 8.30am-1am Mon-Thur; 8.30am-
1.30am Fri, Sat. **Average** €34. **Prix fixe** €30.50
(dinner only). **Lunch menu** €29, €16.50. **Credit**
AmEx, DC, MC, V. **Map** p405 G9.

This famous art-deco brasserie is always buzzing
with an eclectic crowd of Parisians, suburbanites
and tourists. Service is good-natured, with wise-
cracking waiters, so you're guaranteed a great
atmosphere. Truffled scrambled eggs make a good
starter and for mains think seafood: you could spend
an hour tackling a plate-sized crab. It's fun, and a
people-watching treat.

Les Dix Vins

57 rue Falguière, 15th (01.43.20.91.77). M° Pasteur.
Open noon-2.30pm, 7-11.30pm Tue-Sat. **Prix fixe**
€16. **No credit cards. Map** p405 E9.

This friendly neighbourhood restaurant with its
punning name is a good place for a budget meal in
the Montparnasse area. The €16 blackboard *menu*
includes such dishes as spinach, poached egg and
bacon salad, and plate-sized skate wings with a
punchy butter and over-emphatic garlic mash. The
cheese is first-rate and wine reasonable, leaving you
with change from €50 for a meal for two.

La Régalade

49 av Jean-Moulin, 14th (01.45.45.68.58).
M° Alésia. **Open** noon-2pm, 7pm-midnight Tue-Fri;
7pm-midnight Sat. Closed Aug. **Prix fixe** €30.
Credit MC, V. **Map** p405 G10.

Yves Camdeborde's cooking is better than ever and
his *menu prix fixe* remains one of the great-value
bargains of Paris. Camdeborde is a native of the
Béarn region and its tradition of hearty eating comes
through in starters like apple stuffed with black pudding or a sauté of squid with garlic and parsley on
a bed of rice, prepared with squid ink. He's equally
capable of elegant modern dishes like truffle-topped,
foie gras-stuffed ravioli. Make sure that you book
well in advance.

Ti-Jos

*30 rue Delambre, 14th (01.43.22.57.69). M° Edgar
Quinet or Vavin.* **Open** 11.30-2.30pm, 7pm-12.30am
Mon, Wed-Fri; noon-2.30pm Tue. Closed three
weeks in Aug, Christmas/New Year. **Average** €14.
Prix fixe €11 (Mon-Fri). **Credit** AmEx, MC, V.
Map p405 G9.

Behind the basket of fresh eggs on the counter of
this Breton outpost, the cook turns out golden-
brown, frilly-edged crêpes filled with saucisse,
andouillette, roquefort etc. The evening menu has
non-crêpe options such as moules marinières, and
Friday nights often feature live Breton music.

Contemporary/trendy

Le Café des Délices

*87 rue d'Assas, 6th (01.43.54.70.00). M° Vavin or
RER Port Royal.* **Open** noon-2.30pm, 7.30-11.30pm
Mon-Fri . Closed Aug. **Average** €32. **Credit** AmEx,
MC, V. **Map** p405 G7.

Gilles Choukroun is forging his own identity with
this casual restaurant near Montparnasse. Roast
pièce de boeuf comes with a risotto-like mix of wheat
and mimolette cheese, and crisp-skinned sea bream
is accompanied by white coco beans cooked with
anchovies, coriander and lemon. Choukroun's signature dessert of sliced dates with orange, crunchy
pistachios, mint leaves and lemon sorbet is wonderfully refreshing.

Fish

La Cagouille

*10-12 pl Constantin-Brancusi, 14th (01.43.22.09.01/
www.la-cagouille.fr). M° Gaîté.* **Open** 12.30-2.30pm,
7.30-10.30pm daily. **Average** €50. **Prix fixe** €23,
€38. **Credit** AmEx, DC, MC, V. **Map** p405 F9.

Amid marble-topped tables, stubbly walls and a few
ropes and pulleys owner-chef Gérard Allemandou
prepares simple, quality fish dishes – grilled, fried
or steamed with few garnishes except perhaps
chopped parsley, sea salt or a drizzle of olive oil. The
daurade royale (sea bream) in a buttery cockle stock
is near perfection and there are chocolatey desserts.

Eat, Drink, Shop

Bars, Cafés & Tearooms

Find your own sweet bar named desire, pause for tea and sustenance or strike a pose on a terrace and pretend you're waiting for Godard.

Eat, Drink, Shop

Sartre made a habit of popping down to his local, the Café de Flore, to keep his chillblains at bay; it wasn't just the heated conversation that kept him there, it was the heaters. While apartments might be warmer nowadays, cafés retain their living-room allure. People drop in for a heart-starting espresso, a gossip or a session of tongue-wrestling between bites of *croque monsieur*. You can grab a beer at a '*zinc*', alongside with genuine regulars at a genuine zinc bar in an old-style café, or throw back a cocktail, and your head, in slick designer dens and indulge in the ancient art of staring. And don't forget that while you're drinking in the sights and sounds, people will be doing likewise, to you. *Santé!* Note that prices are generally lowest standing at the bar, slightly higher seated inside and highest on the terrace outside; and that prices often go up after 10pm. Many cafés also do full-scale meals, particularly at lunch time. For further listings see the *Time Out Paris Eating & Drinking Guide*.

The Islands

Cafés

Le Flore en l'Ile
42 quai d'Orléans, 4th (01.43.29.88.27). M° Pont Marie or Hôtel de Ville. **Open** 8am-2am daily. **Credit** MC, V. **Map** p400 D5.
Pricey but perfectly positioned, with its view from the tip of Ile-St-Louis over the spidery apse of Notre-Dame, this dressed-up café-brasserie is particularly popular on hot summer afternoons, as the dessert menu features ice creams and sorbets from famous *glacier* Berthillon. Inside is a calm den of wood panelling and wafting classical music.

Tearooms

La Charlotte en l'Ile
24 rue St-Louis-en-Ile, 4th (01.43.54.25.83). M° Pont Marie. **Open** noon-8pm Thur-Sun. Tea and puppet show by reservation only, Wed; piano tea Fri 6-8pm. Closed July and Aug. **Credit** V. **Map** p406 K7.
Poetess and chocolatier Sylvie Langlet has been spinning sweet fantasies here for years. In the miniscule front room she sells superb dark chocolate and candied fruit sticks, while at six round tables she offers magical desserts and 36 teas of quality.

The Louvre, Palais-Royal & Les Halles

Bars

Le Fumoir
6 rue de l'Amiral-de-Coligny, 1st (01.42.92.00.24/ www.lefumoir.com). M° Louvre-Rivoli. **Open** 11am-2am daily. Closed one week in Aug. **Credit** AmEx, MC, V. **Map** p406 H6.
Even the bar staff seem to have been included in the interior decorator's sketches at this sleek bar positioned directly opposite the Louvre. A sleek crowd sipping martinis or browsing the papers at the long mahogany bar gives way to young professionals in the restaurant and pretty young things in the 3000-book library. *Wheelchair access.*

Harry's New York Bar
5 rue Daunou, 2nd (01.42.61.71.14/ www.harrys-bar.fr). M° Opéra. **Open** 11am-3am daily. **Credit** AmEx, DC, MC, V. **Map** p401 G4.
Harry's claims to have invented the Bloody Mary; it's certainly been the origin of some bloody awful hangovers. White-coated waiters chat with tourists, local businessmen and American alumni.

Le Tambour
41 rue Montmartre, 2nd (01.42.33.06.90). M° Les Halles. **Open** 24 hours daily. Credit MC, V. **Map** p402 J4.
Châtelet is hardly lacking in all-night bars, but this place is a welcome alternative to the generally tacky boozers. This is not the home of the intellectual elite: although many of the drinkers have strongly expressed, often incoherent, opinions.

Cafés

Bar de l'Entr'acte
47 rue Montpensier, 1st (01.42.97.57.76). M° Palais Royal. **Open** 10am-2am Tue-Fri; noon-midnight Sat, Sun. **Credit** AmEx, MC, V. **Map** p402 H5.
Finding a table can be tricky during peak hours as this casual drinking hole is popular with theatregoers and the local boho chic. The *jardin d'hiver*, a cellar done up with theatre scenery and red curtains, is best visited after several drinks.

Café Marly
93 rue de Rivoli, cour Napoléon du Louvre, 1st (01.49.26.06.60). M° Palais Royal. **Open** 8am-2am daily. **Credit** AmEx, DC, MC, V. **Map** p401 H5.

All set for action at **Café Marly** in the Louvre. *See left.*

LE SANTAL

Gastronomie Vietnamienne

Savour authentic Vietnamese cuisine
from Saigon, Hanoi and Hué.

Chef-proprietor NGUYEN-LEE and her team are pleased
to welcome you to the "Le Santal" restaurants, recommended
by Gault et Millau and other European restaurant guides.

A warm welcome and quality service.

Le Santal - Opéra	Le Santal - Côté Mer	Escale a Saigon
8 rue Halévy, 9th	6 rue de Poissy, 5th	Le Santal des neiges
M° Opéra	M° Maubert-Mutualité	107 av Laurier (ouest)
Tel: 01.47.42.24.69	Tel: 01.43.26.30.56	Montréal - Québec
www.le-santal.com	Fax: 01.42.71.51.82	Tel: 001.514.272.3456
		Fax: 001.514.272.7304
		as found on: www.restaurant.ca
Paris, France	Paris, France	Canada

Opened in 1994 as part of the Grand Louvre, Café Marly is another Costes brothers success. The terrace, ensconced in the stone balcony of the Cour Napoléon, has a privileged view of the glass pyramid. Inside features regal red and gold panelling. Dine on modern brasserie fare or sip cocktails and spot celebs.

La Coquille

30 rue Coquillière, 1st (01.40.26.55.36). M° Les Halles. **Open** 7am-10pm Mon-Sat. **Credit** MC, V. **Map** p402 J5.
This down-to-earth 1950s shoebox café is a local favourite. The bar has a good selection of cheap wines and the budget food runs from *entrecôtes* to giant salads. Admire the Portuguese owner's gravy boat collection over a glass of *vinho verde*.

Le Dénicheur

4 rue Tiquetonne, 2nd (01.42.21.31.01). M° Etienne-Marcel. **Open** 12.30-3.30pm, 7pm-midnight Tue-Thur; 12.30-4pm, 7pm-2am Fri, Sat; 12.30-4pm, 7pm-2am Sun. Closed two weeks in Aug. **No credit cards. Map** p402 J5.
Just a street or so away from the tourist-fleecing joints of Les Halles, here's a place where you can pick up an affordable light lunch, supper or Sunday brunch. The lunch menu could include a huge salad followed by a crunchy homemade apple crumble.

Tearooms

Jean-Paul Hévin

231 rue St-Honoré, 1st (01.55.35.35.97). M° Tuileries. **Open** 10am-7.30pm Mon-Sat. Closed one week in Aug. **Credit** AmEx, DC, MC, V. **Map** p401 G5.
If black minimalist à la Gucci is your cup of tea, and you have a cocoa habit you have no intention of fighting, then Jean-Paul Hévin is your man. His dark chocolate desserts gleam like edible accessories against the silver and dark-wood furnishings of his shop, and upstairs is a surprisingly warm tea room with dark wood and wicker chairs.

The best Terraces

Café de Flore
An oldie but a goldie. *See p231.*

Café de la Nouvelle Mairie
Latin Quarter secret. *See p229.*

Pause Café
Bastille's best posing. *See p223.*

Le Rostand
Get out your sunglasses. *See p233.*

Le Soleil
Heterogeneity reigns. *See p223.*

Opéra & the Grands Boulevards

Bars

De La Ville Café

34 bd Bonne-Nouvelle, 10th (01.48.24.48.09). M° Bonne Nouvelle. **Open** 11am-2am Mon-Sat; 3pm-2am Sun. **Credit** MC, V. **Map** p402 J4.
De La Ville is a recent addition to the art-squat-as-style-statement gang. The upstairs looks like a turn-of-the-(last)-century church hall and the apothecary-and-cobbler-sharing-office-space corner is a weird design concept. The comfy rattan sofas, brilliant service, and genial punters make this a top place to apéro.

Cafés

La Cave Drouot

8 rue Drouot, 9th (01.47.70.83.38). M° Richelieu-Drouot. **Open** 7am-9pm Mon-Sat. **Credit** MC, V. **Map** p402 H4.
Three seating options await the visitor to La Cave Drouot: bar, brasserie and restaurant, but if you just want to try the excellent Beaujolais (bottled on the premises), then line up at the bar with the porters and antique dealers who pop in here from Drouot and get slurping, chum.

Tearooms

Ladurée

16 rue Royale, 8th (01.42.60.21.79). M° Madeleine or Concorde. **Open** 8.30am-7pm Mon-Sat; 10am-7pm Sun. **Credit** AmEx, DC, MC, V. **Map** p401 F4.
Avoiding someone's eye when they're desperately seeking yours is an art that French waiters have perfected, and Ladurée staff do it exceptionally well. Regulars devour macaroons by the mound. **Branches**: 21 rue Bonaparte, 6th (01.44.07.64.87); 75 av des Champs-Elysées, 8th (01.40.75.08.75); Printemps, 64 bd Haussmann, 9th (01.42.82.40.10); Franck et Fils, 80 rue de Passy, 16th (01.44.14.38.80).

Beaubourg & the Marais

Bars

La Belle Hortense

31 rue Vieille-du-Temple, 4th (01.48.04.71.60). M° St-Paul or Hôtel-de-Ville. **Open** 5pm-2am daily. **Credit** MC, V. **Map** p406 K6.
Bookshop, literary salon, wine bar and off-licence meet at this unusual Marais spot. Good wines by the glass include a strong contingent of Rhône wines by Guigal. It's standing room only at the bar, but the non-smoking reading room at the back is guaranteed to enhance your intellectual credibility.

Eat, Drink, Shop

INTERNATIONAL BARFLIES, SANK ROO DOE NOO, STRAW VOTE AND LOGOS THEREOF ARE

SANK ROO DOE NOO, STRAW VOTE AND LOGOS THEREOF ARE REGISTERED

REGISTERED TRADEMARKS OF HARRY'S NEW YORK BAR S.A.

Harry's New-York Bar ®

Europe's Traditional Cocktail Bar.®
Est. 1911 - Paris - Sank Roo Doe Noo®

Opened Thanksgiving Day 1911.
Original Harry's New York bar.
Rendez-vous of American and French intellectuals.
Birthplace of many cocktails such as the "Bloody Mary,
White Lady, Blue Lagoon and Side Car".
Light Lunch noon - 3pm. Air Conditioned
Piano Bar 10pm-2am

5 rue Daunou - Paris, 2nd.
Daily 10.30am-4am.
www.harrys-bar.fr

HARRY'S NEW YORK BAR, HARRY'S BAR, HARRY'S, HARRY'S NEW YORK BAR, HARRY'S, INTERNATIONAL BARFLIES,

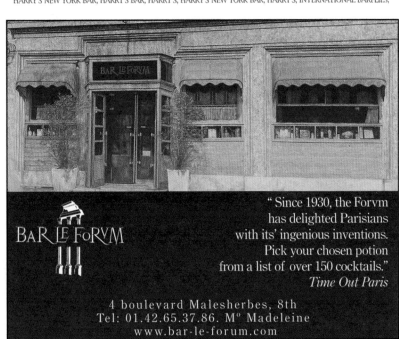

BAR LE FORVM

" Since 1930, the Forvm
has delighted Parisians
with its' ingenious inventions.
Pick your chosen potion
from a list of over 150 cocktails."
Time Out Paris

4 boulevard Malesherbes, 8th
Tel: 01.42.65.37.86. M° Madeleine
www.bar-le-forum.com

Artfully arrayed: **L'Etoile Manquante**. *See below.*

Le Pick-Clops

16 rue Vieille-du-Temple, 4th (01.40.29.02.18).
Mº Hôtel-de-Ville or St-Paul. **Open** 8am-2am Mon-Sat , 9am-2am Sun. **Credit** MC, V. **Map** p406 K6.
This popular corner bar is shamelessly 70s, with top-to-toe pink neon, furniture in clashing colours and a wonderfully awful clock with bauble-adorned hands. Retro chicks vie with Marais trendsters for space at the bar from which to survey passers-by.

Stolly's

16 rue Cloche-Perce, 4th (01.42.76.06.76/www.hip-bars.com). Mº Hôtel de Ville or St-Paul. **Open**
4.30pm-2am daily. **Credit** MC, V. **Map** p406 K6.
Proving that size really doesn't matter, Stolly's packs a large crowd into a small space. The hard-core cocktails, friendly staff and loud music create a welcoming atmosphere. Stolly's is a great place to watch the football or the rugby.

Cafés

L'Apparemment Café

18 rue des Coutures-St-Gervais, 3rd
(01.48.87.12.22). Mº Filles du Calvaire or St-Paul.
Open noon-2am Mon-Fri ; 4pm-2am Sat; noon-midnight Sun. **Credit** MC, V. **Map** p406 L6.
This cosy café across from the Picasso museum is decorated like the front room of an eccentric booze fiend. All the comforts of home with, of course, a bill. Drinks are a little steep but will keep you fuelled for longer than most. Arrive early for meals.

Baz'Art Café

36 bd Henri IV, 4th (01.42.78.62.23). Mº Sully
Morland or Bastille. **Open** 8am-midnight daily.
Credit AmEx, MC, V. **Map** p406 L7.
This light, airy and very spacious café offers good-quality fare and a relaxed, stylish atmosphere. The sandy yellow walls, red velvet chairs and jazzy soundtrack make a fabulosa backdrop and the service couldn't be friendlier. Plenty of market-fresh salads – or check out the great-value Sunday brunch.

Le Petit Marcel

65 rue Rambuteau, 4th (01.48.87.10.20).
Mº Rambuteau or RER Châtelet-Les Halles. **Open**
Mon-Sat 7am-midnight. Closed first three weeks in Aug. **No credit cards. Map** P406 K6.
This tiny *belle époque* bar comes from the Parisian school of authentic faded charm, with its cracked painted ceiling and vintage bar. The sizzling in the corner kitchen might yield up a lunch of steaks, omelettes, pasta, salads, crumble and brownies.

L'Etoile Manquante

34 rue Vieille-du-Temple, 4th (01.42.72.48.34/
www.cafeine.com). Mº Hôtel de Ville or St-Paul.
Open 9am-2am daily. **Credit** MC, V. **Map** p406 K6.
Xavier (Petit Fer à Cheval, Belle Hortense) Denamur's latest artwork-filled endeavour is worth a visit even if you only use the loo. As you relieve yourself, an electric train circulates beneath a photo of a block of flats by night. Then don't forget to smile as you wash your hands and see yourself recorded on the screen reflected in the mirror. The menu features original salads and ice cream from Christian Constant.

Scratch 'n' snifters

Heavenly halfway-houses between the bangin' and the boring, DJ bars will ease you gently into the high-bpm frenzy that awaits you at the business end of the evening. *See also* **Le Cithéa** *(p333)* and chapter **Clubs**.

The Lizard Lounge

18 rue du Bourg-Tibourg, 4th (01.42.72.81.34). Mº Hôtel-de-Ville. **Open** noon-2am daily. Closed one week in Aug. **Credit** MC, V. **Map** p406 K6.
The Anglophone/phile crowd indulges in serious flirting over lethal cocktails. Trip hop and house music help everything along on the small dance floor in the cellar. Sunday brunch has cheap Bloody Marys.

Latina Café

114 av des Champs-Elysées, 8th (01.42.89.98.89). Mº George V. **Open** noon-5am daily. **Credit** MC, V. **Map** p400 D4.
The Latina Café is a sexy place. Run in partnership with Radio Latina, the music is streets away from the Ricky Martin/Enrique Iglesias peddled at other 'Latino' joints. Advice to sleazy suits – dance, don't *drague*!

Le Barramundi

3 rue Taitbout, 9th (01.47.70.21.21). Mº Richelieu-Drouot. **Open** noon-3pm,

Slinky pouring at the **Lizard Lounge**.

7.30pm-Closed two week in Aug. **Credit** AmEx, DC, MC, V. **Map** p401 G5.
Firmly on the bandwagon of all things world: think African art, Indian-inspired tunes and global food. Pretty young things disappear into squishy sofas while nursing potent, 'reassuringly expensive' cocktails.

Sanz Sans

49 rue du Fbg-St-Antoine, 11th (01.44.75.78.78). Mº Bastille. **Open** 9am-5am Tue-Sat; 9am-2am Mon; 6pm-2am Sun. **Credit** MC, DC, V. **Map** p407 M7.
You can't drink a double negative, but you can drink in the exuberant atmosphere in this great bar. If the pumping techno isn't enough to get you going, the barmen will by serving up a huge crash on the cymbal lampshades.

Popin

105 rue Amelot, 11th (01.48.05.56.11). Mº Filles du Calvaire. **Open** 6.30pm-1.30am Tue-Sun. **Admission** free. **Credit** AmEx, MC, V. **Map** p402 L5.
Predominantly French, with more than a smattering of students, Popin also attracts savvy young internationals looking for a pint or ten of the old falling down lotion (the beer's cheap). On weekends the tiny downstairs dancefloor heaves as local DJs spin whatever they fancy, from big beat to indie classics.

Wax

15 rue Daval, 11th (01.40.21.16.16). Mº Bastille. **Open** 8pm-2am Mon-Sat. **Credit** AmEx, DC, MC, V. **Map** p407 M7.
Wax is worth it just for orange swirly paintwork and plastic dinner tables. However, you have to spend to be allowed near the comfy white leather sofas. The music is essentially house.

L'Ile Enchantée

65 bd de la Villette, 19th (01.42.01.67.99). Mº Colonel Fabien. **Open** 8am-2am Mon-Fri; 5pm-2am Sat; 10am-2am Sun. **Credit** MC, V. **Map** p407 M7.
This café is designed to work well by both day and night. On the ground floor DJs spin house, electro and minimal techno to a mixed crowd, with a good number of young Asians making it their local. Upstairs has been turned into a mini club where the music is pushed right up after midnight.

Eat, Drink, Shop

L'Imprévu Café
7-9 rue Quincampoix, 4th (01.42.78.23.50).
Mº Rambuteau or RER Châtelet-Les-Halles.
Open noon-2am Mon-Sat; 1pm-2am Sun. **Credit**
AmEx, DC, MC, V. **Map** p402 K5.
Halfway between the edgy *banlieue* vibe of Les
Halles and the tourist mêlée of the Centre Pompidou,
this café is worlds apart from either. Cluttered with
battered but super-comfy sofas and leopard-skin
chairs, it exudes stylish charm and offers friendly,
laidback service. Exotic cocktails range from those
earmarked for *les chérubins* and *les jeunes filles* to
those reserved for *les machos* and *les durs*.

Web Bar
32 rue de Picardie, 3rd (01.42.72.66.55/
www.webbar.fr). Mº République. **Open** 8.30am-2am
Mon-Fri; 11am-2am Sat; 11am-midnight Sun.
Credit MC, V. **Map** p402 L5.
The net-plus ultra of Paris cyberspace is more than
a computer geek's lair. Industrial vibes intensify as
you pass through its wicker-chaired terrace, its mel-
low-lit bar slamming with speed chess, and the
impressive triple-height atrium (a former silver-
smith's atelier). Web activities extend to live web
painting and on-line DJ links.

Tearooms

Le Loir dans la Théière
3 rue des Rosiers, 4th (01.42.72.90.61). Mº St-Paul.
Open 11am-7pm Mon-Fri; 10am-7pm Sat, Sun.
Credit DC, MC, V. **Map** p406 K6.
Alice in Wonderland would love this place, not least
because it's named after her old friend, the dormouse
in the teapot. Huge wrinkled armchairs and battered
poufs crowd around the tables, while ancient prams
and teapots line deep shelves. Besides staples like
darjeeling and earl grey, there are fabulous perfumed teas and scrumptious cakes and tarts.

The Bastille, eastern & north-eastern Paris

Bars

Café de la Plage
59 rue de Charonne, 11th (01.47.00.48.01).
Mº Ledru-Rollin. **Open** noon-2am Mon-Sat; 5pm-2am
Sun. **Credit** DC, MC, V. **Map** p407 N7.
People with boho-(un)coiffed hair prop up the bar,
but there's a refreshingly simple air of socialising at
the reborn beach café. The Peruvian owner's 'pisco
sours' (a nicely potent shake of pisco, lemon juice
and cinammon) may have something to do with it.
In the basement, DJs mix the usual electro-retro suspects in a white-stone alcove. Monday's Eazy soirées
are popular, with chilled-out grooves and slam inter-
ludes; Sunday is slam poetry night, where renegade
rhymesters can win a bottle of booze. 'Oh, there once
was a fellow named Hunt...'

My old **China** (Club). *See below.*

Chai 33
*33 cour St-Emilion, 12th (01.53.44.01.01). Mº Cour
St-Emilion.* **Open** noon-3pm, 6pm-2am daily. **Credit**
AmEx, MC, V. **Map** p407 P10.
The latest offering from the team behind Barfly,
Buddha Bar and Barrio Latino combines lounge bar,
designer restaurant, terrace bistro and wine shop,
set appropriately in an old wine warehouse in Bercy.
Wine comes first, but design has not been forgotten,
with striking mix of surfaces from stainless steel
vats to pink-satin ladies' loos. Upstairs, under a vault
painted with a copy of Michelangelo's *Creation*, sit
along the bar or recline in deckchairs around concrete
tables over an unusual wine cocktail.

China Club
*50 rue de Charenton, 12th (01.43.43.82.02/ www.
chinaclub.com). Mº Ledru-Rollin or Bastille.* **Open**
7pm-2am Mon-Thur, Sun; 7pm-3am Fri, Sat. Closed 20
Jul-20 Aug. **Credit** AmEx, MC, V. **Map** p407 M7.
With leather Chesterfields, low lighting and a sexy
long bar, it's impossible not to feel glamorous here.
Inspired by Hong Kong, it's like an extremely
relaxed gentleman's club with a distinctly colonial
Cohibas-and-cocktails feel. Ideal seduction territory,
but equally good for a raucous gossip session.

La Flèche d'Or
*102bis rue de Bagnolet, 20th (01.43.72.04.23/www.
flechedor.com). Mº Alexandre Dumas.* **Open** 10am-2am
Tue-Sun. **Credit** AmEx, DC, MC, V. **Map** p407 Q6.

Eat, Drink, Shop

www.**FrogPubs**.com

The English Pubs in Paris!

The Frog & Rosbif
116 rue Saint Denis, 2nd
Mº Etienne Marcel
Tel: 01.42.36.34.73

The Frog & Princess
9 rue Princesse, 6th
Mº Mabillon
Tel: 01.40.51.77.38

The Frog at Bercy Village
25 cour Saint Emilion, 12th
Mº Cour St Emilion
Tel: 01.43.40.70.71

**The Frog &
British Library**
114 avenue de France, 13th
Mº Bibliothèque
Tel: 01.45.84.34.26

English
pubs
serving
delicious
**micro-
brewed
beers
made on
site!**

**Happy
Hours!!**

Great food
& snacks
served until
11pm

Live
sports
on big
screens.
Satellite
TV!

Music fans flock to this funky venue, in a former station on the defunct Petite Ceinture railway line, to catch local groups or dig the decidedly alternative media scene that runs from Télébocal community TV and salsa *bals* to impassioned debates on terrifyingly tedious subjects. *Wheelchair access.*

Le Lèche-Vin

13 rue Daval, 11th (01.43.55.98.91). Mº Bastille.
Open 6pm-2am Mon-Sat; 7pm-midnight Sun. **Credit** MC, V. **Map** p407 M7.
The Lèche-Vin raises idolatry to a new level with its bar-as-shrine to the Virgin Mary. Every available nook, cranny and wall offers up a kitsch, often irreverent tribute to the holiest of mothers, and a trip to the toilets will be enough to make you abandon any hope of salvation. On the bright side, you'll be rewarded with some of the cheapest and best drinks around.

La Mercerie

98 rue Oberkampf, 11th (01.43.38.81.30). Mº Parmentier. **Open** 5pm-2am Mon-Fri; 3pm-2am Sat, Sun. **Credit** MC, V. **Map** p403 M5.
It's all too easy to miss the ivy-obscured entrance but, once inside, there's room for hordes of boisterous, arty types, and comfy alcoves for flirting. The distressed decor is typical of the *quartier*, but carefully chosen accoutrements add a certain flavour.

Les Trois Têtards

46 rue Jean-Pierre-Timbaud, 11th (01.43.14.27.37). Mº Oberkampf or Parmentier. **Open** 8pm-2am Mon-Fri; 5pm-2am Sat-Sun. **Credit** MC, V. **Map** p403 M4.
A familiar interior of rickety chairs and murals is presided over by genial staff and a raucous crowd. Everyone seems to know everyone else, or maybe they're just very good with strangers. The eponymous house speciality is an intoxicating combination of vodka, grapefruit juice, mint and a 'secret' ingredient.

Le Zéro Zéro

89 rue Amelot, 11th (01.49.23.51.00). Mº Bastille. **Open** 6pm-2am daily. **Credit** MC, V. **Map** p407 M6.
Part 70s kitsch, part teen-fantasy, the Zéro Zéro attracts a loyal crowd of the hip and the alcoholic hardcore. Don't come here for an intimate assignation – when you're practically sitting on a stranger's lap, it's not surprising you end up talking to him.

Cafés

Bar Fleuri

1 rue du Plâteau, 19th (01.42.08.13.38). Mº Jourdain or Buttes Chaumont. **Open** 7am-9pm Mon-Sat. **Credit** AmEx, V. **Map** p403 N3.
The unofficial annexe for the artists and curators who visit Le Plateau across the street is the sort of ageless one-off that you'd think no longer exists. Inside, you'll soon learn who's boss – neither the elderly couple who run the bar, nor the boxer dog, but the white hen, Jeanne d'Arc by name, who clucks her way between the tables.

Le Bistrot du Peintre

116 av Ledru-Rollin, 11th (01.47.00.34.39). Mº Ledru-Rollin. **Open** 7am-2am Mon-Sat; 9am-midnight Sun. Closed Christmas. **Credit** DC, MC, V. **Map** p407 N7.
This is a fine example of a sophisticated, well-restored art nouveau café, with luscious carved wood, painted vineyard scenes, frosted-glass partitions, tall mirrors and a long zinc bar. Hot dishes, such as *pot-au-feu* or baked sea bream, change daily, while Salers beef, salads and plates of charcuterie are always available, along with good wines.

Chez Prune

71 quai de Valmy, 10th (01.42.41.30.47). Mº République. **Open** 7am-2am Mon-Sat; 10am-2am Sun. **Credit** MC, V. **Map** p402 L4.
This vibrant Canal St-Martin hotspot in the heart of bobo heaven may be just the place for a well-cooked lunch or a *pastis* and an *assiette* of nibbles at night. Everyone seems to know each other, but it's far from cliquey: as long as you look suitably street and have a screenplay to talk about you'll fit right in.

Pause Café

41 rue de Charonne, 11th (01.48.06.80.33). Mº Ledru-Rollin. **Open** 7am-2am Mon-Sat; 9am-8.30pm Sun. **Credit** AmEx, MC, V. **Map** p407 N7.
Mime school graduates have the best chance of getting a waiter's attention at this perennial Bastille hotspot. Still, the setting's funky and bright and the kitchen makes an effort with hot specials and a selection of filling *tourtes*.

Le Rendez-vous des Quais

MK2 sur Seine, 10-14 quai de la Seine, 19th (01.40.37.02.81). Mº Stalingrad or Jaurès. **Open** noon-midnight daily. **Credit** AmEx, DC, MC, V. **Map** p403 M1.
You can easily while away hours at this relaxed café attached to the MK2 multiplex beside the Bassin de la Villette. Film buffs can't miss with the €23 *menu ciné*. The food is a cut above typical café fare. *Wheelchair access.*

Le Soleil

136 bd de Ménilmontant, 20th (01.46.36.47.44). Mº Ménilmontant. **Open** 9am-2am daily. **No credit cards. Map** p403 N5.
Aptly named, as the terrace catches most of the afternoon sun, this café is a standby for local artists, musicians and hipsters and always an interesting place to strike up a conversation.

Le Viaduc Café

43 av Daumesnil, 12th (01.44.74.70.70). Mº Ledru-Rollin or Gare de Lyon. **Open** 9am-4am daily. **Credit** AmEx, DC, MC, V. **Map** p403 M8.
If you're not a regular, the good modern food and unique setting in the vaults of a disused railway viaduct can be let down by occasionally aloof service, but this is nonetheless a fine place for a sophisticated apéritif or nightcap. Sunday brunch is accompanied by jazz.

ホッとします日本の味

来々軒

restaurant laï-laï ken

ラーメン・餃子・点心・中華料理

Next to Place de L'Opéra
Come and try
our Chinese cuisine,
cooked in a Japanese way

7 rue Sainte Anne, 1st. M⁰ Pyramides
Tel: 01.40.15.96.90 Fax: 01.40.15.06.35
Open daily 11.45am-10pm

The Champs-Elysées & west

Bars

L'Endroit
67 pl du Dr-Félix-Lobligeois, 17th (01.42.29.50.00).
M° Villiers. **Open** noon-2am daily. Closed 1 Jan-15
Feb. **Credit** MC, V. **Map** p401 F1.
A slick café on a charming square where well-dressed, well-behaved 30-somethings lounge. Lamps
diffuse soft light over an art deco-style interior featuring spring-loaded barstools that keep the barflies
bouncing. Barmen serve chihuahua pearl and purple
rain cocktails from a motorised bottle carousel.

Freedom
8 rue de Berri, 8th (01.53.75.25.50).
M° George V. **Open** noon-2am Mon-Fri, noon-5am
Sat, Sun. **Credit** AmEx, DC, MC, V. **Map** p400 D4.
The Freedom pulls in gangs of regulars for after-work frolics, lunchtime sessions and some serious
sharking on weekends, when it's packed till 5am
with goodtime girls and boys from the Champs.
There are pub games, decent grub, genuinely friendly staff and some fiercely patriotic decor.

The James Joyce
71 bd Gouvion-St-Cyr, 17th (01.44.09.70.32).
M° Porte-Maillot. **Open** 7am-2am daily. **Credit**
AmEx, DC, MC, V. **Map** p400 B3.
A friendly Irish corner pub (is there such a thing as
an *unfriendly* Irish pub?) where there's always a
football game to catch and a pint of Guinness to be
had. Joyceian memorablia covers the dark wood
panelling and fills the display cases, and the stained-glass windows show colourful scenes from *Ulysses*.
The upstairs restaurant specialises in Irish cuisine.

Lush
16 rue des Dames, 17th (01.43.87.49.46).
M° Place de Clichy. **Open** 4pm-2am Mon-Fri; noon-2am Sat, Sun. **Credit** MC, V. **Map** p401 F2.
At a prime address in upwardly mobile Batignolles,
this recently opened bar is a sleek lair for chilled-out
drinking. Soft grape purples and comfy banquettes
provide a suitable setting to try out well-chosen New
World wines and delicious cocktails.

Polo Room
3 rue Lord-Byron, 8th (01.40.74.07.78/
www.poloroom.com). M° George V. **Open** noon-3pm,
5pm-1am Mon-Thur; Fri, noon-3pm, 5pm-2am Sat;
7pm-1am Sun. **Credit** AmEx, DC, MC, V.
Map p400 D3.
The 'posh' decor mixes ye olde colonial club pieces
with net curtains, laser lights and low tables that
make it look like a drinking den for leprechauns. The
suave and sophisticated drinks list features variations on the martini theme, though avoid the mandarintini, a hair-curling mix of vodka and fizzy
orange. *Wheelchair access.*

Cafés

Café Antoine
*17 rue La Fontaine, 16th (01.40.50.14.30). RER
Kennedy-Radio France.* **Open** 7.30am-11pm Mon-Sat.
Closed two weeks in Aug. **Credit** AmEx, DC, MC, V.
Map p404 A7.
Hector Guimard slipped this adorable café into one
of his famous art nouveau apartment blocks. Inside
is still a strawberries-and-cream idyll of days gone
by: tiles, painted-glass ceiling and blowsy scenes of
horse-racing and rowing. Tiny blackboards announce tempting foie gras, hot *plats* and *charcuterie*.

Bar des Théâtres
6 av Montaigne, 8th (01.47.23.34.63).
M° Alma-Marceau. **Open** 6am-2am daily. **Credit**
AmEx, MC,V. **Map** p401 E4.
Bang opposite the Théâtre des Champs-Elysées, this
popular bar/café is always buzzing after the curtain
falls, and attracts a steady daytime stream of fashionistas. Yet it couldn't be less pretentious. Simple,
though pricey, brasserie fare is served in the café
area or in a slightly more formal restaurant section.

Granterroirs
30 rue de Miromesnil, 8th (01.47.42.18.18).
M° Miromesnil. **Open** 8.30am-8pm Mon-Fri. Closed
three weeks Aug. **Credit** AmEx, V, MC. **Map** p401 F3.
Welcome to snack-time, luxury-style. This gourmet
deli-cum-café is always packed out at lunch with
gaggles of office workers. Don't be deterred. Even if
you have to be shoe-horned on to the benches around
the two large tables, it's always worth sinking your
fangs into a snackette here. *Wheelchair access.*

IN THE HEART OF THE MARAIS

SINCE 1979
TheStudio
R E S T A U R A N T

OPEN DAILY AT NOON EXCEPT MONDAY LUNCH
WEEKEND BRUNCH FROM 12.30 PM TO 3.30 PM
41 RUE DU TEMPLE, 4TH - TEL: 01 42 74 10 38

BAR A TAPAS
Happy Hour
from 5.30 pm to 7.30 pm

McBrides Irish Pub

Follow the lead ...   ...to McBride's

Happy Hour 5pm-8pm
Big Screen TV
SKY Digital / Canal Satellite
Chamipons League / Premiership Matches / Six Nations

All Major Sports Events Shown
Live Music Tuesdays and Sundays
Food served from 10am till 10pm (Sunday 11am-7pm)
Sunday Roast / Traditional Irish Breakfast / Full Menu

54 rue St Denis, 1st. M° Chatelet/Chatelet les Halles
Tel: 01.40.26.46.70 - Fax: 01.40.26.56.31 - www.mcbridesirishpub.com
Credit cards - Visa, mastercard, diners Club, CB - Pool Table, Darts

Montmartre & Pigalle

Bars

Chào-Bà-Café
22 bd de Clichy, 18th (01.46.06.72.90). M° Pigalle.
Open 8.30am-2am Mon-Wed, Sun; 8.30am-4am Thur;
8.30am-5am Fri, Sat. **Credit** MC, V. **Map** p401 G2.
The former Café Pigalle is now a French Indochina
theme bar that blends in seamlessly with the neon
peep show parlours flanking it on the Pigalle strip.
A bust of Ho Chi Minh looks on approvingly as the
thirsty toast and the hungry dine in fine capitalist
style on Franco-Vietnamese food. Oh, the decadence!

La Fourmi
74 rue des Martyrs, 18th (01.42.64.70.35).
M° Pigalle. **Open** 8am-2am Mon-Thur; 8am-4am Fri-
Sat; 10am-2am Sun. **Credit** MC, V. **Map** p402 H2.
With a retro-industrial decor, long zinc bar and
trademark Duchampian bottle-rack chandelier, this
spacious bar in happening Pigalle buzzes all day and
night with a young, arty crowd and even artier staff,
joined by the odd person from the lower orders.

Cafés

La Chope du Château Rouge
40 rue de Clignancourt, 18th (01.46.06.20.10).
M° Château Rouge. **Open** 7am-1am daily.
No credit cards. Map p402 J1.
All sorts rub shoulders here, and that can create a
really friendly atmosphere. It's one of the best places

to catch the last of the evening sun peeking out over
Sacre-Coeur. Beer is gloriously cheap, and free couscous is served on Friday, so make sure you get in
early to grab a table – even if you have to put it out
yourself (the table, that is).

Chez Camille
8 rue Ravignan, 18th (01.46.06.05.78).
M° Abbesses or Pigalle. **Open** 9am-1.30am Tue-Sat;
11am-8pm Sun. Closed Aug. **No credit cards.**
Map p402 H2.
A down-to-earth café on the *butte* Montmartre, complete with chess players (including the waiter, which
doesn't speed up service), a lovely old clock, zinc bar
and tipsy pick-up artist. Perched on the tiny terrace,
you can feast your eyes on a panoramic view to the
left, a bucolic square to the right, while soaking up
a rare slice of Montmartre bohemia.

Le Progrès
7 rue des Trois Frères, 18th (01.42.51.33.33).
M° Abbesses. **Open** 9am-2am daily. **No credit**
cards. Map p402 H2.
A little less body-fascist than some of the imposingly
cool drinking holes around Montmartre, the Progrès
is a jovial joint with friendly, sometimes English-
speaking staff. Huge windows allow you to people
watch and the tobacco-stained walls often display
the work of local photographers. Unexceptional hot
food at lunchtime, and plates of charcuterie or cheese
in the evening. Asthmatics beware, this bar can
reach chemical-warfare levels of smokiness.

The Latin Quarter & the 13th

Bars

Le Crocodile
6 rue Royer-Collard, 5th. (01.43.54.32.37). RER
Luxembourg. **Open** 10.30pm-6am Mon-Sat (closing
variable). Closed Aug. **Credit** MC, V. **Map** p406 H6.
It's worth ignoring appearances – like boarded-up
windows – for a cocktail at Le Crocodile. Young,
friendly regulars line the sides of this small, narrow
bar and try to choose from some 267 options, most
of them marginally less potent than meths. Pen and
paper are provided to note your decision.

La Folie en Tête
33 rue de la Butte-aux-Cailles, 13th (01.45.80.65.99).
M° Corvisart or Place d'Italie. **Open** 5pm-2am
Mon-Sat. Closed 25 Dec-2 Jan. **Credit** MC, V.
Map p406 K10.
On lazy, hazy, crazy summer evenings this throb-
bing bar is reminiscent of a mobile-phone-and-sun-
glasses Mediterranean student hangout where
carefree tenderlings congregate around their
Vespas, shooting the breeze. The four Belgian beers
on tap are good value and happy hour is unbeatable.

The best Only in Paris

Le Bar Fleuri
Come to roost with the chicken. *See p223.*

Bar des Théâtres
Montaigne sans pretension. *See p225.*

Chai 33
Warehouse meets Michelangelo. *See p221.*

La Chope du Château Rouge
Trendsters versus couscous. *See p227.*

Le Crocodile
Den of cocktail iniquity. *See p227.*

Le Dernier Métro
A locals' local. *See p233.*

L'Etoile Manquante
The loo as artwork. *See p219.*

L'Imprévu Café
Unpredictable but friendly. *See p219.*

the DUTCH bar in Paris

Happy Hour 5pm-8pm

Kitchen open 6.30pm-10.30pm
Open from 5pm to 2am every day
Tel: 01 42 71 43 13
Mo Saint Paul - Hôtel de Ville
36 rue du Roi de Sicile
75004 Paris

The Dutch Place to be in the Marais

International crowd

Wide selection of Cocktails and Beers

Come in, enjoy our food, have a drink and let's have a Party

Café KLEIN HOLLAND

www.dutchbars.com

We make you go up•side down !!!

They really paint the town red at **La Palette**. *See p231*.

Eat, Drink, Shop

Cafés

Café de la Nouvelle Mairie
*19-21 rue des Fossés-St-Jacques, 5th
(01.44.07.04.41). RER Luxembourg.* **Open** 9am-8pm
Mon, Wed, Fri; 9am-10pm Tue, Thur. **No credit
cards. Map** p406 J8.
This low-key café has bags of natural style, laidback
staff and a sunny terrace overlooking a pretty
square. Normale Sup students scribble notes at
tables and at lunch it soon fills with a select bunch
of insiders for quiches, soups, excellent *plats du jour*
and scrumptious desserts.

Le Comptoir du Panthéon
*5 rue Soufflot, 5th (01.43.54.75.36).
RER Luxembourg.* **Open** 7.30am-1am Mon-Sat; 9am-
7pm Sun. **Credit** MC, V. **Map** p406 J8.
This café has been stylishly renovated with dark
wood and crimson velvet and abstract art. The well-
dressed students are more likely to be discussing
affaires du coeur, the right approach to make to
papa for another hand-out or the PSG score sheet
than organising the next demo; and it's all the better for it. The terrace gives a stunning view of the
Panthéon, the law faculty and the Mairie du Vème.

Le Verre à Pied
*118bis rue Mouffetard, 5th (01.43.31.15.72).
Mº Censier-Daubenton.* **Open** 8.30am-9pm Tue-Sat;
9am-2.30pm Sun. **No credit cards. Map** p406 J9.
The buzz of rue Mouffetard can wear you out –
thankfully there are places like this where you can
slow things down with a drink. Locals and street

performers crowd in at the small tables for homely
fare as the market shuts down for lunch; there is usually just one hot special. Open since 1870, Le Verre à
Pied featured in smasheroo film *Amélie*.

Tearooms

La Fourmi Aillée
*8 rue du Fouarre, 5th (01.43.29.40.99).
Mº Maubert-Mutualité.* **Open** noon-3pm, 7pm-
midnight daily; shop noon-midnight daily. Evenings
only in July and Aug. **Credit** MC, V. **Map** p406 J7.
Walking into this tea salon-cum-bookshop is like
stepping into a Vanessa Bell painting. The intimate
caramel-coloured interior is packed with books, lamps
and blue and white teapots. Try the Ceylon and China
blend, perfumed with mango or hazelnut, and the
unlikely apple strudel with ceps and custard.

St-Germain & Odéon

Bars

Le Bar Dix
10 rue de l'Odéon, 6th (01.43.26.66.83). Mº Odéon.
Open 5.30pm-2am daily. **No credit cards.**
Map p406 H7.
If you want to converse with the natives, this is the
place to do it. Faded posters cover shabby walls but
a precariously steep staircase leads down to a much
larger, but equally packed, cellar. Spot a space, make
a bolt for it, order a pitcher of the house sangria and
settle in for the duration.

Stingfellows
London Paris

RESTAURANT & LAP DANCING CLUB

Every evening from 9 until 4 in the morning. Stingfellows' Paris angels unveil the excitement of lap dancing in an atmosphere of glamour and intimacy. The angel's cabaret brings you a quality dining experience in the French tradition, from its 55 euros menu.

27 avenue des Ternes, 17th. Closed on Sundays
Tel: 01 47 66 45 00 / Fax: 01 47 66 97 76

Le Comptoir des Canettes

11 rue des Canettes, 6th (01.43.26.79.15).
M° Mabillon. **Open** noon-2am Tue-Sat. Closed Aug,
Christmas. **Credit** MC, V. **Map** p405 G7.
The heart of St-Germain still runs red as wine in this
historic *bar à vins* (aka Chez Georges). Street-level
is filled with local shop owners and residents; downstairs a studenty crowd huddles around long tables.

Fu Bar

5 rue St-Sulpice, 6th (01.40.51.82.00). M° Odéon.
Open 4pm-2am daily. Happy hour 4-9pm Mon, Wed-
Sat; 4pm-2am Tue; 4pm-midnight Sun. **Credit** MC,V.
Map p405 H7.
The tiny Fu Bar is a brilliant addition to any
serious bar hopper's itinerary; it's full of up-for-it
Anglos making inroads into the cocktail list.
Obscene measures and plenty of punter interaction
make this a top choice for a huge night out.

Cafés

Bar du Marché

75 rue de Seine, 6th (01.43.26.55.15). M° Odéon.
Open 7.30am-2am daily. **Credit** MC, V. **Map** p406 H7.
Bar du Marché is the perfect place to contemplate
dinner; you'll find all the ingredients you need in the
market street rue de Buci. Then again, once you get
a table here you might as well hang on to it as the
high standards of food and service have long kept
it popular with both locals and visitors.

Café de Flore

172 bd St-Germain, 6th (01.45.48.55.26).
M° St-Germain-des-Prés. **Open** 7am-1.30am daily.

Credit AmEx, MC, V. **Map** p405 H7.
The haunt of the Surrealists in the 1920s and 30s is
smokier and both rougher and more stylish than Les
Deux Magots nearby, with a perpetual buzz and
insouciant yet charming waiters. The Flore's internationally spun crowd still contains its share of writers, 'intellectuals', filmmakers and artists. Don't
worry – the occasional real person pops in, too.

Les Editeurs

4 carrefour de l'Odéon, 6th (01.43.26.67.76).
M° Odéon. **Open** 8am-2am daily. Food served noon-
2am daily. **Credit** AmEx, MC, V. **Map** p406 H7.
You don't need to be feeling sociable to come here;
the shelves are stacked with books from nearby publishers, which customers are free to peruse if you
fancy a bit of a literary pose. If you're peckish,
there's *choucroute*, roast cod or a club sandwich.

La Palette

43 rue de Seine, 6th (01.43.26.68.15). M° Mabillon
or Odéon. **Open** 8am-2am Mon-Sat. Closed Aug.
Credit MC, V. **Map** p406 H7.
The classic St-Germain artists' café still looks the
part with its *belle époque* interior and oil paintings
and palettes hanging above the bar, though like the
area, its clientele has gone upmarket and now numbers carrier-bag lugging shoppers as well as art students and gallerists. The pavement terrace tends
towards reserved by day and positively wild by night.

Le Rostand

6 pl Edmond-Rostand, 6th (01.43.54.61.58). RER
Luxembourg. **Open** 8am-midnight Mon-Thur, Sun;
8am-2am Fri, Sat. **Credit** AmEx, DC, MC, V. **Map**
p406 J8.

Amsterdam · Andalucia · Barcelona · Berlin · Boston · Brussels

Budapest · Buenos Aires · Chicago · Copenhagen · Dublin · Edinburgh

Florence · Havana · Hong Kong · Istanbul · Las Vegas · Lisbon

London · Los Angeles · Madrid · Miami · Milan · Moscow

Naples · New Orleans · New York · Paris · Patagonia · Prague

Rome · San Francisco · South of France · Stockholm · Sydney · Tokyo

Venice · Vienna · Washington, DC

Time Out
City Guides

www.penguin.com   www.timeout.com

The **Time Out City Guides** spectrum

Available from all good bookshops and at www.timeout.com/shop

The vast, heated terrace looking out on to the Luxembourg gardens draws the international sunglasses brigade, while the classy interior with its wicker chairs and Orientalist paintings is perfect for a breakfast rendez-vous. Decent salads and a wide selection of beers, whiskies and cocktails.

La Tour de Pierre
53 rue Dauphine, 6th (01.43.26.08.93/ www.latouredepierre.com). M° Odéon. **Open** 8am-9pm Mon-Sat. Closed two weeks in Aug. **Credit** MC, V. **Map** p406 H7.
Time stands still in this tiny, award-winning *tabac/ wine bar.* OK, so it might take an age to get served, but what atmosphere. *Wheelchair access.*

Au Vieux Colombier
65 rue de Rennes, 6th (01.45.48.53.81). M° St-Sulpice. **Open** 8am-midnight Mon-Sat; 11am-8pm Sun. **Credit** MC, V. **Map** p405 G7.
Au Vieux Colombier attracts a demographic cross-section of the area. Making colourful cocktails and serving cheapish beer and refreshing snacks with blinding speed, the young staff are friendly and efficient. Full-wall mirrors combat claustrophobia.

Tearooms

La Maison de la Chine
76 rue Bonaparte, 6th (01.40.51.95.16). M° St-Sulpice. **Open** 10am-6.30pm Mon-Sat. **Credit** MC, V. **Map** p405 G7.
This place conspires to make you fall for the East, from the area filled with lacquered furniture, lamps and celadon ceramics to the beautifully decorated tearoom. Four blends are prepared following the ancient ritual of *gongfu cha;* fine blue-green teas are brewed in tiny vessels, then sipped like a liqueur.

The 7th & the 15th

Cafés

Café du Marché
38 rue Cler, 7th (01.47.05.51.27). M° Ecole-Militaire. **Open** 7am-midnight Mon-Sat; 7am-5.30pm Sun. **Credit** MC, V. **Map** p405 E6.
You don't really expect to find a relaxed place like this sandwiched between the Eiffel Tower and Invalides, but this spot located on a busy market street is perfect for resting the tootsies during tourist duties, for a cheap drink or to enjoy one of the copious salads or daily specials. *Wheelchair access.*

Au Dernier Métro
70 bd de Grenelle, 15th (01.45.75.01.23). M° Dupleix. **Open** 6am-2am daily. **Credit** AmEx, DC, MC, V. **Map** p404 C7.
A gem of a café. Old advertising hoardings line the walls and the bar has designated elbow space for each of the habitués, with corresponding floor space for their faithful hounds. The enormous salads and *plats du jour* are always good choices, and the wel-

coming atmosphere means that you're likely to end up talking to the guy next to you about his broken heart or your plans for world domination.

Café des Lettres
53 rue de Verneuil, 7th (01.42.22.52.17/ www.cafedeslettres.com). M° Rue du Bac. **Open** Mon-Sat 10am-midnight; Sun noon-4pm. Closed two weeks at Christmas. **Credit** MC, V. **Map** p405 G6.
Café des Lettres has deeply meaningful abstract art and a smoke-fugged atmosphere. The salon is used by the Maison des Ecrivains for literary discussions and novel-readings. Contrastingly airy, the courtyard is a good place on a summer's afternoon, drawing a swish crowd for Scandinavian-tinged food.

Le Roi du Café
59 rue Lecourbe, 15th (01.47.34.48.50). M° Sèvres-Lecourbe. **Open** 7am-2am daily. **Credit** MC, V. **Map** p404 B10.
This is the perfect address for lazy, warm summer evening. Just sitting on the terrace chills you out in record time. The range of liquor behind the bar means you'll never run out of fancy drinks to try, but the real reason for hanging out here is the worn art deco elegance. OK, maybe it's the drinks, too.

Montparnasse & beyond

Bars

Le Rosebud
11bis rue Delambre, 14th (01.43.20.44.13). M° Vavin or Edgar-Quinet. **Open** 7pm-2am daily. **Credit** MC, V. **Map** p405 G9.
Stepping into this Montparnasse relic is akin to entering a 1950s film set, with a cast of characters is sure to include a few ageing Lotharios, wannable starlets and Indiana Jones lookalikes. The white-jacketed waiters and martini-sipping habitués trade sugar-coated insults in good-natured competition.

Cafés

Café de la Place
23 rue d'Odessa, 14th (01.42.18.01.55). M° Edgar-Quinet. **Open** 7.30am-2am Mon-Sat; 10am-11pm Sun. **Credit** MC, V. **Map** p405 G9.
This café has a warm feel with stripped wood, vintage Ricard jugs and battered 1950s ads. The lively terrace is a perfect location for a summer *apéro* or a plancher of charcuterie with a glass of wine.

Le Select
99 bd du Montparnasse, 6th (01.42.22.65.27). M° Vavin. **Open** 8am-3am daily. **Credit** MC, V. **Map** p405 G9..
As the setting of events in biographies of writers such as Hemingway and Fitzgerald, you might think Le Select would have little need to blow its own trumpet. But no: this *'bar américain'* is swimming in its own nostalgia. It's good, but it won't be great again until it forgets who it used to be.

heavenly hotels,
devilish deals...

...in paris

with up to 50% off standard rates in quality hotels.

We offer a superb range of quality hotels, from 2 star to deluxe in over 70 European cities and coastal resorts.

Booking is extremely easy with **no booking fee** and offered through both our call centre and on our website.

2★ from	£22
3★ from	£28
4★ from	£48

prices are per person per night based on two people sharing a twin/double room with breakfast & taxes included.

book now on:
020 8731 7000
www.hotelconnect.co.uk

hotelconnect
the hotel specialist

Shops & Services

Unearth treasures at a *bouquiniste*, snap up bargain fabrics at Barbès or blow your budget on shiny baubles at the Bon Marché; when in Paris, shop.

Admit it. You came to Paris to shop. An hour in the Louvre is a small price to pay for the pleasure of roaming the *grands boulevards* and back alleys of the chicest city on earth. As the birthplace of couture, Paris has all the usual designer suspects, but these days if you stick to the luxury labels of avenue Montaigne or the rue du Faubourg-St-Honoré you could just as easily be on Bond Street or Madison Avenue. The real pleasure of shopping in Paris reveals itself in tiny boutiques, museum-worthy foodshops and 19th-century covered *passages.*

Instead of an all-out shopping marathon, try the mental image of a scavenger hunt: the first person to find a pair of 1940s-style, mint-green suede shoes and a first edition of Henry Miller wins. Duck into the nooks and crannies, and have a coffee in between. Classic clusters of shops include antiques in the 7th, second-hand and rare books in the 5th. Street chic and lifestyle outlets live side by side in the Marais, while quirky up-and-comers settle in Abbesses or near Canal St-Martin. Those with a shoe fetish should teeter to rue du Cherche-Midi (6th)

and rue de Grenelle (7th); foodies to Bon Marché (7th) and Fauchon (8th). Specialist enclaves include musical instruments on rue de Rome in the 8th, motorbikes and cameras old and new on boulevard Beaumarchais, porcelain and crystal on rue de Paradis. The flea markets at Vanves and Clignancourt are well worth getting out of bed for early at weekends. The listings for shops in this chapter include major branches, but not every outlet.

As always, common sense applies: the further you venture off the tourist track, the less you should look like a tourist. Barbès is a great place for African textiles and exotic spices, but is no place to brandish your hotel map or your new mobile phone.

Although Paris could easily put a large dent in your most generous overdraft, there is plenty of pleasure to be had without upsetting your bank manager. (Hell, they sell 86% cocoa chocolate in the supermarket.) Whether it's a paperback from a *quai*-side *bouquiniste* or a bottle of golden Sauternes, you are sure to return from Paris with something *fabuleux.*

One-stop Shopping

Concept stores

Concept stores have popped up all over town over the past few years, with their fusion of art, fashion and other creative pursuits to result in a fascinating cross-breeding of ideas. Now there's even an anti-concept, concept store.

Castelbajac Concept Store

31 pl du Marché-St-Honoré, 1st (01.42.60.41.55).
Mº Tuileries or Pyramides. **Open** 10.30am-7.30pm daily. **Credit** AmEx, DC, MC, V. **Map** p401 G5.
Aristo designer Jean-Charles de Castelbajac's humorous, colourful world of fashion is showcased in a 230m² gleaming white concept store. As well as his own eclectic fashion collections (men and women) and accessories, there is funky furniture and pieces by invited artists and designers.

Colette

213 rue St-Honoré, 1st (01.55.35.33.90/
www.colette.fr). Mº Tuileries. **Open** 10.30am-7.30pm Mon-Sat. **Credit** AmEx, DC, MC, V. **Map** p401 G4.
Five years on, the original concept/lifestyle store is still the most cutting-edge. Truly, madly minimalist accessories are displayed within clinical glass cases, as if their WOW factor might be a hazard to customers. Clock Finnish glassware, Sony cameras, the Tom Dixon jack stool and the hair and beauty brands själ, Kiehl's or Bliss as you enter the store before browsing the ultra-cool reviews, magazines and photo albums on the mezzanine. What to wear? Find inspiration on the first floor, where dummies are draped with work by new and established fashion artists. And then lunch with a global selection of mineral water in the basement Water Bar.

Surface to Air

46 rue de l'Arbre-Sec, 1st (01.49.27.04.54).
Mº Pont Neuf. **Open** 11am-7.30pm Mon-Sat.
Credit MC, V. **Map** p402 J6.
Seven guys created this indefinable, non-concept concept store, which also acts as a photo and fashion production company. The cult clothing selection takes in cute T-shirt dresses, Sila and Maria's trashy tank tops, Tatty Devine's hair accessories and mens' space-invaders customised Surface to Air sweats. Chill on the sofa and check out the mags and Surface to Air's limited-edition book *Pour la Victoire*.

Gravity Zero

30 rue de Charonne/1 rue Keller, 11th
(01.43.14.06.39/www.gravityzero.fr). Mº Ledru-Rollin. **Open** 4-7.30pm Mon; 11am-1pm, 2-7.30pm Tue-Thur; 11am-7.30pm Fri, Sat. **Credit** MC, V.
Map p407 N7.
This concept store brings fashion, music, photography and art together with the rue Keller site selling an eclectic selection of electronic music. But let's talk clothes. The three-floor Charonne store plays host

to the upper end of the market with innovative and modern collections where form and material are of the essence. Check out the sophisticated cuts and rich fabrics of Yu Feng, the funky bright boiled wool hats by Hut Up as well as Chez Twin Ceric's men's knitwear with asymmetric cuts and irregular stripes. A good choice of shoes is in store too, from the funky street style of Fly to 'babouches' by Chez Babouche. At rue Keller, the look is more playful street with the latest arrival on the jeans scene by Brazilian Ellis. For accessories, there are the inimitable Freitag bags, Air Day and sculptural jewellery.

Spree

16 rue de La Vieuville, 18th (01.42.23.41.40).
Mº Abbesses. **Open** 10am-7.30pm Tue-Sat. Closed Aug. **Credit** MC, V. **Map** p402 H1.
Run by Bruno Hadjadj and Roberta Oprandi (artist/artistic director and fashion designer respectively) with a distinctly Montmartre vibe, Spree mixes fashion, design and contemporary art. Here you'll find a 60s chair draped in the latest fashions by designers such as Preen or Isabel Marant.

Department stores

The revamped *grands magasins* are upping the fashion ante and introducing new, cutting-edge designers and luxury spaces to lure a younger, cooler, yet monied clientele away from concept stores and independent designer boutiques.

La Samaritaine

19 rue de la Monnaie, 1st (01.40.41.20.20/
www.lasamaritaine.com). Mº Pont Neuf. **Open** 9.30am-7pm Mon-Wed, Fri, Sat; 9.30am-10pm Thur.
Credit AmEx, DC, MC, V. **Map** p402 J6.
This venerable store takes its name from the relief of the Good Samaritan on the Pont Neuf. The main building with its elaborate turquoise and gold wrought-ironwork and peacock mosaics around the *verrière* is one of the jewels of the belle époque. New owner LVMH has restored the decor and reorganised the merchandise, giving priority to beauty, decoration, leisure, and especially fashion. You can also get an eyeful of one of the best views over Paris from the restaurant and top-floor café.

BHV (Bazar de l'Hôtel de Ville)

52-64 rue de Rivoli, 4th (01.42.74.90.00/
www.bhv.fr). Tile shop 14 rue du Temple
(01.42.74.92.12); DIY hire annexe 40 rue de la Verrerie (01.42.74.97.23). Mº Hôtel de Ville. **Open** 9.30am-7pm Mon, Tue, Thur, Sat; 9.30am-8.30pm Wed, Fri. **Credit** AmEx, MC, V. **Map** p401 G5.
DIY fiends spend hours in the basement of this hardware heaven, drooling over hinges, screws, nuts and bolts or dithering over paint colours upstairs. There is even a Bricolage Café, decked out like an old tool shed, offering salads and a computer to surf DIY sites. The store has a good range of men's outdoor wear, surprisingly upmarket bedlinen and a 2,000m² space devoted to every type of storage utility.

Eat, Drink, Shop

Spree bah gum (shoes)!

SATELLITE

PARIS

- 15, rue du Cherche Midi, 6th - M° Sèvres Babylone
- 23, rue des Francs Bourgeois, 4th - M° Saint-Paul
- 10, passage du Grand Cerf, 2nd - M° Etienne Marcel
- Galeries Lafayette • Le Printemps • Le Bon Marché

Tel: 01 55 34 95 73 - www.satellite.fr

ANNA LOWE
DESIGNER DISCOUNT

Haute Couture
and Couture at the
lowest price with
personalized service!

Chicago Tribune
*"The best of the off-price shops
is ANNA LOWE..."*

The Washington Post
*"...this is not like any bargain basement
you've ever seen."*

Mon-Sat 10 am to 7pm

Next to the Hotel Bristol
104, rue du Fbg St Honoré, Paris 8th
Métro: Champs-Elysées Clemenceau
Tel: 01 42 66 11 32   Fax: 01 40 06 00 53
E-mail: annaloweparis@aol.com   Website: www.annaloweparis.com

Le Bon Marché
24 rue de Sèvres, 7th (01.44.39.80.00/
www.bonmarche.fr). M° Sèvres-Babylone. **Open**
9.30am-7pm Mon-Sat. **Credit** AmEx, DC, MC, V.
Map p405 G7.
Paris' oldest department store is also the most swish
and user-friendly, thanks to an extensive redesign
by LVMH. The prestigious Balthazar men's section
offers a cluster of designer 'boutiques', while the
Theatre of Beauty provides a comfort zone for
women. Seven luxury boutiques from Dior to Chanel
take pride of place on the ground floor. Escalators
designed by Andrée Putman take you up to the fashion floor, which includes the store's well-cut, own
label cotton shirts. Cool fashion finds include
Catherine Malandrino's rock T-shirts and trousers
as seen on the likes of Madonna, now available in
Paris for the first time. The Grande Epicerie food
hall (01.44.39.81.00/www.lagrandeepicerie.fr; and
open 8.30am-9pm Mon-Sat) is in the adjoining building along with an antiques gallery, bar and restaurant.

Galeries Lafayette
40 bd Hausmann, 9th (01.42.82.34.56/fashion shows
01.42.82.30.25/fashion advice 01.42.82.35.50/
www.galerieslafayette.com). M° Chaussée d'Antin/RER Auber. **Open**
9.30am-7.30pm Mon-Wed, Fri, Sat; 9.30am-9pm Thur.
Credit AmEx, DC, MC, V. **Map** p401 H3.
This vast wedding cake of a department store has
revamped its fashion, beauty and accessories
sections. Le Labo and Trend on the first floor introduce progressive international creators, such as the
cossack-inspired bags and belts by Roucou Paris
and Amaterasu's plastic pumps. Ninety established
designers are spread over the first and second floors
and the store has five fashion and beauty consultants to guide you through the sartorial maze. There
are fashion shows every Tuesday at 11am and also
on Fridays in the high season. As for the household
goods labyrinth on the low-ceilinged upper floors,
save yourself the headache. The new men's fashion
space on the third floor of Lafayette Homme is a
must, with its natty designer corners and 'Club'
space with fax and Internet access. On the first floor,
Lafayette Gourmet offers plenty of places to snack
and the second biggest wine cellar in Paris.

Printemps
64 bd Haussmann, 9th (01.42.82.50.00/
www.printemps.com). M° Havre-Caumartin/
RER Auber. **Open** 9.35am-7pm Mon Wed, Fri, Sat;
9.30am-10pm Thur. **Credit** AmEx, DC, MC, V.
Map p401 G3.
There are six floors of fabulous fashion, in both the
men's and women's stores, covering all possibilities
from underwear to urban. The sleek, white 3,000m²
luxury area in the Printemps de la Mode store
features an impressive array of 41 women's shoe
brands surrounding a selection of exclusive watches in the centre. On the second floor, discover cutting-edge favourites, where French designers such

as A.P.C. and Zadig et Voltaire sit side by side with
the likes of Dolce e Gabbana and Moschino. The fifth
floor Miss Code targets the teen miss and offers a
huge selection of jeans and sportswear. Check out,
too, the Printemps de la Maison store, with its well-
stocked home decoration and furnishings departments and the more conceptual 'function floor', where
knives, saucepans and coffee machines are set out
on steel shelving. Zoom to the 9th-floor terrace
restaurant and take in the art nouveau cupola.

Tati
4 bd de Rochechouart, 18th (01.55.29.52.50/
www.tati.fr). M° Barbès-Rochechouart. **Open** 10am-
7pm Mon-Fri, 9.15am-7.15pm Sat. **Credit** MC, V.
Map p402 J2.
Tati is a Parisian institution, with its pink and white
checked frontage spread out over several shops
along not-so-salubrious boulevard Rochechouart
and matching trashy-cool carrier bags. Almost
unbeatable in its cheapness, you can find anything
from T-shirts and tights to wedding dresses, as well
as jewellery and household goods. Don't expect high
quality, but bargains can be found if you can get
past the hordes who flock like vultures to the bins
which proclaim the promise of 'only €2.99'.
Branches: 172 rue du Temple, 3rd (01.42.71.41.77);
68 av du Maine, 14th (01.56.80.06.80).

Monoprix
Branches all over Paris. (www.monoprix.fr). **Open**
generally 8am-8pm Mon-Sat; some branches open till
10pm, (Champs-Elysées until midnight) including
Roquette, Commerce and Opéra. **Credit** MC, V.
Every *arrondissement* has a couple of these practical stores stocking everything from paper clips to
pâté. The most representative, with its wet fish
counter, cheese and charcuterie displays, bread shop
and fashion department, is on the Champs-Elysées
(No. 52). Some surprisingly good purchases can be
made as Monoprix stocks decent middle-of-the-
range underwear, an extensive range of sexy,
coloured stockings and tights and the funky Bala
Boost jewellery range. Bargain bins with end-of-line
ranges are often put out where you can snap up
cheap and cheerful baubles for as little as one euro.

Fashion & Beauty

Collected designerwear

Kabuki Femme
25 rue Etienne-Marcel, 1st (01.42.33.55.65).
M° Etienne Marcel. **Open** 10.30am-7.30pm Mon-Sat.
Credit AmEx, DC, MC, V. **Map** p402 J5.
On the ground floor there's intrepid footwear and
bags by Costume National, Miu Miu and Prada,
along with Fendi's cult creations. Burberry belts and
Miu Miu sunglasses are also stocked here. Upstairs
houses no-flies-on-me suits by Helmut Lang and
Véronique Leroy, Prada and Costume National.

Maria Luisa

2 rue Cambon, 1st (01.47.03.48.08). M° Concorde.
Open 10.30am-7pm Mon-Sat. **Credit** AmEx, DC,
MC, V. **Map** p401 G4.

Venezuelan Maria Luisa Poumaillou was one of Paris'
first stockists of Galliano, McQueen and the Belgian
fashion elite, and has an unflagging eye for stars in
the making. An ever-expanding series of shops covers fashion (Olivier Theyskens, Diego Dolcini, Jose
Enrique Ona Selfa, Rick Owens and the curve-caress-
ing creations of Adam Jones), accessories (Manolos
and Pierre Hardy shoes, Carel & Rubio's gloves at 4
rue Cambon), mixed streetwear (38 rue du Mont-
Thabor) and menswear (19bis rue du Mont-Thabor).
A must for fashionistas with the means.

Kokon To Zai

48 rue Tiquetonne, 2nd (01.42.36.92.41).
M° Etienne Marcel. **Open** 11.30am-7.30pm Mon-Sat.
Credit AmEx, DC, MC, V. **Map** p402 J5.

Spot-on for uncovering the latest designer creations,
Kokon To Zai is sister to the London version of this
cutting-edge style emporiette. The neon lights and
club atmosphere in the tiny, mirrored space are in
keeping with the dark glamour of its designs.
Unique pieces straight off the catwalk share space
with creations by Alexandre et Matthieu, Marjan
Peijoski and up-and-coming Norwegian designers.

L'Eclaireur

3ter rue des Rosiers, 4th (01.48.87.10.22/
www.leclaireur.com). M° St-Paul. **Open** 11am-7pm
Mon-Sat. **Credit** AmEx, DC, MC, V. **Map** p406 L6.

Set in a dandified warehouse with iron girders,
L'Eclaireur contains the most uncompromising of

Schnap up a Schnabel at **Barbara Bui**.

the über labels' designs, including pieces by Comme
des Garçons, Helmut Lang, Martin Margiela and
Prada. On a more playful note, hurry to snap up the
stunning hand-painted and patchworked T-shirt
creations by the hugely sought-after Lola Schnabel.
Branches: 10 rue Herold, 1st (01.40.41.09.89); men
12 rue Malher, 4th (01.44.54.22.11); Galerie 26 av des
Champs-Elysées, 8th (01.45.62.12.32).

Onward

147 bd St-Germain, 6th (01.55.42.77.56).
M° St-Germain-des-Prés. **Open** 11am-7pm Mon, Sat;
10.30am-7pm Tue-Fri. **Credit** AmEx, DC, MC, V.
Map p405 G6.

Ever hungry for the most far-out design, Onward
has a rapid turnover of young talent. Currently
stocking over 20 established and up-and-coming
designers including the weird and wonderful creations of Hussein Chalayan, The People of the
Labyrinths, Martin Margiela and a good selection of
accessories designers – Tatty Devine, Pièce à
Conviction and Yazbukey, for tasters.

Camerlo

4 rue de Marignan, 8th (01.47.23.77.06).
M° Franklin D Roosevelt. **Open** 11am-1pm, 2-7pm
Mon-Sat. **Credit** AmEx, DC, MC, V. **Map** p401 E4.

Exuberant dressers who frequent this swanky area
rely on Dany Camerlo to fit them out in head-turning
style. Hence her selection of wild ideas from Russian
duo Seredin et Vassiliev or Frenchman Laurent
Mercier. For more low-key happenings she might
suggest Pascal Humbert, Alberta Ferretti or Van der
Straeten, with sleek shoes by Bruno Frisoni.

The best Nifty Nails

Institut de l'Ongle Fahi

34 rue de Ponthieu, 8th (01.42.89.36.91).
M° Franklin D Roosevelt. **Map** p401 E4.
Ten minutes to unique nail creations.

L'Onglerie

162 rue de la Convention, 15th
(01.45.30.33.00), M° Convention. **Map** p404 C9.
Bring out the dragon in you with a bit of
Chinese calligraphy on those talons.

Carlota

16 av Hoche, 8th (01.42.89.42.89).
M° Ternes. **Map** p400 D3.
Sculpture-designed falsies decorated with
fashion house logos or Hello Kitty motifs.

Institut Peggy Sage

73 av de Wagram, 17th (01.44.40.28.90).
M° Ternes. **Map** p400 C3.
Marbling effects at €45 for both hands.

Shine

30 rue de Charonne, 11th (01.48.05.80.10).
M° Bastille. **Open** 11am-7.30pm Mon-Sat.
Credit AmEx, DC, MC, V. **Map** p407 M7.
If you are looking for a funkier, more youthful batch
of cutting-edge clothes than at Maria Luisa, then
Vinci d'Helia has just what you need: sexy T-shirts
with unusual detailing, Luella's stunning chunky
knits and Earl Jeans trousers and jackets. A plethora of original if pricey accessories includes arm-
cuffs by Petite Mademoiselle and Maria Chen's
super-soft three-quarter-length white leather gloves.
Laetitia Casta and Emma de Caunes shop here.

Designer focus

Barbara Bui

23 rue Etienne-Marcel, 1st (01.40.26.43.65/
www.barbarabui.fr). M° Etienne Marcel.
Open 1-7.30pm Mon; 10.30-7.30pm Tue-Sat.
Credit AmEx, DC, MC, V. **Map** p402 J5.
Businesswomen who like to cut to the chase have a
sartorial ally in Barbara Bui. Dressed in her lean,
impeccably cut trousers, figure-hugging shirts and
jackets and dagger heels, your wish is the board's
command. If you want to be able to fit into your new
purchases, though, hold back on the delicious world
food served in her next-door café.
Branches: 43 rue des Francs-Bourgeois, 4th
(01.53.01.88.05); accessories 12 rue des Sts-Pères, 6th;
35 rue de Grenelle, 7th (01.45.44.05.14); 50 av
Montaigne, 8th (01.42.25.05.25).

Marcel Marongiu

203 rue St-Honoré, 1st (01.49.27.96.38/www.marcel-
marongiu.com). M° Tuileries. **Open** 10.30am-7.30pm
Mon-Sat. **Credit** AmEx, MC, V. **Map** p401 G4.
As if expressing his roots, this part-French, part-
Swedish designer's clothes mix sensuality with
spareness. He is fascinated by opposites, seen in his
ineffably poised jersey wool dresses with a jagged
hemline. Most impressive are his black evening
bustier dresses made of dozens of organza squares.

Martin Margiela

25bis rue de Montpensier, 1st (01.40.15.07.55).
M° Palais Royal. **Open** 11am-7pm Mon-Sat. **Credit**
AmEx, DC, MC, V. **Map** p402 H5.
The first Parisian boutique for the Belgian JD
Salinger of the fashion world (he refuses to be pho-
tographed and only gives interviews by fax) is an
immaculate white, unlabelled space. His clothes, too,
bear a blank label and are recognisable by the external white stitching and other visible techniques. Here
you can find the entire line 13, 0- and 0-10 accessories
for men and women; line 6 (women's basics), line 10
(menswear) and selected magazines and shoes.

Jean-Paul Gaultier

6 rue Vivienne, 2nd (01.42.86.05.05/
www.gaultier.fr). M° Bourse. **Open** 10am-7pm Mon-
Fri; 11am-7pm Sat. **Credit** AmEx, DC, MC, V.
Map p402 H4.

Jean-Paul Gaultier's original boutique has been
restyled as 'a modern boudoir with trapunto quilted
peach taffeta walls', where Gaultier will 'provide a
surrealist backlash to the current wave of fashion'.
Men's and women's ready-to-wear, accessories and
the cheaper JPG Jeans lines are sold here, with haute-
couture (by appointment 01.42.97.48.12) upstairs.
Branch: 40 av George V, 8th (01.44.43.00.44).

A-poc

47 rue des Francs-Bourgeois, 4th (01.44.54.07.05).
M° St-Paul. **Open** 10.30am-7.30pm Tue-Sat.
Credit AmEx, DC, MC, V. **Map** p406 L6.
Short for 'A Piece of Cloth', Issey Miyake's lab-style
boutique designed by Erwan and Ronan Bouroullec
takes a conceptual approach to how clothes are man-
ufactured. Alongside ready-to-wear cotton-Lycra
clothes are great rolls of seamless tubular wool jersey which is cut *sur mesure*. Miyake's assistants will
advise you on a unique ensemble. If you're a Miyake
maniac, check out the original shop at 3 place des
Vosges which houses the creations of Naoki
Takisawa, his latest design protégé.

Plein Sud

21 rue des Francs-Bourgeois, 4th (01.42.72.10.60).
M° St-Paul. **Open** 11am-7pm Mon-Sat. **Credit**
AmEx, MC, V. **Map** p406 L6.
Fayçal Amor's glove-tight designs are meant for the
super-waifs of this world, but don't let that faze you
if you're into spiky stilettos, skirts slit to show off
your fishnet tights and a very black, or brown,
wardrobe.
Branches: 2 pl des Victoires, 2nd (01.42.36.75.02);
70bis rue Bonaparte, 6th (01.43.54.43.06).

Maria Luisa – showcase for new designers.

Eat, Drink, Shop

Amin Kader

2 rue Guisarde, 6th (01.43.26.27.37). M° Mabillon.
Open 2-7.30pm Mon; 10.30am-7.30pm Tue-Sat.
Credit AmEx, MC, V. **Map** p406 H7.
This tiny boutique has been the fashion pros' best-kept secret – they keep coming back for the Berber couturier's superbly soft Arran-knit cashmere pullovers, fluid crêpe-de-chine trousers, raincoats dripping with elegance and hand-stitched travel bags. Kader also stocks the divine beauty products sold at the Florentine church Santa Maria Novella.

Lagerfeld Gallery

40 rue de Seine, 6th (01.55.42.75.51). M° Odéon.
Open 11am-7pm Tue-Sat. **Credit** AmEx, MC, V.
Map p407 H6.
Andrée Putman helped create this shrine to King Karl's world of stylish minimalism, where his creations and photography are exhibited. You could, of course, just sneak in to browse the latest fashion, beauty and art press scattered over the handsome round table at the front of the gallery.

Sonia Rykiel

175 bd St-Germain, 6th (01.49.54.60.60/ www.soniarykiel.fr). M° St-Germain-des-Prés.
Open 10.30am-7pm. **Credit** AmEx, DC, MC, V.
Map p406 G6.
Even if her fabrics aren't as super-soft as they once were, the queen of stripes is still producing skinny rib knitwear evoking the Left Bank babes of Sartre's time. Menswear is across the street, while two recently opened boutiques feature the younger, more affordable 'Sonia by Sonia Rykiel' collection (59 rue des Sts-Pères) and children's wear (6 rue de Grenelle – the site of her original 1966 shop).

Martine Sitbon

13 rue de Grenelle, 7th (01.44.39.84.44). M° Rue du Bac or Sèvres Babylone. **Open** 10.30am-7pm Mon-Sat. **Credit** AmEx, MC, V. **Map** p405 G7.
The scent of orange and mimosa lures you into Sitbon's vault-like store. Beneath the vast ceiling, few pieces hang on the railings, but each appears to have a secret history, born of the originality of the fabric and cut and its singular harmony, often inspired by modern art. The men's clothes will tickle you pink, too. If the prices are out of your reach, she has cute accessories and candles for under €50.

Yohji Yamamoto

3 rue de Grenelle, 7th (01.42.84.28.87). M° Sèvres Babylone or St-Sulpice. **Open** 10.30am-7.30pm Mon-Sat. **Credit** AmEx, DC, MC, V. **Map** p405 G7.
One of the few true pioneers working in the fashion industry today, Yohji Yamamoto's masterful cuts and finish are greatly inspired by the kimono and traditional Tibetan costume. His dexterity with form makes for unique shapes and styles, largely in black, but when he does colour, it's a blast of brilliance.
Branches: 47 rue Etienne Marcel, 1st
(01.45.08.82.45); Y's 25 rue du Louvre, 1st
(01.42.21.42.93); 69 rue des Sts-Pères, 6th
(01.45.48.22.56).

Comme des Garçons

*54 rue du Fbg-St-Honoré, 8th (01.53.30.27.27).
M° Madeleine or Concorde.* **Open** 11am-7pm Mon-Sat. **Credit** AmEx, DC, MC, V. **Map** p400 D3.
Rei Kawakubo's juxtaposed design ideas and revolutionary mix of materials have greatly influenced fashion over the past two decades and are superbly showcased in this fire-engine red fibreglass store. Exclusive perfume lines get a futuristic setting at Comme des Garçons Parfums (23 pl du Marché-St-Honoré, 1st/01.47.03.15.03).

Parisian chic

Agnès b

2, 3, 6, 10, 19 rue du Jour, 1st (women 01.45.08.56.56/ men 01.42.33.04.13). M° Les Halles or Etienne-Marcel. **Open** 10am-7pm Mon-Wed, Fri, Sat; 10am-9pm Thur. **Credit** AmEx, MC, V. **Map** p402 J5.
Fashions come and go but Agnès b rarely wavers from her own design vision: pure lines in excellent quality cotton, merino wool and silk. Best buys are shirts, pullovers and cardigans that keep their shape for years. The cool plan is to tour her mini-empire of women, men, children, travel and accessories outlets.
Branches: (baby/child) 83 rue d'Assas, 6th
(01.43.54.69.21); (women) 13 rue Michelet, 6th
(01.46.33.70.20); (children) 22 rue St-Sulpice, 6th
(01.40.51.70.69); (women/beauty/children/men) 6, 10,
12 rue du Vieux-Colombier, 6th (01.44.39.02.60);
(women/men) 17, 25 av Pierre 1er de Serbie, 16th
(01.47.20.22.44/01.47.23.36.69).

Bali Barret

36 rue du Mont-Thabor, 1st (01.49.26.01.75/ www.balibarret.com). M° Concorde. **Open** 2.30pm-7.30pm Mon, 10.30am-7.30pm Tue-Sat. **Credit** AmEx, MC, V. **Map** p401 G5.
This French label opened its first boutique in 2002, featuring four different colour stories each season and offering an androgynous take on classic styles, with a sexy twist. This year's easy-to-wear collection features bright primaries. Look out for the funky belts and bags and the matching stripey knickers, stockings and cotton polo necks. With a mini-menswear collection added in 2001, there are also some great soft, logoed sweatshirts.

Claudie Pierlot

1 rue Montmartre, 1st (01.42.21.38.38). M° Sentier.
Open 11am-7pm Mon-Sat. **Credit** AmEx, MC, V.
Map p402 H4.
For true Parisian chic a black beret is essential, and Claudie Pierlot can always oblige no matter what the season. Wear it with her simple, elegant tank tops and cardigans and little black suits that are so right for the office.
Branch: 23 rue du Vieux-Colombier, 6th
(01.45.48.11.96).

Corinne Cobson

*6 rue du Marché-St-Honoré, 1st (01.42.60.48.64).
M° Tuileries.* **Open** noon-7.30pm Mon; 11am-7.30pm Tue-Sat. **Credit** AmEx, MC, V. **Map** p401 G4.

Where to find the *jeunes créateurs*

Paris fashion is not just about haute couture and the established big name collections. Young designers are springing up all over the place in reaction to the conformity and conveyor-belt fashion of the established labels. If experimentation is the name of your game, then head this way for a guided tour around the best of the new faces.

Start off with the recently inaugurated **rue de la Mode**, on rue des Gardes in the 18th. In an initiative to revamp the Goutte d'Or district and showcase new talent, 14 young designers have been given low-rent space to exhibit their creations. At the moment, most concentrate on women's clothing and accessories, but Sylviane Nuffer plans to branch out into men's clothing soon. Check out her extraordinary corsets at **SN Style** (6bis rue des Gardes, 18th/ 01.42.55.11.80). Sharing her boutique are the Oriental-inspired garments of Katia Lauranti and the more classical wear of Ken Okada. Colourful Brazilian designers Marcia de Carvalho and Pierina Marinelli at No. 2 will bring sunshine back into even the dullest day.

Head up to M° Anvers next and the little boutique of German designer Danielle Telle at **M Le Maudit** (13 rue Gérando, 18th/ 01.44.53.07.23). Along with her own clubby evening wear, Telle has an eclectic, international selection by young designers,

such as the Neoprene handbags of Naoka Hirota, the reversible, shockingly-bright, tulle underwear by Lili T, and unusual jewellery using bike tyres, fluorescent and reflecting materials. Many pieces are limited editions and the prices are surprisingly reasonable.

Heading east to Gare de l'Est, **Pygmées de la Lune** (28 rue des Vinaigriers, 10th/ 01.46.07.13.73) has a range of clothes as crazy as its name for Peter Pan adults and their kids (*pictured below*). The colourful graphic clothes mix street style with infantile fantasy and sporty details.

Next stop Bastille. Run by an interior designer and an artist, **Igrek-bé** (27 rue Keller, 11th (01.49.23.50.13/www.igrek-be.biz) is dedicated to the talents of tomorrow. Many pieces are limited editions or one-offs from designers such as Dice Kayek, Hôtel du Nord and Editu et Raphaël for women, Premiers Symptomes and Impasse 13 for men.

Finally, trek out to **Universal Love** (8 rue de Mont-Louis, 11th, 01.43.48.94.68, Fri only noon-8pm or by appointment), which began as part of the Free Market nights at the Cabaret Sauvage. An exciting mixed bag takes in sexy corsets by Tuga and fabulous, military-inspired zipped jackets by Muzo, while the jewellery by the Japanese designers Kaolu Matsumoto and Aya Roppongui will provide the perfect icing on your fashion cake.

Eat, Drink, Shop

This mirror-covered boutique is frequented by Paris darlings, such as Guillaume Depardieu. Cobson favours simple lines combined with graphic prints. Check out her anti-racism and pro-environment plunge-neck T-shirts and sumptuous chunky jumpers. Photos by her partner, Tanguy Loisance, provide the decor, and humorous designs by Samuel Lebaron take pride of place in the shop window.

Abou d'Abi Bazar

10 rue des Francs-Bourgeois, 3rd (01.42.77.96.98) **Open** 2-7.15pm Mon; 10.30am-7.15pm Tue-Sat; 2-7pm Sun. **Credit** AmEx, MC, V. **Map** p401 G4.
For trendy pieces at reasonable prices, this is the place to come for all manner of creations from tops and jeans to accessories by a variety of designers (including Vanessa Bruno and Stella Forest). Everything is organised by colour, making pick 'n' mix an easy option.

A.P.C.

3, 4 rue de Fleurus, 6th (01.42.22.12.77). *Mᵒ St-Placide.* **Open** 10.30am-7pm Mon-Sat. **Credit** AmEx, MC, V. **Map** p405 G8.
Think of Muji crossed with a rough-cut Agnès b and you get an idea of A.P.C. Jean Toutou's gear is much sought after by the Japanese in-crowd. Men's clothes are at No.4, along with quirky accessories; cross the road to No.3 for the women's collection.

Comptoir des Cotonniers

59ter rue Bonaparte, 6th (01.43.26.07.56). *Mᵒ St-Germain-des-Prés.* **Open** 11am-7pm Mon; 10am-7.30pm Tue-Sat. **Credit** MC, V. **Map** p405 H6.
Sturdy cotton and wool basics for mothers and daughters who like to keep in step with fashion. Trendy touches on trousers and skirts include ruffles, lacy borders, artily distressed seams and asymmetric cutting at prices that won't break the bank. **Branches include:** 29 rue du Jour, 1st (01.53.40.75.77); 18 rue St-Antoine, 4th (01.40.27.09.08); 53 rue de Passy, 16th (01.42.88.06.30).

Diapositive

42 rue du Four, 6th (01.45.48.85.57). Mᵒ Sèvres Babylone. **Open** 10.30am-7pm Mon-Sat. **Credit** AmEx, MC, V. **Map** p406 H7.
A practical yet *soigné* range of grown-up business suits and evening wear that is good value (suits around €380). For a touch of glamour, there are gold lamé-speckled fine wool pullovers and sequin-patterned, long-sleeved T-shirts. **Branches:** 12 rue du Jour, 1st (01.42.21.34.41); 33 rue de Sèvres, 7th (01.42.44.13.00); 20 av des Ternes, 17th (01.43.80.05.87).

Irié Wash

8 rue Pré-aux-Clercs, 6th (01.42.61.18.28). Mᵒ Rue du Bac or St-Germain-des-Prés. **Open** 10.15am-7pm Mon-Sat. Closed three weeks in Aug. **Credit** MC, V. **Map** p405 F7.
Elegantly avant-garde Parisians love this Japanese designer who is constantly researching new methods and materials, including laser cutting, hologram

prints and most recently a polyester and Elastane mix, like an ultra-supple suede (€190 for a dress).

Vanessa Bruno

25 rue St-Sulpice, 6th (01.43.54.41.04). Mᵒ Odéon. **Open** 10.30am-7pm Mon-Sat. **Credit** AmEx, DC, MC, V. **Map** p406 H7.
Bruno's feminine and very individual clothes have a cool and steady Zen-like quality that no doubt comes from her stay in Japan. She also makes great bags, including the sequin-framed canvas totes which are to be seen hanging from the wrists of much of the (female) Parisian cool brigade. **Branch:** 12 rue de Castiglione, 1st (01.42.61.44.60).

Zadig et Voltaire

1 rue du Vieux-Colombier, 6th (01.43.29.18.29). Mᵒ St Sulpice. **Open** 1-7.30pm Mon; 10.30am-7.30pm Tue-Sat. **Credit** AmEx, DC, MC, V. **Map** p405 G7.
Casual wear in moody shades, besides the odd flare of neon pink or other eye-blinking tone of sweater. Currently stocking some fabulously soft silk cargo pants with this season's requisite drawstring ankles for wearing with heels at an affordable €150. **Branches:** 9 rue du 29 Juillet, 1st (01.42.92.00.80); 4, 12 rue Ste-Croix-de-la-Bretonnerie, 4th (01.42.72.09.55/01.42.72.15.20).

Corinne Sarrut

4 rue du Pré-aux-Clercs, 7th (01.42.61.71.60). Mᵒ Rue du Bac or St-Germain-des-Prés. **Open** 10am-7pm Mon-Sat. **Credit** AmEx, MC, V. **Map** p405 F7.
Fans of *Amélie* will be charmed by the work of Corinne Sarrut, who dressed Audrey Tautou for the part. In fact anyone with a weakness for silky 40s silhouette will love her trapeze creations in silky viscose. **Branches:** (previous season) 24 rue du Champ de Mars, 7th (01.45.56.00.65); 7 rue Gustave-Courbet, 16th (01.55.73.09.73); (wedding and evening) 42 rue des Sts Pères, 7th (01.45.44.19.92).

Paul et Joe

62 rue des Sts-Pères, 7th (01.40.28.03.34). Mᵒ Rue du Bac or St-Germain-des-Prés. **Open** 11am-7.30pm Mon-Sat. **Credit** AmEx, DC, MC, V. **Map** p405 G6.
Fashion victims have taken a great shine to Sophie Albou's weathered 40s-style creations (named after her sons), so much so that she has opened a menswear branch and this new flagship, with its out-to-be noticed bubblegum pink gramophone. **Branches:** 46 rue Etienne-Marcel (01.40.28.03.34); (men) 40 rue du Four, 6th (01.45.44.97.70).

Antoine et Lili

95 quai de Valmy, 10th (01.40.37.41.55). Mᵒ Gare de l'Est. **Open** 1am-7pm Mon; 11am-8pm Tue-Fri; 10.30am-8pm Sat; 11.30am-7.30pm Sun. **Credit** AmEx, DC, MC, V. **Map** p402 L3.
These fuschia-pink and apple-green shops are a colour therapist's dream. Vibrant jumpers and neo-hippy skirts hang amid Mexican shrines, Hindu postcards and all sorts of miscellaneous kitsch. The three-shop Canal St-Martin 'Village' has an equally colourful home decoration outlet, florist and café.

Eat, Drink, Shop

No chance of getting your knickers in a twist at **Fifi Chachnil**. *See p250*.

Isabel Marant – positively coated in class.

Branches: 51 rue des Francs-Bourgeois, 4th (01.42.27.95.00); 87 rue de Seine, 6th (01.56.24.35.81); 7 rue d'Alboni, 16th (01.45.27.95.00); 90 rue des Martyrs, 18th (01.42.58.10.22).

Isabel Marant

16 rue de Charonne, 11th (01.49.29.71.55).
Mº Ledru-Rollin. **Open** noon-7pm Mon; 10.30am-7.30pm Tue-Sat. **Credit** AmEx, MC, V. **Map** p407 M7.
Marant's clothes are easily recognisable by their ethno-babe brocades, blanket-like coats and decorated sweaters in luxurious materials, and the in-crowd is in hot pursuit.
Branch: 1 rue Jacob, 6th (01.43.26.04.12); 3 passage St-Sébastien, 11th (01.49.23.75.40).

Ladies & Gentlemen

4 passage Charles-Dallerey, 11th (01.47.00.86.12).
Mº Ledru-Rollin. **Open** noon-7pm Tue-Sat; 2-7pm Sun. **Credit** AmEx, DC, MC, V. **Map** p407 N7.
Amid paintings and minimalist techno, red dummies are lovingly swathed in the classic yet slightly surreal creations of Isabelle Ballu (women's) and Moritz Rogorsky (men's). Most of the clothes are temptingly hidden away in special alcoves.

Street, club & sports wear

These establishments serve the youth that pours out of the RER station, so street and sportswear outlets abound around Les Halles and Etienne-Marcel.

Clery Brice

11 rue Pierre-Lescot, 1st (01.45.08.58.70).
Mº/RER Les Halles. **Open** 11am-1pm, 2-7pm Mon-Sat. **Credit** MC, V. **Map** p402 J5.

Here you pay lofty prices to get limited editions of the coolest trainers six months before the rest of the world finds out they should be wearing them.

Le Vestibule

3 pl St-Opportune, 1st (01.42.33.21.89). Mº Châtelet.
Open 10.30am-7pm Mon-Sat. Open one Sun in every month. **Credit** AmEx, DC, MC, V. **Map** p402 J5.
An eye-popping showcase for the wildest creations of the vintage street wear and club gear genre, including exhibits by mainstream labels such as Dolce e Gabbana, Bikkembergs and Castelbajac. For effortless flash and panache, Cultura, Diesel StyleLab, Replay and its Coca-Cola Ware label are hard to beat.

Kiliwatch

64 rue Tiquetonne, 2nd (01.42.21.17.37/
www.kiliwatch.tm.fr). Mº Etienne Marcel. **Open** 2-7pm Mon; 11am-7pm Tue-Thur; 11am-8.30pm Fri; 11am-7.30pm Sat. **Credit** AmEx, MC, V. **Map** p402 J5.
The original protagonist of the Etienne-Marcel revival is filled to bursting with hoodies, casual shirts and washed-out jeans. Featured brands include G-Star and Kulte, as well as a huge selection of pricey but good-condition second-hand clothes.

Le Shop

3 rue d'Argout, 2nd (01.40.28.95.94). Mº Etienne Marcel. **Open** 1-7pm Mon; 11am-7pm Tue-Sat.
Map p402 J5.
Street-savvy teenagers hang out at this sprawling covered market with its collection of around 25 brands. Male hip-hoppers go for Homecore, Tribal, Body Cult and Triiad (also at 7 rue de Turbigo, 1st), while the girls slip into Lady Soul, Misolka and Oxyde (also at 12 rue de Turbigo).

Shops & Services: Fashion & Beauty

Tokyoïte
12 rue du Roi de Sicile, 4th (01.42.77.87.01).
M° St-Paul. **Open** 1.30-8.30pm Tue-Sun.
Credit MC, V. **Map** p406 K6.
For some Tokyo-living in Paris, check out this cute
and kitschy Goldorak-fronted boutique which specialises in Japanese imports. Ideal for Converse fans
(they stock lots of models you can't get anywhere
else in Paris) and rare Evisu bags.

Marithé et François Girbaud
7 rue du Cherche-Midi, 6th (01.53.40.74.20).
M° Sèvres-Babylone. **Open** noon-7pm Mon; 10am-
7pm Tue-Sat. **Credit** AmEx, DC, MC, V. **Map** p402 J5.
The *soixantehuitard* couple are as pioneering as
ever, producing complex street wear in high-tech
fabrics using laser cutting and welding. This
new shop has four light-filled floors and a vertical
garden of 250 plants.
Branches: 38 rue Etienne-Marcel, 2nd
(01.53.40.74.20); 20 rue Mahler, 4th (01.44.54.99.01); 8
rue de Babylone, 7th (01.45.48.78.86); 49 av Franklin-
Roosevelt, 8th (01.45.62.49.15).

Stealth
42 rue du Dragon, 6th (01.45.49.24.14).
M° St-Germain-des-Prés or St-Sulpice.
Open 2-7.30pm Mon; 10.30am-7.30pm Tue-Sat.
Credit AmEx, MC, V. **Map** p406 H7.
New York record producer and designer Marcus
Klossock is the mastermind behind this cool boutique.
His men's label Aem Kei (the phonetic rendering of
his initials) melds US street style with European
refinement, and his women's line Aem Aya has fresh
ideas. Other urban underground names to discover
here are Tsumori Chisato, Fake London, Haseltine
and the hilariously named Poetry of Sex.

View on Fashion
*27 rue des Taillandiers, 11th (01.43.55.05.03/
www.viewonfashion.com). M° Bastille.* **Open** noon-
7.30pm Mon-Sat. **Credit** DC, MC, V. **Map** p407 M7.
This latest newcomer on the urban fashion scene has
three floors of accessories, footwear, men's streetwear (Kulte, Shai Wear, Aem Kei etc) and women's
wear, with a corner devoted to one designer or brand
that changes every season. The women's selection
includes one-off, reworked vintage pieces, diago-
nally-zipped sweats and cute sweetie-coloured skirts
by Kulte, stunning layered wrap skirts by
Accostages, and Ken Okada's matching woollen
coats and caps. There are also drinks, CDs, international fashion mags and an outside terrace where
you can relax and reexamine your purchases.

Menswear

Admirers of the *BCBG* style should check out
branches of Vercourt and Berteil, or Phist and
Alain Figaret for shirts, and the international
overview of **Le Bon Marché** and **Galeries
Lafayette**. See also **Agnès b**, **Sonia Rykiel**,
Marithé et François Girbaud.

Madelios
23 bd de la Madeleine, 1st (01.53.45.00.00).
M° Madeleine. **Open** 10am-7pm Mon-Sat.
Credit AmEx, DC, MC, V. **Map** p401 G4.
A 4,500m² one-stop-shop for men's fashion over two
floors. The decor is a bit bland but then it's the
clothes that matter, including suits by Paul Smith,
Dormeuil, Givenchy and Kenzo and casuals from
Diesel and Levi's, plus shoes and accessories.

Ron Orb
39 rue Etienne-Marcel, 1st (01.40.28.09.33).
M° Etienne Marcel **Open** 11am-7pm Mon-Sat.
Credit AmEx, MC, V. **Map** p402 J5.
Forward-looking synthetic fabrics for the techno
generation and beyond come courtesy of the Breton
designer. French Touch fans should check out the
jackets with pockets to hold CDs.

L'Eclaireur Homme
12 rue Malher, 4th (01.44.54.22.11). M° St-Paul.
Open 11am-7pm Mon-Sat. **Credit** AmEx, DC,
MC, V. **Map** p406 L6.
Among the exposed ducts of this former printing
works you'll find the usual designer suspects: Prada,
Comme des Garçons, Dries Van Noten, Martin
Margiela. The star label, though, is Italian Stone
Island, whose radical technical clothing features
parkas with a 'steel outer shell' to fight pollution.

Jack Henry
54 rue des Rosiers, 4th (01.44.59.89.44). M° St-Paul.
Open 2.30-8pm daily. **Credit** AmEx, DC, MC, V.
Map p406 K6.
This thirtysomething New Yorker has been honing
his sartorial skills in Paris for over a decade. His
spare, dark suits offer a fine, elongated silhouette,
enhanced by chest-hugging knitwear. The look is
inspired by US combat gear, but this means discipline in hidden details rather than pockets in unlikely places.
Branch: (women) 1 rue Montmartre, 1st
(01.42.21.46.01).

Façonnable
9 rue du Fbg-St-Honoré, 8th (01.47.42.21.18.04).
M° Concorde. **Open** 10.30am-7pm Mon-Sat. **Credit**
AmEx, DC, MC, V. **Map** p401 F4.
The Nice-based label may be largely the domain of
the *BCBG* male, but its timeless city-slicker suits,
striped shirts and country-gent cords are of too good
a quality to be bypassed. Soft suede jackets and
checked shirts are particularly tempting.

Lanvin
15 rue du Fbg-St-Honoré, 8th (01.44.71.33.33).
M° Concorde. **Open** 10am-6.45pm Mon-Sat. **Credit**
AmEx, DC, MC, V. **Map** p401 G4.
Meltdown Prince of Wales checks for a business
suit, anyone? How's about a luxurious number of ply
cashmere sweaters? This is heady, rocking posh-
wear for those infuriating executive dudes who get
all the best chicks. The range has recently been
revamped to celebrate the arrival of Albert Elbaz.

Eat, Drink, Shop

Loft Design by

12 rue du Fbg-St-Honoré, 8th (01.42.65.59.65).
Mº Madeleine or Concorde. **Open** 10am-7pm Mon-
Sat. **Credit** AmEx, DC, MC, V. **Map** p401 F4.
Thirteen years ago, a certain likely lad named
Patrick Frêche hit upon the idea of producing clothes
that were colour-coordinated with the Paris skyline
– that's to say, heavy on the grey and black. This
turned out to be not such a dullsville idea: Loft now
has a cult following with the Paris media and fashion crowd.
Branches include: 12 rue de Sévigné, 4th
(01.48.87.13.07); 56 rue de Rennes, 6th
(01.45.44.88.99).

Slip's Home

6 rue du Grenier-St-Lazare, 3rd, (01.42.77.53.23)
Mº Rambuteau. **Open** 2-7.30pm Mon; 12-7.30pm
Tues-Sat. **Credit** V, MC, AmEx. **Map** p402 K5.
Indeed it does. Gone are the days of the harvest festival (all is safely gathered in) but there'll be thanksgiving when you see this new store that devotes
85m² to men's underwear. The pants range from the
Peter Stringfellowesque G-string to the boxer, with
brands such as Hom and Tom Robinn (his cosmetics line is also on sale here). Adi Hodzic's jewellery
creations can be snapped up here as well as belts
and other stylish accessories. Important lingo: Y-
fronts are '*slip kangourou*'. No peeping joeys, OK?

Eau, behave!

The idea of smelling good has always had a
whiff of luxury about it. In old Persia perfume
was a sign of rank, though not the odorous
kind, while in France the court of Louis XV
was known as the perfumed court – scent
was sprayed about with gay abandon, on skin,
clothes, fans and furniture.

During the 18th century wealthy French folk
set about bathing in *eau de cologne*, taking it
with their wine, plopping it on sugar cubes,
washing out their mouths with it and cleaning
out other bits (it was a popular enema). Even
the Revolution didn't dampen enthusiasm;
that's when people lost their heads to Parfum
à la Guillotine (seriously).

But there really wasn't any such thing as
women's-only or men's-only – the scented
borders blurred. And, let's face it, he-men
thought that perfume was for pussies.

Well, somewhere along the male
evolutionary scent line (circa the swinging
60s) a hint of rosemary, lemon and basil won
the everyman over. In 1966 Christian Dior
launched Eau Sauvage, the original feral
water, designed explicitly for, grrrrrrrr, real
men. Men with muscles finally had a scent,
aside from pheromones, to call their own.

It was Dior's first foray into men's
fragrances and they struck pagan gold. It
went to the top of the men's charts and is
still the number-one bestseller despite all the
new age sensitive guys out there. Forget your
Contradiction, Declaration, Boss, Envy and
Ultraviolet Man, what men want is cave man
savage. Maybe not a mastiff's bone to chew
on but at least an illusion of rawness.

Eau Sauvage is described as a perfect
marriage of crisp citrus top notes and
masculine woody undertones. They forgot to
mention the flowers: creator Edmond

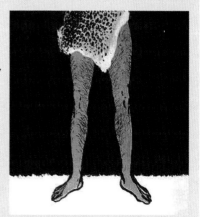

Roudnitska had the audacity to add a flower
scent (hedione, a sweet green fragrance that
occurs naturally in jasmine), which hadn't
been used previously in men's cologne.

Sylvie Husson from Christian Dior Parfums
International in Paris says that Eau Sauvage
is for a real man, an adventurer, a man with
lots of class, a real *séducteur*. So, not so
savage except in his sophistication. Eau
Sauvage is young but it's also a great classic,
she says. It's very popular in Latin countries
as well as France, she adds. And, we all know
the Latin male's reputation for seduction and
liberally slathered aftershave. Eau Sauvage is
also discreet yet truly memorable - and isn't
that how we all wish we were? Its baby
brother Eau Sauvage Extrême, created in
1984, is a more 'ardent' version... 'virile,
assertive with moments of lingering intensity'.
Who needs sex when you have cologne?

Stealth pecs a real punch. *See p247.*

Vintage, designer cast-offs & discount fashion

The craze for vintage fashion has seen second-hand clothes shops flourish, though demand ensures that bargains are rare, so you'll need to be hell-bent on good deal hunting.

Didier Ludot
19, 20 23, 24 galerie Montpensier, 1st (01.42.96.06.56/www.didierludot.com). M° Palais-Royal. **Open** 10.30am-7pm Mon-Sat. *Little black dress 125 galerie Valois, 1st (01.40.15.01.04).* **Open** 11am-7pm Mon-Sat. **Credit** AmEx, DC, V. **Map** p402 H5.
Didier Ludot's series of mini-temples to vintage haute couture have been so successful that he now has a concession in Printemps and in Harrods, his own line of little black dresses and a perfume. There's success for you. Ludot's prices are exorbitant, but then again he has stunning pieces – Molyneux, Balenciaga, Fath, Dior, Pucci, Féraud, Stern and of course Chanel, from the 1940s on.

L'Habilleur
44 rue de Poitou, 3rd (01.48.87.77.12). M° St-Sébastien-Froissart. **Open** 11am-8pm Mon-Sat. **Credit** MC, V. **Map** p402 L5.
Urban warriors prowl this slick store for its severely cut men's and women's wear by Dries Van Noten, Helmut Lang, John Richmond, Plein Sud, Martine Sitbon and Bikkembergs, and dagger-toed shoes by Patrick Cox. All the pieces, which are end-of-line or off-the-catwalk, are 50-70% off.

Alternatives
18 rue du Roi-de-Sicile, 4th (01.42.78.31.50). M° St-Paul. **Open** 11am-1pm, 2.30-7pm Tue-Sat. Closed 15 July-15 Aug. **Credit** V. **Map** p402 K6.
This stylish, if rather cramped, boutique is worth a rummage for designer cast-offs in surprisingly good condition. You might find a man's Burberry coat for around €375, women's Miu Miu high heels €120, along with wearable togs by Jean-Paul Gaultier, Comme des Garçons and Dries Van Noten.

Le Depôt-Vente de Buci-Bourbon
6 rue de Bourbon-le-Château, 6th (01.46.34.45.05). M° Mabillon. **Open** 11am-8pm daily. **Credit** MC, V. **Map** p405 H7.
These two side-by-side boutiques boast an exuberant cocktail of high-quality vintage jewellery, coffee services, wild 1950s shades and men's ties in the first, and good-condition women's retro couture, second-hand modern designer clothes and shoes in the shop next door.

Le Mouton à Cinq Pattes
19 rue Grégoire-de-Tours, 6th (01.43.29.73.56). M° Odéon. **Open** 10.30am-7.30pm Mon-Fri; 10.30am-8pm Sat. **Credit** AmEx, MC, V. **Map** p406 H7.
Designer vintage and last season's collection in mint condition: Vittadini, Klaus Thierschmidt, Buscat, Donn Adriana, Chanel and Lagerfeld. Stock turnover is very quick, so this is no time to have an indecision crisis. Labels are cut out, so make sure you know what you're buying.
Branches: 15 rue Vieille du Temple, 4th (01.42.71.86.30); 138 bd St-Germain, 6th (01.43.26.49.25).

Eat, Drink, Shop

Lingerie & swimwear

Alice Cadolle

14 rue Cambon, 1st (01.42.60.94.94/www.cadolle.fr).
M° Concorde. **Open** 9.30am-1pm Mon-Sat. **Credit**
AmEx, MC, V. **Map** p401 G4.

Five generations of lingerie by appointment are
embodied in this boutique, founded by Hermine
Cadolle, the inventor of the *brassière*. Her great,
great, granddaughter, Poupie Cadolle, continues the
tradition on the belle époque third floor. Poupie's
ready-to-wear speciality is bodices and corsets so
soigné that Christian Lacroix and Thierry Mugler
have made them an intrinsic part of their collections.

Fifi Chachnil

26 rue Cambon, 1st (01.42.60.38.86). M° Madeleine.
Open 11am-7pm Mon-Sat. **Credit** AmEx, MC, V.
Map p401 G4.

Fifi Chachnil offers a modern take on *frou-frou*
underwear in the pin-up and Agent Provacateur tradition. Her chic colour mixes, such as deep red silk
bras with boudoir pink bows and pale turquoise gir-
dles with orange trim, will have you purring with
pleasure. Transparent black babydoll negligées with
an empire-line bust are another favourite.

Sabbia Rosa

73 rue des Sts-Pères, 6th (01.45.48.88.37).
M° St-Germain-des-Prés. **Open** 10am-7pm Mon-Sat.
Credit AmEx, MC, V. **Map** p405 G7.

Settle yourself on the soft green leather sofa in this
lingerie heaven and let Moana Moatti slip on feather-
trimmed satin mules or spread before you satin, silk

and chiffon negligées in delicious shades of tanger-
ine, lemon, mocha, pistachio. All sizes are medium,
others are made *sur mesure*; prices are the cheap side
of extortionate for a slice of exquisite luxury.

Erès

2 rue Tronchet, 8th (01.47.42.28.82). M° Madeleine.
Open 10am-7pm Mon-Sat. **Credit** AmEx, DC, MC,
V. **Map** p401 G4.

Don't be misled by the demure interior of this boutique: the label's beautifully cut, minimalist bikinis
and swimsuits are red-hot and designed to make a
splash. A big advantage for the natural woman is
that the top and bottom can be purchased in different sizes, or you can buy just one piece of a bikini –
should decide you don't want all your bases covered.
Branches: 4bis rue du Cherche-Midi, 6th
(01.45.44.95.54); 40 av Montaigne, 8th (01.47.23.07.26);
6 rue Guichard, 16th (01.46.47.45.21).

Izka

140 rue du Fbg-St-Honoré, 8th (01.43.59.07.07).
M° St-Philippe du Roule. **Open** 10am-7pm Mon-Sat.
Credit AmEx, MC, V. **Map** p400 D3.

Launched in 1999, Gérard Petit's sporty, seamless
lingerie has already been snapped up by Warners.
The ten skimpy sets of bras and pants in microfibre
(one is tempted to collect the whole collection, for
fear of being caught short) have accompanying vests
and you can mix and match the colours and models
to cause gasps of admiration. Prices go from €30
for a seamless bra to around €90 for the seriously
wired model (and let's face it, most models are
seriously wired).
Branch: 74 rue de Rennes, 6th (01.45.49.25.85).

Go on, lose your head at **Ron Orb**. *See p247.*

Eyewear

Traction

6 rue du Dragon, 6th (01.42.22.28.77). Mº St-Germain-des-Prés. **Open** 2-7pm Mon, 10.30-7pm Tue-Sat. **Credit** AmEx, DC, MC, V. **Map** p406 H7.
Gone are the days when glasses were mere devices to help you see; this brand, owned by the Gros family, marries four generations of know-how with a keen sense of modernity. Try the heavy metal specs that are super-light when worn, or the conversation-making frames with quirky details on the shaft (always an ice-breaker, that).

Alain Mikli

74 rue des Sts-Pères, 7th (01.53.63.87.40). Mº Sèvres-Babylone. **Open** 10am-7pm Mon-Sat. **Credit** AmEx, DC, MC, V. **Map** p405 G7.
This wizard French spectacle designer was among the first to inject some vroom into prescription peepers. His signature material is cellulose acetate, a wood and cotton mix sliced from blocks. The Starck-designed boutique has a central glass counter where the colourful frames are laid out like designer sweeties, while upstairs Mikli's collection of 'travel wear' is displayed in an 18th-century setting.
Branch: 1 rue des Rosiers, 4th (01.42.71.01.56).

Lafont

11 rue Vignon, 8th (01.47.42.25.93). Mº Madeleine. **Open** 10am-7pm Mon-Sat. **Credit** AmEx, MC, V. **Map** p401 G4.
Philippe Lafont carries on the impeccable, hand-finished work of his grandfather. The speciality of Philippe's designer wife (that's as in: wife who works as a designer) Laurence is small oval frames that tilt upwards like cat's eyes, perfect, of course, for those small, elfin faces.
Branches: 2 rue Duphot, 1st (01.42.60.01.02); 17 bd Raspail, 7th (01.45.48.24.23).

Hats

Jacques Le Corre

193 rue St-Honoré, 1st (01.42.96.96.40). Mº Tuileries. **Open** 10am-7pm Mon-Sat. **Credit** AmEx, MC, V. **Map** p401 G4.
This flamboyant Breton experiments with textures and pigments to create daywear hats and berets in unusual fabrics. The shopper reaps the rewards of these experiments. Some of his large lambskin bags have bead patterns stamped on them like Braille; others are dyed in fiery red or warm terracotta.

Philippe Model

33 pl du Marché St-Honoré, 1st (01.42.96.89.02). Mº Pyramides. **Open** 10am-7pm Mon-Sat. **Credit** AmEx, DC, MC, V. **Map** p401 H5.
With his exuberant colours and two-tone designs, Model is your man if you're determined to stand out in the wedding, racing or boating crowd. Prices from around €50 for a beret to over €3,000 for a sumptuous, *sur mesure* headdress.

Marie Mercié

23 rue St-Sulpice, 6th (01.43.26.45.83). Mº Odéon. **Open** 11am-7pm Mon-Sat. **Credit** AmEx, DC, MC, V. **Map** p405 H7.
Mercié's inspirations make you wish you were in an era when hat wearing was *de rigueur*. What fun to step out in a creation shaped like curved fingers complete with shocking-pink nail varnish and a pink diamond ring, or a beret like a face with huge turquoise eyes and red lips. Ready-to-wear starts at around €30. Made-to-measure takes ten days.

Tête en l'Air

65 rue des Abbesses, 18th (01.46.06.71.19). Mº Abbesses. **Open** 10.30am-7.30pm Mon-Sat. Closed Aug. **No credit cards. Map** p402 H1.
You know what they say: if you can't fight, wear a big hat. Couture duo Thomas and Anana have been creating wayward hats for attention-seeking Parisians for eight years. Among Anana's favourite creations is a Bacchus-style, overflowing goblet worn by a client at Longchamp. Prices start at around €50.

Jewellery

In this city of artisans there is certainly no lack of jewellery designers. Here is a small selection of the best to suit all tastes and pockets.

Cerize

380 rue St-Honoré, 1st (01.42.60.84.84). Mº Concorde. **Open** 10am-7pm Mon-Sat. **Credit** AmEx, DC. MC V. **Map** p401 G4.
Behind the gaudy window displays, this boudoir-pink boutique has impressively crafted costume jewellery. Look out, too, for the evening bags with embroidery by François Lesage, embroiderer to all the star couturiers, and some seriously eye-popping T-shirts.

Satellite

10 rue Dussoubs, 2nd (01.55.34.95.70). Mº Réaumur-Sébastopol. **Open** 10am-7pm Mon-Sat. **Credit** AmEx, MC, V. **Map** p402 K5.
Stylist Sandrine Dulon uses only the best-quality material from the Czech Republic and Bavaria. We would expect nothing less. The brilliance of the stones and intricacy of the work results in enchanting earrings, bracelet and necklace ensembles. Prices range from €9 to €660.
Branches: 15 rue du Cherche-Midi, 6th (01.45.44.67.06); 23 rue des Francs-Bourgeois, 4th (01.40.29.45.77).

La Licorne

38 rue Sévigné, 4th (01.48.87.84.43). Mº St-Paul. **Open** 12-6.30pm daily. **Credit** AmEx, DC, MC, V. **Map** p406 L6.
The musty smell at La Licorne is perhaps not surprising given it harbours the contents of a costume jewellery factory dating from 1925-30s. Anyway, don't be put off by the whiff (how many times have you heard that, girls?). Besides the abundance of art

Eat, Drink, Shop

deco Bakelite, there is a veritable treasure trove of 50s diamanté, as well as some 19th-century jet. One word of warning - if you're coming from afar, it's always best to ring first.

Galerie Hélène Porée
1 rue de l'Odéon, 6th (01.43.54.17.00). M° Odéon. **Open** 11am-7pm Tue-Sat. **Credit** AmEx, MC, V. **Map** p406 H7.
Around 40 international ultra-minimalist jewellery designers are represented in this starch-white gallery. The French contingent includes Chavent, with his trompe l'oeil pieces, and Schotard, who creates an intriguing mousse-like effect using precious metals.

Irina Volkonski
45 rue Madame, 6th (01.42.22.02.37). M° St-Sulpice. **Open** 10am-7pm Mon-Sat. **Credit** AmEx, MC, V. **Map** p405 G7.
This young Russian creates affordable costume jewellery with a surreal flair, using materials ranging from Plexiglass to wood harvested after the great gale to resin sushi.

Kathy Korvin
13 rue de Tournon, 6th (01.56.24.06.66) M° Odéon. **Open** 10am-7pm Mon-Fri; 11am-7pm Sat. **Credit** AmEx, MC, V. **Map** p406 H7.
This Franco-American jeweller specialises in spider's web-thin silver necklaces and bracelets encircling semi-precious stones, feathers and Swarovski crystals. Her necklaces with nests of fine crocheted gold or silver are particularly elfin. Prices start at around €23 for simple silver earrings.

La Reine Margot
7 quai de Conti, 6th (01.43.26.62.50). M° Pont Neuf. **Open** 10.30am-1pm, 2-7pm Mon-Sat. **Credit** AmEx, DC, MC, V. **Map** p406 H6.
Gilles Cohen, proprietor of this beautiful antiques gallery, invites international jewellers to create modern pieces using ancient stones, amulets and seals. This approach results in some truly exquisite pieces designed by masters of their craft and prices are surprisingly reasonable.

Shoes & bags

Printemps' luxury floor is an excellent source of designer labels, including Hermès shoemaker Pierre Hardy, now making a name solo. Rue du Dragon in the 6th is crammed with boutiques offering young designers' creations.

Christian Louboutin
19 rue Jean-Jacques Rousseau, 1st (01.42.36.05.31). M° Palais Royal. **Open** 10.30am-7pm Mon-Sat. Closed Aug. **Credit** AmEx, DC, MC, V. **Map** p402 J5.
Each of Louboutin's creations, with their hallmark red soles, are displayed in individual frames, like Cinderella's slipper. His Trash mules – incorporating used Métro tickets, glitter, torn letters and

postage stamps – are particularly coveted.
Branch: 38 rue de Grenelle, 7th (01.42.22.33.07).

Rodolphe Menudier
14 rue de Castiglione, 1st (01.42.60.86.27). M° Concorde or Tuileries. **Open** 10.30am-7.30pm Mon-Sat. **Credit** AmEx, MC, V. **Map** p401 G5.
This silver and black cylinder of a boutique is a perfect setting for Menudier's racy designs, which mix moods and materials. Dozens of open, silver-handled drawers display his stilettos laid flat in profile. Mini shopping trolleys are filled with wayward shades of exclusive hosiery made by Gerbé and Chantal Thomass. If that's not pampering enough, then slip upstairs for a RM pedicure or a spot of reflexology and let your feet know just how much you love them.

Alain Tondowski
13 rue de Turbigo, 2nd (01.42.36.44.34). M° Etienne Marcel. **Open** 10.30am-7.30pm Mon-Sat. **Credit** AmEx, MC, V. **Map** p402 J5.
No clumpy shit-crushers here: Tondowski's shoes bring to mind the footnotes of a fashion illustration – a few perfectly executed squiggles. His super-elegant designs (from around €300) have a taut, urban edge, highlighted by the boutique with shoes framed in polished metal and Plexiglass.

Lollipops
60 rue Tiquetonne, 2nd (01.42.33.15.72). M° Etienne Marcel. **Open** 11am-7pm Mon-Sat. **Credit** AmEx, MC, V. **Map** p402 J5.

Eat, Drink, Shop

Millinery magic at **Marie Mercié**. *See p251.*

Eat, Drink, Shop

This fast-growing bag outlet caters for virtually every possible taste, colour and material. There are Manga-inspired retro shoppers with Lichtenstein car prints, crunchy green leather purses and lacy red clutch bags for extra Moulin Rouge flounce. They also have great badges and brooches.

Gelati
6 rue St-Sulpice, 6th (01.43.25.67.44). Mº Odéon.
Open 10am-7pm Mon-Sat. **Credit** MC, V.
Map p405 H7.
If you want your feet to be always in vogue but can't afford designer prices, then go for Gelati. The once-Italian (now French) company offers a stylish range of court and evening shoes in the hippest shapes and colours. Prices start at around €120.

Hervé Chapelier
1 rue du Vieux-Colombier, 6th (01.44.07.06.50). Mº St-Sulpice. **Open** 10.15am-7pm Mon-Fri, 10.15am-7.15pm Sat. **Credit** AmEx, MC, V. **Map** 405 G7.
Number-one stop for the ultimate classic in chic, bi-coloured, hard-wearing totes. Often copied, but never quite equalled, they are available in pretty much every colour under the sun. Choose from a dinky purse at €22, working your way up the size and price range to a stonking weekend bag at €130.

Peggy Huyn Kinh
11 rue Coëtlogon, 6th (01.42.84.83.83). Mº St-Sulpice. **Open** 10am-7pm Mon-Sat. **Credit** AmEx, MC, V. **Map** p405 G7.

This street may not scream fashion, but that does not deter Peggy Huyn Kinh, former creative director for Cartier and other luxury heavyweights, whose bags may use boarskin or python. She does minimalist silver jewellery, too.

Robert Clergerie
5 rue du Cherche-Midi, 6th (01.45.48.75.47). Mº St-Sulpice. **Open** 10am-7pm Mon-Sat. **Credit** AmEx, MC, V. **Map** p405 G7.
Clergerie has thankfully settled back into designing his exquisitely practical daywear. The maestro has even revived that two-tone loafer he created at the start of his career in 1981. Not that he is out of the fashion ring: his stylised 'boxing trainer', Tatoue, knocks the socks off other models.
Branches: 46 rue Croix des Petits Champs, 1st (01.42.61.49.24); 18 av Victor-Hugo, 16th (01.45.01.81.30).

Iris
28 rue de Grenelle, 7th 01.42.22.89.81). Mº Rue du Bac. **Open** 10.30am-7pm Mon-Sat. **Credit** AmEx, MC, V. **Map** p405 F7.
Iris is the Italian manufacturer of shoes by Marc Jacobs, Ernesto Esposito, Alessandro Dell'Acqua and Véronique Branquino: their entire footwear range is in this dazzling white boutique. Esposito's pieces are recognisable by their flower patterns.

Jamin Puech
61 rue de Hauteville, 10th (01.40.22.08.32). Mº Poissonnière. **Open** 10am-2pm, 3-7pm Mon-Sat.

Credit MC, V. **Map** p402 K3.

The full collection of Isabelle Puech and Benoît Jamin's dazzling handbags, which use everything from tapestry and raffia to sequins, are on show in a boho setting complete with antler-horn chairs.

Sandrine Léonard

5 passage Charles-Dallery, 11th (01.47.00.09.94).
M° Ledru-Rollin. **Open** 2-7pm Tue-Sat. **Credit** AmEx, MC, V. **Map** p407 M7.

Slightly off the beaten track, this boutique houses Léonard's classic feminine line and her streetwear offshoot DUP (Déplacements Urbains de Proximité), featuring colourful nylon shoppers and Primary-coloured wool bags with wood handles and contrasting detailing which will brighten any outfit.

Perfume & make-up

By Terry

21 passage Véro Dodat, 1st (01.44.76.00.76).
M° Palais-Royal. **Open** 10.30am-7pm Mon-Sat.
Credit AmEx, MC, V. **Map** p402 H5.

Terry de Gunzburg, the alchemist behind Yves Saint Laurent's cosmetics for 15 years, offers exclusive made-to-measure 'haute couleur' make-up, concocted upstairs by a team of chemists and colourists, who combine high-tech treatments and hand-finished precision. There's also a prêt à porter line.
Branches: 1 rue Jacob, 6th (01.46.34.00.36); 10 av Victor-Hugo, 16th (01.55.73.00.73).

Galérie Noémie

17 rue du Cygne, 1st (01.44.76.06.26/
www.galerienoemie.com). M° Etienne Marcel. **Open** 1-7.30pm Tue-Sat. **Credit** DC, MC, V. **Map** p402 J5

You can tell Noémie is a painter, not just by the name of the boutique but by the way all the make-up is set out in palettes. The products don't just look pretty; they actually do their funky stuff. Little pots of gloss (a very reasonable €7.50) in myriad colours triple as lip gloss, eyeshadow or blusher. This place is proof that God wears make-up.

Stéphane Marais

217 rue St-Honoré, 1st (01.42.61.73.22).
M° Tuileries. **Open** 10.30am-7.30pm Mon-Sat.
Credit AmEx, MC, V. **Map** p401 G5.

The first boutique of the acclaimed make-up artist to the designers may be a bit painfully self-conscious for the casual shopper. These are the risks one takes. Architect-designed, original tubes, pots and compact holders vie for attention with an eclectic selection of contemporary art.

Paris' pulchritude parlours

Come on! Slather on some mud, roll around in seaweed, get hosed down, and who knows; that perfect French silhouette could soon be lurking just beneath that fluffy towel.

Facials are the thing at **Anne Sémonin** (Le Bristol, 108 rue du Fbg-St-Honoré, 8th 01.42.66.24.22/M° Miromesnil), delicious ones with basil, lavender, lemongrass, ginger and plant essences. Try the 'New Package' which includes an energising massage, an absolutely divine facial mask that smells and feels so good you'll have to fight the urge to lick it off, a seaweed bath for your back, plus a reflexologist studying your feet to see how every little thing is holding up. Facial and body treatments €60 to €135.

Institute Pyrène (2 rue Gréffulhe, 8th, 01.42.68.08.10/M° Madeleine) might look a bit clinical, but what do you expect from a place that can break down and liquefy stubborn cellulite lumps (using CelluM6 and ultrasound) and roll them out like a pie crust. They also do permanent make-up application. Treatments start at €54.

Orlane's line of skincare products promises to do to you what the name implies: 'B21'. Splurge on a full day's peeling, remodelling and coiffing at **Institut Orlane** (163 av Victor-Hugo, 16th, 01.47.04.65.00/M° Victor Hugo) and gush at the new head-to-toe you. Prices range from €30 to €370.

Bioline (19 rue Washington, 8th, 01.42.89.65.55/M° George V) takes the natural food store approach to beauty, with its stocks of herbal teas and tonics, specialised body creams and gels and toning machines. Try palpitating, hip-to-toe boots that get the blood going, or sit in a bath of warm water and Dead Sea salts and get a high-pressure hose-down (so rare these days, girls). Treatments €49 to €63.

If you're just looking to get the job done without a lot of hoopla, **Reeva** (10 rue Vivienne, 2nd, 01.47.03.67.00/M° Bourse) is for you. It also boasts some of the lowest prices in town, including hair removal from €8.90 and facials for €29. They also have slimming machines.

Institute Payot (10 rue de Castiglione, 1st, 01.42.60.32.87/M° Concorde, the former home of Countess Castiglione, is as beautifully preserved as its clientele. Created by one of the leading females in French skincare, Payot, it runs the gamut of luxurious face and body treatments. Treatments range from €40 to €80.

L'Artisan Parfumeur

24 bd Raspail, 7th (01.42.22.23.32). M° Rue du Bac.
Open 10.30am-7pm Mon-Sat. **Credit** AmEx, DC,
MC, V. **Map** p405 G7.
Among scented candles, potpourri and charms, you
will find the best vanilla perfume Paris can offer –
Mûres et Musc, a bestseller for over 20 years.

Editions de Parfums Frédéric Malle

*37 rue de Grenelle, 7th (01.42.22.77.22). M° Rue de
Bac.* **Open** 11am-7pm Mon-Sat. **Credit** AmEx, MC,
V. **Map** p405 F6.
Choose from eight perfumes made for Frédéric
Malle, former consultant for Lacroix, Chaumet and
Hermès. This is minimalism taken to the extreme.

Guerlain

*68 av des Champs-Elysées, 8th (01.45.62.52.57/
www.guerlain.fr). M° Franklin D Roosevelt.* **Open**
10.30am-8pm Mon-Sat; 3-7pm Sun. **Credit** AmEx,
MC, V. **Map** p401 E4.
This bijou boutique is one of the last vestiges of
the golden age of the Champs-Elysées, although the
family sold the company to LVMH some years ago.
Head 'nose' Jean-Paul Guerlain is still producing outstanding creations, such as the Aqua Allegorica
range, including the sublime Eau de Pamplun.

Make Up For Ever Professional

*5 rue La Boétie, 8th (01.42.66.01.60).
M° Miromesnil.* **Open** 10am-7pm Mon-Sat. Closed
Sat in Aug. **Credit** AmEx, DC, MC, V.
Map p401 E3.
With truckloads of glitter, nail varnish, lipstick, fake
eyelashes and stick-on tattoos, prepare for a colour
explosion from this outfit beloved of the catwalk
make-up pros.
Branch: 22 rue de Sèvres, 7th (01.45.48.75.97).

Parfums Caron

*34 av Montaigne, 8th (01.47.23.40.82).
M° Franklin D Roosevelt.* **Open** 10am-6.30pm Mon-
Sat. **Credit** AmEx, DC, MC, V. **Map** p401 E4.
In its elegant art deco boutique, Caron sells re-
editions of its classic favourites from 1911-54.

Sephora

*70 av des Champs-Elysées, 8th (01.53.93.22.50/
www.sephora.fr). M° Franklin D Roosevelt.*
Open 10am-midnight Mon-Sat; noon-midnight Sun.
Credit AmEx, MC, V. **Map** p401 E4.
The flagship of this cosmetic supermarket chain carries 12,000 French and foreign brands of scent and
slap. Sephora Blanc (14 cour St-Emilion, 12th/
01.40.02.97.79) features ethnic beauty products.

If you want to feel real nice just ask the Ayurvedic reflexologist's advice.

White, bright and minimalist **Nu Light** (9 rue
Elzevir, 3rd, 01 42.72.66.61/M° Chemin
Vert) specialises in hair removal by Epilight,
a machine that uses light impulses — a less
painful and longer-lasting alternative to waxing
(€76-€610). Nu Light's 'pure vitamin'
concoctions are designed to isolate 'pure'
Vitamin E to keep youthful juices in, and
'fresh' Vitamin C to keep wrinkles out. A
'complete facial' lasts about 90 minutes and
costs €91. You can also de-stress with an
Ayurvedic massage (€76).
    Massages are the name of the game at
Lancôme (29 rue du Fbg-St-Honoré, 8th,
01.42.65.30.74/M° Madeleine). Try the
'Mineral Treatment' featuring a massage with
flat, smooth Arizona desert stones that have
been warmed and rubbed in oil, or 'Flash
Bronzer', a massage using self-tanning
creams. Facials €68 to €136, body

▶

Children

Stylish, well-made clothes for children under 15, with plenty of the fancy buckles, funky pockets, Velcro and clever details that appeal to kids.

Children's clothes & shoes

Young urban sophisticates head for Gap, Agnès b, Zara and **Bill Tornade Enfants** (or Baby Dior and Gucci if you've got the dosh). For classic French *BCBG*, rush to Bonpoint or **Jacadi**; for cheap-and-cheerful try **Du Pareil au Même** and Tout Compte Fait. There are clusters of shops on rue du Faubourg St-Antoine, rue Bréa and rue Vavin.

Les Petits Bourgeois

35 rue de Turenne, 3rd (01.48.04.38.88). M° St Paul. **Open** 10am-7pm daily. **Credit** AmEx, MC. **Map** p406 L6.

Classy clothes and shoes (Burberry, Timberland, Charabia etc). Prices range from expensive to extortionate, with a few cheaper (and funkier) options.

Jean Bourget

167 rue St-Jacques, 5th (01.44.07.03.48). RER Luxembourg. **Open** 10am-7pm Mon-Sat. **Credit** MC, V. **Map** p406 J8.

Bill Tornade Enfants

32 rue du Four, 6th (01.45.48.73.88). M° St-Germain des Prés. **Open** 10.30am-7pm Mon-Fri, 10.30am-7.30pm Sat. Closed Aug. **Credit** AmEx, MC, V. **Map** p405 H7.

Designer Sylvia Rielle's sophisticated children's wear in shiny modern fabrics is more for trendy parties than everyday rolling around on the floor.
Branch: 1 rue de Turbigo, 3rd (01.42.21.35.52).

Jacadi

76 rue d'Assas, 6th (01.45.44.60.44/www.jacadi.fr). M° Vavin. **Open** 10am-7pm Mon-Sat. **Credit** MC, V. **Map** p405 G8.

Jacadi's well-made child and babywear – pleated skirts, smocked dresses, dungarees and fair isle knits – are a favourite with well-to-do parents, and there's some funkier party stuff too.
Branches include: 9 av de l'Opéra, 1st (01.49.27.06.29); 4 av des Gobelins, 5th (01.43.31.43.90).

Petit Bâteau

26 rue Vavin, 6th (01.55.42.02.53). M° Vavin. **Open** 10am-7pm Mon-Sat. **Credit** MC, V. **Map** p405 G8.

▶ Paris' pulchritude parlours

treatments €74 to €149.

Staff at **Saranah** (1 rue Bosio, 16th, 01.40.50.12.05/M° Michel-Ange Auteuil) mix up honey and citrus fruits into a gooey mass that they then plop on and pull off repeatedly, along with unwanted hairs. The 'Oriental technique' has several advantages compared to traditional waxing. It's all natural, which means less ingrown hairs, breakouts, and irritation. Hair removal €16 to €77.

Die-hard fashionistas trust **Carlota** (15 rue de Sablonville, Neuilly-sur-Seine, 01.47.47.12.12/M° Porte Maillot) to make their digits dazzle. As well as manicures and pedicures, they also do numerous other body treatments. Manicures €34 to €84.

Anne Villard (105-109 rue du Fbg-St-Honoré, 8th, 01.56.88.12.13/M° St-Philippe du Roule) offers the total experience: a boutique at street level, a hair salon on the mezzanine, and downstairs, behind the golden doors, face and body treatments. If you're a Sisley fan, try the 'botanique' facial (€105). Treatments range from €67 to €130.

Le Amak (45 av George V, 8th (01.40.73.40.73/M° George V) is the anti-stress address in Paris. This Zen den with wood and bamboo furnishings, palm trees and trickling water offers a variety of

massages, including a 'holistic' one based on a reading of your tarot cards. Try the full body exfoliation with a mix of salt, lime, and tequila, followed by an ultra-relaxing massage with essential oils. Face and body treatments range from €54 to €153.

Wander up the cobblestones at **32 Montorgueil** (32 rue Montorgueil, 1st (01.55.80.71.40 M°/RER Les Halles) for a €300 revamp by hair-on-film guru John Nollet, or a €160 cut by an underling. Then proceed to Spa Nuxe for their all-natural '4F Radiance Booster' (€55) which features fruits, fibres, flowers and foliage. Facials cost €40-€99, body treatments €65-€150.

It's a man's world at **Nickel** (48 rue des Francs-Bourgeois, 3rd, 01.42.77.41.10/ M° Rambuteau). They do numerous boys-only face and body treatments, including 'Corps de Glace' which is designed to soothe muscles after too many gym jaunts. Treatments cost €10-€55.

Hammams

Acclimatise gently in the main room, then sweat it out in the hotter steam room or sauna for as long as you can bear it. Follow your sweat session with a *gommage* (exfoliation with a rough mitt), then a massage. Hammams are normally single-sex – for mixed days take a swimming costume. Towels, flip-flops and

Petit Bâteau is the place for comfy cotton T-shirts, vests and other separates in a myriad of colours and cuts (also currently seen adorning the bodies of the rich and famously thin).
Branches: 81 rue de Sèvres, 7th (01.45.49.48.38); 116 av des Champs-Elysées, 8th (01.40.74.02.03).

Bonton

82 rue de Grenelle, 7th (01.44.39.09.20). M° Rue du Bac. **Open** 10am-7pm Mon-Sat. **Credit** AmEx, DC, MC, V. **Map** p401 F6.
A new kind of concept store for kids and their trendy parents has been set up by Irène and Thomas Cohen in this well-designed loft space. T-shirts, skirts and trousers come in rainbow colours, but the prices are a little steep. There is also a selection of kids' furniture, gadgets, bedlinen, Indian jewellery and hair accessories, plus a children's hairdresser on site.

Six Pieds Trois Pouces

223 bd St-Germain, 7th (01.45.44.03.72). M° Solférino. **Open** 10am-7pm Mon-Sat. Closed Mon in Aug. **Credit** AmEx, V. **Map** p405 F6.
An excellent range of children's and teens' shoes goes from classics by Startrite, Aster and Little Mary to trendy Reeboks and Timberlands, as well as shoes under its less expensive own label.

Branches include: 85 rue de Longchamp, 16th (01.45.53.64.21); 78 av de Wagram, 17th (01.46.22.81.64).

Du Pareil au Même

15-17 rue des Mathurins (Maison at 23), 8th (01.42.66.93.80). M° Havre-Caumertin/RER Auber. **Open** 10am-7pm Mon-Sat. **Credit** MC, V. **Map** p401 G3.
Colourful, hard-wearing basics (three months to 14 years) at remarkably low prices; although note that sizes tend to run small. DPAM Maison or DPAM Bébé serving 0 to three months is great for gifts.
Branches include: 122 rue du Fbg-St-Antoine (Maison at 120), 12th (01.43.44.67.46); 6 rue de l'Ouest (Maison at 15), 14th (01.43.20.59.51).

Toy & book shops

Cosy traditional toyshops abound in Paris. Department stores all provide animated windows and gigantic toy floors at Christmas. The best sources of children's books in English are WH Smith and Brentano's (*see p261*).

La Grande Récré

27 bd Poissonnière, 2nd (01.40.26.12.20). M° Grands Boulevards. **Open** 10am-7.30pm Mon-Sat. **Credit** AmEx, MC, V. **Map** p402 J4.

robes are sometimes given on entry.
Hammam de la Grande Mosquée *1 pl du Puits-de-l'Ermite, 5th (01.43.31.18.14). M° Censier Daubenton.* **Open** (women) 10am-9pm Mon, Wed, Sat; 2-9pm Fri; (men) 2-9pm

Tue; 10am-9pm Sun. Hammam €15; *gommage* €10; massage €10. **Credit** DC, MC, V. Admidst murmuring voices and Arabic music, clients are steamed, scrubbed and massaged in this 1920s mosque.
Hammam Med Centre *43-45 rue Petit, 19th (01.42.02.31.05/www.hammammed.com.). M° Ourcq.* **Open** (women) 11am-10pm Mon-Fri; 10am-8pm Sun; (mixed) 10am-8pm Sat. Hammam and *gommage* €34. 'Forfait florale' €119. **Credit** MC, V. The hammam experience here is hard to beat – spotless, mosaic-tiled surroundings; flowered sarongs and even a pool – but the reason to come is Sonia Benothman, their pioneering masseuse, who literally wraps you in rose petals in her 'Rose de Nuit' treatment, using rare *huile d'Argan* from Morocco.
Les Bains du Marais *31-33 rue des Blancs-Manteaux, 4th (01.44.61.02.02/ www.lesbainsdumarais.com). M° Archives.* **Open** (women) 11am-8pm Mon; 11am-11pm Tue; 10am-7pm Wed; (men) 11am-11pm Thur; 10am-8pm Fri; 10am-8pm Sat; (mixed) 7-11pm Mon; 11am-11pm Sun. Hammam only €30; massage and *gommage* €30. **Credit** V. This chic hammam and spa mixes modern (showers) and traditional (lounging beds and mint tea). Facials, waxing and essential oil massages are also available. Hey, you deserve it!

Eat, Drink, Shop

Bags of fashion at **Hervé Chapelier**. *See p253.*

The French toy supermarket (local rival to Toys R Us) may lack the charm of more trad compatriots but its shelves are packed high: pink and plastic for girls, guns and cars for boys, plus craft sets and Playdoh, Gameboys, Pokémon spin-offs and the like.

Chantelivre

13 rue de Sèvres, 6th (01.45.48.87.90). M° Sèvres-Babylone. **Open** 1-7pm Mon; 10am-7pm Tue-Sat. **Credit** MC, V. **Map** p405 G7.

This specialist children's bookshop leads from teen reads to picture books and a baby section. There are publications on children's health and psychology for parents, a small English-language section, plus CDs, videos, paints, stationery and party supplies.

Fnac Junior

19 rue Vavin, 6th (01.56.24.03.46). M° Vavin. **Open** 10am-7.30pm Mon-Sat. **Credit** AmEx, MC, V. **Map** p405 G8.

The Fnac group has turned its hand to books, toys, videos, CDs and CD-roms for under-12s. Many things take an educational slant but there are fun basics, too. The shop lays on storytelling and activities (mainly Wed, Sat) for three-year-olds and up. **Branches:** cour St-Emilion, 12th (01.44.73.01.58); 148 av Victor-Hugo, 16th (01.45.05.90.60).

Pain d'Epices

29 passage Jouffroy, 9th (01.47.70.08.68). M° Grands Boulevards. **Open** 12.30-7pm Mon; 10am-7pm Tue-Thur; 10am-9pm Fri, Sat. **Credit** MC, V. **Map** p402 H4.

Everything a self-respecting doll would need, from cutlery to toothpaste. There are also dolls' house kits or the finished thing, and trad dolls and teddies.

Apache

84 rue du Fbg-St-Antoine, 12th (01.53.46.60.10/ www.apache.fr). M° Ledru-Rollin. **Open** 10am-8pm Mon-Sat. **Credit** MC, V. **Map** p407 M7.

The shape of toyshops to come. A brightly lit, colourful two-storey space with an activities studio and cyber-café. Equally colourful goodies go from marbles and soft toys to fancy dress, space hoppers and videos. There's also furniture and bath gear.

La Maison du Cerf-Volant

7 rue de Prague, 12th (01.44.68.00.75). M° Ledru-Rollin. **Open** 10am-7pm Tue-Sat. **Credit** V. **Map** p407 M7.

Every kind of kite: dragons, galleons, scary insects and acrobatic stunt kites. If it flies, it's here.

Les Cousines d'Alice

36 rue Daguerre, 14th (01.43.20.24.86). M° Denfert-Rochereau. **Open** 10am-1.30pm, 2.30-7.15pm Mon; 10am-7.15pm Tue-Sat; 11am-1pm Sun. Closed three weeks in Aug. **Credit** MC, V. **Map** p405 G10.

This shop is crammed with soft toys, well-selected books and construction games. There are also plenty of inexpensive pocket-money treats.

Pylones

57 rue St-Louis-en-l'île, 4th (01.46.34,05.02). M° Pont Marie. **Open** 10.30am-7.30pm daily. **Credit** AmEx, MC, V. **Map** p406 K7.

Hilarious gadgets and knick-knacks for kids and kids-at-heart. Furry pencil cases, painted bike bells, Ben baby bottles, animated postcards and Wallace and Gromit toothbrushes.

Home & Gifts

Antiques & flea markets

Knowing who specialises in what is essential for antique buying in Paris, so here are a few tips. Classy traditional antiques can be found in the **Louvre des Antiquaires** (*see p83*), **Carré Rive Gauche**, **Village Suisse** (*see p132*) and Fbg-St-Honoré, art deco in St-Germain, 1950s-70s retro plastic around rue de Charonne in the 11th, antiquarian books and stamps in the covered passages, in the *bouquinistes* along the quais, or at **Parc Georges Brassens** (*see p135*). Don't forget the flea markets, and auction house **Drouot** (recorded information on 01.48.00.20.17), as well as Sotheby's and Christie's. There are also frequent *brocantes* and *braderies* – antiques and collectors' markets, especially in spring and autumn.

Marché aux Puces d'Aligre
pl d'Aligre, 12th. M° Ledru-Rollin.
Open 9am-noon Tue-Sun. **Map** p407 N7.
This flea market has origins going back before the French Revolution. Remaining true to its junk tradition, you'll find a handful of *brocanteurs* peddling books, kitchenwares and knick-knacks at what seem optimistically astronomical prices. Be ready to bargain.

Marché aux Puces de Vanves
av Georges Lafenestre and av Marc-Sangrier, 14th. M° Porte de Vanves. **Open** 7.30am-7pm Sat, Sun.
The smallest and friendliest of the Paris flea markets is good for collectors of dolls, 1950s costume jewellery, glass, crystal, old photographs, magazines, eau de cologne bottles, lace, linens and buttons.

Marché aux Puces de St-Ouen (Porte de Clignancourt)
outside M° Porte de Clignancourt, 18th. **Open** 7am-7pm Mon, Sat, Sun.
This enormous market, reputedly the largest flea market in Europe – with over 2,000 stands and ten miles of walkways – is made up of arcades of semi-permanent shops as well as stands. There are, in theory, rare and quality items to be found here, but the market is overrun with tourists, hence the steep prices. It's divided into ten different markets specialising in everything from art nouveau and decorative objects (Marché Serpette) to expensive retro clothing in the Marché Dauphine.

Marché aux Puces de Montreuil
93100 Montreuil-sous-Bois, M° Porte de Montreuil. **Open** 7.30am-7pm Sat, Sun, Mon.
Like one vast car boot sale, this market disgorges mountains of second-hand clothing, parts for cars, showers and sundry machines, and a jumble of miscellaneous rubbish from its dusty, grungy bowels. You'll find little pre-1900, but there are fun collectables like branded *pastis* water-jugs.

Design, furniture & tableware

Christophe Delcourt
125 rue Vieille-du-Temple, 3rd (01.42.78.44.97). M° Filles du Calvaire. **Open** 10am-7pm Mon-Fri; 11am-7pm Sat. **Credit** V. **Map** p402 L6.
Delcourt's art-deco influenced geometrical lines are given a contemporary edge by their combination of stained wood with waxed black steel.

Bô
8 rue St-Merri, 4th (01.42.72.84.64). M° Hôtel de Ville. **Open** 11am-8pm Mon-Sat; 2-8pm Sun. **Credit** AmEx, MC, V. **Map** p406 K6.
Pared-back contemporary style: candlesticks, vases, unusual lights, new-agey incense burners and elegant grey Limoges porcelain. All *très bô*.

Yves Delorme
8 rue Vavin, 6th (01.44.07.23.14). M° Vavin. **Open** noon-7pm Mon; 10.30am-1.30pm, 2.30-7pm Tue-Sat. **Credit** AmEx, MC, V. **Map** p405 G8.
Extravagant thread-counts with prices to match. The ludicrously soft sheets in tastefully muted tones are ideal for four-posters and futons alike. **Branch:** 96 rue St-Dominique, 7th (01.45.55.51.10).

Kartell Flagship Shop
242 bd St-Germain, 7th (01.45.48.68.37). M° Rue du Bac. **Open** 10am-1pm, 2-7pm Tue-Sat. **Credit** MC, V. **Map** p405 G6.
The Italian plastic furniture pioneer stocks stuff by such names as Philippe Starck, Piero Lissoni and Antonio Citterio; office lines are displayed upstairs and lollipop-colours downstairs.

CFOC
170 bd Haussmann, 8th (01.53.53.40.80). M° St-Philippe-du-Roule. **Open** 10am-7pm Mon-Sat. **Credit** AmEx, DC, MC, V. **Map** p401 E3.
La Compagnie Française de l'Orient et de la Chine is full of eastern promise, from Chinese teapots and celadon bowls, to Iranian blown glass.
Branches include: 163, 167 bd St-Germain, 6th (01.45.48.00.18); 65 av Victor-Hugo, 16th (01.45.00.55.46).

Le Bihan
41 rue du Fbg-St-Antoine, 11th (01.43.43.06.75). M° Bastille. **Open** 2-7pm Mon; 10am-7pm Tue-Sat. **Credit** AmEx, V. **Map** p407 M7.
In case you thought the Faubourg was now entirely clothes shops or mock Louis XV, check out Le Bihan, a three-floor 800m² showcase for the best of modern design. Furniture and lighting from Perriand, Gray and Van der Rohe to Pesce, Santachiara Pillet, Morrison, Arad et al. It also organises sporadic exhibitions and other happenings.

Caravane Chambre 19
19 rue St-Nicolas, 12th (01.53.02.96.96/ www.caravane.fr). M° Ledru-Rollin. **Open** 11am-7pm Mon-Sat. **Credit** AmEx, MC, V. **Map** p407 M7.

Eat, Drink, Shop

Ethno-posh at **Caravane Chambre 19**. *See p259.*

This offshoot of Françoise Dorget's original Marais shop makes you want to pack your bags and move in. The goodies found here include exquisite hand-sewn quilts from West Bengal (€380), Cambodian travel mats, crisp cotton and organdie tunics, Berber scarves and the trademark deep lounging sofas and daybeds (around €2,000). There are also chic travel accessories such as silk sheet sleeping bags and stripey neckrests with matching eyemasks.
Branch: 6 rue Pavée, 4th (01.44.61.04.22).

Florists

Christian Tortu
6 carrefour de l'Odéon, 6th (01.43.26.02.56). Mº Odéon. **Open** 10am-8pm Mon-Sat. Closed two weeks in Aug. **Credit** AmEx, DC, MC, V. **Map** p405 H7.
Paris' most celebrated florist is famous for combining flowers, twigs, bark and moss into still lifes. You can buy his vases at 17 rue des Quatre-Vents.

Champ Libre
104 av Ledru-Rollin, 11th (01.49.29.99.22) Mº Ledru-Rollin **Open** 10am-8.30pm daily. **Credit** AmEx, DC, MC,V. **Map** p407 M8.
Whether it is a bouquet of autumn leaves and crab apples or velvety roses so red they're almost black, you're sure to be wooed at this delectable florist's. Easter week showcases chicks and baby bunnies in the window.

Kitchen & bathroom

E Déhillerin
18 rue Coquillière, 1st (01.42.36.53.13). Mº Les Halles. **Open** 9am-12.30pm, 2-6pm Mon; 9am-6pm Tue-Sat. **Credit** MC, V. **Map** p402 J5.
Suppliers to great chefs since 1820, this no-nonsense warehouse has every kitchen utensil there is.

Bains Plus
51 rue des Francs-Bourgeois, 4th (01.48.87.83.07). Mº RER Hôtel de Ville. **Open** 11am-7.30pm Tue-Sat; 2.30-7.30pm Sun. **Credit** AmEx, MC, V. **Map** p406 K6.
The ultimate gents' shaving shop: duck-shaped loofahs, seductive dressing gowns, chrome mirrors, bath oils and soaps.

Résonances
13 cour St-Emilion, 12th (01.44.73.82.82). Mº Cour St-Emilion. **Open** 11am-9pm daily. **Credit** AmEx, MC, V. **Map** p407 P10.
Résonances stocks an eclectic but well-chosen array of supplies and gadgets for the home. DIY enthusiasts will appreciate the tape measures, paints and brushes (get a life, guys) and interior design books; sybarites will dig the bath products.
Branch: 3 bd Malesherbes, 8th.

Kitchen Bazaar
11 av du Maine, 15th (01.42.22.91.17). Mº Montparnasse-Bienvenüe. **Open** 10am-7pm Mon-Sat. **Credit** AmEx, MC, V. **Map** p405 F8.

A festival of chrome gadgetry and modish accessories, Kitchen Bazaar is perfect for luxury items. Bath Bazaar Autrement (6 av du Maine, 15th/01.45.48.89.00), across the street, sells bathroom goodies.
Branches: 23 bd de la Madeleine, 1st.

Salles de Bains Rétro
29-31 rue des Dames, 17th (01.43.87.88.00/ www.sbrparis.com). Mº Place de Clichy. **Open** 11am-6pm Tue-Sat. **No credit cards.** Map p401 F2.
Marble baths, swan-shaped taps and crystal atomisers evoke a belle époque tart's boudoir while in the workshop next door, craftsmen restore Heath-Robinson showers and English porcelain.
Showroom: 27 rue Benjamin Franklin, 16th (01.47.27.14.50).

Leisure

Books

See also Fnac and Virgin Megastore in **Music & CDs.**

Galignani
224 rue de Rivoli, 1st (01.42.60.76.07). Mº Tuileries. **Open** 10am-7pm Mon-Sat. **Credit** MC, V. **Map** p401 G5.
Opened in 1802, Galignani was reputedly the first English-language bookshop in Europe, and at one point even published its own daily newspaper. Today it stocks fine and decorative arts books and literature in both French and English.

WH Smith
248 rue de Rivoli, 1st (01.44.77.88.99/ www.whsmith.fr). Mº Concorde. **Open** 9am-7.30pm Mon-Sat; 1-7.30pm Sun. **Credit** AmEx, MC, V. **Map** p401 G5.
If you're feeling homesick, this is just like being back in Blighty; over 70,000 titles and a huge crush around the magazine section.

Brentano's
37 av de l'Opéra, 2nd (01.42.61.52.50). Mº Opéra. **Open** 10am-7.30pm Mon-Sat. **Credit** AmEx, MC, V. **Map** p401 G4.
A good address for American classics, modern fiction and bestsellers, plus an excellent array of business titles. The children's section is in the basement.

Librarie Scaramouche
161 rue St-Martin, 3rd (01.48.87.78.58). Mº Rambuteau. **Open** 11am-1pm, 2-7.30pm Mon-Sat. **Credit** MC, V. **Map** p402 K5.
This shrine to celluloid, from the most obscure movies to box-office blockbusters, is packed with film posters, stills and books in French and English.

Bouquinistes
Along the quais, especially quai de Montebello, quai St-Michel, 5th. Mº St-Michel. **Open** times depend on stall, Tue-Sun. **No credit cards.** **Map** p406 J7.

Eat, Drink, Shop

Vulgar? Me? Yep.

Even Paris, the temple of chic, does a line in kitsch – the thrifty might say reasonable-priced quality – souvenirs. Here's our pick of the litter. Right in the shadow of Notre-Dame, **Au Jongleur de Notre Dame** (*8 rue du Cloître Notre Dame, 4th*) has some magnificent items honouring its Gothic neighbour. OK, some of them are in plastic, but don't forget that the plastic option wasn't available to the architects of the original structure, so what you can find here are new horizons in ecclesiastica. Care for a ceramic bread roll embedded with baguette-handled pâté knives, Eiffel-Tower-embossed thimbles, or a headless woman in a flouncy frock? Just around the corner, **Galerie Notre-Dame** (*23 rue d'Arcole, 4th*), has shiny white sculptures of old dinkle-boots Napoléon, the Venus de Milo, Buddha (he was originally from Paris, right?) and Rodin's *The Thinker* as well as an Egyptian cat. You could start a whole collection of glorious pieces here. Homely souls might prefer **Notre Dame Cadeaux** (*19 rue d'Arcole, 4th*) with its miniatures of quintessential French street scenes (well, they don't focus on the anti-*Front National* riots) next to the incongruous chicken-shaped tea cosies, which, strangely, don't feature on any of the mini café tables. Cross the Pont Neuf and you will happen upon the magic mile of souvenirs, rue de Rivoil in the 1st. **La Vie en Rose** (No. 238) stocks every china pill box imaginable, including one topped with both the Eiffel Tower and a painter at his easel. The sleeping cat on a sofa pillbox at close to handbag size is perfect for horse pills or some appropriately large and essential capsule – you know, suppositories and the like. There are also *fleur-de-lys* handbags and floppy dolls with heads in the shape of Paris monuments. Next door, **Mademoiselle France** has classy items like Mona Lisa dinner plates – won't Mona look a treat with mashed potato ears and a sausage on her hooter? Finally, if you want something that says me, me, me and your name on a mug just doesn't cut it, try **Au Coeur Immaculé de Marie** (*8 pl des Petits Pères, 2nd*) where they have tiny saintly name plaques – St Bernard, St Anne, etc – complete with suitably naive depictions. With that little lot, you'll have nothing to declare at the customs of good taste.

The green boxes along the *quais* are a Paris institution. Ignore the nasty postcards and rummage through the stacks of ancient paperbacks for something existential. Be sure to haggle.

Librairie Gourmande
4 rue Dante, 5th (01.43.54.37.27). Mº St-Michel. **Open** 10am-7pm Mon-Sat. **Credit** DC, MC, V. **Map** p406 J7.
Chefs from all over hunt out Geneviève Baudon's bookstore dedicated to cooking, wine and, of course, table arts.

Shakespeare & Co
37 rue de la Bûcherie, 5th (01.43.26.96.50). Mº Maubert-Mutualité/RER St-Michel. **Open** noon-midnight daily. **No credit cards. Map** p406 J7.
George Whitman founded this Paris institution in 1951. His eccentric creation consists of three floors of books stuffed into every nook and cranny. Struggling ex-pat writers who live in upstairs rooms calmly play chess while you browse in their bedrooms.

La Chambre Claire
14 rue St-Sulpice, 6th (01.46.34.04.31). Mº Odéon. **Open** 10am-7pm Tue-Sat. **Credit** MC, V. **Map** p406 H7.
A hommage to Barthes, this bookshop/gallery specialises in photography and also holds exhibitions.

Gibert Joseph
26, 30 bd St-Michel, 6th (01.44.41.88.88). Mº St-Michel. **Open** 10am-7.30pm Mon-Sat. **Credit** MC, V. **Map** p406 J7.
Best known as a bookshop for the Left Bank learning institutions, as well as a place to flog text books; Gibert Joseph also has stationery, office supplies and CD/DVD emporia further up the street.

La Hune
170 bd St-Germain, 6th (01.45.48.35.85). Mº St-Germain des Prés. **Open** 10am-11.45pm Mon-Sat; 11am-7.45pm Sun. **Credit** AmEx, MC, V. **Map** p405 G7.
A Left Bank institution, La Hune boasts an international selection of art and design books and a suberb collection of French literature and theory.

Tea and Tattered Pages
24 rue Mayet, 6th (01.40.65.94.35) Mº Duroc. **Open** 11am-7pm Mon-Sat; noon-6pm Sun. **Credit** MC, V. **Map** p405 F8.
A gentle and friendly American-style tea salon-cum-bookshop where you can browse through 15,000 second-hand, mainly paperback, books in English whilst sipping a steaming-hot cuppa.

Village Voice
6 rue Princesse, 6th (01.46.33.36.47). Mº Mabillon. **Open** 2-8pm Mon; 10am-8pm Tue-Sat; 2-8pm Sun. **Credit** AmEx, DC, MC, V. **Map** p406 H7.
The city's best selection of new fiction, non-fiction and literary magazines in English. It also holds literary events and poetry readings if you fancy a game of spot the luvvie.

Bookstorming

24 rue de Penthièvre, 8th (01.42.25.15.58/
www.bookstorming.com) M° Miromesnil or Champs-
Elysées-Clemenceau. **Open** 1-7pm Tue-Sat and by
appointment. **Credit** MC, V. **Map** p401 E3.
This new arrival to the arts scene boasts an impressive space – more than 280m² of books and catalogues on contemporary art, including limited
editions, plus a collection of 300 videos.

Institut Géographique National

107 rue La Boétie, 8th (01.43.98.85.00). M° Franklin
D Roosevelt. **Open** 9.30am-7pm Mon-Fri.
Credit AmEx, MC, V. **Map** p401 E4.
Paris' best cartographic shop stocks international
maps, detailed guides to France, wine, cheese, walk-
ing and cycling maps and historic maps of Paris.

Artazart

83 quai de Valmy, 10th (01.40.40.24.00/
www.artazart.com) M° Jacques-Bonsergent. **Open**
11am-8pm Mon-Fri; 2-7pm Sat, Sun. **Credit** MC, V.
Map p402 L4.
A bright yellow beacon along trendy Canal St- Martin, this bookshop and gallery has cutting-edge publications on fashion, art, architecture and design.

Gifts & eccentricities

Métro et Bus Paris, objets du Patrimoine boutique

In the Salle des échanges at RER Chatelet-les Halles,
next to the entrance to the line 4 and the Place Carrée
exit, 1st. **Open** 8am-7.30pm Mon-Fri.
Métro-focussed souvenirs including T-shirts with
the Métro map for €15.10 or a bath towel which
looks like a large, fluffy Métro ticket at €20.

Nature et Découvertes

Carrousel du Louvre, 99 rue de Rivoli, 1st
(01.47.03.47.43). M° Palais Royal. **Open** 10am-8pm
daily. **Credit** AmEx, MC, V. **Map** p401 H5.
Camping and stargazing accessories, musical
instruments, art supplies, divining rods and games.
Kids' play space, and workshops Wed afternoon.
Branches include: Forum des Halles, rue Pierre
Lescot, 1st (01.40.28.42.16).

Papeterie Moderne

12 rue de la Ferronnerie, 1st (01.42.36.21.72).
M° Chatelet. **Open** 9am-12.30am, 1.30-6.30pm Mon-
Sat. **No credit cards. Map** p402 J5.
Source of those enamel plaques that adorn Paris
streets and forbidding gateways *(Attention: chien*
bizarre – ideal Chrimbo present for the mother-in-
law) for a mere €7.

Vache and Cow

12 rue de la Ferronnerie, 1st (01.40.26.60.36).
M° Chatelet. **Open** noon-7.30pm Mon-Sat. **Credit** V.
Map p406 J5.
For all cowophiles, this shop has almost everything
you could possibly want, with a cow on it (or in the
shape of a cow). It's very moooooooving.

L'Art du Bureau

47 rue des Francs-Bourgeois, 4th (01.48.87.57.97)
M° St-Paul. **Open** 10.30am-7.30pm Mon-Sat; 2pm-
6.30pm Sun. **Credit** Amex, CD, MC, V.
Map p406 L6.
This boutique in the heart of the Marais sells sleek,
modern and, yes, sexy desk accessories.

Paris-Musées

29bis rue des Francs-Bourgeois, 4th
(01.42.74.13.02). M° St-Paul. **Open** 2pm-7pm Mon;
11am-7am Tue-Sat; 11am-6.30pm Sun.
Credit AmEx, DC, MC, V. **Map** p406 L6.
Run by Ville de Paris museums, this shop showcases
funky lamps and ceramics by young designers, along
with reproductions from the city's museums.

Robin des Bois

15 rue Ferdinand-Duval, 4th (01.48.04.09.36).
M° St-Paul. **Open** 10.30am-7pm Mon-Sat;
2-7.30pm Sun. **Credit** MC, V. **Map** p406 L6.
Robin Hood is linked to an ecological organisation
of the same name. Everything is made with recycled
or ecologically sound products.

Diptyque

34 bd St-Germain, 5th (01.43.26.45.27).
M° Maubert-Mutualité. **Open** 10am-7pm Mon-Sat
Credit: AmEx, MC, V. **Map** p405 G6/K7.
Diptyque's divinely scented candles in 48 different
varieties are the best you'll ever come across.

Deyrolle

46 rue du Bac, 7th (01.42.22.30.07). M° Rue du Bac.
Open 10am-6.45pm Mon-Sat. **Credit** AmEx, MC, V.
Map p405 G6.
Established in 1831, this dusty shop overflows with
stuffed animals. Have your own pet stuffed (€500
for a cat) or even hire a beast for a few days.

Madeleine Gély

218 bd St-Germain, 7th (01.42.22.63.35) M° Rue du
Bac. **Open** 9.30am-7pm Tue-Sat. **Map** p405 G6.
Short or long, plain or fancy, there's an umbrella or
cane here to suit everybody, including 400 styles of
walking sticks. Umbrellas can also be made to order.

Sennelier

3 quai Voltaire, 7th (01.42.60.72.15).
M° St-Germain-des-Prés. **Open** 2-6.30pm Mon;
9.30am-12.30pm, 2-6.30pm Tue-Sat. **Credit** AmEx,
DC, MC, V. **Map** p406 H6.
Old-fashioned colour merchant Sennelier has been
supplying artists since 1887. Oil paints, watercolours and pastels include rare pigments, along
with primered boards, varnishes and paper.

Paris Accordéon

80 rue Daguerre, 14th (01.43.22.13.48).
M° Denfert-Rochereau or Gaîté. **Open** 9am-noon,
1-7pm, Tue-Fri; 9am-noon, 1-6pm Sat.
Credit AmEx, MC, V. **Map** p405 G10.
This joint brims with accordions, from simple
squeeze-boxes to the most beautiful tortoise-shell
models, both second-hand and new.

Eat, Drink, Shop

Megastore, mega staircase: **Virgin Megastore.**

Music & CDs

There are clusters of specialist record shops around Les Halles (1st) and rue Keller (11th); second-hand outlets are concentrated in the 5th.

Monster Melodies

9 rue des Déchargeurs, 1st (01.40.28.09.39). M° Les Halles. **Open** 11am-7pm Mon-Sat. **Credit** MC, V. **Map** p402 J5.
The owners will help you hunt out treasures, and with over 10,000 second-hand, well-priced CDs of all species, it's just as well.

Papageno

1 rue de Marivaux, 2nd (01.42.96.56.54). M° Richelieu-Drouot. **Open** 1.30-7.30pm Tues-Fri, 11am-7.30pm Sat. **Credit** MC, V. **Map** p402 H4.
Specialises in rare opera finds on vinyl, some of which date back to the beginning of the century, as well as the usual large selection of CDs.

Blue Moon Music

84 rue Quincampoix, 4th (01.40.29.45.60). M° Rambuteau. **Open** 11am-7pm Mon-Sat. **Credit** V. **Map** p406 J6.
Specialising in reggae and ragga, this is the place to come for some authentic Jamaican sounds as they receive new imports on a weekly basis.

Paul Beuscher

15-17, 23-29 bd Beaumarchais, 4th (01.44.54.36.00). M° Bastille. **Open** 2pm-7pm Mon; 10.15am-7pm Tue-Sat. **Credit** V. **Map** p406 M6.
Music superstore, with premises on both sides of the river, stocking guitars, pianos and percussion, as well as accessories. North of the river, there are instruments to hire and a music school; whilst on the Left Bank, you'll find a musical bookshop with sheet music and loads of teaching material.
Branch: 66 av de la Motte-Piquet, 15th.

Crocodisc

40-42 rue des Ecoles, 5th (01.43.54.47.95). M° Maubert-Mutualité. **Open** 11am-7pm Tue-Sat. Closed two weeks Aug. **Credit** MC, V. **Map** p406 J7.
An excellent, albeit slightly expensive, range includes pop, rock, funk, African, North-African country music and classical. For jazz, blues and gospel you should try its specialised branch Crocojazz (64 rue de la Montagne Ste-Geneviève, 5th/01.46.34.78.38).

La Flute de Pan

49, 53, 59 rue de Rome, 8th (01.44.70.91.68). M° Europe. **Open** 10am-6.30pm Mon, Tue, Thur-Sat; 2.30-6.30pm Wed. **Credit** MC, V. **Map** p401 E1.
Here you'll find sheet music for strings, wind and orchestra, plus learning material at number 49; brass, sax, percussion and jazz at number 52 and piano, organ, harpsichord and singers at number 59.

Fnac

74 av des Champs-Elysées, 8th (01.53.53.64.64/ www.fnac.com). M° George V. **Open** 10am-midnight Mon-Sat; noon-midnight Sun. **Credit** AmEx, MC, V. **Map** p400 D4.
Fnac's musical range is tame but wide-reaching – the African section being particularly reliable. Fnac also stocks books, computers, stereo, video and photography equipment, as well as being Paris' main concert box office.
Branches: Forum des Halles, 1st (01.40.41.40.00); 136 rue de Rennes, 6th (01.49.54.30.00); 4 pl de la Bastille, 12th (01.43.42.04.04) music only.

Virgin Megastore
52-60 av des Champs-Elysées, 8th (01.49.53.50.00).
Mº Franklin D. Roosevelt. **Open** 10am-midnight
Mon-Sat; noon-midnight Sun. **Credit** AmEx, DC, MC,
V. **Map** p401 E4.
The luxury of perusing the latest CDs till midnight
makes this a choice spot. Not only that, but the listening system allows you to play any CD by its bar-
code. Videos and books are also on offer.
Branches: Carrousel du Louvre, 99 rue de Rivoli, 1st
(01.49.53.50.00); 5 bd Montmartre 2nd (01.40.13.72.13),
15 bd Barbès 18th (01.56.55.53.70).

Bimbo Tower
5 passage St-Antoine, 11th (01.49.29.76.70).
Mº Ledru-Rollin. **Open** 2pm-7pm Mon-Sat.
No credit cards. Map p407 M7.
Rather wonderfully named, Bimbo stocks all manner of new underground, counter-culture music from
concrete music to sonic poetry and performance, rare
discs, independent labels, auto-produced records
and the latest Japanese imports.

Born Bad
17 rue Keller, 11th (01.48.06.34.17). Mº Ledru-Rollin.
Open 12pm-8pm Mon-Sat. **Credit** AmEx, DC, MC, V.
Map p407 M6.
Everything from punk, rock and hardcore to ska and
soul can be found in this indie record shop. New and
second-hand CDs and vinyl are available for around
€10-€12.

Sport & fitness

For general sports equipment and clothes, the
chains Go Sport and Decathlon have branches
all over the city.

Au Vieux Campeur
*main shop 48 rue des Ecoles, 5th (01.53.10.48.48/
www.au-vieux-campeur.com). Mº Maubert-Mutualité.*
Open: 11am-7.30pm Mon-Tue, Thur-Fri; Wed 11am-
9pm; Sat 9.30-7.30pm. **Credit** AmEx, MC, V.
Map p406 J7.
A Parisian institution, Au Vieux Campeur runs 19
specialist shops between rue des Ecoles and the bd
St-Germain. The group deals with just about all
sports you can do in public, from scuba diving to
skiing – except golf, which it considers too bourgeois. Despite such rampant thought policing, staff
are knowledgeable and friendly.

Citadium
*50-55 rue Caumartin, 9th (01.55.31.74.00). Mº Havre
Caumartin.* **Open** 10am-8pm Mon-Wed, Fri, Sat; 10am-
9pm Thurs. **Credit** AmEx, DC, MC, V.
Map p401 G3.
This is one of France's biggest sports stores, and it's
fast gaining cult status. The latest surf 'n' skater
vids blast out into the four themed circular floors
('urban street', 'glide', 'athletic' and 'outdoor'), all of
which are manned by expert staff. Citadium stocks
everything from designer watches to cross-country
skis and travel books.

Regal rock shop

Elvis' death was in some ways a good
career move. Twenty-five years after his
demise, he sells more records than most
living acts ever manage to. He's also the
first performer to headline a live concert
tour while, ahem, not actually living.

Strangely, the late-phase living Elvis
battled the same foes as most middle-
aged Parisian women: the bulge, bad
clothes, bad hair and the difficulty of
tracking down nice, white trouser suits that
don't show the cellulite. That is clearly why
– *quelle surprise* – the second-most
important Elvis fan club in the world is in
li'l old France. Its main place of worship is,
in fact, a Parisian shop.

Club President Jean-Marie Pouzenc saw
the King's car pull away from a Paris kerb
in 1959 and, in that epiphanic moment, a
passion began. In 1992 Pouzenc created
the subtly-named association Elvis My
Happiness and began publishing a
quarterly *Elvis* magazine. All good religions
go commercial in the end and now there's
even an **Elvis My Happiness** (EMH)
boutique (*9 rue Notre Dame des Victoires,
2nd/01.49.27.08.43*) if you're in need of
a King-sized fix. Sadly, at least for those
of us addicted to overblown Elvis, there
are no racks of rhinestone jump-suits, no
fried food bar, no 'jungle den' thick with
shag pile; no, it's all very sedate,
corporate rather than corpulent. That
means stacks of vinyl, CDs (that-hard-to
find *Elvis for Baby* collection), DVDs,
videos, *Elvis* monthly mag, books,
baseball caps and shirts, mugs, clocks,
playing cards and fridge magnets. A small
glass clothes 'museum' houses a cropped
white leather jacket, karate top, and blue
shirt with spiffy yellow scarf. Admittedly,
perhaps, this does not represent his most
memorable garb but it's touched by
Elvisian style.

At this shop, themed squarely in the
ghetto of good taste, Elvis is forever young,
handsome and brimming with talent, not at
all the demented porker with a mania for
white cotton underwear and an appetite for
Danish porn and all things fried and true
that some infidels pretend he became.
To visit Elvis My Happiness and not come
away all shook up with emotion, you'd
have to be nuthin' but a hound dog with a
wooden heart. Uh-huh-huh.

Food & Drink

Every Parisian neighbourhood has its market and speciality shops where the faithful wait patiently in slow-moving queues for rustic corn-fed chicken, farmhouse camembert or briny oysters fresh from Brittany. Supermarkets and suburban *hypermarchés* are indeed a force to be reckoned with but the latest food scares have produced a renewed attention to quality and a willingness to pay a little extra.

Bakeries

Poilâne

8 rue du Cherche-Midi, 6th (01.45.48.42.59/ www.poilane.com). M° Sèvres Babylone or St-Sulpice. **Open** 7.15am-8.15pm Mon-Sat. **No credit cards. Map** p405 F8.

The charismatic Lionel is no more after a helicopter crash in November 2002, but the Poilâne name lives on. Nowhere will you find a fresher version of his famous, dark-crusted *miche* than at this tiny, old-fashioned shop, where bakers toil aréound the clock before a wood-burning oven. The buttery apple tarts almost better the bread.
Branch: 49 bd de Grenelle, 15th (01.45.79.11.49).

L'Autre Boulange

43 rue de Montreuil, 11th (01.43.72.86.04). M° Nation or Faidherbe-Chaligny. **Open** 7.30am-1.30pm, 4-7.30pm Mon-Fri; 7.30am-12.30pm Sat. Closed Aug. **No credit cards. Map** p403 P3.

Michel Cousin rustles up 23 kinds of organic loaves in his wood-fired oven, including the *flutiot* (rye bread with raisins, walnuts and hazelnuts), the *sarment de Bourgogne* (sourdough and a little rye) and a spiced cornmeal bread ideal for foie gras. There are also great croissants and *chaussons* for superior snacking.

Moisan

5 pl d'Aligre, 12th (01.43.45.46.60). M° Ledru-Rollin. **Open** 7am-1.30pm, 3-8pm Tue-Sat; 7am-2pm Sun. **No credit cards. Map** p407 N7.

An organic baking pioneer, Michel Moisan lovingly turns out crunchy *boules de levain*, fragrant *petits pains*, gorgeous orange-scented brioches and flaky apple tarts.
Branch: 4 av du Général Leclerc, 14th (01.43.22.34.13).

Max Poilâne

87 rue Brancion, 15th (01.48.28.45.90/ www.max-poilane.fr). M° Porte de Vanves. **Open** 7.30am-8pm Tue-Sat, 10am-7pm Sun. **No credit cards. Map** p404 D10.

Using the venerable Poilâne family recipe, the lesser-known Max produces bread that easily rivals that of his more famous brother, the late Lionel.
Branches: 29 rue de l'Ouest, 14th (01.43.27.29.91); 42 pl du Marché-St-Honoré, 1st (01.42.61.10.53).

Moulin de la Vierge

166 av de Suffren, 15th (01.47.83.45.55). M° Sèvres-Lecourbe. **Open** 7am-8pm Mon-Sat.
No credit cards. Map p404 C6.

Basile Kamir learned breadmaking after falling in love with an old abandoned bakery. His naturally leavened country loaf is dense and fragrant.
Branches include: 82 rue Daguerre, 14th (01.43.22.50.55); 105 rue Vercingétorix, 14th (01.45.43.09.84); 77 rue Cambronne, 15th (01.44.49.05.05).

Raking in the dough at **Moulin de la Vierge.**

Boulangerie au 140

140 rue de Belleville, 20th (01.46.36.92.47/
www.au140.com). M° Jourdain. **Open** 7.30am-8pm
Tue-Sat; 7.30am-1.30pm, 4-8pm Sun. **Credit** MC, V.
Map p403 O3.

A great baguette is an all-too-rare thing in Paris –
so head up the hill to this bakery, where Pierre
Demoncy handles *levain* (natural yeast) with an
artist's touch that has earned him the city's 'best
baguette' award.

Pâtisseries

Finkelsztajn

27 rue des Rosiers, 4th (01.42.72.78.91). M° St-Paul.
Open 11am-7pm Mon; 10am-7pm Tue-Sun. Closed
Aug. **No credit cards. Map** p406 L6.

Filled with poppy seeds, apples or cream cheese, the
dense Jewish cakes in this motherly shop pad the
bones for the Parisian winter.

A Lerch

4 rue du Cardinal Lemoine, 5th (01.43.26.15.80).
M° Cardinal Lemoine. **Open** 8am-7.30pm Wed-Sun.
No credit cards. Map p406 K8.

With its wedding cake ceiling, this is a dream *pâtisserie* for those who like their tarts rustic. The speciality is Alsatian fruit tarts, with five or six seasonal
varieties on display at any given time.

Gérard Mulot

76 rue de Seine, 6th (01.43.26.85.77). M° Odéon.
Open 6.45am-8pm Mon, Tue, Thur-Sun. Closed Aug.
No credit cards. Map p406 H7.

Picture-perfect cakes – bitter chocolate tart and the
mabillon, caramel mousse with apricot marmalade
– attract local celebrities.

Pierre Hermé

72 rue Bonaparte, 6th (01.53.67.66.65).
M° St-Sulpice. **Open** 9am-7.30pm Mon-Sat; 9am-
6.30pm Sun. **Credit** DC, MC, V. **Map** p405 G7.

Pastry superstar Pierre Hermé attracts the crème de
la crème of St-Germain: sumptuous '2000 feuilles'
and *la cerise sur le gâteau*, the ultimate chocolate
cake are among the reasons.

Branches: 33 rue Marbeuf, 8th (01.53.89.93.95); 185
rue de Vaugirard, 15th (01.47.83.29.72).

Sadaharu Aoki

35 rue de Vaugirard, 6th (01.45.44.48.900.
M° St-Placide. **Open** 11am-7pm Tue-Sun. **Credit** DC,
MC, V. **Map** p405 G8.

This discreet Japanese pastry chef, who opened his
minimalist boutique in 2001, has achieved perfection with his green tea éclairs and the astounding
vanilla and chocolate millefeuille.

Peltier

66 rue de Sèvres, 7th (01.47.34.06.62). M° Duroc or
Vaneau. **Open** 9am-7.30pm Mon-Sat; 9am-6.30pm
Sun. **Credit** MC, V. **Map** p405 F7.

Philippe Conticini was hired in 2002 to whisk this
historic pastry shop into the 21st century. Alongside
conventional cakes are sultry mousses filled with
pear chutney or dried apricot jam.

Cheese

The sign *maître fromager affineur* denotes
merchants who buy young cheeses from farms
and age them on their premises. *Fromage
fermier* and *fromage au lait cru* signify farm-
produced and raw milk cheeses respectively.

Eat, Drink, Shop

Ice 'n' easy does it every time

OK, what makes your cone groan with pleasure? Is it creamy, calorie-crammed double chocolate tiramisu, or is it more in the blackcurrant sorbet line? Chances are you can get it at one of the ice cream parlours scattered around the city.

Amorino

47 rue St-Louis-en-l'Ile, 4th (01.44.07.48.08). Mº Cité. **Open** noon-midnight daily. €3 a scoop. **Map** p406 K7.
This new Italian ice cream shop has style. *Limone* and *lampone* (raspberry) is a winning combination, if you can resist the more calorific creamy varieties. Order a cone, and staff will present you with an ice cream rose.

Berthillon

31 rue St-Louis-en-l'Ile, 4th (01.43.53.31.61). Mº Cité. **Open** 10am-8pm, Wed-Sun Closed Aug. €2 a scoop. **Map** p406 K7.
The most famous ice cream maker in Paris, so beware: hot, sunny summer days mean long queues of over-heated tourists waiting to sit by the river with a double cone. The selection has all the basics, although the more unusual flavours change according to what's in season.

Octave

138 rue Mouffetard, 5th (01.45.35.20.56). Mº Censier Daubenton. **Open** 10am-7.30pm Mon-Thur, Sun; 10am-midnight Fri, Sat (Nov-Feb closed Sun). €2 a scoop. **Map** p406 J9.
Always packed in summer, with a prime sunning spot on the terrace. It's the 30 mouth-watering ice-cream-based deserts that have created this parlour's reputation. Ice cream specialities include quince and liquorice; the dark chocolate ice cream is every bit as dreamy as it sounds.

Le Bac à Glaces

109 rue du Bac, 7th (01.45.48.87.65). Mº Rue du Bac. **Open** 11am-7pm Mon-Sat. €2 a scoop. **Map** p405 F7.
A traditional ice cream counter for takeaway ice cream with very few tables. The brave can

try avocado, camembert or roquefort, which are sold to restaurants as a starter, and there is a good selection of alcohol-based sorbets.

Spécial Comptoir

123 rue Oberkampf, 11th (01.43.38.06.55). Mº Ménilmontant. **Open** noon-midnight daily. €1.50 a scoop. **Map** p403 M5.
It's easy to miss this tiny stand among the gaudy neon lights of the street. There are more than 50 flavours of ice cream and sorbet to choose from, all made locally with natural ingredients, and the staff let you have as many tasters as you like (our advice: go for it). As well as all the usual fruit sorbets, there are savoury flavours such as cucumber, basil and thyme. The black chocolate sorbet is a must, as is the marron-glacé ice cream. The only problem is there is nowhere nearby to sit. Try to be brave.

Raimo

59-61 bd de Reuilly, 12th (01.43.43.70.17). Mº Daumesnil. **Open** 9am-midnight Mon-Sat. €2.50 a scoop. **Map** p407 P9.
This Right Bank café hasn't been redecorated since 1963. On Saturdays, pensioners put on their best frocks, poof up their poodles and idle away the afternoon flirting with the strictly uniformed waiters while tucking away at whipped-cream-covered deserts. The flavours change according to season. As well as the more traditional flavours, there are specialities such as honey- or pepper-flavoured ice cream. There are no takeaway ice creams.

Calabrese

15 rue d'Odessa, 14th (01.43.20.31.63). Mº Montparnasse-Bienvenüe. **Open** 9am-11pm daily. €2.50 a scoop. **Map** p405 G9.
This traditional Italian ice cream parlour is in a 1950s time-warp, from the black-and-white photos on the wall to the metallic ice cream making machines churning away on the counter. Luigi Calabrese and his wife run the show, serving clients scoops in metallic bowls and takeaway cones. The ice creams are much better than the sorbets, which are all a little bland and have an intriguing texture.

Eat, Drink, Shop

Marie-Anne Cantin

12 rue du Champ-de-Mars, 7th (01.45.50.43.94/ www.cantin.fr). M° Ecole Militaire. **Open** 8.30am-7.30pm Mon-Sat. **Credit** DC, MC, V. **Map** p404 D6.
Cantin, a vigorous defender of unpasteurised cheese, is justifiably proud of her dreamily creamy st-marcellins, aged chèvres and nutty beauforts. The cheeses are ripened in her cellars.

Laurent Dubois

2 rue de Lourmel, 15th (01.45.78.70.58). M° Dupleix. **Open** 9am-1pm, 4-7.45pm Tue-Thur; 9am-7.45pm Fri; 8.30am-7.45pm Sat; 9am-1pm Sun. Closed Aug. **Credit** MC, V. **Map** p404 C7.
Nephew of the famous cheese specialist Alain Dubois, Laurent Dubois is a master in his own right and may be beginning something of a Dubois cheese dynasty. Especially impressive are his nutty two-year-old comté and crackly vieille mimolette.

Alain Dubois

80 rue de Tocqueville, 17th (01.42.27.11.38). M° Malesherbes or Villiers. **Open** 9am-1pm, 4-8pm Tue-Fri; 8.30am-8pm Sat; 9am-1pm Sun. Closed first and two weeks in Aug. **Credit** MC, V. **Map** p401 E2.
Dubois, who stocks some 70 varieties of goats' cheese plus prized, aged st-marcellin and st-félicien, is the darling of the superchefs.
Branch: 79 rue de Courcelles, 17th (01.43.80.36.42).

Alléosse

13 rue Poncelet, 17th (01.46.22.50.45). M° Ternes. **Open** 9am-1pm, 4-7pm Tue-Sat; 9am-1pm Sun. **Credit** MC, V. **Map** p400 C2.
People cross town for the cheeses – wonderful farmhouse camemberts, delicate st-marcellins, a choice of *chèvres* and several rareties.

Chocolate

Cacao et Chocolat

29 rue de Buci, 6th (01.46.33.77.63). M° Mabillon. **Open** 10.30am-7.30pm Tue-Sat. **Credit** AmEx, MC, V. **Map** p405 H7.
Opened in 1998, this shop decorated in burnt-orange and ochre recalls chocolate's ancient Aztec origins with spicy fillings (honey and chilli, nutmeg, clove and citrus), chocolate masks and pyramids.
Branch: 63 rue St Louis en l'Ile, 4th (01.46.33.33.33).

Christian Constant

37 rue d'Assas, 6th (01.53.63.15.15). M° St-Placide. **Open** 8.30am-9pm Mon-Fri; 8am-8.30pm Sat; 8.30am-7pm Sun. **Credit** MC, V. **Map** p405 G8.
A true master chocolate maker and *traiteur,* Constant is revered by *le tout Paris.* Trained in the arts of pâtisserie and chocolate, he scours the globe for new and delectable ideas. Ganaches are subtly flavoured with verbena, jasmine or cardamom.

Jean-Paul Hévin

3 rue Vavin, 6th (01.43.54.09.85). M° Vavin. **Open** 10am-7.30pm Mon-Sat. Closed Aug. **Credit** MC, V. **Map** p405 G8.

Chocolatier Jean-Paul Hévin dares to fill his chocolates with potent cheeses, to be served with wine as an apéritif. Even more risqué are his aphrodisiac chocolates.
Branches: 231 rue St-Honoré, 1st (01.55.35.35.96); 16 av de La Motte-Picquet, 7th (01.45.51.77.48).

Debauve & Gallais

30 rue des Saints-Pères, 7th (01.45.48.54.67). M° St-Germain-des-Prés. **Open** 9am-7pm Mon-Sat. Closed Aug. **Credit** DC, MC, V. **Map** p405 G7.
This former pharmacy, with a facade dating from 1800, once sold chocolate for medicinal purposes. Its intense tea, honey or praline-flavoured chocolates do, indeed, heal the soul.
Branches: 33 rue Vivienne, 2nd (01.40.39.05.50); 107 rue Jouffroy d'Abbans, 17th (01.47.63.15.15).

Richart

258 bd St-Germain, 7th (01.45.55.66.00/ www.richart.com). M° Solférino. **Open** 10am-7pm Mon-Sat. **Credit** MC, V. **Map** p405 F6.
Each chocolate ganache has an intricate design, packages look like jewel boxes and each purchase comes with a tract on how best to savour chocolate.

La Maison du Chocolat

89 av Raymond-Poincaré, 16th (01.40.67.77.83/ www.lamaisonduchocolat.com). M° Victor-Hugo. **Open** 10am-7pm Mon-Sat. **Credit** AmEx, MC, V. **Map** p400 B4.
Robert Linxe opened his first Paris shop in 1977 and has been inventing new chocolates ever since. Using Asian spices, fresh fruits and herbal infusions he has won over the most demanding chocolate-lovers.
Branches: 19 rue de Sèvres, 6th (01.45.44.20.40); 225 rue du Fbg-St-Honoré, 8th (01.42.27.39.44); 52 rue François 1er, 8th (01.47.23.38.25).

Regional specialities

La Cigogne

61 rue de l'Arcade, 8th (01.43.87.39.16). M° St-Lazare. **Open** 8.30am-7pm Mon-Fri. Closed Aug. **Credit** AmEx, DC, MC, V. **Map** p401 F4.
Hearty Alsatian fare at La Cigogne includes scrumptious tarts, strüdel, beravecka fruit bread plus sausages laced with pistachios.

Charcuterie Lyonnaise

58 rue des Martyrs, 9th (01.48.78.96.45). M° Notre-Dame de Lorette. **Open** 9am-1.30pm, 4.30-8pm Tue-Sat; 9am-2pm Sun. **Credit** AmEx, DC, MC, V. **Map** p401 H2.
Jean-Jacques Chrétienne prepares Lyonnais delicacies *quenelles de brochet, jambon persillé* and *hure* (pistachio-seasoned tongue).

Treats & traiteurs

Torréfacteur Verlet

256 rue St-Honoré, 1st (01.42.60.67.39). M° Palais Royal. **Open** shop 9.30am-7.30pm Mon-Sat; tea shop 9.30am-6.30pm daily. **Credit** MC, V. **Map** p401 G5.

Eat, Drink, Shop

The freshly roasted coffee in this gem of a shop smells as heavenly as the priciest perfume. Eric Duchaussoy roasts rare beans to perfection – sip a *petit noir* at a wooden table, or treat yourself to the city's best coffee at home.

Goutmanyat

3 rue Dupues, 3rd (01.44.78.96.74). M° Temple
Open 2-8pm Mon-Sat. **Credit** AmEx, DC, MC, V.
Map p402 L5.

Jean-Marie Thiercelin's family has been in the spice business since 1809, and his new, spacious location is a treasure trove of super-fresh flavourings. Star chefs come here for Indonesian *cubebe* pepper, gleaming fresh nutmeg, long pepper (an Indian variety) and Spanish and Iranian saffron.

L'Epicerie

51 rue St-Louis-en-l'Ile, 4th (01.43.25.20.14).
M° Pont Marie. **Open** 11am-8pm daily.
Credit DC, MC, V. **Map** p406 K7.

A perfect delicatessen gift shop crammed with pretty bottles of blackcurrant vinegar, five-spice mustard, orange sauce, tiny pots of jam, honey with figs and indulgent boxes of chocolate snails.

Jean-Paul Gardil

44 rue St-Louis en l'Ile, 4th (01.43.54.97.15). M° Pont Marie. **Open** 9am-12.45pm, 4-5.45pm Tue-Sat; 8.30am-12.30pm Sun. **Credit** MC, V. **Map** p406 K7.

Rarely has meat looked so beautiful as in this fairytale shop, where geese hang in the window and a multitude of plaques confirm the butcher's skill in selecting the finest meats, such as milk-fed veal and lamb, *coucou de Rennes* chickens, Barbary free-range ducklings, and Bresse poulard and geese. Staff are pleasant, unlike some of the fur-coated clients.

La Maison des Trois Thés

33 rue Gracieuse, 5th (01.43.36.73.84). M° Place Monge. **Open** 11.30am-6pm Wed-Fri; 2-7pm Sat, Sun. **Credit** MC, V. **Map** p406 K8.

Yu Hui Tseng, one of world's ten leading tea experts, has moved to larger premises which suit her to a tee. A reverential hush reigns as connoisseurs dip their lips into teas costing up to an incredible €500,000 a kilo, though the average is €10 to €500 a kilo.

La Maison de la Vanille

18 rue du Cardinal Lemoine, 5th (01.43.25.50.95). M° Cardinal Lemoine. **Open** 11.30am-6pm Wed-Fri; 2-7pm Sat, Sun. **Credit** V. **Map** p406 K8.

All the vanilla in this soothingly scented shop and tea room comes from Réunion Island – buy it powdered for baking, liquid for milkshakes or whole to flavour a *crème anglaise* (that's 'custard' to the more civilised among us).

Huilerie Artisanale Leblanc

6 rue Jacob, 6th (01.46.34.61.55). M° St-Germain-des-Prés. **Open** 2.30-7.30pm Mon; 11am-7.30pm Tue-Sat. Closed two weeks in Aug. **No credit cards.**
Map p405 H6.

The Leblanc family started out making walnut oil from its family tree in Burgundy and selling to its neighbours before branching out skilfully to press pure oils from hazelnuts, almonds, pine nuts, grilled peanuts, pistachios and olives.

Fauchon

26-30 pl de la Madeleine, 8th (01.47.42.60.11).
M° Madeleine. **Open** 9.30am-7pm Mon-Sat. **Credit** AmEx, DC, MC, V. **Map** p401 F4.

Paris' most famous food store is like every specialist deli rolled into one. There's a museum-like prepared-food section, cheese, fish and exotic fruit counters, an Italian deli, fine wines in the cellar, chocolates and a plush tea room for refreshment.

Hédiard

21 pl de la Madeleine, 8th (01.43.12.88.88/ www.hediard.fr). M° Madeleine. **Open** 8.30am-9pm Mon-Sat. **Credit** AmEx, DC, MC, V. **Map** p401 F4.

The first establishment to introduce exotic foods to the Parisians, Hédiard specialises in rare teas and coffees, unusual spices, imported produce, jams and candied fruits. The original shop, dating from 1880, has a posh tea room upstairs.
Branches include: 126 rue du Bac, 7th (01.45.44.01.98); 70 av Paul-Doumer, 16th (01.45.04.51.92); 106 bd des Courcelles, 17th (01.47.63.32.14).

La Maison de la Truffe

19 pl de la Madeleine, 8th (01.42.65.53.22/ www.maison-de-la-truffe.com). M° Madeleine.
Open 9am-8pm Mon; 9am-9pm Tue-Sat. **Credit** AmEx, DC, MC, V. **Map** p401 F4.

Come here for truffles worth more than gold – Piedmontese white truffles from Alba cost a cool €4,573 a kilo – or for the more affordable truffle oils, sauces and vinegars.

Allicante

26 bd Beaumarchais, 11th (01.43.55.13.02/ www.allicante.com). M° Bastille. **Open** daily 10am-7.30pm **Credit** AmEx, DC, MC, V. **Map** p406 M6.

A paradise of oily delights, including rare olive oils from Liguria, Sicily and Greece, fragrant pine nut, pistachio and almond varieties, and oils extracted from apricot, peach and avocado pits. Wow your guests with pricey argania oil, pounded by hand by Berber women in Morocco (your being able to wow your guests is what gives the women such tremendous job satisfaction).

Poissonnerie du Dôme

4 rue Delambre, 14th (01.43.35.23.95). M° Vavin. **Open** 8am-1pm, 4-7pm Tue-Sat; 8am-1pm Sun. **Credit** MC, V. **Map** p405 G9.

Jean-Pierre Lopez's tiny shop is probably the best fishmonger in Paris. His fish are individually selected, many coming straight from small boats off the Breton coast. Each one is bright of eye and sound of gill. Try the drool-inducing (but bank-breaking) turbot, the giant crabs or the scallops, when in season.

Thriller in vanilla: La Maison de la Vanille.

International

Kioko
46 rue des Petits-Champs, 2nd (01.42.61.33.65).
Mº Pyramides. **Open** 10am-8pm Tue-Sat; 11am-7pm
Sun. **Credit** MC, V. **Map** p402 H4.
Everything you need to make sushi (or good ready-
made sushi for the lazy), plus sauces, snacks, sake,
Japanese beer, tea and kitchen utensils. There's a 10
per cent reduction at weekends.

Izraël
30 rue François-Miron, 4th (01.42.72.66.23).
Mº Hôtel de Ville. **Open** 9.30am-1pm, 2.30-7pm Tue-
Fri; 9-7pm Sat. Closed Aug. **Credit** MC, V.
Map p406 K6.
Spices and other delights from as far afield as
Mexico, Turkey and India – juicy dates, feta cheese,
tapenades and lots of spirits.

Pasta Linea
9 rue de Turenne, 4th (01.42.77.62.54). Mº St-Paul.
Open 11am-9pm Mon-Fri; 11am-8pm Sat, Sun.
Credit MC, V. **Map** p406 L6.
Artichoke ravioli with truffle cream sauce or fresh
linguine with tomato and rocket are among the heavenly hot pastas you might find here, or buy top-qual-
ity dried pastas and prepared sauces to eat at home.

Mexi & Co
*10 rue Dante, 5th (01.46.34.14.12). Mº Maubert-
Mutualité.* **Open** noon-11pm daily. **Credit** V.
Map p406 J7.
Everything you need for a fiesta, including mari-
nades for fajitas, dried chillies, South American
beers, cachaça and tequilas.

Jabugo Iberico & Co.
11 rue Clément Marot, 8th (01.47.20.03.13).
Mº Alma-Marceau or Franklin D. Roosevelt. **Open**
10am-8pm Tue-Sat. **Credit** MC, V. **Map** p401 E4.
This shop specialises in Spanish hams with the
Bellota-Bellota label, meaning the pigs have feasted
on acorns. Manager Philippe Poulachon compares
the complexity of his cured hams (at €95 a kilo) to
the delicacy of truffles.

Sarl Velan Stores
87 passage Brady, 10th (01.42.46.06.06).
Mº Château d'Eau. **Open** 8.30am-9.30pm Mon-Sat.
Credit AmEx, DC, MC, V. **Map** p402 K4.
Situated in an passage of Indian cafés and shops,
this is an emporium of spices and vegetables
shipped from Kenya and India.

Tang Frères
48 av d'Ivry, 13th (01.45.70.80.00). Mº Porte d'Ivry.
Open 9am-7.30pm Tue-Sun. **Credit** AmEx, MC, V.
Chinatown's biggest Asian supermarket is great for
flat, wind-dried duck and all sorts of unidentifiable
fruit and veg between your chopsticks.

Pick a *pecora* from **Pasta Linea**'s counter.

Les Délices d'Orient
52 av Emile Zola, 15th (01.45.79.10.00).
Mº Charles-Michels. **Open** 7.30am-9pm Tue-Sun.
Credit MC, V. **Map** p404 B8.
Shelves here brim with houmous, stuffed auber-
gines, halva, Lebanese bread, felafel, olives and all
manner of Middle Eastern delicacies.
Branch: 14 rue des Quatre-Frères Peignot, 15th.

Merry Monk
87 rue de la Convention, 15th (01.40.60.79.54).
Mº Boucicaut. **Open** 10am-7pm Mon-Sat; 11am-7pm
Sun. **Credit** V. **Map** p404 B9.
As tidy as your granny's larder, this shop stocks
expats' essentials such as ginger biscuits and loose
tea, with a section dedicated to South Africa.

Wine, beer & spirits

Most *cavistes* happily dispense advice, so ask if
you have a specific wine or menu in mind. To
buy direct from producers, visit the Salon des
Caves Particulières at Espace Champerret in
March and December.

Legrand Filles et Fils
1 rue de la Banque, 2nd (01.42.60.07.12).
Mº Bourse. **Open** 11am-7pm Mon, Wed-Fri; 10am-
7.30pm Thur; 10am-7pm Sat. **Credit** AmEx, MC, V.
Map p402 H4.
This old-fashioned shop offering fine wines and
brandies, chocolates, teas, coffees and bonbons has

now opened a showroom for its huge selection of tasting glasses and gadgets, housed within Galerie Vivienne. Free wine tastings take place on Thursday evenings, with visiting experts to show you what to sip and what to spit out.

Ryst Dupeyron

79 rue du Bac, 7th (01.45.48.80.93/ www.dupeyron.com). M° Rue du Bac. **Open** 12.30-7.30pm Mon; 10.30am-7.30pm Tue-Sat. Closed one week in Aug. **Credit** AmEx, MC, V. **Map** p405 F7. The Dupeyron family has sold Armagnac for four generations. You'll find bottles dating from 1868 (and nearly every year since) in this listed shop. Treasures include some 200 fine Bordeaux, vintage Port and rare whiskies. Labels can be personalised on the spot, which may be helpful when your purchases send you into oblivion.

Les Caves Augé

116 bd Haussmann, 8th (01.45.22.16.97). M° St-Augustin. **Open** 1-7.30pm Mon; 9am-7.30pm Tue-Sat. **Closed** Mon in Aug. **Credit** AmEx, MC, V. **Map** p401 E3. The oldest wine shop in Paris – Marcel Proust was a regular customer – is serious and professional, with sommelier Marc Sibard advising.

Les Caves Taillevent

199 rue du Fbg-St-Honoré, 8th (01.45.61.14.09/ www.taillevent.com). M° Charles-de-Gaulle-Etoile or Ternes. **Open** 2-8pm Mon; 9am-8pm Tue-Fri; 9am-7.30pm Sat. Closed first three weeks in Aug. **Credit** AmEx, DC, MC, V. **Map** p400 D3. Half a million bottles make up the Taillevent cellar. The three head sommeliers supervise the Sunday tastings. Wines start from €3.65 a bottle.

La Maison du Whisky

20 rue d'Anjou, 8th (01.42.65.03.16/ www.whisky.fr). M° Madeleine. **Open** 9.30am-7pm Mon; 9.15am-8pm Tue-Fri; 9.30am-7.30pm Sat. **Credit** AmEx, V. **Map** F4. Jean-Marc Bellier is fascinating as he explains which whisky matches which food or waxes lyrical about different flavours such as honey and tobacco. He also hosts a whisky club.

Bières Spéciales

77 rue St-Maur, 11th (01.48.07.18.71). M° St-Maur. **Open** 4-9pm Mon; 10.30am-1pm, 4-9pm Tue-Sat. **Credit** AmEx, DC, MC, V. **Map** p403 M3. Single bottles and cans from 16 nations (at last count) neatly cover the walls. Belgium might dominate but you'll also find Polish, Scottish, Corsican, Portuguese and Chinese brews.

Les Domaines qui Montent

136 bd Voltaire, 11th (01.43.56.89.15). M° Voltaire. **Open** 10am-8pm Mue-Sat. Lunch served noon-2.30pm. **Credit** MC, V. **Map** p407 M5. This is not only a wine shop but a convivial place to have breakfast, lunch or tea. Wines cost the same as they would at the producer's. Saturday tastings with up-and-coming producers are featured in the shop.

Markets

Nothing tells you more about the French way of shopping – and living – than food markets. At a single street market, you might choose from a dozen shades of honey, buy sunflower-yellow unpasteurised butter for scrambling a free-range goose egg, take a chance on 'trumpets of death' (a sinister-looking wild mushroom) and order your chestnut-stuffed capon for Christmas. Quality comes at a price, but arrive as the market is shutting down and you can pick up bargain crates of fruit and vegetables. In an effort to fit in with working hours, the city is introducing afternoon and evening markets, complete with a child-minding service and home delivery. The pioneer market is **place Baudoyer**, in front of the mairie of the 4th *arrondissement*, now open on Wed from 3-8pm. Recently reopened is the city's oldest street market, the **Marché des Enfants Rouges** (*rue de Bretagne, 3rd. M° Temple*), with plans to make it a true farmers' market. Market streets and covered markets open from 8am-1pm and 4-7pm Tue-Sat; 8am-1pm Sun. Roving markets set up at 8am and vanish in a flurry of green street-sweeping trucks at 2pm.

Market streets

Rue Montorgueil, 2nd. M° Sentier.
Rue Mouffetard, 5th. M° Censier-Daubenton.
Rue Cler, 7th. M° Ecole Militaire.
Place d'Aligre, 12th. M° Ledru-Rollin.
Rue Daguerre, 14th. M° Denfert-Rochereau.
Rue Poncelet, 17th. M° Ternes.

Roving markets

Place Monge, 5th. M° Monge. Wed, Fri, Sun.
Saxe-Breteuil, 7th. M° Ségur. Thur, Sat.
Richard Lenoir, 11th. M° Bastille. Thur, Sun.
Cour de Vincennes, 12th. M° Nation. Wed, Sat.
Bd Auguste Blanqui, 13th. M° Place d'Italie. Tue, Fri, Sun.
Av Président Wilson, 16th. M° Pont de l'Alma. Wed, Sat.
Pyrénées, 20th. M° Jourdain. Thur, Sun.

Organic roving markets

Bd Raspail, 6th. M° Rennes. Sun.
Place Brancusi, 14th. M° Gaîté. Sat.
Rue St-Charles, 15th. M° Dupleix. Fri.
Bd des Batignolles, 17th. M° Villiers. Sat.

Eat, Drink, Shop

Discover the Show of the Most Famous Cabaret in the World !
Dinner & Show at 7pm from €130 • Show at 9pm: €92, at 11pm: €82
Montmartre - 82, boulevard de Clichy - 75018 Paris
Reservations: 01 53 09 82 82 - www.moulin-rouge.com

Prices valid from 1.11.02 to 31.10.03

Arts & Entertainment

Feature boxes

Festivals & Events

Wine, rebellions, the Bible – all valid reasons for a knees-up. There's also blazing saddles, new balls, please, and sandcastles by the Seine.

When it comes to gatecrashing another city's culture, Paris has a knack for making you feel like you're making a rather cool entrance. Traditional French street parties, such as Fête de la Musique, are easy to join in, while smaller dos allow you to spy on local rituals.

The biggest cultural events migrate to the South in summer, but an extensive open-air season is lined-up for those left in Paris. Mayor Delanoë's 'Paris Plage' and 'Nuit Blanche' initiatives are lined up to continue, and have been hailed as the best things since sliced baguette (knife attacks on the Mayor excepted).

The *Time Out Paris* section inside *Pariscope* covers events each week. Selected museum shows are previewed in the **Museums** chapter; further annual events and festivals are covered in the **Arts & Entertainment** chapters.

Public holidays

On *jours fériés* banks, many museums, most shops and some restaurants close; public transport runs as on Sunday. New Year, May Day, Bastille Day and Christmas are the most fully observed holidays. Full list: New Year's Day (Jour de l'An); Easter Monday (Lundi de Pâques); May Day (Fête du Travail); VE Day (Victoire 1945) 8 May; Ascension Day (Jour de l'Ascension); Whit Monday (Lundi de Pentecôte); Bastille Day (Quatorze Juillet) 14 July; Feast of the Assumption (Jour de l'Assomption) 15 Aug; All Saints' Day (Toussaint) 1 Nov; Remembrance Day (L'Armistice 1918) 11 Nov; Christmas Day (Noël).

Spring

end Feb-mid Mar: Festival EXIT
Maison des Arts et de la Culture de Créteil, pl Salvador Allende, 94000 Créteil (01.45.13.19.19/ www.maccreteil.com). M° Créteil-Préfecture. **Tickets** €7-€18.
This modern, international festival sets contemporary dance and theatre against new technology.

end Mar: Salon de l'Agriculture
Paris-Expo, pl de la Porte de Versailles, 15th. M° Porte de Versailles. **Information** 01.49.09.60.00/ www.salon-agriculture.com. **Admission** €6-€10.
France's farmers meet to show off beautiful beasts and prize crops. There's also regional food and wine.

Mar-Apr: Banlieues Bleues
Seine St-Denis area (01.49.22.10.10/ www.banlieuesbleues.org). **Admission** €11-€15.

Five weeks of French and international jazz, blues, R&B, soul, funk, flamenco, world and gospel.

20-21 Mar: La Nuit des Publivores
Grand Rex, 1 bd Poissonnière, 2nd. M° Bonne-Nouvelle. **Information** 01.44.88.98.00/ www.miko.fr/publivores. **Admission** €34.
This all-night ad-fest elevates commercial breaks to cult status. A pantomime atmosphere pervades.

end Mar-early May: Foire du Trône
pelouse de Reuilly, 12th (01.46.27.52.29/ www.foiredutrone.com). M° Porte Dorée. **Admission** free; rides €1.50-€4.
France's biggest funfair boasts stomach-churning rides, bungee jumping, freak shows and candyfloss.

Good Friday: Le Chemin de la Croix
square Willette, 18th. M° Anvers or Abbesses. **Information** Sacré-Coeur (01.53.41.89.00).
Crowds follow the Archbishop of Paris from the bottom of Montmartre up the steps to the Sacré-Coeur, as he performs the stations of the cross.

24 Mar-1 Apr: Festival du Film de Paris
Various venues. **Information** 01.45.72.96.40/ www.festivaldufilmdeparis.com. **Admission** €6-€7.
Public previews of international films, plus mingling with directors, actors and technicians. British film-making is celebrated in 2003.

1 Apr: Poisson d'Avril
Watch your back as pranksters attempt to stick paper fish on to each other as an April Fool's gag.

6 Apr: Marathon de Paris
starts around 9am, av des Champs-Elysées, first runners finish around 11am, av Foch. **Information** 01.41.33.15.68/www.parismarathon.com.
The Paris marathon takes in many of the city's personal bests. There's also a half-marathon in March.

beg May: Foire de Paris
Paris-Expo, pl de la Porte de Versailles. M° Porte de Versailles. **Information** 01.49.09.60.00/ www.comexpo-paris.com. **Admission** €9.15.
This enormous lifestyle salon includes world crafts and foods, plus the latest health and house gizmos.

1 May: Fête du Travail
Labour Day is ardently maintained. All museums and sights (except the Eiffel Tower) close, while unions stage a colourful march through working-class eastern Paris via the Bastille. Lilies of the valley are sold on street corners and given to mum.

Tour de France: the most gruelling sporting event in the world. *See p278.*

23-25 May: Le Printemps des rues

Information 01.47.97.36.06/
www.leprintempsdesrues.com. **Admission** free.
Street performance, exhibitions, and music around
Bastille, Bercy, République, Nation and La Villette.

mid May-end July: Paris Jazz Festival

*Parc Floral de Paris, Bois de Vincennes. M° Château
de Vincennes.* **Information** 01.55.94.20.20/
www.parcfloraldeparis.com. **Admission** park €1.50.
Free outdoor jazz concerts on hot weekend afternoons, in the charming Parc Floral.

mid May-end June: Festival de St-Denis

Various venues in St-Denis. M° St-Denis Basilique.
Information 01.48.13.06.07/www.festival-saint-
denis.fr. **Admission** €9-€55.
The Gothic St-Denis Basilica and other historic
buildings host classical concerts.

Summer

26 May-8 June: French Tennis Open

*Stade Roland Garros, 2 av Gordon-Bennett, 16th
(01.47.43.48.00/www.frenchopen.org). M° Porte
d'Auteuil.* **Admission** €21-€53.
Showbiz stars fill the stands at the glitzy Grand
Slam tournament to watch the balls fly.

beg June: Journées de la Maison Contemporaine

Various venues. **Information** 01.53.90.19.30/
www.maisonscontemporaines.com. **Admission** free.
Modern architects open up the sleek abodes they've
designed for public inspection.

beg June: Les Cinq Jours de l'Objet Extraordinaire

*rues du Bac, des Sts-Pères, de l'Université, quai
Voltaire, 7th. M° Rue du Bac.* **Information**
01.42.60.70.10/www.carrerivegauche.com.
Admission free.
Chic antique dealers each showcase one exciting find.

5 June-6 July: Foire St-Germain

*pl St-Sulpice and other venues in St-Germain des
Prés, 6th. M° St-Sulpice.* **Information**
01.43.29.61.04/www.foiresaintgermain.org.
Concerts, theatre, lectures and workshops. In the
square there's an antiques fair and poetry salon.

mid June-mid July: Festival Chopin à Paris

*Orangerie de Bagatelle, parc de Bagatelle, Bois de
Boulogne, 16th. M° Porte Maillot, then bus 244.*
Information 01.45.00.22.19/www.frederic-
chopin.com. **Admission** €16-€31.
The romance of the piano is promised, with candle-
lit evening concerts complementing the mood.

21 June: Fête de la Musique

All over France. **Information** 01.40.03.94.70/
www.fetedelamusique.fr. **Admission** free.
Dancing in the streets as free concerts invade the city.
The music is incredibly varied.

28 June: Gay Pride March

Information Centre Gai et Lesbien (01.43.57.21.47/
www.gaypride.fr).
Outrageous floats and costumes parade towards
Bastille. Followed by an official *fête* and club events
(*see p280*, **Pink, proud and politicised**).

Arts & Entertainment

23-29 June: Festival de Jazz Django Reinhardt

Samois-sur-Seine, Ile de Berceau. SNCF Fontainebleau/Avon. **Information** 01.64.24.86.45/ www.django.samois.free.fr. **Admission** €15-€50.
Django Reinhardt retired to Samois-sur-Seine, where gypsy jazz fans mark the 50th anniversary of his death at 2003's festival.

beg July: La Goutte d'Or en Fête

square Léon, 18th. M° Barbès-Rochechouart. **Information** 01.46.07.61.64/ www.gouttedorenfete.org. **Admission** free.
Established names play raï, rap and reggae alongside local talent in the up-and-coming, largely Arab and African Goutte d'Or neighbourhood.

beg July-end Aug: Le Cinéma en Plein Air

Parc de la Villette, 19th (01.40.03.76.92/www.la-villette.com). M° Porte de Pantin. **Admission** free.
Settle back in a deckchair as night falls over the park and take in classic films projected onto the big screen.

13, 14 July: Le Quatorze Juillet (Bastille Day)

The French national holiday commemorates the storming of the Bastille prison on 14 July 1789, start of the French Revolution and a foretaste of bloodier events to come (*see chapter* **History**). On the evening of 13 July, Parisians dance at place de la Bastille. More partying takes place at firemen's balls: the stations in rue de Sévigné, rue du Vieux-Colombier, rue Blanche and bd du Port-Royal are particularly renowned (usually 13 and 14 July). There's a big gay ball on quai de la Tournelle (5th). At 10am on the 14th, crowds line the Champs-Elysées as the President reviews a military parade from the Arc de Triomphe to Concorde. (Note: Métro stops on the Champs are closed.) In the evening, thousands gather on the Champ de Mars for fireworks at Trocadéro.

14 July: Miss Guinguette

38 quai Victor Hugo, Ile du Martin Pêcheur, Champigny sur Marne. RER Champigny sur Marne. **Information** 01.49.83.03.02. **Admission** €7.50.
A hunt to find the light-footed queen of the open-air dance hall scene, on this river island venue.

mid July-mid Aug: Paris, Quartier d'Eté

Various venues. **Information** 01.44.94.98.00/ www.quartierdete.com. **Admission** free-€15.
A lively series features classical and jazz concerts, dance and theatre performances in outdoor venues like the Tuileries and the Palais-Royal.

mid July-mid Aug: Paris-Plage

quai Henri IV to quai des Tuileries. M° Sully Morland. **Information** 08.20.00.75.75/www.paris.fr. **Admission** free.
Mayor Bertrand Delanoë brings sand to the masses, with this city-to-seaside metamorphosis. Sunbathers laze by the Seine on (France's smallest) beaches, under the shade of fake palm trees. Rollerbladers, cyclists and walkers have free run of the *quais*.

July: Le Tour de France

finishes av des Champs-Elysées, 8th. **Information** 01.41.33.15.00/www.letour.fr.
Spot the yellow jersey as cyclists speed along the Champs-Elysées to the finish line of this epic endurance test.

Aug: Cinéma au clair de lune

Various venues. **Information** 01.44.76.62.18/ www.forumdesimages.net. **Admission** free.
Reels on wheels provide open-air screenings of films set in Paris, near the locations where they were shot.

15 Aug: Fête de l'Assomption

Cathédrale Notre-Dame de Paris, pl Notre-Dame, 4th (01.42.34.56.10). M° Cité. **Admission** free.
Notre-Dame becomes again a place of religious rather than touristic pilgrimage, with a parade around the Ile de la Cité behind a statue of the Virgin. A national public holiday.

end Aug-beg Sept: L'Etrange Festival

Forum des Images, Porte Saint-Eustache, Forum des Halles, 1st. M° Les Halles. **Information** 01.44.76.62.00. **Admission** €4.50-€6.
Get your freak on with this celebration of weird celluloid, including all-night 'Nuits Freakshows'.

31 Aug: Fête du Seigneur Ganesha

starts at Temple Sri Manicka Vinayakar Alayam, 72 rue Philippe de Gérard, 18th. M° La Chapelle. **Information** 01.40.34.21.89. **Admission** free.
A lively annual procession celebrates the Hindu child-god Ganesha Chaturthi.

Autumn

mid Sept: Jazz à La Villette

211 av Jean-Jaurès, 19th (08.03.07.50.75/ 01.44.84.44.84/www.la-villette.com). M° Porte de Pantin. **Admission** €13-€16.
One of Paris' best jazz fests. The line-up is stacked with big names and up-and-coming talents.

13 Sept: Techno Parade

Information 01.42.47.84.76/www.technopol.net.
BPM junkies get their annual headrush with this parade (usually finishing at place de la Bastille). Marks the start of Rendez-vous Electroniques.

mid-Sept: Rendez-vous Electroniques

Information www.technopol.net.
Paris becomes a magnet for all things electronic. Most clubs put on some kind of event, there's also VJing, films and multimedia installations.

Hey, guys, let's do the **Techno Parade** right here! *See above.*

mid-Sept: Fête de L'Humanité
Probably Parc de La Corneuve, Seine-St-Denis.
Information 01.49.22.72.72/www.humanite.presse.fr.
Admission €10.
L'Humanité, French Communist Party newspaper, has run this popular festival since 1930. A (very Parisian) mix of world music, jazz and heated debate.

3rd weekend in Sept: Journées du Patrimoine
All over France. **Information** CNMHS, Hôtel de Sully, 62 rue St-Antoine, 4th (01.44.61.20.00/ www.jp.culture.fr).
This is the weekend when thousands queue to see the parts the public cannot reach. It's an exercise in faux state glasnost, but no less interesting for that. The longest waits are for the Palais de l'Elysée (home of the President), Matignon (home of the PM), Palais-Royal (Ministry of Culture, Conseil d'Etat) and Palais du Luxembourg (Senate). If you don't like waiting, seek out more obscure embassies, ministries or opulent corporate headquarters: the Marais and Fbg-St-Germain are particularly ripe for historic mansion-hopping. *Le Monde* and *Le Parisien* publish info.

mid Sept-end Dec: Festival d'Automne
Various venues. **Information** 156 rue de Rivoli, 1st (01.53.45.17.00/www.festival-automne.com).
Admission €9-€30.

Keeping Paris at the cutting edge, this festival features challenging contemporary theatre, dance and modern opera, and is committed to bringing non-Western culture into the French consciousness.

Sept: La Journée sans voitures
An attempt to save the environment by getting the French to leave their cars at home for the day.

end Sept: Portes Ouvertes à la Garde Républicaine
18 bd Henri IV, 4th (01.49.96.13.26).
M° Sully Morland. **Admission** free.
The public is allowed a rare glimpse of the uniforms, arms and gleaming mounts of the Presidential Guard.

Oct: Open Studios
Bastille, 11th, 12th (Artistes à la Bastille 01.53.36.06.73; Génie de la Bastille 01.40.09.84.03); Ménilmontant, 11th, 20th (01.40.03.01.61); 13ème Art, 13th (01.45.86.17.67). **Admission** free.
Artists open their studios to the public around the Bastille, Ménilmontant and the 13th.

early Oct: Fête des Vendanges à Montmartre
rue des Saules, 18th. M° Lamarck-Caulaincourt. Mairie du XVIIIème, 1 pl Jules-Joffrin, 18th. M° Jules-Joffrin. **Information** 01.46.06.00.32.
Music, speeches, locals in costume and a parade celebrate the Montmartre grape harvest.

Pink, proud and politicised

The Mayor, trade unions, nightclub floats, rainbow flags, multi-coloured balloons, flamboyant costumes and 650,000 people... welcome to the March of Lesbian, Gay, Bi and Trans Prides. Or if you can get your tongue round this mouthful in French, *la Marche des fiertés lesbiennes, gaies, bi et trans.*

Known as 'Gay Pride' during the late 1980s and early 1990s, it was renamed again in 2001 to include the bisexual, transsexual and transgender communities.

Held on a Saturday afternoon towards the end of June (28th in 2003), the parade attracts drag queens, men wearing nothing but a G-string and leather boots with five-inch-high heels, and topless women with painted breasts. Music from the different floats blares out as thousands of people dance their way through the streets of Paris to proclaim the right to sexual diversity and equality.

The event is organised by the umbrella association Inter-LGBT (*Interassociative lesbienne, gaie, bi et trans*) and last year 98 groups participated. The SNEG (the National Union for Gay Businesses) teamed up with

Queen nightclub for a joint float, and other participants included Amnesty International, the League of Human Rights, Pink TV, Durex, SIDA Info, and the nightclubs Pulp and Folies Pigalle. The march won support from the Socialist Party, the French Communist Party and the Green party.

Far more than a fun festival, the march is a highly political event. Its organisers have three main objectives. 'The march is for the adoption of children by couples of the same sex; it is for marriage rights for gay couples. Even if they're "pacsed" – the PACS is a civil union for gay couples – their rights are very limited compared to those of married couples. We also seek the condemnation of homophobic comments,' explains Thomas Lamandé, director of the march.

Launched in 1971 by 300 people, the march places its origins in the Stonewall riots in New York in 1969 and the revolutionary movement in France following May 1968. Both militant and fun, the March of Lesbian, Gay, Bi and Trans Prides is one of the most colourful dates on the Parisian calendar.

Arts & Entertainment

4-5 Oct: Prix de l'Arc de Triomphe

Hippodrome de Longchamp, Bois de Boulogne, 16th (01.49.10.20.30/www.france-galop.com). Mᵒ Porte d'Auteuil, plus free shuttle bus. **Admission** free-€8.
France's richest flat race attracts the elite of horse racing amid much pomp and ceremony.

early Oct: Nuit Blanche

Information 08.20.00.75.75/www.paris.fr.
Admission free.
Delanoë's initiative keeps the city up all night with culture by moonlight. Events marry unusual venues with big names: 2002 saw artist Sophie Calle sleeping at the top of the Eiffel Tower.

mid Oct: Festival America

Various venues, Vincennes. Mᵒ Château de Vincennes. **Information** 02.23.21.06.21/www.festival-america.com. **Admission** €5-€12.
New literary hob-nobbing fest celebrates writing from the Americas. Previous guests have included Arthur Miller and Margaret Atwood.

end Oct: Salon du Chocolat

Venue to be confirmed (01.45.03.21.26).
Admission €5-€10.
Chocolatiers from around the world gather to show off their mastery of the art of chocolate-making.

end Oct: FIAC

Paris-Expo, Porte de Versailles. 15th. Mᵒ Porte de Versailles. **Information** OIP (01.41.90.47.80/www.fiaconline.com). **Admission** €14.
Well-respected international contemporary art fair.

1 Nov: All Saints' Day

1 Nov is an important date for traditionalists – a day for visiting cemeteries and remembering the dead.

early Nov: Festival Fnac-Inrockuptibles

La Cigale, Divan du Monde and other venues.
Information www.fnac.fr. **Admission** varies.
Originally indie-centred, Inrocks has lately admitted trance, techno and trip hop. Still the place to discover the next big thing.

11 Nov: Armistice Day

Arc de Triomphe, 8th. Mᵒ Charles de Gaulle-Etoile.
At the remembrance ceremony for the dead of both World Wars, wreaths are laid by the President at the Tomb of the Unknown Soldier under the Arc de Triomphe. The remembrance flower is not the poppy but the *bleuet* (cornflower) after the colour of the *pantalons* worn by World War I infantry. *See also p350,* **Compiègne**.

20 Nov: Fête du Beaujolais Nouveau

The arrival of Beaujolais Nouveau on the third Thursday in November is no longer hyped, but wine bars and cafés still throng (some from midnight on Wednesday, but especially Thursday evening) as customers 'assess' the new vintage.

Winter

Dec-Mar: Patinoire de l'Hôtel de Ville

pl de l'Hôtel de Ville, 4th. Mᵒ Hôtel de Ville.
Information 08.20.00.75.75/www.paris.fr.
Admission free (skate hire €4.50).
Take to the ice on the fir-tree-lined outdoor rink in front of the city hall, the perfect way to warm yourself up on a frosty evening. Watch out for the pros.

end Dec: Africolor

Various venues, St-Denis (01.47.97.69.99/www.africolor.com). Mᵒ St-Denis Basilique.
Admission €13.
The African music festival features traditional and new musical trends from the African continent, with a spirited end-of-festival party.

24, 25 Dec: Christmas

Christmas is a family affair in France, with a dinner on Christmas Eve, normally after mass, that traditionally involves foie gras or oysters, goose or turkey and a rich Yule log (*bûche de Noël*). Notre-Dame cathedral is packed for the 11pm service. Children put out shoes for Father Christmas.

31 Dec: New Year's Eve

On the *Réveillon,* or Fête de la St-Sylvestre, thousands crowd the Champs-Elysées and let off bangers. New Year is almost bigger than Christmas in France and nightclubs and restaurants put on expensive soirées. More foie gras and bubbly.

1 Jan: La Grande Parade de Paris

Venue to be confirmed. **Information** 03.44.27.45.67/www.parisparade.com.
Extravagant and colourful floats, giant balloons, bands and dancers parade along the streets.

6 Jan: Fête des Rois (Epiphany)

Pâtisseries sell *galettes des rois*, cakes with frangipane filling in which a *fève* or tiny charm is hidden. Whoever finds it dons a cardboard crown, becomes king or queen for a day, and chooses a consort.

Jan: Commemorative Mass for Louis XVI

Chapelle Expiatoire, 29 rue Pasquier, 8th (01.42.65.35.80). Mᵒ St-Augustin.
On the Sunday closest to 21 January, anniversary of the beheading of Louis XVI in 1793, France's aristocracy gather with die-hard royalists and other far-right crackpots to mourn the end of the monarchy. Firm republicans are supposed to mark the day by eating *tête de veau*.

Jan/Feb: Nouvel An Chinois

Around av d'Ivry and av de Choisy, 13th. Mᵒ Porte de Choisy or Porte d'Ivry.
Lion and dragon dances and martial arts demonstrations in celebration of the Chinese New Year. Some restaurants offer special menus. Festivities take place on the nearest weekend(s) to the actual date.

Cabaret, comedy & circus

Roll up, roll up (or should that be *croissant* up?). Rib-tickling raconteurs, twinkling, leggy lovelies and gigantic titters. Oh, be still, our beating beret!

You want saucy? We've got saucy. After all, this is the place that launched frilly drawers, fishnet stockings and lingerie that twangs to the rhythm of the cancan – and that's just what the guys wear. You can still join the joyous throng at one of Paris' glamour cabarets, where traditional high-kicks combine with snazzy effects and couples sip Champagne and admire the 'interpretive dancing' together. But don't kid yourself that those legs are homegrown – they are more likely to hail from Paris Texas than Paris France with a smattering of Lancashire lasses thrown in. Those who are offended by that kind of showbiz should be aware that traditional Paris cabaret is still very much a get-your-glitz-out-for-the-boys genre.

All things circus are lapped up big-top style in Paris. The **parc de la Villette** alone boasts three venues and offers the best in ground-breaking circus extravaganza, from operatic acrobats to equestrian robots. Fans of the more traditional circus number – poodle-pushing-pram hilarity – fret not: it's all on offer all-year-round in what is fast becoming the critics' choice circus capital of the world.

Paris may not be known as the comedy capital of the world (the idea of French stand-up

makes some people want to sit down), but there's plenty of choice for those who fancy a Gallic giggle. For an all-in fee, many venues serve up satire, songs, plays or sketches with a meal and multiple bottles of wine. A clutch of bars and restaurants offer *café-théâtre* in its purest form: performance round your ear-holes and free of charge.

Cabaret

Crazy Horse Saloon

12 av George V, 8th (01.47.23.32.32). M° Alma-Marceau or George V. **Shows** 8.30pm, 11pm Mon-Fri, Sun; 7.30pm, 9.45pm, 11.50am Sat. **Tickets** €69-€90 for two drinks & show; €20 extra for Champagne. **Credit** DC, MC, V. **Map** p400 D4.
Lithe 'sculptural dancers' with names such as Choochoo Night Train cavort about the stage in an entirely captivating and inoffensive manner. Worth a visit if only to check out the shop, where you can buy such must-haves as Crazy Horse dressing gown.

Le Lido

116bis av des Champs-Elysées, 8th (01.40.76.56.10/ www.lido.fr). M° George V. **Dinner** 7.30pm. **Shows** 10pm Mon-Thur, Sun; 10pm and midnight Sat. Tickets with Champagne-€90; dinner & show €130-€160. **Credit** AmEx, DC, MC, V. **Map** p400 D4.
The 60 Bluebell Girls shake their booty in a classy show with plenty of special effects including a fire-breathing dragon and an ice-rink. *Wheelchair access.*

Moulin Rouge

82 bd de Clichy, 18th (01.53.09.82.82/www.moulin-rouge.com). M° Blanche. **Shows** 7pm, 9pm, 11pm daily, dinner two hours before. **Tickets** €82-€92 Champagne & show; €130-€160 dinner & show. **Credit** AmEx, DC, MC, V. **Map** p401 G2.
Untouched by Lurhmannesque influence, the Pigalle venue is the most traditional of the glitzy cabarets and still relies on feathers, breasts and sparkling grins as the 60 Dorriss girls cancan across the stage.

La Nouvelle Eve

25 rue de la Fontaine, 9th (01.48.78.37.96). M° Blanche. **Open** Apr-Dec. **Shows** 6.30pm, 9.45pm daily. **Tickets** €75 show and half-bottle of Champagne, €111 dinner and show. **Credit** AmEx, MC, V. **Map** p401 H2.
Small fry compared to the big-name cabarets, La Nouvelle Eve offers a more intimate peek, some would say flash, at Pigalle traditions. Handy for those who eschew the headmaster's warning.

Au Bec Fin

6 rue Thérèse, 1st (01.42.96.29.35). M° Pyramides.
Shows daily, matinees for children Wed, Sat, Sun.
call for start times. Closed Aug. **Tickets** €14; €12
students; €8 children, €36 dinner & show. **Credit**
MC, V. **Map** p401 H5.
The owner's very proud of it: this is the oldest *café-
théâtre* venue in Paris, claiming a 300-year-old pedigree. Dine in the restaurant then head upstairs to a
'compact' theatre to see everything from Chekhov to
a cheesy version of Robin Hood for the little 'uns.
Open mike on Mondays for the confident or the -
deluded always provides a giggle.

Café de la Gare

*41 rue du Temple, 4th (01.42.78.52.51/
www.cafe-de-la-gare.fr.st). M° Hôtel de Ville or
Rambuteau.* **Shows** 8pm or 10pm Wed-Sun.
Tickets €18. **Credit** MC, V. **Map** p406 K6.
Up and running since the revolutionary days of 1968
and the most famous *café-théâtre* in Paris, this
atmospheric venue has 300 stage-hugging seats and
hosts quality French stand-up and raucous, irreverent comedies in the 'Carry On' line.

Le Point Virgule

*7 rue Ste-Croix-de-la-Bretonnerie, 4th
(01.42.78.67.03). M° Hôtel de Ville.* **Shows** 7.30pm,
9pm, 10pm daily. **Tickets** €15, €12 students.
No credit cards. Map p406 K6.

Bar none

The term *café-théâtre* now covers everything
from 400-seat comedy venues to whistling
waiters. It's at its purest in the handful of
bars where brave new theatre is put on
round the tables, in your face and free of
charge. No-one dishes it up with more
panache than **Compagnie l'Abribus**
(*pictured right*, 01.42.26.31.21), which has
been entertaining drinkers in various
establishments with short and snappy
musical comedies since 2001. Shows start
when the bar's full and involve audience
interaction (of the friendliest variety – and
don't worry if your French isn't top-notch). And
it's free, with a hat passed round at the end.

The thought of someone thrusting their
party piece on you while you're trying to get
harmlessly wrecked may not appeal, and
these are not the places to go for Andrew
Lloyd Webber populism. But the French have
that 'let's do the show right here' attitude in
spades, and *théâtre dans les bars* – they do
love their sub-genres – is a valid fringe scene
for up-and-coming talent. It's a tradition that
goes back to the artistic experimentation of
the 60s, and is related to French *chanson*,
so don't be perturbed if the performers
frequently break into impassioned song.
What's more, the artistic natural selection
that's at play is usually a guarantee of high
standards: with the exit door *and* a person
selling alcohol both a matter of metres away,
a mediocre show won't stick the circuit long.
Similar conditions at the Comédie Française
would have the actors quaking in their
posture-enhancing boots.

La Patache (60 rue de Lancry, 10th/
01.42.08.14.35; M° Jacques Bonsergent)
is a well-established venue for bar theatre. Not

palatial and certainly smokey (just how
Parisians like it), it has shows most nights of
the week and Sunday afternoons. **La Grosse
Caisse** (6 rue de la Main d'Or, 11th/
01.49.23.05.91; M° Ledru Rollin) has a
regular slot on Sunday evenings for theatre
(7.30pm-ish) and snacks on the bar. For a
good, reasonably priced meal, a serious
selection of wines and music or theatre at no
extra cost, head for **La Part des Anges** (51 rue
de la Fontaine au Roi, 11th/06.12.40.09.41;
M° Goncourt). To find out what's going on in a
bar or bistro near you, try www.zingueurs.com.

Arts & Entertainment

This small Marais theatre is one of the few to stay open in summer. Shows are slick and professional and attract vibrant crowds regularly. Look out for the popular autumn comedy festival.

Le Tartuffe
46 rue Notre-Dame-de-Lorette, 9th (01.45.26.21.37). M° St Georges or Pigalle. **Shows** 7.30pm Mon-Sat. **Tickets** dinner and all three shows €26-€29; €16 with a drink after 9pm. **Credit** MC, V. **Map** p402 H3.
True comic cabaret with great atmosphere. Three acts per night culminate in audience participation and certain embarrassment.

Le Zèbre
63 bd de Belleville, 20th (01.47.99.40.40). M° Père Lachaise. **Open** varies. **Tickets** vary. **Map** p403 N4.
Circus impresario Francis Schoeller came to the rescue of the art deco Zèbre last year, kicking off with the superbly surreal Cirque Cruel (*pictured, p282*). This year it's changed its tack slightly, promising comic cabaret and *chanson*.

Comedy in English

Laughing Matters
Info (01.53.19.98.88/www.anythingmatters.com). Shows normally take place at the Hôtel du Nord, 102 quai de Jemmapes, 10th. M° République or Jacques Bonsergent. **Tickets** €15; €12 students. **No credit cards. Map** p402 L3.
This, in case you were wondering, is the Hôtel du Nord of the Marcel Carné film. Nowadays, its rafters are rocked by titters inspired by big-name Anglophone mirthsters who wander over for a jolly and provide many a memorable show. To come in 2003: Johnny Vegas, Ed Byrne and Ardal O'Hanlon.

Circus

Traditional circuses

For full circus listings consult *Cirque* in the children's section of *Pariscope*. Several troupes move into town for the Christmas season, and it's always worth checking out the giant Cirque Pinder, which is generally around from mid-November to early January (01.45.90.21.25/www.cirquepinder.com).

Le Cirque du Grand Céleste
13 av de la Porte des Lilas, 19th (01.53.19.99.13/ www.grandceleste.com). M° Porte des Lilas. **Open** Oct-Apr. **Shows** matinees Wed, Sat, Sun (times are variable, so phone to check); 8.45pm Fri, Sat (Wed-Sun in school holidays). **Tickets** €20-€26, €13 for children. **No credit cards**.
An impressive traditional circus without the tacky showbiz feel of some. In an intimate, relaxed atmosphere the performers mingle with the audience before the show starts. Why not take some sausages and get friendly with the fire eater?

Cirque d'Hiver Bouglione
110 rue Amelot, 11th (01.47.00.12.25/ www.cirquedhiver.com). M° Filles du Calvaire. **Shows** vary. **Tickets** €10-€35. **Credit** V. **Map** p402 L5.
The beautiful winter circus was built by Hittorff. Bouglione mounts an extravaganza twice a year, with animals, cabaret and international performers.

Cirque de Paris
115 bd Charles de Gaulle, 92390 Villeneuve la Garenne (01.47.99.40.40). M° Porte de Clignancourt + Bus 137 (Zone Industriel Nord) or RER St Denis + bus 261. **Open** Oct-June 10am-5pm Wed, Sun. **Shows** 3pm. **Tickets** (day of circus) €35-€4 adults, €30-€34 children; (show only) €11-€24 adults, €7-€15 children. **Credit** MC, V.
Definitely one for circus addicts. Spend the day fulfilling circus dreams, learn the tricks of the trade and even have lunch with the stars before the show.

Romanès Cirque Tsigane
12 rue Paul-Bert, 11th (01.40.09.24.20). M° Faidherbe-Chaligny. **Open** Oct-Feb. **Shows** vary. **Tickets** €17, €9 students, under 18s. **No credit cards. Map** p407 N7.
Traditional brilliance from the Romanès family circus. A gypsy band accompanies trapeze, juggling, contortionism and songs in the tiny *chapiteau* that moves back here whenever they're in town.

Contemporary circus venues

Cabaret Sauvage
Parc de la Villette, 19th (01.40.03.75.15/ www.cabaretsauvage.com). M° Porte de la Villette. **Shows** vary. **Tickets** €12-€20. **Credit** MC, V. **Map** p403 inset.
Housed in an old circus venue, a mixture of tent, Western saloon and hall of mirrors provides a stage for jugglers, acrobats and other performers, plus concerts and *bals*.

Espace Chapiteaux
Parc de la Villette, 19th (01.40.03.75.15/ www.villette.com). M° Porte de Pantin or Porte de la Villette. **Shows** Wed-Sat 8.30pm; Sun Matinees 4pm. **Tickets** €17; €14 students, under 25s; €8 under 12s. **Credit** MC, V. **Map** p403 inset.
Parc de la Villette's impressive premiere venue boasts a jam-packed calendar. Cirque Plume are regulars and 2003 sees the return of Carles Santos' opera-circus hybrid *Sama Samaruck Suck Suck*.

Olé Bodega
square Victor, rue Lucien Bossoutrot, 15th (01.53.02.90.85/www.olebodega.com). M° Balard. **Open** 8.30-2am Wed-Sat. **Shows** around 9.30pm. **Admission** free, but shows for diners only. **Credit** AmEx, MC, V. **Map** p404 A10.
A jamboree of astonishing acrobatic displays and spirited partying. Catch the spinning, twisiting performers over dinner, before they make way for zealous gaggles of teenagers trampling the circular wooden dancefloor to pop and French *chanson*.

Children

It's official: Paris loves kids. The city is bulging with activities that will keep children engrossed, amused and – if only temporarily – at bay.

Parisians have model children. None of the hair-pulling, chocolate-smeared faces and diva stroppiness that the rest of us have to put up with. How do they do it? Easy: they keep their kids busy – the Paris calendar is packed with infant-friendly events. You'll hear the firecrackers cracking when Chinese New Year (in February) rolls along: thousands head down to the 13th *arrondissement* to see Chinatown's floats, dragons, martial arts displays and beautiful costumes. The *Fête de la Musique* (21 June) and Bastille Day (14 July) are excuses for colourful parades, music and dancing, and new kid in the *quartier*, Halloween, has taken off in a big way. At Christmas, the big department stores arrange wonderful animated window displays, and ice-rinks appear at Hôtel de Ville and Montparnasse. All-year-round carousels reside near most tourist draws and mini-playgrounds are everywhere. Funfairs like the Foire du Trône (*see p286* **Babes in the wood**) and a mini-version in the Tuileries pop up regularly, and circuses (*see chapter* **Cabaret, Comedy & Circus**) and puppet shows are always on somewhere. Most museums, theatres and venues pride themselves on cultivating young egg-heads: programming, workshops and demonstrations abound. If that's not enough to exhaust them, get the wains to burn off surplus energy by taking them for a frolic in one of Paris' many parks and playgrounds. Older kids benefit from a bit of biking or boating in the *bois* (*see p286* **Babes in the wood**), and you're never too young to start rollerblading – the Roller Squad Institut (01.56.61.99.61/www.rsi.asso.fr) organises roller tours for six-to-tens on Sundays. Paris has great outdoor pools (*see chapter* **Sport & Fitness**). If the weather's iffy, hit indoor Aquaboulevard (4 rue Louis Armand, 15th/01.40.60.10.00).

To see what's on offer, get hold of a *Pariscope* (www.pariscope.fr). Drop into the *mairie* (town hall) of any *arrondissement* for some free advice and guide books for kids' activities, or visit the **Espace du Tourisme** in the **Carrousel du Louvre**. The website www.iledenfance.com is another good source of ideas, as is the bi-monthly *Paris-Mômes* which comes with the *Libération* newspaper, at the tourist office and at various other locations (call 01.49.29.01.21 for more details).

Getting around

Public Transport

Paris is a city made for walking, and if you can substitute a stroll by the Seine for a Métro ride, do. If you have very young children, getting into, out of and through Métro stations can be literally an uphill battle. Like the city-folk they are, Parisians will blithely ignore you as you struggle with children, a pushchair and a bag of shopping – but if you do decide to take the challenge, try to travel between 10am and 5pm, to avoid the rush hour. Children might prefer the mostly overground lines: Line 6 (Nation-Charles de Gaulle-Etoile) and Line 2 (Nation-Porte Dauphine), both of which offer attractive views. However, the bus service in Paris is excellent, and a much more pleasant alternative. As for prices, under-fours travel free on public transport, while four-to-ten-year-olds are eligible for a *carnet* (ten tickets) at half-price. These tickets can be used on the whole Paris network (Métro, RERs and buses) – including the

Babes in the wood

Paris has wonderful woods, and they make a real change from inner-city parks. The **Bois de Vincennes**, on the eastern border of Paris, boasts acres of space. The nearby **Parc Zoölogique** has 60 species of beast, and its cages have been replaced by landscaped confines in this marvellously designed zoo. Seal feeding times attract a crowd of eager young onlookers tugging knackered parents that extra yard (you can always do the rounds on the small train).

The **Parc Floral de Paris** offers many free activities: table-tennis, butterfly gardens, libraries, exhibitions, concerts and puppet shows. You can play mini-golf through the monuments of Paris, hire a quadricycle, hop on a miniature train, go swimming or see a play at the Théâtre Astral. There's even a festival dedicated to three-to-tens: *Les Pestacles* runs from the beginning of May to the end of December and offers free shows for kids at 2.30pm most afternoons.

The **Bois de Boulogne**, on the other side of Paris, has many of the same features as Vincennes, but do note that it becomes a prostitutes' prowling ground in the evenings. The Lac Supérieur, with its waterfalls joining the Lac Inférieur, is the perfect place for a stroll, and boat hire is a popular option. Apart from donkey rides and bowling, kids might also be interested in the Jardin de Bagatelle, the famous rose garden, which is good for a run around. Another plus is the **Jardin d'Acclimatation**, an all-in-one day-of-fun, with kids' museums, craft workshops, funfair attractions, zoo and donkey-rides. All kinds of games are available, including mini-golf, table football, billiards and bowling, as well as energy-burning godsends such as rollercoasters, trampolines and a mini racing circuit. The interactive science museum, **Explor@dome** (*see p290* **Children of the (digital) revolution**) is button-pushing fun.

Groovy greenery

Bois de Vincennes

12th. Mº Porte-Dorée or Château de Vincennes.

Parc Zoölogique de Paris *53 av de St-Maurice, 12th (01.44.75.20.10/00). Mº Porte Dorée.* **Open** *Apr-Sept* 9am-6pm daily; *Oct-Mar* 9am-6pm daily. **Admission** €8; €5 4-16s, students, over-60s; free under-4s. **Credit** MC, V. **Wheelchair access.**

Parc Floral de Paris *(01.55.94.20.20/ www.parcfloraldeparis.com). Mº Château de Vincennes.* **Open** *summer* 9.30am-8pm; *winter* 9.30am-6pm. **Admission** €0.75 6-18s, over-60s; €1.50 adults. **No credit cards.** **Théâtre Astral in the Parc Floral** *(01.43.71.31.10).* **Tickets** €5.50; free under-6s. Reservation necessary. **No credit cards. Wheelchair access** (call ahead). **Bike hire** (01.47.47.76.50).

Bois de Boulogne

16th. Mº Porte Maillot or Porte Daupine.

Jardin d'Acclimatation *(01.40.67.90.82/ www.jardindacclimatation.fr). Mº Les Sablons or Porte Maillot then Petit Train (€4.60 every 15 mins from L'Orée du Bois restaurant, includes admission).* **Open** *winter* 10am-6pm daily; *summer* 10am-7pm daily. **Admission** €2.30; free under-3s. Carnet of tickets €35 for 20. **Credit** MC, V.

Bowling de Paris in the Jardin d'Acclimatation *(01.53.64.93.00).* **Open** 9am-3pm daily. €2.45-€6.10, depending on time of day. Reduced rate for under-20s. Shoe hire €1.50. **Credit** AmEx, DC, MC, V.

Boat hire *(01.45.25.44.01).* **Open** 11am-6pm Mon-Fri; 9am-6pm Sat-Sun; hours vary in winter (phone to check). €9.50/hour, deposit €30. **No credit cards.**

Little boats with big ideas in the **Bois de Vincennes**.

Arts & Entertainment

Montmartrobus minibus, the Montmartre funicular and the Balabus (Apr-Sept, Sun and holidays), which takes in most of the sights (see www.ratp.fr for details of routes).

Taxis

Parisian taxi drivers are not known for their sunny personalities, but the sight of a child will frequently touch the hearts of the bitter old misanthropes. Taxi drivers usually take only three people, but they will generally take a family of four, as long as one of the travellers is under ten (under-tens count as half, no matter how much noise they're making). There may be a small cover charge (around €1) for a pushchair.

Did you know?

There is an alternative to train, bus and taxi for getting around Paris: the boat. Batobus (01.44.11.33.99/www.batobus.com) links seven prime targets for visitors, such as the Eiffel Tower, St Germain-des-Prés and the Louvre between April and November, on a regular route, where boats pass every 20 minutes or so. The two-day ticket is good value at €12.50, with children under 12 travelling for €6.50, and there is no restriction on the number of journeys.

Help & babysitting

The American Church

65 quai d'Orsay, 7th (01.40.62.05.00/ www.americanchurchparis.org). M° Invalides. **Open** 9am-10pm Mon-Sat; 9am-2pm Sun. **Map** p401 E5.
The free noticeboard in the basement is a major source of information on recommended English-speaking baby-sitters and au pairs.

Baby Sitting Services

(01.46.21.33.16/www.babysittingservices.com). **Open** 24-hrs daily. **Babysitting** €5.90/hr + €9.90 tax Mon-Sat 8am-10pm; €6.60/hr + €15.90 tax Mon-Sat 10pm-8am, Sun and bank holidays. **Credit** MC, V.
This set-up offers not only baby-sitting at short notice, but also accompanied visits to museums, cinema etc, tuition, activities and children's parties.

Inter-Service Parents

(01.44.93.44.93). **Lines open** 9.30am-12.30pm, 1.30-5pm Mon, Tue, Fri; 9.30am-12.30pm Wed; 1.30-5pm Thur.
Free state-funded advice service lists babysitting agencies as well as giving advice on schools, child psychologists and family lawyers.

Message

(01.46.60.01.81/www.messageparis.org).
English-speaking support and network group for mothers and mothers-to-be of all nationalities living in Paris. This non-profit organisation gives advice and classes, as well as leisure activities for mothers. Its useful book, *ABCs of Motherhood in Paris*, costs €18 to non-members (€12 members).

Swings & roundabouts

Many public gardens offer mini playgrounds and concrete ping-pong tables – even the posh place des Vosges has small slides and rocking horses. Any Parisian park worth its sandpit has its own *théâtre de Guignol* (puppet theatre). There is a lot of frantic audience participation, and language usually isn't much of a barrier to the general shrieking. Bigger parks afford more freedom: the Bois de Vincennes and Bois de Boulogne provide picnic areas, boating lakes and cycle paths (*see left* **Babes in the wood**). Park-keepers seem to have got a little more lenient since the Berlin Wall came down, but the grass is still strictly out of bounds in the Luxembourg (except for one lawn), Tuileries, Monceau and Palais-Royal parks.

Parc des Buttes-Chaumont

19th (01.42.02.91.21). M° Buttes Chaumont or Botzaris. **Open** *May, June, Sept, Oct* 6.30am-10pm; *July, Aug* 6.30am-11pm; *Nov-Apr* 6.30am-9pm. **Map** p403 N2.
A fabulous place for exploring. The view from the top of this hillside park is as good as the one from Sacré Coeur – and arguably better because there aren't so many tourists in the way. As if temples, suspension bridges, grottoes and waterfalls weren't enough, there are all the usual attractions: puppet shows, donkey rides and playgrounds.

Jardin des Enfants aux Halles

105 rue Rambuteau, 1st (01.45.08.07.18). M° Châtelet-Les Halles. **Open** 9am-noon, 2-4pm Tue, Thur, Fri; 10am-4pm Wed, Sat; 1-4pm Sun (until 6pm Apr-June). *July, Aug* 10am-7pm Tue-Thur, Sat, Sun; 2-7pm Fri. **Admission** €0.35 one-hour session. **No credit cards**. **Map** p402 K5.
Underground tunnels, rope swings, secret dens and lost cities promise all kinds of fun at this well-supervised adventure playground. It's perfect for seven-to-elevens, and useful for parents who want to pop into the Forum des Halles without dragging kids underground. Under-sevens are welcome on Saturday mornings if accompanied by an adult: the rest of the time, it's a no-grown-up zone, except for the play leaders (who are reliable and of various nationalities, so there are always some English speakers).

Jardins du Luxembourg

pl Edmond-Rostand, pl Auguste-Comte, rue de Vaugirard, 6th (01.42.34.20.00/www.mairie-paris.fr). RER Luxembourg/M° Odéon or St-Sulpice. **Open** *winter* 8am-one hour before sunset; *summer* 7.30am-one hour before sunset. **Map** p405 H8.
The quintessential urban park has very little wild nature and not much grass that you can legally play on, but it does have a small, well-equipped adventure playground with enough springy animals, slides and climbing frames to satisfy even the most frenzied toddler. There are also swing boats, an adorable old-fashioned merry-go-round, toy boats on the pond, pony rides and marionette shows.

Arts & Entertainment

Parc de la Villette

211 av Jean Jaurès, 19th (01.40.03.75.03/ www.villette.com). M° Porte de Pantin or Porte de la Villette. **Open** 6am-1am daily. **Map** p403 inset.

A series of themed parks, some specially designed for kids. Le Jardin des Miroirs is a walk through a strange reflected landscape, and weirder still is the Jardin des Frayeurs Enfantines, which uses music to produce the spooky atmosphere of fairy-tale forests. Le Jardin des Voltiges has an obstacle course with trampolines and rigging, and the dragon slide in the Jardin du Dragon is always popular.

Museum mayhem

Egyptian mummies at the **Louvre**, Dali's surrealist sense of fun at the **Espace Dalí**, the intricate *Lady and the Unicorn* tapestries at the **Musée National du Moyen Age**, the animal statues on the parvis at **Musée d'Orsay**, jets and space shuttles at the **Musée de l'Air et de l'Espace**. Get a load of that! There's plenty to capture children's imagination and interest in Paris museums, and, nine times out of ten, under-18s can get in free or for practically nothing (*see chapter* **Museums**). Many museums (**Orsay, Monnaie, Arts et Traditions Populaires, Gustave Moreau, Halle St-Pierre**) provide free activity sheets.

Centre Pompidou – Galerie des Enfants

4th (01.44.78.49.13/www.centrepompidou.fr). M° Hôtel de Ville/RER Châtelet-Les Halles. **Open** *exhibition* 11am-7pm Mon, Wed-Sun; *workshops* most Wed and Sat afternoons. Museum entry includes the Galerie des Enfants: €5.50; €3.50 under 25s/students; under-18s free. **Workshop & exhibition** €8. **Map** p402 K5.

Beautifully thought-out exhibitions by top artists and designers introduce children to modern art, design and architecture, with hands-on workshops for six-to-12s. One Sunday a month (11.15am-12.30pm), *Dimanche en famille* explores painting and sculpture in a family visit to the museum.

Grévin

10 bd Montmartre, 9th (01.47.70.85.05/ www.musee-grevin.com). M° Grands Boulevards. **Open** 10am-7pm daily. **Admission** €15; €12 students; €9 children €9. **Map** p402 H4.

Star-struck kids can have their picture taken with Zinédine Zidane (well, maybe not for long) or Lara Croft, but this waxworks museum is as educational as it is sensational. Here you can see the heads of state, artists, writers, and prominent figures who have featured in the history of France.

Musée de la Curiosité

11 rue St-Paul, 4th (01.42.72.13.26). M° St-Paul or Sully-Morland. **Open** 2-7pm Wed, Sat, Sun; daily during school holidays. **Admission** €7; €5 3-12s; free under-3s. **Map** p406 L7.

At last, a museum that you don't have to drag kids to kicking and screaming. Even in the queue, a magician is pulling scarves out of ears. Children love the regular conjuring shows, and the whole museum takes a strictly hands-on approach to optical illusions, psychic phenomena and magic props – including boxes for sawing ladies in two.

Muséum National d'Histoire Naturelle

36 rue Geoffrey-St-Hilaire/2 rue Bouffon, pl Valhubert/57 rue Cuvier, 5th (01.40.79.30.00/ www.mnhn.fr). M° Gare d'Austerlitz or Jussieu. **Admission** varies from €3-€7. **Open** 10am-5pm or 6pm, Mon, Wed-Sun. **Credit** MC, V. **Map** p406 K9.

Not actually one museum but several, gathered together over the Jardin des Plantes' botanical garden. The enormous Grande Galerie de l'Evolution is always a big hit with children, particularly for its famous Noah's Ark-like stream of animals. The displays here are fantastic, and children will enjoy using the microscopes and playing the interactive games in the small Espace Découverte. The Galerie d'Anatomie comparée et de Paléontologie is a cert to capture the imagination of older children, with its jars of eerie pickled samples, labelled in faded copperplate. However, the skeletons of pretty much every creature you can imagine are the main attraction, and a pretty awe-inspiring sight they are, too. It's also worth a visit to the Galerie de Minéralogie, de Géologie et de Paléobotanique; kids will enjoy the giant crystals and the hunks of meteorite.

Musée de la Poupée

Impasse Berthaud, 3rd (01.42.72.73.11). M° Rambuteau. **Open** 10am-6pm Tue-Sun. **Admission** €6; €4; €3 under 18s. **No credit cards.** **Map** p402 K5.

This small, private museum hosts a collection of 300-plus dolls, some going back more than 150 years. Interested kids will get a kick out of the minute detail involved in the clothes, the furniture and the accessories.

Animal magic

See also p286 **Babes in the wood.**

Aquarium at the Musée des Arts d'Afrique et d'Océanie

293 av Daumesnil, 12th (01.44.74.84.80/recorded information 01.43.46.51.61). M° Porte Dorée. **Open & admission** call for details. **Credit** (shop) MC, V.

The collection of African and Oceanic art has gone, but the crocs in the basement are still there. Entry includes the first floor murals.

Espace Rambouillet

Route de Clairefontaine, 78000 Rambouillet (01.34.83.05.00/www.onf.fr/espaceramb). By car A13 direction St Quentin – Rambouillet, then D27 direction Clairefontaine. **Admission** €7.70; €6.10 3-12s. **Open** *Apr-Oct* 9am-6pm Mon-Fri; 9am-6.30pm Sat-Sun; *Nov-Mar* 10am-5pm Tue-Sun.

Arts & Entertainment

It's worth taking a small detour to the château town of Rambouillet to let the kids explore these 250 hectares of natural woodland, home to some 30 species including deer, squirrels, boars and eagles. Between March and November you can see demonstrations of bird-handling with birds of prey.

Ferme du Piqueur

Domaine National de St-Cloud, 92210 St-Cloud (01.46.02.24.53). M° Boulogne-Pont de St-Cloud/ RER Garches-Marne la Coquette. **Open** 10am-12.30pm, 1.30-5.30pm Sat, Sun, school holidays and daily in Aug. **Admission** €2. **No credit cards.**
Cows, chickens, pigs and even rabbits provide educational fun at this small farm within the Parc de St-Cloud. Let's hope the rabbits behave.

La Ménagerie

57 rue Cuvier, 5th (01.40.79.30.00/www.mnhn.fr). M° Gare d'Austerlitz or Jussieu. **Open** *winter* 10am-5.30pm daily; *summer* 10am-6.30pm. **Admission** €6; €3.05 4-18s, students, over-60s; free under-4s. **No credit cards. Map** p406 K8.
The Ménagerie, the zoo in the Jardin des Plantes, is over 200 years old. Although a far cry from the safari park ideal of modern zoos (you won't be bursting into a chorus of *Born Free*), it still offers plenty of vultures, monkeys, cats and reptiles, and it's on a perfect scale for younger kids. An added attraction for older kids is the Microzoo, a unique look at the weird and wonderful mini-universe visible only through a microscope.

Musée Vivant du Cheval

60631 Chantilly (03.44.57.13.13/03.44.57.40.40). SNCF Chantilly from Gare du Nord. By car 40km from Paris by A1, exit 7. **Open** *Apr-Oct* 10.30am-5.30pm Mon, Wed-Sun (plus 2-5pm Tue July, Aug); *Nov-Mar* 2-5pm Mon, Wed, Fri; 10.30am-5.30pm Sat, Sun. **Admission** €8; €7,50 over-60s; €6,50 13-17s; €5,50 4-12s; free under-4s. **Credit** MC, V.
Home to more than 40 breeds of horse and pony, the historic stables of the Château de Chantilly are a real treat for every little girl or boy with equestrian dreams. Every day at 11.30am, 3.30pm, 5.15pm (winter 3.30pm), there are *haute-école* presentations, and children are able to stroke the animals.

Parc de Thoiry

78770 Thoiry-en-Yvelines (01.34.87.52.25/ www.thoiry.tm.fr). By car A13, A12 then N12 direction Dreux until Pont Chartrain, then follow signs. 45km west of Paris. **Open** *winter* 11am-5pm daily; *summer* 10am-6pm daily. **Admission** park €16.70; €13.30 over-60s; €12.70 3-12s, students under 26; château €4; €3 9-18s. **Credit** MC, V.
One of the first European safari parks and still one of the best, Thoiry is a clever mix of sussed conservation and witty marketing. As you drive round the château grounds, zebras come up and smear their noses all over your windscreen, lions laze innocently under the trees and bears amble past down a forest track (call us old-fashioned, but our advice is keep the doors closed and locked, the roof down and the windows shut). A second section contains a zoo

The biggest *boule* in the world at **Parc de la Villette**.

that's accessible on foot. Here there are rare species, including gigantic Komodo dragons and lions that can be viewed close-up. Latest additions to the park are a baby hippo (altogether now, aaaah) and some Przewalski horses (just like those in cave paintings).

Theme parks outside Paris

Disneyland Paris/Walt Disney Studios

Marne-la-Vallée (01.60.30.60.30); from UK 0990 030 303. RER A or TGV Marne-la-Vallée-Chessy. By car 32km by A4 Metz-Nancy exit 14. **Open** *Apr-June* 9am-8pm daily; *July, Aug* 9am-11pm daily; *Sept-Mar* 10am-6pm Mon-Fri; 9am-8pm Sat, Sun. **Admission** high season €36; €29 3-11s; free under-3s; low season €29; €25 3-11s; free under-3s. **Credit** AmEx, DC, MC, V.

Disneyland Paris' pink portals are the entrance to a great place to take kids. There's a range of rides from the fast and furious to the slow and gentle. Fantasyland and Adventureland are the best all-rounders, but don't miss the 3D interactive movie, *Honey I Shrunk the Audience*. Disneyland now has a second theme park, Walt Disney Studios. Aimed at the eight-to-15 age bracket, young film-fanatics enter via the Front Lot, and are confronted by a water tower featuring a certain pair of trademark ears. The Animation Courtyard is particularly fascinating for children as they can learn some of the methods behind the animation process before trying their hand at the art at interactive play stations. Other star turns are Animagique, a show in which classic scenes from Disney cartoons are acted out in Czech 'black light' theatre mode and the Flying Carpets Over Agrahbah, where an actor playing the genie from *Aladdin* turns film director, using visiting children as his cast. Older kids might be interested in seeing theme park meet reality at the Walt Disney Television Studios. The Back Lot has special effects and stunts, along with such treats as the Rock 'n' Roller Aerosmith rollercoaster. Kerrang!

France Miniature

25 route du Mesnil, bd André Malraux, 78990 Elancourt, Saint-Quentin-en-Yvelines (01.30.16.16.30/www.franceminiature.com). SNCF

Children of the (digital) revolution

If the lambkins have been overdoing the Playstation, remind them what legs are for and get them to some of Paris' poppet-oriented science museums. The **Cité des Enfants** is a fine place to get brain-cells boogying. Its section for younger children is a visual and tactile journey, encouraging imitation, repetition and comparison to build awareness. The most fun is a tie between the water works, where small sou'westered ones divert water channels and splash about, and the mini-building site (cute yellow hard-hat mandatory), where children work together to build houses, using sponge bricks, ropes and pulleys, cranes and wheelbarrows. The animal section has kids chasing rats and pretending to be scorpions, and there are also activity groups, where you can make something to take home. The other half of the museum is for five-to-12s, and turns science into a hands-on-fun-fest. It's so popular that visits are limited to 90-minute sessions at pre-arranged times.

Paris' original science museum, the **Palais de la Découverte**, is great. Fascinating facts, illusions and games show how the sciences can apply to life. Regular live experiments attract a wide-eyed crowd – but children who can't read or understand French might have difficulties here, given the more traditional museum style and layout.

Explor@dome is an experience designed to make learning make sense. Inside a futuristic dome in the children's paradise of the Jardin d'Acclimatation, children can learn how tornados form, play with optical illusions, build bridges and more. Several one-hour workshops back up the exhibitions (10.30am, 2pm & 4pm; reservation recommended) and there are loads of packages to encourage little ones to get involved, such as the short multimedia courses that teach the basics of the Internet, how to scan and manipulate images, create webpages and create i-movies (anything from €8-€75, depending on the number of sessions). Explor@dome can even give parents a day off in the school holidays: daily multimedia mornings are partnered with golfing afternoons – and lunch is included!

Gentle experimentals

Cité des Enfants

*Level One of the **Cité des Sciences et de l'Industrie**, 30 av Corentin-Cariou, 19th (01.40.05.80.00/www.cite-sciences.fr). Mº Porte de la Villette.* **Open** for 90-minute visits 9.45am, 11.30am, 1.30pm and 3.30pm Tue, Thur-Fri; at 10.30am, 12.30pm, 2.30pm and 4.30pm Wed, Sat-Sun. Times may vary in the school holidays. **Admission** €5 per session. **Credit** MC, V. **Map** p403 inset.

La Verrière from Gare Montparnasse, then bus 411. By car A13, then A12 direction St-Quentin-en-Yvelines/Dreux, then Elancourt Centre. **Open** *Apr to mid-Nov* 10am-7pm daily (July, Aug 10am-11.30pm Sat). **Admission** €12.50; €8.80 4-16s; free under-4s. **Credit** AmEx, MC, V.

Do the rounds of France's most famous monuments without having to trek all over the country. Europe's biggest miniature park features more than 200 models including the châteaux of the Loire and Mont St-Michel. Dan Ohlman's miniature interiors will also have kids entranced. *Wheelchair access.*

Une Journée au Cirque

Cirque de Paris, 115 bd Charles de Gaulle, 92390 Villeneuve la Garenne (01.47.99.40.40). M° Porte de Clignancourt + Bus 137 (Zone Industriel Nord) or RER St Denis + bus 261. **Open** *Oct-June* 10am-5pm Wed, Sun. **Shows** 3pm circus performance. **Tickets** (day of circus) €36.50-€41 adults, €29-€34.50 children; (show only) €11-€24 adults, €7-€14.50 children. **Credit** MC, V.

Children threatening to run away and join the circus? Encourage them in their dreams/get it out of

Palais de la Découverte

av Franklin D Roosevelt, 8th (01.56.43.20.21/ www.palais-decouverte.fr). M° Franklin D Roosevelt. **Open** 9.30am-6pm Tue-Sat; 10am-7pm Sun. **Admission** €5.60; €3.65 5-18s, students; free under-5s; for planetarium add €3.05 (no under-7s). **No credit cards**. **Map** p401 E5.

Explor@dome

Jardin d'Acclimatation, Bois de Boulogne, 16th (01.53.64.90.40/www.exploradome.com). M° Pont de Neuilly. **Open** 10am-6pm daily. **Admission** €4.50; €7 includes workshop.

their system at this interactive day run by celebrated red-nose Francis Schoeller. Tightrope-walking, juggling, clowing and dressage (not lion taming, strangely enough) are some of the skills taught and there's a fairground museum and trips backstage,. Then have lunch with the stars before the show.

La Mer de Sable

La Mer de Sable, 60950 Ermenonville (03.44.54.18.44/48/www.mer-de-sable.com). By car A1, exit 7, direction Ermenonville. RER B CDG1 Roissy, then special shuttle (10.30am, return 6.10pm Apr, May, Jun, Sep; 10am and 11.20am, return 5.25pm and 6.45pm Jul, Aug). **Open** *Mar-Sep* 10.30am-6.30pm Mon-Fri, 10.30am-7pm Sat-Sun. **Admission** €15; €13 3-11s

This popular Wild West theme park in a geological curiosity (the sea of sand) in the middle of a forest has as much to offer adults as it does kids, including live action shows (and shoot outs), and equestrian acrobatics. There are rides a-plenty, from calming carousels to stomach-lurching log flumes.

Parc Astérix

60128 Plailly (03.44.62.34.34/www.parcasterix.fr). RER B Roissy-Charles de Gaulle 1, then shuttle (9.30am-1.30pm, 4.30pm-closing time). By car A1 exit Parc Astérix. **Open** *Apr to mid-Oct* 10am-6pm daily; *July, Aug* 9.30am-7pm daily. **Closed** mid Oct-Mar; ring to check extra closures. **Admission** €30; €22 3-11s; free under-3s. **Credit** AmEx, MC, V.

The feisty little Roman-basher has his own theme park, split into historical zones that cover Ancient Greece, the Roman Empire, the Middle Ages and 19th-century Paris. A priority must be Astérix's own topsy-turvy village, where you'll meet actors dressed up as, among others, Getafix, Obélix and our hero himself. Daredevils should try Goudurix, a terrifying loop-the-loop, or the log flume frenzy that is La Petite Tempête; the delicate of stomach should try something like La Descente du Styx, a water journey through the Greek Underworld. Remember that children under one metre in height have to be accompanied by an adult, and for the more challenging rides there is a minimum height restriction of 1.2m.

Entertainment

Fairytales, La Fontaine's fables, musical stories and anything to do with witches and wizards are all favourites in the numerous productions for children staged at theatres and *café-théâtres*, especially on Wednesdays and weekends (for details look in *Pariscope*). Productions for very young children involving music, clowning puppets and dance are often accessible for children with little or no French. Over-eights with good French may enjoy Ecla Company's performances of Molière and other classics (01.40.27.82.05/www.ecla-theatre.com). A profusion of circuses pass through Paris, especially at Christmas (*see chapter* **Cabaret, Comedy & Circus**), and proto-clubbers can

Taking the Mickey at **Disneyland Paris**. *See p290.*

try the monthly Sunday afternoon 'Bal grenadine' at the **Divan du Monde** (*see chapter* **Clubs**). As for movies, most kids' films will be dubbed into French. The Champs-Elysées and Odéon are best for catching the latest Disney or Dreamworks extravaganza, and normally show VO (original version) after 6pm. These are busy areas, so don't lose sight of your child. Alternatively see what you can catch at the film library at **Forum des Images** (01.44.76.63.44/47/www.forumdesimages.net), which also organises children's showings and talks on Wednesdays (€3.50). The huge screen shows at the futuristic **Dôme Imax** cinema at La Défense (08.36.67.06.06) or at **La Géode** at La Villette (01.40.05.79.99/ www.lageode.fr) are enough to keep kids goggle-eyed without needing to follow the commentary.

The American Library

10 rue du Général-Camou, 7th (01.53.59.12.60/ www.americanlibraryinparis.org). M° Ecole Militaire/ RER Pont de l'Alma. **Open** 10am-7pm Tue-Sat (Aug noon-6pm Tue-Fri; 10am-2pm Sat). **Membership** €120 family; €37 under-12s. **Map** p404 D6.
Storytelling sessions in English for members: three-to-fives Wed; one-to-threes first and last Thur of month; for six-to-eights, monthly (day varies).

Concerts du Dimanche Matin

Châtelet, Théâtre Musical de Paris, 1 pl du Châtelet, 1st (01.40.28.28.40/children's programme 01.42.56.90.10/www.chatelet-theatre.com). M° Châtelet. **Tickets** concerts €10 children, €20 adults; children's workshops free. **Map** p406 J6.

While parents attend the 11am classical concert on Sundays, four-to-nine-year-olds can explore instruments; budding warblers can join the choir; hoofers can do some hoofing and wannabe DJs can make straight for the decks.

La Croisière Enchantée

Bateaux Parisiens, Port de la Bourdonnais, 7th (01.44.11.33.44). M° Bir-Hakeim. **Trips** *Oct-June* 1.45pm, 3.45pm Sat, Sun, public holidays; daily school holidays. **Admission** €9.15. **Credit** MC, V. **Map** p404 C6.
Two elves take three-to-ten-year-olds, and their parents, on an enchanted boat trip up the Seine, with songs and games laid on (in French, but it's all good fun no matter what level of linguistic skill you have). This is what you might call a national elf service.

Forum des Images

2 Grande Galerie, Porte St-Eustache, Nouveau Forum des Halles, 1st (01.44.76.62.00/ www.forumdesimages.net). RER Châtelet-Les Halles. **Après-midi des enfants** 3pm Wed, Sat. **Admission** €3.50 (€5.50 adults). **Credit** MC, V. **Map** p402 J5.
Movies go from previews to *Spider-Man*. Check to see if it is in VO (original language) or VF (French).

Théâtre Dunois

108 rue du Chevaleret, 13th (01.45.84.72.00). M° Chevaleret. **Tickets** €9.15; €6.10 3-15s. **No credit cards.** **Map** p407 M10.
Adventurous theatre, dance and musical creations will widen expectations of culture for kids. This is the place to turn your little darling into a luvvie. *Wheelchair access (call ahead).*

Clubs

With a mega club perched on the Périphérique the hit of 2002, Paris is dancing till way past dawn, Ibiza-style. Here's where to shake your booty.

Corporate clubbing has finally reached France, with large-scale venues fighting to attract the 100,000 clubbers in the city and its outskirts.

The most talked-about newcomer is **Studio 287**, a mega-club on the outskirts of Paris attracting thousands of hedonists on Friday and Saturday nights and equal numbers for their Sunday morning afters. The other surprising newcomer is **Wagg**, financed by Terence Conran and London's superclub Fabric, which has brought more British-style clubbing to Paris. **La Loco** has also been transformed from a rather downmarket mainstream club into a temple to house and techno with three dance-floors featuring local and international DJs. The third large-scale competitor is **Red Light**, previously l'Enfer, which has re-opened hoping to attract a new, more festive, clientele.

These clubs are pretty much house-bound, with the occasional techno night or headline DJ. Drum'n'bass enthusiasts have to content themselves with Massive, one Wednesday a month at **Rex**, one-offs on Péniche Concorde Atlantique and Une Nuit Autour de La Jungle, monthly at **Divan du Monde**. Trance fans meet every Wednesday, Thursday and Friday at **Le Gibus**, and occasional one-offs organised by Gaïa Tribe. UK Garage hasn't caught on at all in France but R'n'B is becoming a regular feature at house and mainstream nights.

Large-scale clubs are being pushed toward the edges of town, but dozens of smaller clubs play chart music and French classics. Many of these are on the Left Bank, attracting students, tourists and, in the case of a few more select clubs, a 'champagne' clientele.

Paris has a large Latin American community which organises regular jazz, Latino concerts and dances in clubs such as **Le Divan du Monde**, **La Java**, **Les Etoiles**, **Glaz'art** and **Le Cabaret Sauvage**.

The recreation of the village *bal* has also proved popular, with huge school disco-like affairs being held at **l'Elysée Montmartre** (Le Bal) and **Glaz'art** (Le Bal des Ringards). Village atmosphere also reigns at *guinguettes*.

The alternative party or 'free' phenomenon has become a hot media topic with a recent law being passed to restrict the number of Teknivals, or Frees, in the French countryside. Squat parties or nights in unusual locations are ever popular in Paris, since clubs are quite conservative about the music they play. US/French collective InFact have been organising regular unofficial events over the past three years. Clubs and bars such as **Le Gibus**, **Nouveau Casino**, **Flèche d'Or**, **Glaz'art** and **Main d'Oeuvres** (*see p327*) hold events with players from the alternative scene.

USEFUL ADVICE

The only people who arrive at a club before midnight are English. Parisian clubs don't really get going until 2am as people often have a drink in a DJ bar beforehand. Many clubbers visit several clubs in one night and finish their evening at an after party on Sunday morning. This can be expensive but free passes can often be found hidden amongst flyers in shops or handed out outside clubs. On weekdays clubs often hold free nights with quality DJs so going out in Paris need not be expensive.

Girls on top

Club nights with a girl DJ theme have been spreading like teenage acne, and no fashion do is complete without a *belle* behind the decks. Female journalists, models, promoters and actresses all wanting a piece of the record-shaped cake are diversifying and digging out their childhood 45s (bought the Sunday before at Porte de Clignancourt). The press can't get enough of the phenomenon, resulting in any all-female DJ event getting guaranteed coverage. Local club promoters are seeing euro signs pop up every time a girl gets behind the decks, but interestingly almost all exclusively female events are organised and promoted by men.

Fabrice Lamy, promoter of Girly Party at **Mezzanine**, couldn't believe the success of his monthly all-female DJ night with 'real' DJs, celebs and ex-porn star Dragixia. DJ Aurore has taken the theme to its crux by releasing a compilation CD, *Vanity Case, Record Bag*, while TV personality Béatrice Ardisson has done a compilation for the TV show *Paris Dernière*. But there are musical as well as aesthetic reasons for the all-female DJ line-up, and, reluctant though girl DJs might be to be pigeonholed, the theme has the advantage of allowing them the freedom to mix different musical styles in one night. Indeed, the all-female DJ line-up has practically become a musical genre in itself. 'I don't really like doing the whole girly DJ thing,' says Maud from Scratch Massive, 'but if I didn't I would play a lot less and the promotion makes it worthwhile.'

The most popular all-girl nights

Girly Party (featuring Dragixia and Chloé) monthly, Mezzanine Alcazar. **Parisjuana** (featuring Laura Palmer, Eliza) every two months, Nouveau Casino. **Girls in the City** (featuring Lt Ripley) monthly, Folies Pigalle. **Mon DJ Préféré est une femme** (featuring Miss Chrysalide), every Wed, Café de la Plage. **Girls at Work**, Wed, Man Ray. Nights with female residents that don't use it as a selling point include **Naked** (featuring Maud) monthly, Pulp; **Panik** (featuring Chloé) monthly, Elysée Montmartre; **Massive** (featuring Eliza do Brazil, Miss Ficel), Rex Club; **Basement Lounge** (featuring Dinahbird and Princess Lea), Fri, Project 101.

10 CLUBBING COMMANDMENTS FOR GETTING IN:

1) Be confident: walk straight in with a polite hello to the bouncer.
2) Trainers can often be used as a pretext to deny entrance; if in doubt wear shoes.
3) Avoid baseball caps and tracksuit bottoms: for a bouncer this spells trouble.
4) A total look or a killer accessory such as a snakeskin coat offers instant access.
5) Speak English loudly in the queue – tourists mean money.
6) Don't arrive in a group unless you are a group of girls dressed to kill (in which case you may get in for free).
7) If you're a model just walk in; if you're not, find one – they're an excellent accessory.
8) Order a bottle at the door, this often means you don't have to pay an entrance fee, you get VIP treatment and access to your own table.
9) Find out the *physionomiste* (door person)'s first name and kiss them hello as you walk in; they might not remember that they don't actually know you.
10) As you leave say goodbye and thank you to the bouncers and *physionomiste*: they'll be so surprised that they might even remember you the next time you want to get in.

INFO AND GETTING HOME

Radio FG's Plans Capitaux (98.2 FM, throughout the day) and Radio Nova's Bons Plans (101.5 FM 6pm, 7pm, weekdays) as well as www.france-techno.fr and www.novaplanet.com provide up-to-date clubbing information. Shops such as Le Shop and Kiliwatch around rue Etienne-Marcel (*see p246*) have flyers with club details; also try the bars and shops around rue Keller in the 11th. Getting home between the last (around 12.45am) and first Métro (5.45am) can be difficult. The best bet is a taxi but there are *bus de nuit* (night buses), which run between Châtelet and the suburbs; maps are available at Métro stations.

LA PLAG

Technotrain

EXPOSITION DE TRAINS FRANCILIENS
CONCOURS DE MIX TECHNO EN PRÉSENCE D'ARIEL WIZMAN

DU 18 AU 22 SEPTEMBRE 02
A LA GARE DE L'EST

Cool clubs

Most are mixed gay and heterosexual although some nights are essentially gay. Trainers are acceptable, although often racist bouncers use this as a pretext for denying entrance. Check out flyers and listings as the programme can vary from one extreme to another.

Rex Club

5 bd Poissonnière, 2nd (01.42.36.28.83). M° Bonne Nouvelle. **Open** 11pm-dawn Wed-Fri; 11.30pm-dawn Sat. **Admission** free-€16. **Drinks** €5-€12. **Credit** AmEx, MC, V. **Map** p402 J4.

The Rex prides itself on its quality DJs, so arrive early when big-name guests play. Friday's Automatik is one of Paris' few authentic techno nights.

Wagg

62 rue Mazarine, 6th (01.55.42.22.00). M° Odéon. **Open** 11pm-5am Wed-Sun. **Admission** €5 Wed, Sun; €10 Thur; €12 Fri, Sat. **Drinks** €8. **Credit** AmEx, MC, V. **Map** p406 H7.

A new Left Bank club part-owned by London's Fabric. Weekends host Fabric residents and local DJs playing underground house; Wednesdays, Thursdays and Sundays are dedicated to local promoters' labels and magazine nights.

Le Queen

102 av des Champs-Elysées, 8th (08.92.70.73.30). M° George V. **Open** midnight-dawn daily. **Admission** €12 Mon; €10 Tue-Thur, Sun; €20 Fri, Sat. **Drinks** €8-€18. **Credit** AmEx, DC, MC, V. **Map** p400 D4.

The mythical, mostly gay superstar has lost much of its clientele to La Loco and Studio 287 but still has a faithful Sunday and Monday disco crowd. Every second Friday is Ministry of Sound night.

Folies Pigalle

11 pl Pigalle, 9th (01.48.78.25.26). M° Pigalle. **Open** midnight-dawn Tue-Sat; 6am-noon, 6pm-midnight Sun. **Admission** €20 Tue-Sat; €17 (after), €7 (BBB) Sun. **Drinks** €10-€16. **Credit** V. **Map** p401 G2.

This ex-strip joint attracts an assortment of weirdos and transsexuals. Some have speculated that they pump poppers through the air-conditioning: that could explain a lot. Resident DJs spin house at weekends and after-parties are always packed.

Pulp

25 bd Poissonniere, 9th (01.40.26.01.93). M° Grands Boulevards. **Open** midnight-5am Wed-Sat. **Admission** free-€12. **Drinks** €5-€9. **Credit** MC,V **Map** p402 J4.

Pulp is a lesbian club at weekends but Wednesdays and Thursdays see top DJs and collectives drawing in a mixed crowd. This has become the (un)official music business hang-out.

Le Gibus

18 rue du Fbg-du-Temple, 11th (01.47.00.78.88/www.gibus.fr). M° République. **Open** midnight-dawn Wed-Sat. **Admission** free Wed-Thur; €13-€18 Fri, Sat. **Drinks** €9-€11. **Credit** AmEx, DC, MC, V. **Map** p402 L4.

The Gibus can never quite decide where it's going. This year it has gone trance with free nights on Wednesdays and Thursdays, paying on Fridays. Saturday is home to Israeli-style pumping house.

Nouveau Casino

109 rue Oberkampf, 11th (01.43.57.57.40/www.nouveaucasino.net). M° Parmentier or St-Maur. **Open** Mon-Wed, Sun 9pm-2am; Thur-Sat 9pm-5am (but programme varies). **Admission** €7-€15. **Drinks** €5-€11. **Credit** MC, V. **Map** p403 M5.

Tucked away behind Café Charbon, Nouveau Casino is starting to make its mark as prime concert venue and specialist in German-style minimal house and techno. The programming remains quite eclectic as outside organisers bring their sound and clientele.

Batofar

facing 11 quai François-Mauriac, 13th (01.56.29.10.00). M° Bibliothèque. **Open** 9pm-3am Tue-Thur; 9pm-4am Fri, Sat. **Admission** €6.50-€9.50. **Drinks** €3-€8. **Credit** V. **Map** p407 N10.

This waterborne club is a quayside complex with a restaurant and bar on deck and the club on board with a chill-out room. Evenings start with live music, followed by DJs playing anything from electronica to drum'n'bass. New management is taking over, which means that anything may happen.

Arts & Entertainment

La Coupole

102 bd du Montparnasse, 14th (01.43.20.14.20).
M° Vavin. **Open** 10.30pm/11.30pm-4.30am Tue-Sat.
Admission €8-€16. **Drinks** €8.40-€10.65. **Credit**
AmEx, DC, MC, V. **Map** p405 G9.
The 1920s ballroom beneath the famous brasserie
was one of the first venues in Paris to risk dancing
the tango. Now it is home to house and garage nights
such as *Cheers* on Fridays and salsa on a Tuesday.

Red Light

34 rue du Départ, 14th (01.42.79.94.94).
M° Montparnasse. **Open** Thur-Sun 11pm-6am.
Admission €20. **Drinks** €10. **Credit** AmEx, DC,
MC, V. **Map** p405 F9.
L'Enfer has changed its name and, it hopes, its clien-
tele. This huge club with two dancefloors under the
Tour Montparnasse runs pumping-house gay nights
on Saturdays and softer house and R'n'B on Fridays.

Le Divan du Monde

75 rue des Martyrs, 18th (01.44.92.77.66).
M° Pigalle. **Open** 8.30pm/midnight-dawn daily.
Admission free-€18. **Drinks** €4-€7. **Credit** MC, V.
Map p402 H2.
A concert venue and club with Brazilian, raï and
salsa nights as well as drum'n'bass and gay pumping house events. It's a cheap and cheerful option
with a relaxed dress code in the often overpriced and
over sexed Pigalle area.

Elysée Montmartre

72 bd de Rochechouart, 18th (01.44.92.45.38).
M° Anvers. **Open** 11pm-5am Fri, Sat. **Admission**
€10-€18. **Drinks** €7-€12. **Credit** AmEx, DC, MC, V.
Map p402 J2.
This erstwhile concert venue holds regular month-
ly nights at weekends such as gay night Scream, Le
BAL, Open House and Panik. If the music's right the
atmosphere can be banging.

Studio 287

33 av de la porte d'Aubervilliers, 18th
(01.48.34.00.00). **Open** 11pm-5am Tue-Sat; 6am-
noon Sat, Sun. **Admission** €10-€16. **Drinks** €8-
€16. **Credit** AmEx, MC, V.
The revelation of 2002. With a capacity of 2,000, the
287 has brought Ibiza-style clubbing to Paris, with

a terrace, car park, shuttle service and taxi reim-
bursement on the door. The Sunday morning after,
Kit Kat Forever, has put this club on the map.

Le Glaz'art

7-15 ave de la Porte de La Villette, 19th
(01.40.36.55.65). M° Porte de La Villette.
Open 8.30pm-2am Thur (sometimes Weds);
10pm-5am Fri, Sat. **Admission** €8-€12.
Drinks €5-€9. **Credit** MC, V. **Map** p403 inset.
From the outside this ex-Eurolines bus station looks
like a scout hut on the side of a motorway. The low
ceilings make the venue a little claustrophobic, but
this must be the only club with a garden. Music
varies from dub to *chanson*, disco to techno.

Latino, jazz & world

Parisians do Latino clubs well. Dress up: red
frocks and high heels are the norm (for ladies);
the men wear drainpipes, white socks and
loafers. Many Latino clubs provide classes for
those who need to brush up on their foot work.

Caveau de la Huchette

5 rue de la Huchette, 5th (01.43.26.65.05).
M° St-Michel. **Open** 9.30pm-2.30am Mon-Thur, Sun;
9.30pm-3.30am Fri, Sat. **Admission** €10-€13.
Drinks from €4.60. **Credit** MC, V. **Map** p406 J7.
Enduringly popular with ageing divorcées and
wannabe Stones during the week, at weekends this
jazz club attracts a mixed bunch who boogie to soulful jazz or enjoy live rock 'n' roll.

Les Etoiles

61 rue du Château d'Eau, 10th (01.47.70.60.56).
M° Château d'Eau. **Open** 9pm-4am Thur-Sat.
Admission €10. **Drinks** €3-€6. **Credit** V.
Map p402 K3.
Top-notch musicians electrify a soulful crowd here.
There is not much space, but that doesn't stop the
night-owl crowd from giving it some. Women are
unlikely to be left standing for more than a couple
of minutes, and veterans dish out footwork advice.

La Java

105 rue du Fbg-du-Temple, 10th (01.42.02.20.52).
M° Belleville. **Open** 10pm-2am Thur; 9pm-5am Fri,

Paris puts a serious spin on drum'n'bass.

Sat; 2-7pm Sun. **Admission** €6 Thur; €16 Fri, Sat;
€5 Sun. **Drinks** €5.50-€8. **Credit** AmEx, DC, MC, V.
Map p403 M4.
Hidden away in an old Belleville market, DJs and live
bands play anything Latino, with other eclectic additions such as digeridoo. Sunday is a *bal-musette*.

Le Balajo
9 rue de Lappe, 11th (01.47.00.07.87). M° Bastille.
Open 9pm-2am Wed; 2.30-6.30pm, 10pm-5am Thur;
11.30pm-5.30am Fri, Sat; 2.30-6.30pm, 9pm-1am Sun.
Admission €7-€16. **Drinks** €8-€10. **Credit**
AmEx, DC, MC, V. **Map** p407 M7.
Bal-à-Jo (as it used to be called) has been going for
over 60 years. Wednesday's rock 'n' roll, boogie and
swing session attracts some colourful customers,
but these days it's starting to look a bit washed out.

La Chapelle des Lombards
19 rue de Lappe, 11th (01.43.57.24.24). M° Bastille.
Open 10.30pm-dawn Thur-Sat; concerts Thur

8.30pm. **Admission** €15-€18.50. **Drinks** €5-€12.
Credit AmEx, MC, V. **Map** p407 M7.
Tourists and Latino and African residents sweat it
out in this cramped venue. DJ Natalia La Tropikal
mixes salsa, merengue, zouk and tango at weekends.

Mainstream
These clubs attract a mixed crowd. Dress: clean
and casual. Avoid trainers, baseball caps, etc.

La Galerie
161 rue Montmartre, 2nd (01.40.26.92.00)
M° Sentier. **Open** 7pm-1am Thur, 11pm-5am Sat.
Admission €8-€15. **Drinks** €10. **Credit** MC, V.
Map p402 J4.
The ex-Black Bear has kept its early-bird Thursday
rendez-vous Seven2One, ever popular with weary
office workers getting prepared for Casual Friday.
Every other Saturday is taken over by house promoters Velvet, attracting an interesting combination
of posey clubbers in designer trainers and a more
commercial crowd in loafers.

L'Atlantis
32 quai d'Austerlitz, 13th (01.44.23.24.00).
M° Quai de la Gare. **Open** 11pm-dawn Fri-Sat,
public holidays. **Admission** €16. **Drinks** €10.
Credit MC, V. **Map** p407 M9.
One of the most popular French Caribbean clubs
specialising in R'n'B, soukous and zouk, as well as
a sprinkling of commercial hip-hop hits. Those who
like to erect barriers around their personal body
space, be warned: dancing is always close-contact.

Posh & posey
Where teenybopping aristos clink glasses with
superannuated sugar daddies and their
surgically-enhanced wives, straining for a
glimpse of the stars.

Les Bains
7 rue du Bourg-l'Abbé, 3rd (01.48.87.01.80).
M° Etienne-Marcel. **Open** Mon-Sat 11pm-5am.
Admission €16-€20. **Drinks** €14. **Credit** AmEx,
MC, V. **Map** p402 J5.

Arts & Entertainment

Stars still hang out at Les Bains but since the Guettas left the club to start their own strip joint they have taken most of the clientele with them. Wednesday's Be-Fly still attracts a crowd who look as though they have stepped out of an R'n'B video (many of them actually have), and Monday's Don't tell my Booker is nubile fashion model heaven.

Club Castel

15 rue Princesse, 6th (01.40.51.52.80). Mᵒ Mabillon. **Open** 9pm-dawn Tue-Sat. **Admission** free (members and guests only). **Drinks** €15. **Credit** AmEx, DC, MC, V. **Map** p405 H7.
A private club reserved for a selected few. TV personalities do the locomotion with advertising interns and underage starlets. St-Tropez comes to Paris.

Le Monkey Club

67 rue Pierre-Charron, 8th (01.58.56.20.50). Mᵒ George V. **Open** 11.30pm-dawn Tue-Sat. **Admission** €10 Tue-Thur; €20 Fri, Sat. **Drinks** €10. **Credit** AmEx, DC, MC, V. **Map** p400 D4.
A newcomer to the 8th attracts a BCBG clientele with nights organised for private business schools. The music goes from chart to hip-hop. The loos with pebbles in the sinks and mysterious monkey noises are worth a visit.

Le VIP Room

76 av des Champs-Elysées, 8th (01.56.69.16.66). Mᵒ George V. **Open** midnight-5am Tue-Sun. **Admission** free. **Drinks** €20. **Credit** AmEx, DC, MC, V. **Map** p400 D4.
Let there be no confusion, the name says it all. This club aims to attract the stars and does record, film and magazine launches galore.

Duplex

2bis av Foch, 16th (01.45.00.45.00). Mᵒ Charles de Gaulle-Etoile. **Open** 11pm-dawn Tue-Sun. **Admission** €15 (girls free before midnight Tue-Thur, Sun). **Drinks** €11. **Credit** AmEx, MC, V. **Map** p400 C3.
The Duplex caters for young wannabes and privileged youths. Regulars look as though they have raided a parent's wardrobe. A sultry restaurant upstairs is transformed into a chill-out room where champagne flows in rivers.

DJ bars are an important part of the Paris club scene. *See also p220* **Scratch 'n' snifters**.

Mezzanine/Alcazar

62 rue Mazarine, 6th (01.53.10.19.99). Mᵒ Odéon. **Open** 7pm-2am Tue-Sat. **Admission** free. **Drinks** €10. **Credit** AmEx, DC, MC, V. **Map** p405 H7.
The laid-back mezzanine bar draws Parisian yuppies. 'Personalities' and DJs are invited to play a downtempo personal selection on Friday's Lounge night.

Man Ray

34 rue Marbeuf, 8th (01.56.88.36.36). Mᵒ Franklin D Roosevelt. **Open** 6pm-2am daily. **Admission** free. **Drinks** €7-€11. **Credit** AmEx, MC, V. **Map** p400 D4.
With its be-seen restaurant, Man Ray is at the heart of the Champs-Elysées revival. From midnight onwards DJs spin house, trip-hop and techno.

Project 101

44 rue de La Rochefoucault, 9th (project101@ifrance.com). Mᵒ Pigalle or St-Georges. **Open** 9pm-2am Wed, Fri, occasional Suns. **Admission** €10 non-members; €8 members. **Drinks** free. **No credit cards. Map** p402 H3.
Not strictly a bar or club, Project 101 has a laid-back living-room atmosphere, where DJs and VJs perform to an arty crowd, lubricated by the free bar.

Café Chéri(e)

44 bd de la Villette 10th (01.42.02.07.87). Mᵒ Belleville. **Open** daily 8am-2am. **Admission** free. **Drinks** €2.30-€6. **Credit** AmEx, MC, V.
A full programme fills this venue to the brim. At night the bar transforms into a packed dance floor with house blaring from the over-used speakers.

La Fabrique

53 rue du Fbg-St-Antoine, 11th (01.43.07.67.07). Mᵒ Bastille. **Open** 11am-5am daily. **Admission** free Mon-Thur; €7.60 Fri, Sat. **Drinks** €3.50-€9. **Credit** AmEx, DC, MC, V. **Map** p407 M7.
A bar which gets into serious club mode at the weekend. Top local DJs attract a trendy Bastille crowd, and you can slip behind enticing curtains for a decent meal. Bouncers take very little gip.

// 05/10/2002 // GLOBO, PARIS

Arts & Entertainment

Café de la Plage
59 rue de Charonne, 11th (01.47.00.48.01).
M° Ledru-Rollin. **Open** noon-2am Mon-Sat; 5pm-2am
Sun. **Admission** free. **Drinks** €4-€9. **Credit** DC,
MC, V. **Map** p407 N7.
The basement of the re-born 'beach café' is a chilled
out club. Monday's Eazy brings anything from re-
mixed harmonica to belly dancing.

Cithéa
114 rue Oberkampf, 11th (01.40.21.70.95). M°
Parmentier. **Open** 10pm-5am daily. **Admission** free-
€10. **Drinks** €5-€10. **Credit** MC, V. **Map** p403 N5.
This late-night haunt is now a kitsch rococo lounge
bar with multi-media events and quality jazz.

Wax
15 rue Daval, 11th (01.40.21.16.16). M° Bastille.
Open 8pm-2am daily. **Admission** free. **Drinks**
€4-€9. **Credit** AmEx, DC, MC, V. **Map** p407 M6.
The mainly house soundscape is a little passé but
the vibrant colour scheme here makes up for it.

Guinguettes

For a taste of authentic dance-floor style, head
to the *guinguette* dance halls along the Marne.

Chez Gégène
162bis quai de Polangis, 94340 Joinville-le-Pont
(01.48.83.29.43). RER Joinville-le-Pont. **Open** *Apr-*
Oct 9pm-2am Fri, Sat (live band); 7pm-midnight Sun.
Admission €32 (dinner); €14. **Credit** AmEx, MC, V.
This is the classic *guinguette*, packed with elderly
French dance fiends, dapper *monsieurs*, multi-
generational families and young Parisians. Dine
near the dance floor and you can get up for a fox-
trot, tango or rock 'n' roll number between courses.

Guinguette du Martin-Pêcheur
41 quai Victor-Hugo, 94500 Champigny-sur-Marne
(01.49.83.03.02). RER Champigny-sur-Marne.
Open *Apr to Oct* 8pm-2am Tue-Sat; noon-8pm Sun;
Nov-23 Dec Fri-Sat 8pm-2am. **Admission** free Tue-
Sat; €7 Sun. **Drinks** €3-€4. **No credit cards**.
The newest (built in the 1980s) and hippest of the
dance halls, on a tiny, tree-shaded island reached by
raft. There's a live orchestra Sat and Sun afternoon.

The promoters

Parisian night birds don't stick to one club
but follow their favourite promoters. Each
has its own style, DJs and mailing list.

Black Label
Drum'n'bass record shop in Bastille which
has been organising drum'n'bass nights
regularly over the past five years.

Breakfastisback
The team behind Project 101 specialise in
audio-visual events mixing musical styles
and audiences.

Büro
Specialised in electronica events and
concerts with a monthly night at Pulp. They
organise the annual Placard event with a
week's non-stop music in France and Tokyo.

Chérie
Chérie began by organising invite-only
events combining world music and house.
Now they have their own bar, and organise
more mainstream house events.

Gaïa
The main trance promoters in Paris with
regular nights at le Gibus and Cabaret
Sauvage (Parc de la Villette, 19th,
01.42.09.03.09) Their fetish group is
Highlight Tribe who are regularly invited to
perform their marathon live trance sets.

Kwality
Run by Fabrice Lamy, responsible for the
essentially lounge programming at
Mezzanine, and Superstars at Studio 287.

Open House
What began as a non-profit organisation is
now a successful business. They organise
the monthly Open House with resident DJ
Paco at Elysée Montmartre.

Wake Up
Wake Up organises the gay Scream at Red
Light, Welcome2theClub and Club BPM at
la Loco. Renowned for pumping house,
gogo dancers, extravagant décor and huge
glossy flyers.

Yakooza Factory
Yakooza specialises in hard techno, hard
core and drum'n'bass. They organise the
Périf Summer Festival at Glaz'art and work
closely with record label Krysalid.

Arts & Entertainment

Dance

Not dancing? Too, too shy or merely tutu shy? You've got ten tapping toes, and modesty's just excess baggage, so let's dance together, chic to chic.

At the customs of terpsichorean achievement, Paris would simply have to declare its reputation as a host to major international names in classical and contemporary dance. The city has a particular reputation for excellence in the latter genre; the big event in 2003 is dance giant Merce Cunningham's 50th anniversary career celebrations.

If tapping or twinkling across the boards is more your thing than watching others do it, you've come to the right place: Paris offers more dance classes per *danseur dévoué* than any other European city. Nervous about po-faced Parisians observing your technique? Just remember Martha Graham's dictum – 'Nobody cares if you can't dance well. Just get up and dance.' The *Buena Vista*-inspired Latino phenomenon is aflame, with ever-more salsa and tango clubs, bars and classes springing up. Summer dancing on the *quais* near the Institut du Monde Arabe has become an institution: take your pick from tango, salsa, *capoeira* and rock 'n' roll and and drop a few *sous* in a hat for the loan of the ghetto-blaster.

Some of the most exciting contemporary dance is to be found at festivals. Some to look out for, all of which feature big names alongside lesser known experimentalists, are **Paris Quartier d'été** (www.quartierdete.com, July-Aug), the **Festival d'Automne** (www.festival-automne.com, Sept-Dec), **Rencontres Chorégraphiques de Seine-Saint-Denis** (www.rencontreschoregraphiques.com, May-June), the **Agora** festival at Centre Pompidou's Ircam (www.ircam.fr, June), the **Onze Bouge** season (www.festivalonze.org, June) and street-dance led **Rencontres** at La Villette (www.villette.com, Oct-Nov).

Major dance venues

Ballet de l'Opéra National de Paris
Palais Garnier *pl de l'Opéra, 9th. M° Opéra*. Opéra de Paris Bastille *pl de la Bastille, 12th. M° Bastille*. **Box office** (08.92.69.78.68 /www.opera-de-paris.fr). In person 11am-6.30pm Mon-Sat. Closed 15 July-Aug. **Tickets** €6-€67. **Credit** AmEx, MC, V. **Map** p407 M7.
Highlights of the classical season at the two opera houses are Kenneth MacMillan's realist treatment of *L'Histoire de Manon*. Modern movement offerings include the return of Nederlands Dans Teater, show-

casing new works by Jirí Kylian and Paul Lightfoot, and a collaboration between the caustic humour of Mats Ek and the optical illusions of Saburo Teshigawara in *Appartement* and a new piece. *Wheelchair access (call ahead on 01.40.01.18.08)*.

Théâtre des Champs-Elysées
15 av Montaigne, 8th (01.49.52.50.50/ www.theatrechampselysees.fr). M° Alma-Marceau. **Box office** 1-7pm Mon-Sat; phone bookings 10am-noon, 2-6pm Mon-Fri. Closed mid-July, Aug. **Tickets** €10-€55. **Credit** AmEx, MC, V. **Map** p400 D5.
This elegant hall was made famous by free dance pioneer Isadora Duncan and hosted the riotous first performance of *Rite of Spring* when 'Nails' Nijinsky tried to deck members of the audience. It still rocks, with big box office performances such as the *Gala des Etoiles du XXIe siècle* and, in June, Ballet Angelin Preljocaj's version of *Roméo et Juliette*.

Théâtre National de Chaillot
1 pl du Trocadéro, 16th (01.53.65.30.00/ www.theatre-chaillot.fr). M° Trocadéro. **Box office** 11am-7pm Mon-Sat; 11am-5pm Sun; telephone bookings 9am-7pm Mon-Sat; 11am-5pm Sun. Closed July-Aug. **Tickets** €9.50-€30. **Credit** MC, V. **Map** p400 C5.
Chaillot is rapidly becoming Paris' prime forum for Latin American and Spanish dance, with the return of the Tango festival and several flamenco shows in May. European contemporary dance is not being neglected as demonstrated by one of France's best-kept secrets: the Ballet du Nord, led by Maryse Delente, will perform *A la Recherche de Mister K*, a burlesque project for adults who refuse to grow up. A must-see is the interrogative choreography of Christophe Haleb's *Strates et Sphères* which, using technology and dancers, translates dance's immediate future to the stage. *Wheelchair access*.

Théâtre de la Ville
2 pl du Châtelet, 4th (01.42.74.22.77/ www.theatredelaville-paris.com). M° Châtelet-Les Halles. **Box office** 11am-7pm Mon; 11am-8pm Tue-Sat; telephone bookings 11am-7pm Mon-Sat. Closed July-Aug. **Tickets** €11-€29. *Tickets jeunes* for students and under 27s. **Credit** MC, V. **Map** p406 J6.
Paris' leading contemporary dance forum is still at the cutting edge. This season book well in advance for works by Anne Teresa De Keersmaeker, Carolyn Carlson (the self-defined messenger of light) and the inimitable Pina Bausch. Its sister, Théâtre des Abbesses (31 rue des Abbesses, 18th) programmes mainly ethnic dance. *Wheelchair access*.

La Casa del Tango

11 allée Darius-Milhaud, 19th (01.40.40.73.60/
www.lacasadeltango.net). Mº Ourcq or Laumière.
No credit cards. Map p407 P2.
New centre devoted to all things tango in a space
reminiscent of Buenos Aires. Classes, workshops,
concerts, *bals*, poetry and exhibitions are planned.

Centre Mandapa

6 rue Wurtz, 13th (01.45.89.01.60). Mº Glacière.
Box office 30min before performance or by phone.
Tickets €13.50; €9 students; €6 under 16s.
No credit cards. Map p406 J10.
This space is dedicated largely to traditional Indian
dance and music. It hosts visiting companies and
has some excellent classes in Kathak and other clas-
sical Indian dances. *Wheelchair access (call ahead).*

L'Etoile du Nord

16 rue Georgette-Agutte, 18th (01.42.26.47.47).
Mº Guy-Môquet. **Box office** 1-6pm Mon-Fri. Closed
July-Aug. **Tickets** €19; €13 students, over 65s; €8
under-26s. **Credit** MC, V.
This theatre provides a much-needed platform for
the contemporary multi-media dance scene. Les
Jaloux (27 Mar-5 Apr) promotes short works by
young dancemakers.

Le Regard du Cygne

210 rue de Belleville, 20th (01.43.58.55.93/
http://redcygne.free.fr). Mº Télégraphe. Closed Aug.
Tickets €5-€15. **No credit cards. Map** p403 Q3.
Created in 1983 to promote choreographic research,
this remains one of the few truly alternative spaces
in Paris. In most cases dance companies rent the
space, handling the ticketing themselves. During
Spectacles Sauvages (20 Feb-12 Mar and 23-25 May),
for a symbolic fee (nearly) anybody can present a
ten-minute piece to the public.

Studio CND

15 rue Geoffroy-l'Asnier, 4th (01.42.74.44.22/
www.cnd.fr). Mº Pont-Marie or St-Paul. **Box office**
2-7pm Mon-Fri. **Tickets** €9; €8 under-26s. **No**
credit cards. Map p406 K6.
Prior to the opening of the Centre National de la
Danse (1 rue Victor Hugo, 93500 Pantin/
01.41.83.27.27) in autumn 2003, catch up on young
choreographers at its Paris studio .

Théâtre de la Cité Internationale

21 bd Jourdan, 14th (01.43.13.50.50/
www.theatredelacite.ciup.fr). RER Cité Universitaire.
Box office 2-7pm Mon-Sat. Closed July-Aug.
Tickets €18; €12.50 concessions; €9.50 under-26s
and Mon. **Credit** MC, V.
The theatre of the Cité-U hosts performances from
the Festival d'automne and is an established contemporary dance venue. Mark Tompkins visits in May.

Georges Momboye: Paris' premier
evangelist of African dance. *See p303.*

Arts & Entertainment

Dancing in the streets

The music's pumping. They're all at it, you know. No longer marginalised to ghetto kids, street dance is everywhere from swanky theatre stages to, well, the street itself.

Hip-hop first hit France in the 1980s. Since then it has exploded, making France the second-biggest hip-hop consumer (music, dance, graffiti, etc) after the States, although to many hardcore b-boys and girls it has gone over-the-top commercial, losing its original meaning. Who cares? Many of the dance classes in Paris offer an amalgamation of different hip-hop styles: what you see on the streets incorporates breaking (the spins and freezes you see on the floor), top dancing, poppin and lockin and elements of martial arts, such as Brazilian *capoeira*.

All but the most traditional dance schools now offer some training in street dance, so whether you see this as a more exciting alternative to aerobics or as the natural completion to the multi-faceted hip-hop culture which you practice along with your tagging and DJing, there's a class for everyone. Steffy from the **Centre de Danse du Marais** offers courses in hype and breakdancing, while Mohamed at the **Académie des Arts Chorégraphiques** offers old-school-ish hip-hop. Lionel Amadoté

teaches groove at **Studio Harmonic** where the famous Franco-American dancer, Mr Freeze, has also been known to pop in. The **Moving** chain of fitness studios offers exclusive classes in Ragga-Jam, a kind of Afro-Jamaican version of hip-hop. To find your nearest class, call 01.44.37.09.10. If it's a real workout you're after, then try Laure's classes at **Espace Vit'Halles** (*48 rue Rambuteau, 3rd, 01.42.77.21.71/Mº Rambuteau*). This French hip-hop champion favours top dancing, also known as hype (the latest thing in hip-hop incorporating a variety of ethnic dance influences and what you tend to see in MTV clips). And don't forget **Blanca Li**'s studio (*7 rue des Petites-Ecuries, 10th, 01.53.34.04.05/Mº Château d'Eau*). This is the Spanish dancer and choreographer who brought the hip-hop musical *Le Défi* to our screens in 2002. The **F.A.M.E.** school (*81 rue Marcadet, 18th Mº Jules Joffrin 01.42.23.68.40/www.studiofame.net*) offers classes in hip-hop, breakdancing, poppin and boogaloo both to wannabe professionals on its degree course and to interested others. Of course, if you wanna 'keep it real, maaan', unfurl your lino and get out on the streets. The management accepts no responsibilty for injuries sustained whilst poppin.

Dance classes

Académie des Arts Chorégraphiques

4bis Cité Véron, 18th (01.42.52.07.29). M° Blanche.
Classes €13; ten classes €115.
The friendly, recently renovated Académie offers classes in ballet, jazz, hip hop, salsa, capoiera and tango. Gypsies *manqués* should head here too for some real *danse tzigane*.

Association Carnet de Bals

Info: (01.40.24.10.21/www.carnetdebals.com).
Classes €30 membership plus €125 for 14 three-hour classes; day-courses €30.
Step back in time as you learn the dances of the 19th century as well tips on kitting yourself out to avoid anachronistic howlers for the *grand bals* organised.

Association Irlandaise de Paris/ Mission Bretonne – Ti ar Vretored

22 rue Delambre, 14th (Association Irlandaise 01.47.64.39.31/www.fredmathis.net/assirl; Mission Bretonne 01.43.35.26.41/www.tav.trad.org). M° Vavin. **Classes** Irish €25 membership plus €185 a year; Breton €31 membership plus €31 a term.
The Irish and their Celtic cousins share this Paris HQ, where you'll find set dancing classes and ceilidhs, step-dancing for the Flateley-footed and Breton steps to impress them at your next *fest-noz*.

Centre des Arts Vivants

4 rue Bréguet, 11th (01.55.28.84.00/ www.le-centre-des-arts.com). M° Bastille. **Classes** €14-€33; carnet of five classes €65, ten classes €120.
This studio complex provides training for amateurs and pros alike in modern and funky jazz, ballet, tap, contemporary, African dance, hip hop and more.

Centre de Danse du Marais

41 rue du Temple, 4th (01.49.23.40.43/ www.parisdanse.com). M° Rambuteau. **Classes** €15; four for €56; eight for €94; twelve for €120.
One of the 'famous three' dance schools in Paris. Big name choreographers and teachers flock to this school with an extensive list of classes from Afro-jazz to Qi Gong.

Centre International Danse Jazz

54 bis rue de Clichy, 9th (01.53.32.75.00/ www.centre-rick-odums.com). M° Liège or Place de Clichy. **Classes** €12; carnet of ten €98.
A laid-back American-style school with an emphasis on jazz with a good dose of hip hop thrown in for good measure and good calves.

Centre Momboye

25 rue Boyer, 20th (01.43.58.85.01/ www.ladanse.com/momboye). M° Gambetta. **Classes** €28 membership, plus €12 a class; *carnets* available.
Only centre in France to devote itself entirely to teaching African dance (which, in Momboye's book, includes hip-hop, too). Classes, in mirrored studios, are taught to live drumming and you can also learn percussion and singing.

Ecoles des Danses Latines et Tropicales

170bis rue du Fbg-St-Antoine, 12th (01.43.72.26.26/ www.salsadanse.com). M° Faidherbe Chaligny or Reuilly Diderot. **Classes** trial €10; €25 membership, plus €240 for six months of classes; €380 one year.
There are five levels of salsa classes, and many other hip-swinging delights on offer. The ambiance is friendly, but salsa is a serious business here and smiles will not be exchanged if you lie to get in the top class, and then can't tell your taps from your twirls. Multi-dance cards are available.

Espace Oxygène

168 rue St-Maur, 11th (01.49.29.06.77). M° Goncourt or Belleville. **Classes** one lesson €6-€12; ten lessons €76-€100.
This studio offers an exotic variety of classes from capoeira to Egyptian. Tango classes are taught by some of the best teachers in Paris.

Flamenco en France

33 rue des Vignolles, 20th (01.43.48.99.92). M° Avron or Buzenval. **Classes** membership €45; ten lessons €115.
Right next to the Socio-Anarchist Party is this very authentic school, where La Juana will take you through the stamping and attitude you'll need to put some *olé* into your dance moves.

French Country and Western Dance Association

13 passage de Lagny, 20th (01.46.45.27.89/ http://country.france.free.fr/FCWDA).
Yep folks, these Frenchies like to dosie-do their pardners, too. This (cowboy) outfit has the low-down on line, square and partner dancing in Paris. Yeeeha!

Smoking et Brillantine

13 rue Guyton de Morveau, 13th (01.45.65.90.90/ www.smoking-brillantine.com). M° Corvisart.
Classes membership €31, plus €77 for ten lessons.
Specialises in partner dance, including rock 'n'roll and acrobatic rock as well as salon dances, salsa and tango. Ballet, tap and hip hop classes and special *soirées* are also available.

Studio Harmonic

5 passage des Taillandiers, 11th (01.49.23.40.43/ www.studioharmonic.fr). M° Ledru-Rollin. **Classes** €32 membership, plus €13 one class, €102 ten classes.
If you've ever dreamed of being in *Fame* (the original, not *à la* Halliwell), this is the place for you. Teaching and facilities are superb and class variety huge, but if you haven't danced much before the atmosphere and posturing can be a bit much.

Swingtap

21 rue Keller, 11th (01.48.06.38.18/ www.swingtap.com). M° Bastille or Voltaire. **Classes** €24 membership, plus €15 one class; €156 a term.
The location in the back end of a shoe shop is suitably zany; the tap as serious as you like with seven levels of skill taught by pros led by Victor 'The talking feet of Paris' Cuno.

Film

Site of the world's first film show and a melting pot of the art form's current delights, Paris offers an impeccably balanced diet to film-lovers.

'See a film': not an objective high up on the average tourist's plan of campaign. But with the movies as with so many other things, Paris isn't the average tourist destination, and no one who professes even mild interest in the flicks should pass up the opportunity to sample the film-going delights of this eminently cinematic city.

Paris is not so much a moveable feast as a movie feast – a year-long spread of new and recent releases from around the world, regular retrospectives of directors both venerated and under-rated, pick'n'mix packages of *courts-métrages* (short films), open-air screenings under the stars and time-warp programmes of silents made when Monsieur Hulot was barely a glint in Jacques Tati's eye. This, after all, is the city that held the first public screening (in 1895 – Lumière's *Sortie d'usine*); today it has the densest concentration of screens and probably the most open-minded, curious and discerning audiences in the world. You only need go to a news kiosk and peruse the film-related magazines to understand how much movies matter here: the readership is large enough to sustain not only illustrious monthlies such as *Les Cahiers du Cinéma* and *Positif*, but also titles such as *Repérages*, *Synopsis*, *Traffic*, and the more populist *Première* and *Studio* – to name only the best-known. In short, Paris is the place where the medium's claim to artform status seems most credible.

New releases – sometimes as many as 15 – hit the screens every Wednesday. Hollywood is well represented, of course, but Paris audiences balance their blockbuster diet with an insatiable appetite for international product – films made anywhere from Thailand to Tadjikistan. Then there are the 150-plus annual releases funded or part-funded with French money – not only the talkative, 'serious' films for which France is renowned, but in recent years crowd-pleasers in growing numbers. What's more, while French cinema has long dominated art house circuits abroad, now even its large-scale, broad-appeal films are clocking up exceptional international sales: in Quebec in 2002, for example, *Astérix & Obélix: Mission Cléopâtre* trounced both *Spider-Man* and the latest episode in the *Star Wars* saga. Mainstream American movies still

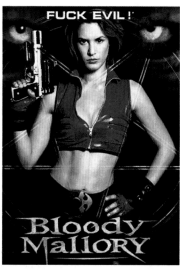

represent the French film industry's biggest rival for market share; though while the French moan about Hollywood's muscle and corrosive cultural influence, they're still happy to 'borrow' US recipes for success (sometimes with embarrassing results – *see picture*).

Even if you're only in town for a short stay, you'll find treats that you won't get back home; and if you take up residence here, the screen's your oyster. If it's blockbusters you're after, there are plenty of screens with the requisite hi-spec facilities; equally, if mapping the human heart is more the kind of thing that fluffs your rice, you can choose from dozens of passionate art house venues where talk about *cinéma d'auteur* won't earn you a lot of funny looks. For venues, times and prices, see the *Cinéscope* section of weekly listings mag *Pariscope* (every Wed, €0.40) – if you're a serious buff, dive into the array of Welles, Ford, Pasolini, Mizoguchi, Truffaut and Renoir in the *'Reprises'* (re-releases) and *'Festivals'* sections. New titles are listed under *'Films Nouveaux'*, with films on general release under *'Exclusivités'*; foreign films are screened in 'VO' (original language with French subtitles) or 'VF' (dubbed into French).

Paris in the pictures

Hôtel du Nord
(Marcel Carné, 1938)
The iron footbridge and the Canal St-Martin lock it spans were recreated in the studio by legendary production designer Alexandre Trauner, and the Hôtel du Nord opposite the real thing is now a national monument. On the bridge, national icon Arletty gives suitor Louis Jouvet the brush-off with the immortal 'Atmosphère! Atmosphère! Est-ce que j'ai une gueule d'atmosphère?'

Les 400 Coups
(François Truffaut, 1959)
Emblematic brat on the run Antoine Doisnel (the young Jean-Pierre Léaud in his first role) gets around a lot of Paris, helping to launch the *Nouvelle Vague* on the way. His biggest troubles start when he catches his mum in an adulterous clinch on place de Clichy. Well, it's never pleasant, is it, seeing your mum sucking some bloke's face?

Le Samourai
(Jean-Pierre Melville, 1967) Supercool trenchcoated hitman Jeff Costello (Alain Delon), the eponymous antihero of Melville's gangster flick, is released from custody at police headquarters on quai des Orfèvres – just one of hundreds of film characters who work or spend time at the address.

Baisers Volés
(François Truffaut, 1968)
The opening shot – a slow pull back from the entrance to the Cinémathèque – is probably the cinéphile's ultimate Paris-on-film moment. The further adventures of Antoine Doisnel see him working as a hotel watchman at 39 avenue Junot and in a shoeshop (where he beds the owner's wife).

Les Ripoux (Le Cop)
(Claude Zidi, 1984)
Loveably roguish cop Philippe Noiret inducts scrupulous rookie Thierry Lhermitte into the fine art of police corruption on their Barbès beat. Free meals at the local bistro, a gratis gigot from the butcher and some buckshee shades from a market stall under the *métro aérien* are all in a day's work – just hope the internal affairs guys aren't watching.

Les Amants du Pont Neuf
(Leos Carax, 1991)
The *folie de grandeur* that was this story of down-and-out romance (starring Juliette Binoche and Denis Lavant) was, like *Hôtel du Nord*, filmed on another mocked-up bridge – this time the Pont Neuf, reconstructed on a lake near Montpellier at infamously budget-bursting cost.

La Fille sur le pont
(Patrice Leconte, 1999)
Circus knife-thrower Daniel Auteuil saves Vanessa Paradis from drowning after she throws herself off the passerelle Debilly in Leconte's sumptuous modern fairytale. Don't feel tempted to copy her, kids: the Seine is nothing like as clean as the underwater footage suggests, and there's a strong chance no-one would leap in and help you.

Le Fabuleux Destin d'Amélie Poulain (Amélie)
(Jean-Pierre Jeunet, 2001)
Amélie's Montmartre stamping ground includes her place of employment, the Café des Deux Moulins at 15 rue Lepic. The place is now a tourist attraction in its own right, though its owners have so far resisted the temptation to rename it Café Amélie.

Ciné showcases

Le Cinéma des Cinéastes
7 av de Clichy, 17th (01.53.42.40.20). M° Place Clichy. **Tickets** €6.60; €5.40 Wed, students, under-12s, over-60s. **Map** p401 G2.
Decorated to evoke old-fashioned film studios, this three-screen showcase of world cinema holds meet-the-director sessions, and festivals of classic, foreign, gay and documentary films. It accepts *cartes illimitées* (season tickets). *Bar-restaurant. Wheelchair access.*

Gaumont Grand Ecran Italie
30 pl d'Italie, 13th (08.92.69.69.69). M° Place d'Italie. **Tickets** €9.50 (big screen); €7.80 (other screens); €5.50 under-12s. **Map** p406 J10.
The huge complex boasts the biggest screen (24m x 10m) in Paris: here blockbusters like *Minority Report* and *Lord of the Rings* really do bust blocks. *Wheelchair access.*

La Géode
26 av Corentin-Cariou, 19th (08.92.68.45.40). M° Porte de la Villette. **Tickets** €8.75; €6.75 students. **Credit** MC, V. **Map inset** p407.
An OMNIMAX cinema housed in a glorious, shiny geodesic dome at La Villette. Most films feature 3D plunges through dramatic natural scenery. Booking is advisable. *Wheelchair access (reserve ahead).*

Le Grand Rex
1 bd Poissonnière, 2nd (08.36.68.05.96). M° Bonne Nouvelle. **Tickets** €7.80; €6.10 students, over-60s; €5.95 under-12s. **Map** p406 J4.
The blockbuster programming of this huge art deco cinema matches the vast screen. Competition from the multiplexes has caused attendance to dwindle steadily in the past few years but if you want the 30s cinema experience complete with roll-down screen this is the place. *Wheelchair access.*

Max Linder Panorama
24 bd Poissonnière, 9th (01.48.24.88.88/ 08.36.68.50.52). M° Grands Boulevards. **Tickets** €8; €6 students, under-20s Mon, Wed, Fri. **Map** p406 J9.
A state-of-the-art screening facility (THX sound). The walls and seating are all black, to prevent even the tiniest twinkle of reflected light distracting the audience from what's happening on the screen. Look out for all-nighters and one-offs such as rare vintage films. *Wheelchair access.*

MK2 sur Seine
14 quai de la Seine, 19th (08.36.68.14.07). M° Stalingrad. **Tickets** €8.10; €6 Mon, Wed, students; €5.50 under-12s. **Map** p407 M2.
The stylish six-screen flagship of the MK2 group offers an all-in-one night out, complete with restaurant and exhibition space. The MK2 chain is a paradigm of imaginative programming. Voracious film fans can invest in the *Carte Le Pass*, which offers unlimited access for €18 per month. *Wheelchair access.*

UGC Ciné Cité Les Halles
7 pl de la Rotonde, Nouveau Forum des Halles, 1st (08.92.70.00.00). M° Les Halles. **Tickets** €8.80; €5.95 students, over-60s; €5.50 under-12s. **Map** p406 J5.
This ambitious 16-screen development screens art movies as well as mainstream, and holds meet-the-director-screenings. UGC has gone two screens better at the Ciné Cité Bercy (2 cour St-Emilion, 12th/08.36.68.68.58/M° Cour St-Emilion), and launched its *UGC Illimitée* card – unlimited access for €16.46 per month. *Internet café. Wheelchair access.*

Art cinemas

Action
Action Christine *4 rue Christine, 6th (01.43.29.11.30). M° Odéon.* **Tickets** €7; €5.50 students, under-20s. **Map** p406 J7.
Action Ecoles *23 rue des Ecoles, 5th (01.43.29.79.89). M° Maubert-Mutualité.* **Tickets** €6; €4.50 students, under-20s. **Map** p406 J8.
Grand Action *23 rue des Ecoles, 5th (01.43.29.44.40). M° Cardinal-Lemoine.* **Tickets** €6.50; €5 students, under-20s. **Map** p406 K8.
A Left Bank feature since the early 80s, the Action group is renowned for screening new prints of old movies. Heaven for those nostalgic for 1940s and 50s Tinseltown classics and American independents, with anything from Cary Grant to Jim Jarmusch.

Accattone
20 rue Cujas, 5th (01.46.33.86.86). M° Cluny La Sorbonne. **Tickets** €6.50; €5 Wed, students, under-20s. **Map** p406 J8.
Named after Pasolini's first film and housed in what was once the venue for France's first strip show, this temple to art house screens films by Robert Bresson, Oshima, Wenders and the like to an earnest crowd.

Le Balzac
1 rue Balzac, 8th (01.45.61.10.60). M° George V. **Tickets** €7; €5.50 Mon, Wed, students, under-18s, over-60s. **Map** p400 D4.
Built in 1935 with a mock ocean-liner foyer, Le Balzac scores high for design and programming. Genial manager Jean-Jacques Schpoliansky welcomes punters in person before every screening.

Le Cinéma du Panthéon
13 rue Victor-Cousin, 5th (01.40.46.01.21). RER Luxembourg. **Tickets** €7; €5.50 Mon, Wed, students, 13-18s; €4 under-13s. **Map** p406 J8.
Paris' oldest surviving movie house (founded in 1907 in the Sorbonne gymnasium) is still a place to catch new, often obscure international films.

Le Denfert
24 pl Denfert-Rochereau, 14th (01.43.21.41.01). M° Denfert-Rochereau. **Tickets** €6.10; €4.60 students, over-60s; €4.30 under-15s. **Map** p406 H10.
This valiant, friendly little spot was founded in 1933. Its eclectic repertory selection ranges from François Ozon and Kitano to short films and new animation, as well as new foreign films. *Wheelchair access.*

Studio 28: bright lights, small *ciné*.

L'Entrepôt

7-9 rue Francis de Pressensé, 14th (08.36.68.05.87).
M° Pernéty. **Tickets** €6.70; €5.40 students, over-60s.
€4 under-12s. **Credit** MC, V. **Map** p405 F10.
The number of films screened each week is quite
modest, but the programme is wide-ranging: new
and Third World directors, shorts, gay cinema and
regular debate sessions. *Café. Restaurant.*

La Pagode

57bis rue de Babylone, 7th (01.45.55.48.48). M° St-
François-Xavier. **Tickets** €7.30; €5.80 Mon, Wed,
students, under-21s. **Map** p405 F7.
The 7th *arrondissement* may have only one cinema,
but wowser, what a cinema: two screens housed in a
19th-century replica of a Far Eastern pagoda that
was given Historic Monument status in 1986.

Studio 28

10 rue Tholozé, 18th (01.46.06.36.07). M° Abbesses.
Tickets €6.80; €5.60 under-12s. **Map** p405 H1.
Montmartre's historic Studio 28 was the venue for
Cocteau's scandalous *L'Age d'Or*. Today it offers a
decent repertory mix of classics and recent movies.

Public repertory institutions

Auditorium du Louvre

entrance through Pyramid, Cour Napoléon, 1st
(01.40.20.51.86/www.louvre.fr). M° Palais Royal.
Tickets €4.57; €3.35 under-18s. **Map** p406 H5.
This 420-seat auditorium was designed by IM Pei.
Film screenings are sometimes related to the exhi-
bitions; silent movies with live music are regulars.

Centre Pompidou

rue St-Martin, 4th (01.44.78.12.33/
www.centrepompidou.fr). M° Hôtel de Ville.
Tickets €5; €3 students. **Map** p406 K6.
Themed series, along with experimental and artists'
films and a weekly documentary session, give a
flavour of what's on. There's also the *Cinéma du Réel*
festival of rare and restored films. *Wheelchair access.*

La Cinémathèque Française

Palais de Chaillot, 7 av Albert-de-Mun, 16th
(01.56.26.01.01/www.cinemathequefrancaise.com).
M° Trocadéro. **Tickets** €4.73; €3 students.
Map p404 C5.
Grands Boulevards, 42 bd Bonne-Nouvelle, 10th
(01.56.26.01.01). M° Bonne Nouvelle. **Tickets** €4.73;
€3 students, membership available. **Map** p404 J4.
The Cinémathèque was vital in shaping the New
Wave directors in the late 1950s. It continues to hold
seasons devoted to directors of all stripes.

Forum des Images

2 Grande Galerie, Porte St-Eustache, Forum des
Halles, 1st (01.44.76.62.00/ www.forumdesimages.net).
M° Les Halles. **Open** 1-9pm Tue, Wed, Fri-Sun;
1-10pm Thur. Closed 2 weeks in Aug. **Tickets** €5.50
per day; €4.50 students, under-30s, membership
available. **Map** p406 J5.
This archive is dedicated to Paris on celluloid.
2003 topics include 'Faith', 'Alter Ego' and 'The
Underworld'. The Forum also screens the *Ren-*
contres Internationales du Cinéma (*see below*), the
trash treats of *L'Etrange Festival* and films from the
critics' selection at Cannes.

Festivals & special events

Côté Court

Ciné 104, 104 av Jean Lolive, 93500 Pantin
(01.48.46.95.08). M° Eglise de Pantin. **Dates** Mar-Apr.
A great selection of new and old short films.

Festival du Film de Paris

Gaumont Marignan, 27 ave des Champs-Elysées, 8th
(01.45.72.96.40). M° Franklin. **Dates** Apr.
The 18th edition of the annual Paris film festival will
go ahead without Mairie de Paris support. The festival's low international profile has been reflected in
lacklustre programming and star presence.

Festival International de Films de Femmes

Maison des Arts, pl Salvador-Allende, 94040 Créteil
(01.49.80.38.98). M° Créteil-Préfecture. **Dates** Mar-Apr.
An impressive selection of retrospectives and new
international films by female directors.
Wheelchair access (reserve ahead).

Rencontres Internationales du Cinéma

Forum des Images (see above). **Dates** Oct-Nov.
A global choice of new independent features,
documentary and short films, many screened in the
presence of their directors.

Arts & Entertainment

Galleries

Paris' gallery scene takes a bit of delving out, but once there, you'll find a wildly international range of artists on show in every medium from paint to sound.

Paris has hundreds of galleries, but fortunately, like-minded galleries tend to cluster together. For innovative work and international names head for the northern Marais and the streets near the Centre Pompidou, where historic *hôtels particuliers* may well be the haven for video and installation art, or to 'Louise', the growing nucleus of young galleries in the 13th. Galleries around St-Germain-des-Prés, home of the avant-garde in the 1950s and 60s, largely confine themselves to traditional sculpture and painting. Galleries near the Champs-Elysées present big modern and contemporary names.

There's a symbiosis between commercial galleries and public institutions. Anyone interested in the gallery scene should watch what's going on at the **Centre Pompidou, Musée d'Art Moderne de la Ville de Paris, Site de Création Contemporaine, Centre National de la Photographie, Le Plateau** and **Fondation Cartier**. But it is the gallery that will follow an artist over the long term. There is also a growing number of artist-run and alternative spaces, which often work on one-off projects with young artists or encourage artistic collaborations. The international art fair **FIAC** in October gives a quick fix on the gallery scene, and has made an effort to keep up with the times by adding a video section.

There are numerous chances to visit artists' studios. The Génie de la Bastille, Ménilmontant and 13ème Art are the best known, but there are also *'portes ouvertes'* (often in May or October) in Belleville, St-Germain, the 10th, 14th and 18th *arrondissements* and the suburbs.

Local publications include monthlies *Beaux Arts, L'Oeil,* bilingual *Art Press* and the fortnightly *Journal des Arts,* as well as hip quarterly fashion/art/sex volume *Purple.* The *Galeries Mode d'Emploi* (Marais/Bastille/Louise-Weiss/www.artsiders.com) and *Association des Galeries* listings foldouts (Left and Right Bank/suburban cultural centres) and flyers can be picked up inside galleries. Most galleries close from late July to early September.

Beaubourg & the Marais

Galerie Chantal Crousel
40 rue Quincampoix, 4th (01.42.77.38.87/ www.crousel.com). M° Rambuteau/RER Châtelet-Les Halles. **Open** 11am-7pm Tue-Sat. **Map** p406 J6.
Crousel focuses on the hottest of the new generation, including Abigail Lane, Rikrit Tiravanija, politically inspired installations by Thomas Hirschhorn, video works by Graham Gussin and Albanian-born Parisian Anri Sala, and the interactions with science by Melik Ohanian. A maze of dark cellars makes for atmospheric video viewing.

Galerie Cent 8
108 rue Vieille-du-Temple, 3rd (01.42.74.53.57). M° Filles du Calvaire. **Open** 10.30am-1pm, 2.30-7pm Tue-Sat. **Map** p406 L5
Serge Le Borgne puts on stimulating, varied shows. Look out for the genetics/anthropological explorations of Christine Borland, the anguished text/drawing/film work of Valérie Mréjen and photos by Seton Smith. There's an extension at 13 rue Saintonge.

Galerie de France
54 rue de la Verrerie, 4th (01.42.74.38.00). M° Hôtel de Ville. **Open** 11am-7pm Tue-Sat. **Map** p406 K6.
This is one of the rare galleries to span the entire 20th century. Shows have included Brancusi sculpture, Surrealist Meret Oppenheim and Raysse's Pop,

Sam Samore sees green at Galerie Anne de Villepoix.

Arts & Entertainment

as well as contemporary artists Alain Kirili and Rebecca Horn and artist/stage director Bob Wilson.

Galerie Marian Goodman
*79 rue du Temple, 3rd (01.48.04.70.52). M°
Rambuteau.* **Open** 11am-7pm Tue-Sat. **Map** p406 K6.
The New York gallerist has an impressive Paris outpost in the beautiful 17th-century Hôtel de Montmor. Alongside established names, including Thomas Struth, Jeff Wall and Lothar Baumgarten, she has snapped up brilliant young Brit videomaker Steve McQueen and fab Finn Eija-Liisa Ahtila.

Galerie Karsten Greve
*5 rue Debelleyme, 3rd (01.42.77.19.37/
www.artnet.com/kgreve). M° Filles du Calvaire or
St-Paul.* **Open** 11am-7pm Tue-Sat. **Map** p402 L5.
Cologne gallerist Karsten Greve's Paris outpost is the venue for retrospective-style displays of top-ranking artists, such as Jannis Kounellis and Louise Bourgeois, and begins 2003 with the first show for a decade by painter Pierre Soulages.

Galerie Laage-Salomon
*57 rue du Temple, 4th (01.42.78.11.71). M° Hôtel
de Ville.* **Open** 2-7pm Tue-Fri; Sat 11am-7pm.
Map p406 K6.
Laage-Salomon alternates painters including Philippe Cognée and art photography from the likes of Hannah Collins, Claudia Hoffe and Axel Hütte.

Galerie Yvon Lambert
*108 rue Vieille-du-Temple, 3rd (01.42.71.09.33).
M° Filles du Calvaire.* **Open** 10am-1pm, 2.30-7pm
Tue-Fri; 10am-7pm Sat. **Map** p402 L5.

Probably France's most important art gallery (and after its expansion in March 2003 Paris' largest), Lambert continues to pull out the stops, whether it's the latest production by a major international name, such as Anselm Kiefer, Nan Goldin or Christian Boltanski, new installation by Claude Levêque or the pick of the young video generation.

Gilles Peyroulet & Cie
*80 rue Quincampoix, 3rd (01.42.78.85.11).
M° Rambuteau or Etienne Marcel.* **Open** 2-7pm
Tue-Sat. **Map** p402 K5.
Peyroulet is at its strongest with photo-based artists including Marin Kasimir and Nick Waplington, but also cleverly bridges the gap between fine art and design, with items commissioned from young designers, such as Frédéric Ruyant and Matali Crasset (generally shown across the street at No 75, Espace #2), and archival-type shows of 20th-century pioneers such as Eileen Gray and Alvar Aalto.

Galerie Rabouan-Moussion
*121 rue Vieille-du-Temple, 3rd (01.48.87.75.91/
www.artnet.com). M° Filles du Calvaire.* **Open**
10am-7pm Mon-Sat. **Map** p402 L5.
The undoubted star at Moussion is Pierrick Sorin, the funniest video artist around, but it might also feature Chrystel Egal, dealing with gender and sexuality, French support-surface artist, Jean Degottex, and radical Russian Oleg Kulik.

Galerie Thaddaeus Ropac
*7 rue Debelleyme, 3rd (01.42.72.99.00/
www.ropac.net). M° St-Sébastien-Froissart or St-Paul.*

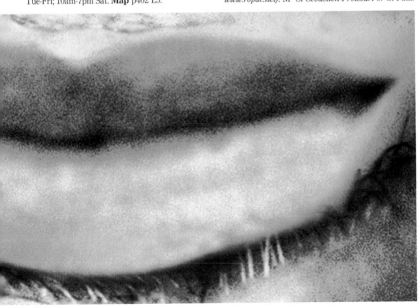

Arts & Entertainment

Open 10am-7pm Tue-Sat. **Map** p402 L5.

The Austrian-owned gallery is strong on American Pop, neo-Pop and neo-Geo (Warhol, Baechler, Fleury, Taaffe, Sachs), but also features major artists Kabakov, Gilbert & George, Balkenhol, Gormley, Sylvie Fleury, photographers Adam Fuss and Bettina Rheims, as well as quirky theme shows.

Galerie Templon

30 rue Beaubourg, 3rd (01.42.72.14.10). M° *Rambuteau.* **Open** 10am-7pm Mon-Sat. **Map** p402 K5.
Templon mainly shows well-known painters, which is perhaps why his gallery is a favourite with the French art establishment. David Salle, Jean-Marc Alberola, Claude Viallat, Vincent Corpet are regulars along with eternally youthful Raymond Hains and he's recently added some young German artists.

Galerie Chez Valentin

9 rue St-Gilles, 3rd (01.48.87.42.55). M° Chemin Vert. **Open** 2.30-7pm Tue-Sat. **Map** p407 L6.
A sense of urban angst pervades the work here. Look for the creeping detritus installations and videos of Véronique Boudier, photos by Nicolas Moulin and videos by François Nouguiès.

Galerie Anne de Villepoix

43 rue de Montmorency, 3rd (01.42.78.32.24/ www.annedevillepoix.com). M° Rambuteau. **Open** 10am-7pm Tue-Sat. **Map** p402 K5.
In her spacious new quarters near the Centre Pompidou, Anne de Villepoix's generational mix takes in established US names John Coplans, Sam Samore and Chris Burden, and a younger conceptual set including Franck Scurti, Gillian Wearing, Jean-Luc Moulène and Valérie Jouve.

Galerie Anton Weller

57 rue de Bretagne, 3rd (01.42.72.05.62). M° Temple or Arts et Métiers. **Open** 2-7pm Tue-Sat. **Map** p403 M5.
Galerie Anton Weller is currently sharing its space with the Sous-Sol (01.48.87.21.92, mainly photo artists) and Galerie Bernard Jordan (01.42.77.19.61, mainly painting). Recent finds include young artists Isabelle Lévénez and Christelle Familiari, who use video and installation to deal with sexuality.

Galerie Zurcher

56 rue Chapon, 3rd (01.42.72.82.20). M° Arts et Métiers. **Open** 11am-7pm Tue-Sat; 2-6pm Sun. **Map** p402 K5.
Young artists with a new take on painting and video include Camille Vivier, Gwen Ravillous, Philippe Hurteau and Dan Hays. *Wheelchair access.*

Bastille & Northeast Paris

Liliane et Michel Durand-Dessert

28 rue de Lappe, 11th (01.48.06.92.23/ www.lm.durand-dessert.com). M° Bastille. **Open** 11am-7pm Tue-Sat. **Map** p407 M7.
Durand-Dessert has long been committed to artists associated with *arte povera* (Pistoletto, Mario Merz),

major French names (Morellet, Garouste, Lavier) and photographers (Wegman, Burgin, Rousse, Burckhardt) presented in an industrial space. There's also an excellent art bookshop.

Galerie Alain Gutharc

47 rue de Lappe, 11th (01.47.00.32.10). M° Bastille. **Open** 2-7pm Tue-Fri; 11am-1pm, 2-7pm Sat. **Map** p407 M7.
Gutharc talent spots young French artists. Check out Delphine Kreuter's fetishistic, colour-saturated slice-of-life photos, the quirky text pieces of Antoinette Ohanassian and the videos of Joël Bartolomméo and former fashion stylist François-Xavier Courrèges.

Galerie Maisonneuve

24-32 rue des Amandiers, 20th (01.01.43.66.23.99/ www.saintmonday.net). M° Père Lachaise. **Open** 2-7pm Tue-Sat.
Grégoire Maisonneuve started with projects on the web before opening his gallery in 2002, with an adventurous programme beginning with Italian dancer/installation artist Claudia Triozzi.

Champs-Elysées

Galerie Lelong

13 rue de Téhéran, 8th (01.45.63.13.19). M° Miromesnil. **Open** 10.30am-6pm Tue-Fri; 2-6.30pm Sat. **Map** p401 E3.
Lelong shows bankable, post-1945, international names including Alechinsky, Bacon, Hockney, Kounellis, Scully. Branches in New York and Zurich.

Galerie Jérôme de Noirmont

38 av Matignon, 8th (01.42.89.89.00/ www.denoirmont.com). M° Miromesnil. **Open** 10am-1pm, 2.30-7pm Mon-Sat. **Map** p401 E4.
The location could arouse suspicions that Noirmont sells purely business art. Not a bit of it – eye-catching shows by A R Penck, Clemente, Jeff Koons, Pierre et Gilles and Shirin Neshat make this gallery worth the trip. Noirmont opened a second space, Noirmont Prospect, in 2002 (15 rue Jean-Mermoz, 8th/01.40.75.00.34, open noon-7pm Tue-Sat) offering first Paris shows to young talents.

St-Germain-des-Prés

Galerie 1900-2000

8 rue Bonaparte, 6th (01.43.25.84.20/ www.galerie1900-2000.com). M° St-Germain-des-Prés. **Open** 2-7pm Mon; 10am-12.30pm, 2-7pm Tue-Sat. **Map** p406 H7.
Marcel and David Fleiss show a strong predilection for Surrealism, Dada, Pop art and Fluxus, with works on paper by anyone from Breton and De Chirico to Lichtenstein, plus the occasional photo show.

Galerie Jeanne Bucher

53 rue de Seine, 6th (01.44.41.69.65). M° Mabillon or Odéon. **Open** 9am-6.30pm Tue-Fri; 10am-12.30pm, 2.30-6pm Sat. **Map** p406 H7.

Arts & Entertainment

Made in Paris?

France may be wildly protective when it comes to French cinema or the French language but, when it comes to art, it displays a magnanimity that means it's easy to get a fix on what's going on internationally, perhaps less so of the home scene. Whereas if you visit galleries in London, 80% of shows will probably be of British artists, with a few Americans thrown in for good measure (and there's a similar situation in New York), Paris galleries sometimes come under fire for not encouraging native production enough. Does it matter? After all, art today is highly international: most of the bright young things of contemporary art are part of networks exhibiting from Paris to London, New York, Tokyo or Berlin (and why not Sao Paolo as well?), and it's only right that galleries put on what's interesting, regardless of where it is produced. But on the down side, this keeps Paris' art scene fairly small and enclosed.

While cinema actors, novelists and, even (to their peril),

French footballers, are all sure of plentiful media coverage, not so artists. Pierre Huyghe's film installation for the 2001 Venice Biennial was widely acclaimed but he's hardly on the map here (something that may change, now he co-designed the latest Costes brothers restaurant Etienne Marcel). When the Site de Création Contemporaine opened at the Palais de Tokyo in January 2002, the event received (rare) TV coverage on the TF1 8pm news, but did it mention Melik Ohanian, Franck Scurti, Beat Streuli or other artists involved? No, rather the French world cup footballer whose companion had works on show (no name mentioned, another opportunity missed) or Chiara Mastroianni who happened to be in the crowd. France now has the Prix Marcel Duchamp, donated by the ADIAF, an association of collectors, to try and do for creation in France what the Turner Prize has done in the UK (2001 winner Thomas Hirschhorn, 2002 Dominique Gonzalez-Foerster), and the Prix Ricard for young artists (2000 winner Natacha Lesueur, 2001 Tatiana Trouvé) – but they've yet to achieve widespread publicity. Low profile, then, but not inactive, there are thousands of artists working here. Whether from France, China, former Eastern Europe or the rest of the world, Paris remains a magnet for artists to work, though may just as well be tapping away at a computer in a tiny room as daubing paint in a draughty studio (or both); you only have to go to the *vernissages* at rue Louise-Weiss or the Musée d'Art Moderne de la Ville de Paris to see them out in force. The best way then to discover the artists for yourself is to visit the galleries, for a dynamic young scene that may take you from shopping (Mathieu Laurette) to hairstyles (Natacha Lesueur), the city streets (Jean-Luc Moulène) to the bathroom cabinet (Delphine Kreuter), crochet (Christelle Familiari), porn (Clarisse Hahn) to outer space (Melik Ohanian).

Natacha Lesueur hams it at Galerie Praz-Devallade.

Arts & Entertainment

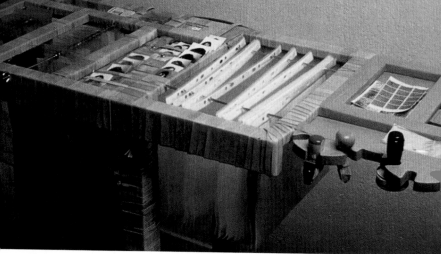

Tatiana Trouvé archives an artist's life chez Galerie G-P & N Vallois.

Based on the Left Bank since 1925, Bucher specialises in postwar abstract (De Staël, Viera da Silva, Rebeyrolle) and Cobra painters.

Galerie Maeght
42 rue du Bac, 7th (01.45.48.45.15/ www.galeriemaeght.com). M° Rue du Bac. **Open** 10am-6pm Mon; 9.30am-7pm Tue-Sat. **Map** p405 G6.
The gallery founded by Aimé Maeght in 1946 is now run by his grandchildren, but pales against a past that included Léger, Chagall, Giacometti and Miró.

Galerie Denise René
196 bd St-Germain, 7th (01.42.22.77.57/ www.deniserene.com). M° St-Germain-des-Prés or Rue du Bac. **Open** 10am-1pm, 2-7pm Tue-Fri; 11am-1pm, 2-7pm Sat. **Map** p406 H7.
Denise René is a Paris institution and has remained committed to kinetic art, Op art and geometrical abstraction ever since Tinguely first presented his machines here in the 1950s.
Branch: 22 rue Charlot, 3rd (01.48.87.73.94).

Galerie Darthea Speyer
6 rue Jacques-Callot, 6th (01.43.54.78.41). M° Mabillon or Odéon. **Open** 11am-12.45pm, 2-7pm Tue-Fri; 11am-7pm Sat. **Map** p406 H6.
Colourful, representational painting and sculpture and naïve artists are the speciality here. It can be kitsch, but at best features the political expressionism of Golub or American dreams of Paschke.

Galerie G-P & N Vallois
36 rue de Seine, 6th (01.46.34.61.07). M° Mabillon or Odéon. **Open** 10.30am-1pm, 2-7pm Mon-Sat. **Map** p406 H7.
G-P & N Vallois sticks out as the only truly contemporary gallery left in St-Germain, but is worth the detour for *nouveau réaliste* torn-poster veteran Jacques Villeglé, and a clutch of young artists: installations by Gilles Barbier, urban interventions by Alain Bublex, polders by Tatiana Trouvé.

Galerie Lara Vincy
47 rue de Seine, 6th (01.43.26.72.51). M° Mabillon or St-Germain-des-Prés. **Open** 2.30-7.30pm Mon; 11am-12.30pm, 2.30-7.30pm Tue-Sat. **Map** p406 H7.
Lara Vincy is one of the few characters to retain something of the old St-Germain spirit and sense of 1970s Fluxus-style 'happenings'. Interesting theme and solo shows include master of the epigram, Ben, and artists' text, music, performance-related pieces.

Scène Est: rue Louise-Weiss

&:
10 rue Duchefdelaville, 13th (gb agency 01.53.79.07.13; in SITU 01.53.79.06.12; Christophe Daviet-Thery 01.53.79.05.95). M° Chevaleret. **Open** 11am-7pm Tue-Sat. **Map** p407 M10.
This gallery is shared in rotation between Fabienne Leclerc's in SITU, whose artists include Mark Dion, Gary Hill, Florence Paradeis and Patrick Corillon and young painter Bruno Perramant, gb agency, which works principally with young artists, and artists' book publisher Christophe Daviet-Thery.

Air de Paris
32 rue Louise-Weiss, 13th (01.44.23.02.77/ www.airdeparis.com). M° Chevaleret. **Open** 2-7pm Tue-Sat. **Map** p407 M10.
This gallery is named after Duchamp's bottle of air. Shows tend to be highly experimental, if not chaotic. Neo-conceptual experiences mix video, performance, photo, objects and a regularly changing artist's mural. A young international stable includes Philippe Parreno, Liam Gillick, Pierre Joseph, Carsten Höller, Bruno Serralongue and fashion photographer Inez van Lamsweede.

Galerie Almine Rech
127 rue du Chevaleret, 13th (01.45.83.71.90/ galeriealminerech.com). M° Chevaleret. **Open** 11am-7pm Tue-Sat. **Map** p407 M10.

Arts & Entertainment

Almine Rech has moved to larger space up the street, with a programme that includes elegant photographer Philip Lorca di Corcia, light maestro James Turrell, installations by Ugo Rondinone and drawings and videos by Rebecca Bournigault.

Galerie Jennifer Flay
20 rue Louise-Weiss, 13th (01.44.06.73.60). M°
Chevaleret. **Open** 11am-7pm Tue-Sat. **Map** p407 M10.
Flay picks up on interesting artists. As well as installation, photo and video from French thirtysomethings Xavier Veilhan, Claude Closky and Dominique Gonzalez-Foerster, and the slice-of-life photos of Richard Billingham, a batch of interesting painters includes John Currin, Chantal Joffe and Lisa Milroy.

Jousse Entreprise
24 and 34 rue Louise-Weiss, 13th (01.53.82.13.60/
www.jousse-entreprise.com). M° Chevaleret. **Open**
11am-1pm, 2-7pm Tue-Sat. **Map** p407 M10.
Philippe Jousse joined the Louise-Weiss strip in 2001, bringing with him Serge Comte, Matthieu Laurette and Thomas Grünfeld. He also features the 1950s avant-garde furniture of Jean Prouvé and lighting of Serge Mouille as a sideline.

Galerie Kréo
22 rue Duchefdelaville, 13th (01.53.60.14.68). M°
Chevaleret. **Open** 11am-7pm Tue-Sat. **Map** p407 M10.
Design gallery Kréo combines retrospectives and an agency commissioning limited-edition pieces. Look for international names Ron Arad, Marc Newson and Jasper Conran, as well as native Radi Designers, Martin Szekely and hotshots, the Bourrellec brothers.

Galerie Emmanuel Perrotin
5 and 30 rue Louise-Weiss, 13th (01.42.16.79.79/
www.galerieperrotin.com). M° Chevaleret.
Open 11am-7pm Tue-Sat. **Map** p407 M10.
Perrotin is the best place to catch up on the provocative young Japanese generation including Noritoshi Hirakawa, manga maniac Takashi Murakami and glossy cyber-punkette Mariko Mori. Among French artists look out for the fashion/body photos of Nicole Tran Ba Vang and painter Bernard Frize.

Galerie Praz-Devallade
28 rue Louise-Weiss, 13th (01.45.86.20.00). M°
Chevaleret. **Open** 11am-7pm Tue-Sat. **Map** p407 M10.
A varied selection includes the crazy drawings of Los Angeles artist Jim Shaw and the elaborate food-meets-feminism photos of Natacha Lesueur.

Artist-run & alternative spaces

Galerie Eof
15 rue St-Fiacre, 2nd (01.53.40.72.22). M° Bonne-
Nouvelle. **Open** call for details. **Map** p402 J4.
This artist-run space puts on shows that vary from solo shows by individual painters to multi-media collaborations with other organisations.

Glassbox
113bis rue Oberkampf, 11th (01.43.38.02.82/

www.icono.org/glassbox). M° Parmentier.
Open 2-7pm Wed-Sat. **Map** p403 N5.
Glassbox's politically oriented shows have included art, poetry, design and exchanges with other artists' collectives from Glasgow to Quebec.

Immanence
21 av du Maine, 15th (01.42.22.05.68/www.art-
immanence.org). M° Montparnasse-Bienvenüe.
Open 2-7pm Thur-Sat. **Map** p405 F8.
Created by two artists in 2000 in a picturesque alley of old Montparnasse artists' studios, Immanence features installations and photo shows, including exhanges with other artist-run spaces.

Paris Project Room
19 rue de l'Echiquier, 10th (06.64.24.63.73).
M° Strasbourg-St-Denis. **Open** 4-9pm Mon, Tue, Fri-Sun. **Map** p402 K4.
Pairs off artists to collaborate on collective works.

Photography

The following galleries specialise in photography, but photoworks of all sorts have become an integral part of contemporary art and can also be found in many other galleries (*see above*), and at branches of Fnac. The bienniel citywide Mois de la Photo (next in Nov 2004) covers both historic and contemporary photography, as does the annual Paris Photo salon in the Carrousel du Louvre (every Nov).

Galerie 213
213 bd Raspail, 14th (01.43.22.83.23). M° Raspail.
Open 11am-7pm Tue-Sat. **Map** p405 G9.
Photographers, often with a fashion world link (Elaine Constantine, Camille Vivier), are shown upstairs. Downstairs, there's a photography bookshop in a listed art nouveau dining room.

Michèle Chomette
24 rue Beaubourg, 3rd (01.42.78.05.62).
M° Rambuteau. **Open** 2-7pm Tue-Sat. **Map** p402 K5.
Classical and experimental photography. Alain Fleischer, Eric Rondepierre, Lewis Baltz, Felten & Massinger, Bernard Plossu, are regulars, shown alongside historic masters.

Galerie Kamel Mennour
60 rue Mazarine, 6th (01.56.24.03.63/
www.galeriemennour.com). M° Odéon.
Open 10.30am-7.30pm Mon-Sat. **Map** p405 H6/H7.
This recently established gallery is attracting buyers with an oh-so fashionable, often provocative, list that includes Nobuyoshi Araki, Peter Beard, Kriki, David LaChapelle, filmmaker Larry Clark and photographer Annie Leibovitz.

Galerie Françoise Paviot
57 rue Ste-Anne, 2nd (01.42.60.10.01). M° Quatre
Septembre. **Open** 2.30-7pm Tue-Sat. **Map** p402 H4.
Paviot presents contemporary and historic photographers with an emphasis on the great Surrealists.

Arts & Entertainment

Gay & Lesbian

Hairy bears, succulent slices of ostrich and feminist fatales posing over pool tables. You see all shades of the pink rainbow in gloriously gay Paris.

Media, shopping, politics – many crucial sectors of French society are taking on a pink hue. To instance the televisual arena; in 2002, the French version of *Big Brother*, *Loft Story*, produced an on-screen coming out by eventual winner Thomas X. Thomas, incidentally, cut the ribbons at the opening of the Louvre Virgin Megastore's My Beautiful Megastore, the first lesbian and gay section in a major high street store in Paris. And just to show that gaydom knows no political boundaries even in France, a prominent member of the conservative Gaullist party, Jean-Luc Romero, was outed by a gay magazine and remained on the government benches. (M. Romero then revealed that he was HIV positive.) The new visibility of French homosexuals, however, has not been without cost, the most highly publicised and unsettling example being the attack on Bertrand Delanoë as he schmoozed with night owls during the *Nuit Blanche* (*see chapter* **Paris Today**). That said, for yer average Arthur, Martha or subtle combination of the two, Paris is an ever-better place in which to be gay. All listings are by order of *arrondissement*.

Associations

CGPif (Fédération sportive gaie et lesbienne Paris Ile-de-France)

(01.48.05.55.17/www.cgpif.org).
Still buffing up the medals plucked from the 2002 Gay Games in Sydney, this body organises Paris' 20 gay and lesbian sports associations.

SNEG (Syndicat National des Entreprises Gaies)

59 rue Beaubourg, 3rd (01.44.59.81.03).
M° Rambuteau. **Open** 2-6pm Mon-Fri. **Map** p402 K5.
The gay and lesbian business group unites more than 1,000 companies across France.

Act Up Paris

45 rue Sedaine, 11th (answerphone 01.48.06.13.89/ www.actupp.org). M° Bréguet-Sabin. **Map** p406 L6.
The Paris branch of the worldwide anti-Aids group has become increasingly politically active and was key to the organised resistance to Le Pen's re-emergence on the political scene in the spring of 2002. Meetings are held Tuesdays at 7pm in amphitheatre 1 of the Ecole des Beaux-Arts (*14 rue Bonaparte, 6th/M° St-Germain-des-Prés*).

Centre Gai et Lesbien

3 rue Keller, 11th (01.43.57.21.47/www.cglparis.org).
M° Ledru-Rollin. **Open** 4-8pm Mon-Sat. **Map** p406 L7.
A valued community resource providing information and a meeting space, a library (2-6pm Fri, Sat), legal and other advice services. The *Association des Médecins Gais* (gay doctors) mans (or, rather, persons) a phone line (6-8pm Wed; 2-4pm Sat/ 01.48.05.81.71). The Centre also houses l'Association des Parents et Futurs Parents Gais et Lesbiens, again contactable by phone (8-10pm Mon/ 06.16.66.56.91/www.apgl.aso.fr). This association advises gay parents (as well as fighting for their rights) and, among its many worthy deeds, organises probably the cutest contribution to the annual Gay Pride march, the children's parade.

Gay bars & cafés

Banana Café

13 rue de la Ferronnerie, 1st (01.42.33.35.31).
M° Châtelet. **Open** 6pm-dawn daily. **Credit** AmEx, MC, V. **Map** p402 J5.
Can you guess from the subtlety of its name just how cruisey, queeny and *joie de diva*-y this place is? For those who just have to sing, sing, sing, there's the opportunity to mangle a few show tunes in the cellar bar. *Wheelchair access.*

Le Tropic Café

66 rue des Lombards, 1st (01.40.13.92.62).
M° Châtelet. **Open** noon-dawn daily. **Credit** AmEx, MC, V. **Map** p405 G6.
Somewhere you can actually feel glad to be gay, this bright, upbeat bar is going through a renaissance with some groovy bashes that draw a loyal band of party poppers. *Wheelchair access.*

Le Duplex

25 rue Michel-le-Comte, 3rd (01.42.72.80.86).
M° Rambuteau. **Open** 8pm-2am daily. **Credit** MC, V. **Map** p402 K5.
Smoky and atmospheric it may look, but it scores a conservative eleven on a one-to-ten cruisiness scale.

Amnesia

42 rue Vieille-du-Temple, 4th (01.42.72.16.94).
M° Hôtel de Ville. **Open** 10am-2am daily.
Credit DC, MC, V. **Map** p406 K6.
A warm meeting place with comfy sofas and easy-going staff who decorate the facade with ferns and hay bales. It's not all about pulling in here. Intercourse of the social kind is high priority.

Hairless whispers? No – a great big 'NON' to the policies of Le Pen.

Pink prandial pleasures

Paris has its comforts for the ageing gay person (by 'ageing' we mean 20 or over), not the least of which is the thriving restaurant scene. Goodbye dinner of illicit substances followed by a night's grinding on some subterranean dancefloor, hello middle-class comforts and dinner in a restaurant. And, of course, posh noshing isn't just a function of age. As the gay world goes more mainstream, wily entrepreneurs, desperate for a whiff of the euro, have seen the light.

Queen of the scene is **l'Amazonial** (3 rue-Ste-Opportune, 1st/01.42.33.53.13). This is Paris' largest gay restaurant, and, to prove that size plays a not insignificant role in the process of attraction, it has just got even bigger thanks to what you might call a terrace-enhancement procedure. The French cuisine nosh is fine and the feelgood feel feels, er, good. An entire corner of the Marais has undergone a transformation with the arrival of **Maison Rouge** (13 rue des Archives, 4th/01.42.71.69.69). The name takes its cue from the prestigious Masion Blanche on deeply bourgeois avenue Montaigne. Cheeky. Despite its slightly sombre-sounding name, Maison Rouge is brightly lit with a matching switched-on Anglophile menu. There's a slim-line, minimalist cellar in the basement, a perfect setting for a raucous boys' or girls' night out. Interestingly, the general chitter-chatter level can rise in vols to drown out the rowdiest gaggle of screaming queens. Most importantly, the atmosphere is mega-friendly.

If you fancy a nibble of typical gay Marais gastronomy, try **Le Carré** (35 rue du Temple, 4th/01.44.59.38.57). This is self-consciously designer, with bright design 'objects' adorning the walls – some are animate, some are works of art and some look vaguely human. If you're watching your waist, linger a while at the busy bar, where you'll see a cross-section of gay flora fawning over itself.

Just around the corner is the more modest **X** (10 rue St Merri, 4th/01.48.87.06.00). As the classical scholars among you will know, 'X' is the Roman numeral representing 'ten'; as the linguists will be aware, the French for 'ten' is *dix*. The knowing among you will have spotted the joke. X dishes up fixed-price, good quality French menus on square plates. It's fine and dandy enough, and you'll have a great time here, but it doesn't quite live up to the dazzle promised by the mirrored mosaic counter. Further north is the new **Si** (4 rue Charlot, 3rd/01.42.78.02.31), where the decoration is understated and the attentive staff is more conspicuously decorative. The food follows an Italian theme, running (screaming) from antipasto and tagliatelli with vegetables all the way to rabbit in gorgonzola and a fine flank of ostrich. That's right, dear reader: ostrich. Well, you don't come to Paris for a fish finger sandwich, do you?

Well red, well fed at **Maison Rouge**.

Arts & Entertainment

Le Bar du Palmier

16 rue des Lombards, 4th (Ol.42.78.53.53).
Mº Hôtel de Ville. **Open** 5pm-5am daily.
Credit AmEx, MC, V. **Map** p406 J6.
The bar gets busy late, but is also good during happy hour (6-8pm). It has a pseudo-tropical decor and a nice terrace. This is one of the gay places where women are welcomed as the goddesses they are.

Le Central

33 rue Vieille-du-Temple, 4th (01.48.87.99.33).
Mº Hôtel de Ville. **Open** 4pm-2am Mon-Fri; 2pm-2am Sat, Sun. **Credit** MC, V. **Map** p406 K6.
One of the city's oldest gay hangouts, Le Central still passes muster against its sprightly neighbours.

Coffee Shop

3 rue Ste-Croix-de-la-Bretonnerie, 4th
(01.42.74.24.21). Mº Hôtel de Ville. **Open** 10am-2am daily. **No credit cards.** **Map** p406 K6.
The laid-back Coffee Shop (not laid back like the ones in Holland) is great for a frothy coffee and a gossip.

Le Cox

15 rue des Archives, 4th (01.42.72.08.00).
Mº Hôtel de Ville. **Open** 1pm-2am daily. **No credit cards.** **Map** p406 K6.
Not, as you first thought, a shop where you can buy rowing equipment, but one of the hottest Marais gay bars. Afternoons are relatively calm, but evenings are a glitterball of promises often fulfilled.

Open Café

17 rue des Archives, 4th (01.42.72.26.18). Mº Hôtel de Ville. **Open** 11am-2am Mon-Thur, Sun; 11am-4am Fri, Sat. **Credit** MC, V. **Map** p406 K6.
The Open Café has become an HQ for gay boys meeting up before heading off into the night. The management also runs the extended Open Bar Coffee Shop at 12 rue du Temple.

Quetzal

10 rue de la Verrerie, 4th (01.48.87.99.07/www. quetzalbar.com). Mº Hôtel de Ville. **Open** 5pm-5am daily. **Credit** MC, V. **Map** p406 K6.
The cruisiest bar in the Marais, Quetzal attracts a crowd of Muscle Marys. The venue is at the end of rue des Mauvais-Garçons ('Bad Boys' street').

Le Thermik

7 rue de la Verrière, 4th (01.44.78.08.18). Mº Hôtel de Ville. **Open** 7pm-2am daily. **No credit cards.** **Map** p406 K6.
This is a friendly, intimate place for those whose eardrums need a break from crowded cruising bars.

Gay clubs & discos

Club 18

18 rue de Beaujolais, 1st (01.42.97.52.13).
Mº Palais Royal. **Open** 11pm-dawn Thur-Sat; 5pm-dawn Sun. **Admission** free Thur, Sun; €11 Fri, Sat. **Credit** AmEx, MC, V. **Map** p402 H5.
You won't come in here for the latest techno, drino, tech-hop, hip-replacement or whatever the generic

for the sound of the moment is, but you will come in to gyrate to classic discovations.

L'Insolite

33 rue des Petits-Champs, 2nd (01.40.20.98.59).
Mº Pyramides. **Open** 11pm-5am daily. **Admission** free Mon-Thur, Sun; €7.70 Fri, Sat. **Credit** MC, V. **Map** p402 H4.
Bright and brassy with a distinctly disco vibe, this place pumps out dance classics.

Le Dépôt

10 rue aux Ours, 3rd (01.44.54.96.96).
Mº Rambuteau. **Open** noon-7am daily.
Admission €10 Mon-Thur, Sun; €12 Fri, Sat.
Credit MC, V. **Map** p402 K5.
The decor is all jungle netting and exposed air ducts. Please note that the Gay Tea Dance on Sundays is not as restrained as its name suggests.

Le Tango

13 rue au Maire, 3rd (01.42.72.17.78).
Mº Arts et Métiers. **Open** Thur 8pm-2am, Fri, Sat 10.30pm-5am; 6.30pm-2am Sun. **Admission** €9 Thur (with concert), €5 after 10.30pm; €6.50 Fri, Sat. **No credit cards.** **Map** p402 K5.
Le Tango has returned to its dancehall roots for dancing *à deux*, with a mixed clientele. Hey, chaps, tired of vacuous hedonism? Then why not try the accordion concert on Thursdays?

Le Queen

102 av des Champs-Elysées, 8th (08.92.70.73.30).
Mº George V. **Open** midnight-dawn daily.
Admission €12 Mon; €10 Tue-Thur, Sun; €20 Fri, Sat. **Drinks** €8-€18. **Credit** AmEx, DC, MC, V. **Map** p400 D4.
Still the pick of the crop, though being challenged by the Red Light (*see below*). Sundays and Mondays are the nights when this is Paris' classic gay club.

Folies Pigalle

11 pl Pigalle, 9th (01.48.78.25.26). Mº Pigalle. **Open** midnight-dawn Tue-Sat; 6am-noon, 6pm-midnight Sun. **Admission** €20 Tue-Sat; €17 (after), €7 (BBB) Sun. **Credit** V. **Map** p401 G2.
Come here for Paris' most popular gay tea dance, the Black Blanc Beur (BBB) (6pm-midnight Sun). You'll find a mix of world music dancing.

Scorp

25 bd Poissonnière, 9th (01.40.26.28.30).
Mº Grands Boulevards. **Open** midnight-6.30am Wed-Sun. **Admission** free Wed, Thur, Sun; €10 Fri, Sat. **Credit** AmEx, MC, V. **Map** p402 J4.
Shortened in name and sharpened in style, the former Scorpion is another *grande dame* of *gai Paris*.

Red Light

34 rue du Depart, 14th (01.42.79.94.94).
Mº Montparnasse. **Open** Thur-Sun 11pm-6am.
Admission €20. **Drinks** €10. **Credit** AmEx, DC, MC, V. **Map** p405 F9.
L'Enfer has changed its name and, it hopes, its clientele. This huge club runs gay house nights on Saturdays. Is this the pretender to Queen's throne?

Men-only clubs

Le Transfert
3 rue de la Sourdière, 1st (01.42.60.48.42).
Mº Tuileries. **Open** midnight-dawn Mon-Fri,
6.30pm-midnight Sat, Sun. **Credit** AmEx, MC, V.
Map p401 G5.
Small-but-serviceable leather/SM bar.

Univers Gym
20 rue des Bons Enfants, 1st (01 42 61 24 83).
Mº Palais Royal. **Open** noon-2am daily. **Credit**
AmEx, DC, MC, V. **Map** p401 H5.
Univers is the busiest Parisian sauna. Trailing
round in a tanga is entirely acceptable, but if it's only
your pores you want opening, do beware: darned hot
action lies behind those loin cloths.

Bear's Den
6 rue des Lombards, 4th (01.42.71.08.20/
www.bearsden.fr). Mº Châtelet. **Open** 4pm-2am
daily. **Credit** AmEx, MC. **Map** p406 K6.
Brimming with butch bearded blokes and strangers
bearing General Haig moustaches, the atmosphere
is evocative of the sort of thing you'd expect to find
if you went down to the woods today.

QG
12 rue Simon-le-Franc, 4th (01.48.87.74.18/
www.qgbar.com). Mº Rambuteau. **Open** 4pm-6am
Mon-Fri; 2pm-8am Sat, Sun. **Credit** V. **Map** p406 K6.
No entrance fee, cheap beer, late opening and a sense
of humour guarantee success. Things get rough
downstairs; don't even ask what the bath is for, especially if you don't like it up the tap end.

Le Trap
10 rue Jacob, 6th (unlisted telephone).
Mº St-Germain des Prés. **Open** 11pm-4am daily.
Admission free Mon-Thur, Sun; varies Fri, Sat.
No credit cards. Map p406 H6.
Le Trap has been packing them in for nearly 20
years and is hip with the fashion crowd. Brace your-
self for naked dancing (Mon, Wed).

Gay shops & services

Hôtel Saintonge
16 rue de Saintonge, 3rd (01.42.77.91.13). Mº Filles
du Calvaire. **Rates** single €105; double €115. **Credit**
AmEx, DC, MC, V. **Map** p402 L5.
Although this hotel is open to everyone, its owners
cultivate a gay clientele. All rooms have a shower,
hairdryer, minbar, safe and TV.

Lionel Joubin
10 rue des Filles-du-Calvaire, 3rd (01.42.74.37.51).
Mº Filles du Calvaire. **Open** 11am-8pm Tue-Sat.
Closed Aug. **Credit** MC, V. **Map** p402 L5.
Famous for its extravagant window displays, florist
Joubin decorates floats for Gay Pride. Just the place
to get a handful of pansies.

Space Hair
10 rue Rambuteau, 3rd (01.48.87.28.51).
Mº Rambuteau. **Open** noon-10pm Mon; 9am-11pm
Tue-Fri; 9am-10pm Sat. **Credit** DC, MC, V.
Map p402 K5.
This flamboyant Marais barber has become an insti-
tution on the Paris gay scene (and even featured in
the recent film *Ay, si j'étais riche*). So successful is
the coiffage that it has expanded next door to Space
Hair Classic.

Boy'z Bazaar
5, 38 rue Ste-Croix-de-la-Bretonnerie, 4th
(01.42.71.94.00). Mº Hôtel de Ville. **Open** noon-9pm
Mon-Thu; noon-11pm Fri, Sat; 2pm-9pm Sun. **Credit**
AmEx, DC, MC, V. **Map** p406 K6.
No 5 caters for Boyz' essential pectastically tight
T-shirts, sportswear and classics, while No 38 serves
up titillating videos.

Hôtel Central Marais
33 rue Vieille-du-Temple, 4th (01.48.87.56.08).
Mº Hôtel de Ville. **Rates** double €84; appt €100-
€122; breakfast €6. **Credit** MC, V. **Map** p406 K6.
Paris' only strictly gay hotel (above gay bar Le Central) has seven rooms (no private bathrooms spoil-
ing the fun), plus an apartment (€100-€122). Book in
advance. English is spoken and each room has double glazing and a telephone..

Les Mots à la Bouche
6 rue Ste-Croix-de-la-Bretonnerie, 4th
(01.42.78.88.30). Mº Hôtel de Ville.
Open 11am-11pm Mon-Sat; 2-8pm Sun.
Credit MC, V. **Map** p406 K6.
This book shop stocks gay-interest literature from
around the world. There's an excellent English-
language section.

Wigging out over wandering hands.

Pause Lecture
61 rue Quincampoix, 4th (01.44.61.95.06/
www.pauselecture.com). Mº Rambuteau. **Open** 11am-
midnight Mon-Sat; 1pm-midnight Sun. **Credit** DC,
MC, V. **Map** p406 J6.
A very cool environment in which to buy your
tomes. You can pose your day away in well-uphol-
stered comfy chairs, have a vada at the exhibitions
and cultivate that intellectual look (in your dreams).

IEM
208 rue St-Maur, 10th (01.42.41.21.41/
www.iem.fr). Mº Goncourt. **Open** 10am-7.30pm Mon-
Sat. **Credit** AmEx, MC, V. **Map** p403 M4.
Scores of videos, clothes, books and condoms.
Upstairs houses all things leather and rubber for a
thrustingly good night out.
Branches: 43 rue de l'Arbre-Sec, 1st (01.42.96.05.74);
33 rue de Liège, 9th (01.45.22.69.01); 16 rue Ste-Croix
de la Bretonnerie, 4th (01.42.74.01.61.).

Lesbian Paris

Over the past two years, Paris' lesbian
community has created a thriving culture, with
an increasing number of lesbian-friendly
restaurants, bars and club nights. The
nightclub **Pulp** has led the way, putting lesbian
journalists, DJs and promoters into the media
limelight. Names to look out for are promoter
and film-maker Anna La Chocha, journalist
Axelle Le Dauphin (also known as DJ Tampax),
Techno DJ of the moment, Jennifer, and Pulp's
ex-toilet attendant, personality and creator of
the web site www.damepipi.com, Yvette Neliaz.

The gay magazine *Têtu* includes articles and
sections with a lesbian focus while the cable
channel Pink TV has regular programmes for
the lesbian community. *La Maison des Femmes*
(01.43.43.41.13/http://maisondesfemmes.free.fr)
is also home to several feminist and lesbian
groups. The annual film festival *Quand Les
Lesbiennes font du Cinema* (information:
01.48.70.77.11), usually held in late October or
early November, specialises in documentaries,
films and experimental videos by lesbian
filmmakers from around the world.

For up-to-date information on events see
www.citegay.com, a website specialising in gay
and lesbian life in all major French towns.

Associations

Les Archives, Recherches, Cultures Lesbiennes (ARCL)
*Maison des Femmes, 163 rue de Charenton 12th
(01.43.43.41.13/01.43.43.42.13). Mº Reuilly-Diderot.*
Open 7-9.30pm Tue. Closed Aug
ACRL produces audio-visual documentation and
bulletins on lesbian and women's activities with
archives of lesbian and feminist documents.

Are you kidding?

As France as a nation seems to be limping
ever further away from the '*égalité*' bit of
its much-vaunted national republican
motto, the question of gay couples having
the right to adopt children is being pressed
with ever more vigour.

It seems as if the establishment, having
granted same-sex couples the right to
register their partnership (oh, how
romantic) under the 1999 social union (or
PACS) law, feels that it has done enough
for the meantime in answering calls for gay
human rights. At any rate, Jacques Chirac
has stated that he feels that every child
needs a father and a mother 'to construct
his identity'. So there's the leader of the
nation's attitude.

Enter Philippe Fretté, a teacher, who
brought France before the European Court
of Human Rights, alleging that the country
was breaking the European convention by
disallowing him from adopting children on
the grounds that he's gay, or, in the legal
gobbledegook, because of his 'choice of
lifestyle'. Lifestyle? What an elegant,
homophobic euphemism.

In February 2002, the European Court
upheld France's decision – despite support
for Mr Fretté from Austria, Britain and
Belgium – that, although French law says
that any adult over 28 can apply to adopt,
France could be cut a little slack in
discriminating against gays while the
country's psychiatrists and sociologists
make their minds up on the impact of
same-sex parents on a child's
development. To be a prospective adoptive
parent in France, as well as being at least
28, you have to be of good reputation and
good physical and mental health (these are
established by rigorous social enquiries
and medical checks). To asume that being
gay automatically means that you cannot
satisfy the above requirements seems a
lot like discrimination.

The fact that the matter of gay adoption
rights has been raised and that it has
generated a high-profile court case
probably bodes well for the eventual
success of Fretté and his supporters. It
certainly appears strange that an openly
gay man can be Mayor of the capital city of
a country that believes that his 'choice of
lifestyle' renders him unfit to adopt a child.

Plucking *belle*.

the corner from the Centre Pompidou. There is a pool table attracting a studenty crowd who sing along to the classic pop songs played at full volume on the sound system. Sundays are calmer with board games and cards provided at the bar.

Le Mixer
23 rue Ste-Croix-de-la-Bretonnerie, 4th (01.48.87.55.44). M° Hôtel de Ville. **Open** 7pm-2am Daily. **Credit** AmEx, MC, V. **Map** p406 K6.
Mixed gay, lesbian and straight, this techno and house DJ bar has become the meeting point for younger crowds before going on to a club. A monthly programme includes big-name DJs and bedroom DJs mixing house, tek-house and techno.

Les Scandaleuses
8 rue des Ecouffes, 4th (01.48.87.39.26). M° St Paul. **Open** 6pm-2am daily. **Credit** MC, V. **Map** p406 K6.
The happy hour from 6pm to 8pm makes this central Marais bar an after-work meeting place. The cellar provides a dancing area with a music policy featuring mainly chart music and 80s rock. Art shows are held here regularly.

Café Chéri(e)
44 bd de la Villette 10th (01.42.02.07.87). M° Belleville. **Open** 8am-2am daily. **Credit** AmEx, MC, V. **Map** p403 M4.
The high percentage of lesbian waitresses and bar maids has made this the pre-club lesbian hang out for the younger clubbing generation of girls. On Monday nights a female DJ is invited to mix her selection of favourite tunes.

Lesbian restaurants

Le Petit Picard
42 rue Ste Croix de la Bretonnerie, 4th (01.42.78.54.03). M° Hôtel de Ville. **Open** noon-2pm, 7.30pm-11pm Tue-Sun. **Credit** MC, V. **Map** p406 K6.
This bistro is always packed, as it is one of the cheapest places to eat in the area. A friendly atmosphere with plenty of inter-table chatter.

Au Feu Follet
5 rue Raymond Losserand, 14th (01.43.22.65.72). M° Pernety. **Open** noon-2pm, 7.30pm-11pm, Mon-Sat. **Credit** MC, V. **Map** p405 E10.
This restaurant serves cuisine from the south-west of France. The crowd is mixed but mainly lesbian.

Lesbian bars and cafés

La Champmesie
4 rue Chabanais, 2nd (01.42.96.85.20). M° Pyramides. **Open** 2pm-2am daily. **No credit cards. Map** p402 H4.
Open for the past 20 years, this bar has become the pillar of the lesbian community with regular cabaret nights and art shows.

Unity Bar
176-178 rue St-Martin 3rd (01.42.72.70.59). M° Rambuteau. **Open** 4pm-2am daily. **No credit cards. Map** p402 K5.
You can't miss this huge colourful bar just around

Lesbian nightclubs

Le Pulp
25 bd Poissonière, 2nd (01.40.26.01.93). M° Grands Boulevards. **Open** midnight-5am Wed-Sat. **Admission** free Wed-Thur; €12 Fri-Sat. **Credit** MC, V. **Map** p402 J4.
The upstairs part of the male gay club Scorp has become one of the trendiest clubs in Paris. The mixed Thursday night events have become the meeting place for Paris' younger media personalities. This hasn't driven the lesbian crowd away, though; on the contrary it has attracted a new generation of lesbians who found the club rather uninviting before. Friday and Saturday nights are women-only with DJs spinning house and techno on Fridays and chart music and new wave for those with more varied tastes on Saturdays.

Girls Zone at Le Dépôt
For address and details, see Le Dépôt p317.
Le Dépôt is essentially a gay nightclub and back room (careful where you venture, ladies: you know what the chaps can be like), but every Wednesday night Girls Zone takes over one floor with resident DJ Miss Attica mixing house to a very responsive lesbian crowd.

Arts & Entertainment

Music: Classical & Opera

With the rivalry between the Opéra National and the Théâtre du Châtelet as a spur to quality, Paris' classical scene is back hitting the high notes.

Paris' classical music scene drips down from the city's main opera house, so a change of direction at the **Opéra National de Paris** causes shock waves. Hugues Gall's reign has been marked by consistency, especially from music director James Conlon, who has conducted a record number of new productions but who has also hogged the limelight, with few challenging guest conductors. The new broom will be the Belgian Gérard Mortier, whose success in raising the status of La Monnaie in Brussels is highly creditable. Mortier takes over in 2004, and opera buffs will be fastening their seatbelts for some challenging listening.

It would be unfair to suggest that Gall has not encouraged contemporary creation, and this year sees a major première from Pascal Dusapin, and a revival of last year's successful *K...* by Philippe Manoury, which showed that an opera can be resolutely of its time, yet enjoyable and relevant to the general public. Otherwise the **Cité de la Musique** and **IRCAM** continue to promote new works, but with less ideologically exclusive programming than when under the directorial hand of Pierre Boulez. Boulez is back in town, conducting the Vienna Philharmonic at the **Théâtre des Champs-Elysées** this season.

It would be too much to hope that Mortier could integrate his programming with the Opéra National's arch revival, the **Théâtre du Châtelet**, stylishly run by the Paris Mairie and their imaginative director Pierre Brossman. This year it presents an exciting season of Russian operas, but two separate productions of *Eugène Onegin* in the same year reveals unnecessarily competitive programming.

Christoph Eschenbach has galvanised the **Orchestre de Paris** into the capital's leading band and Myung-Whun Chung's formidable technique is working wonders for the **Orchestre Philharmonique de Radio France**. Only the **Orchestre National de France** has had a tough time, owing to the illness of its musical director elect, Kurt Masur. The German conductor has now arrived and prospects for this season look fab. Local soloists to watch are the pianist Alexandre Tharaud, violinist Augustin Dumay, soprano Véronique Gens and mezzo-soprano Nora Gubisch.

Record sales of Early Music in France are a bright spot in a flat market. Local star Marc Minkowski now conducts everything from Monteverdi to Debussy, while Malgoire, Jacobs and Christie stick to their fields of predilection. Christie has been invited by Sir Simon Rattle to be the first guest conductor under his reign of the Berlin Philharmonic, where he will perform Rameau. The Baroque guru may be relieved to rejoin his **Arts Florissants** for performances at the **Palais Garnier** of Rameau's *Les Boréades* later in the season.

Lovers of church music in an authentic setting will be happy to discover the Festival d'Art Sacré (01.44.70.64.10), which celebrates religious music in the weeks before Christmas. Les Grands Concerts Sacrés (01.48.24.16.97) and Musique et Patrimoine (01.42.50.96.18) offer concerts at various venues, including the Eglise St-Roch, Palais Royal, Eglise des Billettes, Eglise St-Julien-le-Pauvre, Eglise St-Séverin, the Madeleine and the Val-de-Grâce, while music in Notre-Dame is taken care of by Musique Sacrée à Notre-Dame (01.44.41.49.99/tickets 01.42.34.56.10).

INFORMATION AND RESOURCES

For listings, see *Pariscope*. The monthly *Le Monde de la Musique* and *Diapason* also list classical concerts, while *Opéra International* provides the best coverage of all things vocal. *Cadences* and *La Terrasse*, two free monthlies, are distributed outside concerts. Many venues and orchestras offer cut-rate tickets to students (under-26) an hour before curtain-up. For **La Fête de la Musique**, on 21 June, events are free, as are some concerts at the **Maison de Radio France**, the **Conservatoire de Paris** and churches. Good general websites are www.arpeggione.fr and www.concertclassic.com.

Orchestras & ensembles

Les Arts Florissants

(01.43.87.98.98/www.arts-florissants.com).
William Christie's 'Arts Flo' remains France's most highly regarded Early Music group. A recent initiative of the ensemble is 'Le Jardin des Voix', which trains and promotes young artists.

Concerts Pasdeloup

Based at the Salle Gaveau, Théâtre Mogador and the Cirque d'Hiver.

Modestly effective orchestra with conservative lollipop programming under Patrice Fontanarosa. Occasional star soloists, such as French pianist Anne Queffélec, are the only serious attractions.

Ensemble InterContemporain

(www.ensembleinter.com). Based at the Cité de la Musique and the Centre Pompidou.

The contemporary music ensemble now performs under Jonathan Nott, but spiritually remains the creation of Pierre Boulez. The standard remains consistently high, with a series of Ligeti-meets-Mahler concerts scheduled for May 2003.

Ensemble Orchestral de Paris

(www.ensemble-orchestral-paris.com). Based at the Théâtre des Champs-Elysées.

American John Nelson presides over this vastly improved chamber orchestra. This season guest conductors include the dynamic Italian Baroque specialist Fabio Biondi and French maestro Yann-Pascal Tortelier, while soloists include the fine French pianists François-René Duchâble and Jean-Yves Thibaudet, and superstar violinist Joshua Bell.

Orchestre Colonne

(01.42.33.72.89/www.orchestrecolonne.fr). Based at Théâtre Mogador and the Salle Gaveau.

Pointillism at **Opéra Bastille**. *See p324.*

This orchestra often fails to live up to its glorious past. The excellent series of educational 'Concerts Eveil' has moved to the newly restored Salle Gaveau, an ideal venue to introduce young listeners to the symphony orchestra. Even kids might find higher standards of playing more tempting, though.

Orchestre Lamoureux

(01.58.39.30.30/www.orchestrelamoureux.com). Based at the Théâtre des Champs-Elysées.

The Lamoureux has found a home in the Théâtre des Champs-Elysées. All credit to the conductor Yutaka Sado for bringing challenging 20th- and 21st-century works into his programmes.

Orchestre National de France

(01.40.28.28.40/www.radio-france.fr). Based at the Maison de Radio France and Théâtre des Champs-Elysées.

The arrival of Kurt Masur as musical director was long overdue. The German repertoire is in safe hands with a cycle of Beethoven symphonies and a Mendelssohn celebration for 2002/2003, not to mention a jazz concert with Wynton Marsalis. Will the great conductor swing? The list of visiting conductors includes Muti, Krivine and Järvi.

Orchestre de Paris

(01.45.61.65.60/www.orchestradeparis.com). Based at Théâtre Mogador.

Christoph Eschenbach leads the orchestra from strength to strength. This season the band is based in the Théâtre Mogador, and the Berlioz 2003 celebrations will reach their climax. A new addition is a series of ten free lunchtime concerts called *Croq'notes* featuring promising young artists.

Orchestre Philharmonique de Radio France

(www.radio-france.fr). Based at the Maison de Radio France.

Myung-Whun Chung has taken over the mantle from the mighty Janowski. His credentials as a former director of the Opéra National are impeccable, and his performances of the mainstream Romantic repertoire this season look tempting.

Les Talens Lyriques

(www.lestalenslyriques.com).

Christophe Rousset's spin-off from Les Arts Florissants has established its own personality and a soaring reputation. Rousset is no musical purist, and, alongside his Early Music activities, will also be conducting a programme of 18th-century Spanish *zarzuelas* with soprano Maria Bayo in April 2003.

Venues

Bibliothèque Nationale de France

Quai François-Mauriac, 13th (01.53.79.40.45/ reservations 01.53.79.49.49/www.bnf.fr). M° *Bibliothèque or Quai de la Gare.* **Box office** 10am-7pm Tue-Sat; noon-7pm Sun. **Tickets** prices vary. **Credit** MC, V. **Map** p407 M10.

The new library has a fine concert space. After a long series of concerts exploring French melodies, the new season kicked off with an intellectual exploration of the work of that great and neglected French Wagnerite Vincent d'Indy. What do you mean, you've never heard of him? *Wheelchair access.*

Théâtre des Bouffes du Nord
37 bis bd de la Chapelle, 10th (01.46.07.34.50).
M° La Chapelle. **Box office** 11am-6pm Mon-Sat.
Tickets €12-€18.50. **Credit** AmEx, MC, V.
Map p402 L2.
Peter Brook and Stéphane Lissner take the musical element of their programming seriously. This season more than 30 concerts cover eclectic styles and periods in one of the city's most attractive theatres.

Châtelet - Théâtre Musical de Paris
1 pl du Châtelet, 1st (01.40.28.28.40/www.chatelet-theatre.com). *M° Châtelet.* **Box office** 11am-7pm daily; telephone 10am-7pm Mon-Sat. Closed July-Aug. **Tickets** €8-€106. **Credit** AmEx, MC, V.
Map p406 J6.
This year the emphasis is on the Russian repertoire with rarities such as *The Demon* by Rubinstein, *The Golden Cockerel* by Rimsky Korsakov, and none other than Placido Domingo turning up for Tchaikovsky's *Queen of Spades* conducted by Gergiev. Alongside the operas are a series of orchestral concerts, stellar piano recitals and a fine ballet season. *Wheelchair access.*

Cité de la Musique
221 av Jean-Jaurès, 19th (recorded information 01.44.84.45.45/reservations 01.44.84.44.84/ www.cite-musique.fr). *M° Porte de Pantin.* **Box office** noon-6pm Tue-Sun; phone 11am-7pm Mon-Sat, 11am-6pm Sun. **Tickets** €4-€33; reduced prices under-26s, over-60s. **Credit** MC, V. **Map** p403 inset.
The complex is undoubtedly one of the most successful of Mitterrand's *grands projets*, and the site of the former city abattoir has never sounded so good. The museum has a smaller concert space (*see p176*) for demonstrating instruments from the collection, while the adjacent Conservatoire (01.40.40.45.45) is host to world-class performers and features many free concerts. *Wheelchair access.*

IRCAM
1 pl Igor-Stravinsky, 4th (01.44.78.48.16/ www.ircam.fr). *M° Hôtel de Ville.* **Open** times vary. **Tickets** prices vary. **Credit** AmEx, MC, V.
Map p406 K6.
The underground bunker has finally begun to participate in the musical mainstream. Concerts are now performed both here and in the main hall of the adjoining Centre Pompidou. A chance to look into the future (and perhaps emerge preferring the past).

Auditorium du Louvre
Entrance through Pyramid, Cour Napoléon, 1st (01.40.20.51.86/reservations 01.40.20.84.00/ www.louvre.fr). *M° Palais Royal.* **Box office** 9am-7.30pm Mon, Wed-Fri. Closed July, Aug. **Tickets** €18-€23. **Credit** MC, V. **Map** p401 H5.

Summer notes

In summer, music, like most of Paris, goes on vacation, taking itself off to festivals such as **Aix-en-Provence** (opera), **La Roque d'Anthéron** (piano) and **Prades** (chamber music). But, while most Paris theatre and concert halls lock up for the summer, there are plenty of chances to enjoy music in the open air. The main, multidisciplinary festival of the summer is **Paris Quartier d'Eté** (mid-July to mid-Aug/ www.quartierdete.com). While its more off-beat offerings have included a 'multimedia opera' and Stravinsky's *The Soldier's Tale* performed by an orchestra plus acrobats and film clips, the festival also collaborates with the Orchestre National d'Ile-de-France to give free concerts in Parc André Citroën. Throughout August and September the parc Floral in the Bois de Vincennes has concerts at 4.30pm every Saturday and Sunday forming its **Festival Classique au Vert** (01.55.94.20.20/ www.parcfloraldeparis.com). Soloists have included Patrice Fontanarosa and flautist Cécile Daroux and the music ranges from troubadours' songs to contemporary compositions. In the Orangerie de la Bagatelle, Bois de Boulogne, there is the annual **Festival Chopin** (23 June to 15 July/01.45.00.22.19/www.frederic-chopin.com) with its romantic candle-lit concerts, followed by the **Octuor de France** (17 July- 15 Aug/01.42.29.07.83/ www.octuordefrance.com) performing chamber music in the same location. July also sees the **Festival Musique en l'Ile** (01.44.62.00.55) which supplements the rather sugary diet of music in churches with some serious choral works in and around the Ile de la Cité and Ile St-Louis, and the **Festival Jeunes Talents** (01.40.20.09.34/www.jeunes-talents.org), a chance to hear budding stars in the Hôtel de Rohan. Venturing beyond the Périphérique you can enjoy chamber music in a setting that started out as a concert venue for Louis XIV. Violinist Alfred Loewenguth launched the **Festival de l'Orangerie de Sceaux** (July-Sept, 01.46.60.07.79/www.festival.orangerie.fr ee.fr) 34 years ago and it's still going strong, though now that Paris in summer isn't quite the musical desert it once was concerts are only at weekends.

A fine series is offered at the Louvre: not only musical presentations of silent films, but a full season of chamber music. This year there is a homage to the late Iannis Xenakis, a series of Haydn string quartets, and woodwind concerts, alongside more conventional song recitals.

Maison de Radio France

116 av du Président-Kennedy, 16th (01.42.30.22.22/concert information 01.42.30.15.16/ www.radiofrance.fr). M° Passy/RER Kennedy Radio France. **Box office** 11am-6pm Mon-Sat. **Tickets** free-€20. **Credit** MC, V. **Map** p404 A7.
Radio station France Musique programmes an impressive range of classical concerts, operas and ethnic music here. The main venue within the cylindrical building is the rather charmless Salle Olivier Messiaen, but the quality of music-making featuring two of the capital's leading orchestras compensates. Under-26s can obtain a *Passe Musique*, which gives admission to concerts for the bargain price of €7.50. Watch out for free events. *Wheelchair access.*

Musée National du Moyen Age (Cluny)

6 pl Paul-Painlevé, 5th (01.53.73.78.00). M° Cluny-La Sorbonne. **Tickets** prices vary. **No credit cards. Map** p406 J7.
The museum presents medieval concerts that are in keeping with the collection, in a setting that inspires authenticity.

Musee d'Orsay

62 rue de Lille, 7th (014049 48 14/ www.musee-orsay.fr). M° Solférino/RER Musée d'Orsay. **Tickets** €18-€23. **Credit** MC, V. **Map** p405 G6.
The museum runs stimulating occasional programmes of themed chamber music. It kicked off its last season with a particularly successful look at Spanish music, featuring top artists such as violinist Shlomo Mintz.

Opéra Comique/Salle Favart

pl Boïeldieu, 2nd (01.42.44.45.40/reservations 01.42.44.45.46/www.opera-comique.fr). M° Richelieu-Drouot. **Box office** 14 rue Favart 11am-7pm Mon-Sat; telephone 11am-6pm Mon-Sat. **Tickets** €7-€90. **Credit** AmEx, DC, MC, V. **Map** p402 H4.
The projected season is not ambitious, but not without a few points of interest: Péniche Opéra's review *Le Souriceau*, Renard, Shostakovich, Stravinsky et al... could be fun, and Savary's own production of Offenbach's *La Vie Parisienne* will fill the coffers. Look out for a well-cast revival of Rossini's *Le Comte Ory*, and a rare appearance by the great Spanish mezzo Teresa Berganza in the series 'Les Grandes Voix s'amusent'. *Wheelchair access.*

Opéra National de Paris Bastille

pl de la Bastille, 12th (08.36.69.78.68/ www.opera-de-paris.fr). M° Bastille. **Box office** 130 rue de Lyon 11am-6.30pm Mon-Sat/telephone 9am-7pm. **Guided visits** 01.40.01.19.70. **Tickets** €8-€109; concerts €7-€39. **Credit** AmEx, MC, V. **Map** p407 M7.

From the disused main entrance to the unfinished *salle modulable* via the falling fascia tiles, it all evokes a poor international airport. The acoustics are as Orwellian as the rest, but under Hugues Gall's management and James Conlon's baton, operatic superstars strut their stuff to a high standard. All may change when controversial director Gérard Mortier takes over in 2004. This year's offerings include an important world première from Pascal Dusapin, *Perelà, l'homme de fumée* (Feb/March), and two new productions of French versions of Italian operas – Rossini's apple shooting drama *Guillaume Tell* (March/April) and Verdi's *Les Vêpres Siciliennes* (June/July) starring veteran bass Samuel Ramey. *Wheelchair access (01.40.01.18.08, strictly two weeks in advance).*

Opéra National de Paris Garnier

pl de l'Opéra, 9th (08.36.69.78.68/www.opera-de-paris.fr). M° Opéra. **Box office** 11am-6.30pm Mon-Sat; telephone 9am-7pm. **Visits** 10am-4.30pm daily; guided visits (01.40.01.22.63). **Tickets** €6-€109; concerts €6-€15. **Credit** AmEx, MC, V. **Map** p401 G4.
The restored Palais Garnier is the jewel in Paris' crown, but the Opéra National favours the high-tech of the Bastille for most new productions. A building of over-the-top grandeur, designed for unabashed people-watching, it has poor (sometimes virtually zero) visibility from some side seats, but still, an evening here is a privilege. This season's most prestigious event is a run of Rameau's *Les Boréades* con-

Arts & Entertainment

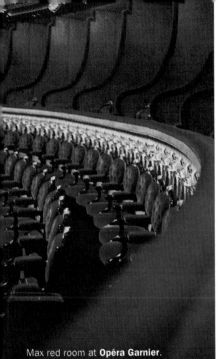
Max red room at **Opéra Garnier**.

ducted by William Christie with the Arts Florissants and produced by the resourceful Robert Carsen in March/April. *Wheelchair access (01.40.01.18.08, strictly two weeks in advance).*

Péniche Opéra
Facing 42 quai de la Loire, 19th (01.53.35.07.76/ www.penicheopera.com). M° Jaurès. **Box office** 10am-7pm Mon-Fri; telephone 01.53.35.07.77. **Tickets** prices vary. **Credit** MC, V. **Map** p403 M1.
An enterprising boat-based opera company producing a programme of Chamber-scale rarities, directed by the indefatigable Mireille Larroche. Bigger shows come ashore to the Opéra Comique, while aboard ship there is much educational work and concerts from the Carpe Diem ensemble.

Salle Cortot
78 rue Cardinet, 17th (01.47.63.85.72). M° Malesherbes. **No box office. Tickets** phone for details. **Map** p400 D2.
This intimate concert hall in the Ecole Normale Supérieure de Musique has an excellent acoustic for chamber music.

Salle Gaveau
45 rue La Boétie, 8th (01.49.53.05.07). M° Miromesnil. **Box office** 11am-6pm Mon-Fri. **Tickets** €20-€50. **Credit** AmEx, MC, V. **Map** p401 E3.
The atmospheric Salle Gaveau is finally profiting from its recent facelift. In addition to chamber music it can now accommodate full orchestral concerts,

without losing its essential intimacy. All that is needed now is a more effective marketing policy to win back the public.

Salle Pleyel
253 rue du Fbg-St-Honoré, 8th (01.45.61.53.01/www.salle-pleyel.fr). M° Ternes. Closed for renovation until spring 2004.

Théâtre des Champs-Elysées
15 av Montaigne, 8th (01.49.52.50.50/ www.theatrechampselysees.fr). M° Alma-Marceau. **Box office** 1pm-7pm Mon-Sat; telephone 10am-noon, 2-6pm Mon-Fri. **Tickets** €5-€110. **Credit** AmEx, MC, V. **Map** p400 D5.
This beautiful theatre, with bas-reliefs by Bourdelle, witnessed the première of Stravinsky's *Le Sacre du Printemps* in 1913. Director Dominique Meyer is rightly proud of the theatre's unsubsidised status and has continued the tradition of high-quality programming. This season includes visits from the San Francisco Symphony and the Vienna Philharmonic, while visiting maestri include Boulez, Muti and rising Teutonic star Christian Thielemann. The operatic highlight looks like being the appearance of sumptuous Alaskan mezzo-soprano Vivica Genaux in Rossini's *La Cenerentola* in April/May 2003.

Théâtre Mogador
25 rue Mogador, 9th (01.53.32.32.00/ www.mogador.net). M° St-Lazare. **Tickets** phone for details. **Map** p401 G3.
With the closing of the Salle Pleyel for renovation the Théâtre Mogador has come to the rescue as a serious venue for classical music. Originally built as a music hall by the Englishman Sir Alfred Butt Loue as a celebration of the *entente cordiale*, the theatre went on to become a rival to the Châtelet, producing big-scale musicals and operettas. If this new space with its 'improved' acoustics catches on, Paris may have found an important new concert space.

Théâtre du Tambour-Royal
94 rue du Fbg-du-Temple, 11th (01.48.06.72.34). M° Belleville or Goncourt. **Box office** 6.30-8pm Tue-Sat; telephone 10am-8pm Mon-Sat. **Tickets** €13 to €20. **Credit** MC, V. **Map** p402 M4.
This is a good place to hear the potential stars of tomorrow; this year's long run of Offenbach's *La Périchole* should reveal some exciting new talent, but standards are inevitably hit-and-miss.

Théâtre de la Ville
2 pl du Châtelet, 4th (01.42.74.22.77/ www.theatredelaville-paris.com). M° Châtelet. **Box office** 11am-7pm Mon; 11am-8pm Tue-Sat; telephone 11am-7pm Mon-Sat. **Tickets** €15. **Credit** MC, V. **Map** p406 J6.
The concerts in this vertiginously raked concrete amphitheatre feature hip classical outfits like the avant-garde Kronos Quartet and Fabio Biondi. This year it celebrates the 50th birthday of the great viola player Yuri Bashmet. *Wheelchair access.*

Arts & Entertainment

Music: Popular Music

France may have the reputation of being to pop what Burkina-Faso is to bobsleigh, but Paris is chock-a-block of rock'n'pop'n'roots'n'raï'n'reggae'n'all that jazz.

If you judged French music only by the tragic parade of MOR-singing celebrities who appear regularly on TV here, you'd never guess that there's a wealth of talent and diversity currently abounding. That said, the big musical success story of 2001/2 was TV's *Star Academy*, a diabolical genre-splice of *Big Brother* and *Popstars* that spawned the musical careers of such gifted performers as Jenifer and Jean-Pascal. Anyway, the show came back for a second series in the autumn of 2002 (argh! the undead!), to unleash more talent.

At street-level, thankfully, the reality is different. The variety and quantity of musical events available in Paris every night is dizzying. The capital is still a stop-off for any British or US rock band, or jazz maestro, on a European jaunt, while more than ever the currents of African, South American, Indian and Eastern European folk traditions flow hither. Another fab aspect of musical life in Paris is the opening up of dialogue with other disciplines and artforms; Les Mains d'Oeuvres encourages interaction between musicians, dancers, photographers and conceptual artists, while at **La Maroquinerie**, sweaty gigs and literary debate go harmoniously hand-in hand.

One of the musical forms most closely associated with romantic Paris is, of course, French *chanson*. It's booming. If the return of the old generation is exemplified by the comeback of swinging Henri Salvador (aged 85, and the ninth most popular person in France in 2002), then it's partly thanks to younger bucks that the *chansonniers* have been revived. The songwriting partnership of Keren Ann and Benjamin Biolay, responsible for Salvador's smash, *Jardin d'Hiver*, are at the forefront of this new generation. Arguably the main man of the whole scene, Biolay combines a craftsman's seriousness with glamour-boy appeal. For now, this freshly minted take on old themes is a breath of fresh air, and the music produced all smacks reassuringly of a time when French pop music was to be cherished. The resuscitation of *chanson* is a reactionary stand, though, and it remains to be seen whether the revival will function as a necessary recapitulation before the next big step, or merely prove to be another example of pop eating itself. Meanwhile, those who prefer to hear the sound of tomorrow today

would be wise to check out French rap renaissance acts like TTC, Caution and La Rumeur; they stretch the sonic and lyrical possibilities of the genre and produce some of the most vital music on the market. In terms of jazz the word is that it's going underground again, so seek out those unmarked doors and venues where smoke gets in your eyes.

Generally, prices for admission to the venues in this chapter have not been included, as the amount usually varies according to the particular group or musician. You can expect to be forking out €10 or under for extremely cult concerns, up to €25 for more established names and about €50 for an act such as Destiny's Child or Kylie. Occasionally, though, your devotion could be tested by sums of up to €90. For ticket agencies, *see p386*.

Stadium venues

Palais Omnisports de Paris-Bercy
8 bd de Bercy, 12th (08.03.03.00.31/www.bercy.fr).
M° Bercy. **Box office** 9am-8pm Mon-Sat. **Credit**
MC, V. **Map** p407 N9.
A veritable kaleidoscope of talent performs here, but you have to get in quick for the better acoustics and superior comfort of the upper tiers. *Wheelchair access* (but phone to arrange).

Zénith
211 av Jean-Jaurès, 19th (01.42.08.60.00/
www.le-zenith.com). M° Porte de Pantin. **No box**
office. Credit MC, V. **Map** p403 inset.
This amphitheatre built its reputation on rock gigs. Dinkier than Bercy, though you wouldn't think it from the sound the system generates. This was the scene of Bob Dylan's magisterial 2002 return to Paris; not only did he talk to the crowd, but he revealed his new dance and biggest cowboy hat so far. *Wheelchair access (call in advance).*

Rock venues

L'Olympia
28 bd des Capucines, 9th (01.55.27.10.00/
reservations 01.74.42.25.49/www.olympiahall.com).
M° Opéra. **Box office** 9am-7.30pm (9.30pm concert nights) Mon-Sat. **Credit** MC, V. **Map** p401 G4.
They've all played here: the Beatles, the Stones, Quo, Sinatra, Hendrix and, of course, the real giants, Hallyday and Piaf. It's always worth checking out who's performing here while you're in town.

Arts & Entertainment

The **Bilboquet**: still swingin' after all these years. *See p333.*

Les Etoiles

61 rue du Château d'Eau, 10th (01.53.19.98.88/
reservations: www.anythingmatters.com). M° Château
d'Eau. **Credit** MC, V. **Map** p402 K4.
This wonderful old music hall (and the first place in
Paris to show talkies) is now the venue for acoustic
concerts organised by the Laughing Matters/Music
Matters outfit. Recent unforgettable sets have been
delivered by Ryan Adams and Chris Smither.

Le Bataclan

50 bd Voltaire, 11th (01.43.14.35.35/www.bataclan.fr).
M° Oberkampf. **Box office** 10.30am-7pm Mon-Fri,
11am-7pm Sat. **Concerts** 8pm. Closed two weeks in
Aug. **Credit** MC, V. **Map** p403 M5.
This charming old theatre hosts a varied bill of
French and foreign acts for seated or standing/
dancing concerts. *Wheelchair access.*

Café de la Danse

5 passage Louis-Phillipe, 11th (01.47.00.57.59/
www.cafedeladanse.com). M° Bastille. **Box office**
noon-6pm Mon-Fri. **Concerts** from 7.30pm.
No credit cards. Map p407 M7.
Overseas pop/rock acts dominate the bill at this
medium-sized former dance hall. Half the seating is
removed on boogie nights for that rarest of sights:
a French crowd grooving. *Wheelchair access.*

La Cigale/La Boule Noire

120 bd de Rochechouart, 18th (01.49.25.89.99).
M° Pigalle. **Box office** noon-7pm Mon-Sat. Closed
15 July-15 Aug. **Map** p402 H2.
One of the most reliably groovy venues in Paris. The
old horseshoe-shaped vaudeville house holds up to
1,900 punters for local and international acts. Seats
are removed for dancier occasions. Downstairs, La
Boule Noire hosts up-and-coming bands.

Le Divan du Monde

75 rue des Martyrs, 18th (01.44.92.77.66).
M° Pigalle. **Concerts** 7.30pm Mon-Sat; 5pm Sun.
Credit AmEx, MC, V. **Map** p402 H2.
A healthy dose of world music, a twist of electro-
dance, a dollop of hip-hop and a sprinkle of indie
rock/pop keeps this venue at the cutting edge.

Elysée Montmartre

72 bd de Rochechouart, 18th (01.55.07.06.00/
www.elyseemontmartre.com). M° Anvers.
Concerts 7.30pm most nights. Closed Aug.
No credit cards. Map p402 J2.
This spacious venue offers tango to techno and vin-
tage reggae, and often attracts overseas artists.
There's plenty of fine music in fine surroundings.
Wheelchair access (call in advance).

Le Trabendo

211 av Jean-Jaurès, 19th (01.49.25.89.99).
M° Porte de Pantin. **Concerts** from 8pm, days vary.
No credit cards. Map p403 inset.
Formerly the Hot Brass jazz club, Le Trabendo has
been done up in a more contemporary manner. The
venue now stages largely underground rock, world
and electro-jazz concerts, and there are frequent
visits from overseas acts such as Nightmares on
Wax and Supergrass. *Wheelchair access.*

Mains d'Oeuvres

1 rue Charles Garnier, St Ouen 93400
(01.40.11.25.25/www.mainsdoeuvres.org).
M° Garibaldi. **Concerts** 8.30pm. **Admission** €8.
Credit MC, V.
This new interdisciplinary centre has 4000m2 of performance and exhibition space. As well as hosting
musicians from the fringes of rock, rap, electronica
and jazz, it has dance and recording studios.

Rock in bars

Le Cavern
21 rue Dauphine, 6th (01.43.54.53.82). M°Odéon or Pont Neuf. **Bar** 7pm-3am Tue-Thur; 7pm-5am Fri, Sat. Closed Aug. **Admission** free. **Credit** MC, V. **Map** p406 H7.
A godsend for young groups seeking an audience, and therefore a good place to spot up-coming stars.

House of Live
124 rue La Boétie, 8th (01.42.25.18.06). M° Franklin D Roosevelt. **Bar/restaurant** 9am-5am daily. **Concerts** times vary. Gospel concerts 11.30pm Tue-Thur; noon Fri, Sat. **Admission** free. **Credit** AmEx, MC, V. **Map** p401 E4.
Music can seem secondary to bizarre mating rituals, but it does run from quiffed-up rock and posey pop to Sunday blues and soulful gospel.

Le Réservoir
16 rue de la Forge Royal, 11th (01.43.56.39.60/ www.reservoirclub.com). M° Ledru-Rollin. **Bar** 8pm-2am Mon-Thur; 8pm-dawn Fri-Sat; noon-5pm Sun (jazz brunch). **Admission** free. **Credit** AmEx, MC, V. **Map** p407 N7.
Live acts range from soul, funk, groove to world, reggae, trip hop and house. This venue boasts celebrity visits and a juicy Sunday jazz brunch.

La Scène
2bis rue des Taillandiers, 11th (01.48.06.50.70/ reservations: 01.48.06.12.13/www.la-scene.com). M° Ledru-Rollin. **Bar/restaurant** 8pm-2am. **Concerts** 9.30pm Mon-Thur; 11pm Fri, Sat. Closed Sun. **Admission** free. **Credit** AmEx, MC, V. **Map** p407 M7.
This superbly designed bar and split-level restaurant has a relaxed, earthy feel thanks to its cool, stone interior and low lights.

Le Bee Bop
64 rue de Charenton, 12th (01.43.42.56.26/ www.bee-bop.cityvox.com). M° Ledru-Rollin. **Bar** 4pm-6am daily. **Admission** free. **Credit** AmEx, DC, MC, V. **Map** p407 M7.
A French-run, English-style pub that serves up a banquet of local bands. Rock, blues, funk, world, *chanson* – the programme is wide open and predominantly electric. Cheap pints. *Wheelchair access.*

La Flèche d'Or
102bis rue de Bagnolet, 20th (01.43.72.42.44/ www.flechedor.com). M° Gambetta. **Bar/restaurant** 6pm-2am Tue; 10am-2am Wed-Sun. **Concerts** 9pm Tue-Sat; 5pm Sun. **Admission** free. **No credit cards. Map** p407 Q6.
This ex-train station is home to old hippies and new alternatives. Music is an eclectic feast of world, ska, reggae and rock. *Wheelchair access.*

Le Gambetta
104 rue de Bagnolet, 20th (01.43.70.52.01). M° Gambetta. **Bar** 9.30am-2am daily. **Concerts** 9pm. **Credit** MC, V. **Map** p407 Q6.

This unpretentious rock and rumble haunt has an edgy student-union feel and bands that thump and rattle. Punk, rock, alternative electric guitar, plus regular world music nights. *Wheelchair access.*

Chanson

Not all *chanson* involves impassioned, aged crooners singing covers from 30 years ago. The following venues offer an eclectic mix of new singer-songwriters, jazz, gypsy music and poetry, but the spiritual home of the form will always be **L'Olympia** (*see p326*).

Sentier des Halles
50 rue d'Aboukir, 2nd (01.42.61.89.96). M° Sentier. **Concerts** 8pm, 10pm Mon-Sat. Closed Aug. **Admission** €9-€12. **No credit cards. Map** p402 J4.
This celebrated cellar seats 120 people for a wide variety of acts (many of them big cheeses), from *chanson* to camembert reggae and roquefort rap.

L'Attirail
9 rue au Maire, 3rd (01.42.72.44.42). M° Arts et Métiers. **Bar/restaurant** 10am-2am daily. **Concerts** 9pm. **Admission** free. **Credit** AmEx, DC, MC, V. **Map** p402 K5.
This low-key Algerian bar offers chanson, plus occasional world music and theatre. Sitting in the back section with the musicians, you will be encouraged not to smoke too much.

Le Limonaire
18 cité Bergère, 9th (01.45.23.33.33/ www.limonaire.free.fr). M° Grands Boulevards. **Bar** 6pm-1am Tue-Sun. **Concerts** 10pm Tue-Sat; 7pm Sun. **Admission** free. **Credit** MC, V. **Map** p402 J4.
Down an atmospheric passageway this *bistro à vins* takes its *chanson* seriously – don't come here for a drink and a chat as the room becomes wrapped in reverent silence while the artistes perform. And don't come here to do your Inspecteur Clouseau impressions either. The venue does accordion *bals* and silent movies with piano accompaniment.

Chez Adel
10 rue de la Grange-aux-Belles, 10th (01.42.08.24.61). M° Jacques Bonsergent. **Bar** 11.30am-2am Mon-Thur; 6pm-2am, Fri, Sat; noon-2am Sun. **Admission** free. **Credit** MC, V. **Map** p402 L3.
What a place to whoop it up. Great sangria, frescoed walls, good-value meals (homemade Syrian at weekends) and a cosy audience. French, folk and gypsy tunes add to the warm and welcoming little village vibe. *Wheelchair access.*

Le Magique
42 rue de Gergovie, 14th (01.45.43.21.32). M° Pernéty. **Bar/restaurant** 8pm-2am Wed-Sun. **Concerts** 9.30pm Wed-Sat; 10.30pm Fri-Sat. **Admission** free. **No credit cards. Map** p405 F10.
Enjoy politically incorrect *chanson*, gypsy swing or

Arts & Entertainment

All you need is luvvies

Anglophones frequently prefer their recording artists to be idiot-savants of the Noel Gallagher variety. With the merest suspicion that the person may actually have a clue, that there might be some part of contrivance involved in the creative process, come the accusations of not being 'for real' enough. So the idea of serious writers turning their hands to music is, frankly, on a plane of pretentiousness that we're really not prepared to deal with. Not so the French!

Over here, the worlds of literature and popular song have long enjoyed a fruitful and shameless partnership. Jacques Prévert, Boris Vian and Raymond Queneau all penned or contributed to 'pop' ditties that were both broadly appealing in their tunefulness and literary in their intent. The status of Prévert's *Les Feuilles Mortes* as a classic of French *chanson* doesn't stop it being considered a valid part of his poetic oeuvre. (Stop smirking now, please). The relationship also works the other way – the lyrics of Gainsbourg, Brel and Brassens are highly regarded and available to buy as stand-alone texts.

Now, with *chanson* (and French pop in general) experiencing a revival of fortunes, it's not surprising that this kind of cross-medium crossover is back. Also, many of today's authors have grown up getting their kicks from rock and techno and subsequently litter their prose with pop references. It is often claimed that all music journalists are failed musicians – but what if that were true of our novelists, too? What if the only thing Bret Easton Ellis ever really wanted to do was dance on stage like a hypnotised chicken in a fake leopard-skin leotard? Actually, it appears that Ellis might have a penchant for French

Touch. In September of last year, the magazine *Chronic'art* hosted an evening of collaborations between writers and recording artists at La Cigale. Ellis' rumoured dalliance with Cassius and Daft Punk's Thomas Bangalter failed to manifest itself, but Will Self, Jonathan Coe and Hubert Selby Jr all showcased their own musical projects.

Also involved was the 'the French Phil Spector', Parisian Bertrand Burgalat, who, through his Tricatel label, was responsible for producing literary naughty boy Michel Houellebecq's first musical forays, and has also released an intriguing album by British writer Coe. Paris has got it going on as far as the rock/lit interface goes. But could any non-masochist listen to the results?

Whereas Vian and Prévert wrote lyrics that were intended to be sung, and that were crafted respecting the form and register of popular songs, their contemporary counterparts are more often content to set short monologues, or extracts of already published work, to an appropriate soundscape and leave it at that. Lots of ego, not so much hard graft. Listening to Maurice Dantec (*pictured*) reciting Nietzsche over prog-techno probably isn't most people's idea of rocks-off fun, and you have to wonder if anything is gained in either musical or literary terms. On the other hand, Serge Gainsbourg proved that there's nothing wrong with being a mumbling pseudo-bohemian passing for a singer – as long as you're in France.

Tracklisting:

Michel Houellebecq *Présence humaine* Tricatel 2001
Jonathan Coe *9th & 11th* Tricatel 2001
Richard Pinhas & Maurice G *Dantec Shitzotrope III Le Pli* Emma 2001.

Arts & Entertainment

hypnotico-futurist song before or after a palatable, discount meal. Donations €5 minimum.

Le Pataquès

8 rue Jouye-Rouve, 20th. No telephone. M° Pyrénées.
Bar 10am-midnight Tue-Fri and every second Mon; 10pm-1am Sat, Sun. **Concerts** 7.30-10.30pm **Admission** free. **No credit cards. Map** p403 N4.
Enter the retro timewarp and savour the alternative ambience or dance the java with strange and/or friendly locals. Le Pataquès has built up a reputation for slam poetry nights but occasionally has music and off-beat theatre too.

Barges

Batofar

quai François-Mauriac, 13th (01.56.29.10.00/ www.batofar.org). M° Quai de la Gare/Bibliothèque.
Bar 5pm-2am Tue-Sat. **Admission** free-€10. **Credit** MC, V. **Map** p407 N10.
An unsinkable pleasure fest for those who can stomach writhing to electro-modern music such as techno, house and dub with a fair bit of wave motion underfoot. New management may change the programme. *See also chapter* **Clubs**.

La Balle au Bond

(01.40.46.85.12/www.laballeaubond.fr). (Oct-Mar) 55 quai de la Tournelle, 5th, M° Maubert-Mutualité; (Apr-Sept) quai Malaquais, 6th. M° Pont Neuf.
Bar 11am-2am Mon-Sun. **Admission** €7. **Credit** AmEx, MC, V. **Map** p402 K7.
Mainstream commotion on mid-river. Come over all 'hello, sailor' as you swing and sway to the party-honk of rock, pop, jazz and *chanson*.

Péniche Déclic

Porte de la Gare, Quai de la Gare, 13th (01.45.32.57.63/www.penichedeclic.free.fr). M° Jussieu/Gare d'Austerlitz. **Bar** 9pm-midnight Thur-Sun. **Concerts** 9pm. Closed Aug. **Admission** €7. **No credit cards. Map** p402 L8.
This modest little packet, no larger than a dingo's donger, is home to an unpretentious crowd of hipsters for didgeridoo and rootsy rhythm nights.

Péniche El Alamein

quai François-Mauriac, 13th (01.45.86.41.60). M° Quai de la Gare/Bibliothèque. **Bar** 7pm-2am daily. **Concerts** 9pm. **Admission** €7. **No credit cards. Map** p407 N10.
For all you sea-legged lovebirds. Serenades are predominantly *chanson*, with the odd pop-rock or ragga-reggae mutiny. *Wheelchair access.*

Blues bars

See also **New Morning**, *p333.*

Utopia

79 rue de l'Ouest, 14th (01.43.22.79.66). M° Pernéty. **Concerts** 10pm Mon-Sat. **Admission** €8-€11. **Credit** MC ,V. **Map** p401 F10.

Bluesmen from home and away dig deep into the soulful territory of their predecessors. Country blues, delta blues, swing and blues rock are laid down with gusto as any considerations of Gallic cool are swept aside by the power of the form.

Quai du Blues

17 bd Vital-Bouhot (Ile de la Jatte), Neuilly sur Seine, (01.46.24.22.00). M° Pont de Levallois. **Bar/ restaurant** 8.30pm-2am. **Concerts** 10.30pm Thur-Sat. Closed July-Aug. **Admission** €16; €12 under 25s (Thur); €40 (dinner & show). **Credit** AmEx, V.
This atmospheric refurbished garage invites only genuine Afro-American artists to grace its stage. The positively discriminatory policy is clearly a quality-control measure, and it usually pays off.

World & traditional music

Théâtre de La Ville

(01.42.74.22.77/ www.theatredelaville-paris.com). 2 pl du Châtelet, 4th. M° Châtelet. 31 rue des Abbesses, 18th. M° Abbesses. **Box office** 11am-7pm Mon; 11am-8pm Tue-Sat; 11am-7pm Mon-Sat (telephone). **Concerts** 8.30pm Mon-Fri; 5pm, 8.30pm Sat. Closed July-Aug. **Credit** MC, V. **Map** p402 J6.
At the Châtelet theatre and its Abbesses offshoot the musical programme presents and celebrates rare and exotic forms – rare and exotic to us blinkered westerners, that is. *Wheelchair access.*

Institut du Monde Arabe

1 rue des Fossés-St-Bernard, 5th (01.40.51.38.38/ www.imarabe.org). M° Jussieu. **Box office** 10am-5pm Tue-Sun; 7.30-9pm show nights. **Concerts** 8.30pm Fri, Sat. **Admission** €16; €13 students, over-60s; €10 under-25s. **Credit** AmEx, MC, V. **Map** p402 K7.
A quality auditorium with wonderful, lounge-like leather seats. The institute is lucky enough to be able to attract a great number of top-class performers from the Arab world.

La Vieille Grille

1 rue du Puits-de-l'Hermite, 5th (01.47.07.22.11/ http://vieille.grille.free.fr). M° Place Monge. **Restaurant** 7 30pm-12.30am Tue-Sat. **Bar** 6pm-1am Tue-Sun. **Admission** €10 (6.30pm concert); €16 (9pm concert). **No credit cards. Map** p402 K8.
A cute, café-théâtre style niche. Regular Latin and Klezmer nights (Klezmer is eastern-European Jewish music that's great for a knees-up) alternate with traditional jazz, world music and text readings (ah well, that's Paris) at weekends.

Kibélé

12 rue de l'Echiquier, 10th (01.48.24.57.74). M° Bonne Nouvelle. **Restaurant** noon-3pm, 7pm-2am Mon-Sat. **Concerts** 9.30pm Wed-Sat. **Admission** free. **Credit** AmEx, MC, V. **Map** p402 K4.
Dine in the friendly Turkish restaurant and then drop down to the snug cellar and drift to the sounds of Eastern Europe and North Africa.

A bit more bass at **Studio des Islettes**. *See p333.*

Satellit' Café

44 rue de la Folie-Méricourt, 11th
(01.47.00.48.87/www.satellit-cafe.com).
M° Oberkampf. **Bar** 8pm-4am Tue-Thur; 10pm-6am
Fri-Sat. **Concerts** 9pm Tue-Thur. **Admission** €8.
Credit AmEx, MC, V (credit cards taken if you buy
two or more tickets). **Map** p403 M5.
Sizzling, blues-tinged delights provide the sounds to
send you into a nocturnal orbit to remember.

Centre Mandapa

6 rue Wurtz, 13th (01.45.89.01.60). M° Glacière.
Box office *(*telephone) 11am-7pm Mon-Sat.
Concerts 8.30pm. Closed July-mid-Sept.
No credit cards. Map p402 J10.
If you have never experienced the hypnotic beauty
of the live *sitar* or *tabla* in full flight, this is where
you get your ticket. *Wheelchair access (call ahead).*

Cité de La Musique

221 av Jean-Jaurès, 19th (01.44.84.44.84/
www.cite-musique.fr). M° Porte de Pantin.
Concerts Tue-Sat, times vary. **Admission** €6-€33.
Credit MC, V. **Map** p403 inset.
The auditorium at the La Villette complex attracts
first-class world, jazz and classical musicians and,
during the Rendezvous Electroniques, electro music
and video too.

La Maroquinerie

23 rue Boyer, 20th (01.40.33.30.60). M° Gambetta.
Restaurant 11.30am-1.30am Mon-Sat. **Bar** 11am-
1am. **Concerts** 8.30pm. **Map** p403 Q5.
A happening locale for world, rock, jazz and country, poetry and debate. That's right: debate.

Jazz

Le Baiser Salé

58 rue des Lombards, 1st (01.42.33.37.71).
M° Châtelet. **Bar** 5pm-6am daily. **Admission** €8-€18.
Credit AmEx, DC, MC, V. **Map** p406 J6.
This little club offers 'happy concerts' of pop, 70s
soul, funk or *chanson*, followed by Afro-jazz. Artists
range from Captain Mercier to Louis Winsberg.

Duc des Lombards

42 rue des Lombards, 1st (01.42.33.22.88).
M° Châtelet. **Bar** 8pm-2am Mon-Sat. **Closed** two
weeks in Aug. **Admission** €13-€20. **Credit** V.
Map p406 J6.
No frills but plenty of atmosphere. You're practically on top of the many jazz acts, so you get a great
vibe and a nice earful.

Le Petit Opportun

15 rue des Lavandières-Ste-Opportune, 1st
(01.42.36.01.36). M° Châtelet. **Bar** 9pm-5am Tue-
Sat. **Admission** €13-€16. **Concerts** 6pm, 10.30pm-
2.30am Tue-Sat. **No credit cards. Map** p406 J6.
Top French jazzers go for the high notes in this tiny
medieval cellar that is especially atmospheric when
it's packed.

Le Slow Club

130 rue de Rivoli, 1st (01.42.33.84.30). M° Châtelet.
Bar 10pm-3am Tue, Thur; 10pm-4am Fri, Sat.
Concerts 10pm. **Admission** €10-€13; €8 students
Tue, Thur. **Credit** MC,V. **Map** p406 J6.
A little cellar with big beat boogie-woogie orches-
tras, R&B, washboard jazz and swing bands.

Arts & Entertainment

French pop: crap, pap or tip-top?

What drives someone to it? Why would anyone from outside the Gallic hexagon ever find French pop music worthy of investigation? We've all heard the horrors. We've all grimaced at strange, sometimes grotesque, monikers like Hallyday, Goldman, Bruel and Daniel Balavoine. Yet some braver souls do persevere, for they have heard other names, names that evoke a more glorious past – Hardy, Gainsbourg, Aznavour, Ferré, Dutronc, Polnareff. If Good French Pop Music existed once, they reason, then surely it could again.

These optimists are not as nuts as you might think. There *is* popular music currently being made in France that's universally recognised as decent – the success of Daft Punk, Air, Kid Loco et al has ensured that a certain proportion of the country's musical output is on the 'in' list for the first time in over 30 years. The bar has been raised, and the ambition has returned. French groups are now forging an identity that goes beyond merely apeing British and American successes. Those influences are now fully digested and, combined with the legacy of the country's last 'cool' epoch, they can result in some unexpectedly wonderful new sounds.

Throughout the 70s, 80s and some of the 90s, though, the picture was a very different one. It was dashed ugly, and it turned many anglophones off the idea of French pop for good. Which is, of course, wonderful news for intrepid pop explorers. Think about it: even the megastars of French music are virtually unheard of in Britain and the U.S. Approximately 99.8% of NME-reading teenagers would, if asked, find it impossible to name one of Johnny Hallyday's records. Now *that's* obscurity, and it goes double for

most 'alternative' French artists. Anyone who gets a bit sniffy when their favourite band becomes too popular needn't worry where Dionysos or Etienne Charry are concerned.

Beyond such elitist concerns, the appeal of quality frog-pop also lies in its ability to come over as sophisticated and effortlessly cool, just by virtue of being French. It may be an illusion, and one that relies on clichéd misconceptions of life in foreign parts, but it works. English group St-Etienne was clearly aware of the wistfully romantic images a French name would conjure up for the

average Brit; for most French people, St-Etienne is merely synonymous with a once great, now useless, football team. This cross-Channel mirage can also function in reverse; take French band Aston Villa (*pictured*). In Villa's homeland, the name would be considered mundane, but who knows what kind of misty associations it sets off in the mind of the Parisian music fan?

So, something is definitely gained in translation; fortunately there's also a fair amount that's lost. Even with a high level of fluency in the language, you're still likely to have trouble deciphering each one of Mylène Farmer's breathy syllables, or grasping every nuance of a French rapper's diatribe. This can be a blessing. Approximative understanding of song lyrics can improve one's listening experience immeasurably. Euro-goth babe Farmer's lyrics might be immature sixth-form doggerel, but magnified by the charm of a helium-and-lipstick French female voice, and filtered through the language sieve, they become altogether more alluring – just as long as you don't sit down with your Micro-Robert (that's a dictionary, not a euphemism) and a copy of the lyrics.

Arts & Entertainment

Le Sunset/Le Sunside

60 rue des Lombards, 1st (01.40.26.46.60
Sunset/01.40.26.21.25 Sunside). M° Châtelet. **Bar**
9.30pm-2am Mon-Sat. **Conce**rts 10pm (Sunset).
Admission €8-€20. **Credit** MC, V.
Map p406 J6.
One of the major jazz venues in Paris, Le Sunset concentrates on electric jazz and world music with
names such as Jeff 'Tin' Watt. Le Sunside focuses
on acoustic with biggies such as Nguyen Lê.

Les 7 Lézards

10 rue des Rosiers, 4th (01.48.87.08.97). M° St-Paul.
Bar 6pm-2am daily. **Concerts** 9.30pm. **Admission**
€9-€12; €7 Wed. **No credit cards. Map** p406 L6.
A jazz hubbub of locals, ex-pats and visiting US
maestros. Prepare yourself for the frenzy of the
bippidy-boppidy fury.

Café Universel

267 rue St-Jacques, 5th (01.43.25.74.20). RER
Luxembourg. **Bar** 9am-2am Mon-Sat. **Concerts**
9.30pm. Closed Aug. **Admission** free. **Credit**
AmEx, MC, V. **Map** p406 J8.
Friendly bar showcases local bebop, modern, Afro
and Latin acts to a student and ex-pat crowd.

Caveau de la Huchette

5 rue de la Huchette, 5th (01.43.26.65.05).
M° St-Michel. **Concerts** 9.30pm daily. **Admission**
€9-€13 Mon-Thur, Sun; €11 Fri-Sat; €8 students
Mon-Thur. **Credit** MC, V. **Map** p406 J7.
Set in the tourist trap part of the Latin Quarter but
worth every euro. The venue is a hit in itself.

Le Bilboquet

13 rue St-Benoît, 6th (01.45.48.81.84).
M° St-Germain-des-Prés. **Concerts** 10.pm-2.am
Mon-Sun. **Admission** €21 (incl one drink).
Credit AmEx, MC, V. **Map** p405 H6.
Its 50s heyday (Miles Davis played here) may be
over but it's still groove enough for the likes of David
Bowie and Zee Zee Top.

Caveau des Oubliettes

52 rue Galande, 5th (01.46.34.23.09) M°/RER
St Michel. **Concerts** Jam sessions 5pm-2am Sun-
Thur; concerts 10pm-2am Fri-Sat. **Admission** free
Sun-Thurs; €8 Fri-Sat. **Credit** AmEx, MC, V.
Map p406 J7.
Explore the secret passage under St. Michel or jump
up on stage for an improvised jazz sesh. Weekends
bring the pros in for a skid-bopitty showdown

New Morning

7-9 rue des Pétites-Ecuries, 10th (01.45.23.51.41/).
M° Château d'Eau. **Box office** 4.30pm-7.30pm Mon-
Fri. **Concerts** 9.pm daily. **Credit** V. **Map** p402 K3.
This prestigious venue attracts a rapt audience with
top-end jazz, blues and world music artists from
Archie Shepp to Julien Lorau.

Le Cithéa

114 rue Oberkampf, 11th (01.40.21.70.95/
www.cithea.com). M° Parmentier/Ménilmontant.

Bar 5pm-5.30am. **Concerts** 11pm daily.
Admission €6. **Credit** MC, V. **Map** p403 N5.
The Cithéa has had a make-over turning it from
scuzzy pub to Gallic seduction den, but the crowd is
a rowdy as ever. Amateur jazz(y) musicians fuse
Afro, Latin, soul-funk, hip hop and dance styles. DJs
follow into the small hours with groove and reggae.

Parc Floral de Paris

Bois de Vincennes, 12th (01.55.94.20.20/
www.parcfloraldeparis.com). M° Château de
Vincennes. **Concerts** May-July 4.30pm Sat, Sun.
Admission €1.50. **No credit cards.**
The cream of the international jazz world congre-
gates every summer at this little gazebo in the park.

Petit Journal Montparnasse

13 rue du Commandant-Mouchotte, 14th
(01.43.21.56.70). M° Gaîté. **Concerts** 10pm. Closed
mid-July-mid-Aug. **Admission** €15-€46 (with concert);
€58-€60 (with dinner). **Credit** MC, V. **Map** p405 F9.
This jazz brasserie offers R&B, soul-gospel, Latin
and Afro-fusion in a harmonious atmosphere.

Lionel Hampton Jazz Club

81 bd Gouvion-St-Cyr, 17th (01.40.68.30.42).
M° Porte Maillot. **Bar** 7am-2am daily. **Concerts**
10.30pm, 2am daily. **Admission** €23-€25 (incl one
drink). **Credit** AmEx, DC, MC, V. **Map** p400 B2.
Here you'll find R&B, soul and gospel. 75% of acts
are from America, but local talent gets to swing, too.

Studio des Islettes

10 rue des Islettes, 18th (01.42.58.63.33).
M° Barbès-Rochechouart. **Open** 8pm-1am Mon-Sat.
Jam sessions/concerts 9pm. Closed Aug.
Admission €6 Mon-Thurs; €8 Fri-Sat. **No credit
cards. Map** p402 J2.
Jazz chart wallpaper and a loose, blues-used feel help
pro or amateur musicians get in the groove and
home in on the source. *Wheelchair access.*

Arts & Entertainment

Sport & Fitness

You want to be sleek, slim and tight-calved, right? But Parisian form dictates a raw steak and a ripe camembert at lunch. The only solution: *du sport*!

OK, let's be grown up about this. Let us not crow about France's savage humiliation in the 2002 football World Cup: three matches, three defeats is a tragedy, not something to harp on about, especially in light of the nation's certainty that they would win the competition. So we will say no more. And, please: let there be no gloating references to hubris so swiftly followed by nemesis. How thoughtful of Chirac to have written the team a letter of condolence.

Let us instead focus on how 1998's World Cup left Paris with a wide range of facilities. This sport-friendly municipality caters for plenty of alternatives, so talcum-powder your swim-cap and get with *les nouveaux sportifs*.

The best source of information for sport in Paris is the *Guide du Sport à Paris*, published annually by the Mairie de Paris and available from the town hall of each *arrondissement*. To use certain sports centres, you will need a *carte* for which you must show an identity card or passport (take an extra photo, too).

Spectator sports

A number of first-class international sporting events are held in the city throughout the year (*see p338,* **The sporting year 2003**). For international events, the usual venue is the Stade de France (rue Francis de Pressensé, 93210 St-Denis/0892.700.900 for tickets, programme and visits/www.stadedefrance.fr). Alternatively, the Palais Omnisports de Paris-Bercy (8 bd de Bercy, 12th, Mº Bercy/0892.692 300 for reservations/www.popb.fr) hosts everything from martial arts to indoor jet skiing. Tickets are available online or at branches of Fnac, Virgin Megastore and Galeries Lafayette.

Basketball

Paris Basket Racing

Stade Pierre de Coubertin, 82 ave Georges Lafont, 16th (01.45.27.79.12/www.ifrance.com). Mº Porte de St-Cloud.
Basketball is very popular in France, and the French first division, the Pro A, is of an admirable level – by European standards, that is. Paris Basket Racing is a consistent mid-table performer, whose moment of glory was – steady yourself – making the final of the 1956 French cup.

Football

Paris St-Germain

Parc des Princes, 24 rue du Commandant-Guilbaud, 16th (01.42.30.03.60/www.psg.fr). Mº Porte d'Auteuil. **Tickets** by Internet or phone (08.25.07.50.78). Prices range from €9-€83.
Paris' only top-division football team, Paris St-Germain has had difficulty in consistently living up to its fans' high expectations. Matches are held at the 48,000-seat Parc des Princes. Post-mortems on what went wrong are frequently held in the dressing room.

Horse racing

There are seven racecourses in the Paris area. *France Galop* publishes a full racing list (01.49.10.20.30/www.france-galop.com) in its *Calendrier des Courses*. **Auteuil**, Bois de Boulogne, 16th (01.40.71.47.47/Mº Porte d'Auteuil), steeplechasing. **Chantilly** (41km from Paris/03.44.62.41.00/train from Gare du Nord), flat racing. **Enghien** (18km from Paris/01.34.17.87.00/train from Gare du Nord), steeplechasing and trotting. **Longchamp**, Bois de Boulogne, 16th (01.44.30.75.00/Mº Porte d'Auteuil, then free bus), flat racing. **Maisons-Laffitte** (1 av de La Pelouse, 78600 Maisons-Laffitte/01.39.62.90.95/RER A Maisons-Laffitte and then bus), flat racing. **St-Cloud** (1 rue du Camp Canadien, 92210 St-Cloud/01.47.71.69.26/RER A Rueil-Malmaison), flat racing. **Paris-Vincennes** Bois de Vincennes, 12th (01.49.77.17.17/ Mº Vincennes/RER Joinville le Pont), trotting.

Rugby

Stade Français CASG

Stade Jean-Bouin, 26 av du Général-Sarrail, 16th (01.46.51.00.75/www.stade.fr). Mº Porte d'Auteuil. **Tickets** €5-€35.
Le Stade Français has put Paris on the national rugby map. The arrival of coach Bernard Laporte was a turning point for the club. Under his guidance the team earned promotion to the first division and went on to be champions in 1998. Since 1999 the side has been managed by Georges Coste; as 2002 turned into 2003, they were hovering near the top of their league.

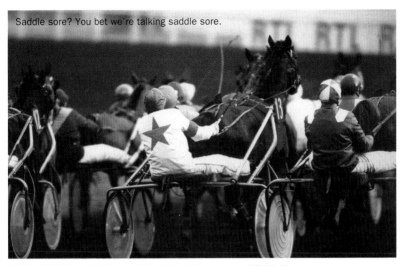

Saddle sore? You bet we're talking saddle sore.

Arts & Entertainment

Gyms & fitness

The city has a relatively small number of *clubs de forme*. Nonetheless, they are well equipped, with a broad range of activities available and helpful staff. For outdoor fitness there are 13 *Sport Nature* points in Paris' parks (Buttes-Chaumont, Georges Brassens, Montsouris) which hold free aerobics and fitness sessions every Sunday (except July and August) from 9am-noon. For full details and addresses log onto the website www.paris-france.org (in French only under *animations sportives*).

Club Quartier Latin

19 rue de Pontoise, 5th (01.55.42.77.88/ www.clubquartierlatin.com). M° Maubert-Mutualité. **Open** 9am-midnight Mon-Fri; 10am-7pm Sat, Sun. **Membership** Fitness section annual €540. **Credit** MC, V. **Map** p406 K7.
The gym has plenty of well-maintained machines, together with a range of stretch, cardio and other classes. There's also a squash membership which grants you access to the centre's four squash courts (in varying states of repair). The club does, however, get crowded at peak times. Both memberships include access to the Piscine Pontoise.

Club Med Gym

30 locations in and around Paris; visit www.clubmedgym.com for the full list. **Membership** approximately €75 per month. **Credit** AmEx, MC, V.
The gymnasium uber-franchise offers rowing and cycling machines and cardio-training equipment, and some branches have pools. Courses include aerobics, step, stretching and water-based workouts. It's George Michael's 1980s hairdo incarnate.

Espace Vit'Halles

48 rue Rambuteau, 3rd (01.42.77.21.71). M° Rambuteau. **Open** 8am-10.30pm Mon-Fri; 10am-7pm Sat; 10am-6pm Sun. **Membership** annual €750, student €600; one month €140, student €125; one visit €15. **Credit** AmEx, MC, V. **Map** p402 K5
The gym here is good, the changing rooms are clean and the crowd is non-posey. A range of classes from Tai Chi to pump is run by friendly instructors.

Ken Club

100 av du Président Kennedy, 16th. M° Passy (01.46.47.41.41). **Open** 7am-10pm Mon-Wed; 7am-midnight Thur; 9am-8pm Fri-Sun. **Membership** €700 in entry credits, valid for life; €2,500. **Credit** AmEx, MC, V.
Surprisingly not named after Barbie's dinky boyfriend, this is the ultimate in luxury gymming, with pools, a spa, hammams, solarium and even an on-site hairdresser and restaurant. A wide variety of classes is available from yoga to bums 'n' tums and afterwards there is a special nutritional buffet available so that the spare tyre doesn't reappear.

Activities & team sports

All-round sports clubs

The **Standard Athletic Club** (Route Forestière du Pavé de Meudon, 92360 Meudon-la-Forêt/01.46.26.16.09) is a private, non-profit-making club aimed at English speakers living in Paris. Full membership is €625 per year, plus an initial joining fee. It fields a cricket side (May-Sept), hockey and football teams. There are eight tennis courts, two squash courts, a heated outdoor pool and billiards table. Some top-level French clubs also run teams in various sports, such as **Racing Club de France** (01.45.67.55.86/www.racingclubdefrance.org), **Paris Université Club** (01.44.16.62.62/ www.puc.asso.fr) and **Le Stade Français** (01.40.71.33.33).

American football

Though there are no teams in Paris itself, there are 15 teams in the area. Many teams have some Americans in them, whether players or coaches. Contact the **Fédération Française de Football Américain** (01.43.11.14.70/ www.ffa.org or www.efaofficiating.org for those interested in learning how to referee) to find the club nearest you.

Athletics & running

Paris has many municipal tracks (including eight indoor ones) which are generally of a good standard. To find the track nearest you, consult the *Guide du Sport* or call Paris Infos Mairie. For an open-air run, the **Bois de Boulogne** and the **Bois de Vincennes** are the only large green expanses in Paris, although most of the parks (try Buttes-Chaumont in the 19th) as well as the banks of the Seine and the canals attract a fair number of joggers. Be aware that the Bois de Boulogne is a cruising spot.

Baseball

Baseball clubs are predictably Americanised and many of the players are English speakers. The best way to find a team near you is to contact the **Fédération Française de Baseball, Softball et Cricket** (01.44.68.89.30/www.ffbsc.org).

Basketball

Basketball is very popular in Paris, and virtually every municipal sports centre has a court and club. The **Comité Parisien de Basketball** (01.53.94.27.90/www.basketfrance. com) lists clubs, public and private, including **Racing Club de France and Paris Université Club**. There are also a number of public courts in the city where anyone can play. Popular spots include two courts under the Métro tracks near the Glacière stop in the 13th *arrondissement* and at Mᵒ Stalingrad in the 19th.

Bowling & boules

The Paris region has more than 25 tenpin bowling centres. The two we list below are among the most pleasant; both rent out shoes

and have restaurants, games rooms and late hours. There are eight lanes at the centrally located and lively **Bowling-Mouffetard** (73 rue Mouffetard, 5th/01.43.31.09.35/ Mᵒ Place Monge/open 3pm-2am Mon-Fri, 10am-2am Sat, Sun). The **Bowling de Paris** (Jardin d'Acclimatation, Bois de Boulogne, 16th/01.53.64.93.00/Mᵒ Les Sablons/open 9am-3am Mon-Fri; 9am-5am Sat, Sun) has 24 lanes, pool, billiards and video games. Bear in mind that you have to pay €2 to get into the Jardin d'Acclimatation before you get to the centre. You can play *boules* or *pétanque* in most squares. There are also some *boulodromes* at **Jardins du Luxembourg**.

If you feel like shooting some balls of the coloured kind, then the **Cercle Clichy Montmartre** (84 rue de Clichy/ Mᵒ Place de Clichy/01.48.78.32.85/www.academie-billard.com) is a superb place to come, with frescoes, bars and tables a-plenty. Young and old mingle from 10am-6am. Prices range from €7.90 per hour for pool to €10 for American billiards. The largest pool hall, at 400m², is the **Academy Billard** at 32 rue Linois, Mᵒ Charles-Michels (01.45.79.67.23/www.academy-billard.com). Open until 5am at the weekend, you get to play to the tunes of a live DJ.

Climbing

The wall at the **Centre Sportif Poissonnier** (2 rue Jean-Cocteau, 18th/01.42.51.24.68/ Mᵒ Porte de Clignancourt) is the largest municipal facility (there are six others in Paris) and has a little 'real rock' section, as well as a 21m-high unlit outside wall. To use any of the state-owned facilities, you need to get a personal ID card. To get one, take a photo, your passport, proof of valid insurance and €3.05 per month to the centre you want to use. For more of a workout and an even closer acquaintance with fear, there is the privately run **Mur Mur** (55 rue Cartier Bresson, 93500 Pantin/ 01.48.46.11.00/Mᵒ Aubervilliers-Pantin Quatre Chemins), said to be the best climbing wall in Europe, with 1,500m² of wall, 10,000 holds and an even greater number of ways of falling off. It costs €9.15-€12.20 for adults, €5.30-€6.20 for under-12s per session, though there is a joining fee of €23 for adults and €10 for under-12s. There is kit for hire and tuition on offer. Newly added is a section to practise ice-climbing (or 'dry-tooling', as they so picturesquely call it).

If you prefer real rock, you can train on the huge, slightly surreal boulders strewn around the forêt de Fontainebleau. Contact **l'Association des amis de la forêt de Fontainebleau** (01.64.23.46.45/www.aaff.org). You might also want to check out the **Club**

Arts & Entertainment

Martialing those inner resources

For traditional Chinese martial arts and various options for zenning out, try **Les Temps du Corps** (10 rue de l'Echiquier, 10th, 01.48.01.68.28/M° Strasbourg St Denis). There's a variety of stages and lessons on offer at non-extortionate prices. If you want to be all exclusive, try the **Kajyn Club** (13 rue Faidherbe, 11th, 01.55.25.29.29/M° Faidherbe-Chaligny), which offers such gems as the Indian kalaripayatt or artistic karate. For some authentic Indian duelling, try **Soleil D'Or** (146 rue Raymond-Losserand, 14th, 01.45.43.50.12/www.membres.lycos.fr/soleildor/M° Plaisance). Here you can try Varma Kalai, a traditional Indian sport that is fought barehanded and with white sticks, alongside Indian dance classes and yoga. If you want celeb-cachet, Pilates is the way to go (and get a flat stomach). Working around the principles of using the body as resistance, pilates class devotees are the sport's best advertisement with their lithe dancers' bodies. Try it for yourself at **Studio Pilates** (39 rue du Temple, 4th, 01.42.72.91.74/www.obtpilates.com/M° Hôtel-de-Ville). Three trial lessons will set you back €23 and it costs €190 for 10 group lessons. Annual membership is also available. If you want the ultimate in relaxation, but also top-notch for increasing

mobility whilst lowering stress levels, the gentle Feldenkrais method, invented – as we all know – by the doctor of physics of the same name, is beloved by artists, sportsmen and women worldwide. **Anne Candardjis** (01.40.09.94.07) teaches at Unesco as well as holding classes in the 11th (25 av Philippe Auguste, M° Nation, Thur 6.30-7.30pm and 8-9pm) and the 1st (34 rue des Archives, M° Rambuteau, Wed 10.30-11.30am and 7-8pm). Trial lessons are free, after which it's €14 per lesson or you can pay per term. For the best place to do Wing Chun in Paris (the only place really, once you've seen the rest!), check out Didier Beddar's WWLKFA-affiliated **Wing Chun Academy** (3 rue des Vignolles, 20th, 01.43.56.36.12/M° Réaumur-Sébastopol). Yogaholics can choose from classes in most of the sports clubs in Paris. Also worth a try is the **Centre de Yoga Sivananda** (23 bd de Sébastapol, 2nd, 01.40.26.77.49/www.sivananda.org/paris). This is one of 30 centres throughout the world with daily lessons for beginners, intermediates and open classes. Prices start at €16 per class, and meditation and positive thinking courses are also offered. For the low down on all yoga classes and styles on offer in Paris, contact the **Fédération Francaise de Yoga** (01.47.00.28.20/www.wanadoo.fr/yoga).

Arts & Entertainment

The sporting year 2003

January
Horse racing Prix d'Amérique, Hippodrome de Paris-Vincennes. France's glitzy trotting race.

February
Judo International tournament at Bercy (www.popb.fr). **Rugby** France take on their rivals in the Six Nations Cup. Matches are held at the Stade de France in February, March and April. **Tennis** Open Gaz de France at the Stade Pierre de Coubertin (82 av Georges-Lafont, 16th/01.44.31.44.31/ Mº Porte de St-Cloud). Stars of the women's circuit compete at this WTA indoor event. Information and tickets 0825.811. 812/www.gazdefrance.fr/open. **Dance** Salon dancing competition with salsa, hip-hop, Latin American on show.

March
Athletics half-marathon on 9 March to warm up for full marathon in April. Details on www.parismarathon.com. **Gymnastics** Internationaux de France at the Palais Omnisports de Paris-Bercy. **Jet-Skiing** International indoor jet-skiing antics at Bercy. **Showjumping** Jumping International de Paris, at Bercy. Tickets and details for both events via www.ticketnet.fr.

April
Athletics Paris Marathon. Information or entry forms on www.parismarathon.com. **Horse racing** Prix du Président de la République, top steeplechase at Auteuil, third Sun of April.

May
Table Tennis World championships at Bercy. **Tennis** France's Grand Slam event, the French Open, is held at the Stade Roland-Garros (01.47.43.48.00) at the end of May/early June www.frenchopen.org.

June
Rugby The domestic season reaches its climax with the final of the Championnat de France at the Stade de France. **Horse racing** The Prix de Diane Hermès, French equivalent of the Derby, at Chantilly.

July
Athletics IAAF Gaz de France meeting at the Stade de France, a Golden League event. **Cycling** The Tour de France arrives in Paris for a grand finale on the Champs-Elysées on 27 July (information 01.41.33.15.00/ www.letour.fr). **European Youth Olympics** end July/beg. August, various venues. **Golf** The French Women's Open at the Paris International Golf Club, 18 route du Golf, 95160 Baillet-en-France (01.34.69.90.00) in mid-July.

August
Athletics The 9th world athletics championships to be held in Seine St-Denis on 22-31 August. Information on www.paris2003saintdenis.org

September
Golf The Trophée Lancôme, at Golf de St-Nom-la-Brétèche, 78860 St-Nom-la-Brétèche. Information and ticket reservations 0803.804.000. www.trophee-lancome.com.

October
Horse-racing Flat race and society event Prix de l'Arc de Triomphe takes place at Longchamp. **Tennis** BNP Masters end October/ beginning of November.

November
Tennis The Paris Open, a top-ranking international men's indoor tournament, at Bercy. **Skating** Lalique Skating Trophy at Bercy. International ice champions and contenders. **Supercross** Mud, high jumps, wheel flangers, superskids and all those other things you're not allowed to do on the roads: do all of this and more vicariously at Bercy.

December
Go-karting This is no longer a hobby for geeky wannabees in skid-lids. Karting is now officially cool. Formula One drivers get into smaller-than-usual vehicles and race each other round an indoor track at Bercy in the Elf Masters. **Showjumping** Concours Hippique International at Paris-Expo, Porte de Versailles, 15th, in association with the annual Salon du Cheval, du Poney et de l'Ane.

Arts & Entertainment

Alpin Francais (01.42.18.20.00/
www.clubalpin.idf.free.fr) who organise
climbing excursions within the Ile de France
every weekend and occasional trips away.

Cycling

Bike lanes have been expanded by Mayor
Delanoë, and increasing numbers of cyclists are
taking to the streets. In fact, every Sunday and
on public holidays many areas are shut off to
cars to allow pedestrians and cyclists free
wheel. The quais de Seine and the Canal St-
Martin are the nicest, but the Bois de Boulogne
and the Bois de Vincennes offer good cycling.

Paris has many cycling clubs, both in the
competition-based and more leisurely
categories. You can find your nearest club
by phoning the **Fédération Française de
Cyclotourisme** (01.44.16.88.88/www.ffc.fr).
The **Stade Vélodrome Jacques-Anquetil**
(Bois de Vincennes, 12th/01.43.68.01.27) is a
functional racing track open to cyclists on a
regular basis. The **Maison du Vélo** (11 rue
Fénélon, 10th/01.42.81.24.72) sells and repairs
all types of bikes. There are also companies
offering bike tours in and around Paris and the
MDB (01.43.20.26.02/www.mdb-idf.org)
(movement for the defence of the bicycle)
organises rides for its members. Membership
costs €10 for the year.

Diving

For a diving shop, try **Plongespace**
(80 rue Balard, 15th/ 01.45.57.01.01/
www.plongespace.fr). **The Club de Plongée
du 5ème Arrondissement** (01.43.36.07.67) is
a friendly club where you can train for the
French licence. It organises trips to the Med and
meets at the **Piscine Jean-Taris** (*see below*).
There are well-qualified, friendly and
experienced instructors at **Surplouf**
(06.14.10.26.11/ 01.42.21.18.14), which offers
courses in English. Courses for beginners,
including textbooks, insurance and gear rental,
cost €250 for the French licence or €280 for the
more universally useful PADI.

Fencing

Many of the city gyms organise fencing classes
or play host to fencing clubs. For a full list of
clubs consult www.escrime-ffe.fr. **The Racing
Club de France**'s (5 rue Eblé, 7th,
01.45.67.55.86/www.racingclubdefrance.org)
fencing section is a good bet for leisure or
competition with 12 fencing masters and 18
pistes, leaving you ample room to practise those
flèches. All levels, weapons and ages are catered

for. Annual subscription is €435 which includes
your licence and insurance. The **Association
Sportive de la Préfecture de Police
(ASPP)** (4 rue de la Montagne-Ste-Geneviève,
5th/01.42.34.54.00) is worth checking out too,
especially as the police sections often work out
cheaper than many of the other public and
private clubs at €180 for one year's
participation in one activity (other sports are
also on offer).

Football

Those expecting to find a grass pitch for a
kickabout will be disappointed. The city's 80
public pitches tend to be either dirt, artificial
turf, or a place where grass once grew. To find a
pitch near you, consult the *Guide du Sport* or
call Paris Infos Mairie. To find an amateur team
to play for, call the **Ligue Ile de France de
Football** (01.42.44.12.12/www.ffr.fr) and ask
for a contact number in your *arrondissement*.

Golf

There are no courses in central Paris, but scores
in the Paris region. For a full list, contact the
Fédération Francaise de Golf (68 rue
Anatole France, 92309 Levallois Perret/
01.41.49.77.00/www.ffg.org). The **Golf
Clément Ader** (Domaine du Château Péreire,
77220 Gretz Armainvilliers/01.64.07.34.10/
SNCF Gretz Armainvilliers) is challenging. The
Golf Disneyland Paris Marne-la-Vallée
(77777 Marne-la-Vallée/01.60.45.68.90/
www.disneylandparis.com/RER Marne-la-
Vallée-Chessy then taxi) has everything. Closer
to central Paris is the **Académie de Golf de
Paris** at the Paris Country Club, Hippodrome
de St-Cloud (1 rue du Camp Canadien, 92210 St-
Cloud/01.47.71.39.22/SNCF Suresnes
Longchamp), which has a nine-hole course
within its horse-racing track.

Horse riding

Both the Bois de Boulogne and the Bois de
Vincennes are beautiful riding areas. Excellent
clubs to join are: **La Société d'Equitation de
Paris** (01.45.01.20.06), the **Centre Hippique
du Touring** (01.45.01.20. 88) or the **Cercle
Hippique du Bois de Vincennes**
(01.48.73.01.28). Beginners can learn in the
unpretentious **Club Bayard Equitation**
(Bois de Vincennes, Centre Bayard/UCPA de
Vincennes, av de Polygone, 12th/01.43.65.46.87).
Membership runs for three months (€220) or
you can do a five-day course in July or August
(€250). The **Haras de Jardy** (bd de Jardy,
92430 Marnes-la-Coquette /01.47.01.35.30) is a

lovely equestrian centre near Versailles, which organises group rides. If you want to train to compete in dressage and jumping, then the Centre Equestre du Bois de Boulogne might be the one for you. Getting up to scratch doesn't come cheap though; it's €75 to join the club, €130 annual fee, €25-€40 for the licence and €65 a month for one hour's instruction per week.

Ice skating

In winter the **place de l'Hôtel de Ville** is transformed into an open-air ice rink. If temperatures drop extremely low, there is skating on Lac Supérieur in the **Bois de Boulogne**. Indoor all-year round rinks include the **Patinoire de Boulogne** (1 rue Victor Griffuelhes, Boulogne Billancourt/ 01.46.94.99.74/M° Marcel Sembat) and the **Patinoire d'Asnières-sur-Seine** (bd Pierre de Coubertin, 92600 Asnières/ 01.47.99.96.06/ M° Gabriel Péri/Asnières-Gennevilliers). The **Sonja Henie** rink (Palais Omnisports de Paris-Bercy, 01.40.02.60.60) was opened to the public last October. It was previously only available for shows and to various clubs. Protection, helmets and skates are all available for hire (€3) and admission starts at €3.

Rollerblading

The Paris rollerblading scene is the most fully developed flowering of the *liberté, égalité, fraternité* ideal. Simply everybody's doing it. Parisian skaters have been braving both the potential disgrace of a spectacular fall and the wrath of infringed pedestrians for several years now. If, on a Friday evening stroll, you notice traffic at a standstill and rabid drivers honking their horns, you'll be witnessing the effects of 40,000 roller maniacs on their Friday Night Fever run. This free weekly roll averages 25km and the route changes each week, passing along the Champs-Elysées once every two months. Paris isn't flat, so knowing how to stop on a steep slope is a must. However, the Pari Roller team staff in their bright yellow T-shirts are on hand at all times to deal with mishaps. The starting point is at 40 av d'Italie, 13th, M° Place d'Italie, at 7.45pm and the run finishes here three hours later. The route is announced on Thursday on the Pari Roller website: www.pari-roller.com (01.43.36.89.81).

A more sedate beginner's skate takes place every Sunday at 2.30pm, organised by **Roller et Coquillage** and meeting at the **Nomades** shop just off place de la Bastille (37 bd Bourdon, 4th/M° Bastille/01.44.54.94.42/ www.rollers-coquillages.org). The nervous neophyte, crawling along with all the grace of a new-born foal and

Rollerblading: the wheel thing.

emitting banshee wails, is accorded as much respect as some Nureyev-on-wheels.
The Roller Squad Institute (www.association.rsi.free.fr) organises lessons for young and old, beginners and advanced alike. They offer variations on the theme with fitness, street, slalom and hockey blading all available. To book a place, call 01.56.61.99.61 48 hours in advance. For renting skates, the best place to go is **Vertical Line** (01.47.27.21.21/www.vertical-line.com), where they have 350 pairs from size 28 to 48. They also do repairs and custom-made skates. Not to be missed if the weather is not standing up to its side of the bargain is Rollerparc Avenue (01.47.18.19.14/www.rollerparc.com), the largest indoor roller centre in Europe with 6,000m² full of different tracks. Entrance is only €10 and you can hire skates for €4.

Rowing & watersports

You can row, canoe and kayak (Wed, Sat; equipment is provided) in the 600m x 65m basin at the **Base Nautique de la Villette** (15-17 quai de la Loire, 19th/ 01.42.40.29.90/M° Jaurès). You need to reserve a week in advance and have proof of your residence in Paris. Waterskiing, wakeboarding and the like are all possible at the **Club Nautique du 19ème** (28 ave Simon-Bolivar), Sunday 3-6.30pm. Prices start at €8. Call 01.42.03.25.24 or 06.03.91.96.92 to reserve. La Défense-based **Société Nautique de la Basse Seine** (26 quai du Président Paul Doumer, 92400 Courbevoie/01.43.33.03.47) has both competitive and recreational sections; or you can hire boats on Lac Daumesnil and Lac des Minimes in the **Bois de Vincennes** or on Lac Supérieur in the **Bois de Boulogne**.

Rugby

Top-level rugby goes on at **Racing Club de France**. For a good club standard try the **Athletic Club de Boulogne** (Saut du Loup, route des Tribunes, 16th), which fields two teams. The **British Rugby Club of Paris** (01.40.55.15.15/ 01.39.16.33.56) fields two teams in the corporate league.

Skateboarding

Paris is a skater's dream. Whether you're strapping on your wheels in order to show off, practise your ollies or bag yourself a cute skater, here are a few tips on where to hang out. (Bladers and roller-skaters are generally welcome, too.) There are always skaters a-plenty by the fountain near **Les Halles** (1st) shopping centre, but the standard of talent generally doesn't offer much in the way of a challenge (and if you're too good, be careful you don't get your face pushed in). Other popular spots to strut your stuff in front of the tourists are **Palais Royal** (1st) and the esplanade at **Trocadéro** (16th) where there are ramps available. **Bercy** (12th) is extremely popular because it is so huge and has some excellent flights of steps. If it's too cold for you outside (you wimp), head off to one of Paris' only indoor skate parks at **Balard** (Wasteland, 15th). And if slalom and jumps are more your thing, then the only place to go is **La Défense** (the site is managed by the Roller Team La Défense association, and there's training every Sat and Sun after 3pm.) For information, call 06.60.41.42.12.

Squash

You can play at **Club Quartier Latin** or the **Standard Athletic Club**, or try **Squash Montmartre** (14 rue Achille-Martinet, 18th/ 01.42.55.38.30/Mº Lamarck-Caulaincourt). Membership is €520 per year or €140 for three months, or you can pay each time you visit (€12 per hour).

Vicious cycles

2003 is the centenary year of the Tour de France. Founded as a publicity stunt by a hack named Henri Desgrange as part of a circulation war between two French cycling magazines, the event has grown into what is generally regarded as the most testing sporting event in the world. (In the wider cultural sense, incidentally, the Tour was also crucial in 'elevating' sportsmen into media figures.)

Until the early 1960s, the Tour was dominated by French, Belgian and Italian cyclists. It took the Englishman Tom Simpson to kick open the doors to competitors from other nations (the same Tom Simpson who died of exhaustion on Mount Ventoux in Provence while taking part in the 1967 race). At the moment, the Tour is dominated by an American, Lance 'The Boss' Armstrong, who has won it for the last four years, simultaneously staging a recovery from cancer.

In its modern form, the race takes in the six cities of Paris, Lyon, Marseille, Toulouse, Bordeaux and Nantes in a maximum of 24 stages (the course changes slightly every year), over a distance of 4,000km. A great amount of its appeal as a spectator event lies in the fact that it is not safe: only a lunatic would participate. It takes even the fittest cyclists to the edge; placards line its route, exhorting the riders to 'give us something to dream about'. Maybe the mental and physical pressures explain why the Tour is dogged by rumours of drug abuse. The 1998 race was the nadir of substance use. A car belonging to the Festina team was found to contain massive quantities of performance-enhancing drugs. This led to police raids on all competitors' hotel rooms, which in turn led to a riders' strike, the withdrawal of six teams, the cancellation of an entire stage and, eventually, a clean-up of the sport. Whatever the rights and wrongs of riders' behaviour, in our play-safe world there's something compelling about an event that brings out the win-at-any-cost spirit. You can be sure that whoever wins at the Champs-Elyseés on 27 July 2003 will have confronted the limits of his physical and mental endurance.

Arts & Entertainment

Swimming

If you were planning on making an entrance in style, don't forget that you will usually have to contend with the fetching addition of a swim cap. And no hiding behind baggy, boxer-style surfer shorts; for blokes it's nut-hugging trunks or no entry. Hygenic, perhaps, but not the best look for every figure type. This isn't going to be a fashion parade, then; still, only the most confident should turn up in water wings.

Public pools

Paris's state-run pools are generally of a good standard; they're clean and cheap. They cost €2.50 for adults and €1.35 for children. You can also buy *carnets* of 10 entries which work out a couple of euros cheaper. With varying opening hours due to school use, it's best to check availability in advance.

Piscine Jean-Taris

16 rue Thouin, 5th (01.43.25.54.03). M° Cardinal Lemoine. Map p406 G8.
Look on to the Panthéon from this lovely 25m pool.

Piscine du Marché St-Germain

12 rue Lobineau, 6th (01.43.29.08.15). M° Mabillon. Map p405 H7.
This is a deeply hip, underground 25m pool in St-Germain.

Piscine Butte-aux-Cailles

5 pl Paul-Verlaine, 13th (01.45.89.60.05). M° Place d'Italie.
One main pool (33m) and two outdoor pools built in the 1920s.

Piscine Didot

22 av Georges-Lafenestre, 14th (01.42.76.78.14). M° Porte de Vanves.
This 25m pool welcomes diving clubs and practitioners of aquagym as well as individual swimmers.

Piscine Emile-Anthoine

9 rue Jean-Rey, 15th (01.53.69.61.59/ 01.42.76.78.18). M° Bir-Hakeim. Map p404 C6.
This large, modern pool has a fabulous view of the Eiffel Tower.

Private pools

These often offer extra attractions, and have longer opening hours. Check these out:

Aquaboulevard

4 rue Louis-Armand, 15th (01.40.60.15.15). M° Balard. Admission six hours in peak periods €20, under-11s €9. Map p404 A10.
This extravagant indoor-outdoor complex is great fun for kids. Its tropical lagoon makes you feel as if you're the Mayor of Suave County.

Piscine Georges-Hermant

4-6 rue David d'Angers, 19th,(01.42.02.45.10) M° Danube. Admission €4, €3 under-16s.
This is Paris' biggest pool, at 50m x 20m. It's uncovered in summer and there's a great atmosphere.

Tennis

The **Jardins du Luxembourg** (6th/ 01.43.25. 79.18/ M° Notre-Dame-des-Champs/ RER Luxembourg) is a great place to play. The **Centre Sportif La Falguère** (route de la Pyramide, Bois de Vincennes, 12th/ 01.43.74. 40.93/M° Château de Vincennes) has 21 acrylic courts. **Centre Sportif Henry-de-Montherlan**t (30-32 bd Lannes, 16th/ 01.40.72.28.33/M° Porte-Dauphine) has seven hard courts. To use these courts you need to get hold of the Paris tennis card. All you need to do is to turn up at a tennis centre with a copy of your passport and two photos. That'll get you your card, and then then you only pay for the time spent on court (€5.75 per hour for an outside court and €11.40 for an inside court). The private **Tennis de Longchamp** (19 bd Anatole-France, 92100 Boulogne/ 01.46.03.84.49/ M° Boulogne-Jean Jaurès) has 20 hard courts. **Club Forest Hill** (4 rue Louis-Armand, 15th/01.40.60.10.00/M° Balard/ RER Boulevard Victor) has 14 branches in the Paris region. For **table tennis** fans, there are tables on the quais at Stalingrad, and all the clubs in Paris are listed on www.tennis-de-table.com.

A couple of ball breakers.

Theatre

Oh, how deep Paris minstrels delve! And what emerges from their collective leotard? Musicals, classics and the, er, fruits of Stephen Berkoff's loins.

Nothing thrills a thesp like the whiff of a government subsidy, and Parisian theatreland is an aromatic place indeed. Following the vogue for block-busting musicals, this year brings the musical version of Saint-Exupéry's *Le Petit Prince*, brought to life by Richard Cocciante of *Notre Dame de Paris* fame. Of course, those with a bent for the classics will always find satisfaction here: Racine, Molière and Anouilh are never off the boards, and Paris attracts top-class productions from all over the world, often in their original language. The **Théâtre de la Cité Internationale**, **Odéon**, and the **Sudden Theatre** pride themselves on their international outlook, and Paris festivals attract quality touring theatre to rival anything at Avignon – drama junkies should time their trip to catch the *Festival d'Automne* (September to December) or the springtime *Festival de l'Imaginaire*. Top-notch directors are in town: there's Peter Brook at the **Bouffes du Nord**, and Ariane Mnouchkine at the **Théâtre du Soleil**. For those with an appetite for the truly innovative, it does have to be said that mainstream Parisian theatre fare can be a bit stodgy compared with the kind of risk-taking productions that flourish elsewhere in Europe. Sometimes it's worth taking a trip out of the centre to find some of the more interesting productions: try out the Théâtre Gérard Philipe (01.48.13.70.00/www.theatregerardphilipe.com) in Saint-Denis, MC93 (01.41.60.72.72/

www.mc93.com) in Bobigny or Nanterre's Théâtre des Amandiers (www.tem-nanterre.com). For something more alternative, *café-théâtre* (*see chapter* **Cabaret, Comedy & Circus**) offers underground productions – but you have to be pretty fluent to keep up. There's plenty of high-quality theatre in English in Paris (*see p344* **When in Paris, act English**), and for all-singing theatre fun in English don't discount some of the amateur theatre groups. The International Players (01.34.62.02.19) usually put on two short-run productions a year in St-Germain-en-Laye and play to packed houses. Still on the Brit theme, a surprise hit of 2002 was *Les Pythons* at the Palais des Glaces, a bundle of Monty Python sketches re-hashed by an all-French cast. A whole new generation of geekster anoraks doing silly walks and complaining about dead parrots? Tuff tights.

National theatres

Comédie Française
Salle Richelieu *pl Colette, 1st (01.44.58.15.15/ www.comedie-francaise.fr). M° Palais Royal.* **Box office** 11am-6pm daily. **Tickets** €11-€30; €10 under-27s (1hr before play). **Credit** AmEx, MC, V. **Map** p406 H5. **Théâtre du Vieux-Colombier** *21 rue du Vieux-Colombier, 6th (01.44.39.87.00/ www.comedie-francaise.fr). M° St-Sulpice.* **Box office** 1-6pm Mon, Sun; 11am-7pm Tue-Sat. **Tickets** €26; €19 over-60s; €13 under-27s. **Credit** MC, V. **Map** p405 G7. **Studio Théâtre** *Galerie du*

Arts & Entertainment

When in Paris, act English

It can be difficult to find new or controversial drama in Paris. Theatre-goers are, in general, served a diet of tried-and-tested 'classics'. Nothing wrong with that, of course, but it's no surprise that groups like **Dear Conjunction**, **Glasshouse** and **On Stage** have sprung up to bring rarely performed plays to new audiences. What might be more surprising (though the names could be a give-away) is that they operate mainly in English. Helen Later, co-founder of Glasshouse, explains: 'We just want to do theatre that we get really excited about and that we think other people will get really excited about – and that wasn't being done over here.' This is a woman who clearly didn't catch the recent musical version of the life of De Gaulle.

Glasshouse (01.40.36.55.83) is run by two women. In the past three years, they have staged Atkins' *Vita & Virginia*, McAvera's *Picasso's Women* and the European première (in English) of Quebec author Normand Chaurette's *The Queens*. Glasshouse doesn't rely on stock-in-trade; most of their plays are chosen because they have never been seen by a Paris audience. In 2003 the company is having a bash at *Little Women*, apparently in a 'pantomime version'.

Bridging the lingo gap, Anglo-Franco-American company **Dear Conjunction** (01.42.41.69.65) has brought a range of French theatre to Anglophone audiences. In 2002, they created the first-ever English version of Francis Weber's *The Dinner Game* (*Le Dîner des Cons*, pictured). Alternating the commercial pieces with more controversial work, the group has tackled the subject of the Holocaust, introduced French audiences to Berkoff's *Brighton Beach Scumbags* (their level of gratitude for that one can only be guessed at) and featured the work of new authors such as Helen Edmonson. For a more mainstream mix of modern and contemporary, Nick Calderbank's **On Stage Theatre Company** (06.81.39.12.21), based in the tiny Théâtre de Nesle (8 rue de Nesle, 6th/01.46.34.61.04; Mº Odéon), stages plays by Pinter, Mamet, Albee and Ayckbourn in English. *Marry Me!*, an original play penned by Calderbank, which tells the tale of what happens when an English teacher in Paris falls in love with a French girl, clearly struck a chord with audiences, and this year sees the sequel, *For Better or For Worse*.

The newest addition to the scene is the mighty **One World** (01.48.28.00.46/www.oneworld actors.com), a mob of cultural missionaries who not only lay before their salivating public a weekly platter of English-language belters (8.15pm, Monday nights, Théâtre Espace Cardin, 1 av Gabriel, 8th; Mº Concorde) but also arrange 'holistic' personal development courses, body-awareness programmes and on-stage language training.

Always on shoestring budgets and often with no stable base to work from, non-French theatre companies are constantly fighting to get by – but that doesn't affect the amount of good product and talent that their efforts bring to Paris. They enliven the scene and they fill a niche. Perhaps that's the answer – don't subsidise the arts and only the worth-seeing will survive. So, if you ever find yourself all Racined out or you're tired of the old Anouilh, let them entertain you.

Arts & Entertainment

Carrousel (99 rue de Rivoli), 1st (01.44.58.98.58/
www.comedie-francaise.fr). M° Palais Royal. **Box
office** 5.30pm on day (Mon, Wed-Sun). **Tickets**
€13; €7.50 under-27s. **Credit** MC, V. **Map** p405 H5.
The Comédie Française is an obligatory pit-stop for
theatre aficionados, and if marble and pillars are
your thing you won't be disappointed by the historic
Salle Richelieu. The stern faces of the high priests
of French theatrical tradition watch as you go in, and
you can even see the chair in which Molière died during a performance of *Le Malade imaginaire* (incidentally, back on the programme for 2003). The
celebrated *pensionnaires*, who sound like old fogeys
but are in fact an acting troupe, are performing the
usual repertoire classics but look out for a new production of Racine's Old Testament tragedy *Esther*,
and Alexander Ostrovsky's most famous play, *La
Fôret*. The Left Bank Théâtre du Vieux-Colombier,
founded in 1913 by Jacques Copeau to 'combat the
cowardice of commercial theatre', came under the
wing of the Comédie Française in 1986, but nonetheless it has tried to preserve the *auteur* mentality. One
of the highlights this year is sure to be Gao
Xingjian's *Quatre Quatuors pour un week-end*
(*Weekend Quartet*) directed by the Nobel prize-
winning author himself. The latest addition to the
family is the much smaller Studio Théâtre in the
Carrousel du Louvre, which offers a range of classic
and contemporary plays and readings, and hosts
early evening short plays (6.30pm) and salons.
Wheelchair access (call ahead).

Odéon, Théâtre de L'Europe
Temporary address (until autumn 2004):
Aux Ateliers Berthier, 32 bd Berthier, 17th
*(01.44.41.36.36/www.theatre-odeon.fr). M° Porte de
Clichy.* **Box office** 11am-6.30pm Mon-Sat; *telephone*
11am-7pm Mon-Sat (Sun if play on). **Tickets** €13-
€26. **Credit** MC, V. **Map** p401 E1.
One of the more adventurous venues in terms of
repertoire, this beautiful neo-classical theatre is currently undergoing an exhaustive overhaul – but the
show must go on, and for the occasion an ex-ware-
house on boulevard Berthier has been converted into
a 500-seat theatre. One of today's top French directors, Patrice Chéreau, will be taking Racine's *Phèdre*
in hand this season, and there's also a chance to see
Gorky's rarely-staged *Les Barbares*. *Wheelchair
access (call ahead).*

Théâtre National de Chaillot
Palais de Chaillot, 1 pl du Trocadéro, 16th
(01.53.65.30.00/www.theatre-chaillot.fr).
M° Trocadéro. **Box office** 11am-7pm Mon-Fri; 1pm-
5pm Sun; *telephone* 11am-7pm Mon-Sat. **Tickets**
€18-€30; €15.50-€25 concessions; €9.50-€17.50
under-26s. **Credit** MC, V. **Map** p404 B5.
Popular, accessible plays (classic and modern),
dance and musical theatre are programmed for
Chaillot's mammoth 2,800-seat, 1930s theatre, while
more experimental fare can be found in its smaller
theatre space. 2003 looks set to be a winning season,
thanks to two collaborations between director

Deborah Warner and actress Fiona Shaw – *Medea*
and an adaptation of Jeanette Winterson's *The
Power Book*. *Wheelchair access (call ahead).*

Théâtre National de la Colline
*15 rue Malte-Brun, 20th (01.44.62.52.52/
www.colline.fr). M° Gambetta.* **Box office** 11am-6pm
Mon-Tue; 11am-7pm Wed-Fri; 1pm-7pm Sat; 2-5pm
Sun if play on; *telephone* Mon-Sat only. **Tickets**
€24.50; €20 over-60s; €12 under-30s; €17 Tue.
Credit MC, V. **Map** p403 Q5.
This is the place to come for contemporary drama.
Productions to look forward to in 2003 include
Eugene O'Neill's *Dynamo*, as well as several intrigu-
ing and topical recent plays such as the future-
philosophical *Anthropozoo* and *Algérie 54-62*, Jean
Magnan's poetic portrait of the one-time French
colony. *Wheelchair access (call ahead).*

Right Bank

Théâtre de la Ville/Les Abbesses
*2 pl du Châtelet, 4th (01.42.74.22.77/
www.theatredelaville-paris.com). M° Châtelet.*
Box office 11am-7pm Mon; 11am-8pm Tue-Sat;
telephone 11am-7pm Mon-Sat. **Tickets** €15-€22;
half-price on day under-27s. **Credit** MC, V.
Map p406 J6.
The Théâtre de la Ville mixes dance productions
with cutting edge contemporary theatre, varying
from first-rate to well, controversial. Highlights this
year include *Mangeront-ils?* by Victor Hugo, and
a brief visit from Jan Lauwer's Needcompany. At
Les Abbesses (31 rue des Abbesses, 18th), its
Montmartre spin-off, don't miss two Dan Jemmet
gems: his version of Middleton's *The Changeling*
(rebaptised *Dog Face*) and *Shake*, in which five
actors and a ventriloquist's dummy take on the
bard's *Twelfth Night*.

Bouffes du Nord
*37bis bd de la Chapelle, 10th (01.46.07.34.50/
www.bouffesdunord.com). M° La Chapelle.* **Box
office** 11am-6pm Mon-Sat. **Tickets** €8-€24.50.
Credit MC, V. **Map** p406 K2.
True theatre worshippers cannot come to Paris without paying tribute to legendary director Peter Brook,
whose experimental company the CICT is based
at this famously unrenovated venue. Stéphane
Lissner's co-direction has added classical and opera
to the ever-innovative programme, and although
Brook's *Hamlet* this year will be in French, it's still
worth the effort to see a master at work.

Théâtre de la Bastille
*76 rue de la Roquette, 11th (01.43.57.42.14/
www.theatre-bastille.com). M° Bastille/Voltaire.*
Box office 10am-6pm Mon-Fri; 2-6pm Sat, Sun.
Tickets €19; €12.50 under-26s, over-60s. **Credit**
AmEx, MC, V. **Map** p407 N6.
Imbued with the young, fun ambience of the surrounding Bastille area, this is the place where those
in search of something a bit different can explore
experimental theatre, music and dance (full marks

for daring, though quality can be hit or miss). *Wheelchair access (lower theatre only).*

Cartoucherie de Vincennes

Route du Champ de Manoeuvre, bois de Vincennes, 12th. M° Château de Vincennes, then shuttle bus or bus 112. Each theatre operates independently. **Théâtre du Soleil** *(01.43.74.24.08/ www.theatre-du-soleil.fr).* **Théâtre de l'Epée de Bois** *(01.48.08.39.74).* **Théâtre de la Tempête** *(01.43.28.36.36/www.la-tempete.fr).* **Théâtre de l'Aquarium** *(01.43.74.99.61/ www.theatredelaquarium.com).* **Théâtre du Chaudron** *(01.43.28.97.04).*

Deep in the Bois de Vincennes, near the Parc Floral, this batch of ex-army munitions warehouses now shelters five independent theatres. Ariane Mnouchkine's famed Théâtre du Soleil draws an arty crowd; the Théâtre de l'Epée de Bois and the Théâtre du Chaudron are often overlooked despite their excellent, if smaller-scale programming. The Théâtre de la Tempête always features a top-class programme. This season Jez Butterworth's *Mojo* is rubbing shoulders with Molière and Ibsen amongst other past and present classics. At the Théâtre de l'Aquarium, Chekhov's *Uncle Vanya* (in French) looks set to be the season highlight, in a production by the theatre's own director, Julia Brochen.

Théâtre de l'Athénée-Louis Jouvet

7 rue Boudreau, sq de l'Opéra-Louis-Jouvet, 9th (01.53.05.19.19/www.athenee-theatre.com). M° Opéra. **Box office** 1-7pm Mon-Sat. **Tickets** €6-€26. **Credit** MC, V. **Map** p401 G4.

A long-established theatre celebrated for its illustrious past, which does French and foreign classics in a beautiful Italianate main *salle*, while the studio upstairs caters for smaller contemporary works. Make a date for *Ritter, Dene, Voss* (*Wittgenstein's Nephew*) and *Antoine et Cléopâtre*. *Wheelchair access (call ahead).*

La Bruyère

5 rue La Bruyère, 9th (01.48.74.76.99/ www.ddo.fr/labruyere). M° St-Georges. **Box office** 11am-7pm Mon-Sat. **Tickets** €13-€32. **Credit** MC, V. **Map** p401 H2.

This is where feelgood box-office smashes can meet a French audience – previous long-runners have included *Popcorn* and *Visiting Mr Green*.

Left Bank

Théâtre Lucernaire

53 rue Notre-Dame-des-Champs, 6th (01.45.44.57.34). M° Notre-Dame-des-Champs. **Box office** 2-9pm Mon-Sat. **Tickets** €10-€20. **Credit** AmEx, MC, V. **Map** p405 G9.

This ex-factory turned bustling arts centre is a favourite haunt for the students, housing two 130-seat theatres, a cinema, a café and various exhibitions. The repertoire occasionally features new work from contemporary authors, but usually reverts to reliable commercial successes.

Théâtre de la Huchette

23 rue de la Huchette, 5th (01.43.26.38.99). M° St-Michel. **Box office** 5-9pm Mon-Sat. **Tickets** €16 one play, €25 both plays; €12.50 students under 25, €19 both plays. **Credit** MC, V. **Map** p406 J7.

Home to Nicolas Bataille's original production of Ionesco's *La Cantatrice chauve* for more than 50 years, this tiny venue is often crowded out with students wanting to see their set texts in the flesh. *Wheelchair access.*

Théâtre de la Cité Internationale

21 bd Jourdan, 14th (01.43.13.50.50/ www.theatredelacite.ciup.fr). RER Cité Universitaire. **Box office** 2-7pm Mon-Sat. **Tickets** €18; €12.50 over-60s; €9.50 students, under-26s, Mon. **Credit** MC, V.

This well-equipped modern theatre favours experimental theatre and dance from around the world, with a decided emphasis on the intellectual. The cheap rate for all on Mondays is cool, as is the friendly student snack bar. This season, Samuel Beckett's *La dernière Bande* (*Krapp's Last Tape*) is sure to be a crowd-puller.

Guichet-Montparnasse

15 rue du Maine, 14th (01.43.27.88.61). M° Montparnasse-Bienvenüe. **Box office** *telephone* 2-7pm Mon-Sat. **Tickets** €17; €12 students, over-60s, Mon. **No credit cards. Map** p405 F9.

In a minute 50-seat auditorium, this lively fringe venue features everything from the grand classics to new writing, showcasing small companies and new directing and acting talent. Several short productions are shown each night, offering a perfect taster of French theatre.

Good booking

For details of programmes see the **Time Out Paris** section of *Pariscope*. There are also plenty of useful websites, such as **www.passion-theatre.org**, with up-to-date info (in French). Tickets can be bought direct from theatres, or at agencies (*see* chapter **Directory**). Specialists include **Agence Chèque Théâtre** (33 rue Le Peletier, 9th/01.42.46.72.40; open 10am-7pm Mon-Sat) and **Kiosque Théâtre** (opposite 15 pl de la Madeleine, 9th, and in front of Gare Montparnasse, 15th; open noon-8pm Tue-Sun) which sells same-day tickets at half-price. Tickets are also available at **Fnac** stores and at the **Virgin Megastore** on the Champs-Elysées; and on websites, notably **www.theatreonline.com**, where subscribers also benefit from half price tickets and free invites. Many private theatres offer 50% reductions on previews and students can also get same-day deals.

Arts & Entertainment

Trips Out
of Town

Trips Out of Town

Tired of the big-city buzz? Aching for the meadowsweet and hollyhocks, snow-drops and forget-me-nots? Hit the road, Jacques, and get outta town.

Stately Châteaux

Versailles

Versailles – and Voltaire's description of it as 'a masterpiece of bad taste and magnificence' supports the comparison – is very much the Essex Girl of châteaux. It was the result of Louis XIV's decision to transform a simple hunting lodge, in a fit of envy after seeing Vaux-le-Vicomte, the château of his finance minister, Nicolas Fouquet (*see p353*). Painter Charles Le Brun transformed the château, while André Le Nôtre set about the gardens, turning marshland into terraces, pools and paths.

In 1678 Jules Hardouin-Mansart took over as principal architect and dedicated the last 30 years of his life to adding the two main wings, the Cour des Ministres and Chapelle Royale. In 1682 Louis moved in and thereafter rarely set foot in Paris. The palace could house the entire court and its entourage – some 20,000 people in all. The nobility had no choice but to leave their provincial châteaux or Paris mansions and spend years in service at court, at great personal expense. In the 1770s, Louis XV chose his favourite architect Jacques Ange Gabriel to add the sumptuous Opéra Royal, sometimes used for concerts by the Centre de Musique Baroque (01.39.20.78.10). With the fall of the monarchy in 1792, most of the furniture was dispersed and after the 1830 Revolution Louis-Philippe saved the château from demolition.

Versailles is way over the top, yet you can't help but be impressed at the architectural purity of the vast classical facades, the 73m-long Hall of Mirrors, the King's Bedroom, where Louis held his celebrated *levées* in the presence of the court; the Apollo Salon, and the Queen's Bedroom, where queens gave birth in full view of courtiers, there to confirm the sex of the child and to ensure no substitutes were slipped in.

The **gardens** stretch over 815 hectares comprising formal *parterres*, ponds, wooded parkland and sheep-filled pastures, as well as the recently restored Potager du Roi, the king's vegetable garden. Statues of the seasons, elements and continents, many commissioned by Colbert in 1674, are scattered throughout,

and the spectacular series of fountains is served by an ingenious hydraulic system, pumping water from a 20km radius.

The main palace being a little unhomely, in 1687 Louis XIV had Hardouin-Mansart build the **Grand Trianon** in the north of the park, a pretty, but still hardly cosy palace of stone and pink marble, where Louis stayed with Mme de Maintenon. Napoléon Bonaparte also stayed there with his second Empress, Marie-Louise.

The **Petit Trianon** is a perfect example of Neo-Classicism, and was built for Louis XV's mistress Mme de Pompadour, although she died before its completion. Marie-Antoinette, however, played out her milkmaid fantasies at the nearby **Hameau de la Reine**, a mock farm arranged around a lake.

Each Sunday afternoon from April to October (plus Sat July, Aug, Sept) the great period fountains in the gardens are set in action, to music, in the Grandes Eaux Musicales, while seven times a year the extravagant Grandes Fêtes de Nuit capture something of the splendour of the celebrations of the Sun King.

Château de Versailles

78000 Versailles (01.30.83.76.20/ www.chateauversailles.com). **Open** *Apr-Sept* 9am-6pm Tue-Sun; *Nov-Mar* 9am-5pm Tue-Sun. **Admission** €7.60; €5.30 after 3.30pm; free under-18s. Jump the queues: Gate D takes you direct to the Grands Appartements and Appartements Privés: call ahead to reserve (01.30.83.77.43). All inclusive 'Passport' tickets are available for €20 (€14.50 Nov-Mar) from RER stations.

Grand Trianon/Petit Trianon

Open *Apr-Oct* noon-6pm daily; *Nov-Mar* noon-5pm daily. **Admission** €5; free under-18s.

Gardens

Grand Parc **Open** dawn-dusk daily. **Admission** free (Grandes Eaux €5; free under 10s). **Petit Parc Open** *Apr-Oct* 9am-6pm. **Admission** €3; free in winter, when most statues are protected by a tarpaulin. **Potager du Roi** (01.39.24.62.62). **Open** *Apr-Oct* 10am-6pm daily (guided tours only Sat, Sun). **Admission** €4.50; guided tours €6.50.

Where to eat

Le Chapeau Gris (5 rue Hoche/01.39.50.10.81) has a good €26 *menu*. Les Trois Marches (Hôtel Trianon Palace, 1 bd Reine, 01.39.50.13.21) is for a splurge.

Getting there

By car
20km from Paris by A13 or D10.

By RER
RER C Versailles-Rive Gauche.

Chantilly

In the middle of a lake, cream-coloured
Chantilly with its domes and turrets looks like
the archetypal French Renaissance château. In
fact, the fanciful main wing is a largely 19th-
century reconstruction, as much of the original
was destroyed during the Revolution. Restored
by the eccentric Duc de Condé, Chantilly is
notable for the Duc's remarkable art collection,
including three paintings by Raphael, Filippino
Lippi's *Esther and Assuarus* and the *Très
Riches Heures du Duc de Berry* medieval book
of hours (facsimile only usually on show).

Today, Le Nôtre's park is rather dilapidated,

but still contains an extensive canal system, an
artificial 'hamlet' predating that of Versailles
and a 19th-century 'English garden'.

The town of Chantilly is also an equestrian
centre, with many racing stables and a major
racetrack (*see chapter* **Sport**). The 18th-century
Great Stables once housed 240 horses, 500 dogs
and almost 100 palfreys and hunting birds, and
today contain the Musée Vivant du Cheval (*see
chapter* **Children**).

South of the château spreads the **Forêt de
Chantilly**. A pleasant walk of around 7km
circles the four small Etangs de Commelles
lakes and passes the 'Château de la Reine
Blanche', a mill converted in the 1820s into a
pseudo-medieval hunting lodge.

Senlis, 9km east of Chantilly, has been
bypassed since its glory days as the town where
Hugues Capet was elected king in 987. Its
historical centre contains several quaint, half-
timbered streets, some handsome mansions, a
Gothic cathedral and the remains of the Gallo-
Roman amphitheatre and city wall.

Trips Out of Town

Château de Chantilly

Musée Condé, 60500 Chantilly (03.44.62.62.62/ www.chateaudechantilly.com). **Open** *Mar-Oct* 10am-6pm Mon, Wed-Sun; *July-Aug* 10am-6pm daily; *Nov-Feb* 10.30am-12.45pm, 2-5pm Mon, Wed, Sun; 10.30am-5pm Sat and public holidays. **Admission** €7; €6 12-17s; €2.80 4-12s; *park only* €3; €2 4-11s; free under 4s. **Credit** MC, V.

Where to eat & stay

La Carrousel du Musée Vivant du Cheval (03.44.57.19.77) has an excellent €10 set meal.

Getting there

By car

41km from Paris by A1, exit Chantilly or N16 direct.

By train

SNCF Chantilly from Gare du Nord (30 mins), then 30-min walk or short taxi ride.

Compiègne & Pierrefonds

North of Paris on either side of the substantial hunting forest of Compiègne stand two very different châteaux, each with an Imperial stamp.

On the edge of the old town of Compiègne, the **Château de Compiègne** is a monument to the French royal family's obsession with hunting. The château was given its present form by Jacques Ange Gabriel, who created a classical pleasure palace for Louis XV. Most of the interior was ruthlessly remodelled by Napoléon for his second wife Marie-Louise and is stuffed with Imperial eagles, bees, palms and busts of the great self-publicist.

Napoléon III also left his mark at Compiègne, where he and Empress Eugénie hosted lavish house parties every autumn. His most popular legacy was the highly efficient heating system which still works today and makes a visit to the château bearable even in the depths of winter. In one wing, the **Musée de la Voiture** is devoted to early transport, from Napoléon I's state coach to an 1899 Renault and the 1899 Jamais Contente electric car.

In the forest 4km from Compiègne by D973 is the **Clairière de l'Armistice**, a memorial to the site where the Germans surrendered to Maréchal Foch, ending World War I, on 11 November 1918 (it is also where in 1940 the French surrendered to the Germans). The clearing features the spot where the combatants' two railway lines met, a statue of Foch and a reconstruction of his railway-carriage office.

At the opposite edge of the forest, a sudden dip in the land gives a view of strange turrets. At first sight, the neo-medieval **Château de Pierrefonds** is so clearly a fake it's almost grotesque. Yet it deserves a detour. Napoléon had bought the ruins of a 14th-century castle, and in 1857, Napoléon III asked Viollet-le-Duc to restore one tower as a hunting lodge. But the project grew and the fervent medievalist ended up reconstructing the whole edifice, in part using the remaining foundations, in part borrowing elements from other castles, or simply inventing his own fantastical brand of 'medieval revival'. Grand baronial halls harbour elaborately carved Gothic chimneypieces. The magnificent Salle des Preuses has a fireplace sculpted with nine ladies (one a likeness of Empress Eugénie). Another fantasist, Michael Jackson, once expressed interest in buying Pierrefonds but it was not for sale.

Château de Compiègne

5 pl du Général-de-Gaulle, 60200 Compiègne (03.44.38.47.00) **Open** 10am-5pm Mon, Wed-Sun. **Admission** €5.50 château and museum; €4 château only; €3 18-25s; free under 18s. **No credit cards.**

Château de Pierrefonds

60350 Pierrefonds (03.44.42.72.72). **Open** *1 Sept-14 May* 9.30am-12.30pm, 2-6pmMon-Sat; 9.30am-6pm Sun; *15 May-1 Sept* 9.30am-6pm daily. Closed public holidays. **Admission** €5.50; €3.50 17-25s; free under 17s. **No credit cards.**

Clairière de l'Armistice

route de Soissons (03.44.85.14.18). **Open** (museum) *Apr-Oct* 9am-12.15pm, 2-6pm daily; *Oct-Mar* 9-11.45am, 2-5pm Mon, Wed-Sun. **Admission** €2; €1 7-14s; free under 7s. **No credit cards.**

Where to eat & stay

In Compiègne, **Rive Gauche** (13 cours Guynemer/ 03.44.40.29.99) does inventive cuisine (*menus* €30-€35). The **Hôtel Les Beaux-Arts** (33 cours Guynemer/03.44.92.26.26, double €72) is a cosy hotel.

Getting there

By car

Compiègne is 80km from Paris by A1. To reach Pierrefonds from Compiègne take the N31 towards Soissons, then follow signs.

By train

From Gare du Nord.

Fontainebleau

Fontainebleau's congenial atmosphere today is the product of two big-time local establishments – first, the sumptuous royal palace which dominates the town centre and second, INSEAD business school (the 'European Harvard') on the

'Joe le public's gonna love it,' thought Louis.

edge of the forest, which adds a distinctly cosmopolitan touch. In 1528 François 1er brought in Italian artists and craftsmen – including Rosso and Primaticcio – to help architect Gilles le Breton transform what was a neglected royal lodge into the finest Italian Mannerist palace in France. This style is noted for its grotesqueries, contorted figures and crazy fireplaces, still visible in the Ballroom and Long Gallery. Much of the palace's charm comes from its very disunity. Henri IV added a real tennis court, Louis XIII built the celebrated double-horseshoe entrance staircase, Louis XIV and XV added further classical trimmings, and Napoléon redecorated in Empire style before leaving France for exile from the front courtyard, known ever since as the Cour des Adieux.

With its ravines, rocky outcrops and mix of forest and sandy heath, the Forest of Fontainebleau (*see also p355,* **Barbizon**), where François 1er liked to hunt, is the wildest slice of nature near to Paris and now popular with Parisian weekenders for walking, cycling, riding and rock climbing. The GR1 is a popular hiking trail signposted straight from the station at Bois-le-Roi, 30 minutes from Gare de Lyon. Don't miss the fabulously atmospheric Café de la Gare, doubling as a museum of advertising (chiefly for booze and cigarettes).

Château de Fontainebleau

77300 Fontainebleau (01.60.71.50.70). **Open** *Oct-May* 9.30am-5pm Mon, Wed-Sun; *June-Sept,* 9.30am-6pm Mon, Wed-Sun. Closed 1 Jan, 1 May, 25 Dec. **Admission** €5; €4 18-25s; free under 18s. **Credit** V.

Where to eat & stay

Thanks to the MBA set, Fontainebleau is stuffed with lively eateries — everything from Cuban to Libyan, Tex-Mex and *très français*. **Le Caveau des Ducs** (24 rue Ferrare/01.64.22.05.55, *menus* €18-€33) does good, simple French food in a vaulted 17th-century cellar. Pedestrianised rue Montebello is lined with restaurants. **Jungle House** at no.5 (01.64.22.15.66) serves excellent, authentic African and Afro-Indian dishes. Lunches by chef William Lesaulnier at **Au Délice Impérial** (1 rue Grande/ 01.64.22.20.70, €7-€18) are inventive and stylish. Some rooms at the **Hôtel de Londres** (1 pl Géneral de Gaulle/01.64.22.20.21/ www.hoteldelondres.com) have balconies overlooking the château.

Getting there

By car
60km from Paris by A6, then N7.

By train
Gare de Lyon to Fontainebleau-Avon (35 mins), then bus marked Château.

Vaux-Le-Vicomte

This sumptuous country château shows the risks of outdoing your master. Nicolas Fouquet (1615-1680), protégé of the ultra-powerful Cardinal Mazarin, bought the site in 1641. In 1653 he was named *Surintendant des Finances*, and set about building himself an abode to match his position. He assembled three of

Fontainebleau: scene of Napoléon's longest *adieu*.

France's most talented men for the job: painter Charles Lebrun, architect Louis Le Vau and landscape gardener André Le Nôtre.

In 1661 Fouquet made the fatal mistake of inviting the Sun King to a huge inaugural soirée. Guests were entertained by jewel-encrusted elephants and spectacular Chinese fireworks. Lully wrote music for the occasion, and Molière a comedy. The King, who was 23 and ruling for the first time, was outraged by his minister's show of grandeur. Shortly afterwards Fouquet was arrested, and his embezzlement of state funds exposed in a show trial. His personal effects were taken by the crown and the court sentenced him to exile; Louis XIV commuted the sentence to solitary confinement. Fouquet is sometimes mooted as the infamous 'Man in the Iron Mask', privy to damaging state secrets and locked away for life.

As you round the moat, the relatively sober frontage gives way to the stunningly Baroque rear aspect. The most telling symbol of the fallen magnate is the unfinished, domed ceiling in the elliptical Grand Salon, where Lebrun only had time to paint the cloudy sky and one solitary eagle. Fouquet's *grand projet* did live on in one way, however: it inspired Louis XIV to build Versailles – using Fouquet's architect and workmen to do it.

The spectacular fountains spout from 3-6pm on the second and last Saturday of the month, Apr-Oct. The biggest draw, though, are the candlelit evenings, which transform the château into a palatial jack-o-lantern.

Vaux-Le-Vicomte

77950 Maincy (01.64.14.41.90). **Open** *29 Mar-11 Nov* 10am-6pm daily (château closed 1-2pm Mon-Fri). **Admission** €10; €8 6-16s, students, over-60s; free under-6s. **Candlelit visits** *3 May-11 Oct* 8pm-midnight Sat. **Admission** €13; €11.50 6-16s, students, over-60s; free under-6s. **Credit** MC, V.

Getting there

By car
60km from Paris by A6 to Fontainebleau exit; follow signs to Melun, then N36 and D215.

By coach
Paris-Vision (01.42.60.30.01) runs half-day and day trips from Paris.

Châteaux of the Loire

Seat of power of the Valois kings, who preferred to rule from Amboise and Blois than Paris (more game, fewer strikes), the Loire valley became the wellspring of the French Renaissance. François 1er was the main instigator, bringing architects, artists and craftsmen from Italy to build his

palaces, and musicians and poets to keep him amused. Royal courtiers followed suit with their own elaborate residences.

First up is the enormous **Château de Chambord** (02.54.50.40.00; 02.54.50.40.28 for events), François 1er's masterpiece, probably designed in part by Leonardo da Vinci. Built in the local white stone, it's a magnificent but also rather playful place, from the ingenious double staircase – it was possible to go up or down without crossing someone coming the other way – to the wealth of decoration and the 400 draughty rooms. The curious flock to the huge, forested park in late September/early October to hear the annual stag rut at night. Nice.

In total contrast of scale is the charming **Château de Beauregard** (02.54.70.40.05) nearby at Cellettes. Its main treasure is the unusual panelled portrait gallery, depicting in naïve style 327 famous men and women. The park contains a modern colour-themed garden designed by Gilles Clément.

From here the road to Amboise follows an attractive riverside stretch, under the looming turrets of the **Château de Chaumont** (02.54.51.26.26) past roadside wine cellars dug into the tufa cliffs (with numerous opportunities to indulge). The grounds of Chaumont are used for an innovative garden festival (02.54.20.99.22; June-Oct) when international garden designers, artists and architects create gardens on a theme.

The lively town of Amboise, not far from Tours, grew up at a strategic crossing point on the Loire. The **Château Royal d'Amboise** (02.47.57.00.98) was built within the walls of a medieval stronghold, although today only a (still considerable) fraction of Louis XI's and Charles VIII's complex remains. The château's interiors span several styles from vaulted Gothic to Empire. The exquisite Gothic chapel has a richly carved portal, vaulted interior and, supposedly, the tomb of Leonardo da Vinci.

It's a short walk up the hill, past several cave dwellings, to reach **Clos Lucé** (02.47.57.62.88), the Renaissance manor where Leonardo lived at the invitation of François 1er for the three years before his death in 1519. There's an enduring myth of a (so far undiscovered) tunnel linking it to the château. The museum focuses on Leonardo as Renaissance Man: artist, engineer and inventor, with models of his inventions (sadly not functional). An oddity just outside town is the 18th century pagoda of Chanteloup, built when *chinoiserie* was all the rage.

South of Amboise, the **Château de Chenonceau** (02.47.23.90.07) occupies a unique site spanning the river Cher. Henri II gave the château to his beautiful mistress Diane de Poitiers, until she was forced to give it up to a jealous Catherine de Médicis, who commissioned

Philibert Delorme to add the three-storey gallery that extends across the river. Chenonceau is packed with tourists in summer, but its watery views, original ceilings, fireplaces, tapestries and paintings (including *Diane de Poitiers* by Primaticcio) are well worth seeing.

Rising magically from an island in the river Indre west of Tours, **Azay-le-Rideau** (02.47.45.42.04) is the quintessential fairytale castle, especially during the nocturnal garden visits in summer. Built 1518-27 by the king's treasurer, it combines the turrets of a medieval fortress with the true Italian Renaissance style.

Villandry (02.47.50.02.09) is famous for its spectacular Renaissance knot gardens. Most unusual is the colourful and appetisingly aromatic *jardin potager*, where the patterns created with artichokes, cabbages and pumpkins compose the ultimate kitchen garden.

Where to stay

At the heart of the park in Chambord, the **Hôtel Restaurant du Grand St-Michel** (pl St-Louis/02.54.20.31.31, double €49-€64) faces the château. Amboise is a pleasant, centrally placed stopping-off point. In town, try the **Lion d'Or** (17 quai Charles Guinot/02.47.57.00.23, double €48-€70) or the grander **Le Choiseul** (36 quai Charles Guinot/02.47.30.45.45/www.le-choiseul.com, double €70-€260), both of which have restaurants. For a taste of château life, try the **Château de Pray** (02.47.57.23.67/www.praycastel.online.fr, double €89-€160) at Chargé, 3km outside town. There are more hotels and restaurants in Tours.

Getting there

By car
By far the best way to explore the region. Take the A10 to Blois (182km), or leave at Mer for Chambord. An attractive route follows the Loire from Blois to Amboise and Tours, along the D761.

By train
Local trains from Gare d'Austerlitz run to Amboise (2hrs) and Tours (2$\frac{1}{2}$ hours); the TGV from Gare Montparnasse to Tours takes 70 mins.

Artists' Haunts

Auvers-sur-Oise

Auvers-sur-Oise has become synonymous with Van Gogh, who rented a room at the **Auberge Ravoux** on 20 May 1890 (*see p357*, **Auvers and out**). A well-prepared video and the tiny attic room where he lodged for 3.5 francs a day give an evocative sense of the artist's stay.

Van Gogh was not the only painter to be

attracted by Auvers. The **Atelier de Daubigny** was built by the successful Barbizon school artist in 1861 and decorated with murals by Daubigny, his son and daughter and his friends Corot and Daumier. There is also a museum dedicated to the artist.

Auvers retains a surprising degree of rustic charm. Illustrated panels around town let you compare paintings to their locations today, such as the town hall and medieval church. Cézanne also stayed here for 18 months in 1872-74, not far from the house of Doctor Gachet, doctor, art collector and amateur painter, who was himself painted by both Cézanne and Van Gogh.

The 17th-century **Château d'Auvers** offers an audiovisual display about the Impressionists, while the **Musée de l'Absinthe** is devoted to their favourite drink, long-since banned but recently revived in muted form.

Atelier de Daubigny
61 rue Daubigny (01.34.48.03.03). **Open** *Easter-1 Nov* 2-6.30pm Thur-Sun. **Admission** €4.50; free under-12s.

Auberge Ravoux
pl de la Mairie (01.30.36.60.60). **Open** 10am-6pm Tue-Sun, mid-Mar to mid-Nov. **Admission** €5; free under-18s.

Château d'Auvers
rue de Léry (01.34.48.48.50). **Open** 10.30am-6pm Tue-Fri; 10.30am-6.30pm Sat, Sun. **Admission** €10; €6 6-25s; free under-6s. **Credit** AmEx, MC, V.

Musée de l'Absinthe
44 rue Callé (01.30.36.83.26). **Open** *mid-June to mid-Sept* 11am-6pm Wed-Sun; *mid-Sept to mid-June* 11am-6pm Sat, Sun and public holidays. **Admission** €4.50; €3.80 students; free under 15s.

Musée Daubigny
Manoir des Colombières, rue de la Sansonne (01.30.36.80.20). **Open** 2-6pm Wed-Sun. **Admission** €3.50; €2 students; free under-12s.

Where to eat

Auberge Ravoux (pl de la Mairie/01.30.36.60.60, *menu* €25-€32) does good, simple food (no rooms).

Getting there

By car
35km north of Paris by A15 exit 7, then N184 exit Méry-sur-Oise for Auvers.

By train
Gare du Nord or Gare St-Lazare direction Pontoise, change at Persan-Beaumont or Creil, or RER A Cergy-Préfecture, then bus (marked for Butry).

By coach
Paris-Vision (01.42.60.30.01) runs tours from Paris.

By chimney, it's **Chambord**. *See p353.*

Monet at Giverny

In 1883, Claude Monet moved his large personal entourage (one mistress, eight children) to Giverny, a rural retreat west of Paris. He died in 1926, having immortalised both his flower garden and the water lilies beneath his Japanese bridge. Though beseiged by busloads of tourists and annexed to an enormous gift shop, the natural charm of the pink-brick house and the rare glory of the gardens, especially the water garden with its weeping willows and punt, survive intact. Arrive at 10am to avoid the crowds. Up the road, the **Musée Américain Giverny,** devoted to the American artists who followed the Impressionists, also has a wide-ranging programme of temporary exhibitions.

Fondation Claude Monet
27620 Giverny (02.32.51.28.21). **Open** *Apr-Oct* 10am-6pm Tue-Sun. **Admission** €5.50; €1.50 house only, €4 gardens; €3 students, over 60s; free under-7s. **Credit** (shop) AmEx, MC, V. *Wheelchair access.*

Musée Américain Giverny
99 rue Claude Monet (02.32.51.94.65). **Open** *Apr-Nov* 10am-6pm Tue-Sun (Thur-Sun Nov). **Admission** €5; €4 students, over 60s; €3 12-18s; free under 12s. **Credit** AmEx, MC, V. *Wheelchair access.*

Where to stay
Chambre d'hôte Le Bon Maréchal (1 rue du Colombier/02.32.51.39.70, double €46-€62) is a comfy bed and breakfast.

Getting there

By car
80km west of Paris by A13 to Bonnières and D201.

By train
Gare St-Lazare to Vernon (45 mins); then taxi or bus.

Millet at Barbizon

A rural hamlet straggling along a lane into the forest of Fontainebleau, Barbizon was an ideal sanctuary for painters Corot, Théodore Rousseau, Daubigny and Millet, who from the 1830s on showed a new concern with peasant life and landscape, paving the way for Impressionism. The main sights are all on the Grande Rue and, although now very chic (the village has a friendly local Porsche dealer), some of the atmosphere remains. Plaques point out who lived where.

Other artists soon followed. Many stayed at the **Auberge du Père Ganne**, painting on the walls and furniture of the long-suffering (or perhaps far-sighted) Ganne, in lieu of rent. After years of dilapidation, the inn today is a rather over-sanitised museum, where the artists' charming sketches and paintings can still be seen *in situ*. The **Office du Tourisme** is in the former house of Théodore Rousseau. Prints and drawings by Millet and others can be seen in the **Maison-atelier Jean-François Millet**, where Millet moved in 1849 to escape cholera in Paris. Millet and Rousseau are both buried at nearby Chailly-en-Bière.

In the woods not far from Barbizon, but light-years away artistically, is an extraordinary 20th-century monster. The **Cyclop** (open Sat, Sun, May-Oct, visits every 45 mins from 11am), is a huge clanking confection of mirrors and iron cogs, the work of the Swiss artist Jean Tinguely, who began it in 1969, in a rare collaboration with Nikki de Saint Phalle and others. It was finished after his death and opened to the public in 1994. Kids love it, but the under-10s are not allowed into the monster's innards.

Musée de l'Auberge du Père Ganne
92 Grande Rue (01.60.66.22.27). **Open** 10am-12.30pm, 2-5.30pm Mon, Wed-Sun. **Admission** €4.50; €2.30 12-25s, students; free under 12s. **Credit** MC, V.

Maison-atelier Jean-François Millet
27 Grande Rue (01.60.66.21.55). **Open** 9.30am-12.30pm, 2-5.30pm Mon, Wed-Sun. **Admission** free.

Trips Out of Town

Auvers and out

Everybody was worried about Van Gogh. When Vince lost his best mate, Paul Gauguin (who'd decided that Tahiti was the only place far enough away from barmy, razor-wielding Vince), VVG's brother, Theo, decided to install the Goghster in the Auberge Ravoux, Auvers. This would be close enough to Paris for Theo to keep an eye on Vincent, but also far enough away to give One-eared V the serenity he craved. Auvers was also home to Doctor Gachet, who Theo believed would not only be able to take medical care of Vincent, but would also be something of a soul mate to his brother, as they were both gingers. What seemed a winning plan on paper fell apart in the Auvers wheat fields: after a few calm and extremely productive months, on 27 July 1890, Vincent took himself out into the countryside, where he had recently painted his gloomy masterpiece *Cornfields with Flight of Birds*, and shot himself in the chest. It took Van Gogh two days to die of his self-inflicted injuries. Six months later, Theo was dead, too. Both repose in the Auvers cemetery.

Debate has raged for more than a century over what exactly loosened Vincent's grasp on sanity. The seductively romantic view, that he was driven mad by the sheer intensity of his own artistic vision, has more recently been challenged by the suggestion that he was pushed over the edge by a massive consumption of alcohol, particularly the tipple of choice for all self-respecting tortured artists in turn-of-the-century France, absinthe.

Some historians even claim that he was such a committed soak that he drank his own paint thinner. A kinder view suggests that he was in fact epileptic, and the medicines that he took to calm his seizures gradually poisoned him. For all the theories, the truth is obscure; Van Gogh, who attempted to become a clergyman in his twenties, took a rather moralistic view on drinking, and was unlikely to have admitted to his full intake. However, his letters do express regret at his abuse of alcohol and tobacco. If he couldn't even handle a couple pints of thinner and a few fags, the question begs to be asked: was Vincent Van Gogh merely the art world's greatest lightweight?

The Auberge Ravoux – scene of Vincent's last innings.

Office du Tourisme

55 Grande Rue, 77630 Barbizon (01.60.66.41.87).
Open 10am-12.30pm, 2-5pm Mon, Wed-Sun.

Where to eat

La Bohème (35 Grande Rue/01.60.66.48.65) has a
good-value €27 *menu*. **The Auberge Manoir du St
Hérem** (29 Grande Rue/01.60.66.42.42) has €22-€30
menus and double rooms for €46-€57.

Getting there

By car
57km from Paris by A6, then N7 and D64.

By train
Gare de Lyon to Melun, then taxi (12km).

Beside the Seaside

Dieppe & Varengeville

Le Touquet may call itself 'Paris-Plage', but
Dieppe (an important port since the middle
ages) is in fact the nearest seaside town to
Paris, ideal for a dip and a fish meal. The
charming area around the harbour along quai
Henri IV is prettier than ever now that ferries
from Britain go to a new container port and the
old railway terminal has been demolished. At
one end the Tour des Crabes is the last remnant
of fortified wall. The maze of old streets
between the harbour and the newer quarters
fronting the promenade contains numerous
brick sailors' houses and the fine Gothic
churches of St-Jacques, once a starting point for
pilgrims to Compostella, and St-Rémi.
The beach is shingle except at low tide, but
the seafront offers plenty of activities for kids,
with mini-golf, pony rides, a children's beach
and lawns filled with kite flyers (the
international kite festival is in September). The
beach is overlooked from the clifftop by the
gloomy **Château de Dieppe** (02.35.84.19.76),
now the municipal museum, which has a
collection of alabasters and paintings by
Pissarro and Braque.
Leave town by the D75 for a twisting,
breathtakingly scenic drive along the cliffs all
the way to Etretat. This is the so-called
Alabaster Coast, its many moods immortalised
by Monet. Just outside Dieppe is Varengeville-
sur-Mer, celebrated for its clifftop churchyard
where Cubist painter Georges Braque (who also
designed the stained-glass in the church) and
composer Albert Roussel are buried. Here too is
the **Parc du Bois des Moustiers**
(02.35.85.10.02), planted by Lutyens and

Gertrude Jekyll, famed for its rhododendrons
and views; the unusual 16th-century **Manoir
d'Ango** (02.35.85.14.80) has a fascinating
galleried courtyard and unusual dovecote.
8km south of Dieppe is the decorative early
17th-century **Château de Miromesnil**
(02.35.85.02.80) where the writer Guy de
Maupassant was born in 1850. The building has
a fascinating historic kitchen garden. Nearby,
dominating a little hill at Arques la Bataille, are
the ruins of a 10th-century castle.

Where to eat

In Dieppe, head towards the harbour, along quai
Henri IV. Here you'll find countless little fish
restaurants offering endless variations on mussels,
skate and sole, plus the delicious local cider.

Getting there

By car
Dieppe is 170km north-west from Paris. Take the
A13 to Rouen and then the A151.

By train
From Gare St-Lazare (2½ hours).

Tourist information

Office du Tourisme de Dieppe
Pont Jehan Ango, 76204 Dieppe (02.32.14.40.60).
Open *July, Aug* 9am-1pm, 2-8pm Mon-Sat, 10am-
1pm, 3-6pm Sun; *Sept-June* 9am-1pm, 2-7pm Mon-Sat.

Baie de Somme

Although the Somme remains forever
synonymous with the horror and carnage of
theWorld War I, the area is, by nature, quite
beautiful. The estuary region boasts a rich
variety of wildlife and has a gentle, ever-
changing light that has attracted artists and
writers. There are many picturesque villages
and a wild, beautiful coastline that varies from
long beaches and rolling dunes to pebbles and
cliffs. The bay has an astounding 2,000 hectares
of nature reserves and France's first maritime
reserve was created here in 1968, with some 200
bird species, notably winter migrants, recorded
at the **Parc Naturel du Marquenterre**.
A popular tourist steam train, the **Chemin de
Fer de la Baie de Somme** (03.22.26.96.96)
tours the bay in summer between Le Crotoy,
Noyelles, St-Valéry-sur-Somme and Cayeux.
The panorama around the bay at the small
fishing port of **Le Crotoy** inspired Jules Verne
to write *20,000 Leagues Under the Sea* and
drew Colette, Toulouse-Lautrec and Arthur
Rimbaud. It boasts the only south-facing sandy
beach in northern France and as such is a busy

Trips Out of Town

resort, with hotels, guest houses and campsites, plus restaurants serving excellent fresh fish; there are opportunities for watersports (03.22.27.04.39), hunting, fishing and tennis.

Across the bay, **St-Valery-sur-Somme**'s well-preserved medieval upper town has a commanding position, and plenty of history. It was from here that William the Conqueror set sail in 1066, and Joan of Arc passed through as a prisoner in 1430. The upper town contains a Gothic church and château, part of the former abbey. A small chapel overlooking the bay houses the tomb of St-Valéry. In the lower town, the **Ecomusée Picarvie** recreates aspects of traditional village life. Strolling from the port to the bay, you can see some impressive late-19th-century villas. Consult tide times: at low tide the sea goes out nearly 14km; it comes back again in less than five hours.

At the tip of the bay, **Le Hourdel** consists of a few fishermen's houses and a dock where the fishing boats sell their daily catch. Here is your best chance to see seals from the largest colony in France. Lying below sea-level, **Cayeux**, three miles south, was a chic resort in the early 1900s. It has beautiful sand beaches at low tide, often almost completely deserted. The seafront is captivatingly dressed with wooden cabins and planks in a 2km promenade.

Ecomusée Picarvie

5 quai du Romeral, St-Valéry-sur-Somme (03.22.26.94.90). **Open** *Apr-Sept* 2-6pm. **Admission** €4; €2.50 4-14s.

Parc Naturel du Marquenterre

(03.22.25.03.26). **Open** *Apr-Sept* 9.30am-5pm daily; *Oct-Nov* 10am-4pm daily. **Admission** €9.50; €7 6-18s, students, disabled.

Where to eat & stay

In St-Valery-sur-Somme, **Le Nicol's** (15 rue de la Ferté/03.22.26.82.96, *menu* €13-€29) does excellent fare. The **Relais Guillaume de Normandie** (46 quai Romeral/03.22.60.82.36, double €49-€50) is a welcoming hotel.

Getting there

By car

Le Crotoy is 190km from Paris by N1 or A15 and N184, then A16 motorway (exit Abbeville Nord).

By train

The closest train station is Noyelles-sur-Mer, just after Abbeville, about 2 hours from Gare du Nord.

Getting around

Limited local buses serve villages on the bay. Bikes can be hired at St-Valery-sur-Somme (03.22.26.96.80).

Tourist information

Offices de Tourisme: Le Crotoy

1 rue Carnot, 80550 Le Crotoy (03.22.27.05.25). **Open** *Sept-June* 10am-noon, 2-6pm Mon, Wed-Sun; *July, Aug* 10am-7pm daily.

St-Valery-sur-Somme

2 pl Guillaume le Conquérant, 80230 St-Valery-sur-Somme (03.22.60.93.50). **Open** *May-Sept* daily 9.30am-12.30pm, 2-6pm .

Cathedral Cities

Beauvais

Beauvais is one of the strangest and most impressive of French cathedrals. It has the tallest Gothic vault in the world and a spectacular crown of flying buttresses. The cathedral had a very challenging nativity: first the choir had to be rebuilt – you can still see where an extra column was added between the arches – and then the spire collapsed, while the nave was never built at all. Left of the choir is a curious astrological clock, made in the 1860s by local watchmaker Lucien-Auguste Vérité; around the corner is a 14th-century clock.

Next to the cathedral, a medieval gateway leads into the 16th-century bishop's palace, now the **Musée Départemental de l'Oise** (03.44.11.43.83), which traces the region's illustrious heritage in sculptures rescued from destroyed houses and churches, Nabis paintings and art nouveau furniture, plus the tapestries for which Beauvais was famed. The tapestry industry reached its peak in the 18th century, then stopped when the factory was evacuated to Aubusson in 1939, but it has recently been revived at the **Manufacture Nationale de la Tapisserie** (24 rue Henri Brispot/ 03.44.05.14.28) where you can watch weavers working under natural light (2-4pm Tue-Thur).

Most of Beauvais was well and truly flattened by bombing during World War II, but the centre was rebuilt not unpleasantly in the 1950s in a series of low-rise squares and shopping streets. One other impressive medieval survivor remains, the **Eglise St-Etienne**, a curious mix of Romanesque and Gothic styles, with elaborate gargoyles sticking out in the centre of a traffic island.

Where to eat

Two reliable addresses are restaurant-bar **Le Marignan** (1 rue Malherbe/03.44.48.15.15), and a branch of Alsatian brasserie chain **Taverne du Maître Kanter** (16 rue Pierre Jacoby/03.44.06.32.72).

Sea-faring fo'c's'le really dig **Dieppe**. See p357.

Getting there

By car
75km from Paris by A16 or N1.

By train
From Gare du Nord.

Tourist information

Office du Tourisme
1 rue Beauregard, 60000 Beauvais (03.44.15.30.30).
Open 10am-1pm, 2-6pm Mon; 9.30am-6.30pm Tue-Fri; 10am-6pm Sat; 10am-1.30pm Sun.

Chartres

Chartres cathedral was described by Rodin, with admirable understatement, as the 'French Acropolis'. Viewed from afar, the building, with its mismatched spires, looms mysteriously over the lonely plains of the Beauce. Up close, the sublime stained glass and doorways bristling with sculpture embody a complete medieval world view, with earthly society and civic life reflecting the divine order.

Chartres was a pilgrimage site long before the cathedral was built, ever since the Sacra Camisia (said to be the Virgin Mary's lying-in garment) was donated to the city in 876 by the Carolingian King Charles I. When the church caught fire in 1194, locals had a whip round to raise the necessary funds to reconstruct it, taking St-Denis as the model for the new west

front, 'the royal portal' with its three richly sculpted doorways. The stylised, elongated figure columns above geometric patterns still form part of the door structure.

Inside, another era of sculpture is represented in the lively 16th-century scenes of the life of Christ that surround the choir. Note, too, the circular labyrinth of black and white stones in the floor. Such mazes used to exist in most cathedrals, but most have been destroyed.

The cathedral is, above all, famed for its stained-glass windows depicting Biblical scenes, saints and medieval trades in brilliant 'Chartres blue', punctuated by rich reds. If you want to decipher the medieval messages that lie behind the windows and sculpture alike, take one of the educational, erudite and entertaining tours given in English by Malcolm Miller (02.37.28.15.58/€10, €5 students)

The cathedral may dominate the town from a distance, but once in the town's narrow medieval streets, with their overhanging gables, glimpses of it are only occasional. Wander past the iron-framed market hall, down to the river Eure, crossed by a string of attractive old bridges, past the partly Romanesque Eglise St-André and down the rue des Tanneries, which runs along the bank. There's more fine stained glass in the 13th-century Eglise St-Pierre.

There's a good view from the Jardin de l'Evêché, located at the back of the cathedral and adjoining the **Musée des Beaux-Arts** (29 Cloître Nôtre-Dame/02.37.36.41.39). Housed in the former Bishop's palace, the collection

Trips Out of Town

includes some fine 18th-century French paintings by Boucher and Watteau, as well as some distinctly creepy medieval sculpture.

Chartres' other main tourist attraction is a reminder that the surrounding Beauce region is known as the 'bread basket of France' thanks to its prairie-like expanses of wheat. The **COMPA** (pont de Mainvilliers/02.37.36.11.30) in a converted engine shed near the station gives a lively presentation of the history of agriculture and food (and consequently society) from 50,000BC to today, with the emphasis on the machinery, from vintage tractors and threshing machines to old fridges.

Where to eat & stay

La Vieille Maison (5 rue au Lait/02.37.34.10.67) has good classical cooking (*menu* €26). Facing the cathedral, the **Café Serpente** (2 Cloître Notre Dame/02.37.21.68.81) triples as café, tearoom and restaurant.

Getting there

By car

88km from Paris by A10, then A11.

By train

From Gare Montparnasse.

Tourist information

Office du Tourisme

pl de la Cathédrale, 28000 Chartres (02.37.18.26.26). **Open** *Apr-Sept* 9am-7pm Mon-Sat; 9.30am-5.30pm Sun; *Oct-Mar* 10am-6pm Mon-Sat; 10am-1pm, 2.30-4.30pm Sun.

Lille

Selected as European City of Culture for 2004, Lille is buzzing, with a lively mix of popular and high culture, and the futuristic Eurolille showcase business complex. One of the great wool towns of medieval Flanders, it became part of France in 1667. Lille is a crossroads between the Netherlands, France, Belgium, Germany and Britain. Come for La Braderie on the first weekend in September. Dating back to medieval times, the wonderfully anarchic 'great clear-out' attracts two million visitors annually and sees streets lined with jumble and antiques stalls, while mussel shells pile up outside cafés.

Up a lazy river

Paris is high-density, low-greenery. Stay a week, and you soon realise that Not Much is very hard to do. So why not take a breather? Follow the Seine upstream to where the villages of Chartrettes, Fontaine-le-Port, Héricy, Vulaines and Samois-sur-Seine line up along a truly idyllic stretch of river, offering tranquility, picnic spots and some highly romantic rural retreats. Famous as the home of gipsy jazzman Django Reinhardt, **Samois** welcomes Rom musicians and international jazz aficionados to its annual festival on the willow-shaded Ile du Berceau the last weekend of June (01.64.24.86.45). A stroll along the Seine takes in sumptuous and cranky houseboats, and some stunning riverside residences. River trips (06.73.61.70.51/€60 for two hours upstream to Bois-le-Roi and back) afford views of more so-called '*affolantes*' – fanciful country piles built by eminent Parisians. Styles range from Venetian palatial to Scots-Baronial-meets-Deauville-seafront and art deco suntraps. In July and August, foot passengers can step aboard the *passeur*, a quaint river ferry that plies between Samois and Héricy (crossings on the half-hour from Héricy, on the hour from Samois/€1.25 one

way). From **Héricy**, it's a tranquil stroll 2km upriver to **Vulaines** and the riverside home and garden of the poet Stéphane Mallarmé, now a museum (4 quai Stéphane Mallarmé/01.64.23.73.27). Walkers and cyclists can hop off the train at **Fontaine-le-Port** and cross the river for the delightful 4km forest track along the Seine's left bank to Samois. You can also swim in this tranquil stretch of river. But if you just can't quench that need for speed, try waterskiing from the marina at **Chartrettes** (beginners' sessions on weekends in July/Aug).

Where to eat & stay

The broad, grassy riverbanks of Fontaine-le-Port (after the bridge to the left of the station), Héricy and Vulaines are perfect for picnics and, provided you're *très discrèt*, camping wild. Close to the Musée Mallarmé in Vulaines, two reliable restaurants have (as the French say) their feet in the water: the recently-revamped **L'Anneau de Mallarmé** (8 quai Stéphane Mallarmé/01.64.23.71.61, *menus* €18.50-€38) serves inventive French cooking on a charming riverside terrace, while the **Ile aux Truites** (6 chemin Basse

In Vieux Lille, Renaissance houses have been renovated, including the 1652-53 Vieille Bourse on the Grand' Place at the historic heart of the city. The adjoining place du Théâtre has the 19th-century Nouvelle Bourse, a pretty opera house and the rang de Beauregard, a row of late 17th-century houses. The tourist office is in the Gothic Palais Rihour started in 1454 by Philippe Le Bel, Duc de Bourgogne. Nearby is Lille's finest church, the Gothic **Eglise St-Maurice**.

The **Musée de l'Hospice Comtesse** (32 rue de la Monnaie/03.20.49.50.90) contains displays of Flemish art, furniture and ceramics. Nearby on place de la Treille is Lille's cathedral, begun 150 years ago, after a public subscription and only completed in 1999. Visit the modest brick house where **De Gaulle** was born (9 rue Princesse/03.28.38.12.05).

You'll find one of France's best art collections at the palatial **Musée des Beaux-Arts** (pl de la République, 03.20.06.78.00), including works by Rubens, Jordaens, El Greco, Goya, David, Delacroix and Courbet. The **Musée d'Art Moderne** (1 allée du Musée, Villeneuve d'Ascq, 03.20.19.68.68) houses works by Picasso, Braque, Derain and Modigliani amid a

Chartres... golly Goth. *See p359.*

landscaped sculpture garden. In nearby Roubaix, the new **Musée d'Art et d'Histoire** (23 rue de l'Espérance, Roubaix, 03.20.69.23.60) occupies a stunning art deco swimming pool.

Varenne/01.64.23.71.87) is almost absurdly idyllic, with a simple menu of grills and freshly caught trout (you can catch your own in streams running through the garden). On the opposite bank, at Samois, the surprisingly named **Country Club** (say 'Coontree Clurb') at 11 quai Franklin Roosevelt (01.64.24.60.34, double €60-91) is a fine *belle époque* hotel facing the river. On the D39 in Chartrettes, the **Château de Rouillon** (01.60.69.64.40) offers *chambres d'hôtes* in an 18th-century château, with gardens overlooking the Seine.

Getting there

By car
N6 from Paris to Melun (50km). From here, the D39 follows the right bank of the Seine through Chartrettes, Fontaine-le-Port, Héricy and Vulaines (follow signs for the Seine and quai Mallarmé).

By train
Fontaine-le-Port is 40 mins from Gare de Lyon (trains to Montereau) and may involve a change at Melun.

Where to eat & stay

Bistros line rue de Gand. Try chic **L'Huîtrière** (3 rue des Chats-Bossus/03.20.55.43.41), or brasserie **Alcide** (5 rue des Debris-St-Etienne/03.20.12.06.95). Stop for tea at the pâtisserie **Méert** (27 rue Esquermoise/03.20.57.07.44). **Hôtel de la Treille** (7-9 pl Louise de Bettignies/03.20.55.45.46, double €69-€74) is a pleasant modern hotel; otherwise try the simple **Hôtel de la Paix** (46bis rue de Paris/03.20.54.63.93, double €73-€78).

Getting there

By car
220km from Paris by A1; 104km from Calais.

By train
TGV from Gare du Nord (1hr) or 2hrs by Eurostar from London.

Tourist information

Office du Tourisme
pl Rihour, 59002 Lille (03.20.21.94.21). **Open** 9.30am-6.30pm Mon-Sat; 10am-noon, 2-5pm Sun.

Reims

The **Cathédrale Notre-Dame** is cherished by
French Royalists as the coronation church of
most French monarchs since Clovis in 496. The
present church was begun in the 13th century
and its rich Gothic decoration includes
thousands of figures on the portals; the Kings of
Judea high above the rose window show how
sculptural style developed over the centuries.
Heavy shelling in World War I, together with
erosion, means that many of the carvings have
been replaced by copies; the originals are on
show next door in the Palais de Tau, the
Bishop's palace. One bonus of the destruction is
the superb 20th-century stained glass by Marc
Chagall, behind the high altar. It is possible that
some of the masons from Chartres also worked
on Reims, but the figures generally show more
classical influence in their drapery and
expressivity. Look out for the winsome 'smiling
angel' sculpture and St Joseph on the west front,
and the elaborate foliage on the capitals inside.

A few streets south of the cathedral, the
Musée des Beaux-Arts (8 rue Chanzy/
03.26.47.28.44) has some wonderful portraits of
German princes by Cranach, 26 canvases by
Corot and the famous *Death of Marat* by Jean-
Louis David. From the museum, head down rue
Gambetta to the Basilique St-Rémi, which
honours the saint who baptised Clovis. Built
1007-49, it is a fascinating complement to the
cathedral. Subsequent alterations allow you to
see how the Romanesque style evolved into the
Gothic. Don't miss the ten remarkable 16th-
century tapestries depicting the life of St-Rémi
in the **Musée St-Remi** (53 rue Simon/
03.26.85.23.36) next door.

Reims is also, of course, at the heart of the
Champagne region. Many leading producers of
the famous bubbly are based in the town and
offer cellar visits, an informative insight into the
laborious and skilful process. The **Champagne
Pommery** cellars (03.26.61.62.56/tours mid
Mar-mid Nov daily) occupy Gallo-Roman chalk
mines 30m below ground and are decorated with
art nouveau bas-reliefs by Emile Gallé.
Taittinger (03.26.85.84.33) doesn't look like
much until you descend into the *cave*: on the first
level are the vaulted Gothic cellars of a former
monastery; below are the strangely beautiful,
Gallo-Roman chalk quarries.

Where to eat

Haute-cuisine mecca is Gérard Boyer's **Château des
Crayères** (64 bd Henri-Vanier/03.26.82.80.80) in a
Second Empire château southeast of town. His
former partner, chef Fabrice Maillot runs the lively
bistro **Au Petit Comptoir** (17 rue de Mars/

Medieval **Troyes** will shiver your timbers.

03.26.40.58.58); another Boyer-trained chef is at the
good-value **La Vigneraie** (14 rue de Thillois/
03.26.88.67.27). There are numerous brasseries,
restaurants and cafés on place Drouet d'Erlon.

Getting there

By car
150km by A4.

By train
From Gare de l'Est about 90 mins.

Tourist information

Office du Tourisme
*2 rue Guillaume-de-Machault, 51100 Reims
(03.26.77.45.25).* **Open** *mid-Apr-mid-Oct* 9am-7pm
Mon-Sat; 10am-6pm Sun; *mid-Oct-mid-Apr* 9am-6pm
Mon-Sat; 10am-5pm Sun.

Rouen

The capital of Normandy features a historic
centre with lots of drunken half-timbered
buildings and narrow streets, while the port
areas by the Seine were almost totally
destroyed by bombing during World War II
and were reconstructed in the 1950s. Begun at
the start of the 13th century, the **Cathédrale
Notre-Dame**, depicted at all times of the day

Trips Out of Town

by Monet in a famous series of paintings, spans the Gothic period, from the early north tower to the flamboyant late 15th-century Tour de Beurre. Nearby, the tourist office occupies a fine Renaissance house, while the Gros Horloge gateway, with its famous ornamental clock, spans the busy medieval rue du Gros-Horloge, leading to still more picturesque streets of half-timbered houses.

Two more Gothic churches are worth a visit, the **Abbatiale St-Ouen** and the **Eglise St-Maclou**, as well as the fanciful Flamboyant Gothic Palais de Justice. Near the Abbatiale St-Ouen, the **Musée de l'Education** (185 rue Eau-de-Robec/02.32.82.95.95) presents a lively view of French education since the 15th century over two floors of a half-timbered house. The striking, contemporary **Eglise Ste-Jeanne d'Arc**, adjoining a funky modern market hall on place du Vieux-Marché, is a boat-shaped structure with a swooping wooden roof and stained glass windows recovered from a bombed city church. The **Musée des Beaux Arts** (1 pl Restout/02.35.71.28.40) numbers masterpieces by Gérard David, Velázquez, Perugino and Caravaggio, some wonderful oil studies by Géricault (a native of Rouen) and several Monets and Sisleys.

Where to eat and stay

Best-known gourmet stop is **Restaurant Gill** (9 quai de la Bourse/02.35.71.16.14), home to fish specialist Gilles Tournadre (*menus* €38-€73), who also runs the less formal **37** (37 rue St-Etienne des Tonneliers/02.35.70.56.65). Among the many bistros on place du Vieux-Marché are local favourite **Les Maraîchers** (No.37, 02.35.71.57.73) and La Couronne (No.31, 02.35.71.40.90), which claims to be the oldest inn in France. **Hôtel de la Cathédrale** (12 rue St Romain/02.35.71.57.95/www.hotel-de-la-cathedrale.com, double €53-€61) and **Hôtel du Vieux-Carré** (34 rue Ganterie/02.35.71.67.70, double €51-€55) are two attractive, central hotels.

Getting there

By car
137km west of Paris by A13.

By train
From Gare St-Lazare. Check times: fast trains take about an hour; slow ones about $2^{1}/_{2}$ hours.

Tourist information

Office du Tourisme
25 pl de la Cathédrale, 76000 Rouen (02.32.08.32.40). **Open** *May-Sept* 9am-7pm Mon-Sat; 9.30am-12.30pm, 2.30-6.30pm Sun; *Oct-Apr* 9am-6.30pm Mon-Sat;10am-1pm Sun.

Troyes

Troyes is fast-expanding, and none too prettily at that, but its remarkably preserved medieval core remains delightful. Stroll along rue Champeaux and don't miss the ruelle des Chats, an atmospheric narrow lane which leads up to the **Eglise Ste-Madeleine**, the city's oldest church. Nearby, the **Basilique St-Urbain** was built in 1262-86 on the orders of Pope Urban IV, a native of Troyes, and represents an early apogee of Gothic architecture.

Heading down rue Champeaux, pass through café-lined place du Maréchal-Foch, with the handsome 17th-century Hôtel de Ville, and cross a canal into the oldest part of the city around the **Cathédrale St-Pierre St-Paul**. Part of the impressive facade is by Martin Chambiges, who also worked on the cathedrals at Sens and Beauvais. The triforium of the choir was one of the first in France to be built with windows instead of blind arcading.

Nearby, the **Musée d'Art Moderne** (pl St-Pierre/03.25.76.26.80) is a must for lovers of early 20th-century art, and for André Derain fans in particular. The **Maison de l'Outil** (7 rue de la Trinité/ 03.25.73.28.26) has a fascinating array of craftsmen's tools. Next to the cathedral in the Abbaye St-Loup, the **Musée des Beaux-Arts et d'Archéologie** (4 rue Chrétien de Troyes/03.25.76.21.68) has some fine Gallo-Roman bronzes and a fantastic treasure of arms and jewellery from a fifth-century Merovingian tomb.

Troyes' equally famous factory outlets draw fashion cognoscenti for top clothing (including Cacharel, Armani, Levis and Calvin Klein) and crockery/kitchenware at knock-down prices. From the city centre, follow the unmissable hoardings to the McArthur Glen complex.

Where to eat

At **Le Clos Juillet** (22 bd du 14 Juillet/ 03.25.73.31.32) chef Philippe Colin specialises in modernised regional dishes.

Getting there

By car
150km southeast of Paris by A6 and A5.

By train
From Gare de l'Est (75 mins).

Tourist information

Office du Tourisme
16 bd Carnot, 10000 Troyes (03.25.82.62.70). **Open** 9am-12.30pm; 2-6.30pm Mon-Sat.

Trips Out of Town

FARES YOU CAN GET HOLD OF

PARIS

From

£37

EURO-
APEX
RETURN

NO NEED TO BOOK MONTHS AHEAD.

Book 7 days in advance and pay just £37 return. Book within 7 days before travel and the most you'll pay is £55 return.

CHOOSE FROM UP TO 5 DAILY SERVICES.

08705 143219 GoByCoach.com eur❍lines

Fares shown are from Victoria Coach Station, London and are valid until 31/03/2004 (excluding the following travel dates within this period: 1/7-31/8 and 15/12- 3/1). A £2 booking fee per person applies to all bookings. Conditions apply.

EUROPE'S EXPRESS COACH NETWORK

GOLDEN AIR

LUXURY VAN SERVICE

ONLY €17

PARIS

per person

Airport Transfert

We commit ourselves to make your trips pleasant moments

any service you need, all our drivers speak English.

■ Versailles ■ Giverny
■ Loire Castles

■ City Tour ■ Normandy
■ Bruges

www.goldenair.net
Phone : 33 (0)1 47 37 06 56

Directory

Directory

Getting Around

By air

Roissy-Charles-de-Gaulle airport

Most international flights arrive at Roissy-Charles-de-Gaulle airport, 30km north-east of Paris. Its two main terminals are some way apart, so it's important to check which is the right one for your flight if you are flying out. 24-hr information service in English: 01.48.62.22.80/ www.adp.fr (under 'flight schedules'). The **RER B** is the quickest and most reliable way to central Paris (about 35 minutes to Gare du Nord; 45 minutes to Châtelet-Les Halles, €7.60 single). A new station gives direct access from Terminal 2 (including Air France flights); from Terminal 1 you take the free shuttle bus. RER trains run every 15 minutes, 5.24am-11.56pm daily. SNCF information: 01.53.90.20.20. **Air France buses** (€10) leave every 15 minutes, 6am-10.30pm daily, from both terminals, and stop at Porte Maillot and pl Charles-de-Gaulle (35-50 min trip). Air France buses also run to Gare Montparnasse and Gare de Lyon (€11.50) every 30 minutes (45-60 minute trip), 7am-9.30pm daily. There is also a bus between Roissy and Orly (€15.50) every 20-30 minutes, 6am-11pm daily. Information: 08.92.35.08.20/ www.cars.airfrance.fr. The RATP **Roissybus** (€8.08) runs every 15 minutes, 5.45am-11pm daily, between the airport and the corner of rue Scribe/rue Auber, near pl de l'Opéra (at least 45 minutes); tickets are sold on the bus. Information: 08.36.68.77.14. **Paris Airports Service** is a door-to-door minibus service between the airports and hotels, running 24hrs daily. It works on a 'the more passengers the less you pay' system. Roissy prices

from €23 for one person to €11.25 each for eight people sharing; Orly €19 for one to €6.37 each for eight sharing (reserve ahead on 08.21.80.08.01/ www.parisairportservice.com). **Airport Connection** (01.44.18.36.02/www.airport-connection.com; reservations 7am-8pm) runs a similar service, 4am-8pm, at €24 per person, €13.50-€14.50 each for two or more. **Taxis** are the least reliable and most expensive means of transport. A taxi to central Paris can take 30-60 mins depending on traffic and your point of arrival. Expect to pay €26-€45, plus €1 per piece of luggage. **Km2** (01.45.16.28.56) runs **motorbike taxis** aimed largely at executives. Roissy-Charles de Gaulle to Versailles about €60; Orly to La Défense about €50.

Orly airport

French domestic and several international flights use Orly airport, 18km south of the city. It also has two terminals: Orly-Sud (mainly international flights) and Orly-Ouest (mainly domestic flights). English-speaking information service on 01.49.75.15.15, 6am-midnight daily. **Air France buses** (08.92.35.08.20/www.cars.airfrance.fr; €8) leave both terminals every 20 minutes, 6.30am-10.30pm Mon-Fri, 7am-10.30pm Sat, Sun, and stop at Invalides and Montparnasse (30-45 minutes). The RATP **Orlybus** at Denfert-Rochereau leaves every 15 minutes, 5.35am-11.05pm daily (30-minute trip); tickets (€5.50) are available on the bus. Information: 08.36.68.77.14. The high-speed **Orlyval** shuttle train runs every 7 minutes (6am-8.30pm Mon-Sat; 7am-11pm Sun) to RER B station Antony (Orlyval and RER together cost €8.65); getting to central Paris takes about 35 minutes. Alternatively, catch the courtesy bus to RER C station Pont de Rungis, where you can get the **Orlyrail** to central Paris

(€5.15). Trains run every 15 minutes, 5.45am-11.10pm daily; 50-minute trip. A **taxi** into town takes 20-40 minutes and costs €16-€26, plus €1 per piece of luggage. The minibus and Km2 services listed above also run to and from Orly.

Paris Beauvais airport

Beauvais, 70km from Paris, is served by **Ryan Air** (03.44.11.41.41/www.ryanair.com) flights from Dublin and Glasgow, **Mytravellite** (01.55.69.81.66/ www.mytravellite.com) from Birmingham, and **Goodjet** (03.44.11.41.44/www.goodjet.com) from Norway and Sweden. A bus service (€10) between the airport and Porte Maillot leaves 20 mins after each arrival and 2hrs 45 mins before each departure. tickets can be bought at the arrival lounge or from the Beauvais shop at 1 bd Pershing, 17th. Information: 01.58.05.08.95/ www.aeroportbeauvais.com.

Airline contacts

Aer Lingus 01.55.38.38.55/ www.aerlingus.com.
Air France 08.20.82.08.20/ www.airfrance.fr.
American Airlines 08.10.87.28.72/ www.americanairlines.com.
bmibaby +44 (0)870 264 2229/ www.bmibaby.com.
British Airways 08.25.82.54.00/ www.britishairways.fr.
British Midland 01.41.91.87.04.
Continental 01.42.99.09.09/ www.continental.com.
Easyjet 08.25.08.25.08/ www.easyjet.com.
KLM & NorthWest 08.10.55.65.56/www.klm.com.
United 08.10.72.72.72/ www.united.com.

By car

For travelling between France and the UK by car, options include tunnel **Le Shuttle** (Folkstone-Calais 35mins)

(01.43.18.62.22/08.10.63.03.04/
www.eurotunnel.com); seacat
Hoverspeed (Dover-Calais,
Newhaven-Dieppe) (03.21.46.14.00/
www.hoverspeed.com); ferry
Brittany Ferries (08.25.82.88.28/
www.brittany-ferries.com), **P&O
Stena Line** (08.20.01.00.20/
www.posl.com) and **SeaFrance**
(08.25.04.40.45/www.seafrance.com).

Shared journeys

Allô-Stop *8 rue Rochambeau,
9th (01.53.20.42.42/
www.ecritel.fr/allostop).* **Open**
10am-1pm, 2-6.30pm Mon-Fri;
10am-1pm, 2-5pm Sat. **Credit** MC,
V. Call several days ahead to be put
in touch with drivers. There's a
fee (€4 under 200km; up to €10 over
500km), plus €0.34 per km to the
driver. Routes most travelled:
Cologne, Lyon, Marseille, Nantes,
Rennes, Toulouse.

By coach

International coach services arrive
at the Gare Routière Internationale
Paris-Galliéni at Porte de
Bagnolet, 20th (M° Galliéni).
For reservations (in English) call
Eurolines on 08.36.69.52.52
(€0.34 min), or in the UK 01582-
404511/www.eurolines.fr.

By rail

The **Eurostar** train between
London and Paris takes three
hours. You must check in at least
30 minutes in advance. Passports
must be carried on the Eurostar.
Eurostar trains from London
Waterloo (01233-617575/
www.eurostar.com) arrive at Gare
du Nord (08.92.35.35.39,
€0.34/min; www.sncf.fr), with
easy access to public transport.
Bicycles can be transported as
hand luggage provided they are
dismantled and carried in a bike
bag. You can check them in at
the Eurodispatch depot at
Waterloo (Esprit Parcel Service:
08705-850850) or the Sernam
depot at Gare du Nord
(08.25.84.58.45) up to 24 hours in
advance. A Eurostar ticket must
be shown and the service costs
£20 or €45.75.

Travel agencies

Havas Voyages

*26 av de l'Opéra, 1st
(01.53.29.40.00/
www.havasvoyages.fr). M° Opéra.*
Open 10am-7.30pm Mon-Sat.
Credit AmEx, V. General travel
agent with more than 15 branches
in Paris.

Nouvelles Frontières

*13 av de l'Opéra, 1st
(08.25.00.08.25/www.nouvelles-
frontieres.fr). M° Pyramides.* **Open**
9am-8pm Mon-Sat. **Credit** MC, V.
Agent with 16 branches in Paris.

USIT *6 rue de Vaugirard, 6th
(01.42.34.56.90/08.25.08.25.25/
www.usitconnections.fr). M° Odéon.*
Open 10am-7pm Mon-Fri; 10am-
6pm Sat. **Credit** MC, V. Coach,
air and train tickets for under-26s
and others.

Maps

Free maps of the Métro, bus and
RER systems are available at
airports and Métro stations.
Other brochures from Métro
stations are *Paris Visite – Le
Guide*, with details of transport
tickets and a small map, and the
Plan de Paris, a fold-out map that
also indicates *Noctambus* night
bus lines. Useful maps sponsored
by Galeries Lafayette and
Printemps can be picked up at
most hotel receptions. A Paris A-Z
(also called *Plan de Paris*) can be
bought from newsagents or
stationers (*papeteries*).

Public transport

The public transport system
(**RATP**) consists of bus routes,
the Métro (underground), the **RER**
suburban express railway (which
interconnects with the Métro
inside Paris) and two suburban
tramways. Paris and its suburbs
are divided into eight travel zones;
zones 1 and 2 cover the city centre.
Information 6am-9pm daily,
08.36.68.77.14/in English
08.36.68.41.14 (€0.34/ min);
www.ratp.fr. **SNCF**, the state
railway system, serves the
French regions and international
(*Grandes Lignes*) and the suburbs
(*Banlieue*). Information:
08.36.35.35.35/www.sncf.com.

Fares & tickets

RATP **tickets** and passes are
valid on the Métro, bus and
RER. Tickets and *carnets* can be
bought at Métro stations, tourist
offices and *tabacs* (tobacconists);
tickets can be bought on the bus.
Keep your ticket in case of spot
checks and to exit from RER
stations. Individual tickets cost
€1.30; it's more economical to buy
a *carnet* of ten tickets for €9.60.
Carte Orange travel passes
(passport photo needed) offer
unlimited travel in the relevant
zones for a week or month. A
Coupon Mensuel (valid from the
first day of the month) zones 1-2
costs €46.05. A weekly *Coupon
Hebdomadaire* (valid Mon-Sun
inclusive) zones 1-2 costs €13.75
and is better value than *Paris
Visite* passes – a three-day pass
for zones 1-3 is €18.25; a five-day
pass is €26.65, with discounts on
some tourist attractions. A one-
day Mobilis pass goes from €5 for
zones 1-2 to €17.95 for zones 1-8
(not including airports).

Métro & RER

The Paris **Métro** is at most times
the quickest and cheapest means
of travelling around the city.
Trains run daily 5.30am-12.40am.
Individual lines are numbered,
with each direction named after
the last stop. Follow the orange
correspondance signs to change
lines. Some interchanges, notably
Châtelet-Les Halles,
Montparnasse-Bienvenüe and
République, involve a long walk.
The exit (*sortie*) is indicated in
blue. The high-speed Line 14,
Météor, links the new Bibliothèque
Nationale to Madeleine and by the
end of 2003 will have reached Gare
St-Lazare. Pickpockets and bag-
snatchers are rife on the Métro –
pay special attention as the doors
are closing. The five **RER** lines
(A, B, C, D and the new Eole) run
5.30am-1am daily across Paris and
into commuter land. Within Paris,
the RER is useful for making
faster journeys – for example,
Châtelet-Les Halles to Charles de
Gaulle-Etoile is only two stops on
the RER compared with eight on
Métro Line 1. The €1.30 Métro
tickets are valid for RER journeys
within zones 1-2.

Directory

Buses

Buses run from 6.30am until
8.30pm, with some routes
continuing until 12.30am, Mon-
Sat, with a more limited service
on selected lines on Sundays and
public holidays. You can use a
Métro ticket, a ticket bought from
the driver (€1.30) or a travel pass.
Tickets should be punched in the
machine next to the driver; passes
should be shown to the driver.
When you want to get off, press
the red request button, and the
arrêt demandé (stop requested)
sign above the driver will light up.

Night buses

After the Métro and normal
buses stop, the only public
transport – apart from taxis –
is the 18 **Noctambus** lines,
between place du Châtelet and
the suburbs (hourly 1.30am-
5.35am Mon-Thur; half-hourly
1am-5.35am Fri, Sat). Routes A
to H, P, T and V serve the Right
Bank and northern suburbs; I to
M, R and S serve the Left Bank
and southern suburbs. Look out
for the owl logo on bus stops.
A ticket costs €2.40 and allows
one change; travel passes are valid.

River transport

Batobus (www.batobus.com).
River buses stop every 15-20 mins
at: Eiffel Tower, Musée d'Orsay,
St Germain-des-Prés (Quai
Malaquais), Notre-Dame, Jardin
des Plantes, Hôtel de Ville, Louvre,
Champs-Elysées (Pont Alexandre
III). They run June-Sept 10am-
9pm; Apr-Oct 10am-7pm. A single
ticket costs €3.50 for one stop, €2
for each stage thereafter; one-day
pass €10, (€5.50 children, €8
students, €6.50 Carte Orange
holders); two-day pass €12.50
(€6.50, €9, €9); season-ticket €42.
Tickets can be bought at Batobus
stops, RATP ticket offices and the
Office de Tourisme.

Trams

Two modern tramlines operate in
the suburbs, running from La
Défense to Issy-Val de Seine and
from Bobigny Pablo Picasso to
St-Denis. They connect with the
Métro and RER and fares are the
same as for buses.

Rail services

Several attractions in the suburbs,
notably Versailles and Disneyland
Paris, are served by the RER. Most
locations farther from the city are
served by the SNCF state railway;
there are few long-distance bus
services. The TGV high-speed
train has revolutionised journey
times and is gradually being
extended to all the main regions.

SNCF Reservations/Tickets

SNCF national reservations
and information: 08.36.35.35.35
(€0.34 per min) www.sncf.com.
Open 7am-10pm daily.

SNCF information (no
reservations) in the Ile de
France: 01.53.90.20.20. **Open** 6am-
10pm daily.

Tickets can be bought at any
SNCF station (not just the one
from which you'll be travelling),
SNCF shops and travel agents. If
you reserve online or by phone,
you can pay and pick up your
tickets from the station or have
them sent to your home. SNCF
automatic machines (*billeterie
automatique*) only work with
French credit/debit cards. Regular
trains have both full-rate White
and cheaper Blue periods. You can
save on TGV fares by purchasing
special cards. Carte 12/25 gives
under-26s a 25%-50% reduction;
without it, under-26s are entitled
to 25% off. Pensioners over 60
benefit from similar terms with a
Carte Senior. Before you board
any train, validate your ticket in
the orange *composteur* machines
located by the platforms, or you
might have to pay a hefty fine.

Paris mainline
stations

Gare d'Austerlitz: Central
and SW France and Spain.
Gare de l'Est: Alsace,
Champagne and southern
Germany.
Gare de Lyon: Burgundy, the
Alps, Provence, Italy.
Gare Montparnasse: West
France, Brittany, Bordeaux, the
Southwest.
Gare du Nord: Northeast France,
Channel ports, Eurostar, Belgium
and the Netherlands.
Gare St-Lazare: Normandy.

Taxis

Paris taxi drivers are not known
for their charm, nor for infallible
knowledge of the Paris street plan
– if there's a route you would
prefer, say so. Taxis can also be
few and far between, especially at
rush hour or early in the morning.
Your best bet is to find a taxi rank
(*station de taxis*) – on major roads,
crossroads and at stations –
marked with a blue sign. The
white light on a taxi's roof
indicates the car is free. A glowing
orange light means the cab is
busy. Taxi charges are based on
area and time: A (7am-7pm Mon-
Sat, €0.60 per km); B (7pm-7am
Mon-Sat, all day Sun; 7am-7pm
Mon-Sat suburbs and airports,
€1.00 per km); C (7pm-7am daily
suburbs and airports, €1.20 per
km). Most journeys in central
Paris average €6-€12; there's a
minimum charge of €5, plus €0.90
for each piece of luggage over 5kg
or bulky objects, and a €0.70
surcharge from mainline stations.
Most drivers will not take more
than three people, although they
should take a couple and two
children. Don't feel obliged to tip,
although rounding up by €0.30-
€0.70 is polite. Taxis are not
allowed to refuse rides because
they are too short and can only
refuse to take you in a particular
direction during their last half-
hour of service – however, in
practice these rules are blatantly
ignored. If you want a receipt, ask
for *un reçu* or *la note* (compulsory
for journeys of €15.25 or more).
Complaints should be made in
writing to the **Bureau de la
réglementation publique de
Paris**, 36 rue des Morillons,
75732 Paris Cedex 15.

Phone cabs

The following accept telephone
bookings 24-hrs. However, you
also pay for the radioed taxi to get
to where you are and there is no
guarantee they will actually turn
up. If you wish to pay by credit
card, mention this when you order.

Credit cards over €15.24:
Alpha 01.45.85.85.85. **Artaxi**
01.42.03.50.50/www.artaxi.fr; **G7**
01.47.39.47.39/01.41.27.66.99 (in
English); **Km2** (motorbikes)
01.45.16.28.56/www.k-m-2.com

(Mon-Fri 7.30am-7pm);
Taxis Bleus (01.49.36.10.10/
www.taxis-bleus.com).

Driving

If you bring your car to France,
you will need to bring the
registration and insurance
documents – an insurance green
card, available from insurance
companies and the AA and RAC
in the UK, is not compulsory but
is advisable. As you come into
Paris you will inevitably meet the
Périphérique, the giant ring road
that carries traffic in, out and
around the city. Intersections,
which lead onto other main roads,
are called *portes* (gates). Driving
on the Périphérique is not as hair-
raising as it might look, even
though it's often congested,
especially during rush hour and at
peak holiday times. The key word
is confidence. If you've come to
Paris by car, it can be a good idea
to park at the edge of the city and
use public transport. A few hotels
have parking spaces which can be
paid for by the hour, day or by
various types of season tickets.
In peak holiday periods, the
organisation Bison Futé hands out
brochures at the motorway *péages*
(toll stations), suggesting less-
crowded routes. French roads are
divided into *Autoroutes*
(motorways, with an 'A' in front
of the number), *Routes Nationales*
(national 'N' roads), *Routes
Départementales* (local, 'D'
roads) and tiny, rural *Routes
Communales* ('C' roads).
Autoroutes are toll roads (*péages*),
although some sections, including
most of the area immediately
around Paris, are free. Motorways
have a speed limit of 130km/h
(80mph), though this is not
adhered to with any degree of zeal
by many French motorists. The
limit on most *Routes Nationales* is
90km/h (56mph); within urban
areas the limit is 50km/h (30mph),
30km/h (20mph) in selected
residential zones.

**Traffic information for the
Ile-de-France:**
01.48.99.33.33/www.bison-
fute.equipement.gouv.fr.

Breakdown services

The AA or RAC do not have
reciprocal arrangements with an
equivalent organisation in France,
so it is advisable to take out
additional breakdown insurance
cover, for example with *Europ
Assistance* (01.41.85.85.41/
www.europ-assistance.co.uk).
If you don't have insurance, you
can use its service (01.41.85.85.85)
but it will charge you the full
cost. Other 24-hour breakdown
services in Paris include
Action Auto Assistance
(01.45.58.49.58); **Adan Dépann
Auto** (01.42.66.67.58).

Driving tips

• At intersections where no
signposts indicate the right of
way, the car coming from the right
has priority. Many roundabouts
now give priority to those on the
roundabout. If this is not indicated
(by road markings or a sign with
the message *Vous n'avez pas la
priorité*), priority is for those
coming from the right.
• Drivers and all passengers
must wear seat belts.
• Children under ten are not
allowed to travel in the front of a
car, except in special babyseats
facing backwards.
• You should not stop on an
open road; pull off to the side.
• When drivers flash their lights
at you, this means that they will
not slow down and are warning
you to keep out of the way.
• Friendly drivers also flash their
lights to warn you when there are
gendarmes lurking in the vicinity.
• Try to carry plenty of change, as
it's quicker – and less stressful –
to make for the exact-money line
on *péages*; but, if you are caught
short, cashiers do give change and
péages accept credit cards.

Parking

There are still a few free on-street
parking areas left in Paris, but
they are often full. If you park
illegally, you risk getting your
car clamped or towed away (*see
below*). It is forbidden to park in
zones marked for deliveries
(*livraisons*) or taxis. Parking
meters have now been replaced by
horodateurs, pay-and-display

machines, which either take coins
or cards (€15 or €30 available
from *tabacs*). Parking is often free
at weekends, after 7pm, and in
August. There are numerous
underground car parks in central
Paris. Most cost €2.30 per hour;
€18.30 for 24 hours; some offer
lower rates after 6pm and many
offer various types of season
ticket. Information:
www.saemes.com

Clamps & car pounds

If you've had your car clamped,
contact the local police station.
There are eight car pounds
(*préfourrières*) in Paris. You'll
have to pay a €91.50 removal fee
plus €4.60 storage charge per day,
and a parking fine of €35 for
parking in a no-parking zone.
Bring your driving licence and
insurance papers. But before you
can pay, you need to find that
treasured vehicle – not a small
task given the labyrinth that
represents the world of
impounded cars in Paris and the
affability of those who run it. Here
goes. Once clamped, your car will
first be sent to the *préfourrière*
closest to where it was snatched.
The six *préfourrières* correspond
– roughly – to the following
districts: **Les Halles** 1st, 2nd,
3rd, 4th (01.40.39.12.20); **Bercy**
5th, 12th, 13th, 14th
(01.53.46.69.20); **Pantin** 10th,
11th, 19th, 20th (01.44.52.52.10);
Balard 6th, 7th, 14th, 15th, 16th
(01.45.58.70.30); **Foch** 8th, 16th,
(01.53.64.11.80); **Poucet** 9th, 17th,
18th (01.53.06.67.68). After a 72-hr
spell in the *préfourrière*, if no-one
comes to claim it your car will be
sent to one of the following two
fourrières (pounds): **Paris Nord
Macdonald** 1st-4th, 8th-10th,
16th-19th (01.40.37.79.20); **Paris
Sud Bonneuil** 5th-7th, 11th-15th,
20th (01.45.13.61.40). But, if your
car is deemed not necessarily
worth retrieving, it will be sent to
one of the following *fourrières*:
Paris Nord La Courneuve
1st-4th, 8th-10th, 16th-19th
(01.48.38.14.81); **Paris Sud
Clichy** 5th-7th, 11th-15th, 20th
(01.47.31.22.15). Information:
www.prefecture-police-
paris.interieur.gouv.fr.

Directory

PARIS

L'OpenTour

UNIQUE

**Get an eyeful
of Paris from
the open top deck.
Complete freedom!**

- 1 or 2 day pass
- Commentary
  in English and French
- 3 routes

*Information:
13, rue Auber - 75009 Paris
01.42.66.56 .56
www.paris-opentour.com*

**More than 40 hop-on
hop-off bus stops !**

CLUB QUARTIER•LATIN

- **Piscine Pontoise:** 33x15m pool.
  Open daily, 4.30pm-11.45pm.
  Sat-Sun 10am-7pm.
- **Fitness Club:** Open 9am-midnight.
  Sat-Sun, 9.30am-7pm.
  Gym, Step, Pump, Body Sculpt,
  Weight lifting, Cardio training.
- **Squash:** 4 courts. Open 9am-midnight.
  Sat-Sun, 9.30am-7pm.
- **Cafeteria**

For more information and detailed rates:
Tel: 01.55.42.77.88. Fax: 01.55.42.77.90

19 rue de Pontoise, 5th
M° Maubert-Mutualité
http://www.clubquartierlatin.com

CLUB
QUARTIER • LATIN

Car hire

To hire a car you must normally be 25 or over and have held a licence for at least a year. Some agencies accept drivers aged 21-24, but a supplement of €20-€22 per day is usual. Take your licence and passport with you.

Hire companies

Ada 01.45.54.63.63/08.25.16.91.69/ www.ada-location.fr.
Avis 08.20.05.05.05/www.avis.com.
Budget 08.25.00.35.64/ www.budget-rentacar.com.
Calandres 04.93.76.03.50. Has a *flotte prestige* of luxury cars from cabriolets to Ferraris (for those who've held a licence for at least five years). **EasyRentacar** www.easyRentacar.com.
Europcar 01.30.43.82.82. **Hertz** 01.39.38.38.38/www.hertz.com.
Rent-a-Car 01.45.22.28.28/ 08.36.69.46.95/www.rentacar.fr.
Valem 01.43.14.79.79/ www.valem.fr.

There are often good weekend offers (Fri evening to Mon morning). Week-long deals are better at the bigger hire companies – with Avis or Budget, for example, it's around €240 a week for a small car with insurance and 1,750km included. The more expensive hire companies allow the return of a car in other French cities and abroad. Bargain companies may have an extremely high charge for damage, so read the small print before signing on the dotted line.

Chauffeur-driven cars

First Limousine
(01.41.40.84.84/www.carey-first.com). **Open** 24 hours daily. **Prices** from €135 sedan airport transfer; €222 for four hours. **Credit** AmEx, DC, MC, V.

International Limousines
(01.41.66.32.00/www.inter-limousines.com). **Open** 24 hours daily. **Prices** from €47.79/hr + €15.25 meal allowance for a chauffeur-driven car (minimum 4 hrs); half-day guided tours from €228.31. **Credit** AmEx, DC, MC, V.

Cycling

Since 1996, the Mairie de Paris has been promoting cycling in the city. There are now almost 200km of

bike lanes and there are even plans for a bicycle 'Périphérique' circling Paris. Mayor Delanoë has continued with predecessor Jean Tiberi's enthusiasm, although his big summer 2002 splash, the 3km of the Right Bank closed for cyclists, rollerbladers and pedestrians beside Paris-Plage, was clearly aimed at leisure rather than commuter cyclists. The Itinéraires Paris-Piétons-Vélos-Rollers – scenic strips of the city that are closed to cars on Sundays and holidays – have been consistently multiplied; the city website (www.paris.fr/Parisweb/ fr/recherch.htm) can provide you with an up-to-date list of them and a downloadable map of cycle lanes. A free *Paris à Vélo* map can also be picked up at any Mairie or from bike shops. Cycle lanes *(pistes cyclables)* run mostly N-S and E-W. N-S routes include rue de Rennes, av d'Italie, bd Sébastopol and av Marceau. E-W routes take in the rue de Rivoli, bd St-Germain, bd St-Jacques and av Daumesnil. Lanes are at the edge of the road or down *contre-allées*. You could be fined (€22) if you don't use them, which may seem a bit rich considering the lanes are often blocked by delivery vans, scooters and pedestrians and the €137.20 fine for obstructing a cycle lane is barely enforced. The Bois de Boulogne and Bois de Vincennes offer paths away from traffic although they are still criss-crossed by roads. Cycling in Paris is no more frightening than in any other big city, but don't let the Parisians' blasé attitute to helmets and lights convince you it's not worth using them. Be confident, make your intentions clear and keep moving are the best words of advice, and beware of scooter-mounted bag-snatchers and (believe it or not) bum-pinchers. If the thought of peddling around alone in a city known for the verve of its drivers fazes you, consider a guided bike or tandem tour *(see p372,* **Guided Tours**).

Cycles & scooters for hire

Note that bike insurance may not cover theft: be sure to check before you sign on the dotted line.

Atelier de la Compagnie *57 bd de Grenelle, 15th (01.45.79.77.24).* **Open** 5.30am-7pm Mon-Fri. Closed 3 weeks in Aug. **Credit** MC, V. A scooter for €30 per day or €130 per week. Deposit of €1,200, plus passport, required.

Maison Roue Libre *1 passage Mondétour, 1st (08.10.44.15.34). M° Châtelet. Plus (Mar-Oct) four RATP cyclobuses at Stalingrad, pl du Châtelet, porte d'Auteuil and parc Floral in the Bois de Vincennes (01.48.15.28.88/www.citefutee.com/ sortir/roue_libre.php).* **Open** 9am-7pm daily. **Credit** MC, V (for weekend hire only). Bike hire costs €3.10 an hour; €17.50 a weekend. Helmets come free. Passport and €150 deposit required.

Paris-Vélo *2 rue du Fer-à-Moulin, 5th (01.43.37.59.22/www.paris-velo-rent-a-bike.fr). M° Censier-Daubenton. Also (15 Apr to 15 Oct) in the Bois de Boulogne (rond-pont du Jardin d'Acclimatation) and the Bois de Vincennes (av Daumesnil, by lac Daumesnil).* **Open** 10am-7pm daily. **Credit** MC, V. Good selection of mountain bikes *(VTT)* and 21-speed models for hire. Five hours costs €12, a weekend €30, a month €116. Passport and €300 deposit required.

Walking

Exploring by foot is the very best way to discover Paris; just remember that to anything on wheels (and this includes cyclists and in-line roller skaters), pedestrians are the lowest form of life. Crossing Paris' multi-lane boulevards can be lethal to the uninitiated, as the 3,000 or so pedestrians who finish up in hospital – or worse – each year learn. Brits, of course, must realise that traffic will be coming in an opposite direction from the one to which they are used. By law, drivers are only fully obliged to stop when there is a red light. Even then, a lot of drivers will take a calculated risk (your personal safety is not likely to be a high factor in that calculation). Where there is a crossing, whether or not it has a flashing amber light or a sign saying *Priorité aux Piétons,* most drivers will ignore pedestrians and keep going. Safety in numbers can help – or use the Métro underpass if there is one.

Guided tours

Boat trips

Bateaux-Mouches *pont de l'Alma, Rive Droite, 8th* (01.42.25.96.10/recorded info 01.40.76.99.99/www.bateaux-mouches.fr). M° Alma-Marceau. **Departs** *summer* every 30 min 10am-8pm; every 20 min 8-11pm daily; *winter* 11am, 2.30pm, 4pm, 6pm and 9pm. **Tickets** €7; €4 4-12s; free under-4s; €50 lunch (€25 under-12s); €85 dinner. **Credit** MC, V. *Wheelchair access.*

Bateaux Parisiens *Tour Eiffel, port de la Bourdonnais, 7th* (01.44.11.33.55/www.bateauxparisiens.com). RER *Pont de l'Alma.* **Departs** *Easter-Oct* every 30 min (except 12.30pm and 5.30pm) 10am-11pm daily; *Nov-Easter* every hr (every half hr at peak times) 10am-10pm daily. **Tickets** €8.50-€9; €4.10 under-12s; €125 dinner. **Credit** AmEx, DC, MC, V. *Wheelchair access.*

Bateaux Vedettes de Paris *port de Suffren, 7th* (01.47.05.71.29/www.vedettesdeparis.com). M° Bir-Hakeim. **Departs** every 30 min *Apr-Oct* 10am-10pm Mon-Fri, 10am-11pm Sat, Sun; *Nov-Mar* 11am-7pm Mon-Fri, 11am-9pm Sat, Sun. **Tickets** €8; €3 under-12s. Also offers a Bacchus cruise and a chocolate cruise. **Credit** AmEx, DC, MC, V.

Bateaux Vedettes du Pont-Neuf *square du Vert Galant, 1st* (01.46.33.98.38/www.pontneuf.net). M° Pont-Neuf. **Departs** *Mar-Oct* approx every 30 min 10.30am-10.30pm daily; *Nov-Feb* approx every 45 min 10.30am-10pm daily. **Tickets** €9; €4.50 under-12s. **No credit cards.**

Canal trips

Canauxrama (01.42.39.15.00/www.canauxrama.com). **Departs** *Canal St-Martin trip:* from Bassin de la Villette, 13 quai de la Loire, 19th, M°Jaurès, 9.45am, 2.45pm daily; from Port de l'Arsenal, opposite 50 bd de la Bastille, 12th, M° Bastille, 9.45am, 2.30pm daily. *Bords de Marne trip:* from Port de l'Arsenal 9am daily (Thur, Sat, Sun in July & Aug). **Tickets** Canal St-Martin (2½hrs) €13; €10 over-60s

and students; €8 6-12s (no reductions Sat, Sun afternoons and holidays). Bords de Marne (day cruise) €33 (children discouraged). **No credit cards.** Cruises on the romantic Canal St-Martin and past the *guinguettes* on the banks of the Marne with commentary (in English if sufficient demand).

Paris Canal (01.42.40.96.97/www.pariscanal.com). Musée d'Orsay (M° Solférino) to Parc de la Villette (M° Porte de Pantin) or reverse. **Departs** *mid-Mar to mid-Nov* Musée d'Orsay 9.30am daily; Parc de la Villette 2.30pm daily; *mid-Nov to mid-Mar* depends on numbers. **Tickets** €16; €12 12-25s, over-60s; €9 4-11s; no reductions Sun, bank holidays. **No credit cards.** Three-hour trip with commentary in French and English. Reservation required.

Coach tours

Cityrama *4 pl des Pyramides, 1st* (01.44.55.61.00/www.cityrama.com). M° Palais Royal. **Departs** *summer* 9.45am, 10.45am, midday, 1.45pm, 3pm, 7.30pm daily; *winter times differ.* **Tickets** €24; free under-12s. **Credit** AmEx, DC, MC, V. *Wheelchair access.*

Les Cars Rouges (01.53.95.39.53/www.lescarsrouges.com). **Departs** 9.30am-7pm every 10-15 min daily. **Tickets** 2-day pass €21; €10 4-12s. **Credit** AmEx, DC. Recorded commentary in English. Hop-on, hop-off at any of nine stops (including Eiffel Tower, Notre-Dame, Louvre, Opéra). *Wheelchair access.*

Paris Vision *214 rue de Rivoli, 1st* (01.42.60.30.01/www.parisvision.fr). M° Tuileries. **Trips** (2hr) 9.30am, 10.30am, 2.30pm, 3.30pm daily. Full day tours also available. **Tickets** €24; free 4-11s. **Credit** AmEx, MC, DC, V.

Cycle tours

Mike's Bike Tours
(01.56.68.10.54/www.mikesbiketoursparis.com). Meet Eiffel Tower, Pilier Sud, Champ de Mars, 7th. M° Bir-Hakeim. **Departs** *Mar, Apr, mid-Aug to Oct* 11am daily; 7pm Tue, Thur, Sun; *May to mid-Aug* 11am, 3.30pm, 7pm daily (no night tour

Sat); *Nov-Feb* by appointment. **Tours** day €22/$19; night €26/$23. **No credit cards but US dollars accepted.** Day and night tours in English hit the major sights. They go rain or shine and provide wet-weather gear.

Paris à vélo, c'est sympa!
37 bd Bourdon, 4th (01.48.87.60.01/www.parisvelosympa.com). M° Bastille. **Departs** *Apr-Oct* Mon, Fri, Sat 10am, 3pm, 8.30pm; Wed 3pm; Sun 6am (May-Sept only) 10am, 3pm, 8.30pm. *Nov-Mar* Sat, Sun 10am, 2pm. **Tickets** (incl bike hire) €30; €26 under-26s; €16 under-12s. **Credit** MC, V. Multilingual guided tours follow a variety of routes and themes, including Paris at dawn. Reservation required. *Handbikes for handicapped riders.*

Tandem services
Parking St-Germain l'Auxerrois, pl du Louvre, 1st (01.42.60.66.55/www.tandem-services.org). M° Palais Royal. **Departs** 24hr daily (with reservation in advance). **Tours** approx €15/hr, or €1 per km. **No credit cards.** This enterprising company has a fleet of two-seaters that double up as taxis and sightseeing transport. Sling your leg over behind one of the knowledgeable drivers and watch Paris whisk past you in a totally different light (they provide most of the leg power).

Walking tours

Guided walks in French are listed weekly in *Pariscope* under 'Promenades'. Walks in English are usually listed in the *Time Out Paris* section in *Pariscope* and the guides below can organise group walks on request. Prices exclude entrance fees for sights.

Paris Contact
Jill Daneels (01.42.51.08.40/www.realfrance.com). **Tickets** €12; €10 students, over-60s; €8 children. 2-hr tours by appointment daily, minimum four people (or €48 solo).

Paris Walking Tours
Oriel and Peter Caine (01.48.09.21.40/www.pariswalkingtours.com). Choice of 2-hr tours daily. **Tickets** €10; €7 students; €5 children.

Resources A-Z

Addresses

Paris *arrondissements* are reflected in the postal code, eg. the 5th *arrondissement* 75005, the 12th 75012. The 16th *arrondissement* is subdivided into two sectors, 75016 and 75116. Some business addresses have a more detailed postcode, followed by a Cedex number which indicates the *arrondissement*. *Bis* or *ter* is the equivalent of 'b' or 'c' after a building number.

Age restrictions

You must be 18 or over to drive, and 18 in order to consume alcohol in a public place. There is no age limit for buying cigarettes. The age of consent for heterosexuals and homosexuals is 15.

Attitude and etiquette

Parisians take manners seriously and are generally more courteous than their reputation may lead you to believe. If someone brushes you accidentally on the Métro they will more often than not say '*pardon*'; you can do likewise, or reply '*C'est pas grave*' (don't worry). In shops

it is normal to greet the assistant with a '*Bonjour madame*' or '*Bonjour monsieur*' when you enter and say '*au revoir*' when you leave. The question of '*vous*' and '*tu*' is a difficult one for English speakers. Strangers, people significantly older than you and professional contacts should be addressed with '*vous*'; friends, relatives, children and dogs as '*tu*'. Among themselves young people often launch straight in with '*tu*'.

Business

The best first stop in Paris for initiating business is the CCIP (*see* **Useful Organisations**, *below*). Banks can refer you to lawyers, accountants and tax consultants. Other US and British banks provide expatriate services.

Conventions & conferences

The world's leading centre for international trade fairs, Paris hosts over 500 exhibitions a year.

CNIT *2 pl de la Défense, BP 321, 92053 Paris La Défense (01.46.92.28.66/www.parisexpo.fr). Mº/RER Grande Arche de La Défense.* Mainly computer fairs.

Palais des Congrès *2 pl de la Porte-Maillot, 17th (01.40.68.22.22/ www.palaisdescongres-paris.com). Mº Porte-Maillot.*

Paris-Expo Porte de Versailles *15th (01.43.95.37.00/ www.parisexpo.fr). Mº Porte de Versailles.* Paris' biggest expo centre, from fashion to pharmaceuticals.

Parc des Expositions de Paris-Nord Villepinte *SEPENV 60004, 95970 Roissy-Charles de Gaulle. (01.48.63.30.30/ www.expoparisnord.com). RER B Parc des Expositions.* Trade fair centre near Roissy airport.

Courier services

Chronopost (*Customer service: 08.25.80.18.01/www.chronopost.com*). **Open** 9am-8pm Mon-Fri; 9am-1pm Sat. **Credit** MC, V. This overnight delivery offshoot of the state-run post office is the most widely used service for parcels of up to 30kg.

DHL *59 av d'Iéna, 16th (08.00.20.25.25). Mº Iéna.* **Open** 9am-7.30pm Mon-Fri; 9am-5pm Sat. **Credit** MC, V. Big name in international courier service.

Europstar (*01.43.44.13.12*). **Open** 8.30am-7.30pm Mon-Fri, deliveries until 9pm. **No credit cards**. A local bike messenger company with later operating hours than most.

Secretarial services

ADECCO International *14 pl de la Défense, 92974 Paris La Défense (01.49.01.94.94/ www.adecco.fr). Mº Grande Arche de La Défense.* **Open** 8.30am-12.30pm, 2-6.30pm Mon-Fri. Large international employment agency specialises in bilingual secretaries and office staff – permanent or temporary.

Translators & interpreters

Certain documents, from birth certificates to loan applications, must be translated by certified legal translators, listed at the CCIP (*see below*) or embassies. For business translations there are dozens of reliable independents.

Climate

Month	Average monthly Temperature:		Average monthly Rainfall:	
	Centigrade	Fahrenheit	mm	inches
January	7.5º	45.5º	56	2.0
February	7.1º	44.8º	42	1.7
March	10.2º	50.4º	36	1.4
April	15.7º	60.3º	40	1.6
May	16.6º	61.9º	56	2.2
June	23.4º	74.1º	52	2.0
July	25.1º	77.2º	58	2.3
August	25.6º	78.1º	60	2.4
September	20.9º	69.6º	53	2.1
October	16.5º	61.7º	48	1.8
November	11.7º	53.1º	48	1.8
December	7.8º	46.0º	48	1.8

Directory

Association des Anciens Elèves de L'Esit *(01.44.05.41.46).* **Open** by phone only 9am-6pm Mon-Fri. A translation and interpreting cooperative whose 1,000 members are graduates of L'Ecole Supérieure d'Interprètes et de Traducteurs.

International Corporate Communication *3 rue des Batignolles, 17th (01.43.87.29.29). M° Place de Clichy.* **Open** 9am-1pm, 2-6pm Mon-Fri. Translators of financial and corporate documents plus simultaneous translation.

Useful organisations

American Chamber of Commerce *104 rue Miromesnil, 8th (01.53.89.11.00/ www.faccparisfrance.com). M° Villiers.*

British Embassy Commercial Library *35 rue du Fbg-St-Honoré, 8th (01.44.51.34.56/ www.amb-grandebretagne.fr). M° Concorde.* **Open** 10am-1pm, 2.30-5pm Mon-Fri, by appointment. Stocks trade directories, and assists British companies that wish to develop or set up in France.

CCIP (Chambre de Commerce et d'Industrie de Paris) *16 rue Châteaubriand, 8th. M° George V. (01.55.65.55.65/ www.ccip.fr).* **Open** 9am-5pm Mon-Fri. This huge organisation provides a variety of services for people doing business in France and is particularly useful for small businesses. Pick up the free booklet *Discovering the Chamber of Commerce* from the head office (above). **Branch:** *Bourse du Commerce, 2 rue de Viarmes, 1st (01.53.40.46.00). M° Louvre-Rivoli or Chatelet.* **Open** 9am-1pm, 2-5.30pm Mon-Fri. Contains a free library and bookshop. **Branch:** *2 rue Adolf Jullien, 1st. M° Louvre-Rivoli or Châtelet.* **Open** 8.30am-12.30pm, 1.30-4.35pm. Support for businesspeople wishing to export their goods and services to France. **Free legal advice line:** 01.55.65.75.75. **Open** 9am-5.30pm Mon-Thur; 9am-noon Fri.

Chambre de Commerce et d'Industrie Franco-Britannique *31, rue Boissy d'Anglas, 8th (01.53.30.81.30/ fax 01.53.30.81.35/ www.francobritishchamber.com). M° Madeleine.* **Open** 2-5pm Mon-Fri. This organisation promotes contacts through conferences and social/cultural events. It publishes

its own trade directory as well as *Cross-Chanel*, a trade magazine.

INSEE (Institut National de la Statistique et des Etudes Economiques) **Salle de consultation:** *195 rue de Bercy, Tour Gamma A, 12th (01.41.17.66.11/www.insee.fr). M° Bercy.* **Open** 9.30am-12:30pm, 2-5pm Mon-Thu, 9.30-12.30pm, 2-4pm Fri. The mother of seemingly every statistic that dissects French economy and society. Visit the reading room or search the website for free stats.

US Commercial Service *US Embassy, 2 av Gabriel, 8th (01.43.12.28.14/fax 01.43.12.21.72/ www.buyusa.gov/france). M° Concorde.* **Open** 9am-6pm Mon-Fri, by appointment. Aids US companies looking to export to France. Advice by fax and e-mail.

Customs

There are no limits on the quantity of goods you can take from one EU country to another for personal use, provided tax has been paid in the country of origin.

Quantities accepted as being for personal use are:

• 800 cigarettes, 400 small cigars, 200 cigars or 1kg loose tobacco.

• 10 litres of spirits (over 22% alcohol), 90 litres of wine (under 22% alcohol) or 110 litres of beer.

For goods from outside the EU:

• 200 cigarettes, 100 small cigars, 50 cigars or 250g loose tobacco.

• 1 litre of spirits (over 22% alcohol) or 2 litres of wine and beer (under 22% alcohol)

• 50g perfume

• 500g coffee

Visitors can carry up to €7,600 in currency (www.finances.gouv.fr).

Tax refunds

Non-EU residents can claim a refund (average 12%) on VAT if they spend over €175 in any one day and if they live outside the EU for more than six months per year. At the shop ask for a *bordereau de vente à l'exportation*, and when you leave France have it stamped by customs. Then send the stamped form back to the shop. *Détaxe* does not cover food, drink, antiques, services or works of art.

Disabled travellers

An excellent English-language guide, *Access in Paris*, by Gordon Couch and Ben Roberts (Quiller Press), is available for £6.95 (including UK postage) from RADAR, Unit 12, City Forum, 250 City Road, London EC1V 8AS (+44 (0)207 250 3222). *J'accède* is a new monthly listings magazine for disabled people in France, available by subscription (€24) from SARL Bernic Editions, 47bis bd Richard Lenoir, 11th (01.48.06.18.46). It also publishes an annual guide to accessible places and runs a good web portal, www.jaccede.com. *Time Out* guides include wheelchair access in listings, but it's always wise to check beforehand. Other places are accessible to wheelchair users but do not have adapted toilets.

APAJH (Association pour Adultes et Jeunes Handicapés) *26 rue du Chemin Vert, 11th (01.48.07.25.88/www.apajh.org). M° Chemin Vert.* **Open** 9.30am-noon, 2pm-5pm Mon-Fri. Advice for disabled people living in France.

Association des paralysés de France *22 rue du Père-Guérain, 13th (01.44.16.83.83). M° Place d'Italie.* **Open** 9am-12.30pm, 1.30-6pm Mon-Fri (closes 5pm Fri). Publishes *Guide 98 Musées, Cinémas* (€3.81) listing cinemas and museums accessible to those with limited mobility, and a guide to restaurants and monuments.

Platforme d'accueil et d'information des personnes handicapées de la Marie de Paris has a Freephone 08.00.03.37.48 which gives advice (in French) to disabled persons living in or visiting Paris. The Office de Tourisme's website **www.parisbienvenue.com** gives information for disabled visitors.

Getting around

Neither the Métro nor buses are wheelchair-accessible, except Métro line 14 (Météor), bus lines 20, PC (Petite Ceinture) and some No 91s. Forward seats on buses are intended for people with poor mobility. RER lines A and B and some SNCF trains are wheelchair-accessible in parts. All Paris taxis are obliged by law to take

Directory

passengers in wheelchairs. The following offer adapted transport for the disabled. You should book 72hrs in advance.

Aihrop (01.41.29.01.29). **Open** 8am-noon, 1.30-6pm Mon-Fri. Closed Aug. Transport to and from the airports.

GiHP 24 av Henri Barbusse, 93000 Bobigny (01.41.83.15.15/ www.gihpidf.asso.fr). **Open** 6.30am-7pm Mon-Fri.

Drugs

French police have the power to stop and search anyone; it's always wise to keep any prescription drugs in their original containers, and, if possible, to carry copies of the original prescriptions. If you're caught in possession of illegal drugs you can expect a prison sentence and/or a fine. **Centre DIDRO** (01.45.42.75.00/www.didro.net) is an excellent source of advice for young people with drug problems. See also **Health**, **Helplines**.

Electricity & gas

Electricity in France runs on 220V. Visitors with British 240V appliances can change the plug or use an adapter (adaptateur). For US 110V appliances, you will need to use a transformer (transformateur) available at the Fnac and Darty chains or in the basement of BHV. Gas and electricity are supplied by the state-owned Electricité de France-Gaz de France. Contact EDF-GDF (01.45.44.64.64/www.edf.fr/ www.gazdefrance.com) about supply, bills, or in case of power failures or gas leaks.

Education

Language

Most of the large multinational language schools such as **Berlitz** (www.berlitz.com) have at least one branch in Paris. If you just want conversation practice **Konversando** (01.47.70.21.64/ www.konversando.fr) specialises in organising language exchanges and conversation groups.

Alliance Française 101 bd Raspail, 6th (01.42.84.90.00/

www.alliancefr.org). Mº St-Placide or Notre Dame des Champs. Non-profit French-language school, with beginners and specialist courses starting every month, plus a médiathèque, film club and lectures.

British Institute 11 rue Constantine, 7th (01.44.11.73.83/ www.bip.lon.ac.uk). Mº Invalides. Linked to the University of London, the 4,000-student Institute offers English courses for Parisians, and French courses (not beginner). Also offers a degree course and MAs.

Ecole Eiffel 3 rue Crocé-Spinelli, 14th. (01.43.20.37.41/ www.ecole-eiffel.fr). Mº Pernety. Intensive classes, business French, and phonetics.

Eurocentres 13 passage Dauphine, 6th (01.40.46.72.00/ www.eurocentres.com). Mº Odéon. Intensive classes with emphasis on communication. Has a médiathèque.

Institut Catholique de Paris 12 rue Cassette, 6th (01.44.39.52.68/www.icp.fr). Mº St-Sulpice. Traditional courses in French language and culture. Students must be 18 or above, but don't have to be Catholic.

Institut Parisien 87 bd de Grenelle, 15th (01.40.56.09.53). Mº La Motte Picquet-Grenelle. Dynamic private school offers courses in language and French civilisation, business French, plus evening courses if there's demand.

La Sorbonne – Cours de Langue et Civilisation 47 rue des Ecoles, 5th (01.40.46.22.11 ext 2664 through 75/www.fle.fr/sorbonne). Mº Cluny-La Sorbonne/RER Luxembourg. Classes for foreigners ride on the name of this eminent institution. Teaching is grammar-based. Courses are open to anyone over 18, and fill up quickly.

Specialised

Many of the prestigious Ecoles Nationales Supérieures (including film schools La Fémis and ENS Louis Lumière) offer summer courses in addition to their full-time degree courses – ask for formation continue.

Adult education courses

Information: (08.75.75.20.00/ www.mairie-paris.fr) or from your local Mairie. A huge range of inexpensive adult education classes is run by the City of Paris, including French as a foreign

language, computer skills and applied arts.

American University of Paris 31 av Bosquet, 7th (01.40.62.07.20/www.aup.edu). RER Pont de l'Alma. An international college awarding four-year American liberal arts degrees (BA/BSc). Contact the Division of Continuing Education (102 rue St-Dominique, 7th/01.40.62.06.14) for evening classes and summer school.

Christie's Education Paris Hôtel Salomon de Rothschild, 11 rue Berryer, 8th (01.42.25.10.90). Mº George V. The international auction house offers a one-year diploma, ten-week intensive courses and specialisations. A four-day course in English explores the 'art of living' at the court of Louis XIV.

CIDD Découverte du Vin 30 rue de la Sablière, 14th (01.45.45.44.20). Mº Pernéty. Wine tasting and appreciation courses (some in English) at all levels.

Cordon Bleu 8 rue Léon-Delhomme, 15th (01.53.68.22.50). Mº Vaugirard. Courses range from three-hour sessions on classical and regional cuisine to a nine-month diploma aimed at those embarking on a culinary career.

Ritz-Escoffier Ecole de Gastronomie Française 38 rue Cambon, 1st (01.43.16.31.43/ www.ritzparis.com). Mº Opéra. Offers everything from afternoon demos in the Ritz kitchens to diplomas, but it doesn't come cheap. Courses are in French with English translation.

Ecole du Louvre Porte Jaugard, Aile de Flore, Palais du Louvre. quai du Louvre, 1st (01.55.35.17.35/ www.ecoledulouvre.fr). Mº Palais Royal-Musée du Louvre. Art history and archaeology courses. Foreign students not wanting to take a degree attend lectures.

INSEAD bd de Constance, 77305 Fontainebleau (01.60.72.40.00/ www.insead.edu). Highly regarded international business school offers a ten-month MBA in English. Not a bad place to name-drop on your CV (only if you've actually been here).

Parsons School of Design 14 rue Letellier, 15th (01.45.77.39.66). Mº La Motte-Picquet-Grenelle. Subsidiary of New York art college offers BFA programme in fine art, fashion, photography, marketing and interior design.

Directory

Spéos – Paris Photographic Institute *7 rue Jules-Vallès, 11th (01.40.09.18.58/www.photography-education.com). M° Charonne.* Full-, part-time and summer programmes. Exchange programmes with four art schools, including the Rhode Island School of Design.

Student life

Cartes de séjour and housing benefit

Take a deep breath before you read this lot. Foreign students wishing to qualify for housing benefit or to work legally during their course in Paris must get a *Carte de Séjour* (*see p387*). You may then (note the 'may') be eligible for the ALS (*Allocation de Logement à Caractère Social*), which is handled by four CAFs (*caisses d'allocations familiales*), by *arrondissement*. The '*calculez votre aide au logement*' feature of their website (www.caf.fr) allows you to see how much you'll receive. www.droitsdesjeunes.gouv.fr gives information on your rights.

Centre de Réception des Etrangers (EU and non-EU students) *Hôtel de Police, 114/116 av du Maine, 14th (01.53.71.51.68/ www.prefecture-police-paris. interieur.gouv.fr). M° Gaîté or Montparnasse.* **Open** 9am-4.30pm Mon-Fri (closes 4pm Fri).

CAFs *19 rue Pot de Fer, 5th (01.55.43.80.20), M° Place Monge; 101 rue Nationale, 13th (01.40.77.58.00), M° Nationale; 18 rue Viala, 15th (01.45.75.62.47), M° Dupleix; 67 av Jean-Jaurès, 19th (01.44.84.74.98), M° Laumière.* **Open** 8.30am-4pm Mon-Fri.

Accommodation

The simplest budget accommodation for medium-to-long stays can be found at the **Cité Universitaire** or *foyers* (student hostels). Another option is a *chambre contre travail* – free board in exchange for childcare, housework or English lessons. Look out for ads at language schools and the American Church. For cheap hotels and youth hostels, *see chapter* **Accommodation**. As students often cannot provide proof of income, a *porte-garant* (guarantor) is required who will guarantee payment of rent and bills.

Cité Universitaire *19 bd Jourdan, 14th (01.44.16.64.46/48/www.ciup.fr). RER Cité Universitaire.* **Open** offices 8.30am-7pm Mon-Fri. Foreign students enrolled on a university course, or interns who are also studying, can apply for a place at this campus of halls of residence (but be forewarned: only about 10% of the students that apply get in). Rooms must be booked for the entire academic year. Rents are around €300-€400/month single, €200-€300 per person double. UK citizens must apply to the Collège Franco-Britannique, and Americans to the Fondation des Etats-Unis.

CROUS (Centre régional des oeuvres universitaires et scolaires) *39 av Georges-Bernanos, 5th (01.40.51.36.00/ www.crous-paris.fr). Service du Logement: (01.40.51.55.55). RER Port-Royal.* **Open** 9am-5pm Mon-Fri. Manages all University of Paris student residences, posts ads for rooms and has a list of hostels. Requests for rooms must be made by 1 April for the next academic year. CROUS also runs cheap canteens (listed on website) and is the clearing house for all *bourses* (grants) issued to foreign students. Call the Service des Bourses on 01.40.51.37.35.

UCRIF (Union des centres de rencontres internationales de France) *office: 27 rue de Turbigo, 2nd (01.40.26.57.64/ www.ucrif.asso.fr). M° Etienne Marcel.* **Open** 9am-6pm Mon-Fri. Operates cheap, short-stay hostels from four help centres:
5th (01.43.29.34.80);
12th (01.44.75.60.06);
13th (01.43.36.00.63);
14th (01.43.13.17.00).

Student & youth discounts

To claim the *tarif étudiant* (around €1.52 off some cinema seats, up to 50% off museums and standby theatre tickets), you must have a French student card or an International Student Identity Card (ISIC), available from CROUS, student travel agents and the Cité Universitaire. ISIC cards are only valid in France if you are under 26. Under-26s can get up to 50% off rail travel on certain trains with the SNCF's Carte 12/25 and the same reduction on the RATP with the 'Imagine R' card.

Working

Foreign students can legally work up to 20hrs per week. Non-EU members studying in Paris must apply for an *autorisation provisoire de travail* from the DDTEFT. CROUS's job service (01.40.51.37.52 through 57) places students in part-time jobs.

DDTEFT (Direction Régionale du Travail, d'Emploi et du Formation Professionelle) *109 rue Montmartre, 75084 Paris Cedex 02 (01.44.76.69.30/ www.travail.gouv.fr).*

Useful organisations

CIDJ (Centre d'information et de documentation jeunesse) *101 quai Branly, 15th (01.44.49.12.00/www.cidj.com). M° Bir-Hakeim/ RER Champ de Mars.* **Open** 10am-6pm Mon, Wed, Fri; 10am-7pm Tue, Thur; 9.30am-1pm Sat. Library gives students advice on courses and careers, while the youth bureau of ANPE (Agence Nationale Pour l'Emploi/www.anpe.fr) helps with job applications.

Edu France *173 bd St-Germain, 6th (01.53.63.35.00/ www.edufrance.com). M° St Germain des Près.* **Open** Mon-Fri 9am-6pm (call as hours vary). **Fees** €200-€500. Government-run organisation promotes the French university system abroad and assists foreign students in France. The website has some useful free information.

Maison des Initiatives Etudiantes (MIE) *50 rue des Tournelles, 3rd (01.53.36.77.31/ www.paris.fr).* Offers Paris-based student associations resources such as meeting rooms, grants and on-line computers. Its future plans include creating a radio station for students (Radio Campus Paris).

Socrates-Erasmus Programme
Britain: *UK Socrates-Erasmus Council, RND Building, The University, Canterbury, Kent CT2 7PD (01227-762712).*
France: *Agence Erasmus, 10 pl de la Bourse, 33080 Bordeaux Cedex (05.56.79.44.00/ www.socrates-france.org).* The Socrates-Erasmus scheme enables EU students with reasonable written and spoken French to spend a year of their degree in the French university system. Applications must be made through the Erasmus

co-ordinator at your home university. Non-EU students should find out from their university whether it has an agreement with the French university system. US students can find out more from MICEFA (26 rue du Fbg-St-Jacques, 14th/01.40.51.76.96/www.micefa.org).

Embassies & consulates

There's a full list of embassies and consulates in the *Pages Jaunes* (or www.pagesjaunes.fr) under '*Ambassades et Consulats*'. Consular services are for citizens of that country (passport matters, etc) while a separate visa service operates for foreign nationals applying for visas.

Australian Embassy *4 rue Jean-Rey, 15th (01.40.59.33.00/ www.austgov.fr). M° Bir-Hakeim.* **Consular services** 9.15am-noon, 2-4.30pm Mon-Fri; **Visas** 10am-12am Mon-Fri.

British Embassy
35 rue du Fbg-St-Honoré, 8th (01.44.51.31.00/www.amb-grandebretagne.fr). M° Concorde. **Consular services** *18bis rue d'Anjou, 8th.* **Open** 9.30am-12pm, 2.30-5pm Mon, Wed-Fri; 9.30am-4.30pm Tue. **Visas** *16 rue d'Anjou, 8th (01.44.51.33.01/ 01.44.51.33.03).* **Open** 9am-noon Mon-Fri; by phone 2.30-5pm Mon-Fri. British citizens wanting consular services (new passports etc) should note that the long queue extending along rue d'Anjou is for the visa department – bypass this and walk straight in at no. 18*bis*.

Canadian Embassy *35 av Montaigne, 8th (01.44.43.29.00/ www.amb-canada.fr). M° Franklin D. Roosevelt.* **Consular services** *(01.44.43.29.02).* **Open** 9am-noon, 2-4.30pm Mon-Fri. **Visas** *37 av Montaigne (01.44.43.29.16).* **Open** 8.30-11am Mon-Fri.

Irish Embassy *12 av Foch, 16th.* **Consulate** *4 rue Rude, 16th (01.44.17.67.00). M° Charles de Gaulle-Etoile.* **Open** (consular/visas) 9.30am-noon Mon-Fri; by phone 9.30am-1pm, 2.30-5.30pm Mon-Fri.

New Zealand Embassy
7ter rue Léonard de Vinci, 16th (01.45.01.43.43/www.nzembassy.com/ france). M° Victor-Hugo. **Open** 9am-1pm, 2pm-5.30pm Mon-Fri (closes 4pm Fri). *July, Aug* 9am-1pm, 2-4.30pm Mon-Thur; 9am-2pm

Fri. **Visas** 9am-1pm Mon-Fri (*www.immigration.govt.nz*).

South African Embassy
59 quai d'Orsay, 7th (01.53.59.23.23/www.afriquesud.net). M° Invalides. **Open** by appointment; by phone 8.30am-5.15pm Mon-Fri. **Consulate and visas** 9am-noon.

US Embassy *2 av Gabriel, 8th (01.43.12.22.22.www.amb-usa.fr). M° Concorde.* **Consulate/Visas** *2 rue St-Florentin, 1st (01.43.12.22.22). M° Concorde.* **Open** (consular services) 9am-12.30pm, 1-3pm Mon-Fri. **Visas** phone 08.99.70.37.00 or check website for non-immigration visas.

Emergencies

Most of the following services operate 24 hrs a day. In a real medical emergency such as a road accident, call the Sapeurs-Pompiers, who have trained paramedics.

Police	**17**
Fire (Sapeurs-Pompiers)	**18**
Ambulance (SAMU)	**15**
Emergency (from a mobile phone)	**112**
GDF (gas leaks)	08.10.43.32.75
EDF (electricity)	08.10.33.39 +

number of *arrondissement* (01-20)

Centre anti-poison	01.40.05.48.48

See also **Health: Accident & Emergency, Doctors; Helplines.**

Health

Nationals of non-EU countries should take out insurance before leaving home. EU nationals staying in France are entitled to use of the French Social Security system, which refunds up to 70% of medical expenses. British nationals should obtain form E111 from a post office before leaving the UK (or E112 for those already in treatment). If you are staying for longer than three months, or working in France but still paying NI contributions in Britain, you will need form E128 filled in by your employer and stamped by the NI contributions office in order to get a French medical number. Consultations and prescriptions have to be paid for in full, and are reimbursed on receipt of a completed *fiche*. If you undergo

treatment the doctor will give you a prescription and a *feuille de soins* (statement of treatment). Stick the little stickers from the medication onto the *feuille de soins*. Send this, the prescription and form E111, to the local **Caisse Primaire d'Assurance Maladie**. For those resident in France more and more doctors now accept the Carte Vitale, which allows them to establish a virtual *feuille de soins* and you to pay only the non-reimbursable part of the bill. Information on the health system can be found at www.cnamts.fr. You can track your refunds with Allosecu (08.20.90.09.00/€0.12 per minute).

Accident and emergency

Note that many hospitals specialise in one type of medical emergency or illness. Consult the Assistance Publique's admirable web site (www.ap-hop-paris.fr) for details. Following (in order of *arrondissement*) are Paris hospitals with 24-hour accident and emergency departments:

Adults

Hôpital Hôtel Dieu
1 place du Parvis Notre-Dame, 4th (01.42.34.82.34).

Hôpital St-Louis *1 av Claude Vellefaux, 10th (01.42.49.49.49).*

Hôpital St-Antoine
184 rue du Fbg-St-Antoine, 12th (01.49.28.20.00).

Hôpital Pitié-Salpêtrière
47-83 bd de l'Hôpital, 13th (01.42.16.00.00).

Hôpital Cochin *27 rue du Fbg-St-Jacques, 14th (01.58.41.41.41).*

Hôpital Européen Georges Pompidou *20 rue Leblanc, 15th (01.56.09.20.00).*

Hôpital Bichat-Claude Bernard *46 rue Henri Huchard, 18th (01.40.25.80.80).*

Hôpital Tenon *4 rue de la Chine, 20th (01.56.01.70.00).*

Children

Hôpital Armand Trousseau
26 av du Dr Arnold Netter, 12th (01.44.73.74.75).

Hôpital St Vincent de Paul
82 av Denfert Rochereau, 14th (01.40.48.81.11).

Hôpital Necker *149 rue de Sèvres, 15th (01.44.49.40.00).*

Hôpital Robert Debré *48 bd Sérurier, 19th (01.40.03.20.00).*

Private hospitals

American Hospital in Paris *63 bd Victor-Hugo, 92200 Neuilly (01.46.41.25.25/www.american-hospital.org). M° Porte Maillot, then bus 82.* **Open** 24-hr. English-speaking hospital. French Social Security refunds only a small percentage of treatment costs.

Hertford British Hospital *(Hôpital Franco-Britannique) 3 rue Barbès, 92300 Levallois-Perret (01.46.39.22.22). M° Anatole-France.* **Open** 24-hr. Most of the medical staff speak English.

Complementary medicine

Académie d'homéopathie et des médecines douces *2 rue d'Isly, 8th (01.43.87.60.33). M° St-Lazare.* **Open** 10am-6pm Mon-Fri. Health services include acupuncture, aromatherapy and homeopathy.

Contraception & abortion

To obtain the pill (*la pilule*) or the coil (*stérilet*), you need a prescription, available on appointment from the first two places below or from a *médecin généraliste* (GP) or gynaecologist. Note that the morning-after pill (*la pilule du lendemain*) is available from pharmacies without prescription but is not reimbursed. Spermicides and condoms (*préservatifs*) are sold in pharmacies and supermarkets, and there are condom machines in Métros, club lavatories and on some street corners. If you are considering an abortion (*IVG* or *interruption volontaire de grossesse*) but want to discuss options in detail you may get better information and counselling from the *orthogénie* (family planning) department of a hospital than from the two organisations below (see www.ap-hop-paris.fr for where IVG is offered). While abortion rights are strongly grounded in France, some doctors remain opposed. Ultrasound

examinations to ascertain the exact stage of pregnancy are obligatory.

Centre de planification et d'éducation familiales *27 rue Curnonsky, 17th (01.48.88.07.28). M° Porte de Champerret.* **Open** 9am-5pm Mon-Fri. Free consultations on family planning and abortion. Abortion counselling on demand; otherwise phone for an appointment.

MFPF (Mouvement français pour le planning familial) *10 rue Vivienne, 2nd (01.42.60.93.20). M° Bourse.* **Open** 9.30am-5.30pm Mon-Fri. Phone for an appointment for contraception advice and prescriptions. For abortion advice, turn up at the centre at one of the designated time slots. The approach here, however, is brusque. **Branch:** 94 bd Masséna, 13th (01.45.84.28.25/ open 10am-3.30pm Wed; 11am-4pm Fri).

Dentists

Dentists are found in the *Pages Jaunes* under *Dentistes*. For emergencies contact:

Urgences Dentaires de Paris (01.42.61.12.00). **Open** 8am-10pm Sun, holidays.

SOS Dentaire *87 bd Port-Royal, 13th (01.43.37.51.00). M° Gobelins, RER Port-Royal.* **Open** Call for an appointment as hours vary. Phone service for emergency dental care.

Hôpital de la Pitié-Salpêtrière *(see above,* **Accident & Emergency)** offers 24hr emergency dental care.

Doctors

A complete list of GPs is in the *Pages Jaunes* under *Médecins: Médecine générale.* To get a Social Security refund, choose a doctor or dentist who is '*conventionné*' (state registered). Consultations cost €20 upwards, of which a proportion can be reimbursed. Seeing a specialist costs more.

Centre Médical Europe *44 rue d'Amsterdam, 9th (01.42.81.93.33/dentists 01.42.81.80.00). M° St-Lazare.* **Open** 8am-7pm Mon-Fri; 8am-6pm Sat. Practitioners in all fields, charging minimal consultation fees.

House calls

SOS Infirmiers *(Nurses) (01.43.57.01.26/06.08.34.08.92/ 01.40.24.22.23).* **House calls** 8pm-midnight; daytime Sat-Sun; the cost is generally €22.87.

SOS Médecins *(01.47.07.77.77).* Home visits at least €60 if you don't have French social security; €30 if you do, before 7pm; from €50 after.

Urgences Médicales de Paris *(01.53.94.94.94).* Doctors make house calls around the clock for €31-€55 per visit. Some speak English.

Eyes

Branches of Alain Afflelou (www.alainefflelou.com) and Lissac (www.lissac.com) stock hundreds of frames and can make prescription glasses within the hour. For an eye test you will need to go to an *ophtalmologiste* – ask the optician for a list. Contact lenses can be bought over the counter if you have your prescription details.

Hôpital des Quinze-Vingts *28 rue de Charenton, 12th (01.40.02.15.20).* Specialist eye hospital offers on-the-spot consultations for eye problems.

SOS Optique *(01.48.07.22.00/ www.sosoptique.com).* 24-hr repair service for glasses.

Pharmacies

Pharmacies sport a green neon cross. Paris has a rota system of *pharmacies de garde* at night and on Sunday. A closed pharmacy will have a sign indicating the nearest open pharmacy. Staff can provide basic medical services like disinfecting and bandaging wounds (for a small fee) and will indicate the nearest doctor on duty. *Parapharmacies* sell almost everything pharmacies do but cannot dispense prescription medication. Toiletries, sanitary products and cosmetics are often cheaper in supermarkets.

Night pharmacies

Pharma Presto *(01.42.42.42.50/ www.pharma-presto.com).* **Open** 24-hr. Delivery charge €39 from 8am-6pm; €54 6pm-8am. Delivers prescription medication (non-prescription exceptions can be made). Will also chauffer your ailing pet to the vet.

made). Will also chauffer your ailing pet to the vet.

Pharmacie des Halles *10 bd de Sébastopol, 4th (01.42.72.03.23). Mº Châtelet.* **Open** 9am-midnight Mon-Sat; 9am-10pm Sun.

Dérhy/Pharmacie des Champs *84 av des Champs-Elysées, 8th (01.45.62.02.41). Mº George V.* **Open** 24-hr.

Matignon *2 rue Jean-Mermoz, 8th (01.43.59.86.55). Mº Franklin D. Roosevelt.* **Open** 8.30am-2am Mon-Sat; 91m-2am Sun.

Pharmacie Européenne de la Place de Clichy *1 pl de Clichy, 9th (01.48.74.65.18). Mº Place de Clichy.* **Open** 24-hr.

Pharmacie de la Place de la Nation *13 pl de la Nation, 11th (01.43.73.24.03). Mº Nation.* **Open** 8am-midnight daily.

Pharmacie d'Italie *61 av d'Italie, 13th (01.44.24.19.72). Mº Tolbiac.* **Open** 8am-2am Mon-Sat; 9am-midnight Sun.

STDs, HIV & AIDS

Centre Medico-Sociale (Mairie de Paris) *2 rue Figuier, 4th (01 49 96 62 70). Mº Pont-Marie.* **Open** 1.30-6pm Mon-Fri, 9.30-12.30pm Sat. Free, anonymous tests (*dépistages*) for HIV, Hep B and C and syphillis (wait one week for results). Excellent counselling.

Le Kiosque Info Sida *36 rue Geoffroy l'Asnier, 4th (01.44.78.00.00). Mº St-Paul.* **Open** 10am-7pm Mon-Fri; 2pm-7pm Sat. Youth association offering info on AIDS and health. Face-to-face counselling service.

FACTS *(01.44.93.16.69/www.factsline.com).* **Open** 7-9pm Mon, Wed. English-speaking crisis line gives info and support for those touched by HIV/AIDS and runs groups for friends and relatives.

SIDA Info Service *(08.00.84.08.00).* **Open** 24-hr. Confidential AIDS information in French. English-speaking counsellors 2-7pm Mon, Wed, Fri.

Helplines

SOS Dépression *(01.40.47.95.95).* **Open** 24-hr. People listen and/or give advice. Can send a counsellor or psychiatrist to your home in case of a crisis.

SOS Help *(01.47.23.80.80).* **Open** 3-11pm daily. English-language helpline .

Alcoholics Anonymous in English *(01.46.34.59.65/ www.aaparis.org).* 24-hr recorded message gives details of AA meetings at the American Church or Cathedral (*see p384,* **Religion**).

Narcotics Anonymous *(01.48.58.38.46/01.48.58.50.61/ www.nafrance.org).* Meetings in English three times a week.

The Counseling Center *(01.47.23.61.13).* English-language counselling service, based at the American Cathedral.

SOS Drogue International *(01.43.13.14.35).* Phone service for help with drug problems.

ID

French law demands that some form of identification is carried at all times. Be ready to produce a passport or *Carte de Séjour* in response to that old police refrain *'Papiers, s'il vous plaît'.*

Insurance

See p377, **Health**.

Internet

After a slow start, use has skyrocketed. It is now possible get cable access in most of Paris.

ISPs

Noosnet *(08.25.34.54.74/ 08.00.114.114/www.noos.com).*

America Online *(08.26.02.60.00/www.aol.fr).*

Club-Internet *(08.26.02.70.28/ www.club-internet.fr).*

CompuServe *(03.21.13.49.49/ www.compuserve.fr).*

Microsoft Network *(08.25.82.78.29/www.fr.msn.com)*

Wanadoo *(France Télécom) (08.10.63.34.34/www.wanadoo.fr)*

Internet access

Café Orbital *13 rue de Médicis, 6th (01.43.25.76.77). RER Luxembourg.* **Open** 10am-10pm Mon-Fri; 10am-8pm Sat, Sun.

Clickside *14 rue Domat, 5th (01.56.81.03.00). Mº Maubert-*

Mutualité. **Open** 10am-midnight Mon-Fri; 1pm-11pm Sat-Sun.

Cyber Cube *12 rue Daval, 11th (01.49.29.67.67/www.cybercube.fr). Mº Bastille.* **Open** 10am-10pm daily.

easyEverything *31-37 bd de Sébastopol, 1st (www.easyeverything. com). Mº Châtelet-Les Halles.* **Open** 7.15am-12.15am. **Branches:** *6 rue de la Harpe, 5th, Mº St-Michel* (open 7.15am-12.15am daily); *15 rue de Rome, 8th, Mº St-Lazare* (open 7.30am-midnight daily).

Most hotels offer Internet access, some from your own room.

Language

See p388, **Essential Vocabulary**, and *p184,* **Menu Lexicon**, for food terms.

Legal advice

Mairies can answer some legal enquiries. Phone for times of free *consultations juridiques.*

Direction départmentale de la concurrence, de la consommation, et de la répression des fraudes *8 rue Froissart, 3rd (01.40.27.16.00). Mº St-Sébastien-Froissart.* **Open** 9-11.30am, 2-5pm Mon-Fri. This subdivision of the Ministry of Finance deals with consumer complaints.

Palais de Justice Galerie de Harlay *Escalier S, 4 bd du Palais, 4th (01.44.32.48.48). Mº Cité.* **Open** 9.30am-noon Mon-Fri. Free legal consultation. Arrive early.

SOS Avocats *(08.03.39.33.00).* **Open** 7-11.30pm Mon-Fri. Closed July, Aug. Free legal advice by phone.

Libraries

All *arrondissements* have free public libraries. For a library card, you need ID and evidence of a fixed address in Paris.

American Library *10 rue du Général-Camou, 7th (01.53.59.12.60/ www.americanlibraryinparis.org). Mº Ecole-Militaire/RER Pont de l'Alma.* **Open** 10am-7pm Tue-Sat (shorter hours in Aug). **Admission** day pass 11; annual 87. The largest English-language lending library in continental Europe. Receives 400 periodicals, plus

Bibliothèque Historique de la Ville de Paris *Hôtel Lamoignon, 24 rue Pavée, 4th (01.44.59.29.40). M° St-Paul.* **Open** 9.30am-6pm Mon-Sat. Closed first two weeks in Aug. **Admission** free (bring ID and a passport photo). Reference books and documents on Paris history in a Marais mansion.

Bibliothèque Marguerite Durand *79 rue Nationale, 13th (01.45.70.80.30). M° Tolbiac or Place d'Italie.* **Open** 2-6pm Tue-Sat. Closed 3 weeks in Sept. **Admission** free. 40,000 books and 120 periodicals on women's history and feminism. Collection includes letters of Colette and Louise Michel.

Bibliothèque Nationale de France François Mitterrand *quai François-Mauriac, 13th (01.53.79.59.59/www.bnf.fr). M° Bibliothèque.* **Open** 10am-8pm Tue-Sat; noon-7pm Sun. Closed 2 weeks in Sept. **Admission** day pass €3; annual €30. Books, papers and periodicals, plus titles in English. An audio-visual room lets you browse photo, film and sound archives. *Wheelchair access.*

Bibliothèque Publique d'Information (BPI) *Centre Pompidou, 4th (01.44.78.12.71/www.bpi.fr). M° Hôtel de Ville/RER Châtelet-Les Halles.* **Open** 12am-10pm Mon, Wed-Fri; 11am-10pm Sat, Sun. **Admission** free. Now on three levels, the Centre Pompidou's vast library has a huge international press section, reference books and language-learning facilities. *Wheelchair access.*

BIFI (Bibliothèque du Film) *100 rue du Fbg-St-Antoine, 12th (01.53.02.22.30/www.bifi.fr). M° Ledru-Rollin.* **Open** 10am-7pm Mon-Fri. Closed 2 weeks in Aug. **Admission** €3.50 day pass; €34 annual; €15 students annual. Film buffs' library offers books, magazines film stills and posters, as well as films on video and DVD.

Documentation Française *29 quai Voltaire, 7th (01.40.15.72.72/www.ladocumentationfrancaise.fr). M° Rue du Bac.* **Open** 10am-6pm Mon-Wed, Fri; 10am-1pm Thur. Closed Aug and first week Sept. The official government archive and central reference library has information on French politics and economy since 1945.

Directory

Locksmiths

Numerous 24-hr emergency repair services handle plumbing, locks, car repairs and more. Most charge a minimum €18-€20 call-out (*déplacement*) and €30 per hour, plus parts; more on Sun and at night.

Allô Assistance Dépannage (08.00.00.00.18). No car repairs.

Numéro Un Dépannage (01.40.71.55.55). No car repairs.

SOS Dépannage (01.47.07.99.99). Double the price of most, but claims to be twice as reliable.

Lost property

Bureau des Objets Trouvés *36 rue des Morillons, 15th (01.55.76.20.20/www.prefecture-police-paris.interieur.gouv.fr). M° Convention.* **Open** 8.30am-5pm Mon-Thur; 8.30am-4.30pm Fri. Visit in person to fill in a form specifying details of the loss. This may have been the first lost property office in the world, but it is far from the most efficient. Horrendous delays in processing claims mean that if your trip to Paris is short you may need to nominate a proxy to collect found objects after your return, although small items can be posted. If your passport was among the lost items you will need to go to your consulate to get a single-entry temporary passport in order to leave the country.

SNCF lost property Some mainline SNCF stations have their own lost property offices.

Media

Magazines

Arts & listings

Three pocket-sized publications compete for basic Wed-to-Tue listings information: **Pariscope** (€0.40), the Parisian cinema-goer's bible, which includes **Time Out Paris** in English; the thinner **Officiel des Spectacles** (€0.35); and trendy **Zurban** (€0.80). Linked to Radio Nova, monthly **Nova** gives rigorously multi-ethnic information on where to drink, dance or hang out. **Technikart** tries to mix clubbing with the arts. Highbrow TV guide **Télérama** has good arts and entertainment features and a Paris listings insert. *See also below* **Le Monde** *and* **Le Figaro**.

There are specialist arts magazines to meet every interest. Film titles include intellectual **Les Cahiers du Cinéma**, glossy **Studio** and younger, celebrity-geared **Première**.

Business

Capital, its sister magazine **Management** and the weightier **L'Expansion** are worthwhile monthlies. **Défis** has tips for the entrepreneur, **Initiatives** is for the self-employed.

English

On the local front, **Time Out Paris** is a six-page supplement inside weekly listings magazine **Pariscope**, available at all news stands, covering selected Paris events, exhibitions, films, concerts and restaurants. The quarterly **Time Out Paris Free Guide** is distributed in bars, hotels and tourist centres and **Time Out Paris Eating & Drinking Guide** is available in newsagents across the city. **FUSAC** (France-USA Contacts) is a small-ads free-sheet with flat rentals, job ads and appliances for sale.

Gossip

The French appear to have an almost insatiable appetite for gossip. 1998 saw the arrival of **Oh La!** from Spain's *Hola!* (and UK's *Hello!*) group. **Voici** is France's juiciest scandal sheet whilst **Gala** tells the same stories without the sleaze. **Paris Match** is a French institution founded in 1948, packed with society gossip and celebrity interviews, but still regularly scoops the rest with photo shoots of international affairs. **Point de Vue** specialises in royalty and disdains showbiz fluff. Monthly **Entrevue** tends toward features on bizarre sexual practices. **Perso** presents the stars exactly as they would like to be seen.

News

Weekly news magazines are an important sector in France, taking the place of weighty Sunday tomes and offering news, cultural sections as well as in-depth reports. Titles range from solidly serious **L'Express** and **Le Point** to the traditionally left-wing **Le Nouvel Observateur** and sardonic, chaotically arranged **Marianne**. Weekly **Courrier**

International publishes a fascinating selection of articles from newspapers all over the world, translated into French.

Women, men & fashion

Elle was a pioneer among women's mags and has editions across the globe. In France it is weekly and spot-on for interviews and fashion. Monthly **Marie-Claire** takes a more feminist, campaigning line. Both have design spin-offs (**Elle Décoration**, **Marie-Claire Maison**) and Elle has spawned foodie **Elle à Table**. **DS** aims at the intellectual reader, with lots to read and coverage of social issues. **Vogue**, read both for its fashion coverage and big-name guests, is rivalled when it comes to fashion week by **L'Officiel de la Mode**. The underground go for more radical publications **Purple** (six-monthly art, literature and fashion tome), **Crash**, and the new wave of fashion/lifestyle mags: **WAD** (We Are Different), **Citizen K**, **Jalouse** and **Numéro**. Men's mags include French versions of lad bibles **FHM**, **Maximal**, **Men's Health**, and the naughty **Echo des Savanes**.

Newspapers

The national dailies are characterised by high prices and relatively low circulation. Only 20% of the population reads a national paper; regional dailies hold sway outside Paris. Serious, centre-left daily **Le Monde** is essential reading for business people, politicians and intellectuals, who often also publish articles in it. Despite its highbrow reputation, subject matter is surprisingly eclectic, although international coverage is selective. It also publishes *Aden*, a Wednesday Paris-listings supplement. Founded post-68 by a group that included Sartre and de Beauvoir, trendy **Libération** is now centre-left, but still the read of the *gauche caviar*, worth reading for wide-ranging news and arts coverage and guest columnists. The conservative upper and middle classes go for **Le Figaro**, a daily broadsheet with a devotion to politics, shopping, food and sport. Sales

are boosted by lots of property and job ads and the Wednesday *Figaroscope* Paris listings. Saturday's edition contains three magazines which rockets the price from €1 to €4. For business and financial news, the French dailies **La Tribune**, **Les Echos** and the weekly **Investir** are the tried and trusted sources. Tabloid in format, the easy-read **Le Parisien** is strong on consumer affairs, social issues, local news and events and vox pops, and has a Sunday edition. Downmarket **France Soir** has gone tabloid. **La Croix** is a Catholic, right-wing daily. The Communist Party **L'Humanité** struggles to exist, as does the Party itself. Sunday broadsheet **Le Journal du Dimanche** comes with *Fémina* mag and a Paris. section. **L'Equipe** is a big-selling sports daily with a bias towards football; **Paris-Turf** caters for horse-racing fans.

English papers

The Paris-based **International Herald Tribune** is on sale throughout the city; British dailies, Sundays and **USA Today** are widely available on the day of issue at larger kiosks in the centre. Saturday's issue of **Le Monde** includes a series of articles from the *New York Times* in English.

Satirical papers

Wednesday-published institution **Le Canard Enchaîné** is the Gallic *Private Eye* – in fact it was the inspiration for the *Eye*. It's a broadly left-wing satirical weekly broadsheet that's full of in-jokes and breaks political scandals. **Charlie Hebdo** is mainly bought for its cartoons.

Radio

A quota requiring a minimum of 40% French music has led to overplay of Gallic pop oldies and to the creation of dubious hybrids by local groups that mix some words in French with a refrain in English. Trash-talking phone-in shows also proliferate. Wavelengths are in MHz.

87.8 France Inter State-run, MOR music, international news and concerts by rock newcomers.

90.4 Nostalgie As it sounds.

90.9 Chante France 100% French *chanson*.

91.3 Chérie FM Lots of oldies.

91.7 France Musiques State classical music channel has brought in more *variété* and slush to its highbrow mix of concerts, contemporary bleeps and top jazz.

92.1 Le Mouv' New public station aimed at luring the young with pop and rock music.

93.1 Aligre From local Paris news to literary chat.

93.5/93.9 France Culture Verbose state culture station.

94.8 RCJ/Radio J/Judaïque FM/ Radio Shalom Shared wavelength for Jewish stations.

95.2 Ici et Maintenant/Neo New stations hoping to stir local public debate about current events.

96 Skyrock Pop station with loudmouth presenters. Lots of rap.

96.4 BFM Business and economics.

96.9 Voltage FM Dance music.

97.4 Rire et Chansons A non-stop diet of jokes – racist, sexist or just plain lousy – and pop oldies.

97.8 Ado Music for adolescents.

98.2 Radio FG Gay station also beloved of clubbers for its up-to-the-minute what's on announcements.

99 Radio Latina Great Latin and salsa music.

100.3 NRJ Energy: national leader with the under-30s.

101.1 Radio Classique More classical pops than France Musique.

101.5 Radio Nova Hip hop, trip hop, world, jazz.

101.9 Fun Radio Now embracing techno alongside Anglo pop hits.

102.3 Oui FM Ouï rock you.

103.9 RFM Easy listening.

104.3 RTL The most popular French station nationwide mixes music and talk programmes.

104.7 Europe 1 News, press reviews, sports, business, entertainment. Much the best weekday breakfast news broadcast, with politicians interviewed live.

105.1 FIP Traffic and weather bulletins, what's on in Paris and a brilliantly eclectic mix of jazz, classical, world and pop.

105.5 France Info 24-hr news, economic updates and sports bulletins. As everything gets repeated every 15 minutes, it's guaranteed to drive you mad – good though if you're learning French.

106.7 Beur FM North African music and discussion.

For up-to-date info on TV and radio see www.csa.fr.

English

You can receive the **BBC World Service** (648 KHz AM) for its English-language international news, current events, pop and drama. Also on 198KHz LW, from midnight to 5.30am daily. At other times this frequency carries **BBC Radio 4** (198 KHz LW), for British news, talk and *The Archers* directed at the home audience. **RFI** (738 KHz AM) has an English-language programme of news and music from 7-8am, 2-3pm and 4.30-5pm daily; www.rfi.fr

Television

TF1 The country's biggest channel, and first to be privatised in 1987. Reality shows, dubbed soaps and football are staples.

France 2 State-owned station mixes game shows, chat, documentaries, and the usual cop series and films.

FR3 The more heavyweight of the three state channels offers regional, wildlife and sports coverage, debates and *Cinéma de Minuit*, late-night Sunday classic films in V.O. (original language).

Canal+ Subscription channel shows recent films, exclusive sport and late-night porn. *The Simpsons* and satirical puppets *Les Guignols* are available unscrambled.

Arte/France 5 Intellectual Franco-German hybrid Arte shares its wavelength with educational channel France 5 (3am-7pm).

M6 Imports *Ally McBeal* and the *X-Files*. Homegrown programmes include *Culture Pub* (about advertising) and the phenomenally successful *Loft Story*.

Cable TV & satellite

France offers a decent range of cable and satellite channels but content in English remains limited. CNN and BBC World offer round-the-clock news coverage. BBC Prime keeps you up to date on *Eastenders* (omnibus Sun 2pm), while Teva features original-language comedy *Sex and the City*.

Noostv (08.00.114.114/ www.noos.fr). The first cable provider to offer an interactive video service via Internet. Packages from €19 per month ('Noos Pass').

Money

The euro

On 1 January 2002 euro currency became the official currency in France. If you still have francs left over, only the Banque de France or the Trésor Public now offer free exchanges (coins until 17 Feb 2005, notes until 17 Feb 2012). Foreign debit and credit cards can automatically be used to withdraw and pay in euros, and currency withdrawn in France can be used all over the euro zone. Daylight robbery occurs, however, if you try to deposit a euro cheque from any country other than France in a French bank: they are currently charging around €15 for this service, and the European parliament has backed down on its original decision that cross-border payments should be in line with domestic ones across the euro zone. Good news for Brits though – if you transfer money from the UK to France in euros you'll pay the same charges as if Britain were within the euro zone (watch the exchange rate carefully though).

Useful websites

www.banque-france.fr

www.euro.gouv.fr Official website: information, updates and online franc-euro converter.

www.xe.com/ucc Universal live rate currency converter.

ATMs

Withdrawals in euros can be made from bank and post office automatic cash machines. The specific cards accepted are marked on each machine, and most give instructions in English. Credit card companies charge a fee for cash advances, but rates are often better than bank rates.

Banks

French banks usually open 9am-5pm Mon-Fri (some close at lunch); some banks also open on Sat. All are closed on public

holidays, and from noon on the previous day. Note that not all banks have foreign exchange counters. Commission rates vary between banks. The state Banque de France usually offers good rates. Most banks accept travellers' cheques, but may be reluctant to accept personal cheques even with the Eurocheque guarantee card, which is not widely used in France.

Bank accounts

To open an account (*ouvrir un compte*), French banks require proof of identity, address and your income (if any). You'll probably be required to show your passport, *Carte de Séjour*, an electricity/gas or phone bill in your name and a payslip/letter from your employer. Students need a student card and may need a letter from their parents. Of the major banks (BNP, Crédit Lyonnais, Société Générale, Banque Populaire, Crédit Agricole), Société Générale tends to be most foreigner-friendly. Most banks don't hand out a *Carte Bleue/Visa* until several weeks after you've opened an account. A chequebook (*chéquier*) is usually issued in about a week. *Carte Bleue* is debited directly from your current account, but you can choose for purchases to be debited at the end of every month. French banks are tough on overdrafts, so try to anticipate any cash crisis in advance and work out a deal for an authorised overdraft (*découvert autorisé*) or you risk being blacklisted as '*interdit bancaire*' – forbidden from having a current account – for up to 10 years. Depositing foreign-currency cheques is slow, so use wire transfer or a bank draft in euros to receive funds from abroad.

Bureaux de change

If you arrive in Paris early or late, you can change money at the **Travelex** bureaux de change in the terminals at Roissy (01.48.64.37.26) and at Orly (01.49.75.89.25) airports, which are open 6.30am to 11 or 11.30pm daily. **Thomas Cook** has bureaux de change at the main train stations. Hours can vary. www.travelex.fr

Gare d'Austerlitz 01.53.61.92.40. **Open** 10am-6pm daily.

Gare Montparnasse
01.42.79.03.88. **Open** 8am-7pm daily.

Gare St-Lazare 01.43.87.72.51.
Open 8.30am-7pm Mon-Sat; 9am-5pm Sun.

Gare du Nord 01.42.80.11.50.
Open 6.45am-11.25pm daily.

Gare de l'Est 01.42.09.51.97.
Open Mon-Sat 7am-10pm, 7am-7pm Sun.

Credit cards

Major international credit cards are widely used in France; Visa (in French *Carte Bleue*) is the most readily accepted. French-issued credit cards have a special security microchip (*puce*) in each card. The card is slotted into a card reader, and the holder keys in a PIN number to authorise the transaction. Non-French cards also work, but generate a credit slip to sign. In case of credit card loss or theft, call the following 24-hr services which have English-speaking staff: **American Express** 01.47.77.72.00; **Diners Club** 08.10.31.41.59; **MasterCard/Visa** 08.92.70.57.05.

Foreign affairs

American Express *11 rue Scribe, 9th (01.47.14.50.00/ www24.americanexpress.com/ France). M° Opéra.* **Open** 9am-4.30pm Mon-Fri. **Bureau de change** (01.47.77.77.58). **Open** 9am-6.30pm Mon-Fri; 9am-5.30pm Sat; 10am-4pm Sun. Travel agency, bureau de change, poste restante, card replacement, travellers' cheque refund service, international money transfers and a cash machine for AmEx cardholders.

Barclays *6 rond point des Champs-Elysées, 8th (01.44.95.13.80/www.barclays.fr). M° Franklin D Roosevelt.* **Open** 9.15am-4.30pm Mon-Fri. Barclays' international Expat Service handles direct debits, international transfer of funds, etc.

Chequepoint *150 av des Champs-Elysées, 8th (01.42.56.48.63). M° Charles de Gaulle-Etoile.* **Open** 24-hr. Other branches have variable hours. No commission.

Travelex *52 av des Champs-Elysées, 8th (01.42.89.80.32/ www.travelex.fr). M° Franklin D. Roosevelt.* **Open** 9am-10pm daily. Hours of other branches (over 20 in Paris) vary. Issues travellers' cheques and travel insurance and deals with bank transfers.

Western Union Money Transfer *CCF Change, 4 rue du Cloître-Notre-Dame, 4th (01.40.41.28.46/ www.westernunion.com). M° Cité.* **Open** 9am-5.10pm daily (till 6pm in summer). CCF is an agent for Western Union in Paris, with several branches in the city. 48 post offices now provide Western Union services as well (call 08.25.00.98.98). Money transfers from abroad should arrive within 10-15 minutes. Charges paid by the sender.

Citibank *125 av des Champs-Elysées, 8th (01.53.23.33.60/ www.citibank.fr). M° Charles de Gaulle-Etoile.* **Open** 10am-6pm Mon-Fri. Existing clients get good rates for transferring money from country to country, preferential exchange rates and no commision on travellers cheques.

Opening hours

Standard opening hours for shops are 9am/10am-7pm/8pm Mon-Sat. Some shops close on Mon. Shops and businesses often close at lunch, usually 12.30-2pm. Many shops close in August. While Paris doesn't have the 24-hr consumer culture beloved of some capitals, most areas have a local grocer that stays open until around 9.30 or 10pm, as do larger branches of Monoprix.

24-hr florist Elyfleur *82 av de Wagram, 17th (01.47.66.87.19). M° Wagram.*

24-hr newsagents include: *33 av des Champs-Elysées, 8th. M° Franklin D. Roosevelt; 2 bd Montmartre, 9th. M° Grands Boulevards.*

24-hr tabac Drugstore Publicis *133 av des Champs-Elysées, 8th. M° Charles de Gaulle-Etoile.*

24-hr garage Select Shell *6 bd Raspail, 7th (01.45.48.43.12). M° Rue du Bac.* This round-the-clock garage has a large if pricey array of supermarket standards from the Casino chain. No alcohol sold 10pm-6am.

Photo labs

Photo developing is often more expensive than in the UK or USA.

Fnac Service, Photo Station (www.photostation.fr) and Photo Service (www.photoservice.com) have numerous branches.

Police stations

Trying to bring the police closer to the public, the Préfecture de Police has established 94 different outposts in the city. If you are robbed or attacked, you should report the incident as soon as possible. You will need to make a statement (*procès verbal*) at the *point d'accueil* closest to the site of the crime. To find the nearest one, phone the Préfecture Centrale (08.36.67.22.22) day or night, or consult their website, www.prefecture-police-paris.interieur.gouv.fr. Stolen goods are unlikely to be recovered, but you will need the police statement for insurance purposes.

Postal services

Post offices (*bureaux de poste*) are open 8am-7pm Mon-Fri; 8am-noon Sat. All are listed in the phone book: under Administration des PTT in the *Pages Jaunes*; under Poste in the *Pages Blanches*. Most post offices have automatic machines (in French and English) that weigh your letter, print out a stamp and give change, saving you from wasting time in an enormous queue. You can also buy stamps at a tobacconist (*tabac*). For info see www.laposte.fr

Main Post Office *52 rue du Louvre, 1st (01.40.28.76.00). M° Les Halles or Louvre-Rivoli.* **Open** 24-hr for Poste Restante, telephones, stamps, fax, photocopying and some banking operations. This is the best place to get your mail sent if you haven't got a fixed address in Paris. Mail should be addressed to you in block capitals, followed by Poste Restante, then the post office's address. There is a charge of €0.46 for each letter received.

Recycling & rubbish

The city has a new system of colour-coded domestic recycling bins. A yellow-lidded bin can take paper, cardboard cartons, tins and small electrical items; a white-

Directory

lidded bin takes glass. All other rubbish should go in the green-lidded bins except for batteries (all shops that sell batteries should accept them), medication (take it back to a pharmacy), toxic products (call 08.20.00.75.75 to have them picked up) or car batteries (take them to an official tip or return to garages exhibiting the 'relais verts auto' sign). Green hive-shaped bottle banks can be found on street corners.

Allô Propreté (08.20.00.75.75/ www.paris.fr). **Open** 9-5pm Mon-Fri. Recycling information and collection of cumbersome objects.

Religion

Churches and religious centres are listed in the phone book (*Pages Jaunes*) under *Eglises* and *Culte*. Paris has several English-speaking churches. The *International Herald Tribune*'s Saturday edition lists Sunday church services in English.

American Cathedral
23 av George V, 8th (01.53.23.84.00/ www.us.net/amcathedral-paris). M° George V.

American Church in Paris
65 quai d'Orsay, 7th (01.40.62.05.00/ www.americanchurch.paris.org). M° Invalides.

Emmanuel Baptist Church of Paris 56 rue des Bons Raisins, 92500 Rueil-Malmaison (01.47.51.29.63/www.ebcparis.org).

Kehilat Geisher 10 rue de Pologne, 78100 St Germain-en-Laye (01.39.21.97.19). The Liberal English-speaking Jewish community has rotating services in Paris and the western suburbs.

La Mosquée de Paris
2 pl du Puits de l'Ermite, 5th (01.45.35.97.33).

St George's Anglican Church
7 rue Auguste-Vacquerie, 16th (01.47.20.22.51/ www.stgeorgesparis.com). M° Charles de Gaulle-Etoile.

St Joseph's Roman Catholic Church 50 av Hoche, 8th (01.42.27.28.56/www.stjoeparis.org). M° Charles de Gaulle-Etoile.

St Michael's Church of England 5 rue d'Aguesseau, 8th (01.47.42.70.88/ www.saintmichaelsparis.org). M° Madeleine.

Renting a flat

Northern, eastern and southeastern Paris is generally cheapest for flat rental. Expect to pay roughly €17 per month/m² (€595 per month for a 35m² flat, and so on). Studios and one-bedroom flats fetch the highest prices proportionally; lifts and cellars will also boost the rent.

Flat hunting

Given the shortage of accommodation in Paris, it is a landlord's world out there so you will need to search actively, or even frenetically, in order to find an apartment. The site www.logement.com is a reassuring place to start. In addition to giving reliable information about most aspects of the real estate world, it also provides links to at least 20 other sites that list rental ads. Click on, for example, www.explorimmo.fr, which lists rental ads from *Le Figaro* as well as specialised real estate magazines. Thursday morning's *De Particulier à Particulier* (www.pap.fr) is a standby for those that want to rent directly from the owner, but be forewarned, most apartments go within hours. Fortnightly *Se Loger* (www.seloger.com) is worth checking out also, even though only agencies place ads. Flats offered to foreigners are advertised in the *International Herald Tribune* and English-language fortnightly *FUSAC* (www.fusac.fr); rents tend to be higher than in the French press. There are also assorted free ad brochures that can be picked up from agencies. Private landlords often set a visiting time; prepare to meet hordes of other flat-seekers and have your documents and cheque book on hand. After the success of *Loft Story* and *Friends*, young French people who have traditionally rented a small studio of their own are eagerly getting into the idea of flat-sharing (*colocatatation*). Les Jeudis de la Colocation, is a monthly event organised by the flatshare website www.colocation.fr the first Thursday of every month at Le Vestiaire Café, 64 rue Jean-Pierre Timbaud, 11th (08.92.23.15.15). Would-be flatsharers pay €7 (including a drink) to meet possible flatmates/soulmates.

Rental laws

The legal minimum rental lease (*bail de location*) on an unfurnished apartment is three years; furnished flats are generally one year. During this period the landlord can only raise the rent by the official construction inflation index. At the end of the lease, the rent can be adjusted, but tenants can object before a rent board if it seems exorbitant. Tenants may be evicted for non-payment, or if the landlord wishes to sell the property or use it as his own residence. It is illegal to throw people out in winter. Before accepting you as a tenant, landlords will probably require you to present a dossier with pay slips (*fiches de paie/bulletins de salaire*) showing three to four times the amount of the monthly rent, and, for foreigners in particular, to provide a financial guarantor (someone who will sign a document promising to pay the rent if you scarper without paying). When taking out a lease, payments usually include the first month's rent, a deposit (*une caution*) equal to two month's rent, and an agency fee, if applicable. It is customary for an inspection of the premises (*état des lieux*) at the start and end of the rental, the cost of which (around €150) is shared by landlord and tenant. Landlords may try to rent their flats *non-declaré* – without a written lease – and get rent in cash. This can make it difficult for tenants to establish their rights – which is one reason landlords do it.

Bureau de l'information juridique des proprietaires et des occupants (BIPO)
6 rue Agrippa-d'Aubigné, 4th (01.42.76.31.31). M° Sully-Morland. **Open** 9am-5pm Mon-Fri. Municipal service provides free advice (in French) about renting or buying a flat, housing benefit, rent legislation and tenants' rights.

Centre d'information et de défense des locataires
9 rue Severo, 14th (01.45.41.47.76). M° Pernety or Convention. **Open** By appointment 10am-12.30pm, 2.30-3.30pm Mon-Fri. Will help you sort out problems with landlords, rent increases, etc.

Shipping services

Hedley's Humpers *6 bd de la Libération, 93284 St-Denis (01.48.13.01.02/ www.hedleyshumpers.com). M° Carrefour-Pleyel.* **Open** 9am-1pm, 2-6pm Mon-Fri. Closed 3 weeks in Aug. **Branch:** *102 rue des Rosiers, 93400 St-Ouen (01.40.10.94.00). M° Porte de Clignancourt.* **Open** 9am-1pm Mon, Fri; 9am-6pm Sat, Sun. Specialised in transporting furniture and antiques. **In UK:** *3 St Leonards Rd, London NW10 6SX, UK (0208 965 8733).* **In USA:** *21-41 45th Road, Long Island City, New York NY 11101, USA (1.718.433.4005).*

Smoking

Although smoking seems to represent a quintessential part of French life (and death), the French government and public health groups have recently been trying to wage the war against the cigarette on two fronts. Smoking is now banned in most public spaces, such as theatres, cinemas and public transport and an anti-smoking ad campaign began in summer 2002. Restaurants are obliged to provide a non-smoking area (*espace non-fumeurs*), however, you'll often end up with the worst table in the house, and there's no guarantee other people seated in the section won't light up anyway. For more information about quitting smoking, contact the Tabac Info Service (08.03.30.93.10/www.tabac-info.net). If you are a dedicated smoker, you'll soon learn the hard way that most tabacs close at 8pm. Some bars have cigarettes behind the bar, but they are generally only on sale to customers who stay for a drink.

Telephones

Cellphones

The three companies that rule the cell phone market in France are:

Bouyges Telecom (08.10.63.01.00/ www.bouyguestelecom.fr).

France Telecom/Orange (08.25.00.57.00/www.orange.fr).

SFR (08.05.80.08.05/www.sfr.fr).

A subscription (*abonnement*) will normally get you a free phone if you sign up for a minimum of one year. Two hours' calling time a month costs about €35/month. International calls are not normally included.

Dialing & codes

All French phone numbers have ten digits. Paris and Ile de France numbers begin with 01; the rest of France is divided into four zones (02-05). Mobile phone numbers start with 06. 08 indicates a special rate (*see below*). If you are calling France from abroad leave off the 0 at the start of the ten-digit number. Country code: 33. To call abroad from France dial 00, then country code. Since 1998 other phone companies have been allowed to enter the market, with new prefixes (eg. Cégétel numbers starting with a 7).

France Telecom English-Speaking Customer Service *08.00.36.47.75.* **Open** 9am-5.30pm Mon-Fri. Freephone information line in English on phone services, bills, payment, Internet.

Public phones

Most public phones in Paris use phonecards (*télécartes*). Sold at post offices, tobacconists, airports and train and Métro stations, cards cost €7.40 for 50 units and €14.75 for 120 units. France Telecom now also sells telephone 'tickets' with a PIN code (€7.50-€15), which can be used with any type of telephone, as does Travelex's International Telephone Card, which can be used in more than 80 countries (from Travelex agencies). Cafés have coin phones, while post offices usually have card phones. In a phone box, the digital display screen should read *Décrochez*. Pick up the phone. When *Introduisez votre carte* appears, insert your card into the slot. The screen should then read *Patientez SVP*. *Numérotez* is your signal to dial. *Crédit épuisé* means that you have no more units left. Finally, hang up (*Raccrochez*), and don't forget your card. Some public phones take credit cards. If you are using a credit card, insert the card, key in your PIN number and *Patientez SVP* should appear.

Operator services

Operator assistance, French directory enquiries (renseignements), dial 12. To make a reverse-charge call within France, ask to make a call en PCV.

International directory enquiries 32.12, then country code. €3 per call.

Telephone engineer dial 10.13.

International news (French recorded message, France Inter), dial 08.36.68.10.33 (€0.34 per min).

Telegram all languages, international 08.00.33.44.11; within France 36.55.

Time dial 36.99.

Traffic news dial 01.48.99.33.33.

Weather dial 08.36.70.12.34 (€1.35 then €0.39 per min) for enquiries on weather in France and abroad, in French or English; dial 08.92.68.02.75 (€0.34 per min) for a recorded weather announcement for Paris and region.

Airparif (01.44.59.47.64). Mon-Fri 9am-12.30pm, 1.45-5.45pm. Information about pollution levels and air quality in Paris and Ile-de-France: invaluable for asthmatics.

Telephone directories

Phone books are found in all post offices and most cafés. The *Pages Blanches* (White Pages) list people and businesses alphabetically; *Pages Jaunes* (Yellow Pages) list businesses and services by category. Online versions can be found at www.pagesjaunes.fr.

Telephone charges

Local calls in Paris and Ile-de-France beginning with 01 cost €0.11 for three minutes, standard rate, €0.04 per minute thereafter. Calls beyond a 100km radius (province) are charged at €0.11 for the first 39 seconds, then €0.24 per minute. International destinations are divided into 16 zones. Reduced-rate periods for calls within France and Europe: 7pm-8am during the week; all day Sat, Sun. Reduced-rate periods for the US and Canada: 7pm through to 1pm Mon-Fri; all day Sat, Sun.

Cheap rate providers

The following providers offer competitive rates from France:

Fast Telecom 01.46.98.20.00.

Teleconnect 08.05.10.25.05.

AT&T Direct Local access number: 0800-99-00-11.

Directory

Special rate numbers

08.00 Numéro Vert Freephone.

08.01/08.10 Numéro Azur
€0.11 under 3 min, then €0.04 per min.

08.02/08.20 Numéro Indigo I
€0.118 per min.

08.25 Numéro Indigo II
€0.15 per min.

08.36.64/08.90.64/08.90.70
€0.112 per min.

08.90.71 €0.15 per min.

08.36.67/08.91.67/08.91.70
€0.225 per min.

**08.36.68/08.36.69/08.92.35/
08.92.68/08.92.69/08.92.70**
€0.337 min. This rate applies not just to chat lines but increasingly to cinema and transport infolines.

Special rate information: **10.14**

Minitel

France Telecom's Minitel is a videotext service available to any telephone subscriber, though the Internet has made it virtually reduncant. If you come across one of these beige plastic boxes, dust it off then dial 3611 for Minitel directory in English, wait for the beep, press *Connexion*, type MGS, then *Envoi*. Then type *Minitel en anglais* for the English service.

Ticket agencies

The easiest way to reserve and buy tickets for concerts, plays and matches is from a **Fnac** store. You can also reserve on www.fnac.com or by phone (08.92.68.36.22; 9am to 8pm Mon-Sat) and pick them up at one of their *points de vente* (see site for complete list) or pay with your credit card and have them sent to your home. **Virgin** has teamed up with Ticketnet to create an online ticket office (www.virginmega.fr). Tickets can also be purchased by phone (08.25.02.30.24) and sent to your home for a €5.35 fee.

Fnac Forum des Halles
1st (01.40.41.40.00/www.fnac.com). Mº Les Halles/RER Châtelet-Les Halles. **Open** 10am-7.30pm Mon-Sat. **Credit** AmEx, MC, V.

Virgin Megastore
52 av des Champs-Elysées, 8th (01.49.53.50.00). Mº Franklin D.

Roosevelt. **Open** 10am-midnight Mon-Sat. **Credit** AmEx, DC, MC, V.

Time & seasons

France is one hour ahead of Greenwich Mean Time (GMT). France uses the 24-hr system (eg. 20h for 8pm).

Tipping

Service is legally included in your bill at all restaurants, cafés and bars. However, it is polite to either round up the final amount for drinks, and to leave a cash tip of €1-€2 or more for a meal, depending on the restaurant and, of course, on the quality of service you receive.

Toilets

Automatic street toilets are not as terrifying as they look. You place your coin in the slot, and – open sesame – you're in a disinfected wonderland (each loo is completely disinfected after use, so don't try to sneak in as someone is leaving: you'll

end up covered in bleach). Once in, you'll have 15 minutes in which to do the bizzo. If a space-age-style loo experience doesn't appeal, you can always nip into the loos of a fast-food chain. Café toilets are theoretically reserved for customers' use; some still have coin-op stalls.

Tourist information

Espace du Tourisme d'Ile de France *Carrousel du Louvre, 99 rue de Rivoli, 1st (08.26.16.66.66/ www.paris-ile-de-france.com). Mº Palais Royal.* **Open** 10am-7pm daily. Information showcase for Paris and the Ile-de-France.

Maison de la France/French Travel Centre *178 Piccadilly, London W1J 9AL (0906-824 4123/ www.franceguide.com).* **Open** 10am-6pm Mon-Fri; 10am-5pm Sat. Information on visiting France. Can also reserve train tickets for France and other European countries.

Office de Tourisme et de Congrès de Paris *127 av des Champs-Elysées, 8th (08.92.68. 31.12 (€0.34/min); recorded information in English*

Size Charts

Women's Clothes

British	French	US
4	32	2
6	34	4
8	36	6
10	38	8
12	40	10
14	42	12
16	44	14
18	46	16
20	48	18

Women's Shoes

British	French	US
3	36	5
4	37	6
5	38	7
6	39	8
7	40	9
8	41	10
9	42	11

Men's Suits

British	French	US
34	44	34
36	46	36
38	48	38
40	50	40
42	52	42
44	54	44
46	56	46
48	58	48

Men's Shoes

British	French	US
6	39	7
$7^{1}/_{2}$	40	$7^{1}/_{2}$
8	41	8
8	42	$8^{1}/_{2}$
9	43	$9^{1}/_{2}$
10	44	$10^{1}/_{2}$
11	45	11
12	46	$11^{1}/_{2}$

Directory

and French 08.36.68.31.12/
www.parisbienvenu.com).
M° Charles de Gaulle-Etoile. **Open**
summer 9am-8pm daily; winter
9am-8pm Mon-Sat; 11am-7pm Sun.
Closed 1 May. Information on Paris
and the suburbs, shop, *bureau de
change*, hotel reservations,
phonecards, museum cards, travel
passes and tickets. Multilingal staff.
Branches: *Gare de Lyon, 20 bd
Diderot, 12th.* **Open** Mon-Sat 8am-
8pm. *Tour Eiffel* **Open** 11am-6pm
daily May-Sept.

Visas

European Union nationals do
not need a visa to enter France,
nor do US, Canadian, Australian
or New Zealand citizens for
stays of up to three months.
Nationals of other countries
should enquire at the nearest
French Consulate before leaving
home. If they are travelling to
France from one of the countries
included in the Schengen
agreement (most of the EU, but
not Britain, Ireland, Italy or
Greece), the visa from that
country should be sufficient.
For stays of over three months,
see below, **Cartes de Séjour**.

Weights & measures

France uses only the metric
system; remember that all speed
limits are in kilometres. One
kilometre is equivalent to 0.62
mile (1 mile = 1.6km). Petrol,
like other liquids, is measured
in litres; one UK gallon = 4.54
litres; 1 US gallon = 3.79 litres).

Women's Paris

Paris is not especially
threatening for women,
although the precautions you
would take in any major city
apply: be careful at night in
areas like Pigalle, the rue St-
Denis, Stalingrad, La Chapelle,
Château Rouge, Gare du Nord,
the Bois de Boulogne and Bois
de Vincennes. If you receive
unwanted attention a politely
scathing '*N'insistez pas!*' ('Don't
push it) makes your feelings

clear. If things get too heavy,
go into the nearest shop or café
and ask for help.

CIDFF *7 rue du Jura, 13th*
(01.42.17.12.34). M° Gobelins. **Open**
1.30-5.30pm Tue-Thur (phone 9am-
12.30pm).The Centre d'Information
et de Documentation des Femmes et
des Familles offers health, legal and
professional advice for women.

**Violence conjugale: Femmes
Info Service** *(01.40.33.80.60).*
Open 7.30am-11.30pm Mon-Sat.
Telephone hotline for battered
women, directing them towards
medical aid or shelters.

Viols Femmes Informations
(08.00.05.95.95). **Open** 10am-7pm
Mon-Fri. Freephone in French gives
help and advice to rape victims.

Working in Paris

All EU nationals can work
legally in France, but should
apply for a French social
security number and *Carte de
Séjour*. Some job ads can be
found at branches of the
**Agence nationale pour
l'emploi (ANPE)/**
www.anpe.fr, the French
national employment bureau.
This is also the place to go to
sign up as a *demandeur
d'emploi,* to be placed on file as
available for work and possibly
to qualify for French
unemployment benefits. Britons
can only claim French
unemployment benefit if they
were already signed on before
leaving the UK. Non-EU
nationals need a work permit
and are not entitled to use the
ANPE network without valid
work papers.

CIEE *112ter rue Cardinet, 17th*
(01.58.57.20.50/
www.councilexchanges-fr.org).
M° Malesherbes. **Open** 9am-6pm
Mon-Fri. The Council on
International Educational
Exchange provides three-month
work permits for US citizens at or
recently graduated from university
('Work in France' programme), has
a job centre, mostly for sales and
catering, and a housing placement
service for those participating in the
programme.

**Espace emploi international
(OMI et ANPE)** *48 bd de la
Bastille, 12th* (01.53.02.25.50/

www.emploi-international.org).
M° Bastille. **Open** 9am-5pm Mon,
Wed-Fri; Tue 9am-noon. Provides
work permits of up to 18 months for
Americans aged 18-35 and has a job
placement service.

The Language Network
(01.44.64.82.23/01.43.08.35.19).
Helps to orient native English
speakers who wish to teach.

Job ads

Help-wanted ads sometimes
appear in the *International Herald
Tribune*, in *FUSAC* and on
noticeboards at language schools
and the American Church.
Bilingual secretarial/PA work is
available for those with good
written French. If you are looking
for professional work, have your
CV translated, including French
equivalents for any qualifications.
Most job applications require a
photo and a handwritten letter
(employers often use
graphological analysis).

Cartes de Séjour

Officially, all foreigners, both
EU citizens and non-Europeans,
who are in France for more than
three months must apply at the
Préfecture de Police for a *Carte de
Séjour*, valid for one year. Those
who have had a *Carte de Séjour*
for at least three years, have been
paying French income tax, can
show proof of income and/or are
married to a French national can
apply for a *Carte de Résident*,
valid for ten years.

**CIRA (Centre interministeriel
de renseignements
administratifs)** *(01.40.01.11.01/
www.service-public.fr).* **Open** 9am-
12.30pm, 2-5.30pm Mon-Fri. Advice
on French admin procedures.

**Préfecture de Police de Paris
Service Étrangers** *7-9 bd du
Palais, 4th (01.53.71.51.68/
www.prefecture-police-
paris.interieur.gouv.fr). M° Cité.*
Open 9am-4pm Mon-Fri.
Information on residency and work
permits for foreigners.

**Cosmopolitan Services
Unlimited** *64 bd Malesherbes, 8th*
(01.44.90.10.00/
*www.cosmopolitanservices.com). M°
Villiers.* **Open** 9am-6pm Mon-Thur;
9am-5pm Fri. A good but pricey
relocation company. Services
include getting work permits and
Cartes de Séjour approved.

Directory

Essential Vocabulary

In French the second person singular (you) has two forms. Phrases here are given in the more polite *vous* form. The *tu* form is used with family, friends, young children and pets; you should be careful not to use it with people you do not know sufficiently well. You will also find that courtesies such as *monsieur*, *madame* and *mademoiselle* are used much more than their English equivalents.

General expressions

good morning/afternoon, hello *bonjour;* good evening *bonsoir;* goodbye *au revoir;* hi (familiar) *salut;* OK *d'accord;* yes *oui;* no *non;* How are you? *Comment allez vous?/vous allez bien?;* How's it going? *Comment ça va?/ça va?* (familiar); Sir/Mr *monsieur (Mr);* Madam/Mrs *madame (Mme);* Miss *mademoiselle (Mlle);* please *s'il vous plaît;* thank you *merci;* thank you very much *merci beaucoup;* sorry *pardon;* excuse me *excusez-moi;* Do you speak English? *Parlez-vous anglais?;* I don't speak French *Je ne parle pas français;* I don't understand *Je ne comprends pas;* Speak more slowly, please *Parlez plus lentement, s'il vous plaît ;* Leave me alone *Laissez-moi tranquille;* How much?/how many? *combien?;* Have you got change? *Avez-vous de la monnaie?* I would like… *Je voudrais…* I am going *Je vais;* I am going to pay *Je vais payer;* it is *c'est;* it isn't *ce n'est pas;* good *bon/bonne;* bad *mauvais/mauvaise* small *petit/petite;* big *grand/grande;* beautiful *beau/belle;* well *bien;* badly *mal;* expensive *cher;* cheap *pas cher;* a bit *un peu;* a lot *beaucoup;* very *très;* with *avec;* without *sans;* and *et;* or *ou;* because *parce que* who? *qui?;* when? *quand?;* what? *quoi?;* which? *quel?;* where? *où?;* why? *pourquoi?;* how? *comment?;* at what time/when? *à quelle heure?;* forbidden *interdit/défendu;* out of order *hors service (hs)/en panne;* daily *tous les jours (tlj)*

On the phone

hello (telephone) *allô;* Who's calling? *C'est de la part de qui?/Qui est à l'appareil?;* Hold the line *Ne quittez pas*

Getting around

Where is the (nearest) Métro? *Où est le Métro (le plus proche)?;* When is the next train for… ? *C'est quand le prochain train pour… ?;* ticket *un billet;* station *la gare;* platform *le quai;* entrance *entrée;* exit *sortie;* left *gauche;* right *droite;* straight on *tout droit;* far *loin;* near *pas loin/près d'ici;* street *la rue;* street map *le plan;* road map *la carte;* bank *la banque;* is there a bank near here? *est-ce qu'il y a une banque près d'ici?;* Post Office *La Poste;* a stamp *un timbre*

Sightseeing

museum *un musée;* church *une église;* exhibition *une exposition;* ticket (for museum) *un billet;* (for theatre, concert) *une place;* open *ouvert;* closed *fermé;* free *gratuit;* reduced price *un tarif réduit*

Accommodation

Do you have a room (for this evening/for two people)? *Avez-vous une chambre (pour ce soir/pour deux personnes)?;* full *complet;* room *une chambre;* bed *un lit;* double bed *un grand lit;* (a room with) twin beds *une chambre à deux lits;* with bath(room)/shower a*vec (salle de) bain/douche;* breakfast *le petit déjeuner;* included *compris;* lift *un ascenseur*

At the café or restaurant

I'd like to book a table (for three/at 8pm) *Je voudrais réserver une table (pour trois personnes/à vingt heures);* lunch *le déjeuner;* dinner *le dîner;* coffee (espresso) *un café;* white coffee *un café au lait/café crème;* tea *le thé;* wine *le vin;* beer *la bière;* mineral water *eau minérale;* fizzy *gazeuse;* still *plate;* tap water *eau du robinet/une carafe d'eau;* the bill, please *l'addition, s'il vous plaît*

Behind the wheel

no parking *stationnement interdit/ gênant;* toll *péage;* speed limit 40 *rappel 40;* petrol *essence;* speed *vitesse;* traffic moving freely *traffic fluide*

Shopping

may I try this on? *est-ce que je pourrais essayer cet article?;* do you have a smaller/ larger size? *auriez-vous la taille endessous/au dessus?;* I'm a size 38 *je fais un 38;* I'll take it *je le prends;* does my bum look big in this? *cela me fait-il de grosses fesses?*

The come on

do you have a light? *vous avez du feu?;* what's your name? *comment vous appelez-vous?;* would you like a drink? *vous voulez boire un verre?;* your place or mine? *chez toi ou chez moi?* (nb: you need a certain style to carry the last one off without appearing tragically geeky).

The brush-off

leave me alone *laissez-moi tranquille;* fuck off *va te faire foutre.*

Staying alive

be cool *restez calme;* I don't want any trouble *je ne veux pas d'ennuis;* I only do safe sex *je ne pratique que le safe sex.*

Numbers

0 *zéro;* 1 *un, une;* 2 *deux;* 3 *trois;* 4 *quatre;* 5 *cinq;* 6 *six;* 7 *sept;* 8 *huit;* 9 *neuf;* 10 *dix;* 11 *onze;* 12 *douze;* 13 *treize;* 14 *quatorze;* 15 *quinze;* 16 *seize;* 17 *dix-sept;* 18 *dix-huit;* 19 *dix-neuf;* 20 *vingt;* 21 *vingt-et-un;* 22 *vingt-deux;* 30 *trente;* 40 *quarante;* 50 *cinquante;* 60 *soixante;* 70 *soixante-dix;* 80 *quatre-vingts;* 90 *quatre-vingt-dix;* 100 *cent*

Days & months

Mon *lundi;* Tues *mardi;* Wed *mercredi;* Thur *jeudi;* Fri *vendredi;* Sat *samedi;* Sun *dimanche;* Jan *janvier;* Feb *février;* Mar *mars;* Apr *avril;* May *mai;* June *juin;* July *juillet;* Aug *août;* Sept *septembre;* Oct *octobre;* Nov *novembre;* Dec *décembre*

Further Reference

Books

Non-fiction

Petrus Abaelardus & Heloïse
Letters The full details of Paris'
first great romantic drama.
**Antony Beevor & Artemis
Cooper** *Paris after the Liberation*
Rationing, liberation and
existentialism.
Rupert Christiansen *Tales of
the New Babylon* Napoléon III's
Paris; blood, sleaze and bulldozers.
Vincent Cronin *Napoleon*
A fine biography of the great
megalomaniac.
Noel Riley Fitch *Literary Cafés
of Paris* Who drank where.
Alastair Horne *The Fall of
Paris* Detailed chronicle of the
Siege and Commune 1870-71.
Ian Littlewood *Paris:
Architecture, History, Art* Paris'
history and its treasures.
Patrick Marnham *Crime & the
Académie Française* Quirks and
scandals of Mitterrand-era Paris.
Nancy Mitford *The Sun King;
Madame de Pompadour* Great
gossipy accounts of the courts
of the *ancien régime.*
**Douglas Johnson &
Madeleine Johnson** *Age of
Illusion: Art & Politics in France
1918-1940* French culture in a
Paris at the forefront of
modernity.
Renzo Salvadori *Architect's
Guide to Paris* Plans, illustrations
and a guide to Paris' growth.
Simon Schama *Citizens*
Giant but wonderfully readable
account of the Revolution.
Alice B Toklas *The Alice B
Toklas Cookbook* How to cook fish
for Picasso, by the companion
(and cook) of Gertrude Stein.
Theodore Zeldin *The French*
Idiosyncratic and entertaining
survey of modern France.

Fiction & poetry

Louis Aragon *Paris Peasant*
A great Surrealist view of the city.
Honoré de Balzac *Illusions
perdues; La Peau de chagrin; Le
Père Goriot; Splendeurs et misères
des courtisanes* Some of the most
evocative novels in the 'Human
Comedy' cycle, all set in Paris.

Baudelaire *Le Spleen de Paris*
Baudelaire's prose poems with
Paris settings.
Louis-Ferdinand Céline *Mort
à crédit* Vivid account of an
impoverished Paris childhood.
Simone de Beauvoir *The
Mandarins* Paris intellectuals and
idealists just after the Liberation.
Michel Houellebecq *Platform*
Naughty boy of French literature
tackles sexual tourism.
Victor Hugo *Notre Dame de
Paris* Quasimodo and the romantic
vision of medieval Paris.
Guy de Maupassant *Bel-Ami*
Gambling and dissipation.
Catherine Millet *The Sexual
Life of Catherine M*
Bonkographie par excellence.
Patrick Modiano *Honeymoon*
Evocative story of two lives that
cross in Paris.
Georges Perec *Life, A User's
Manual* Intellectual puzzle in a
Haussmannian apartment building.
Nicolas Restif de la Bretonne
Les Nuits de Paris The sexual
underworld of Louis XV's Paris,
by one of France's most famous
defrocked priests.
Raymond Queneau *Zazie in the
Metro* Paris in the 1950s: bright
and very *nouvelle vague.*
Jean-Paul Sartre *Roads to
Freedom* Existential angst as the
German army takes over Paris.
Georges Simenon The *Maigret*
series All of Simenon's books
featuring his laconic detective
provide a great picture of Paris
and its underworld.
Emile Zola *Nana, L'Assommoir,
Le Ventre de Paris* Vivid accounts
of the underside of the Second
Empire.

The ex-pat angle

Ernest Hemingway *A Moveable
Feast* Big Ern drinks his way
around 1920s writers' Paris.
Henry Miller *Tropic of Cancer;
Tropic of Capricorn* Low-life and
lust in Montparnasse.
Anaïs Nin *Henry & June* More
lust in Montparnasse with Henry
Miller and his wife.
George Orwell *Down & Out in
Paris & London* Orwell's stint as a
lowly Paris washer-up.
Gertrude Stein *The
Autobiography of Alice B Toklas*
Ex-pat Paris, from start to finish.

Film

**Asterix & Obelix: Mission
Cleopatra (2002)**
Wonderful ensemble playing, and
many big titters.
**Carry On Don't Lose Your
Head (1966)**
Brit-pack *Carry On* team's take on
the ins and outs of the revolution.
The Rebel (1960)
Tony Hancock satire on ex-pat
artistes who come to Paris for the
sake of their art. Our hero founds
the *Infantile* school of painting.

Sounds

Couleur Café, *Serge Gainsbourg*
A sixties platter cut before the
booze, drugs and women got hold
of the poor lamb.
**Frank Sinatra and Sextet live
in Paris 1962**
He came, he swung, he conquered,
they dug.
I Love Paris
The compilation that will put you
in the mood for all those special
moments, and subsequently help
you remember them.
Moon Safari, *Air*
Relaxing, ambient beeps and
sonics from that *rara avis,* a
credible French pop group.
Song for Europe, *Roxy Music*
Bryan Ferry croons like a
chansonnier in immaculate heart-
broken Geordie style.
The Paris Concert, *Thelonius
Monk*
A blend of the experimental and
the romantically gentle.

Websites

www.fnac.com
Great for booking tickets to all
sorts of events.
www.leparisien.com
The capital's daily newspaper.
www.paris-touristoffice.com
The organ of the official Paris
Tourist Board (available in
English).
www.timeout.com
A list of the month's current
events, and an extensive guide to
hotels, restaurants and the arts.
Simply the best.

Directory

Index

Index

RESTAURANTS

Note: numbers in italics indicate a photograph; numbers in bold indicate major entries

Institut Parisien

To learn French in Paris

START A CLASS ANY MONDAY AT A LEVEL PERFECTLY SUITED TO YOU

- **Intensive Courses:** 10, 20 or 30 hrs/w, 12 students max/class (all year round).

- **Special "au pair" programme:** $4^{1/2}$ hrs/w (October through June): general and/or specialised language (literature, tourism and hotel industry, Business French). **Preparation for the diplomas of the Paris Chamber of Commerce and the Sorbonne.**

- **Also French Civilisation:** lectures free of charge (1 ^{1}/2 hrs/w), courses on French culinary arts and/or French fashion, French cinema, cultural activities ...

- **Housing service:** host families selected with care, two or three-star-hotels, student hostels, airport transfer

OPEN ALL YEAR ROUND

87 bd de Grenelle, 15th. Tel: 01.40.56.09.53
Fax: 01.43.06.46.30 - www.institut-parisien.com

ECOLE EIFFEL

établissement privé d'enseignement supérieur
FRENCH FOR FOREIGNERS

Flexible Enrollment Schedule
- specialised teachers
- all levels throughout the year
- day & evening courses
- extensive & intensive courses
Minimum 2 weeks

**sample fees: (10 hours a week) 4 weeks: €255
(20 hours a week) 4 weeks: €495**

Accredited by la Formation Continue
Certificate of enrollment provided

**3 rue Crocé-Spinelli, 14th • Mº Pernety (line 13)
Tel: 01.43.20.37.41 or 01.43.20.41.19 • Fax: 01.43.20.49.13
Internet: http://www.ecole-eiffel.fr
e-mail: eiffelfr@club-internet.fr**

Central Paris Maps Key

Place of Interest and/or Entertainment

Hospital or College . . . .

Pedestrians only . . . .

Arrondissement Boundary & Number — 16

Railway Line & Station . . . .

Paris Métro & RER Station . . . . (M) (RER)

Maps

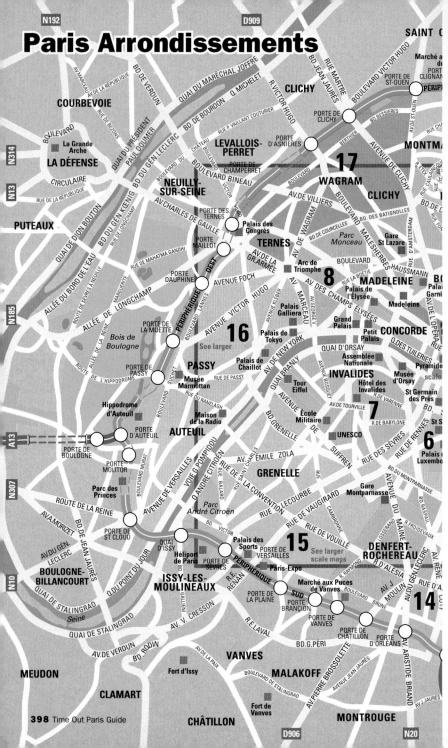

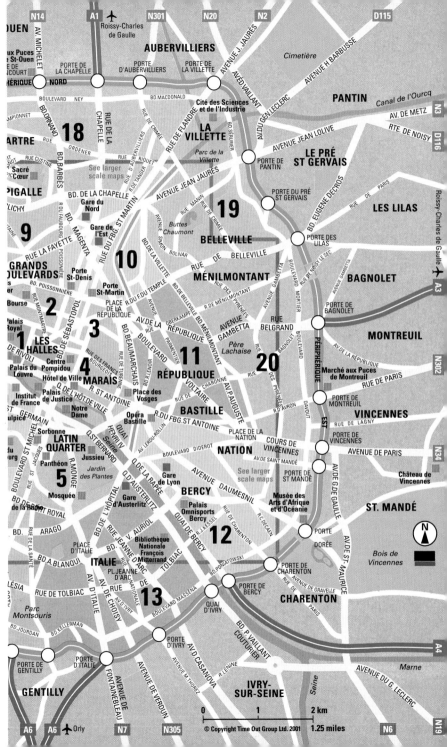

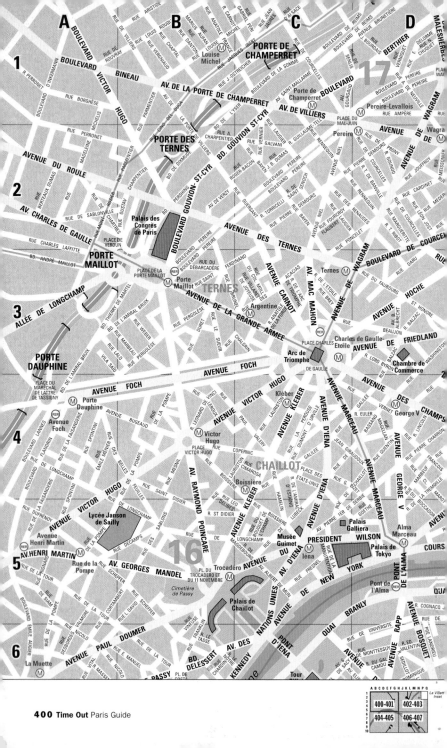

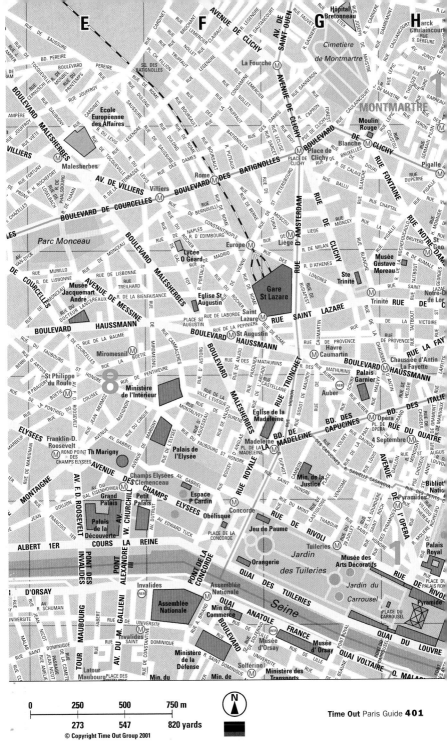

© Copyright Time Out Group 2001

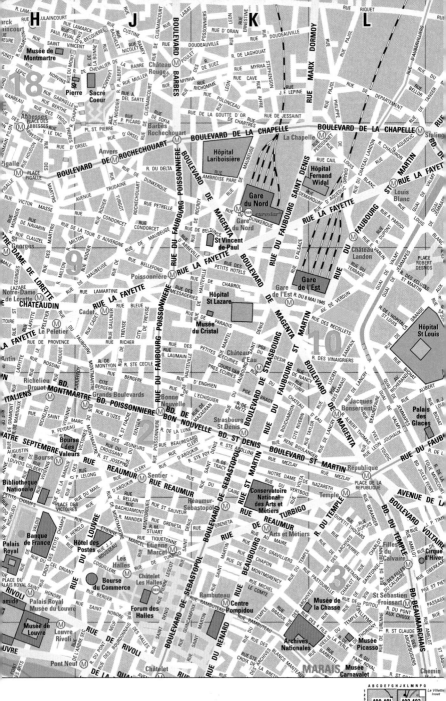

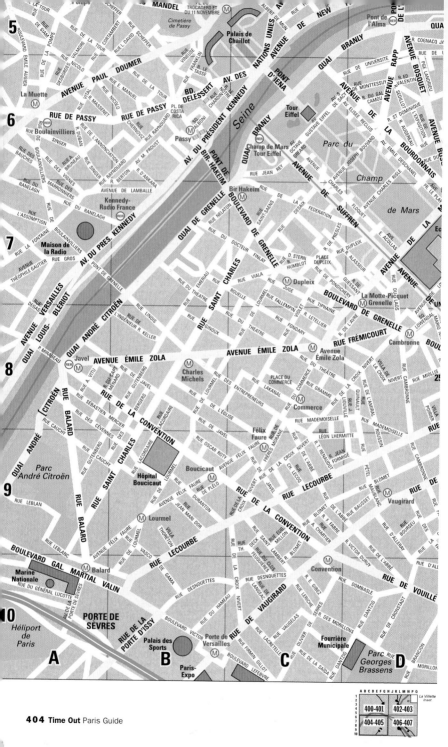

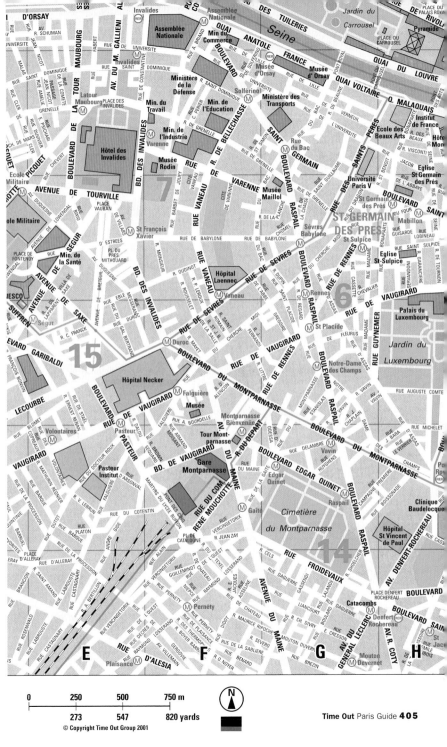

© Copyright Time Out Group 2001

0 250 500 750 m

273 547 820 yards

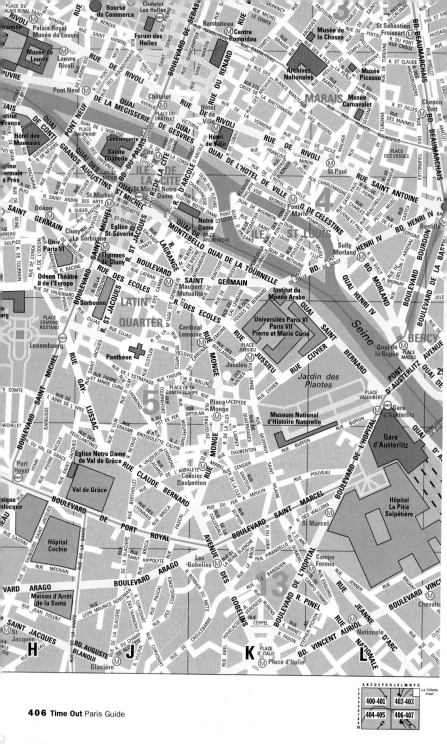

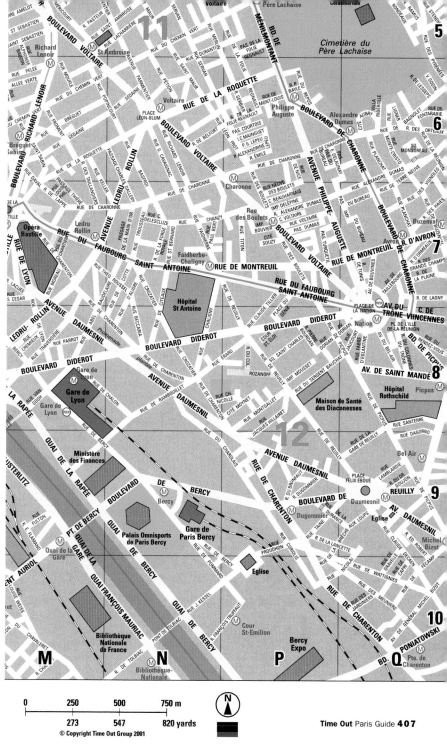

© Copyright Time Out Group 2001

Street Index

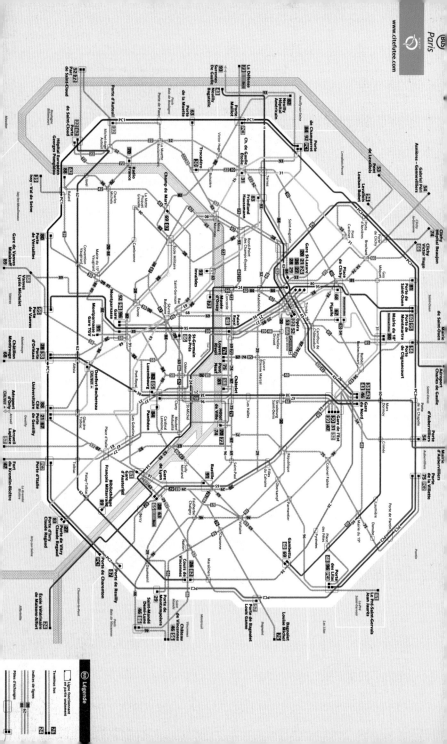

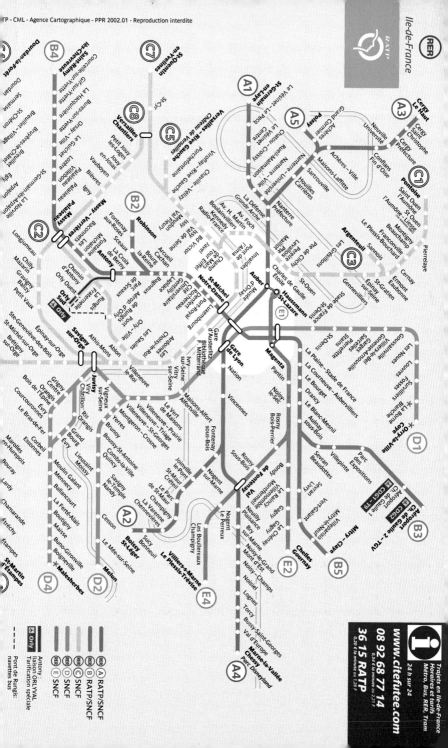

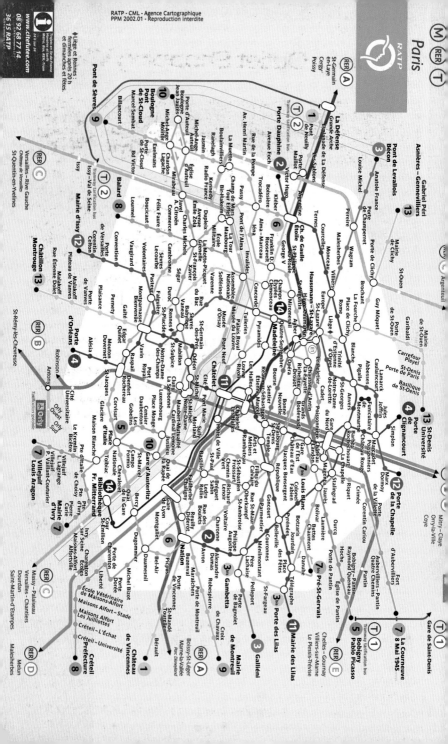